Guide to Computer Forensics and Investigations, Second Edition

By
Bill Nelson, Amelia Phillips, Frank Enfinger, and Christopher Steuart

THOMSON

COURSE TECHNOLOGY

Australia • Canada • Mexico • Singapore • Spain • United Kingdom • United States

Guide to Computer Forensics and Investigations, Second Edition
is published by Course Technology

Managing Editor:
William Pitkin III

Production Editor:
Kristen Guevara

Technical Editor:
Mike McNown

Associate Product Manager:
Sarah Santoro

Compositor:
GEX Publishing Services

Product Manager:
Amy M. Lyon

Senior Manufacturing Coordinator:
Trevor Kallop

Technical Editor:
John Bosco

Editorial Assistant:
Jennifer Smith

Text Designer:
GEX Publishing Services

Developmental Editor:
Lisa M. Lord

Product Marketing Manager:
Gayathri Baskaran

Quality Assurance Testing:
Christian Kunciw, Shawn Day,
Danielle Shaw

Cover Design:
Abby Scholz

Disclaimer
Course Technology reserves the right to revise this publication and make changes from time to time in its content without notice.

ISBN 0-619-21706-5

<small>BRIEF</small> Contents

TABLE OF
Contents

CHAPTER FIVE
Processing Crime and Incident Scenes   151

CHAPTER SIX
Digital Evidence Controls   197

Preface

Recent events throughout the world have changed and influenced how we think about gathering evidence. Soon after the attacks on the World Trade Center in New York City on September 11, 2001, many young men and women volunteered to serve their country in different ways. For those who did not choose the military, options included positions with law enforcement and security organizations. Ultimately, the combination of a renewed emphasis on homeland security with the popularity of mainstream television shows such as *CSI*, *Forensic Files*, and *NCIS* has created a huge demand for highly-educated specialists in the discipline of computer forensics. This demand is now being met by the advent of specialized forensic courses in colleges, universities, and even high schools throughout the United States.

Computer forensics, however, is by no means a new field of endeavor. During the early 1990s, while serving as a Special Agent with the Naval Criminal Investigative Service (NCIS), I realized that personal computers and, more specifically, unsecured personal computers, posed a potential threat to national security. I became involved in conducting forensic investigations involving white collar crime, network intrusions, and telecommunications fraud. Today, most new computer forensics specialists can expect to be involved in a wide variety of investigations, including terrorism counterintelligence, anti-money laundering, intellectual property theft, and electronic discovery issues.

The skill sets computer forensics specialists must have are varied. At a minimum, they must have an in-depth knowledge of the criminal justice system, computer hardware and software systems, and investigative and evidence-gathering protocols. The next generation of "digital detectives" will have to possess the knowledge, skills, and experience to conduct complex, data-intensive forensic examinations involving multiple operating systems and file types.

As time passes, the "hybrid discipline" of computer forensics is slowly evolving into a "hybrid science"—the science of digital forensics. Several colleges and universities in the United States and the United Kingdom are currently creating multidisciplined curriculums that will offer undergraduate and graduate degrees in digital forensics. *Guide to Computer Forensics and Investigations*, now in its second edition, has emerged as a significant authoritative text for the computer and digital forensics communities. It's my belief that this book, designed to be used primarily in an academic setting with an enthusiastic and knowledgeable facilitator, will make for a fascinating course of instruction.

Today, it's not just computers that harbor the binary code of 1s and 0s, but an infinite array of personal digital devices. If one of these devices retains evidence of a crime, it will be up to newly trained and educated digital detectives to find the digital evidence in a forensically sound manner. This book will assist both students and practitioners in accomplishing this goal.

Respectfully,

John A. Sgromolo

As a Senior Special Agent, John was one of the founding members of the NCIS Computer Crime Investigations Group. John left government service to run his own company, Digital Forensics, Inc., and has taught hundreds of law enforcement and corporate students nationwide the art and science of computer forensics investigations. Currently, John serves as a lead investigator in digital forensic investigations for Verizon.

Introduction

Computer forensics has been a professional field for many years, but most well-established experts in the field have been self-taught. The growth of the Internet and the worldwide proliferation of computers have increased the need for computing investigations. Computers can be used to commit crimes, and crimes can be recorded on computers, including company policy violations, embezzlement, e-mail harassment, murder, leaks of proprietary information, and even terrorism. Law enforcement, network administrators, attorneys, and private investigators now rely on the skills of professional computer forensics experts to investigate criminal and civil cases.

This book is not intended to provide comprehensive training in computer forensics. It does, however, give you a solid foundation by introducing computer forensics to those who are new to the field. Other books on computer forensics are targeted to experts; this book is intended for novices who have a thorough grounding in computer and networking basics.

The new generation of computer forensics experts needs more initial training because operating systems, computer hardware, and forensic software tools are changing more quickly. This book covers current and past operating systems, such as Windows 9x, Mac OS, and Linux, and a range of computer hardware, from basic PC workstations to high-end network servers. Although this book focuses on a few forensic software tools, it also reviews and discusses other currently available tools.

The purpose of this book is to guide you toward becoming a skilled computer forensics investigator. A secondary goal is to help you pass the appropriate certification exams. As the field of computer forensics and investigations matures, keep in mind that certifications will change. One of the better known, the International Association of Computer Investigative Specialists (IACIS) certification, is intended primarily for law enforcement. Chapter 3 reviews the certifications that are current at the time of publication, and Appendix A covers them in more detail.

INTENDED AUDIENCE

Although this book can be used by people with a wide range of backgrounds, it's intended for those with an A+ and Network+ certification or equivalent. A networking background is necessary so that you understand how PCs operate in a networked environment and can work with a network administrator when needed. In addition, readers must understand how to use a computer from the command line and how to use popular operating systems, including Windows 9x/2000/XP, Linux, and Mac OS, and their related hardware.

This book can be used at any educational level, from technical high schools and community colleges to graduate students. Current professionals in the public and private sectors can also use this book. Each group will approach investigative problems from a different perspective, but all will benefit from the coverage.

New to This Edition

The chapter flow of this book has been revised so that students are first exposed to what happens in a computer forensics lab and how to set one up before they get into the nuts and bolts. Coverage of several GUI tools has been added to give students a familiarity with some of the popular software. In addition, because of PDAs' impact on the market, an overview of working with them has been included, and a new chapter on network forensics shows security professionals how computer forensics can be used in their field. Historical corrections have been made to the first edition based on feedback from users, and all software packages and Web sites have been updated to reflect what's current at the time of publication.

Chapter Descriptions

Here is a summary of the topics covered in each chapter of this book:

Chapter 1, "Computer Forensics and Investigations as a Profession," introduces you to the history of computer forensics and explains how the use of electronic evidence developed. It also introduces legal issues and compares public and private sector cases.

Chapter 2, "Understanding Computer Investigations," introduces you to an application used throughout the book and shows you how to apply scientific techniques to an investigative case.

Chapter 3, "The Investigator's Office and Laboratory," outlines an ideal view of how computer forensics labs should be equipped, from small private investigators' labs to the regional FBI lab. It also covers certifications for digital investigators.

Chapter 4, "Current Computer Forensics Tools," explores current computer forensics tools, including those that might not be readily available, and evaluates their strengths and weaknesses.

Chapter 5, "Processing Crime and Incident Scenes," explains search warrants and the nature of a typical computer forensics case. It discusses when to use outside professionals, how to assemble a team, and how to evaluate a case.

Chapter 6, "Digital Evidence Controls," emphasizes that digital evidence is fragile and easily changed. The chapter covers how to control a crime scene and secure and verify authenticity of evidence so that it can be used in court.

Chapter 7, "Working with Windows and DOS Systems," discusses the most common operating systems. You learn what happens and what files are altered during computer startup and how each system deals with deleted and slack space.

Chapter 8, "Macintosh and Linux Boot Processes and File Systems," continues the operating system discussion from Chapter 7 by examining Macintosh and Linux operating systems. It also covers CDs, DVDs, and SCSI and RAID systems.

Chapter 9, "Data Acquisition," explains how to prepare to acquire data from a suspect's drive and discusses the tools available for command-line and GUI operating systems.

Chapter 10, "Computer Forensics Analysis," covers investigative plans and explains how to set up your forensic workstation for a specific investigation. It also outlines the step-by-step process for retrieving potential evidence.

Chapter 11, "Recovering Image Files," explains how to recover image files on an evidence disk and examines image recovery tools, data compression, and restoring graphics. It also discusses steganography and copyright issues.

Chapter 12, "Network Forensics," covers tools and methods that can be used for conducting network-centered investigations. It also provides an overview of using network logs to collect evidence of a network intrusion incident or a crime.

Chapter 13, "E-mail Investigations," covers e-mail and Internet fundamentals and examines e-mail crimes and violations. It also reviews some popular e-mail forensic tools.

Chapter 14, "Becoming an Expert Witness and Reporting Results of Investigations," explores the role of expert witnesses, including developing curriculum vitae and tracking your qualifications as you acquire them. It also describes the differences between expert and technical witnesses and explains how to develop oral and written reports for computer forensics investigations.

Appendix A, "Certification Test References," examines the certifications that are currently available.

Appendix B, "Computer Forensics References," contains tables of commands referenced throughout the book, explores scripts and FAT directory structures in more depth, and lists additional reference books for forensic investigators.

Appendix C, "Procedures for Corporate High-Technology Investigations," outlines procedures and checklists for corporate investigations, such as Internet and e-mail abuse investigations, employee terminations, and industrial espionage cases.

FEATURES

To help you fully understand computer and network security, this book includes many features designed to enhance your learning experience:

- **Chapter Objectives.** Each chapter begins with a detailed list of the concepts to be mastered in that chapter. This list gives you a quick reference to the chapter's contents and is a useful study aid.

- **Figures and Tables.** Screenshots are used as guidelines for stepping through commands and forensic tools. For tools not included with the book or that aren't offered in free demo versions, figures have been added to illustrate the tool's interface. Tables are used throughout the book to present information in an organized, easy-to-grasp manner.

- **Chapter Summaries.** Each chapter's material is followed by a summary of the concepts introduced in that chapter. These summaries are a helpful way to review the ideas covered in each chapter.

- **Key Terms.** Following the Chapter Summary, a list of all new terms introduced in the chapter with boldfaced text are gathered together in the Key Terms list, with full definitions for each term. This list encourages a more thorough understanding of the chapter's key concepts and is a useful reference.

- **Review Questions.** The end-of-chapter assessment begins with a set of review questions that reinforce the main concepts in each chapter. These questions help you evaluate and apply the material you have learned.

- **Hands-on Projects.** Although it's important to understand the theory behind computer technology, nothing can improve on real-world experience. To this end, each chapter offers several Hands-on Projects that involve software supplied with this book or free downloads of computer forensics software. You can explore a variety of ways to acquire and even hide evidence. For the conceptual chapters, research projects are provided.

- **Case Projects.** At the end of each chapter are several Case Projects, including two running case examples used throughout the book. To complete these exercises, you must draw on real-world common sense as well as your knowledge of the technical topics covered to that point in the book. Your goal for each project is to come up with answers to problems similar to those you'll face as a working computer forensics investigator.

- **Software and Student Data File CDs.** This book includes two CD-ROMs, which contain the student data files for the Case Projects, and free software demo packages for use with the Hands-on Activities and Case Projects in the chapters. (Additional software demos or freeware are also used in activities and projects, and can be downloaded before you begin.) Three software companies have very graciously agreed to allow us to include their products with our book: Digital Intelligence, including DriveSpy and Image (online registration is neeeded for these programs); Access Data, including Forensics Toolkit, Password Recovery Toolkit, Registry Viewer, and FTK Imager; and X-Ways, X-Ways Forensics. To check for newer versions or additional information, visit Digital Intelligence, Inc. at *www.digitalintelligence.com*, AccessData Corporation at *www.accessdata.com*, and X-Ways Software Technology AG at *www.x-ways.net*.

- **EnCase Demo DVD.** In addition, this book also comes with an exciting DVD from Guidance Software, Inc. This DVD includes a demo version of their EnCase software, a special Case Project and evidence files for use with the demo, as well as the user's manual and other documentation. For more information about EnCase, or to purchase a full version of the software, please visit *www.GuidanceSoftware.com*.

TEXT AND GRAPHIC CONVENTIONS

Where appropriate, additional information and exercises have been added to this book to help you better understand the topic at hand. Icons throughout the text alert you to additional materials. The following icons are used in this book:

The Note icon draws your attention to additional helpful material related to the subject being covered.

Tips based on the authors' experience offer extra information about how to attack a problem or what to do in real-world situations.

The Caution icons warn you about potential mistakes or problems and explain how to avoid them.

Each Hands-on Project in this book is preceded by the Hands-on icon and a description of the exercise that follows.

These icons mark Case Projects, which are scenario-based assignments. In these extensive case examples, you are asked to apply independently what you have learned.

INSTRUCTOR'S MATERIALS

The following additional materials are available when this book is used in a classroom setting. All the supplements available with this book are provided to instructors on a single CD-ROM. You can also retrieve these supplemental materials from the Course Technology Web site, *www.course.com*, by going to the page for this book, under "Download Instructor Files & Teaching Tools."

Electronic Instructor's Manual. The Instructor's Manual that accompanies this book includes the following items: additional instructional material to assist in class preparation, including suggestions for lecture topics; recommended lab activities; tips on setting up a lab for Hands-on Projects; and solutions to all end-of-chapter materials.

ExamView Test Bank. This cutting-edge Windows-based testing software helps instructors design and administer tests and pretests. In addition to generating tests that can be printed and administered, this full-featured program has an online testing component that allows students to take tests at the computer and have their exams automatically graded.

PowerPoint presentations. This book comes with a set of Microsoft PowerPoint slides for each chapter. These slides are meant to be used as a teaching aid for classroom presentations, to be made available to students on the network for chapter review, or to be printed for classroom distribution. Instructors are also at liberty to add their own slides for other topics introduced.

Figure files. All the figures in the book are reproduced on the Instructor's Resources CD. Similar to the PowerPoint presentations, they are included as a teaching aid for classroom presentation, to make available to students for review, or to be printed for classroom distribution.

LAB REQUIREMENTS

The Hands-on Projects in this book help you apply what you have learned about computer forensics techniques. The following sections lists the minimum hardware requirements for completing all the Hands-on Projects in this book. In addition to the items listed, students must be able to download and install demo versions of software.

Minimum Lab Requirements

- Computers that boot to a true command line to run Digital Intelligence's DriveSpy and Image. Windows XP does not allow certain programs to run; as an alternative, a DOS boot disk and the standard external DOS commands for that version of DOS saved to a folder on the forensic drive

- Lab computers that boot to Windows XP or 2000

- Computers that dual boot to Linux or UNIX

- At least one Macintosh computer

The steps and projects in this book are designed with the following hardware and software requirements in mind. The lab in which most of the work takes place should be a typical network training lab with a variety of operating systems and computers available, including a Windows XP, 2000, or 9x computer and a Linux computer.

Operating Systems and Hardware

Windows XP and 2000

Use a standard installation of the Home, Professional, or Server versions. The computer running Windows XP or 2000 should meet the following minimum requirements:

- 3½-inch disk drive

- CD-ROM drive

- VGA or higher monitor

- Hard disk partition of 10 GB or more

- Mouse or other pointing device

- Keyboard

- 128 MB RAM

Windows 9x

Some steps and projects require access to a computer that can boot directly to a DOS prompt. You can also run many GUI programs on these machines, but they might require more memory than what's listed below. The computer running Windows 95 or 98 should meet the following minimum requirements:

- *Windows 95*—8 MB RAM, with 24 MB or more recommended
  Windows 98—16 MB RAM, with 24 MB or more recommended

- Hard disk partition of 1 GB or more

- Other hardware requirements are the same as those listed for Windows XP computers

Note: As mentioned in the minimum lab requirements, you can boot directly from a DOS boot disk as long as the external commands are in a folder on the drive.

Linux

For this book, it's assumed you're using the Red Hat Linux 9 or Fedora standard installation. Some optional steps require the GIMP graphics editor, which must be installed separately in Red Hat Linux 9. Linux can be installed on a dual-boot computer as long as one or more partitions of at least 2 GB are reserved for the Linux OS.

- Hard disk partition of 2 GB or more reserved for Linux

- Other hardware requirements are the same as those listed for Windows XP computers

Computer Forensics Software

This book provides two computer forensics programs: DriveSpy and Image, both developed by Digital Intelligence, Inc. DriveSpy and Image are DOS programs that run from a true DOS prompt rather than from a DOS shell. DriveSpy and Image both run on Windows 98 only. A true DOS prompt require a dual-boot setup that includes Windows 98 if you want to use the software.

This book includes steps and projects that involve the following software, most of which can be downloaded from the Internet as freeware, shareware, or free demo versions. Because Web site addresses change frequently, use a search engine to find the following software online if the addresses are no longer valid:

- *Digital Intelligence's DriveSpy and Image*: If you are a faculty member of an accredited academic institution, please contact Digital Intelligence to inquire about an academic license for DriveSpy and Image software for training purposes. The Web site is *www.digitalintelligence.com*.

- *AccessData Forensic ToolKit (FTK)*: Download the demo version from *www.accessdata.com*. As of the writing of this book, AccessData has an educational package along with instructor training for a fraction of the retail price.

- *EnCase:* From Guidance Software, this tool is used widely by law enforcement.

- *Hex Workshop*: Download the trial version from *www.hexworkshop.com*. You can also use Norton DiskEdit or WinHex instead of Hex Workshop.

- *X-Ways Forensics and X-Ways Replica*: Both are available for download from *www.x-ways.net*.

- *IrfanView*: Download from *www.irfanview.com*.

- *NTFSDOS*: Download from *www.sysinternals.com*.

- *SecureClean*: Download from *www.accessdata.com*.

- *Steganography tools (S-Tools suggested)*: Download from *www.stegoarchive.com*.

- *Tom's Root Boot Kit*: Download the freeware version from *www.tux.org*.

- *WinZip*: Download an evaluation version from *www.winzip.com/download.htm*.

- *JASC Paint Shop Pro*: Download a trial version from *www.jasc.com*.

In addition, you use Microsoft Office Word (or other word processing software) and Excel (or other spreadsheet software). You also need to have e-mail software, such as Microsoft Outlook Express or Eudora, installed on your computer.

About The Authors

Bill Nelson has been a lead computer forensics investigator for a Fortune 50 company for more than eight years and has developed high-tech investigation programs for professional organizations and colleges. His previous experience includes Automated Fingerprint Identification System (AFIS) software engineering and reserve police work. Bill has served as president and vice president for Computer Technology Investigators Northwest (CTIN) and is a member of Computer Related Information Management and Education (CRIME). He routinely lectures at several colleges and universities in the Pacific Northwest.

Amelia Phillips is a graduate of the Massachusetts Institute of Technology with B.S. degrees in astronautical engineering and archaeology and an MBA in technology management. After serving as an engineer at the Jet Propulsion Lab, she worked with e-commerce Web sites and began her training in computer forensics to prevent credit card numbers from being stolen from sensitive e-commerce databases. She designed programs for community colleges in e-commerce, computer forensics, and data recovery. She is currently tenured at Highline Community College in Seattle, Washington. Amelia has recently been awarded a Fulbright Scholarship to teach in this area and conduct research in sub-Saharan Africa.

Frank Enfinger is a tenured professor at North Seattle Community College as well as a computing forensics specialist with a local police department. Before entering the computing industry, Professor Enfinger served a tour of duty in the U.S. Marine Corps. Over the years, he has worked with computer technology for a number of corporate and government entities, including hospitals, ISPs, and environmental protection companies. He has earned a degree and numerous certifications in the field of computer science and continues to work with evolving technologies.

Christopher K. Steuart is a practicing attorney maintaining a general litigation practice, with experience in information systems security for a Fortune 50 company and the U.S. Army. He is General Counsel for Computer Investigators Northwest (CTIN). He has presented computer forensics seminars in regional and national forums, including the American Society for Industrial Security (ASIS), Agora, Northwest Computer Technology Crime Analysis Seminar (NCT), and CTIN.

ACKNOWLEDGMENTS

The team would like to express its appreciation to Managing Editor Will Pitkin, who has given us a great deal of moral support. We would like to thank the entire editorial and production staff for their dedication and fortitude during this project, including Amy Lyon, the Product Manager, and Kristen Guevara, the Production Editor. Our special thanks goes to Lisa Lord, the Developmental Editor, as well as the testers in the Quality Assurance Department: Shawn Day and Danielle Shaw. We also appreciate the careful reading and thoughtful suggestions of the Technical Editors, Mike McNown and John Bosco. We also would like to thank Franklin Clark, an investigator for the Pierce County Prosecutor in Tacoma, Washington, for his input, and Mike Lacey for his photos. In addition, we would like to thank our team of peer reviewers who evaluated each chapter and provided very helpful suggestions and contributions:

Larry Anderson	Metropolitan Community College
Mark Davis	University of Tulsa
Michael Sthultz	Community College of Southern Nevada

Bill Nelson

I want to express my appreciation to my wife, Tricia, for her support during the long hours spent writing. I would also like to express appreciation to my co-authors, Amelia, Chris, and Frank, along with our editors for the team effort in producing this book. And special thanks for the support and encouragement from my computer forensics colleagues: Franklin Clark of the Pierce County Prosecutor's Office, Tacoma, Washington; Detective Mike McNown, retired Wichita PD; Scott Larson and Don Allison of Stoz Friedberg, LLC; Detectives Brian Palmer, Barry Walden, and Melissa Rogers of the King County Sheriff's Office Fraud Unit, Seattle, Washington; and John Sgromolo of Verizon.

Amelia Phillips

My first acknowledgements go to the fabulous group of students who put together the firestarter/arson case project that runs throughout the book. They created it as a response to the number of arson cases that were running rampant in the Seattle area at the time. My thanks go to Travis Scott Anderson, Cesar V. Noche, Jr., Lucas Reber, Eric Apple, Mike Danseglio, and Seth Diaz. I would also like to thank the students from the Seattle area PDs and corporations who attended my classes. They gave me a lot of case histories and insight. I want to thank my co-authors and friends for their fantastic fortitude and good humor throughout the learning experience we have had. And thanks to Lisa Lord, who made this a fun experience.

Frank Enfinger

First, I would like to thank my family for their love, support, and understanding while their "ol' man" took time away from other activities to write a book. To my co-authors, thank you for everything. It has been an honor and a privilege to help write this book with you. To Lisa Lord, a special thank you for all you have done to make this edition a smoother process and all the help you have rendered over the past several months. To all my mentors, you know who you are-thank you! My contribution to this book is a direct result of the training, work, and opportunities you have provided me. Finally, I would like to thank the readers of this book. For all you do and will do in the future with your computer forensics skills, thank you.

Christopher K. Steuart

I would like to express my appreciation to my wife, Josephine, son, Alexander, and daughter, Isobel, for their enthusiastic support of my commitment to *Guide to Computer Forensics and Investigations*, even as it consumed time and energy that they deserved. I would like to thank my parents, William and Mary, for their support of my education and the development of the skills needed for this project. I thank my co-authors, Bill, Amelia, and Frank, for inviting me to join them in this project. I would like to express my appreciation to Lieutenant General (then Captain) Edward Soriano for seeing the potential in me as a young soldier and encouraging me in learning the skills and processes required to administer, communicate with, and command an organization within the structure of law, regulation, and personal commitment. I thank the faculty of Drake University Law School and particularly Professor James A. Albert for encouraging me to think and write creatively about the law.

PHOTO CREDITS

Figure 1-2:   8088 computer courtesy of IBM Corporate Archives

1

COMPUTER FORENSICS AND INVESTIGATIONS AS A PROFESSION

After reading this chapter and completing the exercises, you will be able to:

♦ Understand computer forensics

♦ Prepare for computer investigations

♦ Understand enforcement agency investigations

♦ Understand corporate investigations

♦ Maintain professional conduct

This chapter introduces you to computer forensics and investigations and discusses some of the problems and concerns prevalent in the industry. The field of computer forensics and investigations is still in the early stage of development. This book blends traditional investigation methods with classic systems analysis problem-solving techniques and applies them to computer investigations. An understanding of these disciplines combined with the use of computer forensics tools will make you a highly skilled computer forensics analyst.

UNDERSTANDING COMPUTER FORENSICS

Computer forensics involves obtaining and analyzing digital information for use as evidence in civil, criminal, or administrative cases. The Federal Rules of Evidence (FRED) has controlled the use of digital evidence since 1970; from 1970 to 1985, state rules of evidence, as they were adopted by each state, controlled usage of this type of evidence. Documents maintained on a computer are covered by different rules, depending on the nature of the documents. Many court cases in state and federal courts have further developed and clarified how the rules apply to digital evidence. The **Fourth Amendment** to the U.S. Constitution (and each state's constitution) protects everyone's rights to be secure in their person, residence, and property from search and seizure. Continuing development of the jurisprudence of this amendment has played a role in determining whether the search for digital evidence has established a different precedent, so separate **search warrants** might not be necessary. However, when preparing to search for evidence in a criminal case, to avoid problems many investigators still include the suspect's computer and its components in the search warrant. A significant case addressed by a state supreme court occurred in Pennsylvania. This case (see *Commonwealth v. Copenhefer* 553 Pa. 285, 719 A.2d 242) addressed expectations of privacy and whether evidence is admissible. The case involved a kidnapped woman who was eventually found dead, clearly murdered. Initial investigations by the Federal Bureau of Investigation (FBI), state police, and local police resulted in discovery of a series of hidden computer-generated notes and instructions, each discovery leading to another. The investigation also produced several possible suspects, including one who owned a nearby bookstore and had a history of hostile encounters with the victim and her husband.

In addition to finding physical evidence, investigators also examined a computer the victim's husband had used. They discovered a series of drafts and amendments to the text of a phone call the husband received, a ransom note, a series of other notes, and a detailed plan for kidnapping the victim. On direct appeal, the Pennsylvania Supreme Court concluded that the physical evidence, especially the computer forensics evidence, was sufficient to support the bookstore owner's conviction.

The defendant's argument was that ". . . even though his computer was validly seized pursuant to a warrant, his attempted deletion of the documents in question created an expectation of privacy protected by the Fourth Amendment. Thus, he claims, under *Katz v. United States*, 389 U.S. 347, 357, 88 S. Ct. 507, 19 L. Ed. 2d 576 (1967), and its progeny, Agent Johnson's retrieval of the documents, without first obtaining another search warrant, was unreasonable under the Fourth Amendment and the documents thus seized should have been suppressed."

The Pennsylvania Supreme Court rejected this argument, stating "A defendant's attempt to secrete evidence of a crime is not synonymous with a legally cognizable expectation of privacy. A mere hope for secrecy is not a legally protected expectation. If it were, search warrants would be required in a vast number of cases where warrants are clearly not necessary."

NOTE The United States Department of Justice offers a useful guide to search and seizure procedures for computers and computer evidence at *www.usdoj.gov/ criminal/cybercrime/s&smanual2002.htm.*

Computer Forensics Versus Other Related Disciplines

According to DIBS USA, Inc., a privately owned corporation specializing in computer forensics (*www.dibsusa.com*), computer forensics involves scientifically examining and analyzing data from computer storage media so that the data can be used as evidence in court. You can find similar definitions on the FBI's Web site (*www.fbi.gov/hq/lab/fsc/backissu/oct2000/ computer.htm*) or at *http://whatis.com.* Typically, investigating computers includes securely collecting computer data, examining suspect data to determine details such as origin and content, presenting computer-based information to courts, and applying laws to computer practice.

In general, computer forensics investigates data that can be retrieved from a computer's hard disk or other storage media. Like an archaeologist excavating a site, computer investigators retrieve information from a computer or its component parts. The information you retrieve might already be on the disk, but it might not be easy to find or decipher. In contrast, **network forensics** yields information about how a perpetrator or hacker gained access to a network. Network forensics uses log files to determine when users logged on or last used their logon IDs. A network forensics investigator tries to determine which URLs a user accessed, how he or she logged on to the network, and from what location. In Chapter 12, you explore when and how network forensics should be used in your investigation.

Computer forensics is different from **data recovery**, which involves recovering information from a computer that was deleted by mistake or lost during a power surge, for example. Computer forensics is the task of recovering data that users have hidden or deleted, with the goal of ensuring that the recovered data is valid so that it can be used as evidence. The evidence can be **inculpatory** (in criminal cases, the expression is "incriminating") or **exculpatory**, meaning it might clear the suspect. Investigators often examine a computer disk not knowing whether it contains evidence—they must search storage media, and if they find data, they piece it together to produce evidence. Various software forensic tools on the market can be used for most cases. In extreme cases, investigators can use electron microscopes and other sophisticated equipment to retrieve information from machines that have been damaged or purposefully reformatted. This method is usually cost prohibitive, running from US$3000 to more than US$20,000, so it's not normally used.

Like companies specializing in data recovery, companies specializing in **disaster recovery** use computer forensics techniques to retrieve information their clients have lost. Disaster recovery also involves preventing data loss by using backups, uninterruptible power supply (UPS) devices, and off-site monitoring.

Investigators often work as a team to make computers and networks secure in an organization. The computer investigations function is one of three in a triad that makes up computing security. In the enterprise network environment, the triad consists of the following parts:

- Vulnerability assessment and risk management
- Network intrusion detection and incident response
- Computer investigations

Figure 1-1 shows how these three parts of computing security are related. Each side of the triad represents a group or department responsible for performing the associated tasks. Although each function operates independently, all three groups draw from one another when a large-scale computing investigation is being conducted. By combining these three groups into a team, all aspects of a high-technology investigation are addressed without calling in outside specialists.

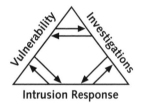

Figure 1-1   The investigations triad

The term **enterprise environment** refers to large corporate computing systems that might include one or more disparate or formerly independent systems. In smaller companies, one group might perform the tasks shown in the investigations triad, or a small company might contract with other companies to perform these tasks.

When you work in the **vulnerability assessment and risk management** group, you test and verify the integrity of standalone workstations and network servers. This integrity check covers the physical security of systems and the security of operating systems (OSs) and applications. People who work in this group test for known vulnerabilities of OSs and applications used throughout the network. This group launches attacks on the network and its computer workstations and servers to assess vulnerabilities. Typically, people performing this task have several years of experience in UNIX and Windows NT/2000/XP administration.

Professionals in the vulnerability assessment and risk management group also have skills in **network intrusion detection and incident response**. This group detects intruder attacks by using automated tools and by monitoring network firewall logs manually. When an attack is detected, the response team tracks, locates, and identifies the intruder and denies him or her further access to the network. If an intruder launches an attack that causes significant or potential damage, this team collects the necessary evidence, which can be used for civil or criminal litigation against the intruders. **Litigation** is the legal process of proving guilt or innocence in court.

If an unauthorized user is using the network or if any user is performing illegal acts, the network intrusion detection and incident response group responds by locating the user or blocking the user's access. For example, someone at a community college sends inflammatory e-mails to other users on the network. The network team quickly realizes that the e-mails are coming from a node on its own network and dispatches a security team to the location. Historically, vulnerability assessment staff contribute significantly to high-end computing investigations.

The **computer investigations** group manages investigations and conducts forensic analysis of systems suspected of containing evidence related to an incident or crime. For complex casework, the computer investigations group draws on resources from those involved in vulnerability assessment, risk management, and network intrusion detection and incident response. This group resolves or terminates all case investigations.

A Brief History of Computer Forensics

Thirty years ago, most people didn't imagine that computers would be an integral part of everyday life. Now computer technology is commonplace, as are crimes in which the computer is the instrument of the crime, the target of the crime, and, by its nature, the location where evidence is stored or recorded.

By the 1970s, electronic crimes were increasing, usually in the financial sector. Most computers in this era were mainframes, used by an exclusive realm of trained or educated people with specialized skills. People who used mainframe computers worked in banks, engineering, and academia. White-collar fraud began when people in those industries saw a way to make money by manipulating computer data.

One of the most well-known crimes of the mainframe era is the one-half cent crime. It was common for banks to track monies in accounts to the third decimal place or more. Banks used and still use the "rounding up" accounting method when paying interest. If the interest applied to an account resulted in a fraction of a cent, that fraction was used in the calculation for the next account until the total resulted in a whole cent. It was assumed that sooner or later every customer would benefit. On more than one occasion, computer programmers corrupted this method by opening an account for themselves and writing programs that diverted all the fractional monies into their accounts. In smaller banks, this practice amounted to only a few hundred dollars a month. In larger banks with branch offices, however, the amount of money reached hundreds of thousands of dollars.

In the 1970s and early 1980s, when crimes such as the one-half cent crime were being committed, most law enforcement officers didn't know enough about computers to ask the right questions or to preserve evidence for trial. Many began to attend the Federal Law Enforcement Training Center (FLETC) programs designed to train law enforcement in recovering digital data.

As PCs gained popularity and began to replace mainframe computers in the 1980s, many different OSs emerged. Apple released the Apple 2E in 1983, and then launched the Macintosh in 1984. Computers such as the TRS-80 and the Commodore 64 were the machines of the day. CP/M machines (the 8088 series) and Zeniths were also in demand.

The disk operating system (DOS) was available in many varieties, including PC-DOS, QDOS, DR-DOS, IBM-DOS, and MS-DOS. Forensic tools at that time were simple, and most were generated by government agencies such as the Royal Canadian Mounted Police (RCMP) in Ottawa, which had its own investigative tools, and the U.S. Internal Revenue Service (IRS). Most of these tools were written in C and assembly language and were not used by the general public.

In the mid-1980s, a new tool called Xtree Gold appeared on the market. It recognized file types and retrieved lost or deleted files. Norton DiskEdit soon followed and became the best tool for finding deleted files. You could use these tools on the most powerful PCs of that time; IBM-compatible computers had 10 MB hard disks and two floppy drives, as shown in Figure 1-2.

Figure 1-2   An 8088 computer

In 1987, Apple produced the Mac SE, a Macintosh that was available with an external EasyDrive hard disk with 60 MB of storage (see Figure 1-3). At this time, the Commodore 64 was a popular computer that still used standard audiotapes to record data, so the Mac SE represented an important advance in computer technology.

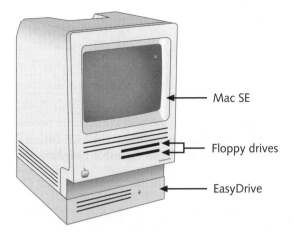

Mac SE

Floppy drives

EasyDrive

Figure 1-3   A Mac SE with an external EasyDrive hard disk

By the early 1990s, specialized tools for computer forensics were available. The **International Association of Computer Investigative Specialists (IACIS)** introduced training on currently available software for forensic investigations, and the IRS created search-warrant programs. However, no commercial software for computer forensics was available until ASR Data created Expert Witness for the Macintosh. This software can recover deleted files and fragments of deleted files. One of the ASR Data partners later left and developed EnCase, which has become a popular computer forensics tool.

As computer technology continued to grow, more computer forensics software was developed. The introduction of large hard disks posed new problems for investigators. Most DOS-based software doesn't recognize a hard disk larger than 8 GB. Because contemporary computers have hard disks of 40 to 100 GB and larger, changes in forensics software are needed. Later in this book, you explore the challenges of using older software and hardware.

Other software, such as iLook, which is currently maintained by the IRS Criminal Investigation Division and limited to law enforcement, can analyze and read special data files that are copies of a disk. AccessData's Forensic Toolkit (FTK) has become a popular commercial product that performs similar tasks in the law enforcement and civilian markets. These tools and others are covered in Chapter 4.

As software companies become more savvy about computer forensics and investigations, they are publishing more forensic tools to keep pace with technology. This book discusses as many tools as possible. You should also refer to trade publications and Web sites such as *www.ctin.org* (Computer Technology Investigators Northwest) or *www.usdoj.gov* (U.S. Department of Justice) to stay current.

Developing Computer Forensics Resources

To be a successful computer forensics investigator, you must be familiar with more than one computing platform. In addition to older platforms, such as DOS and Windows 9*x*, you should be familiar with Linux, Macintosh, and the current Windows platforms.

However, no one can be an expert in every aspect of computing. Likewise, you cannot know everything about the technology you're investigating. To supplement your knowledge, you should develop and maintain contact with computing, network, and investigative professionals. Keep a log of contacts, and record the names of other professionals with whom you have worked, their area of expertise, the last few projects you worked on together, and their particular contribution.

Join as many computer user groups as you can, both in the public and private sectors. In the Pacific Northwest, for example, **Computer Technology Investigators Northwest (CTIN)** meets monthly to discuss problems that law enforcement and corporations face. This nonprofit organization also conducts free training. You can probably locate a similar group in your area, such as the **High Technology Crime Investigation Association (HTCIA)**, an organization that exchanges information about techniques related to computer investigations and security.

User groups can be especially helpful when you need information about obscure OSs. For example, a user group helped convict a child molester in Pierce County, Washington, in 1996. The suspect installed video cameras in all the rooms of his house, served alcohol to young women to intoxicate them, and secretly filmed them playing strip poker. When he was accused of molesting a child, police seized his computers and other physical evidence. The investigator discovered that the computers used CoCoDos, an OS that had been out of use for years. The investigator contacted a local users group, which supplied the standard commands and other information needed to gain access to the system. On the suspect's computer, the investigator found a diary detailing the suspect's actions over the past 15 years, including the molestation of more than 400 young women. As a result, the suspect received a much longer sentence than he would have if he had molested only one child.

Build a network of computer forensics experts and other professionals, and keep in touch through e-mail. Find and cultivate professional relationships with people who specialize in technical areas different from your own. If you are a Windows expert, maintain contact with experts in Linux, UNIX, and Macintosh.

Outside experts can provide detailed information that you need to retrieve digital evidence. For example, in a recent murder case, a husband and wife owned a Macintosh store. When the wife was discovered dead, probably murdered, investigators found that she had wanted to leave her husband, but didn't because of her religious beliefs. The police got a search warrant and confiscated the home and office computers.

When the detective on the case examined the home Macintosh, he found that the hard disk had been compressed and erased. He contacted a Macintosh engineer, who determined the two software programs that had been used to compress the drive. Based on this information, the detective could retrieve information from the hard disk, including text files indicating that the husband had spent $35,000 in business funds to purchase cocaine and prostitution services. This piece of evidence proved crucial in making it possible for the prosecutor to convict the husband of premeditated murder.

Take advantage of news services devoted to computer forensics, which you can access with your e-mail software. You can also post a description of a forensics problem on an electronic mailing list, such as LISTSERV or Majordomo, to solicit advice from experts. These posts are broadcast to everyone on the list. In one case, an Intel computer contained digital evidence, but investigators couldn't access the hard disk without the password, which was hard-coded into the motherboard. When the detectives on the case began to run out of options and time, they posted a description of the problem on a mailing list. Someone responded and told them that a dongle (a mechanical device) would bypass the password problem. As a result, the detectives were able to convict the perpetrator.

PREPARING FOR COMPUTER INVESTIGATIONS

Computer investigations and forensics falls into two distinct categories: public investigations and private or corporate investigations (see Figure 1-4).

Public investigations involve government agencies responsible for criminal investigations and prosecution. Government agencies range from local, county, and state or provincial police departments to federal regulatory enforcement agencies. These organizations must observe items such as Article 8 in the Charter of Rights of Canada and, in the United States, Fourth Amendment issues related to **search and seizure** rules (see Figure 1-5).

The law of search and seizure protects the rights of all people, including people suspected of crimes; as a computer investigator, you must be sure to follow these laws, especially the laws of search and seizure. The Department of Justice (DoJ) updates its information on computer search and seizure on a regular basis (see *www.usdoj.gov/criminal/cybercrime/*).

Public investigations usually involve criminal cases and government agencies; private or corporate investigations, however, deal with private companies, nonenforcement government agencies, and lawyers. These private organizations are not governed directly by **criminal law** or Fourth Amendment issues, but by internal policies that define expected employee behavior and conduct in the workplace. Private corporate investigations also involve litigation disputes. Although private investigations are usually conducted in civil cases, a civil case can escalate into a criminal case, and a criminal case can be reduced to a civil case.

Private or corporate organizations
Company policy violations
Litigation disputes

Government agencies
Article 8 in Charter of Rights of Canada
U.S. Fourth Amendment search
   and seizure rules

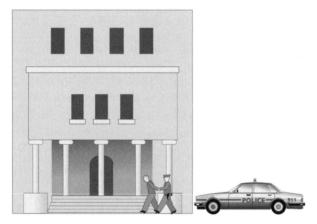

Figure 1-4   Public versus private sector investigations

Understanding Enforcement Agency Investigations

When conducting public computer investigations, you must understand your local city, county, state or province, and federal laws on computer-related crimes, including the standard legal processes and how to build a **criminal case**. In a criminal case, a suspect is tried for a criminal offense, such as burglary, murder, or molestation. To determine whether there was a computer crime, an investigator asks questions such as the following: What was the tool used to commit the crime? Was it a simple trespass? Was it a theft, a burglary, or vandalism? Did the perpetrator infringe on someone else's rights by cyberstalking or e-mail harassment?

Computers and networks are only tools that can be used to commit crimes and are, therefore, no different from the lockpick a burglar uses to break into a house or the slim-jim a car thief uses. For this reason, many states have added specific language to their criminal codes to define crimes that involve computers. That is, many states have expanded the

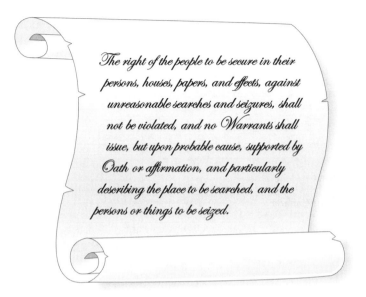

The right of the people to be secure in their persons, houses, papers, and effects, against unreasonable searches and seizures, shall not be violated, and no Warrants shall issue, but upon probable cause, supported by Oath or affirmation, and particularly describing the place to be searched, and the persons or things to be seized.

Figure 1-5   The Fourth Amendment

definition of laws for crimes such as burglary or theft to include taking data from a computer without the owner's permission, therefore making computer theft the same as breaking into someone's house and stealing the silver. Other states have instituted specific criminal statutes that address computer-related crimes, but typically don't include computer-related issues in standard trespass, theft, vandalism, or burglary laws. Until 1993, laws defining computer crimes did not exist. To this day, many have yet to be tested in court.

Computers are involved in many serious crimes. The most notorious are those involving child molestation. Digital images are stored on hard disks, Zip disks, floppy disks, and other storage media and circulated on the Internet. Other computer crimes concern missing children and adults because information about missing people is often found on computers. Drug dealers often keep information about transactions on their computers or personal digital assistants (PDAs). This information is especially useful because it helps law enforcement convict the person they arrested and helps locate drug suppliers and other dealers. In stalking cases, deleted e-mail, digital photos, and other digital evidence stored on a computer can help solve a case.

Following the Legal Processes

When conducting a computer investigation for potential criminal violations of the law, the legal processes you follow depend on local custom, legislative standards, and rules of evidence. In general, however, a criminal case follows three stages: the complaint, the investigation, and the prosecution (see Figure 1-6). Someone files a complaint, a specialist investigates the complaint and, with the help of a prosecutor, collects evidence and builds a case. If a crime has been committed, the case is tried in court.

Figure 1-6   The public-sector case flow

A criminal case begins when someone finds evidence of an illegal act or witnesses an illegal act. The witness or victim (referred to as the "complainant") makes a complaint to the police. Based on the incident or crime, the complainant makes an **allegation**, an accusation or supposition of fact that a crime has been committed.

A police officer or constable interviews the complainant and writes a report about the crime. The police department processes the report, and the department's upper management decides to start an investigation or log the information into a police blotter. The **police blotter** provides a record of clues to crimes that have been committed previously and is an aid for all current and future investigations. Criminals often repeat actions in their illegal activities, and these habits appear in a police blotter. This historical knowledge is useful when conducting investigations, especially in high-technology crimes.

Law enforcement is concerned with protecting the public good. As a result, not every good police officer is a computer expert. Some are computer novices; others might be trained to recognize what they can retrieve from a computer disk. To differentiate the training and experience law officers have, CTIN has established three levels of law enforcement expertise:

- *Level 1*—Acquiring and seizing digital evidence, normally performed by a street police officer.

- *Level 2*—Managing high-tech investigations, teaching the investigator what to ask for, understanding computer terminology and what can and cannot be retrieved from digital evidence. The assigned detectives usually handle the case.

- *Level 3*—Specialist training in retrieving digital evidence, normally performed by a data recovery or computer forensics expert, network forensics, or Internet fraud investigation.

If you are an investigator assigned to a case, recognize the level of expertise of police officers and others involved in the case. You should have Level 3 training to conduct the investigation and manage the case. You start by assessing the scope of the case, which includes the OS, hardware, and peripheral devices. You then determine whether resources are available to process all the evidence. For example, determine whether you have the proper tools to collect and analyze evidence and whether you need to call on other specialists to assist in collecting and processing evidence. After you have gathered the resources you need, your role is to delegate, collect, and process the information related to the complaint.

After you build a case, the information is turned over to the prosecutor. Your job is finished when you have used all known and available methods to extract data from the digital evidence that was seized. As the investigator, you must then present the collected evidence with a report to the government's attorney. Depending on your community and the nature of the crime, the prosecutor can be a prosecuting attorney, district attorney, state attorney, county attorney, Crown attorney, or U.S. attorney. In large organizations, the actual prosecutor is typically a deputy or an assistant attorney to the prosecuting attorney.

In a criminal or public case, if you have enough information to support a search warrant, the prosecuting attorney might direct you to submit an **affidavit**. This sworn statement of support of facts about or evidence of a crime is submitted to a judge to request a search warrant before seizing evidence. Figure 1-7 shows a typical affidavit. It is your responsibility to write the affidavit, which must include **exhibits** (evidence) that support the allegation to justify the warrant. You must then have the affidavit **notarized** under sworn oath, verifying that the information in the affidavit is true.

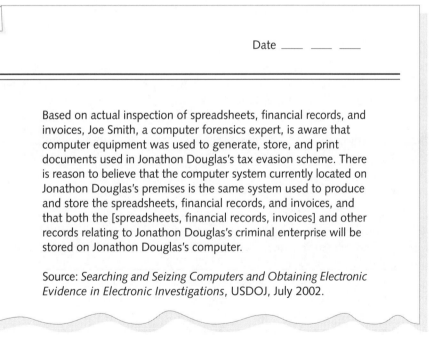

Figure 1-7   Typical affidavit language

After a judge approves and signs a search warrant, it's ready to be executed, meaning that you can collect evidence as defined by the warrant. After you collect the evidence, you process and analyze it to determine whether a crime actually occurred. The evidence is then presented in court, after which a judge, an administrative law judge, or a jury hands down a verdict.

Understanding Corporate Investigations

Private or corporate investigations involve private companies and lawyers who address company policy violations and litigation disputes, such as wrongful termination. When conducting a computer investigation for a private company, remember that business must continue with minimal interruption from your investigation. Because businesses usually focus on continuing their usual operations and making profits, many in a private corporate environment consider your investigation and apprehension of a suspect secondary to stopping the violation and minimizing damage or loss to the business. Businesses also strive to minimize or eliminate litigation, which is an expensive way to address criminal or civil issues. Corporate computer crimes can involve e-mail harassment, falsification of data, gender and age discrimination, embezzlement, sabotage, and **industrial espionage**, which involves selling sensitive company information to a competitor. Anyone with access to a computer can commit these crimes.

Embezzlement is a common computer crime, particularly in small firms. Typically, the owner is busy and trusts one person, such as the office manager, to handle daily transactions. When the office manager leaves, the owner discovers that some clients were overbilled, others were not billed at all, and money is missing. Rebuilding the paper and electronic trail can be tedious. Collecting enough to press charges might be beyond the owner's capabilities.

Corporate sabotage is most often committed by a disgruntled employee. The employee decides to take a job at a competitor's firm and collects critical files on a floppy or Zip disk before leaving. This type of crime can also lead to industrial espionage, which increases every year.

Investigators will soon be able to conduct digital investigations on-site without a lab and without interrupting work on a computer. Suppose that an assisted-care facility has an employee involved in an insurance scam. The person is overcharging the insurance company and then funneling the monies into his or her own bank account. The network server keeps track of patient billing and critical information, such as medication, serious medical conditions, and treatments, for each patient in the facility. To take that system offline for more than a short time could result in harm to one of the patients. Investigators cannot seize the evidence; instead, they acquire a disk image and any other pertinent information and allow the system to go back online as quickly as possible.

Organizations can help prevent and address these crimes by creating and distributing appropriate policies, making employees aware of the policies, and enforcing the policies.

Establishing Company Policies

One way that businesses can avoid litigation is to publish and maintain policies that employees find easy to read and follow. The most important policies are those that set rules for using the company's computers and networks. Published company policies provide the **line of authority** for a business to conduct internal investigations. The line of authority states who has the legal right to initiate an investigation, who can take possession of evidence, and who can have access to evidence.

Well-defined policies give computer investigations and forensic examiners the authority to conduct the investigation. Policies also demonstrate that an organization intends to be fair-minded and objective about how it treats employees and that it will follow due process for all investigations. Without defined policies, a business risks exposing itself to litigation by current or former employees.

Displaying Warning Banners

Another way a private or public organization can avoid litigation is to display a warning banner on its computer screens. A **warning banner** usually appears when a computer starts or connects to the company intranet, network, or virtual private network (VPN) and informs the end user that the organization reserves the right to inspect computer systems and network traffic at will. (An **end user** is a person using a computer workstation to perform routine tasks other than systems administration.) Without explicitly stating this right, employees may have an assumed **right of privacy** when using a company's computer systems and network accesses. With an assumed right of privacy, employees think that their transmissions at work are protected in much the same way that mail sent via the U.S. Postal Service is protected. Figure 1-8 shows a sample warning banner.

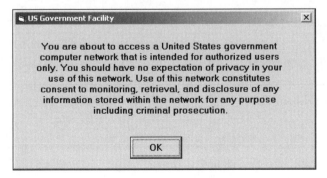

Figure 1-8   A sample warning banner

A warning banner establishes authority for conducting an investigation. By displaying a strong, well-worded warning banner, an organization doesn't need to obtain a search warrant or court order as required under Fourth Amendment search and seizure rules. If a company owns the computer equipment, it doesn't need a search warrant to seize the machinery. In a business with a well-defined policy, this right to inspect or search at will applies both to criminal activity and to company policy violations.

Computer systems users can include employees or guests. Employees can access the intranet, and guests can typically access only the main network. Companies can use two types of warning banners: one for internal employee access (intranet Web page access) and another for external visitor accesses (Internet Web page access). The following lists recommend the items that should be listed in all warning banners. Before applying these warnings, you should consult with the sponsoring organization's legal department for any additional required legal notices for your work area or department.

Depending on the type of organization you are part of, the following text can be used in internal warning banners:

- Access to this system and network is restricted.
- Use of this system and network is for official business only.
- Systems and networks are subject to monitoring at any time by the owner.
- Using this system implies consent to monitoring by the owner.
- Unauthorized or illegal users of this system or network will be subject to discipline or prosecution.

An organization such as a community college might simply state that systems and networks are subject to observation and monitoring at any time because members of the local community who aren't staff or students might use the facilities. A for-profit organization could have proprietary information on its network and use all the suggested text items. Guests such as employees of business partners might be allowed to use the system regularly.

The text that appears when a guest attempts to log on can be similar to the warnings in the following list:

- This system is the property of Company X.
- This system is for authorized use only; unauthorized access is a violation of law and violators will be prosecuted.
- All activity, software, network traffic, and communications are subject to monitoring.

As a corporate computer investigator, make sure a company displays a well-defined warning banner. Without a banner, your authority to inspect might conflict with the user's expectation of privacy, and a court might have to determine the issue of authority to inspect. States' laws vary on the expectation of privacy, but all states accept the concept of a waiver (of the expectation of privacy).

Some might argue that written policies are all that are necessary. However, in the actual prosecution of cases, warning banners have been critical in determining that an individual user of the system did not have a privacy interest in the information stored on the system. A warning banner has the additional advantage of being more easily presented in trial as an exhibit than a policy manual. Government agencies, such as the Department of Energy, Argonne National Labs, and Lawrence Livermore Labs, now require warning banners on all computer terminals on their system. Many corporations also require warning banners as part of the logon/startup process.

Designating an Authorized Requester

As mentioned earlier, investigations must establish a line of authority. In addition to warning banners that state a company's rights of computer ownership, businesses should specify an **authorized requester** who has the power to conduct investigations. Executive management should define this policy to avoid conflicts from competing interests between organizations or departments. In large organizations, competition for funding or management support can become so fierce that people sometimes weave false allegations of misconduct to prevent a competing department from delivering a proposal for the same source of funds.

Executive management must also define and limit who is authorized to request a computer investigation and forensic analysis to avoid trivial or inappropriate investigations. Generally, the fewer groups with authority to request a computing-related investigation, the better. Examples of groups that should be considered to have direct authority to request computer investigations in the corporate environment include the following:

- Corporate Security Investigations
- Corporate Ethics Office
- Corporate Equal Employment Opportunity Office
- Internal Auditing
- The general counsel or Legal Department

All other groups, such as the Human Resources or Personnel departments, should coordinate their requests through the Corporate Security Investigations group. This practice or policy separates the investigative process from the process of employee discipline.

Conducting Security Investigations

Conducting a computer investigation in the private sector is not much different from conducting one in the public sector. During public investigations, you search for evidence to support criminal allegations. During private investigations, you search for evidence to support allegations of abuse of a company's assets and, in some cases, criminal complaints. Three types of situations are common in the enterprise environment:

- Abuse or misuse of corporate assets
- E-mail abuse
- Internet abuse

Most computer investigations in the private sector involve misuse of computing assets. Typically, this misuse is referred to as employee violation of company rules. Computing abuse complaints center on e-mail and Internet misuse by employees, but could involve other computing resources, such as using company software to produce a product for personal profit. Figure 1-9 shows some of the ways employees can abuse their company computer privileges.

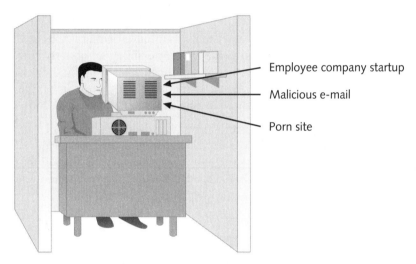

Figure 1-9 Employee abuse of computer privileges

The scope of an e-mail investigation ranges from excessive use of a company's e-mail system for personal use to making threats or harassing others via e-mail. Some of the most common e-mail abuses involve transmitting offensive and lewd messages. These types of messages create a **hostile work environment** that can result in an employee filing a civil lawsuit against a company that does nothing to prevent it (in other words, implicitly condones the e-mail abuse).

In addition to e-mail and general abuse, computer investigators also examine Internet abuse. Abuse of Internet privileges by employees ranges from excessive use, such as spending all day Web surfing, to viewing pornographic pictures on the Web while at work. An extreme situation of Internet abuse is viewing contraband pornographic images online, such as child pornography. Viewing contraband images is a criminal act in most jurisdictions, and the computer investigator must handle this situation with the highest level of professionalism. In later chapters, you learn the procedures and processes for conducting these types of investigations. By enforcing policy consistently, a company minimizes its liability exposure.

The role of a computer investigator is to help management verify and correct abuse problems in an organization.

Be sure to distinguish between a company's abuse problems and potential criminal problems. Abuse problems violate company policy, but might not be illegal if performed at home. Criminal problems involve acts such as industrial espionage, embezzlement, and murder. However, actions that appear to relate to internal abuse could also have criminal or civil liability. Because any civil investigation can become a criminal investigation, you must treat all the evidence you collect with the highest level of security and accountability. Later in this book, you learn the Federal Rules of Evidence, processes to ensure the chain of custody and apply them to computing investigations.

Similarly, your private corporate investigation might seem to involve a civil, noncriminal matter, but as you progress through your analysis, you might identify a criminal matter involved, too. Because of this possibility, you must always remember that your work can come under the scrutiny of the civil or criminal legal system. The Federal Rules of Evidence are the same for civil and criminal matters. By uniformly applying the rules to all investigations, you eliminate any concerns. These standards are emphasized throughout this book.

Corporations often follow the **silver-platter doctrine**, which is what happens when evidence is delivered by a civilian or corporate investigative agent to a law enforcement officer. Remember that a police officer is a law enforcement agent. If you are a corporate investigator, your job is to minimize the risk to your company. After you turn over the evidence to law enforcement and begin working under their direction, you become an agent of law enforcement, subject to the Fourth Amendment restrictions on search and seizure.

Litigation is costly, so after you have assembled evidence, offending employees are usually disciplined or let go with a minimum of fanfare. However, when you discover that a criminal act has been committed involving a third-party victim, generally you have a legal and moral obligation to turn the information over to law enforcement. In the next section, you learn about situations in which criminal evidence must be separated from any corporate proprietary information.

Distinguishing Personal and Company Property

Many company policies distinguish between personal and company computer property. One area that's difficult to distinguish involves PDAs and personal notebook computers. Say that an employee has purchased a PDA and hooks up the device to her company computer. As she synchronizes the information on her PDA with the information in her copy of Microsoft Outlook, she copies some of the data in her PDA to the company network. Because the data is on the company network, does the information on the PDA belong to the company or the employee?

Now suppose that the company gave the employee the PDA as part of her holiday bonus. Can the company claim rights to the PDA? Similar issues come up when an employee brings in a personal notebook computer and hooks it up to the company network. What rules apply? As computers become more entrenched into daily life, these issues are ones you'll encounter more often. These questions are still being debated, and companies are establishing their own policies to handle them. The safe policy is to not allow any personally owned devices to be connected to company-owned resources, thereby limiting the possibility of commingling personal and company data. This policy can be counterproductive; however, the risks must be known and addressed in company policy.

MAINTAINING PROFESSIONAL CONDUCT

Your **professional conduct** as a computer investigation and forensics analyst is critical because it determines your credibility. Professional conduct includes ethics, morals, and standards of behavior. As a professional, you must exhibit the highest level of ethical behavior at all times. To do so, you must maintain objectivity and confidentiality during an investigation, enrich your technical knowledge, and conduct yourself with integrity. By watching any current crime drama, you can see how attorneys attack the character of witnesses. Your character should be beyond reproach.

Maintaining objectivity means you must form and sustain unbiased opinions of your cases. Avoid making conclusions about your findings until you have exhausted all reasonable leads and considered the available facts. Your ultimate responsibility is to find digital evidence to support the allegation or exclude the defendant from the criminal conduct. You must ignore external biases to maintain the integrity of your fact-finding in all investigations. For example, if you are employed by an attorney, do not allow the attorney's agenda to dictate the outcome of your investigation. Your reputation and long-term livelihood depend on being objective in all matters.

You must also maintain an investigation's credibility by keeping the case confidential. Discuss the case only with people who need to know about it, such as other investigators involved in the case or someone in the line of authority asking for an update. If you need advice from other professionals, discuss only the general terms and facts about the case without mentioning specifics. All investigations you conduct must be kept confidential, until you are designated as a witness or required to release a report at the direction of the attorney or court.

In the corporate environment, confidentiality is critical, especially when dealing with employees who have been terminated because they were running home-based businesses at work on company machinery and time. The agreement might have been to lay off the employee without benefits or unemployment compensation in exchange for no bad references. If you give case details and the employee's name to others, your company could be sued for breach of contract.

In rare instances, your corporate case might become a criminal case as serious as murder. Because of the legal system, it could be years before the case gets to trial. If an investigator were to talk about the digital evidence, the case could be damaged because of pretrial publicity. When working for an attorney on an investigation, the attorney–work-product rule and attorney-client privilege apply to all communications. This means you can discuss the case only with the attorney or other members of the team working with the attorney. All communications about the case to other people requires the attorney's approval.

In addition to maintaining objectivity and confidentiality, you can enhance your professional conduct by continuing your training. The field of computer investigations and forensics is changing constantly. You should stay current with the latest technical changes in computer hardware and software, networking, and forensic tools. You should also learn about the latest investigation techniques that you can apply to your cases.

One way to enrich your knowledge of computer investigations is to record your fact-finding methods in a **journal**. A journal can help you remember how to perform tasks and procedures and use tools for both hardware and software. Be sure to include dates and important details that serve as memory triggers. Develop a routine of regularly reviewing your journal to keep your past achievements fresh in your mind.

To continue your professional training, you should attend workshops, conferences, and vendor-specific courses conducted by software manufacturers for their products. You might also need to continue your formal education. You enhance your professional standing if you have at least an undergraduate bachelor's degree in a computing field. If you don't have an advanced degree, consider graduate-level studies in a complementary area of study, such as business law or e-commerce.

Companies often supplement your education in exchange for a commitment to additional employment time.

TIP

In addition to education and training, membership in professional organizations adds to your credentials. These organizations often sponsor training and offer information exchanges of the latest technical improvements and trends in computer investigations. Also, monitor the latest book releases and read as much as possible about computer investigations and forensics.

As a computer investigation and forensics professional, your community expects you to achieve a high public and private standing and maintain honesty and integrity. You must conduct yourself with the highest levels of integrity in all aspects of your life. Any indiscreet actions on your part can embarrass you and give opposing attorneys opportunities to discredit you during your testimony in court or in depositions.

Chapter Summary

- ◻ Computer forensics is the systematic accumulation of digital evidence in an investigation. Computer forensics differs from network forensics, data recovery, and disaster recovery in scope, technique, and objective.

- ◻ Laws relating to digital evidence were established in the late 1960s.

❑ To be a successful computer forensics investigator, you must be familiar with more than one computing platform. To supplement your knowledge, develop and maintain contact with computer, network, and investigative professionals.

❑ Public and private computer investigations differ in that public investigations typically require a search warrant before the digital evidence is seized. The Fourth Amendment to the U.S. Constitution applies to governmental searches and seizures. During public investigations, you search for evidence to support criminal allegations. During private investigations, you search for evidence to support allegations of abuse of a company or person's assets and, in some cases, criminal complaints.

❑ The silver-platter doctrine refers to handing the results of private investigations over to the authorities because of indications of criminal activity.

❑ Computer forensics investigators must maintain an impeccable reputation to protect their credibility.

Key Terms

affidavit — The document, given under penalty of perjury, that an investigator creates detailing his or her findings. In many cases, this document is used to justify issuing a warrant or to deal with abuse in a corporation.

allegation — A charge made against someone or something before proof has been found.

authorized requester — In a corporation or company entity, the person who has the right to request an investigation, such as the chief security officer or chief intelligence officer.

computer forensics — Applying scientific methods to retrieve data and/or information that can be used as evidence.

computer investigations — Detailed examination and collection of facts and data from a computer and its operating system.

Computer Technology Investigators Northwest (CTIN) — A nonprofit group based in the Seattle–Tacoma, WA, area composed of law enforcement members, private corporation security professionals, and individual security professionals whose aim is to improve the quality of high-technology investigations in the Pacific Northwest.

criminal case — A case in which criminal law must be applied.

criminal law — Statutes applicable to a jurisdiction that state offenses against the peace and dignity of the jurisdiction and the elements that define those offenses.

data recovery — A specialty field in which companies retrieve files that were deleted accidentally or purposefully.

disaster recovery — A specialty field in which companies perform real-time backups, monitoring, data recovery, and hot site operations.

end user — The person who uses a software product. In most cases, this person has less expertise than the software designer.

enterprise environment — A large corporate computing system that can include one or more formerly independent systems.

exculpatory — Evidence that indicates the suspect is innocent of the crime.

exhibits — Items used in court to prove a case.

Fourth Amendment — The Fourth Amendment to the United States Constitution in the Bill of Rights dictates that the government and its agents must have probable cause for search and seizure.

High Technology Crime Investigation Association (HTCIA) — A nonprofit association for solving international computer crimes.

hostile work environment — An environment in which a person cannot perform his or her assigned duties because of the actions of others. In the workplace, these actions include sending threatening or demeaning e-mail or a co-worker viewing hate sites.

inculpatory — Evidence that indicates a suspect is guilty of the crime with which he or she is charged.

industrial espionage — Selling sensitive company or proprietary information to a competitor.

International Association of Computer Investigative Specialists (IACIS) — An organization created to provide training and software for law enforcement in the computer forensics field.

journal — A notebook or series of notebooks in which you record the techniques you used and the people who assisted you with specific types of investigations.

line of authority — The people or positions specified in a company policy who have the right to initiate an investigation.

litigation — The legal process leading to a trial with the purpose of proving criminal or civil liability.

network forensics — Monitoring network intrusions and illicit activity, including Internet usage.

network intrusion detection and incident response — Detecting attacks from intruders by using automated tools; also includes the manual process of monitoring network firewall logs.

notarized — Having a document witnessed and a person clearly identified as the signer before a notary public.

police blotter — A journal of criminal activity used to inform law enforcement personnel of current criminal activities.

professional conduct — Behavior expected of an employee in the workplace or other professional setting.

right of privacy — When employees think their transmissions at work are protected.

search and seizure — The legal act of acquiring evidence for an investigation. *See* Fourth Amendment.

search warrants — Legal documents that allow law enforcement to search an office, place of business, or other locale for evidence relating to an alleged crime.

silver-platter doctrine — The policy of submitting to the police by an investigator who is not an agent of the court when a criminal act has been uncovered.

vulnerability assessment and risk management — Determining the weakest points in a system, and then calculating the return on investment to decide which ones have to be fixed.

warning banner — Text that appears on computer screens when people log on to a company computer; this text states the ownership of the computer and appropriate use of the machine or Internet access.

REVIEW QUESTIONS

1. List two organizations mentioned in the chapter that provide computer forensics training.

2. Computer forensics and data recovery refer to the same activities. True or False?

3. Police must use procedures that adhere to:
   a. the Third Amendment
   b. the Fourth Amendment
   c. the First Amendment
   d. none of the above

4. The triad of computing security includes:
   a. detection, response, and monitoring
   b. vulnerability, detection, and monitoring
   c. vulnerability, intrusion response, and investigation
   d. vulnerability, intrusion response, and monitoring

5. List three common types of digital crime.

6. A corporate investigator must follow Fourth Amendment standards when conducting an investigation. True or False?

7. To what does the term "silver-platter doctrine" refer?

8. Policies can refer to items such as:
   a. when you can log on to a company network from home
   b. the Internet sites you can or cannot access
   c. the amount of personal e-mail you can send
   d. any of the above

9. List two items that should appear on an internal warning banner.

10. Warning banners are more likely to stand up in court than policy manuals. True or False?

11. A corporate investigator is considered an agent of law enforcement. True or False?

12. List two types of computer investigations that are typically conducted in the business environment.

13. What are the elements of ethical behavior for a computer investigator?

14. What is professional conduct and why is it important?

15. You can lose your job for violating a company policy, even if you do not commit a crime. True or False?

16. What is the purpose of maintaining a professional journal?

17. iLook is maintained by _____ .

18. The United States _____ maintains a manual on the proper procedures to follow for search and seizure of computers.

19. Laws and procedures regarding PDAs are:
    a. well established
    b. still being debated
    c. on the law books
    d. none of the above

20. Why should companies appoint an authorized requester for computer investigations?

HANDS-ON PROJECTS

Project 1-1

Use a Web search engine such as Google or Yahoo! and search for companies specializing in computer forensics. Select three of them and write a three- to five-page paper comparing what each company does.

Project 1-2

Research the criminal law in your state or province related to computer crime. If laws exist, list the source and how long they have been in existence. Identify cases that have been tried using these laws.

Project 1-3

Locate the computing usage policy for your school or place of work. What surprises you most about the policies? Which are most effective? Which are not enforceable?

Project 1-4

Compare Article 8 of the Charter of Rights of Canada to the U.S. Fourth Amendment. How do they differ? How are they similar? Use sources such as the U.S. Department of Justice Web site to justify your conclusions in a paper at least two pages long.

Project 1-5

Search the Internet for articles on computer crime prosecutions. Find at least two. Write one to two pages summarizing the two articles and identify any landmark decisions you find in your search.

Project 1-6

Is there a high-tech criminal investigation unit in your community? If so, who are the participants? E-mail the person in charge and let him or her know you are taking a course in computer forensics. Ask what the unit's policies and procedures are. Then write one to two pages summarizing your findings.

Project 1-7

Start building a professional journal for yourself. Find at least two electronic mailing lists you can join and three Web sites and read them on a regular basis. The electronic mailing lists should contain areas for OSs, software and hardware listings, people contacted or worked with, user groups, other electronic mailing lists, and the results of any research you have done thus far.

Project 1-8

Examine and list your community, state, or country's rules for search and seizure of criminal evidence. What concerns do you have after reading them?

CASE PROJECTS

Case Project 1-1

A lawyer in a law firm is suspected of embezzling money from a trust account. Who should conduct the investigation? If evidence is found to support the claim, what should be done? Write at least two pages detailing the steps to be taken, who is involved, and what items must be considered.

Case Project 1-2

A private corporation suspects an employee is using password-cracking tools to gain access to other accounts. The accounts include people in the Payroll and Human Resources departments. Write a two- to three-page paper outlining what steps to take, who should be involved, and what should be considered.

Case Project 1-3

An employee is suspected of operating his llama business using a company computer. It's been alleged that he is tracking the sales price of the wool and the cost of feed and upkeep on spreadsheets. What should the employer do? Write at least two pages explaining the tasks an investigator should perform.

2

UNDERSTANDING COMPUTER INVESTIGATIONS

After reading this chapter and completing the exercises, you will be able to:

♦ Prepare a case

♦ Begin an investigation

♦ Understand computer forensics workstations and software

♦ Conduct an investigation

♦ Complete a case

♦ Critique a case

This chapter gives an overview of how to manage a computing investigation. You learn about the problems and challenges examiners face when preparing and processing investigations, including the ideas and questions they must consider. This chapter also introduces you to three software tools (one DOS based and two GUI based) and explains how to use them. Throughout this chapter, you examine the details and differences among software packages and learn how to use the software in different scenarios. You also explore standard problem-solving techniques.

As a basic computer user, you can solve most software problems by working with a graphical user interface (GUI). A forensics professional, however, needs to interact with primary levels of the OS that are more fundamental than a GUI. You should be comfortable working from the command line. In several instances, it's your only alternative. Many computer forensics software tools involve working at the command line, and you should be prepared to learn how to use these tools.

In this chapter, you work with forensic disk images the size of floppy disks to perform the steps and projects in this chapter. After you know how to search for and find data on a small storage device, you can apply the same techniques to a large disk, such as a 40 GB or larger hard disk.

PREPARING A COMPUTER INVESTIGATION

Your role as a computer forensics professional is to gather evidence from a suspect's computer and determine whether the suspect committed a crime or violated a company policy. If the evidence suggests that a crime or policy violation has been committed, you begin to prepare a case, which is a collection of evidence you can offer in court or at a corporate inquiry. To gather the evidence in a computer forensics case, you investigate the suspect's computer and then preserve the evidence on a different computer. Before you begin investigating, however, you must follow an accepted procedure to prepare a case. By approaching each case methodically, you can evaluate the evidence thoroughly and document the chain of evidence, or **chain of custody**, which is the route the evidence takes from the time you find it until the case is closed or goes to court.

The following sections present two sample cases—one involving a computer crime and another involving a company policy violation. Each describes the typical steps of a forensics investigation, including gathering evidence, preparing a case, and preserving the evidence.

Examining a Computer Crime

Law enforcement often finds computers and computer components as they are investigating crimes, gathering other evidence, or making arrests. Computers can contain information that helps law enforcement determine the chain of events leading to a crime or information that provides evidence that's more likely to lead to a conviction. For example, consider the following scenario in which computers were involved in a crime. The police raided a suspected drug dealer's home and found a computer, several floppy disks, a **personal digital assistant (PDA)**, a cell phone, and several thumb drives (also called "key-chain drives") in a bedroom (see Figure 2-1). Two computers were "bagged and tagged," meaning they were placed in evidence bags and then labeled with tags along with the storage media as part of the search and seizure. The lead detective on the case wants you to investigate the computer to find and organize data that could be evidence of a crime, such as files containing the names of the drug dealer's contacts.

The acquisitions officer gives you documentation on items the investigating officers collected with the computer, including a list of the other storage media, such as removable disks, CDs, and DVDs. The acquisitions officer also notes that the computer is a Windows XP system and that the machine was running when they discovered it. Before shutting down the computer, officers photographed all the open windows on the Windows desktop, including one showing Windows Explorer. The acquisitions officer gives you digital photos of the desktop.

As a digital forensics investigator, you're grateful that the officers followed proper procedure when acquiring the evidence. With digital evidence, it's important to realize how easily key data, such as last accessed date, can be altered by an overeager investigator who is first on the scene. The U.S. Department of Justice (DoJ; *www.usdoj.gov*) has a document you can download that reviews proper acquisition of electronic evidence.

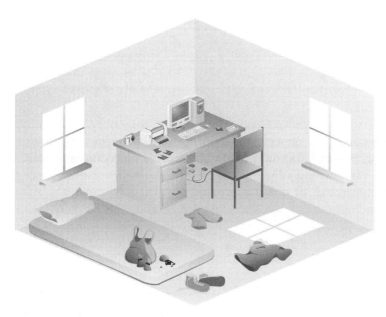

Figure 2-1 The crime scene

In your preliminary assessment, you assume that the floppy disks, hard disk, and other storage media include intact files, such as e-mail messages, deleted files, and hidden files. You have a range of software to use in your investigation. Your office owns Digital Intelligences DriveSpy and Image, Norton DiskEdit, Guidance Softwares EnCase, and AccessData's Forensics Toolkit. This chapter introduces you to these tools. In Chapter 4 you learn the strengths and weaknesses of a multitude of software packages, including the ones introduced in this chapter.

NOTE
Because some cases involve computers running legacy OSs, older versions of tools often need to be used in forensic investigations. For example, Norton Diskedit is an older tool, but you can still find it on the Norton SystemWorks 2004 CD.

After your preliminary assessment, you determine the risks in this case. Because drug dealers don't usually make information about their accomplices readily available, the files on the disks you received are probably **password protected**. You might need to acquire **password–cracking software** or find an expert who can help you crack the passwords.

Now you're ready to list the steps you need to take in the case, including how to address the risks and obstacles. Then you can begin the actual investigation and data retrieval.

Examining a Company Policy Violation

Companies often establish policies for computer use by employees. Employees surfing the Internet, sending personal e-mail, or otherwise using company computers for personal tasks during work hours can waste company time. Because lost time can cost companies millions of dollars, computer forensics specialists are often used to investigate policy violations. For example, consider the following scenario that involves a company policy violation.

George Montgomery has worked at a firm for several years and is now missing. Another employee, Martha, is also missing. No one knows where they are or has seen them in over a week, so Steve (George's supervisor) asks the IT Department to confiscate George's hard drive and all storage media in his work area.

Taking a Systematic Approach

When preparing a case, you can apply standard systems analysis steps to problem solving, which are explained in the following list. Later in this chapter, you apply these steps to cases.

- *Make an initial assessment about the type of case you are investigating*—To assess the type of case you're handling, talk to others involved in the case and ask questions about the incident. Have law enforcement or company security officers already seized the computer, disks, and other components? Do you need to visit an office or other locale? Was the computer used to commit a crime, or does it contain evidence about another crime?

- *Determine a preliminary design or approach to the case*—Outline the general steps you need to follow to investigate the case. If the suspect is an employee and you need to acquire his or her system, determine whether you can seize the employee's computer during working hours or if you have to wait until after office hours or the weekend. If you are preparing a criminal case, determine the information that law enforcement has already obtained.

- *Create a detailed design*—Refine the general outline by creating a detailed checklist of the steps you need to take and an estimated amount of time you need for each step. This outline helps you stay on track during the investigation.

- *Determine the resources you need*—Based on the OS of the computer you're investigating, list the software you plan to use for the investigation, noting any other software or tools you might need.

- *Obtain and copy an evidence disk drive*—In some cases, you might be seizing multiple computers along with Zip disks, Jaz drives, CDs, thumb drives, PDAs, and other removable media. (For the examples in this chapter, you are using only floppy disks.) Make a forensic copy of the disk.

- *Identify the risks*—List the problems you normally expect in the type of case you are handling. This list is known as a standard risk assessment. For example, if the suspect seems knowledgeable about computers, he or she might have set up a logon scheme that shuts down the computer or overwrites the data on the hard disk when someone tries to change the logon password.

- *Mitigate or minimize the risks*—Identify how you can minimize the risks. For example, if you're working with a computer on which convicted criminals or smart engineers have likely password protected the hard drive, you can make multiple copies of the original media before starting. Then if you destroy one or more copies during the process of retrieving information from the disk, you have additional copies.

- *Test the design*—Review the decisions you've made and the steps you've already completed. If you have already copied the original media, a standard part of testing the design involves comparing hash signatures (discussed in Chapter 6) to ensure that you made a proper copy of the original media.

- *Analyze and recover the digital evidence*—Using the software tools and other resources you've gathered, and overcoming the risks and obstacles you identified, examine the disk to find digital evidence. Later in this chapter, you recover data from a floppy disk.

- *Investigate the data you recover*—View the information recovered from the disk, including existing files, deleted files, and e-mail, and organize the files to help prove the suspect's guilt or innocence.

- *Complete the case report*—Write a complete report detailing what you did and what you found.

- *Critique the case*—Self-evaluation is a critical part of professional growth. After you complete a case, review it to identify successful decisions and actions and determine how you could have improved your participation.

The amount of time and effort you put into each step varies depending on the nature of the investigation. For example, in most casework, you need to create a simple investigation plan so that you don't overlook any steps. However, if a case involves many computers with complex issues to identify and examine, a detailed plan with periodic review and updates is essential.

A systematic approach helps you discover the information you need for your case, and you should gather as much information as possible. "Never enough information" should be your credo when you start a computing investigation and begin hunting for a crucial piece of evidence. Eventually, however, you might feel that you have too much information, especially if it's not logically organized. How do you process this information during a computer or network investigation? Where do you start gathering information? Moreover, what exactly are you looking for? These are some of the key questions you must answer during each phase of a computing investigation.

Assessing the Case

Recall that identifying case requirements involves determining the type of case you are investigating. Doing so means you should systematically outline the case details, including the nature of the case, the type of evidence available, and the location of the evidence.

In the previous company-policy violation case, suppose you have been asked to investigate George Montgomery, who is missing and suspected of conducting his own business using a company computer. Recall that Steve Billings, George's supervisor, has confiscated all of George's storage media that might contain evidence about George's business and his whereabouts. By talking to George's co-workers, Steve has learned the nature of George's business. You can begin assessing this case as follows:

- *Situation*—Employee abuse case.

- *Nature of case*—Side business on the employer's business computer.

- *Specifics about the case*—The employee is reportedly conducting a side business on his assigned computer. The business involves registering domain names for clients and setting up their Web sites at local Internet service providers (ISPs).

- *Type of evidence*—Floppy disk.

- *Operating system*—Microsoft Windows XP.

- *Known disk format*—FAT12.

- *Location of evidence*—One 3½-inch floppy disk that a manager recovered from the employee's assigned workstation. The manager has received complaints from the employee's co-workers that he's been spending too much time on his own business and not performing his assigned work duties. Company policy states that all company-owned computing assets are subject to inspection by company management at any time. Employees have no expectation of privacy when operating company computing systems.

Based on these details, you can determine the case requirements. You now know that the nature of the case involves employee abuse of computers, and you're looking for evidence that an employee was conducting his own business using his employer's computers. On the floppy disk Steve retrieved from the employee's computer, you're looking for any information related to Web sites, ISPs, or domain names. You know that the OS of the employee's computer is Windows XP and that the floppy disk the manager retrieved uses the FAT12 file system. To duplicate the floppy disk and find deleted and hidden files, you need a reliable computer forensics tool, such as DriveSpy or Image Acquisition (also called Image), from Digital Intelligence. Because Image and DriveSpy run at the command line, you need to use a Windows 98 workstation to acquire the evidence from the floppy disk. Most computer forensics labs set up dual-boot machines or use forensic boot floppies on newer machines that allow you to boot to the MS-DOS prompt. You will also use two GUI-based tools—AccessData's FTK Imager and Guidance Software's EnCase—to create a forensics image and examine the evidence. (In Chapters 4 and 8, you discover that the OS of the forensics machine is independent of the OS of the suspect's machine.) Because the manager already retrieved the floppy disk, you don't need to obtain the disk yourself.

In Chapter 3 you see the advantages of using older OSs to acquire certain data.

You call this case the Domain Name case and determine that your task is to gather data from the storage media seized to confirm or deny the allegation that George is conducting his own business on company time. Remember that the employee is only suspected of abuse and the evidence you obtain might be exculpatory—meaning it tends to, or helps, prove his innocence. You must always maintain an unbiased perspective and be objective in all your fact-findings. If you are systematic and thorough, you're more likely to produce consistently reliable results.

Planning Your Investigation

Now that you have identified the requirements of the Domain Name case, you can plan your investigation. You have already determined the kind of evidence you need; now you can identify the specific steps to gather the evidence, establish a chain of custody, and perform the forensic analysis. These steps become the basic plan for your investigation and indicate what you should do when. To investigate the Domain Name case, you should perform the following general steps. Most of these steps are explained in more detail in the following sections.

1. Acquire the floppy disk from George's manager.
2. Complete an evidence form and establish a chain of custody.
3. Transport the evidence to your computer forensics lab.
4. Secure your evidence in an approved secure container.
5. Prepare your forensic workstation.
6. Obtain the evidence from the secure evidence container.
7. Make a forensic copy of the **evidence floppy disk**.
8. Return the evidence floppy disk to the secure evidence container.
9. Process the copied floppy disk with your computer forensics tools.

The approved secure container you need in Step 4 should be a locked, fireproof locker or cabinet that has limited access. Limited access means that only you and other authorized people can open the evidence container.

The first rule for all investigations is to preserve the evidence, which means it should not be tampered with or contaminated. Because the IT Department members confiscated the storage media, you need to go to them for the evidence. When you talk to the IT Department manager, he confirms that the storage media has been locked in a secure cabinet since it was retrieved from George's desk. Keep in mind that even though this is a corporate policy matter, many cases are thrown out because the chain of custody cannot be proved or has been broken. When this happens, there's the possibility that the evidence has been compromised.

To document the evidence, you record details about the disk, including who recovered the evidence and when, and who possessed it and when. Use an **evidence custody form**, also called a chain-of-evidence form, which helps you document what has and has not been done with both the original evidence and forensic copies of the evidence.

Depending on whether you are working in law enforcement or private corporate security, you can create an evidence custody form to fit your environment. This form should be easy to read and use. It can contain information for one or several pieces of evidence. Consider creating a **single-evidence form** (which lists each piece of evidence on a separate page) and a **multi-evidence form** (see Figure 2-2), depending on the administrative needs of your investigation.

If necessary, document how to use your evidence custody form. Clear instructions help users remain consistent when completing the form. It also ensures that everyone uses the same definitions for collected items. Standardization helps maintain consistent quality for all investigations and avoid confusion and mistakes about the evidence you collect.

An evidence custody form usually contains the following information:

- *Case number*—The number assigned by your organization when an investigation is initiated.

- *Investigating organization*—The name of your organization. In large corporations with global facilities, several organizations might be conducting investigations in different geographic areas.

- *Investigator*—The name of the investigator assigned to this case. If many investigators are assigned, insert the lead investigator's name.

- *Nature of case*—A short description of the case. For example, in the corporate environment, it might be "Data recovery for corporate litigation" or "Employee policy violation case."

- *Location evidence was obtained*—The exact location the evidence was collected. If you are using a multi-evidence from, a new form should be created for each location.

- *Description of evidence*—Describes the evidence, such as "hard disk drive, 20 GB" or "one 3½-inch floppy disk, 1.44 MB." On a multi-evidence form, write a description for each item of evidence you acquire.

Corporation X					
Security Investigations					
This form is to be used for one to ten pieces of evidence					

Case No.:			Investigating Organization:	
Investigator:				
Nature of Case:				
Location where evidence was obtained:				

	Description of evidence:	Vendor Name	Model No./Serial No.
Item #1			
Item #2			
Item #3			
Item #4			
Item #5			
Item #6			
Item #7			
Item #8			
Item #9			
Item #10			

Evidence Recovered by:		Date & Time:	
Evidence Placed in Locker:		Date & Time:	

Item #	Evidence Processed by	Disposition of Evidence	Date/Time
			Page __ of __

Figure 2-2   A sample multi-evidence form used in a corporate environment

- *Vendor name*—The name of the manufacturer of the computer evidence. List a 20 GB hard disk drive, for example, as a Maxtor, or list a floppy disk as a Floppy Disk Imation 2HD IBM Formatted 1.44MB, for instance. In later chapters, you see how differences among manufacturers can affect data recovery.

- *Model number or serial number*—List the model number or serial number (if available) of the computer component. Many computer components, including hard disk drives, memory chips, and expansion slot cards such as internal modems, have model numbers but not serial numbers.

- *Evidence recovered by*—The name of the investigator who recovered the evidence. The chain of custody for the evidence starts with this information. If you insert your name, for example, you are declaring that you have taken control of the evidence. It is now your responsibility to ensure that nothing damages the evidence and that no one tampers with it. The person placing his or her name here is responsible for preserving, transporting, and securing the evidence.

- *Date and time*—The date and time the evidence was taken into custody. This information establishes exactly when the chain of custody starts.

- *Evidence placed in locker*—Indicates which secure evidence container is used to sort your evidence and when the evidence was placed in the secure locker.

- *Item #/Evidence processed by/Disposition of evidence/Date/Time*—When you or an authorized computing investigator obtain the evidence from the evidence locker for processing and analysis, list the specific item number and your name, and then describe what was done to the evidence.

- *Page*—The forms used to catalog all evidence for each location should have individual page numbers. List the page number, and indicate the total number of pages associated with this group of evidence. For example, if you collected 15 pieces of evidence at one location and your form has only 10 lines, you need to fill out two multi-evidence forms. The first form is filled in as "Page 1 of 2," and the second page is filled in as "Page 2 of 2."

Figure 2-3 shows a single-evidence form. The only major difference is that a single-evidence form lists only one piece of evidence per page. A single-evidence form gives you more flexibility in tracking individual pieces of evidence for your chain-of-custody log. Typically, it has more space for descriptive narrative, which is helpful when finalizing the investigation and creating a case report. Here you can accurately account for what was done to the evidence and what was found.

Use these forms as a reference to all actions taken for your investigative analysis.

Figure 2-3 A single-evidence form

You can use both multi-evidence and single-evidence forms in your investigation. By using two forms, you can keep the single-evidence form with the evidence and the multi-evidence form in your report file. Two forms also provide redundancy that can be used as a quality control for your evidence.

Securing Your Evidence

Computing investigations demand that you adjust your procedures to suit the case. For example, if the evidence for a case includes an entire computer system and associated media, such as floppy disks, Zip and Jaz cartridges, 4 mm DDS digital audio tape (DAT), and USB thumb drive storage devices, you must be flexible when you account for all the items. Some evidence is small enough to fit into an evidence bag. Other items, such as the CPU cabinet, monitor, keyboard, and printer, are too large.

To secure and catalog the evidence contained in large computer components, you can use large **evidence bags**, tape, tags, labels, and other products available from police supply vendors or office supply stores. When gathering products to secure your computer evidence, make sure they are safe and effective to use on computer components. Be cautious when handling any computer component to avoid damaging the component or coming into contact with static electricity, which can destroy digital data. When collecting computer evidence, make sure you use antistatic bags. (Consider using an antistatic pad with an attached wrist strap, too. Both help prevent damage to your computer evidence.)

Be sure to place computer evidence in a well-padded container. Padding prevents damage to the evidence as you transport it to your secure evidence locker, evidence room, or computer lab. Save discarded hard disk drive boxes, antistatic bags, and packing material for computer hardware when you or others acquire computer devices.

Because you might not have everything necessary to secure your evidence, you have to improvise. Securing evidence often requires you to build secure containers. If the computer component is large and contained in its own casing, such as a CPU cabinet, you can use evidence tape to seal all openings on the cabinet. Placing evidence tape over the floppy disk drive opening, power supply electrical cord insert, CD drive, and any other openings ensures the security of your evidence. As a standard practice, you should write your initials on the tape before applying it to the evidence. This practice makes it possible to prove later in court that the evidence hasn't been tampered with because the case could not have been opened nor could power have been supplied to the closed case with this tape in place. If the tape had been replaced, your initials wouldn't be present, which would indicate tampering. If you transport a CPU case, place a new floppy disk into the floppy disk drive to reduce possible damage to the drive while you're moving it.

Computer components have specific temperature and humidity ranges. If it's too cold, hot, or wet, computer components and magnetic media can be damaged. Even heated car seats can damage digital media, and placing a computer on top of a two-way car radio in the trunk can cause damage to magnetic media. When collecting computer evidence, make sure you have a safe environment for transporting and storing it until you reach a secure evidence container.

Understanding Data-Recovery Workstations and Software

Now you know what's involved in acquiring and documenting the evidence. In Chapter 3, you examine a complete setup of a computer forensics lab, or the **data-recovery lab**, which is where you conduct your investigations and where most of your equipment and software are located, including the secure evidence locker. Be aware that some companies that perform computer investigations also do data recovery, which is the more well-known and lucrative side of the business.

NOTE Please note the difference between data recovery and computer forensics. In data recovery, you don't necessarily need a sterile target drive when restoring the forensics image. Typically, the customer or your company just wants the data back. The other key difference is that in data recovery you usually know what you're trying to retrieve. In computer forensics, you might have an idea of what you're searching for, but not necessarily.

To conduct your investigation and analysis, you must have a specially configured personal computer (PC) known as a **computer forensics workstation** (or "forensic workstation"), which is a computer loaded with additional bays and forensics software. Depending on your needs, most computer forensics work can be performed on the following Microsoft OSs:

- MS-DOS 6.22
- Windows 95, 98, or Me
- Windows NT 3.5 or 4.0
- Windows 2000
- Windows XP

TIP Chapters 3 and 4 cover the software resources you need and the forensic lab and workstation in detail. Visit *www.digitalintel.com* to examine the specifications of the Forensic Recovery of Evidence Device (F.R.E.D.) unit.

TIP In addition to the Windows OSs listed, you can use Linux or UNIX to perform your analysis. Several open-source and freeware tools are available for this purpose. Note that Windows server software, such as Windows Server 2003 or Windows 2000 Server, isn't generally used for forensics work.

2

If you start Windows while you are examining a hard disk, Windows alters the evidence disk by writing data to the Recycle Bin file and damages the quality and integrity of the evidence you're trying to preserve. Chapter 7 covers which files Windows automatically updates at startup. Windows XP and 2000 systems also record the serial number of the hard drives and CPUs in a file, which can be difficult to recover.

Of all the Microsoft operating systems, the least intrusive (in terms of changing data) to floppy disks and hard disks is MS-DOS 6.22. Later in this chapter, you create a forensic boot floppy disk. This special bootable floppy disk doesn't alter the data on a suspect's computer disk. When you acquire data from a hard disk, you should start the system from a forensic boot floppy disk. The only exception is when you have installed a write-blocking device on the suspect's hard disk. You can use one of several write-blockers that enable you to boot to Windows without writing any data to the evidence disk.

There are many hardware write-blockers on the market. Some are inserted between the disk controller and the hard disk; others connect to internal cables or other devices. One write-blocker is based on technology from ACARD (*www.acard.com*). ACARD has developed a circuit card that is inserted between the computer's disk controller and the hard disk. Several ACARD models are based on the small computer system interface (SCSI). These SCSI-based devices enable you to connect and access Enhanced Integrated Drive Electronics (EIDE) disks. (See Chapters 7 and 8 for more information on hard disk types.) This special write-blocker circuit card prevents the OS from writing data to the connected disk drive. Other vendors sell write-blocker devices that connect to SCSI cards, FireWire, or USB 2.0 ports. Current vendors include Digital Intelligence with its SCSIBlock, FireBlock, and FireChief; Guidance Software, producer of FastBloc; and Intelligent Computer Solutions (*www.icsforensic.com*), which offers Image MaSSter Solo.

To avoid writing data to a disk, you set up your forensic workstation for Windows 98 so that it boots to MS-DOS rather than Windows 98. You need to use Windows 98 because Windows XP and 2000 can access only a DOS shell; they cannot boot directly to DOS. If you're not already familiar with MS-DOS, the following section introduces you to common MS-DOS commands. MS-DOS is the baseline for all computer forensics analysis. Many computer forensics acquisition tools work in the MS-DOS environment. Although these tools can operate from an MS-DOS window in Windows 98 or from the command prompt in Windows 2000/XP, some of their functions are disabled or generate error messages.

Windows products are being developed that make performing disk forensics easier. However, because Windows has limitations when performing disk forensics, you must still become skilled in acquiring data in MS-DOS. At times, the only way you can recover data is with an MS-DOS tool. Remember that no single computer forensics tool can recover everything. Each has its own strengths and weaknesses. Develop skills with as many tools as possible to become an effective computing investigator.

Setting Up Your Workstation for Computer Forensics

To set up your Windows 98 workstation to boot into MS-DOS, you need to modify the Windows 98 file Msdos.sys. You can add commands to this file so that Windows displays a Startup menu listing options for starting your computer, including booting into MS-DOS.

The C: drive root directory for Windows 98 contains a system file named Msdos.sys. The properties for this file are usually set to Hidden and Read-only so that it can't be changed inadvertently. You can add two commands to this file so that it displays the Windows Startup menu, also called the Startup Boot menu. To add commands to the Msdos.sys file, follow these steps:

1. Start Windows 98, if necessary. Click **Start**, **Run** to open the Run dialog box.

2. In the Open text box, type **msconfig** and then click **OK**. The System Configuration Utility dialog box opens (see Figure 2-4).

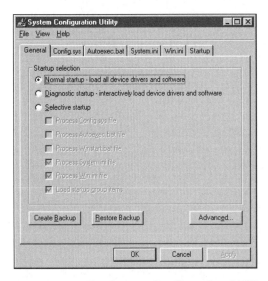

Figure 2-4   The System Configuration Utility dialog box

3. On the General tab, you select startup settings. Configuring the Startup menu is an advanced setting, so click the **Advanced** button to open the Advanced Troubleshooting Settings dialog box (see Figure 2-5).

4. Click the **Enable Startup Menu** check box so that Windows displays the Startup menu when you start the computer.

5. Click **OK** to close the Advanced Troubleshooting Settings dialog box.

6. Click **OK** to close the System Configuration Utility dialog box. Windows modifies the Msdos.sys file by turning on the Boot Menu switch.

Click to have Windows display the Startup menu when you start the computer

Figure 2-5   The Advanced Troubleshooting Settings dialog box

7. If a message appears asking whether you want to restart so that the changes can take effect, click **Yes**. Because the Startup menu has been enabled, ensure that 1. Normal is selected for the boot option, and press **Enter**.

Now you can open the Msdos.sys file, examine its settings, and add a command to the file to extend the amount of time the Startup menu appears before it closes and Windows starts as usual. Before you can modify the Msdos.sys file, you must change its Read-only and Hidden properties. Follow these steps to change those properties and add a command to the Msdos.sys file:

1. If necessary, change the Windows view setting to show hidden files. To do this, double-click **My Computer** on the desktop, and then click **View**, **Folder Options** from the menu. In the Folder Options dialog box, click the **View** tab. Under the Hidden files folder, click the **Show all files** option button, and then click **OK**.

2. In the My Computer window, navigate to the root folder on your hard disk, which is usually C:\. (If the drive where Windows is installed has a different drive letter, use that letter instead of C.) Right-click **Msdos.sys**, and then click **Properties** to open the Msdos.sys Properties dialog box.

3. In the Attributes section, click to clear the **Read-only** and **Hidden** check boxes. Click **OK** to close the Msdos.sys Properties dialog box.

4. Click **Start**, point to **Programs**, point to **Accessories**, and then click **Notepad**.

5. Click **File**, **Open** from the menu to open the Open dialog box. Navigate to the root drive, click **All Files (*.*)**, if necessary, in the Files of type list box, and then double-click **Msdos.sys**. The Msdos.sys file opens in Notepad.

NOTE Note that the BootMenu command is set to 1, which means it's turned on. A setting of 0 means it's turned off. (You might need to scroll to see the BootMenu command in this window.) If your Msdos.sys file contains a BootMenuDelay command, it's also set to 5 seconds by default.

6. If your Msdos.sys file doesn't include a BootMenuDelay line, press **Enter** at the end of the file to add a new line, and then type **BootMenuDelay=59**, as shown in Figure 2-6. If your file does have a BootMenuDelay line, extend the amount of time the Startup menu is displayed by changing the BootMenuDelay setting to **59**, which is the maximum setting for displaying the Startup menu.

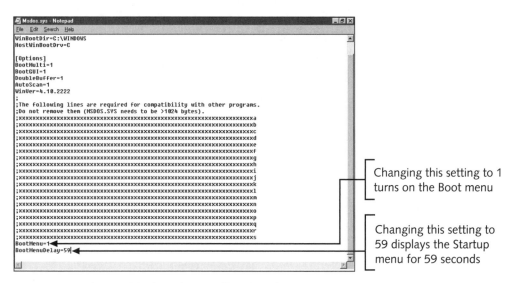

Figure 2-6 The modified Msdos.sys file after the BootMenu command has been turned on

7. Click **File**, **Save** from the menu. Close Notepad.

8. Now you need to restart your computer using the Normal boot option. If you're working in a computer lab, check with your instructor or technical support person to make sure you have permission to restart your computer. Click **Start**, **Shut Down**, **Restart**, **OK**.

Next, you see how to install DriveSpy and Image on your computer. The CD that accompanies this book contains a 120-day license for your computer. You need to contact the vendor for a license key. Please note that the company might take several days for a response—it's not an autoresponder.

1. Your computer should have rebooted to Windows 98. Use Windows Explorer to create folders named **Chap02\Chapter** and **Tools** in the work folder for this book.

TIP

In the "Read This Before You Begin" section of this book, you or your instructor created a folder on your system where you can store your work. This book calls this folder the "work folder," which should be created on a drive that your instructor specifies. Create the Chap02\Chapter and Tools folders in your work folder.

2

2. Using Windows Explorer, copy the following Digital Intelligence files, after you have received them from Digital Intelligence, to the Tools folder in your work folder:

- Drivespy.exe
- Drivespy.hlp
- Drivespy.ini
- Image.exe
- Image.ini

Your instructor will tell you where the files are located on the lab machines. For both Drivespy.exe and Image.exe, you must create a command-line batch file that appends an additional path defining the location for the Digital Intelligence tools so that you can use the forensic tools from any folder on your hard disk. To do so, follow these steps to create a text file in Notepad called Toolpath.bat:

1. To start Notepad, click **Start**, point to **Programs**, point to **Accessories**, and then click **Notepad**.

2. Type the command **SET PATH=%PATH%;C:*work folder*\Tools** to define the path to your forensics tools. Replace *work folder* with the name of the work folder you're using to store your files for this book. C: is the drive where your work folder is located.

3. Click **File**, **Save As** from the menu. In the Save As dialog box, click the **Save in** list arrow, and then navigate to C:\Windows. (If Windows is installed on a different drive, use that drive letter instead of C.) Click the **Save as type** list arrow, and then click **All Files (*.*)**. In the File name text box, type **Toolpath.bat**. Click **Save**.

4. Close Notepad.

5. Shut down your computer by clicking **Start**, **Shut Down**, **Restart**, **OK**.

6. The Windows 98 Startup Menu appears, as shown in Figure 2-7. Use option 1 for a Normal boot to Windows 98 and option 5 for Command prompt only to boot to MS-DOS. You have approximately 59 seconds to respond to the menu. If you do not select one of the numbered mode options, the computer boots to Normal mode (Windows 98).

7. To boot your workstation into MS-DOS mode, at the Enter a choice prompt, type **5** to select Command prompt only and then press **Enter**.

```
Microsoft Windows 98 Startup Menu


    1. Normal
    2. Logged (\BOOTLOG.TXT)
    3. Safe mode
    4. Step-by-step confirmation
    5. Command prompt only
    6. Safe mode command prompt only

Enter a choice: 1          Time remaining: 57







F5=Safe mode   Shift+F5=Command mode prompt   Shift+F8=Step-by-step confirmation [N]
```

Figure 2-7   The Windows 98 Startup menu

Your workstation boots to the root level of your C:\ disk drive and displays a C:\>
command prompt. You have now set up your workstation so that you can perform some
basic computer forensics acquisitions and analysis at the DOS level.

Conducting an Investigation

Now you're ready to return to the Domain Name case. You have created a plan for the
investigation, set up your forensic workstation, and installed the software you need to
examine the evidence. To begin conducting an investigation, you start by copying the
evidence using a variety of methods. Recall that no single method retrieves all the data from
a disk, so using several tools to retrieve and analyze data is a good idea.

Start by gathering the resources you identified in your investigation plan. You need the
following items:

- Original storage media
- Evidence custody form
- Evidence container for the storage media, such as an evidence bag
- Bit-stream imaging tool; in this case, the Digital Intelligence Image utility
- Forensic workstation to copy and examine your evidence
- Secure evidence container

TIP

You use the Digital Intelligence Image utility to copy a floppy disk later in this chapter. For more information on this utility, visit the Digital Intelligence Web site at *www.digitalintel.com*. The PDF file included on the accompanying CD also explains the utility.

2

Gathering the Evidence

Now you're ready to gather evidence for the Domain Name investigation. When you gather evidence, recall that you need antistatic bags and pads with wrist straps to ensure that you are grounded to prevent static electricity from damaging fragile electronic evidence. You also want to make forensic copies that are exact duplicates.

You need to acquire George Montgomery's storage media from the IT Department and then secure the disk in an evidence bag. You perform the following steps to collect the evidence and transport it to your forensic facility:

1. Arrange to meet the IT manager so that you can interview him and pick up the storage media.

2. After interviewing the IT manager, fill out the evidence form, have him sign it, and then sign it yourself.

3. Store the storage media in an evidence bag, and then transport it to your forensic facility.

4. Carry the evidence to a secure container, such as a locker, cabinet, or safe.

5. Complete the evidence custody form. As mentioned earlier, if you're using a multi-evidence form, you can store the form in the file folder for the case. If you're also using single-evidence forms, store them in the secure container with the evidence. Reduce the risk of tampering by limiting access to the forms.

6. Secure your evidence by locking the container.

Understanding Bit-stream Copies

A **bit-stream copy** is a bit-by-bit copy of the original storage medium and is an exact duplicate of the original disk. Recall that the more exact the copy, the better chance you have of retrieving the evidence you need from the disk. A bit-stream copy is different from a simple backup copy of a disk. Backup software can only copy or compress files that are stored in a folder or are of a known file type. Backup software cannot copy deleted files or e-mail messages or recover file fragments.

Bit-streaming literally means that a disk is copied bit by bit, creating an exact image of the disk. A **bit-stream image** is the file that contains the bit-stream copy of all the data on a disk or disk partition. To create an exact image of an evidence disk, copying the bit-stream image to a target work disk that's identical to the evidence disk is preferable (see Figure 2-8). The target disk's manufacturer and model, in general, should be the same as the manufacturer and model of the original evidence disk. The size of both disks should also be the same, although some software tools that create bit-stream images can accommodate a target disk that's a different size than the original evidence disk is. These imaging tools are discussed in Chapter 9. As you'll see, some of the latest versions of forensic tools enable you to work directly from the forensic image.

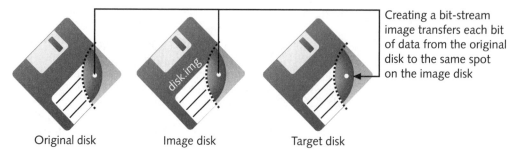

Creating a bit-stream image transfers each bit of data from the original disk to the same spot on the image disk

Original disk   Image disk   Target disk

Figure 2-8 Transfer of data from original to bit-stream image to target

Occasionally, the track and sector maps on the original and target disks don't match, even if you use disks of exactly the same size. Newer tools such as FTK Imager are available that adjust for the target-drive geometry.

TIP

CREATING A FORENSIC BOOT FLOPPY DISK

Recall that your goal when conducting a computer forensics examination is not to alter any portion of the original data on a disk when making a copy or examining the data. The preferred way to avoid modifying evidence data is to never examine the original evidence disk. Thus far, you have learned how to make a copy of a floppy disk so that you can re-create and then examine it. The same principle applies when examining hard disks—you must preserve the original disk and not alter its contents during your examination.

In the following section, you make a boot floppy disk to serve as your forensic boot floppy disk. Whenever a computer is started, it accesses files on the hard disk, even if the computer boots from a floppy disk that contains system files. When the boot process accesses files on the hard disk, it changes their date and time stamps, which can jeopardize an investigation, especially if a goal in the investigation is to determine when the computer was last used. By booting the computer without a specially configured floppy disk, you destroy information important to an investigation. Windows 9x can also alter other files, especially if DriveSpace is implemented on a FAT16 disk drive. The boot floppy disk you create is specially configured so that the boot process doesn't alter any files on the hard disk when the computer is powered on, thus preserving the suspect's disk drive. Having access to a software or hardware write-blocker for the suspect's drive is always a good precaution.

Assembling the Tools for a Forensic Boot Floppy Disk

2

To make a boot floppy disk for forensics data acquisition, you need the following items:

- Disk editor, such as Norton Disk Edit or Hex Workshop, installed on your computer
- Floppy disk containing files you no longer need
- MS-DOS operating system, such as MS-DOS 6.22, Windows 95B (OSR2), or Windows 98 running on your computer, not Windows XP, 2000, Me, or NT
- Computer that can boot to a true MS-DOS level—that is, an MS-DOS 6.22, a Windows 95B (OSR2), or a Windows 98 computer
- Forensics acquisition tool, such as DriveSpy, EnCase, SafeBack, or SnapCopy
- Write-blocking tool to protect the evidence drive

The first task is to make the floppy disk bootable from the MS-DOS prompt, meaning that it contains the system files needed to boot the computer. The following steps use a Windows 98 computer to make the boot floppy disk. The process is similar for Windows 95.

1. Boot into DOS mode. Insert the floppy disk into your computer's floppy disk drive, which is usually drive A.

2. At the C:\> prompt, format the floppy disk by typing **format a: /u /s**, pressing **Enter**, and then pressing **Enter** again when ready. When the system is done formatting, it prompts you for a volume name. Type in **Bootdisk**, and press **Enter**. Next, you're asked if you want to format another disk. Type **n** for no, and press **Enter**.

3. At the DOS prompt, type **attrib –r –h –s a:*.*** and then press **Enter** to remove the Read-only and Hidden attributes for all files on the floppy disk.

4. On the A: drive, delete the Drvspace.bin file by typing **del a:\drvspace.bin** and pressing **Enter**.

To make the floppy disk bootable from Windows Explorer, follow these steps:

1. Boot into Windows 98. (Note: If your workstation's BIOS is set to boot from the A: floppy drive first, remember to remove the bootable floppy disk from the drive before you start Windows.) Insert the floppy disk into your computer's floppy disk drive, which is usually drive A.

2. Open Windows Explorer. Right-click the **3½ Floppy (A:)** icon, and then click **Format**.

3. Click **Full** in the upper pane, and click to enable the **Copy system files** check box in the lower pane. Click **Start**. When you're done, change the file attributes by right-clicking the files and clicking **Properties**. Click to clear the **Hidden** and **Read-only** check boxes, and click **OK**. Click **Close** in the Format Results dialog box, and then click **Close** in the Format dialog box.

4. Right-click the **Drvspace.bin** file, click **Delete**, and then click **Yes** in the Confirm File Delete message box.

After you create a bootable floppy disk, update the operating system files to remove any reference to the hard disk, which is usually the C: drive. This ensures that when you're acquiring a FAT16 or FAT32 evidence disk, your boot floppy disk does not contaminate it. You need to modify the Command.com and Io.sys files to make a forensic boot disk. The following steps show you how to use Hex Workshop for this task. Hex Workshop should already be installed on your computer before you perform these steps. If you're using Norton Disk Edit, first boot your workstation into MS-DOS mode. For further information on how to use Norton Disk Edit, refer to its online help.

1. If necessary, boot your workstation into Windows.

2. Insert the boot floppy disk you created in the previous set of steps into your computer's floppy disk drive.

3. The changes from this point can be done in Windows 98 or in Windows 2000. (Screen shots in these steps were taken using Windows 2000.) In Windows 2000, open Windows Explorer, and click **Tools, Folder Options** from the menu. Click the **View** tab, if necessary, and under the Advanced settings section, click **Show Hidden files and folders**, and then click **OK**. In Windows 98, click **View, Folder Options** from the Windows Explorer menu. Click the **View** tab. Under Hidden files, click the **Show all files** option button (if necessary), and click **OK**.

4. To start Hex Workshop, double-click the **Hex Workshop** icon on your desktop or click **Start**, point to **Programs** (**All Programs** in Windows XP), point to **Hex Workshop**, and then click **Hex Workshop**. The opening window shown in Figure 2-9 might differ slightly from your Hex Workshop window, depending on the version.

5. Click **File, Open** from the menu.

6. In the Open dialog box, navigate to the A: drive. Click **Command.com**, and then click **Open**.

7. To replace references to the hard disk (drive C:) in Command.com, start by clicking **Edit, Replace** from the menu.

8. In the Replace dialog box, click the **Type** list arrow under the Replace section. A list of data you can replace is displayed. Click **Text String**.

9. In the Find text box, type **c:** or the letter of your primary hard disk. In the Replace text box, type **a:** (see Figure 2-10).

10. Click **OK**. The Replace dialog box opens, which you use to search for and replace the specified text. Click the **Replace All** button, and then click **OK**.

11. Click **File, Save** from the bar to save the changes you made to Command.com on the floppy disk. If a message is displayed asking whether you want to make a backup of Command.com, click **No**.

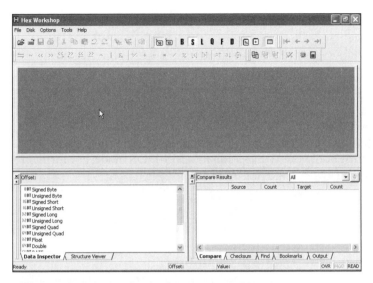

Figure 2-9   The opening window in Hex Workshop

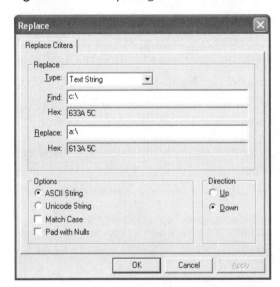

Figure 2-10   Specifying what text to replace in the Command.com file

In the following steps, you modify the Io.sys file to change all references to the C: drive and the DriveSpace utility. You don't want to activate DriveSpace because it can corrupt data.

1. Click **File**, **Open** from the Hex Workshop menu.

2. In the Open dialog box, navigate to the A: drive, and then click **Io.sys**.

3. Click the **Open** button to open the file in Hex Workshop (see Figure 2-11).

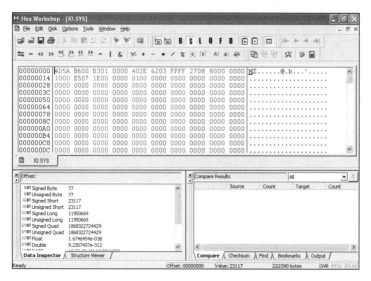

Figure 2-11 Io.sys open in Hex Workshop

4. Click **Edit**, **Replace** from the menu. In the Replace dialog box, click the **Type** list arrow, and then click **Text String**, if necessary. In the Find text box, type **c:**. In the Replace text box, type **a:**, and then click **OK**.

5. In the Replace dialog box, click the **Replace All** button, and then click **OK**.

6. Click **Edit**, **Replace** from the menu. In the Find text box, delete the current text, and then type **.bin**. In the Replace text box, type **.zzz** (see Figure 2-12). Replacing .bin with .zzz prevents Io.sys from referencing DriveSpace. Note that the .zzz extension isn't associated with any program; it's used here simply to change .bin to something else.

7. Click **OK**. In the Replace dialog box, click the **Replace All** button, and then click **OK**.

8. Click **File**, **Save** from the menu to save your changes to Io.sys on the floppy disk. If a message is displayed asking whether you want to make a backup of Io.sys, click **No**.

9. Click **File**, **Exit** from the menu to close Hex Workshop. Restart your machine with the forensic boot floppy disk to test it.

10. Store your forensic boot floppy disk in a safe place.

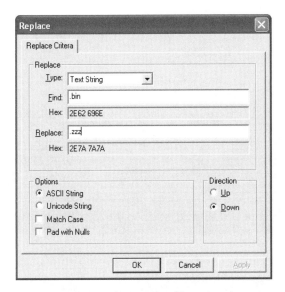

Figure 2-12   Replacing the file extension

Now you can use the floppy disk to boot a suspect's computer without contaminating evidence on the hard disk. Next, you add forensic software to the floppy disk so that you can use it to acquire an evidence disk. The specific forensics software you add to your forensic boot floppy disk depends on the tools you have available. In the following steps, you copy the Digital Intelligence software tools to the forensic boot floppy disk:

1. Access the command prompt on your computer.

2. Navigate to the **Tools** folder in your work folder.

3. Place your forensic boot floppy disk in the floppy disk drive. You need both DriveSpy and Image on the boot disk.

4. At the command prompt, type **copy *.* a:** and press **Enter**.

5. Verify that the files have been copied to the floppy disk by typing **dir a:** and pressing **Enter**.

6. Exit the command prompt.

Now you should make a backup copy of this floppy disk. You can use the MS-DOS Diskcopy command or you can make an image copy with the Digital Intelligence Image utility. You need your original forensic boot floppy disk and an extra blank floppy disk. To make a duplicate disk with Diskcopy, follow these steps:

1. Insert the original forensic boot floppy disk in the floppy disk drive (for example, drive A:).

2. Access a command prompt. Type **diskcopy a: a: /v** and then press **Enter**.

3. Follow the prompts to make the duplicate copy, inserting the blank formatted floppy disk when requested.

Use these steps to make an image copy of the forensics disk with the Image utility:

1. Insert the original forensic boot floppy disk in the floppy disk drive (for example, drive A:).

2. Access a command prompt and navigate to the **Tools** folder located in your work folder, which is where you originally installed the DriveSpy and Image programs.

3. With the forensic floppy disk in the drive, type **image a: for_boot.dat** and press **Enter**.

4. When the command prompt is displayed, remove the forensic boot floppy disk and place the blank disk in the drive.

5. Type **image for_boot.dat a:** and press **Enter** to transfer the files to the new disk. You now have a copy of your forensic boot floppy on a disk and on your hard disk.

Retrieving Evidence Data Using a Remote Network Connection

If you're working on a LAN, you can retrieve bit-stream image copies of disks through a workstation's network connections. An older product called SnapBack originally made it possible to boot a suspect's workstation with a specially configured boot floppy disk that had the appropriate network drivers to connect to a remote server. Other tools, such as EnCase v4, now offer the same feature as SnapBack. R-Tools also allows remote imaging of a drive.

Acquiring a bit-stream image over a LAN can be time consuming, even with a 1000-Mb connection. However, if you have a direct NIC-to-NIC connection with a twisted-pair network cable, you can acquire a bit-stream copy through a network connection in a reasonable amount of time. This feature is available in Guidance Software's EnCase v3 or later.

Copying the Evidence Disk

After you retrieve and secure the evidence, you're ready to copy the evidence disk and analyze the data. The first rule of computer forensics is to preserve the original evidence. Conduct your analysis only on a forensic copy of the original media. A **forensic copy** is an exact duplicate of the original data. To make a forensic copy of a floppy disk, you must create a bit-stream data copy of the disk using an MS-DOS command or a specialized tool, such as the Digital Intelligence Image utility.

Making a Bit-stream Copy of a Floppy Disk Using MS-DOS

One method of making a duplicate copy of your evidence floppy disk is to use the MS-DOS command Diskcopy with the verification switch /v, which verifies that the data is copied correctly. This command copies one floppy disk to another floppy disk. Its only disadvantages are that it does not create a separate image file of the original floppy disk and does not generate a hash value. Use the Diskcopy command only if you have no other tools available to preserve the original data. The Image tool gives you a reliable backup of your floppy disk evidence. It generates a verifiable hash value, but Diskcopy does not generate a hash value that's admissible in court as proof of nontampering. This topic is covered at length in Chapter 6.

To make a bit-stream copy of a floppy disk, retrieve the floppy disk (the storage medium) from your secure evidence container, and write the appropriate information on your evidence custody form. Then complete the following steps at the DOS prompt on your forensics workstation to make a bit-stream copy of a floppy disk using MS-DOS:

1. Because the evidence floppy disk you retrieved from the IT manager is the original storage medium, you must write-protect the floppy disk. Move the write-protect tab on the floppy disk to the open position. (When working with multiple disks, be sure to specify, in your working notes, on which disks you moved the write-protect tab. Some judges have required investigators to return the evidence to the owner in exactly the same condition in which it was seized which includes correct repositioning of the write–protect tabs.)

2. If necessary, boot your forensic workstation to the MS-DOS prompt.

3. Insert the evidence floppy disk into your workstation's floppy disk drive (usually the A: drive). The original disk is your source disk.

4. At the MS-DOS prompt, type the command **diskcopy a: a: /v** and press **Enter**. Recall that the /v switch verifies that the data is copied correctly. You might be prompted to insert the source disk; if you are, insert the disk and press **Enter**.

5. After the disk is copied, you are prompted to place a target disk in the A: drive. This is where you want to store the copy of the evidence disk. Remove the evidence disk and insert a blank unformatted or formatted disk into the floppy drive. The software automatically overwrites everything. Follow the on-screen instructions and proceed with the data copy.

6. As the data is being copied to the target floppy disk, place the original floppy disk into your secure evidence container. When asked whether you want to create another duplicate of the disk, type **n** for no. When asked whether you want to copy another disk, type **n** for no.

7. Place a label on the working copy of the floppy disk, if necessary, and then write **Domain Name working copy #1** on the label.

Always remember to maintain your chain of custody for your evidence.

In a live investigation, you should place the original floppy disk into your secure evidence container as the data is being copied to the target floppy disk.

Acquiring a Bit-stream Copy of a Floppy Disk Using Image

You can also make a bit-stream copy of a floppy disk using Digital Intelligence's Image utility. This tool creates a file that contains every byte of data on a floppy disk, creating an image of the floppy disk rather than just a copy. The unique feature of this tool is that it preserves your data in a compact data file (also called an **image file**) on your disk. After you have created an image file of the floppy disk, you can transfer the forensic image to another floppy disk.

Although newer tools on the market can read directly from the image file, with most computer forensics tools, recall that the image file must be restored to a medium of the same size and type to access the data. In this way, working with image files is similar to restoring a file from a true backup utility that does not merely copy files.

When you use Image, you first acquire a bit-stream copy of a floppy disk and store that copy in a file on your hard disk. You complete this task in the following steps. After that, you'll copy the file from your hard disk to a blank floppy disk, as shown in the following section.

As described earlier, in a live investigation, you first retrieve the original floppy disk or storage medium from your secure evidence container, and then fill out your evidence custody form before performing the following steps at your forensic workstation. Because the image file for this case is in your student data files, you don't need to perform these steps. You can, however, practice the steps using one of your own disks. To acquire a bit-stream copy of a floppy disk using Image, follow these steps:

1. Write-protect the original floppy disk by moving the write-protect tab to the open position.

2. If necessary, boot your computer to MS-DOS command mode.

3. Insert the original floppy disk into your computer's floppy disk drive, which is usually the A: drive. This is the source disk.

4. Change to the Tools folder. Run the Toolpath.bat file by typing in **toolpath** and pressing **Enter**. The system should respond by echoing the path, including the newly added Tools folder.

5. At the command prompt, change to the Chap02\Chapter folder in your work folder on the hard disk by typing **cd c:*work folder*\Chap02\Chapter** and then pressing **Enter**. This command assumes that your work folder is in the root directory and the Chap02 folder is in the work folder. Substitute the names of the folders you're using on your computer, if needed.

6. To acquire data from the original evidence floppy disk, you need to be in the directory you intend to save the image to. Next, type the command **image a: Test.img**, and then press **Enter**. If your disk is in a floppy drive other than A:, substitute that drive letter in the command. Replace *work folder* with the name of the work folder on your hard disk. If the drive letter of your hard disk is not C, substitute that drive letter for C. This command generates the bit-stream copy and stores it in the *work folder*\Chap02\Chapter folder.

7. Remove the original evidence floppy disk. In a live investigation, you would return the original disk to your secure evidence container.

You have now acquired the bit-stream copy of your evidence and stored it on your hard disk in a file called Test.img. The next step is to transfer the image of your evidence to a target disk such as a floppy disk to create a working copy.

Making a Bit-stream Copy of Evidence Using Image

Now that you have created a bit-stream image copy of your original evidence floppy disk, you must create a working copy of the disk, one that you can analyze without contaminating the evidence. When you transfer the contents of the image file you created in the previous steps to a different disk, Image uncompresses the image file and creates an exact duplicate of the disk, including **slack space** and **free space** on the disk. Slack space is the disk area between the end of a file and the allotted space for that file, and free space is any space on the drive not currently assigned to an existing file. (Both terms are covered in detail in Chapters 7 and 8.)

1. If necessary, boot your computer to Windows.

2. Using Windows Explorer or My Computer, find the **C2Chap01.img** file in your student data files.

3. Copy the **C2Chap01.img** file from your student data files to the Chap02\Chapter folder in your work folder on your hard disk.

4. Reboot your computer to MS-DOS mode.

TIP

You can also access the MS-DOS prompt in a window if you're using Windows 98 or from the command line if you're using Windows 2000 or XP.

5. Change to the Tools folder. Run the Toolpath.bat file by typing in toolpath and pressing **Enter**. The system should respond by telling you the Tools folder has been added to the path.

6. At the MS-DOS prompt, change to the *work folder*\Chap02\Chapter directory, if necessary, by typing the command **cd c:*work folder*\Chap02\Chapter** and pressing **Enter**.

7. Place a blank formatted floppy disk into your computer's floppy disk drive (usually drive A:).

8. At the MS-DOS prompt, type the command **image C2Chap01.img a:**, and then press **Enter**.

9. Place a label on the working copy of the floppy disk, if necessary, and then write **Domain Name working copy #2** on the label.

You have now created a working bit-stream copy of your original evidence floppy disk, which contains the same evidence as the original. Next you can analyze the working bit-stream copy of your evidence.

Creating a Bit-stream Image with FTK Imager

There are GUI tools you can use to make a bit-stream or forensic-quality image. The first one you use in this book is AccessData's FTK Imager. Later in this chapter, you see how FTK Imager can convert images to other formats for use with other forensics tools.

In the previous exercise, you transferred the image for the in-chapter exercise to a floppy disk. This time you create a forensics disk image that other applications can read off this disk. Leaving the boot floppy disk in the drive, follow these steps:

1. Start FTK Imager by double-clicking the icon on your desktop.

2. Click **File**, **Image Drive** from the menu. Insert the floppy disk you labeled "Domain Name working copy #2."

3. In the dialog box that opens, click the **A:** drive to select a local drive, and then click **OK**.

4. A wizard opens to walk you through the steps. Accept all the defaults. One of the steps asks you to specify the destination folder. If necessary, create a folder called **Forensics Files**. Name the file **Bootimage.1**.

NOTE

Note that FTK Imager creates two files: a Bootimage.1 file for the image and a Bootimage.txt file containing summary information for that file, including the MD5 hash value for verification.

5. Click **Finish**. After the image has been created, close FTK Imager.

Analyzing Your Digital Evidence

When you analyze digital evidence, your job is to recover the data. If users have deleted or overwritten files on a disk, the disk contains deleted files and file fragments in addition to complete files. Remember that as files are deleted, the space they occupied becomes free space—meaning it can be used for new files that a user saves. The files that were deleted are still on the disk until a new file is saved to the same physical location, overwriting the original file. In the meantime, those files can still be retrieved. Most forensics tools can retrieve deleted files to be used as evidence.

To analyze digital evidence, in this chapter you use another MS-DOS tool from Digital Intelligence called DriveSpy, which is also a command-line tool. Then you use AccessDatas Forensic Toolkit to read the image file directly. Note that in some instances you need to restore the forensic image to a physical drive to run software specific to the case, instead of generic software such as MS Office. (Be aware that applications such as the Forensic Toolkit start the associated programs. MS Office is considered a generic program in this instance because most people own it or StarOffice).

Overview of DriveSpy

DriveSpy is a powerful computer forensics tool compact enough to fit on a floppy disk. It recovers and analyzes data on FAT12, FAT16, and FAT32 disks, which are different formatting techniques Microsoft uses. DriveSpy logs all your actions and copies data from your forensic image disk. It searches for files that have been altered so that they appear to be a different format, and it searches for keywords of interest to your investigation. DriveSpy is designed to work from the DOS command prompt and has limited functionality from a Windows MS-DOS shell. It's best to use DriveSpy from a workstation booted into MS-DOS. If you are running DriveSpy using MS-DOS version 6.22, DriveSpy can read disk drives larger than 8.4 GB and disk partitions larger than 2 GB. If you run DriveSpy in MS-DOS 7.0 or later, you can store recovered data in larger disk partitions. DriveSpy uses the following modes:

- *System mode*—DriveSpy operates at the workstation's BIOS level and enables you to view and navigate to all disk drives connected to the computer.

- *Drive mode*—DriveSpy accesses the physical level of the disk drive. Use this mode when you need to examine a disk not formatted for MS-DOS or Windows 9x. Specifically, Drive mode lets you view the raw data on a disk. (Chapter 4 provides more details about DriveSpy Drive mode.)

- *Part (or Partition) mode*—DriveSpy refers to the logical level of the disk drive. At the logical level, you view the actual file structure of a disk—that is, the disk's partition. In Part mode, DriveSpy can read MS-DOS and Windows 9x disks and shows the directory structures and files for FAT file systems. (FAT is covered in more detail in Chapter 7.)

DriveSpy extracts files and other raw data from a disk, including deleted files and fragments of deleted files that have been partially overwritten. DriveSpy can also generate an exact copy of a drive.

In this chapter, you have used Digital Intelligence's Image, a special utility that creates an exact copy of a floppy disk. Image stores the data from a floppy disk in a compressed data file or a flat (noncompressed) file. Image also duplicates an evidence floppy disk on another floppy disk, which lets you preserve your original evidence. Recall that you should avoid working with the original medium. By creating a bit-by-bit copy, you can perform your forensics examination on the duplicate floppy disk. Image is useless on large drives, however. As a result, there are several commands in the DriveSpy arsenal that can be used, such as the SavePart, SaveSect, and CopySect commands. The CopySect command enables you to save directly from one drive to another. (These commands are covered in Chapter 9.)

Using DriveSpy

Recall that you copied the DriveSpy files to the *work folder*\Tools folder earlier in this chapter. To start DriveSpy, the DriveSpy.exe file must be in the same folder as the DriveSpy.ini and DriveSpy.hlp files.

DriveSpy specifies drives by number, with the first drive being D0. Many systems have multiple partitions and multiple drives, which becomes important in your computer forensics lab where several drives might be connected to the same machine. Although DriveSpy identifies hard disks by number, it does not number the floppy disk and CD drives. With most versions of Windows (although Windows Me can present more challenges to use), you can start DriveSpy from Windows Explorer to access the DOS prompt. To prepare to analyze the bit-stream copy of your evidence disk, follow these steps:

1. Retrieve the forensic copy of your evidence disk (Domain Name working copy #2) from your evidence container, and write-protect the floppy disk by moving the tab to the open position.

2. Start your forensic workstation and boot into MS-DOS or to Windows 98.

3. Under the c:*work folder*\Chap02\Chapter\ folder, use the DOS prompt or Windows Explorer to create two subfolders called **copied** and **unerased**.

4. To run the Toolpath.bat file created earlier, go to the *work folder*\Tools folder (*work folder* is the name of your work folder). At the prompt, type **toolpath.bat** and press **Enter**. You return to a command prompt.

5. Insert the evidence disk you labeled "Domain Name working copy #2" into drive A: of your workstation.

Now you're ready to start DriveSpy. To use DriveSpy to analyze the bit-stream copy of your evidence disk, leave the evidence disk in the floppy drive, and follow these steps:

1. At the MS-DOS prompt, type **drivespy** and then press **Enter**. The opening screen is shown in Figure 2-13. Note that DriveSpy provides a SYS prompt where you can type DriveSpy commands. You can use the DriveSpy Output command to log your actions, which you need for your final report for this examination. The log file keeps track of all the commands you use to obtain data from the forensic disk as well as all the output.

2. At the SYS> prompt, type the command **outputc:*work folder*\Chap02\ Chapter\C2Chap01.log** (substituting for *work folder* if needed) and then press **Enter**.

3. To access the floppy disk with DriveSpy, type **drive a**, and then press **Enter**.

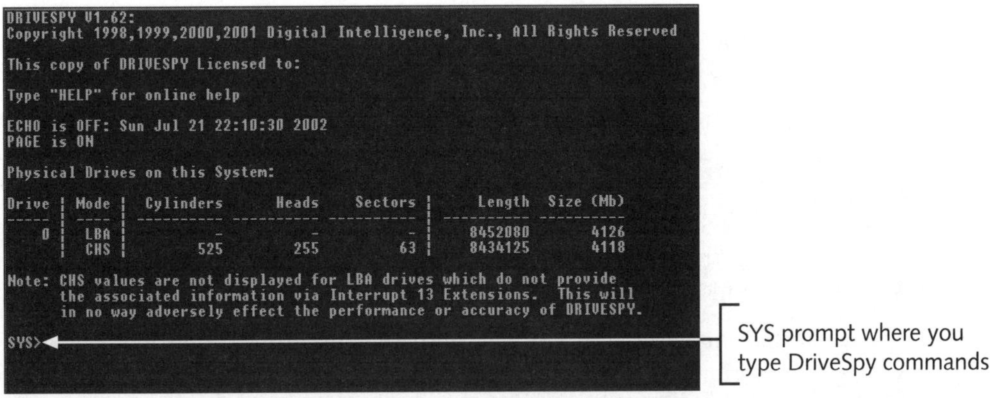

```
DRIVESPY V1.62:
Copyright 1998,1999,2000,2001 Digital Intelligence, Inc., All Rights Reserved

This copy of DRIVESPY Licensed to:

Type "HELP" for online help

ECHO is OFF: Sun Jul 21 22:10:30 2002
PAGE is ON

Physical Drives on this System:

Drive | Mode | Cylinders    Heads    Sectors |   Length   Size (Mb)
----- | ---- | ---------   --------  ------- | --------- ---------
  0   | LBA  |                               |  8452080    4126
      | CHS  |   525        255       63     |  8434125    4118

Note: CHS values are not displayed for LBA drives which do not provide
      the associated information via Interrupt 13 Extensions.  This will
      in no way adversely effect the performance or accuracy of DRIVESPY.

SYS>
```

SYS prompt where you type DriveSpy commands

Figure 2-13   The opening screen for DriveSpy

4. DriveSpy changes to Disk mode and summarizes the disk information for the disk in drive A: (see Figure 2-14). Recall that Disk mode reads the physical level of the disk, and does not show file structures such as directories (or folders) and files.

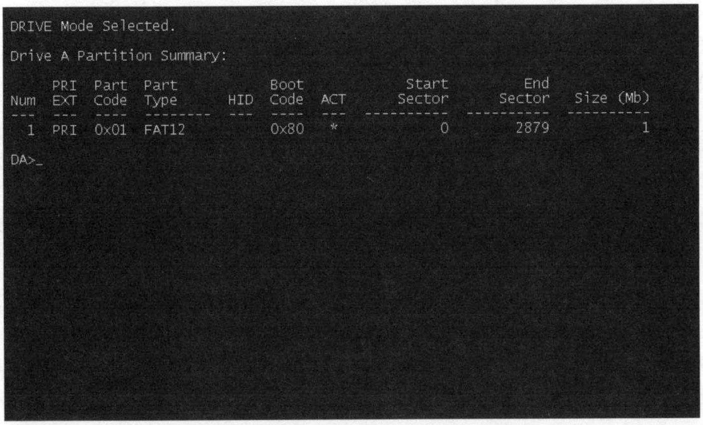

```
DRIVE Mode Selected.

Drive A Partition Summary:

     PRI  Part  Part                Boot               Start      End
Num  EXT  Code  Type      HID  Code  ACT     Sector    Sector   Size (Mb)
---  ---  ----  --------  ---  ----  ---   ----------  ------   ---------
 1   PRI  0x01  FAT12          0x80   *         0        2879        1

DA>_
```

Figure 2-14   Accessing the A: drive with DriveSpy

5. To access Partition mode of the floppy disk, type **part 1** at the DA prompt, and then press **Enter**. Partition information is displayed, as shown in Figure 2-15, including the type of file system used on the disk, the number of sectors per cluster, the total sectors and clusters available in the partition, and its raw and formatted data storage capacity. The information also includes a useful map of where the start and end sectors are for the boot sector of the partition, the first and second FATs (FAT1 and FAT2), the root directory, and the data storage areas of the partition. Chapter 7 discusses these file structures in detail.

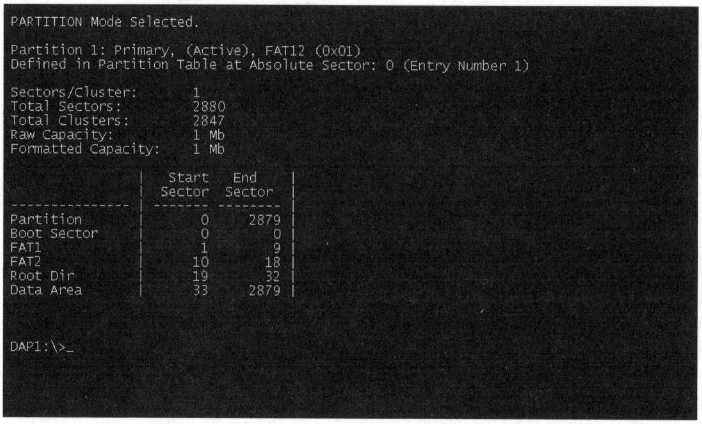

```
PARTITION Mode Selected.

Partition 1: Primary, (Active), FAT12 (0x01)
Defined in Partition Table at Absolute Sector: 0 (Entry Number 1)

Sectors/Cluster:         1
Total Sectors:           2880
Total Clusters:          2847
Raw Capacity:            1 Mb
Formatted Capacity:      1 Mb

                 |  Start    End  |
                 | Sector  Sector |
---------------- | ------- ------ |
Partition        |      0    2879 |
Boot Sector      |      0       0 |
FAT1             |      1       9 |
FAT2             |     10      18 |
Root Dir         |     19      32 |
Data Area        |     33    2879 |


DAP1:\>_
```

Figure 2-15   Accessing the Partition mode of a disk

6. Type **q** and then press **Enter** to exit DriveSpy.

You have successfully explored the investigation disk that contains your evidence. Next, you can run basic commands to navigate to the DriveSpy folder and analyze and extract data from the evidence disk:

1. Restart DriveSpy by typing **drivespy** at the MS-DOS prompt and then pressing **Enter**.

2. At the DriveSpy SYS prompt (indicating System mode), create the log file where DriveSpy can record all the tasks you perform while working in DriveSpy. Type the command **outputc:***work folder***\\Chap02\\Chapter\\Ch2Chap02.log** and then press **Enter**, substituting the name of the work folder on your system if necessary.

3. At the DriveSpy SYS prompt, type **drive a** and press **Enter** to switch to Drive mode.

4. At the DA (Drive A) prompt, type **part 1** and press **Enter** to switch to Partition mode for the A: drive.

5. At the DAP1 (Drive A, Partition 1) prompt, type the command **dbexport c:***work folder***\\Chap02\\Chapter\\C2Chap01.txt** and then press **Enter**, substituting the name of the work folder on your system if necessary. The Dbexport command creates a text file with the name you specify, such as C2Chap01.txt. This text file contains all the entries of directories and files listed in the FAT and is useful in identifying what's on the evidence disk. You can also open this text file in a word processing, spreadsheet, or database program to sort and search for information.

2

6. Next, you copy all the allocated data from the evidence disk. Allocated data is data not deleted from the disk. At the DriveSpy prompt, enter the command **copy *.* /s c:*work folder*\Chap02\Chapter\copied** (replacing the italicized text if necessary), and then press **Enter**. The recursive /s switch copies all the allocated files in any subdirectories that might exist on the evidence disk to the Chap02 folder in your work folder. If a message appears asking whether you want to view the results in page mode because they might be lengthy, press **Y**. (*Note:* Do *not* press Enter because it generates an error message.)

7. To copy all deleted files from the evidence disk, type the command **unerase *.* /s c:*work folder*\Chap02\Chapter\unerased** (replacing the italicized text if necessary), and then press **Enter**. If a message appears asking whether you want to view the results in Page mode because they might be lengthy, press **Y**. (*Note:* Do *not* press Enter because it generates an error message.)

8. At the command prompt, type **q** to exit DriveSpy, and type **exit** to close the command-prompt window.

DriveSpy locates all the deleted files on the evidence disk that have not been overwritten. That is, it searches the FAT for all files in which the file name starts with the MS-DOS delete symbol of a lowercase sigma (σ). Then DriveSpy copies the contents of the deleted files to the specified location, such as the Chap02 folder in your work folder. To analyze the data, follow these steps:

1. Reboot your machine to Windows mode.

2. Use Windows Explorer or My Computer to open the floppy disk, and note how many files it contains.

3. Right-click the first file and then click **Properties**. In the General tab of the Properties dialog box for the file, note the Created, Modified, and Accessed dates and times. List the file name and properties in a separate document or sheet of paper. Put an asterisk next to any times that are during George's working hours (8 a.m. to 5 p.m.). Then close the Properties dialog box. Note the properties for each file on the disk.

4. Open each file. In a separate document or on a sheet of paper, note what each file contains, and then close any open windows.

5. Use Windows Explorer or My Computer to open the *work folder*\Chap02\ Chapter folder and examine the contents. You should see several files in addition to the log and text files. These are the deleted files DriveSpy retrieved.

6. In Notepad, open **C2Chap01.txt** and examine the contents. Depending on your system, you might see the sigma symbol (σ) to represent deleted files or a question mark (?) at the beginning of the file name. Close Notepad.

7. Examine the contents of the deleted files. Determine whether they contain information about George's own business and his whereabouts.

8. In Windows Explorer or My Computer, right-click each file and examine the Created, Modified, and Accessed dates and times in the file's Properties dialog box. Record your findings in a separate document or sheet of paper.

You should find evidence that proves George was working on his own business during company work hours.

Overview of Forensic Toolkit

AccessDatas Forensic Toolkit (FTK) is an easy-to-use GUI application, even for first-time users. FTK is part of a suite of tools that includes FTK Imager, the Registry Viewer, and the Password Recovery Toolkit. With this arsenal, you can usually solve most cases. FTK reads FAT12, FAT16, FAT32, and NTFS files.

Using Forensic Toolkit

FTK (either the demo or licensed version) should be loaded on your lab machine. Earlier you created an image of the boot floppy disk. In this exercise, you use it to become acquainted with FTK. To analyze the data, follow these steps:

1. Start FTK. You should see the opening window shown in Figure 2-16.

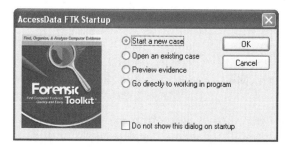

Figure 2-16   The opening window for FTK

2. Click **Start a new case**, and then press **Enter** or click **OK**.

3. In the New Case dialog box (see Figure 2-17), type your name in the Investigator Name text box.

4. In the Case Number text box, type **C2-3**, and in the Case Name text box, type **Boot**.

5. Click the **Browse** button next to the Case Path text box, and select your Chapter 2 work folder. Notice that FTK adds your case name to the end of the location and creates that subfolder for you.

6. Click **Next** in all the remaining dialog boxes until you arrive at the Add Evidence dialog box (see Figure 2-18).

7. Click the **Add Evidence** button, and then verify that the Acquired Image of Drive option button is selected (see Figure 2-19). Click the **Continue** button.

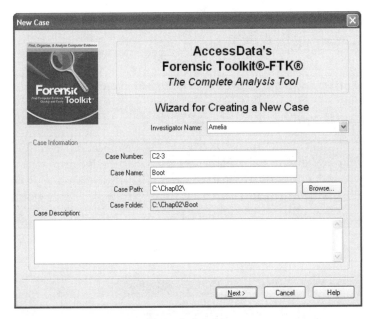

Figure 2-17   The New Case dialog box

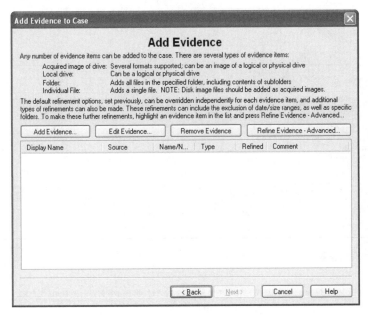

Figure 2-18   The Add Evidence dialog box

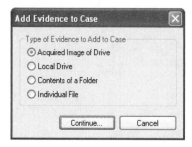

Figure 2-19 The Add Evidence to Case dialog box

8. Click to select **Bootimage.1** and click **Open**. In the Evidence Information dialog box, click **OK**.

9. Click **Next** to get to the Case Summary dialog box shown in Figure 2-20, and then click **Finish**.

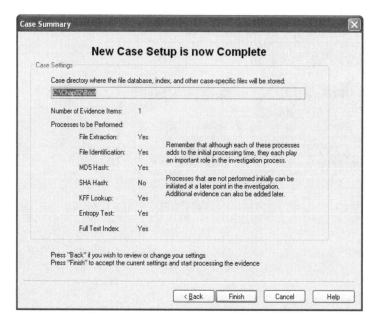

Figure 2-20 The Case Summary dialog box

10. When FTK finishes, explore some of the buttons in this dialog box, such as Executables and Total File Items (see Figure 2-21).

11. Close FTK.

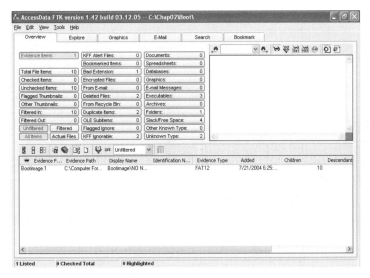

Figure 2-21   FTK's Overview window

COMPLETING THE CASE

After you analyze a disk, you can retrieve deleted files and e-mail, items that have been purposefully hidden, and much more, which you do later in this book. The files on George's floppy disk indicate that he was doing outside work on the company's machine.

Now that you have retrieved and analyzed the evidence, you need to find the answers to the following questions to write the final report:

- How did George's manager acquire the disk?

- Did George perform the work on a laptop, which is his own property? If so, did he perform his business transactions on his break or during his lunch hour?

- At what times of the day was George using the non-work-related files? How did you retrieve that information?

- Which company policies apply?

- Are there any other items that need to be considered?

When you write your report, state what you did and what you found. The log file DriveSpy generates gives you a historical account of all the steps you have taken. As part of your report, depending on guidance you have from your management or legal counsel, include the DriveSpy log file to document your work. In any computing investigation, you should be able to repeat your steps and achieve the same results. Without this ability, your work product has no value as evidence.

> **TIP**
>
> Keep a written journal of everything you do. Your notes can be used in court, so be mindful of what you write or e-mail, even to a fellow investigator. Often these journals start out as handwritten notes, but you can transcribe the notes to electronic format periodically.

Basic report writing involves answering the six Ws: *who, what, when, where, why,* and *how.* In addition to these basic facts, you must also explain computer and network processes. Typically, your reader will be a senior personnel manager, a lawyer, or, on rare occasions, a judge and might have little computer knowledge. Identify your reader and write the report for that person. Provide explanations for processes, the inner workings of systems and their components, and how they work.

Your organization might have predefined templates to use when writing reports. Depending on your organization's needs and requirements, your report must describe the findings from your analysis. The log file generated by DriveSpy lists all your activity in the order you performed your examination and data recovery. Integrating a computer forensics log report will augment your formal report. Consider writing your narrative first and then placing the log output at the end of the report, using references to the log report on your fact-findings. Writing technical reports for your investigations is covered in more detail in Chapter 14.

In the Domain Name case, you would want to show conclusive evidence that George had his own business that registered other people's domain names and would provide the names of his clients and his income from this business. You would also want to show letters he wrote to clients about their accounts. The time and date stamps on the files are during work hours. As the investigator, you eventually hand the evidence file to your supervisor or to Steve, George's boss. They then decide on a course of action.

CRITIQUING THE CASE

After you close the case and make your final report, you need to meet with your department or a group of fellow investigators and critique the case. Ask yourself critical questions such as the following:

- How could you improve your participation in the case?

- Did you expect the results you found? Did the case develop in ways you did not expect?

- Was the documentation as thorough as it could have been?

- What feedback has been received from the requesting source?

- Did you discover any new problems? If so, what are they?

- Did you use new techniques during the case or during research?

Make notes to yourself in your journal about techniques or processes that might need to be changed or addressed in future investigations. Then store your journal in a secure place.

CHAPTER SUMMARY

❑ Always use a systematic approach to your investigations. Determine the type of problem you are dealing with, create a preliminary plan, choose your resources, perform a risk analysis, and then implement the plan.

❑ When planning a case, take into account the nature of the case, the instructions from the requester, what additional tools and expertise you might need, and how you will acquire the evidence.

❑ Criminal cases and corporate-policy violations should be handled in much the same manner to ensure that quality evidence is presented. Both criminal cases and corporate-policy violations can go to court.

❑ When you begin a case, apply standard problem-solving techniques, such as defining the problem, designing a solution, and carrying out that solution.

❑ You should create a standard evidence custody form to track the chain of custody of the evidence related to your case. There are two types of forms—a multi-evidence form and a single-evidence form.

❑ Always maintain a journal to make notes on exactly what you did when handling evidence.

❑ An image file is a bit-by-bit duplicate of the original disk. You should use the duplicate whenever possible.

❑ DriveSpy and Image are command-line forensic tools that can retrieve existing files, deleted files, and file fragments.

❑ You can create bit-stream copies of files by using the Diskcopy DOS utility or the Image tool.

❑ In completing a case, describe what you did, how you did it, and what you found.

❑ You should always critique your own work to determine what improvements you made during each case, what could have been done differently, and how to apply those lessons to future cases.

KEY TERMS

allocated data — Data on a drive that has not been deleted or written over.

approved secure container — A fireproof container that is locked by key or combination.

bit-stream copy — A bit-by-bit copy of the data on the original storage medium.

bit-stream image — The file used to store the bit-stream copy.

chain of custody — The route evidence takes from the time the investigator obtains it until the case is closed or goes to court.

computer forensics workstation — A workstation set up to allow copying of forensic evidence, whether on a hard drive, floppy, CD, or Zip disk. It usually has various software preloaded and ready to use.

data recovery lab — An alternate name for a computer forensics lab.

evidence bag — A nonstatic bag used to transport floppy disks, hard drives, and other computer components.

evidence custody form — A printed form indicating who has signed out and been in physical possession of evidence.

evidence floppy disk — The original disk on which electronic evidence was found.

forensic copy — An exact copy of an evidence disk used during the actual investigation.

free space — Space on a drive that is not reserved for saved files.

image file — A file created by the Image tool from Digital Intelligence.

multi-evidence form — An evidence custody form used to list all items associated with a case. *See also* single-evidence form.

password-cracking software — Software used to match the hash patterns of passwords or simply guess the words by using common combinations or standard algorithms.

password protected — Files and areas of any storage media can have limited access by requiring a password to prevent unintentional use.

personal digital assistant (PDA) — One of several pocket-sized computers that store addresses, notes, and calendars. One popular brand is Palm.

single-evidence form — A form that dedicates a page for each item retrieved for a case. It allows the investigator to add more detail about exactly what was done to the evidence each time it was taken from the storage locker. *See also* multi-evidence form.

slack space — Space on a disk between the end of a file and the allotted space for that file.

REVIEW QUESTIONS

1. List the five standard steps of computer investigations.

2. Digital Intelligence's Image tool is:

   a. a GUI tool

   b. a command-line tool

   c. a Linux tool

   d. none of the above

3. A bit-stream image is the same as a backup copy. True or False?

4. List three items that should be on an evidence custody form.

5. What is involved in planning an investigation?

6. You should always prove the allegations made by the person who hired you. True or False?

7. An evidence bag is typically made of nonstatic material. True or False?

2

8. What is the command you use in Digital Intelligence's Image to copy an image of a disk from your hard drive to a working forensic floppy disk?

9. Who should have access to a secure container?

   a. only the primary investigator

   b. only the investigators in the group

   c. everyone on the floor

   d. only senior-level management

10. Typically, the Image tool creates a file with what extension?

11. Why should your evidence disk be write-protected?

12. Why should you be familiar with command-line software?

13. What does the Drive A (DA) command in DriveSpy do?

   a. accesses the hard drive

   b. accesses the CD-ROM

   c. accesses the floppy disk drive

   d. accesses the secondary hard drive

14. List three items that should be in your case report.

15. Why should you critique your case after it is done?

16. The Image utility is developed by:

   a. Microsoft

   b. Digital Intelligence

   c. Norton

   d. Symantec

17. Diskcopy is:

   a. a utility by AccessData

   b. a standard MS-DOS command

   c. a Digital Intelligence utility

   d. none of the above

18. To access Partition mode information in DriveSpy, you type:

   a. D1

   b. Part 1

   c. Drive A

   d. Partition1

19. The Unerase command in DriveSpy does which of the following?

    a. retrieves allocated files

    b. retrieves partial files

    c. retrieves deleted files that have not been written over

    d. is not a valid command

20. What do you call a list of the people who have had physical possession of the evidence?

HANDS-ON PROJECTS

In the following Hands-on Projects, continue to work at the workstation you set up in this chapter.

HANDS-ON PROJECTS

Project 2-1

In this project, the case involves a murder investigation. You use the Image tool to copy an image file to a blank floppy disk. Assume that the image is a verified copy of a data disk. You now need to copy it to a blank target disk, using the following steps:

1. In Windows Explorer, navigate to the Chap02 folder in your work folder. Create a new subfolder called **Projects**.

2. In the student data files, find the file named **C2Prj01.img** in the Chap02\Projects folder. Copy the file to the **Chap02\Projects** folder in your work folder.

3. Insert a blank, formatted floppy disk in the floppy disk drive.

4. Open a command-prompt window by clicking **Start**, pointing to **Programs**, and then clicking **MS-DOS Prompt**.

5. Navigate to the Chap02\Projects folder in your work folder.

6. Type **image C2Prj01.img a:** and press **Enter**. This command copies an exact image of a disk contained in the C2Prj01.img file to the disk in drive A. If Image does not start, you might need to run the Toolpath.bat file created earlier in the chapter.

7. Type **exit** to close the command-prompt window.

8. Use Windows Explorer to view the files you copied to the floppy disk. In a separate document or on a sheet of paper, list these files.

9. Start DriveSpy.

10. Type **drive a** and press **Enter** to access the floppy disk. To capture the screen, press the **PrtScrn** key to save a copy of the screen to the Clipboard. (Your PrtScrn key

might have a different name, such as Print Screen.) Open a word processing program, such as WordPad, open a new document, and then press **Ctrl+V** to paste the screen image into the document. Print the document and give it to your instructor.

11. In the command-prompt window, type **part 1** and press **Enter** to access the Partition mode. Capture the screen and print a copy of it, as in Step 10.

12. Type **q** to exit DriveSpy.

13. List four items or terms you saw and write their definitions in a separate document or on a sheet of paper. Refer to the Digital Intelligence Web site at *www.digitalintel. com*, if necessary.

14. Examine the files you retrieved from the image. In what way could they be connected to a murder? What other information would you need?

15. Write one to two paragraphs summarizing how you would approach this case.

HANDS-ON PROJECTS

Project 2-2

In this project, you practice making and restoring image files. You restore the image to a floppy disk, create an image of the disk, and then restore it to another disk. Follow these steps to use DriveSpy to compare two disks:

1. Copy **C2Prj02a.img** from the student data files to the Chap02\Projects folder in your work folder.

2. Open a command-prompt window by clicking **Start**, pointing to **Programs**, and then clicking **MS-DOS Prompt**.

3. If you have not run Toolpath.bat during this session at the computer, change to the Tools folder by typing **cd c:*work folder*\tools** from the root and then pressing **Enter**. Type **toolpath.bat** and press **Enter** to make the Image program available in your current directory. Then change to the Chap02\Projects folder in your work folder.

4. Label a blank, formatted floppy disk **Project 2-2 Disk1** and insert it in the floppy disk drive.

5. At the DOS command prompt, type **image C2Prj02a.img a:** and press **Enter**. This places the files sector by sector on the floppy disk.

6. Start Windows Explorer, navigate to the Chap02\Projects folder in your work folder, and note the files that are listed.

7. With the same floppy disk in the drive, at the command prompt, create a new image by typing **image a: C2Prj02b.img** and pressing **Enter**.

8. Label a blank, formatted floppy disk **Project 2-2 Disk2** and insert the second disk in the floppy disk drive.

9. At the DOS command prompt, type **image C2Prj02b.img a:** and press **Enter**.

10. Create two subfolders in the Projects folder called **Disk1** and **Disk2**.

11. Leaving the second floppy disk in the drive, start DriveSpy by typing **drivespy** in the C:*work folder*\\Chap02\\Projects area of your work folder and pressing **Enter**. Type **drive a** and press **Enter,** then type **part 1** and press **Enter** to access the DAP1> prompt.

12. Create a log file for Disk2 by typing the command **outputc:*work folder*\\Chap02\\Projects\\Disk2\\C2Prj02.log** and then pressing **Enter**.

13. Next, use the Dbexport command by typing the command **dbexport c:*work folder*\\Chap02\\Projects\\Disk2\\C2Prj02.txt** and then pressing **Enter**.

14. Copy all the allocated files to the Disk2 folder by typing the command **copy *.* /S c:*work folder*\\Chap02\\Projects\\Disk2** and then pressing **Enter**. If prompted to disable Page mode, press **Y,** but don't press Enter afterward because it generates an error message.

15. Type the command **unerase *.* /S c:*work folder*\\Chap02\\Projects\\Disk2,** and then press **Enter** to retrieve all deleted files. If prompted to disable Page mode, press **Y**.

16. Replace Disk2 with Disk1 and repeat Steps 12 to 15 for Disk1.

17. When you finish, type **q** to exit DriveSpy and **exit** to close the command-prompt window.

18. Use Windows Explorer to compare the two folders and their files. In a word processing document or on a sheet of paper, list the files each folder contains and note any discrepancies.

**HANDS-ON
PROJECTS**

Project 2-3

In this project, you see the problems of using DriveSpy in a DOS shell, or command-prompt window, by attempting to use the Wipe command to overwrite unallocated space on a specified drive with zeroes. This helps ensure that data on a disk does not change during transportation, analysis, or storage. For this project, use a floppy disk that contains files you no longer need and follow these steps in a command-prompt window:

1. In the floppy disk drive, insert a formatted floppy disk containing files you no longer need.

2. Open a command-prompt window.

3. If necessary, navigate to the *work folder*\\Tools folder.

4. To start DriveSpy, type **drivespy** and press **Enter**.

5. Type **drive a** and press **Enter**, and then type **part 1** and press **Enter** to access the Partition mode of the floppy disk in your drive.

6. Type **wipe /free** and press **Enter**. You use the /free switch to specify that DriveSpy should overwrite unallocated disk space with zeroes. An error message is displayed stating that "Windows is running: the Wipe command has been disabled."

7. Exit DriveSpy, and then close the command-prompt window.

8. Reboot your machine to MS-DOS mode.

9. If necessary, navigate to the *work folder*\Tools folder, and start DriveSpy.

10. At the SYS> prompt, type **drive a** and then press **Enter**. Type **part 1** and then press **Enter** to access the Partition mode of the disk.

11. Type **wipe /free** and press **Enter**. When asked if you are sure you want to wipe the disk, type **Y**. Wipe displays the number of unallocated sectors on the floppy disk and then wipes the disk (in other words, fills the unallocated sectors with zeros so that the sectors can't contain any other data).

12. Exit DriveSpy, and then reboot to Windows.

HANDS-ON PROJECTS

Project 2-4

In this project, you explore the Drivespy.ini file, which is a critical file for using the program.

1. Start Notepad.

2. Click **File**, **Open** from the menu. In the Open dialog box, navigate to the *work folder***Tools** folder.

3. Click the **Files of type** list arrow, and then click **All Files (*.*)**.

4. Double-click the **DriveSpy.ini** file to open it.

5. Click **File**, **Print** from the menu. Make sure you are connected to a printer, and then click **OK** to print the file. Refer to the printed copy of this file as you write a report in the following steps.

6. In a separate Notepad document, list the parts of the DriveSpy.ini file—those areas that are in square brackets, such as [License].

7. In the [File Headers] section, select six file types with which you are unfamiliar. In your report, answer the following questions:

   ◻ Is the application still in use today?

   ◻ If so, what version?

   ◻ If not, what applications can still open the file type? For example, WordStar documents can be opened in Microsoft Word.

   ◻ If you needed more information about the application, who in your area would know? Which user groups could you ask?

8. Close Notepad.

Project 2-5

In this project, you take an image created with Digital Intelligences Image utility, restore it to a floppy disk, and then use FTK Imager to create a *.1 file for use in FTK.

1. Obtain a blank floppy disk, and then open a DOS prompt on your machine.

2. Change to the **Tools** folder and run **Toolpath.bat**.

3. Change to the directory containing the files for this chapter, such as C:\Chap02. You should have a file from your student data disk called C2prj05.img. If you don't, copy it from your data disk to this location.

4. Restore the image to the blank floppy disk by typing **image C2Prj05.img a:** and pressing **Enter**. After it has finished, close the command-prompt window.

5. Restart, if necessary, to get to the area where FTK and FTK Imager are located.

6. Start FTK Imager.

7. Click **File**, **Image Drive** from the menu to open a dialog box listing the local drives. Click the **A:** drive and then click **OK**.

8. Make sure the destination folder is C:\Chap02 and the file name is C2Prj05. Keep all the default settings until you reach the final window, and then click **Finish**. When the process is finished, close FTK Imager.

9. Start FTK, and click the **Start a new case** option button.

10. In the New Case dialog box, type in your name as the investigator. Type **C2-5** for the case number and **test conversion** for the case name. Click **OK**.

11. Click **Next**, leaving all the defaults until you reach the Add Evidence dialog box. Click the **Add Evidence** button, click the **Acquired Image of Drive** option button, and then click **Continue**. In the dialog box that opens, click the file you just generated.

12. Click **Next** again to continue to the Case Summary dialog box, and then click **Finish**.

13. When FTK has finished, try exploring the files. After you're done, close FTK.

Project 2-6

In this project, you use FTK to examine a forensic disk image and look for existing and deleted files.

1. Start FTK.

2. Start a new case.

3. Type your name as the investigator.

4. Assign a case number of **C2-6** and a case name of **Shakespeare**.

5. Click **Next** in all the dialog boxes, accepting the default settings.

6. In the Add Evidence to Case dialog box, click the **Add Evidence** button, click the **Individual File** option button, and click to select the **C2Prj06.1** file from your student data files.

7. Click **Open**, click **OK**, and click **Next** to get to the Case Summary dialog box, and click **Finish**.

8. After FTK has finished, click the **Documents** button under File Category. Notice in the lower pane that two of the documents have a red X next to them. They are files that have been deleted.

9. You can click each file and see a preview of it. In Chapter 7, you see how to start the associated programs, such as Microsoft Word, for each file.

10. Close FTK.

CASE PROJECTS

Case Project 2-1

An insurance company has assigned your firm to review a case for an arson investigation. The suspected arsonist has already been arrested, but the insurance company wants to determine whether there's any contributory negligence on the part of the victims. Review the synopsis of the case (refer to the ArsonMemo.doc file in your student data files), and decide what course of action your firm needs to take. Write an outline for how your firm should approach the case.

Case Project 2-2

A young girl is missing after having an argument with her parents. They call the police on May 28. A police investigator shows up the next day to interview them. The officer finds out that the daughter had spent a lot of time on the Internet. The parents agree to let him take her laptop. What should happen next?

Case Project 2-3

Jonathan Simpson owns a construction company. One day a subcontractor calls him, saying that he needs a replacement check for the job he completed at 1437 West Maple Avenue. Jonathan looks up the job on his accounting program and agrees to reissue the check for $12,750.00. The subcontractor says that the original check was for only $10,750.00. Jonathan looks around the office and cannot find the company checkbook or ledger. Only one other person has access to the accounting program. Jonathan calls you to investigate. How would you proceed? Write a one-page report detailing the steps Jonathan needs to take to obtain the necessary evidence and protect his company.

Case Project 2-4

You are the computer forensics investigator for a law firm. The firm acquired a new client, a young woman who was discharged from her job for inappropriate material discovered on her computer. She swears she never accessed that material. What questions should you ask and how should you proceed? Write a one to two-page report detailing the computer the new client could access, who else had access to it, and any other relevant facts that should be investigated.

Case Project 2-5

A desperate employee calls because she has accidentally deleted crucial files from her hard drive and cannot retrieve them from the Recycle Bin. What are your options? Write one to two pages in response that explain your capabilities and list the questions you need to ask her about her system.

3

THE INVESTIGATOR'S OFFICE AND LABORATORY

> **After reading this chapter and completing the exercises, you will be able to:**
>
> ♦ Understand computer forensics lab certification requirements
> ♦ Determine the physical layout of a computer forensics lab
> ♦ Select a basic forensic workstation
> ♦ Build a business case for developing a forensics lab

This chapter details what you need to set up an effective computer forensics laboratory, which is where you examine most of the evidence data you acquire for an investigation. Adjacent to the lab, most computer forensics investigators have a private office where they manage their cases. Whether you are new to computer forensics or are an experienced examiner, your goal is to make your office and lab work smoothly and efficiently for all casework.

Computer forensics examiners must update their labs to keep pace with computer technology changes. The workflow and processes you establish directly affect the quality of evidence you discover. You must balance cost, quality, and reliability when determining the kind of equipment, software, and other items you need to add to your lab. This chapter provides a foundation for organizing, controlling, and managing a safe, efficient computer forensics laboratory.

Understanding Forensic Lab Certification Requirements

A **computer forensics lab** is where you conduct your investigations, store evidence, and do most of your work. You use the lab to house your instruments, current and legacy software, and computer forensics workstations. In general, you need a variety of computer forensics hardware and software to do your work.

The **American Society of Crime Laboratory Directors (ASCLD)** (*www.ascld.org*) provides guidelines for managing a forensics lab and for acquiring official crime-lab certification. ASCLD certifies forensics labs that analyze other criminal evidence, such as fingerprints and DNA samples. Note that this type of forensics lab is different from a computer forensics lab and handles different types of analysis.

The ASCLD offers a detailed and extensive certification program, ASCLD/LAB (*www.ascld-lab.org*), that regulates how crime labs are organized and managed. The ASCLD/LAB program includes specific audits on all functions to ensure that lab procedures are being performed correctly and consistently for all casework. These audits can be applied to computer forensics labs to maintain quality and integrity.

ASCLD has defined what constitutes a professional crime laboratory. The following sections discuss several key guidelines from the ASCLD/LAB program that you can apply to managing, configuring, and auditing your computer forensics lab.

Identifying Duties of the Lab Manager and Staff

The ASCLD states that each lab should have a specific set of objectives that a parent organization and the lab's director or manager determine. The lab manager sets up the processes for managing cases and reviews these procedures regularly. Besides performing general management tasks, such as promoting group consensus in decision making, maintaining fiscal responsibility for lab needs, and encouraging honesty among staff members, the lab manager plans updates for the lab, such as new hardware and software purchases.

The lab manager also establishes and promotes quality-assurance processes for the lab's staff to use, such as what to do when a case arrives, including logging evidence, specifying who can enter the lab, and establishing guidelines for filing reports. To ensure the lab's efficiency, the lab manager also sets reasonable production schedules for processing work.

A typical case for an internal corporate investigation involves seizing a hard disk, making forensic copies of the disk, evaluating evidence, and filing a report. Performing a forensic analysis of a disk 20 GB or larger can take several days and often involves running imaging software overnight and on weekends. This means that one of the forensic computers in the lab is occupied for that time. Evaluating such a disk can take 80 hours or more. Based on past experience, the lab manager can estimate how many cases each investigator can handle and estimate when to expect a preliminary and final report for each case.

The lab manager creates and monitors lab policies for staff and provides a safe and secure workplace for staff and evidence. Above all, the lab manager accounts for all activities the lab's staff conducts to complete its work. Tracking cases such as e-mail abuse, Internet misuse, and illicit activities can justify the funds spent on a lab.

Staff members in a computer forensics lab should have sufficient training to perform their tasks. Staff skill sets include hardware and software knowledge, including OS and file types, and deductive reasoning. Their work is reviewed regularly by the lab manager and peers to ensure quality. The staff is also responsible for continuing technical training to update their investigative and computer skills and maintaining a record of the training they have completed. Many vendors and organizations hold annual or quarterly training seminars that offer certification exams.

The ASCLD Web site summarizes the requirements of managing a computer forensics lab, handling and preserving evidence, performing laboratory procedures, setting personnel requirements, and encouraging professional development. The site also provides a user license for printed and online manuals of lab management guidelines. ASCLD stresses that each lab maintain an up-to-date library of resources in its field. For computer forensics, these resources include software, hardware information, and technical journals.

Lab Budget Planning

To conduct a professional computing investigation, you need to understand the cost of your lab operation. Lab costs can be broken down into daily, quarterly, and annual expenses. The better you understand these expenses, the better you can delegate resources for each investigation. Using a spreadsheet program helps you keep track of past investigation expenses. From past expenses, you can extrapolate expected future costs. Remember, expenses for a lab include computer hardware and software, facility space, and trained personnel. When creating a budget, start by estimating the number of computer cases your lab expects to examine and identifying the types of computers you're likely to examine, such as Windows PCs or Linux workstations.

For example, suppose you work for a state police agency that's planning to provide computing investigation services for the entire state. You could start by collecting state crime statistics for the current year and several previous years. As you examine these statistics, determine how many computers were used to commit a crime and identify the types of computers used in these crimes. Criminal behavior often reflects sales trends for specific computing systems. Because more than 90% of all consumers use Intel and AMD PCs, and 90% of these computers are running a version of Microsoft Windows, the same statistics are likely true of computers used in crimes. Verify this trend by determining how often each type of system is used in a crime. List the number of crimes committed using DOS or Windows computers, Linux or UNIX systems, and Macintosh computers.

If you cannot find detailed information that identifies the types of computers and OSs used in computer crimes, gather enough information to make an educated guess. Your goal is to build a baseline for the types and numbers of systems you can expect to investigate. In addition to the historical data you compile, identify any future trends that could affect your lab, such as a new version of an OS or an increase in the number of computers involved in crime.

After you compile these statistics, estimate how many investigations you might conduct involving computer systems used less frequently. Doing so helps determine how many tools you need to examine these systems. For example, if you learn that on average, one Macintosh computer running OS 9 or earlier is involved in a criminal investigation each month, you probably need only one or two software tools to perform a forensic analysis on Macintosh file systems.

Figure 3-1 shows a table of statistics from a **Uniform Crime Report** that identifies the number of hard disk types, such as IDE or SCSI, and the specific OS used to commit crimes. Uniform Crime Reports are generated at the federal, state, and local levels to show the types and frequency of crimes committed. For federal reports, see *www.fbi.gov/ucr/ucr.htm,* and for a summary of crimes committed at various levels during the 1990s, see *http://fisher.lib. virginia.edu/crime.*

You can also identify which crimes used a computer with specialized software. For example, if you find that many counterfeiters use a certain type of check-writing software, consider adding this specialized software to your inventory.

If you're preparing to set up a computer forensics lab for a private company, you can easily determine your needs because you're working in a contained environment. Start by obtaining an inventory of all known computing systems used in the business. For example, an insurance company often has a network of Intel PCs and servers. A large manufacturing company might use Intel PCs, UNIX workstations running a computer-aided design (CAD) system, super minicomputers, and mainframes. A publishing company might have a combination of Intel PCs and Apple Macintosh systems.

Next, check with your Management, Human Resource, and Security departments to determine the types of complaints and problems reported in the last year. Most companies that have Internet connections, for example, receive complaints about employees accessing the Web excessively or for personal use, which generate investigations of Web use. Be sure to distinguish investigations concerning excessive Web use from inappropriate Web site access involving porn sites or hate sites and e-mail abuse.

Your budget should also take future developments in computing technology into account because disk drive storage capabilities improve constantly. When examining a disk, recall that you need a target disk to which you copy your evidence data. The target disk should be at least one and one-half times the size of the evidence (suspect) disk. For example, a lab equipped with 60 GB disks can effectively analyze 20 GB or 40 GB disks. If your company upgrades its computers to 120 GB disks, however, you need disks that are 200 GB or larger or a central secure server with one or more terabytes of storage.

	IDE Drive	SCSI Drive	Intel PC Platform		MS Other O/S	Linux	Apple Platform		UNIX H/W	Other H/W	Total Systems Examined	Total HDD Examined
			Win9x	WinNT / 2k / XP			OS 9.x & older	OS X				
Arson	5	3	3	1		1					5	8
Assault—Aggravated	78	5	31		1	14				1	47	83
Assault-Simple	180	3	77	6	1	32	44	2		1	163	183
Bribery	153		153								153	153
Burglary	1746		1487	259							1746	1746
Counterfeiting & Forgery	1390	4	543	331		309	21	186			1390	1394
Destruction, Damage, & Vandalism	976	48	142	45	29	127	325	90	217	1	976	1024
Drug, Narcotic	1939	24	1345	213		158	213	10			1939	1963
Embezzlement	1023		320	549		23	87	41		3	1023	1023
Extortion & Blackmail	77		2	61		10	3	1			77	77
Fraud	2002		638	932	9	173	55	190		5	2002	2002
Gambling	4910	5	1509	2634		136	138	498			4915	4915
Homicide	36		5	11	9	1	3	7			36	36
Kidnapping & Abduction	2		1	1							2	2
Larceny Theft	7342	56	2134	3093	5	935	127	982	1	21	7298	7398
Motor Vehicle Theft	1747		231	1508		5	1	2			1747	1747
Child Porn	593	2	98	162		68	105	160	2		595	595
Robbery	33		23	7			2	1			33	33
Sex Offense—Forcible	80		21	45		1	5	8			80	80
Sex Offense—Non-Forcible	900		324	437		6	90	43			900	900
Stolen Property Offenses	2711	10	800	1634	3	169	53	37	1	9	2706	2721
Weapons Violations	203	1	43	89	2	11	28	31			204	204
Totals Per System	28126	161	9930	12018	59	2179	1300	2289	222	40	28037	28287
			HDD FAT/NTFS	22007			HDD Mac O/S X/Linux/ UNIX		2511			

Figure 3-1   Uniform Crime Report statistics

Many businesses replace their desktop computer systems every 18 months to three years. You must be informed of computer upgrades and other changes in the computing environment so that you can prepare and submit your budget for needed resources.

Like computer hardware, OSs also change periodically. If your current computer forensics tool doesn't work with the next release of a Microsoft OS or file system, you must upgrade your software tools. You should also monitor vendor product developments to learn about upgrades. For example, the release of Windows NT caused problems for computer forensics examiners. Windows NT hard disks can use FAT12, FAT16, FAT32, and New Technology File System (NTFS). Windows NT 3.0 through 3.5 can also access IBM OS/2 High Performance File System (HPFS) disk drives. When Windows NT was released, computing forensics software vendors didn't have tools that could analyze and extract data from NTFS or HPFS disks. Microsoft released a disk editor called DiskProbe that enabled users to view NTFS disks on Windows NT 3.5 through Windows XP systems. However, DiskProbe cannot write-block a suspect's disk, making it usable only on copied disks. In this situation, monitor the updates to forensics tools to find a tool that works with Windows NT and NTFS and HPFS disks.

Examining PDAs, USB memory sticks, and cellular telephones is routine now. Types of investigations that demand forensic examination of these devices range from criminal investigation to civil litigation discovery demands. Computer investigators must be prepared to deal with the constant changes in these devices and know what tools are available to safely extract data from them for an investigation. In Chapter 9, you learn how to acquire data from these devices.

Acquiring Certification and Training

To continue a career in computing investigations and forensic analysis, you need to upgrade your skills through appropriate training. Several organizations are currently developing certification programs for computer forensics that usually test you after you have successfully completed one or more training sessions. The certifying organizations range from nonprofit associations to vendor-sponsored groups. All these programs charge fees for certification, and some require candidates to take vendor- or organization-sponsored training to qualify for the certification. More recently, some state and federal government agencies have been looking into establishing their own certification programs that address the minimum skills for conducting computing investigations at various levels.

Before enlisting in a certification program, thoroughly research the requirements, cost, and acceptability in your chosen area of employment. Most certification programs require continuing education credits or reexamination of the candidate's skills, which can become costly.

International Association of Computer Investigative Specialists (IACIS)

Created by police officers who wanted to formalize credentials in computing investigations, IACIS is one of the oldest professional computer forensics organizations. IACIS restricts membership to sworn law enforcement personnel or government employees working as computer forensics examiners. This restriction might change, so visit the IACIS Web site (*www.cops.org*) to verify the requirements.

IACIS conducts an annual two-week training course for qualified members. Students must interpret and trace e-mail, acquire evidence properly, identify operating systems, recover data, and understand encryption theory and other topics. Students must pass a written exam before continuing to the next level. Passing the exam earns the status of **Certified Electronic Evidence Collection Specialist (CEECS)**.

3

The next level of training is completed through a correspondence course lasting up to one year. The IACIS certification process for this level of training consists of examining six floppy disks, a CD, and one hard disk drive in sequence, submitting a thorough report of each examination, and completing a written test. The first four floppy disks must be examined by using a command-line tool. (You cannot use a GUI tool to examine the floppy disks.) The testing agency plants files on the disks that you must find, including items that are easy to find, data in unallocated space, RAM slack, file slack, and deleted files. Other topics include data hiding, determining file types of disguised files, and accessing password-protected files. You might also be asked to draw conclusions on a case based on evidence found on the disks. Proficiency in the use of technical tools and deductive reasoning is necessary. A full and thorough report demonstrating accepted procedures and evidence control must be submitted with each disk before proceeding to the next disk. Candidates who successfully complete all parts of the IACIS test are designated as **Certified Forensic Computer Examiners (CFCEs)**. The CFCE process changes as technology changes. The description here is current as of this writing. IACIS requires recertification every three years to demonstrate continuing work in the field of computer forensics. Recertification is less intense than the original certification, but does test examiners to make sure they're continuing their education and are still active in the field of computer forensics. For the latest information about IACIS and applying for a CFCE certification or membership in IACIS, visit the IACIS Web site.

High-Tech Crime Network (HTCN)

The **High-Tech Crime Network (HTCN)** also provides several levels of certification for applicants. Unlike IACIS, however, HTCN requires a review of all related training, including training in one of its approved courses, a written test for the specific certification, and a review of the candidate's work history. HTCN certification is open to anyone meeting the criteria in the profession of computing investigations. At the time of this writing, the HTCN Web site (*www.htcn.org*) specified the following four levels of certification and the requirements for each.

Certified Computer Crime Investigator, Basic Level

- Candidates have two years of law enforcement or corporate investigative experience or a bachelor's degree and one year of investigative experience.

- Eighteen months of the candidate's experience directly relates to the investigation of computer-related incidents or crimes.

- Candidates have successfully completed 40 hours of training from an approved agency, organization, or training company.

- Candidates must provide documentation of at least 10 cases in which they participated.

Certified Computer Crime Investigator, Advanced Level

- Candidates have three years of law enforcement or corporate investigative experience in any area or a bachelor's degree and two years of investigative experience.
- Four years of the candidate's experience directly relates to the investigation of computer-related incidents or crimes.
- Candidates have successfully completed 80 hours of training from an approved agency, organization, or company.
- Candidates served as lead investigator in at least 20 separate cases during the past three years and were involved in at least 40 other cases as a lead investigator or supervisor or in a supportive capacity. Candidates had at least 60 hours of involvement in cases in the past three years.

Certified Computer Forensic Technician, Basic

- Candidates have three years of investigative experience in any discipline from law enforcement or corporate or have a college degree with one year of experience in investigations.
- Candidates have 18 months of investigative experience in computing investigations from law enforcement or corporate.
- Candidates must have completed 40 hours of computer forensic training from an approved organization.
- Candidates must successfully complete a written examination.
- Candidates must provide documentation of at least 10 computing investigations.

Certified Computer Forensic Technician, Advanced

- Candidates must have three years of experience in any investigation discipline from law enforcement or corporate or possess a college degree and two years of experience in any investigation discipline.
- Candidates must have four years of direct experience related to computer forensics in law enforcement or corporate investigations.
- Candidates must have completed 80 hours of computer forensics training from an approved organization.
- Candidates must have been the lead computer forensics investigator in 20 or more investigations in the past three years and in 40 or more additional computing investigations as lead computer forensics technician, supervisor, or contributor. The candidate must have completed at least 60 investigations in the past three years.

EnCase Certified Examiner (EnCE) Certification

Guidance Software, the creators of EnCase, a computer forensics utility, sponsors the EnCE certification program. EnCE certification is open to the public and private sectors and is specific to the use and mastery of EnCase computer forensics analysis.

Requirements for taking the EnCE certification exam do not depend on taking the Guidance Software EnCase training courses. Candidates for this certificate are required to have a licensed copy of EnCase. For more information on EnCE certification requirements, visit *www.encase.com* or *www.guidancesoftware.com*.

Other Training and Certifications

Other organizations are considering certifications or have related training programs. Non-profit high-technology organizations for public- and private-sector investigations that offer certification and training include the following organizations:

- High Technology Crime Investigation Association (HTCIA), *www.htcia.org*

- SysAdmin, Audit, Network, Security Institute (SANS), *www.sans.org*

- Computer Technology Investigators Northwest (CTIN), *www.ctin.org*

- New Technologies, Inc. (NTI), *www.forensics-intl.com*

- Southeast Cybercrime Institute at Kennesaw State University, *www.certified-computer-examiner.com*

Organizations that offer training and certification only for law enforcement personnel include the following:

- Federal Law Enforcement Training Center (FLETC), *www.fletc.gov*

- National White Collar Crime Center (NW3C), *www.cybercrime.org*

DETERMINING THE PHYSICAL LAYOUT OF A COMPUTER FORENSICS LAB

After you have sufficient training to become a computer forensics investigator, you conduct most of your investigations in a lab. This section discusses the physical requirements of a basic computer investigation and forensics lab. The correct layout of a lab can make it more safe, secure, and productive.

Your lab facility must be physically secure so that evidence is not lost, corrupted, or destroyed. Workspaces should also be set up to prevent or alleviate work-related injuries, such as repetitive-motion injuries. As with hardware and software costs, you must consider what you need to maintain a safe and secure environment when determining physical lab expenses.

You must also use inventory control methods to track all your computing assets, which means you should maintain a complete and up-to-date inventory list of all major hardware and software items you have in the lab. For consumable items such as cables and media, including floppy disks, CDs, and tapes, maintain an inventory list so that you know when to order more supplies.

Identifying Lab Security Needs

All computer investigation and forensics labs need an enclosed room where a forensic workstation can be set up. You should not use an open cubicle because it allows easy access to your evidence. You need a room that you can lock to control your evidence and attest to its integrity. In particular, your lab should be secure during data analysis, even if it takes several weeks to analyze a disk drive. To preserve the integrity of evidence data, your lab should function as an evidence locker or safe, making it a **secure facility** or a secure storage safe.

The following are the minimum requirements for a computer investigation and forensics lab of any size:

- Small room with true floor-to-ceiling walls
- Door access with a locking mechanism, which can be a regular key lock or combination lock; the key or combination must be limited to authorized users
- Secure container, such as a safe or heavy-duty file cabinet with a quality padlock that prevents the drawers from opening
- Visitor's log listing all people who have accessed your lab

For daily work production, several examiners can work together in a large open area, as long as they all have the same level of authority and access need. This lab area should also have floor-to-ceiling walls and a locking door. In many public and private organizations, several investigators share a door to the lab that requires an ID card and an entry code.

As a security practice, computing investigators and forensic examiners must be briefed on the lab's security policy. Share information about a case investigation only with other examiners and personnel who need to know about the investigation.

Conducting High-risk Investigations

High-risk investigations, such as those involving national security or murder, for example, demand more security than the minimum lab requirements provide. As technology improves and information circulates among computer hackers, keeping your investigation secure can be more difficult. For example, detecting computer eavesdropping is difficult and expensive, but sophisticated criminals and intelligence services in foreign countries can use equipment that detects network transmissions, wireless devices, phone conversations, and the use of computer equipment. Instructions for building a sniffing device that can illegally collect computer emanations are available online and are, therefore, available to anyone. These devices can pick up anything you type on your computer.

Most electronic devices emit electromagnetic radiation (EMR). Certain kinds of equipment can intercept EMR, and the EMR can be used to determine the data the device is transmitting or displaying. According to Webopedia (see *www.webopedia.com/DidYouKnow/ Computer_Science/2002/vaneck.asp*), the EMR from a computer monitor can be picked up as far away as a half mile.

To protect your investigations, consider how defense contractors during the Cold War were required to shield sensitive computing systems and prevent electronic eavesdropping of any computer emissions. The U.S. Department of Defense calls this special computer-emission shielding **TEMPEST**. (For a brief description of TEMPEST, see the National Industrial Security Program Operating Manual (NISPOM) DoD 5220.22-M, Chapter 11, Section 1, Tempest, *http://nsi.org/Library/Govt/Nispom.html*.)

Constructing a TEMPEST lab requires lining the walls, ceiling, floor, and doors with specially grounded conductive metal sheets. Typically, copper sheeting is used because it conducts electricity well. TEMPEST facilities must include special filters for electrical power that prevent power cables from transmitting computer emanations. All heating and ventilation ducts require special baffles to trap the emanations. Likewise, telephones inside the TEMPEST facility must have special line filters. A TEMPEST facility usually has two doors separated by dead space. The first exterior door must be shut before opening the interior door. Each door also has special copper molding to enhance electricity conduction.

Because a TEMPEST-qualified lab facility is expensive and requires routine inspection and testing, it should be considered only for large regional computer forensics labs that demand absolute security from illegal eavesdropping. To avoid these financial and maintenance costs, some vendors have built low-emanating workstations instead of TEMPEST facilities. These workstations are more expensive than average workstations but are less expensive than a TEMPEST lab.

Considering Office Ergonomics

Because computing investigations often require hours of processing disk drives for evidence, your workspace should be as comfortable as possible to prevent repetitive-motion injuries and other computer work-related injuries. **Ergonomics** is the study of designing equipment to meet the human need of comfort, while allowing for improved productivity. Ergonomics involves psychology, anatomy, and physiology. Understanding psychology helps designers create equipment that people can easily understand how to use. Ergonomic design considers anatomy to make sure the equipment correctly fits the person using it. Physiology helps determine how much effort or energy the person using the equipment requires.

To ensure an ergonomic workspace, review the following questions and refer to Figure 3-2 when arranging your workspace and selecting lab furniture:

- *Desk or workstation table*—Is the desk placed at the correct height for you? Do you need a chair that's lower or higher than normal to make the desktop easy to reach and comfortable for you? Are your wrists straight when sitting? Is this position comfortable? Are the heels of your hands in a comfortable position? Do they exert too much pressure on the desktop? Do you need a keyboard or mouse pad?

- *Chair*—Does your chair allow you to adjust its height? Is the back of the chair too long or too short for the length of your back? Is the seat portion of the chair too long or too short for the length of your thigh? Are the seat and back of the chair padded enough to be comfortable for you? Can you sit up straight when viewing the computer monitor? Are your elbows in a comfortable position while working? How do your shoulders and back feel while sitting and working at the workstation? Is your head facing the computer's monitor or is it off center because you can't position the chair correctly in front of the desk?

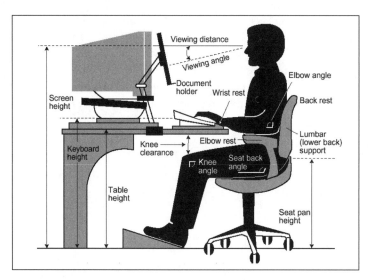

Figure 3-2   Proper ergonomics at a desk

- *Workbench*—Is the workbench for your lab facility at the correct height when you're standing in front of it? Can you easily reach the back of the bench without having to stand on a stool?

Besides furniture, consider the ergonomics of your keyboard and mouse. These two items probably contribute to more repetitive-motion injuries than any other device, primarily because they were designed for moderate but not extensive use. Using the keyboard for several hours at a time can be painful and cause physical problems. As shown in Figure 3-3, make sure your wrists are straight when you're working with a keyboard or mouse, even if these items are ergonomically designed.

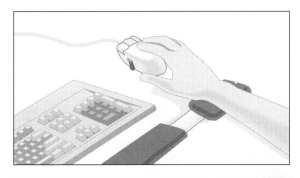

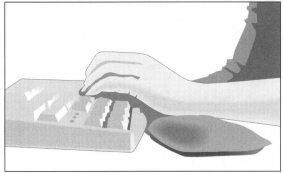

Figure 3-3   Hand and wrist positioning with a wrist pad

If you work with computers for hours in one position, you will injure yourself. No matter how well the furniture, keyboard, or mouse is designed, always take breaks to stretch and rest your body.

Considering Environmental Conditions

Just as the chair, desk, keyboard, and mouse affect your comfort and health, your lab's ventilation and temperature also contribute to your comfort and productivity. Although a typical desktop computer uses standard household electricity, computers get warm as they run. Unless you invest in a liquid-cooled computer case for your forensic workstation, a standard desktop computer generates heat. The more workstations you're running, the hotter your lab. Therefore, you need adequate air conditioning and ventilation for the room. You should consult with your building's facility coordinator to determine whether the room can be upgraded to handle your current and expected computing needs.

Use the following checklist of heating, ventilation, and air-conditioning (HVAC) system questions when planning your computing forensics laboratory:

- How large is the room, and how much air moves through it per minute?
- Can the room handle the increased heat that workstations generate?
- What is the maximum number of workstations the room can handle?

- How many computers will be located in this room immediately?
- Can the room handle the heat output from a small redundant array of independent disks (RAID) server?

Lighting

An overlooked environmental issue for any computer forensics facility is the lighting. Most offices have too many lights at the wrong illumination, causing headaches or eyestrain. Several vendors offer natural or full-spectrum lighting, which is less fatiguing than standard incandescent or fluorescent lights, although it doesn't have any health benefits.

In 1986, the Food and Drug Administration (FDA) issued a Health Fraud Notice regarding "false and misleading" claims and "gross deceptions" by light bulb and lamp manufacturers to consumers on the benefits of full-spectrum lighting (FDA Enforcement Report: Health Fraud Notice, 1986, WL 59812 [F.D.A.]).

If the lighting in your computer forensics lab is a problem, consult with your facility's management and find out what products are currently available that can best meet your needs. For additional information on how to deal with eyestrain, see *www.apple.com/about/ergonomics/vision.html*.

Considering Structural Design Factors

In addition to ergonomic and environmental concerns, consider the physical construction of your computer forensics laboratory. Your lab should be a safe, secure, lockable room. Because it can take anywhere from a few hours to several days or weeks to process a computer disk, your lab needs to be secure for the same amount of time. Evidence on larger disk drives takes even longer to analyze and sort. Often you need to leave computer evidence, such as a suspect's hard disk drive, connected to your workstation overnight to complete a bit-stream image backup, which can take several hours. You need to leave your unattended evidence in a secure location—a room that no unauthorized person can access without your direct control.

The *National Industrial Security Program Operating Manual* (NISPOM), Chapter 5, Section 8, page 1, "Construction Requirements," provides an overview of how to build a secure lab. See *http://nsi.org/Library/Govt/Nispom.html* for details.

To ensure the security of your lab, examine the facility's hardware, walls, ceiling, floors, and windows. Make sure only heavy-duty building material has been used in the construction of your lab. All hardware, such as door hinges on the outside of the lab, should be peened, pinned, brazed, or spot welded to prevent removal.

Walls can be constructed of plaster, gypsum wallboard, metal panels, hardboard, wood, plywood, grass, wire mesh, expanded metal, or other materials offering resistance to and evidence of any unauthorized entry to the lab. If you use insert panels, you also need to install material that can reveal evidence of any attempt to gain entry.

Ceilings, like walls, can be constructed of plaster, gypsum wallboard, acoustic ceiling panels, hardboard, wood, plywood, ceiling tile, or other material that offers some sort of resistance, which makes detection possible if access is attempted. For false ceilings or drop ceilings in which the walls don't extend to the true ceiling because of hanging ceiling tile, the false ceiling must be reinforced with wire mesh or 18-gauge expanded metal that extends from the top of the false wall to the actual ceiling. This wire mesh or expanded metal must overlap adjoining walls and should provide resistance that allows detection of attempted access.

If you have raised floors such as those often found in data centers, look for large openings in the perimeter walls. If you find openings, use the same types of material described for ceilings to make sure the floor provides sufficient resistance and shows evidence of someone attempting to access the lab.

Avoid windows on your lab exterior. If you're assigned a room with exterior windows, install additional material, such as wire mesh, on the inside to improve security. If you're working in an office building and need to place your lab on an exterior wall, locate the lab on an upper floor, not a ground floor. Also, make sure that all computer monitors of your forensic workstations face away from the windows to prevent unauthorized people from spying on you while you're working on a case.

Doors can be wood (solid core) or metal and preferably should not have windows. If your door does have a window, it should have wire mesh in the glass for sufficient resistance to prevent and detect an attempted entry. The door's locking device should have a heavy-duty built-in combination device or a high-quality key-locking doorknob. If you're using a key-locking doorknob, only authorized personnel should have a copy of the key.

Depending on your lab's location, you might need to install intrusion-detection systems and fire alarms. Consult and contract with a bonded alarm company.

Determining Electrical Needs

You need sufficient electrical power to run your workstations and other equipment; 15- and 20-amp service is the preferred setup for electrical outlets. In addition, you should have enough electrical outlets spaced throughout the lab for easy access, eliminating the need for extension cords or electrical plug strips, which are potential fire hazards.

If you have adequate electrical power for your operation, power fluctuations are usually not a problem unless you're in an area with poor electrical service. Most computers are fairly tolerant of power fluctuations, although these fluctuations do cause electrical wear and tear on your computer's components. However, all electrical devices eventually fail, usually because of accumulated electrical voltage spikes, where voltage increases rapidly (that is, surges) or decreases suddenly. If your lab equipment exhibits unexplained failures, consult with your facilities manager to check for problems in electrical power.

As part of any computer forensics lab, UPS (uninterruptible power supply) units must be connected to all forensic workstations. Using UPS units reduces electrical problems with your workstations. If a power failure occurs, a UPS allows you to continue working until you can safely shut down your computer. In addition to giving you time for a safe shutdown of your computer, most UPS systems block or filter electrical fluctuations. This feature helps minimize computer component problems that might corrupt and destroy sensitive magnetic media evidence.

Planning for Communications

When planning voice and data communications, note that each examiner needs a telephone. Unless you're working in a TEMPEST environment, which has special voice and data access requirements, you can install a multiline Integrated Services Digital Network (ISDN) phone system in the lab. ISDN is the easiest way for lab personnel to handle incoming calls.

You also need access to the Internet through a dial-up or broadband Internet service provider (ISP). Computer forensics software vendors often provide software updates and patches on a Web site, so you need to be able to download that software. You also need Internet access to conduct research on evidence you find and to consult with other forensics professionals. However, don't keep your workstation connected to the Internet while conducting your analysis unless it's absolutely required. Internet connections can compromise your system's security. This risk includes systems that have a firewall.

Setting up a network for workstations in a computer forensics lab enables you to easily transfer data to other examiners. Having an internal local area network (LAN) makes operations run more smoothly. For example, you can easily share a RAID file server and printers on a LAN. This setup is especially useful when you have specialty printers connected to a print server. Using a central lab RAID server also saves time and energy when you're copying large data files, such as bit-stream image files.

If your organization is part of a wide area network (WAN), consider having a separate computer used only to connect to your WAN to protect the security of your forensic workstations. By keeping your forensic workstations physically separate from the WAN, you eliminate any intentional or unintentional access to your evidence or output from your work product. For example, although workstations on a WAN can receive notices to upgrade software, doing so while your forensic workstation is connected to your WAN can corrupt evidence. Isolating systems prevents this corruption.

Installing Fire-Suppression Systems

Fire can be a disaster in a computer forensics lab. Any electrical device can cause a fire, although this isn't common in computers. On rare occasions, an electrical short in a computer might destroy a cable. If the power on a low-voltage cable is high enough, it could ignite other combustible items nearby.

Computers can also cause fires if a hard disk's servo-voice coil actuators freeze because of damage to the drive. If these actuators are frozen, the head assembly cannot move. The internal programming of the disk's circuit card then applies more power to the actuators to provide more electrical power to move the head assembly correctly, passing too much electrical power through the disk. The components in the disk can handle only so much power before they fail and overload the cables connecting the drive to the computer. These cables, especially the ribbon type, don't respond well to excessive power. When too much power is applied to these low-voltage cables, especially ribbon cables, sparks can fly, causing a fire.

Most offices are equipped with fire sprinkler systems and dry chemical fire extinguishers (B rated). For most computer forensics lab operations, these fire-suppression systems work well. The standard desktop workstation used for most forensic analysis doesn't require additional protection. However, if your lab facility has raised floors, you might need to install a dry chemical fire-suppression system. If you have any concerns about your fire-suppression needs, contact your facility's coordinator or local fire marshal. For additional information on best practices for fire extinguishers, see *www.pp.okstate.edu/ehs/MODULES/Exting/Intro. htm*. For information on computer room fire-suppression systems, see *www2.fpm.wisc.edu/ safety/gsp/Fire%20Suppression%20Systems.html*.

Using Evidence Containers

The containers you use to store your evidence, also known as evidence lockers, must be secure so that no unauthorized person can easily access your evidence. You must use high-quality locks, such as padlocks, with limited duplicate-key distribution. Also, routinely inspect the content of your evidence storage containers to make sure they store only current evidence. Evidence for closed cases should be moved to a secure off-site facility.

NISPOM Chapter 5, Section 3 (*http://nsi.org/Library/Govt/Nispom.html*) describes the characteristics of a safe storage container. Consult with your facility management or legal counsel, such as corporate or prosecuting attorneys, to determine what your lab should do to maintain evidence integrity. The following are recommendations for securing storage containers:

- The evidence container should be located in a restricted area that's accessible only to lab personnel.

- The number of people authorized to open the evidence container should be kept to a minimum. Maintain records on who is authorized to access each container.

- All evidence containers should remain locked when they are not under the direct supervision of an authorized person.

If a combination locking system is used for your evidence container, implement the following practices:

- Provide the same level of security for the combination as for the container's contents. Store the combination in another equally secure container.

- Destroy any previous combinations after setting up a new combination.

- Allow only authorized personnel to change lock combinations.

- Change the combination every six months, when any authorized personnel leave the organization, and immediately after finding an unsecured container—that is, one that's open and unattended.

If you are using a keyed padlock, use the following practices:

- Appoint a key custodian responsible for distributing keys.

- Stamp sequential numbers on each duplicate key.

- Maintain a registry that lists which key is assigned to which authorized person.

- Conduct a monthly audit to ensure that no authorized person has lost a key.

- Take an inventory of all keys when the custodian changes.

- Place keys in a lockable container accessible only to the lab manager and designated key custodian in the lab.

- Maintain the same level of security for keys as for evidence containers.

- Change locks and keys annually; if a key is missing, replace all associated locks and the key.

- Do not use a master key for several locks.

The storage container or cabinet should be made of steel and include an internal cabinet lock or external padlock. If possible, acquire a safe, which provides superior security and protects your evidence from fire damage. Look for specialized safes, called media safes, designed to protect electronic media. Media safes are rated by the number of hours it takes before the contents are damaged by a fire. The higher the rating, the better the safe protects evidence.

An evidence storage room is also convenient, especially if it's part of your computer forensics lab. Security for an evidence room must integrate the same construction and securing devices as does the general lab. Large computer forensics operations also need an evidence custodian and a service counter with a securable metal roll-up window system to control evidence. With a secure evidence room, you can store large computer components, such as computers, monitors, and other large peripheral devices.

Be sure to maintain a log that lists every time an evidence container is opened and closed. Each time the container is accessed, the log should indicate the date the evidence container was opened and the initials of the authorized person. These records should be maintained for at least three years or longer, as prescribed by your prosecuting or corporate attorneys. Logs are discussed in more detail in Chapter 5.

Overseeing Facility Maintenance

Your lab should be properly maintained at all times to ensure the safety and health of lab personnel. If damage occurs to the floor, walls, ceilings, or furniture, it should be repaired immediately. Also, be sure to monitor—that is, escort—cleaning crews as they work.

Because static electricity is a major problem when handling electrical devices such as computer parts, consider placing special antistatic pads around electronic workbenches and workstations. In addition, floors and carpets should be cleaned at least once a week to help minimize dust that can cause static electricity.

Maintain two separate trash containers, one to store items unrelated to an investigation, such as discarded CDs or magnetic tapes, and the other for sensitive material that requires special handling to ensure that it's destroyed. Using separate trash containers maintains the integrity of criminal investigation processes and protects trade secrets and attorney-client privileged communications in a private corporation. Several commercially bonded firms specialize in disposing of sensitive materials. Your lab should have access to these services to maintain the integrity of your investigations.

Considering Physical Security Needs

In addition to your lab's physical design and construction, you need to enhance your lab's security by setting security policies. How much physical security you implement depends on the nature of your lab. If your lab is a regional computer crime lab, your security needs are high because the lab risks losing, corrupting, or otherwise damaging evidence. The physical security needs of a large corporation are probably not as high because the risk of evidence loss or compromise is much lower. Determining the risk for your organization dictates how much security you integrate into your computer forensics lab.

Regardless of the security risk to your lab, maintain a sign-in log, in a notebook or electronically, for all visitors. The log should list the visitor's name, date and time of arrival and departure, employer's name, purpose of the visit, and name of the lab member receiving the visitor. Consider anyone who's not assigned to the lab to be a visitor, including janitors, facility maintenance personnel, friends, and family. All visitors should be escorted by an assigned authorized staff member throughout their visit to the lab to ensure that they don't accidentally or intentionally tamper with an investigation or evidence. As an added precaution, use a visible or audible alarm, such as a visitor badge, to let all investigators actively working on cases know that a visitor is in the area. If possible, hire a security guard or have an intrusion alarm system with a guard force ensure your lab's security. Alarm systems with guards can be used after business hours to monitor your lab.

Auditing a Computer Forensics Lab

To ensure that all security policies and practices are followed, conduct routine inspections to physically audit your lab and evidence storage containers. Audits should include, but are not limited to, the following facility components and practices:

- Inspect the ceiling, floor, roof, and exterior walls of the lab at least once a month, looking for anything unusual or new.

- Inspect doors to make sure they close and lock correctly.

- Check locks to see if they need to be replaced or changed.

- Review visitor logs to see if they are being used properly.

- Review log sheets for evidence containers to determine when they have been opened and closed.

- At the end of every workday, secure any evidence that's not being processed on a forensic workstation.

Determining Floor Plans for Computer Forensics Labs

How you configure the work area for your computer forensics lab depends on your budget, the amount of available floor space, and the number of computers you might assign to each computing investigator. For a small operation handling two or three cases a month, one forensic workstation should handle your workload. One workstation requires only the area of an average desk. If you're handling many more cases per month, you can probably process two or three computing investigations at a time, which requires more than one workstation. The ideal configuration for multiple workstations is to have two forensic workstations plus one non-forensic workstation that has Internet access.

Because you need plenty of room around each workstation, a work area containing three workstations requires approximately 150 square feet of space, meaning that the work area should be about 10 feet by 15 feet. This amount of space allows for two chairs so that the computing investigator can brief another investigator, paralegal, or attorney on the case.

Small labs usually consist of two forensic workstations, a research computer, a workbench (if space allows), and storage cabinets, as shown in Figure 3-4.

Mid-size computer forensics labs, such as those in a private business, have more workstations. For safety reasons, the lab should have at least two exits, as shown in Figure 3-5. If possible, cubicles or even individual offices should be part of the layout to enforce the need-to-know policy. These labs can usually have more library space for software and hardware storage.

State law enforcement or the Federal Bureau of Investigation (FBI) usually runs most large or regional computer forensics labs. As shown in Figure 3-6, these labs have a separate evidence room, which is typical in police investigations, except this room is limited to digital evidence. One or more custodians might be assigned to manage and control traffic in and out of the evidence room.

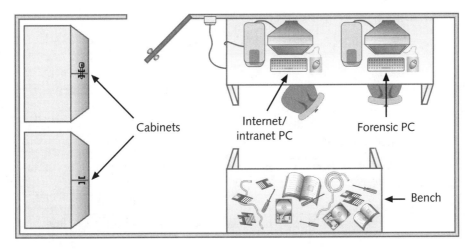

Figure 3-4　Small or home-based lab

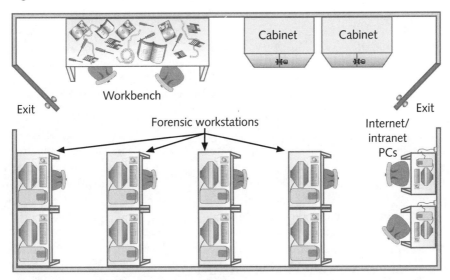

Figure 3-5　Mid-size computer forensics lab

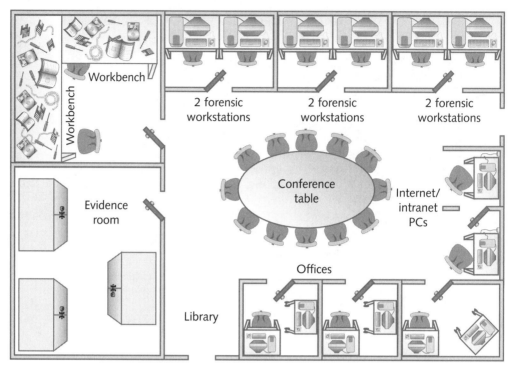

Figure 3-6   Regional computer forensics lab

As discussed earlier, the evidence room needs to be secure. The lab should have at least two controlled exits and no windows. Individual offices for supervisors and cubicles for investigators are more practical in this configuration. Remember that the forensic workstations are connected to an isolated LAN, and only a few machines are connected to the outside WAN or metropolitan area network (MAN).

SELECTING A BASIC FORENSIC WORKSTATION

The computer workstation you use as a forensic analysis system depends on your budget and specific needs. Many well-designed forensic workstations are available that can handle most computing investigation needs. Consider, however, that when you start processing a case, you use a workstation for the duration of the examination. Use less powerful workstations for mundane tasks and multipurpose workstations for the higher-end analysis tasks. Chapter 4 lists several well-known forensic workstation vendors and the features that make them unique.

Selecting Workstations for Police Labs

Police departments in major cities probably have the most diverse needs for computing investigation tools because the communities they serve use a wide assortment of computing systems. Not all computer users have the latest technology, so police departments need older machines and software, such as a Commodore 64, an Osbourne I, or a Kaypro computer running CP/M or Minix, to match their community.

One way to investigate older and unusual computing systems is to keep track of **special-interest groups (SIGs)** that still use these old systems. SIGs can be a valuable source of support for recovering and analyzing uncommon systems. (Search for SIGs on the Web as necessary.) When investigating cases involving unusual computer systems, you can also coordinate with or subcontract to larger computer forensics labs. Like large police departments, a regional computer forensics lab must have diverse systems to serve its community. Regional labs often receive work from smaller labs involving unusual computers or operating systems.

For small, local police departments, the majority of work involves Windows PCs and Apple Macintosh systems. The computer forensics lab of a small police department can be limited to one multipurpose forensic workstation with one or two basic workstations.

The computing systems in a lab should be able to process typical cases in a timely manner. The time it takes to process a typical case usually depends on the size and type of industries in the region. For example, suppose your lab is located in a region with one or more large manufacturing firms that employ 50,000 or more people. Ten percent of those employees might be involved in criminal behavior. One Fortune 500 company investigates an average of one or two murders a year in which law enforcement uses information on the employee's work computer as evidence.

As a general rule, there should be at least one law enforcement computer investigator for every 250,000 people in a geographic region. For example, if your community has 1,000,000 people, the regional computer forensics lab should have at least four computer investigators. Each investigator should have at least one multipurpose forensic workstation with one general-purpose workstation.

Selecting Workstations for Private and Corporate Labs

For the private sector, such as a business conducting internal investigations or a commercial business service providing computer forensics services to private parties, equipment resources are generally easy to determine.

Commercial services providing computer forensics analysis for other businesses can tailor their services to specific markets. They can specialize in one or two platforms, such as an Intel PC running a Microsoft operating system. They can also gather a variety of tools to meet a wider market. The type of equipment they need depends on their specialty, if any. For general computer forensics facilities, a multipurpose forensic workstation is sufficient.

Private companies with their own Internal Computing Investigation departments can determine the type of forensic workstation they need by identifying the types of computers they use. If a business is running only Windows PCs, internal investigators don't need much specialized equipment. If a business uses many kinds of computers, the Internal Forensics Department needs systems and equipment that support the same types of computers. With some of the leading computer forensics programs, you can work from a Windows PC and examine both Windows and Macintosh disk drives.

Stocking Hardware Peripherals

In addition to workstations and software, all labs should have a wide assortment of cables and spare expansion slot cards. Consider stocking your computer forensics lab with the following peripheral devices:

- 40-pin 18-inch and 36-inch IDE cables, both ATA-33 and ATA-100 or faster
- Ribbon cables for floppy disks
- Extra SCSI cards, preferably ultra-wide
- Graphics cards, both Peripheral Component Interconnect (PCI) and Accelerated Graphics Port (AGP) types
- Extra power cords
- A variety of hard disk drives (as many as you can afford)
- At least two 2.5-inch Notebook IDE hard drive to standard IDE/ATA adapter
- Computer hand tools, such as a Phillips screwdriver, socket wrench, flathead screwdriver, and small flashlight

Maintaining Operating Systems and Application Software Inventories

Operating systems are a necessary part of your lab's inventory. You should maintain licensed copies of as many legacy operating systems as possible to handle cases involving unusual systems. Microsoft operating systems should include Windows XP, 2000, NT 4.0, NT 3.5, 98, 3.11, and Microsoft DOS 6.22. Apple Macintosh operating systems should include Mac OS X, 9.x, and 8 or older. Linux operating systems can include Fedora, Caldera Open Linux, Slackware, and Debian.

Although most high-end computer forensics tools can open or display data files created with popular programs, they don't support all programs. Your software inventory should include current and older versions of the following programs. If you deal with both Windows PCs and Apple Macintosh systems, you should have programs for both.

- Microsoft Office XP, 2003, 2000, 97, and 95
- Quicken (if you deal with a lot of financial investigations)

- Programming languages, such as Visual Basic and Visual C++
- Specialized viewers, such as QuickView, ACDSee, ThumbsPlus, and IrfanView
- Corel Office Suite
- StarOffice/OpenOffice
- Peachtree accounting applications

3

Using a Disaster Recovery Plan

Besides planning for equipment needs, you also need to plan for disasters, such as hard disk crashes, lightning strikes, and power outages. A disaster recovery plan ensures that you can restore your workstations and investigation file servers to their original condition if a catastrophic failure occurs, such as a fire, a flood, or a head crash of an important disk drive.

A disaster recovery plan also specifies how to rebuild an investigation workstation after it has been severely contaminated by a virus from a disk drive you're analyzing. Central to any disaster recovery plan is a system for backing up investigation computers. Tools such as Norton Ghost are useful for directly restoring files. As a general precaution, consider backing up your workstation once a week. You can restore programs from the original disks or CDs, but recovering lost data without up-to-date backups is difficult.

Store your system backups where they are easily accessible. You should have at least one copy of your backups on site and a duplicate copy or a previous copy of your backups stored in a safe off-site facility. Off-site backups are usually rotated on a schedule that varies according to your needs, such as every day, week, or month.

In addition to performing routine backups, record all the updates you make to your workstation by using a process called **configuration management**. Some companies record updates in a configuration management database to maintain compliance with lab policy. Every time you add or update software on your workstation, enter the change in the database or in a simple notebook with handwritten entries to document the change.

A disaster recovery plan can also address how to restore a workstation you reconfigured for a specific investigation. For example, if you install a suite of applications, you might not have enough disk space for normal processing needs, so you might encounter problems during reconfigurations or even during simple upgrades. The disaster recovery plan should outline how to uninstall software and delete any files the uninstall program hasn't removed so that you can restore your system to its original configuration.

For labs using high-end RAID servers (such as Digital Intelligence F.R.E.D.C. or F.R.E.D. M.), you must consider methods for restoring large datasets. These large-end servers must have adequate data backup systems available in the event of a major failure of more than one disk drive. When planning a recovery procedure for RAID servers, consider whether the amount of downtime it takes to restore backup data is acceptable to the lab operation.

Planning for Equipment Upgrades

Risk management involves determining how much risk is acceptable for any process or operation, such as replacing equipment. Identify the equipment your lab depends on, and create a schedule to replace that equipment. Also identify equipment that you can replace when it fails.

Recall that computing components are designed to last 18 to 24 months in normal business operations, and new, larger versions of operating systems and applications are released frequently. Therefore, systems periodically need more RAM, disk space, and processing speed. To keep your lab current, schedule hardware replacements at least every 18 months and preferably every 12 months.

Using Laptop Forensic Workstations

Recent important advances in hardware technology offer more flexibility to computer forensics. You can now use a laptop PC with a FireWire (IEEE 1394B standard), USB 2.0, or PCMCIA SATA hard disks to create a lightweight, mobile forensic workstation. Improved throughput speeds of data transfer on laptops also make it easier to create bit-stream copies of suspect disk drives.

However, laptops are still limited as forensic workstations. Even with improved data transfer rates, acquiring data with a data compression-imaging tool such as EnCase or SafeBack creates a bottleneck. The processor speed determines how quickly you can acquire an image file of a hard disk. The faster the CPU on your laptop (or other PC), the faster the image is created in a compressed mode.

BUILDING A BUSINESS CASE FOR DEVELOPING A FORENSICS LAB

Before you can set up a computer forensics lab, you must enlist the support of your managers and other team members. To do so, you build a **business case**, a plan you can use to sell your services to your management or clients. In the business case, you justify acquiring newer and better resources to investigate computer forensics cases.

How you develop your business case depends on the organization you support. If you are the sole proprietor, making a business case is fairly simple. If you need money to buy the tools, you can save your money for the purchase or negotiate with your bank for a loan. For a public entity such as a police department, business requirements change significantly because budgets are planned a year or more in advance. Public agency department managers present their budget proposals to upper managers. If approved, the department makes money available to acquire resources outlined in the budget. Some public organizations might have other funds available that can be spent immediately for special needs. Managers can divert these funds in the case of emergency or unforeseen needs.

3

Keep in mind that a private-sector business, especially a large corporate environment, is motivated by the need to make money. A business case should demonstrate how computing investigations could save money and avoid risks that can damage profits, such as by preventing litigation involving the company. For example, recent court decisions have defined viewing pornographic images in the workplace as creating a hostile environment for other employees, which is related to employee harassment and computer abuse. An employer is responsible for preventing and investigating harassment of employees and non-employees associated with the workplace. A company is also liable if it doesn't actively prevent the creation of a hostile workplace by providing employee training and investigating allegations of computer abuse. A lawsuit, regardless of who wins, can cost an employer several hundred thousand dollars. In your business case, compare the cost of training and conducting computing investigations with the cost of a lawsuit.

The Internet makes it difficult for employers to provide a safe and secure environment for employees. In particular, employees can easily abuse free e-mail services available on the Web. These free services give senders anonymity, enabling an employee to transmit inappropriate e-mail messages, often in the form of sexual harassment. Because training rarely prevents this type of inappropriate behavior, an employer needs to institute an investigation program that involves collecting network logs, such as proxy server logs, and examining computer disks to locate traces of message evidence. Chapter 13 discusses e-mail abuse and using e-mail server and network logs.

Your business case should also show how computing investigations can improve profits, such as by protecting intellectual property, trade secrets, and future business plans. For example, when employees leave one company for a competing company, they can reveal vital competitive information to their new employers. Suppose a fictitious company called Skateboard International (SI) has invested research and development into a new product that improves the stability of skateboards. Its main competitor is Better Skateboard; this company contacts Gwen Smith, a disgruntled SI employee, via e-mail and offers her a job. When Gwen leaves SI, she takes with her the plans for a new product. A few months later, Better Skateboard introduces a product similar to the skateboard Gwen had been researching at SI. SI recognizes that the new improved skateboard is similar to the one Gwen had been developing and consults the noncompete agreement Gwen signed when she was hired. SI thinks that the new technology Gwen might have provided to Better Skateboards belongs to its company. It suspects that Better Skateboard stole its trade secret and intellectual property.

SI could sue Better Skateboard and demand discovery on internal documents. Because Gwen and Better Skateboard corresponded via e-mail, a computing investigator needs to find data related to both hiring and research engineering at Better Skateboard. Better Skateboard can also demand discovery on SI's research records to determine whether any discrepancies in product design could disprove the lawsuit. In this fictitious scenario, computing investigations can allow one company to generate revenue from a new product and prevent the other company from doing so. Information related to profit and loss makes a persuasive argument in a business case.

Preparing a Business Case for a Computer Forensics Lab

It's important to understand the need for planning in the creation and continued maintenance operation of a computer forensics lab. The reason for this demand is the constant cost-cutting efforts of senior managers in all organizations. This behavior is common in all organizations, be they police departments or large private corporations. Because of organizations' tendencies to constantly reduce costs, you must plan ahead to ensure that money is available for facilities, tools, supplies, and training for your computer forensics lab.

The following sections describe some key elements for creating a computer forensics business case. It's a good idea to maintain a business case with annual updates.

Justification

Before you can start, you need to justify to the person controlling the budget the reason a lab is needed. This justification step requires asking the following questions:

- What type of computing investigation service is needed for your organization?

- Who are the potential customers for this service and how will it be budgeted—as an internal operation (police department or company security department, for instance)—or as an external operation (that is, a for-profit business venture)?

- How will you advertise your services to customers?

- Where will the initial and sustaining budget for business operations come from?

No matter what type of organization you work for, operating a computer forensics lab requires constant marketing of its services. That is, for a lab to be successful, effort must be taken to communicate, or advertise, the lab's services to previous, current, and future customers and clients. This need for marketing applies to both public agencies and private businesses. By applying marketing techniques to customers or clients, you can justify future budgets for the lab's operation and staff.

Budget Development

The budget needs to include all the items described in the following paragraphs. You must be as exact as possible when determining the true cost of these items. Making a mistake could cause delays and possible loss of the opportunity to start or improve your lab.

Facility Cost

For a new computer forensics lab, startup costs for a facility might take most of the budget. Depending on how large the lab is, you must determine first how much floor space is needed. As described previously in this chapter, a good rule of thumb is to plan 150 square feet per person. This amount of space might seem a bit larger than necessary, but you must consider how much storage space is needed to preserve evidence and to have enough supplies in stock. Check with your organization's facility manager regarding per-square-foot costs for your area or building. In developing your budget, here are some sample questions to ask. From the answers, you can then start calculating a budget.

- How many computer forensic examiners will use the lab?
- Will there be a need to temporarily accommodate other nonexaminers to inspect the recovered evidence?
- What are the costs to construct a secure lab?
- Is there a suitable room that can be converted into a lab?
- Is there sufficient electrical power and HVAC in the designated room?
- Are there existing telephone lines and network cables in the designated room?
- If not, how much will it cost to install these additional items?
- Is there an adequate door lock on the designated room's door?
- What will the furniture costs be?
- Will you need to install an alarm system?
- Are there any other facility costs, such as janitorial services and facility maintenance service fees?

Computer Hardware Requirements

Determining the types of investigations and data that will be analyzed in your computer forensics lab dictates what hardware equipment you need. For example, if you are the examiner for a mid-size private corporation, identifying the type of computer systems used can help you determine the type of forensic workstation needed for your lab. If your organization is using Intel-based PCs with Microsoft Windows XP, for instance, your forensic workstation should be a high-end Intel-based PC, too. For a small police department, determining the types of computers the public uses is more difficult. The diversity of a community's computer systems requires a police department to be much more versatile in the tools needed to conduct investigations. To determine computer hardware budget needs, here are some questions to consider in your planning:

- What types of investigations and data recovery will be performed in the lab?
- How many investigations can be expected per month of operation?
- Will there be any time-sensitive investigations that will demand rapid analysis of disk data?
- What sizes and how many disk drives will be needed to support a typical investigation?
- Will you need any high-speed backup device system, such as tape backup or DVD burners?
- What is the predominant type of computer system that you will investigate?

Software Requirements

In the past few years, many more computer forensics tools have become available. For the private sector, the cost for these tools ranges from about $300 and up. For the public sector, many computer forensics software vendors offer some discounts. However, just as you select hardware for your computer forensics lab to fit specific needs, you must first determine what type of operating systems and software applications will be investigated and then make purchases that fit. Keep in mind that the more you spend on a computer forensics software package, the more function and flexibility will be available. To determine computer software budget needs, here are some questions to consider in your planning:

- What types of operating systems will be examined?

- For less popular, uncommon, or older operating systems (such as Macintosh OS 9.x, OS/2, and CP/M), how often will there be a need to investigate them?

- What are the minimum needs for forensic software tools? That is, how many copies of EnCase, FTK, DriveSpy, or WinHex will be needed? How often will each tool be used in an average week?

- What types of operating systems will be needed to perform routine examinations?

- Will there be a need for any software such as QuickBooks or Peachtree?

- Is there a budget to purchase more than one forensic software tool, such as EnCase, FTK, or DriveSpy?

- Which disk-editing tool should be selected for general data analysis?

Miscellaneous Cost Needs

For this section of the budget, you need to brainstorm on other items, tools, and supplies to consider purchasing for the lab. They can range from general office supplies to specific needs for daily operations. To determine miscellaneous budget needs, here are some questions to consider in your planning:

- Will there be a need for errors and omission insurance for the lab's operation and staff?

- Will you need a budget for office supplies?

Approval and Acquisition

The approval and acquisition phase for a computer forensics lab is the management function. It's your responsibility to create a business case with a budget to present to your management for approval. As part of the approval process of your business case, you should include a risk analysis describing how a lab will minimize the risk of litigation, which is a persuasive argument for supporting the lab. You also need to make an educated guess of how many investigations are anticipated and how long they will take to complete on average. Remember, part of the approval process requires you to use negotiation skills to justify the business case. You might need to revise your case as needed to get approval.

As part of the business case, acquisition planning requires you to research different products to determine which one is the best and most cost effective. You need to contact several vendors' sales staff and design engineers to learn more about each product and service. Another factor to ask about is any annual maintenance costs. You need to budget for this expense, too, so that you can get support if you run into problems during an investigation. An additional item to research from others in the profession is the vendor's maintenance history. That is, do other computer forensics labs use the same product, and have they had any problems getting support for problems they encounter?

Another consideration is vendors' pricing structures. Vendor pricing isn't based on the cost of creating CDs and putting them into boxes. Product prices are based on cost for development, testing, documentation support, shipping, and research and development for future improvements. In addition, vendors are for-profit organizations; they have investors to pay, too. Keep in mind that for vendors to be around next year to provide products and services for you, they need to make money.

Implementation

After approval and acquisition, you need to plan the implementation of facilities and tools. As part of your business case, you need to describe how implementation of all approved items will be processed. A timeline showing expected delivery or installation dates and expected completion dates must be part of the business case. You should also have a coordination plan for delivery dates and times for arrival of materials and tools. Inspection of facility construction, equipment (including furniture and benches), and software tools should be included in the schedule. Make sure you schedule inspection dates in your business case to ensure that what you ordered arrived and is functional.

Acceptance Testing

Following the implementation scheduling and inspection, you need to develop an acceptance test plan for the computer forensics lab. The purpose of the acceptance test plan is to make sure everything works correctly. When writing the acceptance test, consider the following items:

- Inspect the facility to see whether it meets the security criteria to contain and control digital evidence.

- Test all communications, such as telephone and network connections, to make sure they work as expected.

- Test all hardware to see that it operates correctly; for example, test a computer to make sure it boots to Windows.

- Install and start all software tools; make sure all application software can run on the computers and operating systems you have in the lab.

Correction for Acceptance

The better you plan for your lab, the less likely there will problems. However, any lab operation has some problems during the initial startup. Your business case must anticipate problems that can cause delays in lab production. In the business case, you need to develop contingencies to deal with system or facility failures. That is, you must develop a workaround for problems such as the wrong door locks being installed on lab doors or electrical power needing additional filtering.

Production

After all essential corrections have been taken care of, your computer forensics lab can then go into production. At this time, you implement the lab operations procedures that have been described in this chapter.

NOTE For additional information on how to write a business case, see *www.sba.gov/ starting_business/planning/writingplan.html*. For a good description of how to write a budget for a computer forensics lab, see *www.agilegroup.net/pdf/ papers/OutsourcingForensics.pdf*.

Chapter Summary

▫ A computer forensics lab is where you conduct your investigations, store your evidence, and do most of your work. You use the lab to house your instruments, current and legacy software, and forensic workstations. In general, you need a variety of computer forensics hardware and software to do your work.

▫ To continue a career in computing investigations and forensic analysis, you need to upgrade your skills through training. Several organizations provide training and certification programs for computer forensics that test you after you have successfully completed training. Some state and federal government agencies are also considering establishing their own certification programs that address minimum skill sets to conduct computing investigations at different levels.

▫ Your lab facility must be physically secure so that evidence is not lost, corrupted, or destroyed. Workspaces should also be set up to prevent or alleviate work-related injuries, such as repetitive-motion injuries. As with hardware and software costs, you must balance physical lab expenses with what you need to maintain a safe and secure environment. In building a computer forensics lab, you must consider factors such as structural integrity, access, fire prevention, HVAC, lighting, and ergonomics.

▫ Police departments in major cities need a wide assortment of computing systems, including older, outdated technology. Most computer investigations in small, local police departments involve Windows PCs and Apple Macintosh systems. As a general rule, there should be at least one law enforcement computer investigator for every 250,000 people in a geographic region. Commercial services providing computer forensics analysis for other businesses can tailor their services to specific markets.

❏ Before you can set up a computer forensics lab, you must enlist the support of your managers and other team members by building a business case, a plan you can use to sell your services to your management or clients. In the business case, you justify acquiring newer and better resources to investigate computer forensics cases.

3

KEY TERMS

American Society of Crime Laboratory Directors (ASCLD) — A national society that sets the standards, management, and audit procedures for labs used in crime analysis, including computer forensics labs used by the police, FBI, and similar organizations.

business case — Justification to upper management or a lender for purchasing new equipment, software, or other tools when upgrading your facility. In many instances, a business case shows how upgrades will benefit the company.

Certified Computer Crime Investigator, Basic Level — A certificate awarded by the HTCN upon successful completion of the appropriate exams. Requires a bachelor of science degree, two years of investigative experience, and 18 months of experience related to computer crimes.

Certified Computer Crime Investigator, Advanced Level — A certificate awarded by HTCN upon successful completion of appropriate exams. Requires a bachelor of science degree, three years of investigative experience, and four years of experience related to computer crimes.

Certified Computer Forensic Technician, Basic Level — A certificate awarded by the HTCN upon successful completion of its requirements. Same requirements as the Certified Computer Crime Investigator, Basic Level, but all experience must be related to computer forensics.

Certified Computer Forensic Technician, Advanced Level — A certificate awarded by the HTCN upon successful completion of its requirements. Same requirements as the Certified Computer Crime Investigator, Advanced Level, but all experience must be related to computer forensics.

Certified Electronic Evidence Collection Specialist (CEECS) — A certificate awarded by IACIS upon completion of the written exam.

Certified Forensic Computer Examiner (CFCE) — A certificate awarded by IACIS upon completion of the correspondence portion of testing.

computer forensics lab — A computer lab dedicated to computing investigations; typically has a variety of computers, OSs, and forensic software.

configuration management — The process of keeping track of all upgrades and patches you apply to your computer's OS and applications.

ergonomics — The proper placement of machinery, office equipment, and computers to minimize physical injury or repetitive-motion injuries. It's also the study of designing equipment to meet the human need of comfort while allowing for improved productivity.

High Tech Crime Network (HTCN) — A national organization that provides certification for computer crime investigators and computer forensics technicians.

risk management — Involves determining how much risk is acceptable for any process or operation, such as replacing equipment.

secure facility — A facility that can be locked and provides limited access to the contents of a room.

special-interest groups (SIGs) — Associated with various operating systems, these groups maintain electronic mailing lists and might hold meetings to exchange information about current and legacy operating systems.

TEMPEST — An unclassified term that refers to facilities that have been hardened so that electrical signals from computers, the computer network, and telephone systems cannot be easily monitored or accessed by someone outside the facility.

Uniform Crime Report — Information collected at the federal, state, and local levels to determine the types and frequencies of crimes committed.

REVIEW QUESTIONS

1. An employer can be held liable for e-mail harassment. True or False?

2. Building a business case can involve:
   a. procedures for gathering evidence
   b. testing software
   c. protecting trade secrets
   d. all of the above

3. The ASCLD has direct control over the procedures established for a computer forensics lab. True or False?

4. The manager of a computer forensics lab is responsible for which of the following? (Choose all that apply.)
   a. necessary changes in lab procedures and software
   b. having sufficient training to do the job
   c. knowing the lab objectives
   d. none of the above

5. To determine the types of operating systems needed in your lab, you should _____.

6. Typically, computer systems in corporate North America are replaced every _____ or so.

7. List two popular certification systems.

8. The National Cybercrime Training Partnership is available only to law enforcement. True or False?

9. List three pieces of furniture or hardware components that a small forensics lab should have.

10. If a visitor to your computer forensics lab is a personal friend, it's not necessary to have him sign the visitor's log. True or False?

11. Ergonomics can include the placement of _____, _____, or _____.

12. Large computer forensics labs should have at least _____ exits.

13. Typically, you can find a separate storage area or room for evidence in a(n) _____ lab.

14. Computer forensics facilities always have windows. True or False?

15. The chief custodian of evidence lockers should keep several master keys. True or False?

16. Putting out fires in a computer lab usually requires a type _____ fire extinguisher.

17. What is the purpose of a UPS?

18. A forensic workstation should always have a direct broadband connection to the Internet. True or False?

19. Which organization provides good information on how to build a secure lab?

20. Which organization provides a good reference on how to operate a computer forensics lab?

21. What name refers to the shielding of EMR?

HANDS-ON PROJECTS

HANDS-ON PROJECTS

Project 3-1

You are setting up a small office to do computer forensics work for an attorney. What are the minimum security requirements for maintaining the chain of evidence? Based on what was presented in this chapter and what you can find on the Internet, make a plan to set up a small forensics unit. Write two to three pages describing the equipment and furniture you need, including safes and locks.

HANDS-ON PROJECTS

Project 3-2

Check your workstation at school or home for its ergonomics. On the Internet, research how your back, wrists, eyes, and neck should be positioned. With a partner, take the appropriate measurements to see whether your workstation is healthy for you. Write one to two pages that include the following:

❑ Explain whether your workstation is appropriate for you.

❑ Identify changes you had to make to create an ergonomic workspace.

❑ Sketch the final outcome. Include the position of the chair, desk, mouse, and monitor and indicate other alterations you made.

Project 3-3

Sketch your computer lab. Note where the HVAC system enters the lab and where workstations are placed in relation to the vents. Are certain areas colder or warmer than others? Write a one-page paper noting the areas you think should be altered based on your observations. Turn in your sketch and paper.

Project 3-4

On the Internet, research the effect of poor or high lighting on the eyes. Check reliable sites, such as the FDA, Occupational Safety and Health Administration (OSHA), and American Medical Association (AMA), to find information on the results of viewing monitors and working in fluorescent lighting, full-spectrum lighting, and standard bulbs. What studies have been done and what were their conclusions? What type of lighting do you have in your lab and what type should you have? What precautions can you take? Write two to three pages summarizing the studies and making recommendations for your lab.

Project 3-5

Physical security of a lab must always be maintained. In your network lab, get permission to make observations at different times of the day when classes are and are not in session. Record how many people go in and out for a week. Do you know all the people or can you identify them? Who monitors the lab when classes are not in session? Write one to two pages detailing your observations. If this were a computer forensics lab, what changes would you have to make?

Project 3-6

Write a disaster recovery plan of not more than three pages for your lab. Include backup schedules, note the programs and operating system installed on each machine, and list other information you would have to recover after a disaster. You should also note where the original disks and the backups are located.

Case Projects

Case Project 3-1

Based on your evaluation of the arson case in Case Project 2-1, build a business case for the resources you think you'll need to investigate the arson case for the insurance company. Write a brief paper outlining the resources you'll need, and make sure you justify your needs.

Case Project 3-2

You have acquired the laptop of the kidnapping victim from Case Project 2-2. What resources are needed to analyze a laptop? Conduct a survey of the architectural hardware differences between a laptop and a desktop computer, along with the different tools or equipment that might be needed to perform a forensic image acquisition.

Case Project 3-3

A new version of Windows has been released. What do you need to do to be ready in 6 to 10 months when cases involving the new operating system begin happening? Include research, user groups, and others you need to contact. Write a one-page paper on the procedure.

4

CURRENT COMPUTER FORENSICS TOOLS

> **After reading this chapter and completing the exercises, you will be able to:**
>
> ♦ Understand how to identify needs for computer forensics tools
> ♦ Evaluate the requirements and expectations for computer forensics tools
> ♦ Understand how computer forensics hardware and software tools integrate
> ♦ Validate and test your computer forensics tools

Chapter 3 outlined how to set up an effective computer forensics laboratory. This chapter explores many of the software and hardware tools used during computing investigations and forensic analysis. This chapter doesn't endorse or recommend any specific computer forensics tools; instead, it explains how to select tools for computing investigations based on specific criteria.

Computer forensics products are constantly being developed, updated, patched, revised, released, and marketed. Therefore, it's important to routinely check with vendors' Web sites to see what new features and improvements are available. These improvements might address a difficult or impossible-to-solve problem you're having in an investigation.

Before purchasing any forensic tools, consider whether the tool can save you time during the investigation. If it does, is there a cost to the reliability of the data that's discovered? For example, does the tool enable you to search a drive's contents based on a keyword? And if so, is the search applicable only to file names, or can the tool also search file contents for the keyword? These are the types of questions you need to ask your tool vendors.

Often you'll find yourself trading speed for reliability. For example, many new GUI forensic tools are resource intensive and demand more memory and other resources from your computer. In some cases, they require more resources than what a typical workstation might have because of other applications, such as antivirus programs, running in the background. These background programs compete for resources with a computer forensics program, and a GUI forensic application or the OS itself can stop running or hang, causing delays in your investigation. When planning purchases for your computer forensics lab, determine what a new forensic tool does better than the one you're currently using. In particular, research how well the software performs in validation tests, and then verify the integrity of the data analysis tool's results. Later in this chapter, you learn more about validating forensic tools.

COMPUTER FORENSICS SOFTWARE NEEDS

As described in Chapter 3, you need to develop a business plan to justify the acquisition of computer forensics hardware and software. When researching what to get, strive for versatile, flexible, and robust tools that provide technical support. The goal is to find the best value for as many features as possible. Some questions to ask when evaluating computer forensic tools include the following:

- What OS does the forensic tool work on?
- Is the tool version versatile? For example, will it work on both Windows 98 and XP and produce the same results on both OSs?
- Can the forensic tool analyze more than one file system, such as FAT, NTFS, or Ext2fs?
- Can a scripting language be used with the tool to automate repetitive functions and tasks?
- Does the forensic tool have any automated features that can help reduce the time it takes to analyze data?
- What is the vendor's reputation for providing product support?

As you learn more about computing investigations, you'll have more questions about the available tools for conducting these investigations. When you search for tools, keep in mind what application files you'll be analyzing. For example, if you need to analyze Microsoft Access databases, look for a product designed to read these files. If you're analyzing e-mail messages, look for a forensic tool that can read e-mail message contents.

Types of Computer Forensics Tools

Computer forensics tools are divided into two major categories: hardware forensic tools and software forensic tools. Each category has additional subcategories that are discussed in more depth later in this chapter. The following sections outline some basic principles required and expected of most computer forensics tools.

Hardware Forensic Tools

Hardware forensic tools range from simple single-purpose components to complete computer systems and servers. Single-purpose components can be devices such as the ACARD AEC-7720WP Ultra Wide SCSI-to-IDE Bridge designed to write-block an IDE disk drive connected to a SCSI cable. An example of a complete system is Digital Intelligence F.R.E.D. or DIBS Advanced Forensic Workstation. Later in this chapter, you learn more about these products. Other hardware forensic tools have software, known as **firmware**, programmed into them. These devices have **erasable programmable read-only memory (EPROM)** components that allow for programming upgrades.

Software Forensic Tools

Software forensic tools are grouped into command-line applications and GUI applications. Some tools are specialized to perform one task, such as the command-line disk acquisition tool SafeBack from New Technologies, Inc. (NTI). Other tools are designed to perform many different tasks. For example, Guidance Software's EnCase or AccessData's FTK are GUI tools designed to perform multiple functions. Typically, GUI tools can perform most computer forensic acquisition and analysis functions.

Another aspect of software forensic tools is copying data from a suspect's disk drive to a data file, commonly referred to as an image file. Many GUI acquisition tools can read an image file as though it was the original disk drive. In all appearances. the GUI tool sees all the data structures in the image file as though the file was the actual disk drive. Many analysis tools, such as EnCase, FTK, X-Ways Forensics, iLook, and others, have this capability to analyze image files. Later in this chapter and in Chapter 9, you learn more about these tools.

Tasks Performed by Computer Forensics Tools

All computer forensic tools, both hardware and software, have specific functions they perform. These functions are grouped into five major categories, each with subfunctions that offer additional refinement for data analysis and recovery:

- Acquisition
- Validation and discrimination
- Extraction
- Reconstruction
- Reporting

In the following sections, you learn how these five functions and their associated subfunctions apply to computing investigations.

Acquisition

The first need in computer forensics investigations is to make a copy of the original disk drive. This procedure preserves the original disk to make sure it doesn't become corrupt and damage the digital evidence. In Chapter 7, you learn how to handle digital evidence correctly, and in Chapter 9, you learn how to apply some computer forensics acquisition tools. The subfunctions in the acquisition category are:

- Physical data copy
- Logical data copy
- Data acquisition format
- Command-line acquisition
- GUI acquisition
- Remote acquisition
- Verification

For computer forensics tools that can acquire data—that is, make a bit-stream image backup of a disk drive—there are hardware and software solutions. Some hardware devices, such as the Image MaSSter Solo 2 Forensic unit from Intelligent Computer Solutions, Inc., can work independently to perform a disk copy. As described earlier, these devices have their own built-in software and allow direct copying of data from a suspect disk to a target disk. No other device or program is needed to make a duplicate disk.

Other computer forensics acquisition applications require combining hardware devices and software programs to make disk acquisitions. For example, Guidance Software has a DOS program named En.exe and a function in its Windows application, EnCase, to make data acquisitions. To make a disk acquisition with En.exe requires only a PC running MS-DOS with a 12-volt power connector and an IDE or a SCSI connector cable. The Windows application of EnCase requires a write-blocker device, such as FastBloc, to prevent Windows from accessing and corrupting a suspect disk drive. Later in this chapter you learn more about write-blockers.

In software acquisition, there are two types of data-copying methods: physical copying of the entire disk drive and logical copying of a disk partition. Most software acquisition tools include this option of bit-stream imaging an entire physical drive or just a logical partition.

The formats available for disk acquisitions vary from Raw data to vendor-specific proprietary compressed data. Raw data is a direct copy of a disk drive. An example of a Raw image is output from the UNIX and Linux shell dd command. The Raw imaging data format is a simple bit-for-bit copy of a data file, a disk partition, or an entire disk drive. A Raw imaging tool can copy data from one disk drive to another disk or into one or many segmented data files. Because it's a true unaltered copy, you can view the content of a Raw image file with any hexadecimal editor, such as Hex Workshop or WinHex. Hexadecimal editors, also known as disk editors (such as Norton DiskEdit), provide both a view of the data's hexadecimal values and a plaintext view of the data (see Figure 4-1).

Many acquisition tools can make smaller segmented files. This segmenting feature is typically found in vendor acquisition tools, such as NTI's SafeBack, X-Ways' Replica, and Guidance Software's EnCase. The purpose of segmenting data from a disk drive is to make it easier to store data on smaller media, such as CD-Rs or DVD-Rs. In Chapters 9 and 12, you learn more about data acquisitions.

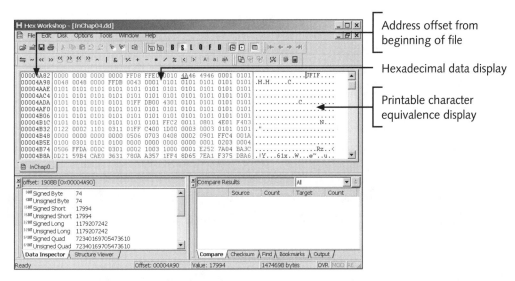

Address offset from beginning of file

Hexadecimal data display

Printable character equivalence display

Figure 4-1 A sample hexadecimal editor

Vendor-specific data formats for acquisition are found in products such as EnCase; SafeBack; ASR Data's SMART; X-Ways WinHex, Forensic, and Replica; Digital Intelligence's floppy disk Image tool; and DriveSpy's SavePart command. Some of these tools can create bit-stream image files, either noncompressed or compressed to reduce the size of data recovered from a suspect's disk drive. Compression can save significant amounts of data storage for an investigation. The typical compression ratio is about 50% or less of the disk drive's original size. For example, a 30 GB disk might compress to approximately 16 or 17 GB. The only time data isn't compressed is when the original data is already compressed, such as Zip, JPEG, or GIF files.

Recent developments in computer forensics have made tools available that can acquire data remotely over a network. These remote acquisition tools make it possible to inspect and acquire data for evidence collection. An important feature of remote acquisitions is rapid response to a suspect computer system over a network connection.

All computer forensics acquisition tools provide a method for verification of the data-copying process to ensure that data was correctly copied from the suspect's disk to the target disk. For example, EnCase prompts you to obtain the MD5 hash value of acquired data, and SafeBack runs an SHA-256 hash while acquiring data. Hardware data acquisition tools, such as Image MaSSter Solo, implement CRC-32 during data copying.

Validation and Discrimination

When dealing with computer evidence, there are two issues. First is ensuring the integrity of data being copied—the *validation* process. Second is the *discrimination* of data, which involves sorting and searching through all investigation data. The process of validating the data is what allows for the discrimination of data. Many forensic software vendors offer three methods for discriminating data values. These are the subfunctions of the validation and discrimination function:

- Hashing
- Filtering
- Analyzing file headers

Validation of data is achieved by obtaining hash values, such as CRC-32, MD5, or Secure Hash Algorithm (SHA-1, SHA-256, SHA-384, and SHA-512). As a standard feature, most forensic tools and even many disk editors provide one or more types of data hashing. How data hashing is applied depends on the investigation's needs. Using one of the preferred hashes, such as CRC-32, MD5, or SHA-1, of the entire original disk drive is usually a good idea. Obtaining hashes for each file on a disk drive is also recommended. Recording hash values of an entire disk and individual files produces a unique hexadecimal value (similar in concept to a fingerprint) for that data set. This unique value is used to make sure the original data hasn't changed since it was first hashed. In later chapters, you learn more about hashes and how to apply these validation techniques to verify data integrity.

The purpose of discriminating is to remove good data from suspicious data. Good data consists of known files, such as OS files and common programs (Microsoft Word, for example). Several computer forensics programs have or can integrate known good file hash sets. These programs compare hash sets to file hashes from a suspect disk to see whether they match. If they don't, the program alerts you to the mismatched values. By comparing known hash values to good files on a suspect's disk drive, you can eliminate large amounts of data to search through, thus minimizing how much data you need to examine to locate and recover evidence.

An additional method of discriminating data is to analyze and verify the header information of known file types. Similar to the hash values of known files, many computer forensics programs include a list of common header data values. For example, the letters "JFIF" are embedded near the beginning of all JPEG files. Some forensic tools allow adding unique header data values. This customizing feature helps improve the data discrimination function in an investigation. By searching and comparing file headers, you can locate files that might have been intentionally altered. In later chapters, you see how to use this function to locate hidden data.

Extraction

The extraction function is the recovery task in a computing investigation and is the most demanding of all tasks for computer investigators to master. In Chapter 2, you learned how system analysis applies to an investigation. Recovery of data is the first step in analyzing an investigation's data. In later chapters, you apply the following subfunctions of extraction to investigations:

- Data viewing
- Keyword searching

- Decompressing

- Carving

- Decrypting

- Bookmarking

4

Many computer forensic tools provide a data-viewing mechanism for digital evidence. How data is viewed depends on the particular tool. DriveSpy, for example, provides a view of a suspect disk drive's logical configuration and a hexadecimal view of the drive's clusters and sectors (covered in more detail in Chapter 7). Tools such as FTK, EnCase, SMART, iLook, ProDiscover, and others offer several different ways to view data, including disk drive logical structures such as folders (directories) and files. They also display allocated file data and unallocated disk areas with special file and disk viewers. Being able to view data in its normal form makes it much easier to analyze and collect clues related to the investigation.

One of the most common tasks in conducting computing investigations is searching for and recovering key data facts. Computer forensics programs have functions that allow searching for key data facts—that is, keywords of interest to the investigation. Using this function speeds up the analysis process for investigators, if used properly. Typically, however, a **keyword search** generates too much information, so to reduce false-positive hits (covered in Chapter 10), determine whether the tool allows combinations of words to be searched at the same time. In addition, determine whether the tool can be selective in what data types to search through, such as searching only e-mail messages. Another function available with some forensic tools is indexing all words on a disk drive. Presently, FTK offers this feature, using the binary index (b-tree) search engine from dtSearch. This feature provides instant lookup for keywords, which speeds up the analysis task of the investigation. FTK can also decompress archive files, such as Zip files, and even Microsoft PST and OST e-mail folders and index their contents. Another tool, iLook, has a limited indexing capability that lists several keywords of interest. This tool creates a b-tree index file that can be viewed after searches for keywords of interest are completed.

As part of the investigation process, it's necessary to reconstruct fragments of files that have been deleted from a suspect's disk drive. In North America, this reconstruction is referred to as "carving"; in Europe, it's referred to as "salvaging." (Carving is covered in more depth in Chapter 11.) The ability to extract data from unallocated disk space has become more common for computing investigators. Locating file header information, as mentioned in the previous section, "Validation and Discrimination," is a reliable method for carving data. Most forensic tools analyze unallocated data areas of a disk drive or bit-stream image file locating fragments or entire file structures that can be carved out and copied into a new file. A tool such as DriveSpy can locate the data but requires manual methods of copying clusters to a new file. More advanced tools, such as EnCase, FTK, ProDiscover, iLook, and other GUI tools, have built-in functions that automate carving. DataLifter and Davory are specifically designed to carve known data types from exported unallocated disk space. DataLifter has a customization feature that enables you to add other unique header data values.

A major challenge to computing investigations is analyzing, recovering, and decrypting data from encrypted files or systems. Encryption can be implemented on a disk drive, a disk partition, or individual files. Many e-mail services, such as Microsoft Outlook, provide encryption protection for PST folders and individual messages. The types of encryption range from platform specific, such as Microsoft Encrypted File System (EFS), to third-party vendors, such as Pretty Good Privacy (PGP) and even GnuPG.

From an investigation perspective, encrypted files and systems are a problem. Many password recovery tools have a feature that allows generating potential lists for a **password dictionary** attack. AccessData's FTK, for example, produces a list of words that have possible relevance to a password for an encrypted file from a suspect's disk. There's a remote chance that the password might have been written to a temporary file or a system file on disk, such as Pagefile.sys. The generated password list from FTK can be loaded into AccessData's Password Recovery Toolkit (PRTK) dictionary. PRTK first runs the password dictionary list you have created against the encrypted file. If it fails to match the password's hash values, it then runs a **brute-force attack** on the encrypted file.

Locating digital evidence is a major part of a computing investigation. After locating the evidence, the next task is to bookmark it. The purpose of bookmarking data is so that you can refer to it. Many forensic tools use bookmarks to insert digital evidence into a report generator, which produces a technical report of the examination's findings. A simple report generator is the output log file you can create in DriveSpy. Because DriveSpy is a command-line shell tool, it can't save keyword searches from the screen, but if you use the Output command, DriveSpy copies the screen output generated from a keyword search to a log file. To view and analyze the search results, you have to exit DriveSpy and open the log file with a text editor. GUI forensic tools, such as FTK, iLook, ProDiscover, or EnCase, have bookmark options that can be applied to digital evidence the investigator identifies. When the report generator is launched in FTK or EnCase, bookmarks are loaded into the report. FTK and iLook produce an HTML report file that can be viewed in any Web browser. EnCase produces an RTF-formatted document file that can be viewed in most word processors.

Reconstruction

The purpose of having a reconstruction feature in a forensic tool is to re-create a suspect's disk drive. It might be necessary to run a suspect's computer to show what happened during a crime or incident. Another reason for duplicating a suspect's disk is to create an identical copy for other computer investigators, who might need a fully functional copy of the suspect's disk drive so that they can perform their own tests and analysis. The copied computer system is usually the original suspect computer. The copied disk is an exact bit-stream duplicate of the suspect's disk drive. These are the subfunctions for reconstruction:

- Disk-to-disk copy
- Image-to-disk copy

- Partition-to-partition copy

- Image-to-partition copy

There are several ways to re-create a forensic bit-for-bit copy of a suspect's disk drive. Under ideal circumstances, the best and most reliable method of forensic disk duplication is obtaining the same make and model disk drive as the suspect's original disk drive. If the drive is recently manufactured, locating an identical drive is fairly easy. However, because computer and disk drive manufacturers use just-in-time delivery systems for parts inventory supplies, it's not uncommon for a disk drive manufactured three months ago to be out of production and unavailable for sale. This makes locating identical older disk drives more difficult.

The simplest method of duplicating a disk drive is using a tool that does a direct disk-to-disk copy from the original disk to the target disk. Many tools can perform this task. One free tool available in Linux distributions and UNIX is the dd shell command. This dynamic tool has one major disadvantage for creating a working duplicate copy of an original drive, however: The target drive being written to must be identical to the original drive, with the same cylinder, sector, and track count. If an identical drive is unavailable, manipulating the drive's cylinders, sectors, and tracks to match the original drive might be possible through the BIOS of your workstation. Be aware, however, that other issues might prevent this technique from working correctly because of the target disk's firmware. To address the problem of matching a suspect's disk, several manufacturers have developed tools that can force a geometry change from a suspect's drive to a target drive. For most forensic disk duplication tools, the target drive must be equal in size to or larger than the original suspect's drive.

For performing a disk-to-disk copy, both hardware and software duplicators are available; hardware duplicators are the fastest way to copy data from one disk to another. The duplicators in the following lists adjust the target disk drive's geometry to match the original disk drive's cylinder, sectors, and tracks:

Hardware duplicators

- Logicube Forensic SF-5000

- Logicube Forensic MD5

- Image MaSSter Solo 2 Forensics Hard Drive Duplicator

Software duplicators

- SafeBack

- SnapCopy

For image-to-disk and image-to-partition copies, many more tools are available, but they are considerably slower in transferring data. Some of the many tools that perform an image-to-disk copy are:

- SafeBack

- SnapBack

- EnCase

All three tools have their own proprietary data formats that can be restored only by the same vendor application that created them. For example, a SafeBack image can be restored only by using SafeBack. The same applies to SnapBack and EnCase. SafeBack and SnapBack restore original bit-stream image files from the MS-DOS level. Restoring an EnCase image requires using the Windows tool EnCase.

There has been a need to demonstrate in court how a suspect's computer performs. For this demonstration, you need a product that shadows a suspect's disk so that it can be used to run demonstrations of criminal activity on a computer. This shadowing technique requires a hardware device such as VOOM Technologies' Shadow Drive. The VOOM Shadow Drive connects the suspect's disk drive to a read-only IDE port and another drive to a read-write port. The read-write port drive is referred to as a "shadow drive." When the VOOM box with drives is connected to a computer, you can access and run applications on the suspect disk drive. All data that would normally be written to the suspect drive is redirected to the shadow drive. This tool saves time and helps solve problems you might encounter when trying to make a working duplicate suspect disk drive.

Reporting

To complete a forensic disk analysis and examination, you need to create a report. Before Windows-based forensic tools were available, this report required copying data from a suspect's disk drive and manually extracting the digital evidence. After extracting the data, the investigator would copy it into a separate program, such as a word processor, to create a report. File data that couldn't be read in a word processor—databases, spreadsheets, and graphics, for example—made it extremely difficult to insert nonprintable characters, such as binary data, into a report. Typically, these reports weren't stored electronically because investigators had to collect printouts from several different applications to consolidate everything into one large paper report.

The newer Windows-based forensic tools can produce electronic reports in a variety of formats, such as word processor documents, HTML Web pages, or Acrobat PDF files. These are the subfunctions for the reporting function:

- Log reports

- Report generator

As part of the validation process for computing investigations, often you need to document what steps you took to obtain data from a suspect's disk drive. Many of the current forensic tools can produce a record of activity, known as a log report, performed by the examiner or investigator. The log report can be added to the investigation's final report as additional documentation of what steps were taken during the examination, which can be useful if it's necessary to repeat the examination. For a case that requires a peer review, log reports confirm what activities were performed and what results were obtained from the original analysis and examination.

These are some of the computer forensics tools that provide log reports:

- FTK
- iLook
- X-Ways Forensic
- DriveSpy

4

The following tools offer report generators that display bookmarked evidence:

- EnCase
- FTK
- iLook
- X-Ways Forensic

Tool Comparisons

To help determine what computer forensics tool to purchase, a comparison table of functions, subfunctions, and vendor products, as described in the previous section, is useful. Cross-referencing functions and subfunctions with vendor products makes it much easier to identify what computer forensics tool best meets your needs.

Table 4-1 is an example of how to compare forensic vendors' tools. Your needs might differ from the functions and subfunctions listed in this table. When developing your own table, add any other functions and subfunctions you think are necessary to help analyze what tool or tools to acquire for an investigation.

Table 4-1 Forensic Tool Functions and Subfunctions Comparison

VENDOR TOOL	AccessData Ultimate Toolkit	Guidance Software EnCase	Digital Intelligence DriveSpy
FUNCTION			
Acquisition			
Physical data copy	√	√	
Logical data copy	√	√	√
Data acquisition formats	√	√	
Command-line process		√	√
GUI process	√	√	√
Remote acquisition		√*	
Verification	√	√	√
Validation and Discrimination			
Hashing	√**	√**	√
Filtering	√	√	√

Table 4-1   Forensic Tool Functions and Subfunctions Comparison (continued)

VENDOR TOOL	AccessData Ultimate Toolkit	Guidance Software EnCase	Digital Intelligence DriveSpy
Analyzing file headers	√	√	
Extraction			
Data viewing	√***	√***	
Keyword searching	√	√	√
Decompressing	√	√	
Carving	√	√	
Decrypting	√		
Bookmarking	√	√	
Reconstruction			
Disk-to-disk copy	√	√	√
Image-to-disk copy	√	√	√
Partition-to-partition copy		√	√
Image-to-partition copy		√	√
Reporting			
Log reports	√	√	√
Report generator	√		

*Must purchase Enterprise Edition for this feature
**Both MD5 and SHA-1
***Supported file formats vary

Other Considerations for Tools

As part of the business planning for your lab, determine which tools offer the most flexibility, reliability, and future expandability to do the job. The software tools you select should be compatible with the next generation of OSs. For example, when Microsoft upgraded from Windows 9x to Windows NT, computing investigators had difficulty examining the disks because the disks used the newly developed NTFS. When FAT32 was introduced with Windows 95B, forensic software vendors revised their software for the new file system. Seek information on any changes included with a new release of hardware or software and those planned for the next release. Because OS vendors don't always provide adequate information about future file system upgrades, it's your responsibility to research and prepare for these changes. You need to develop your own sources for obtaining new specifications if the vendor fails to provide them.

Maintaining a computer forensics lab also involves creating a software library containing older versions of forensic utilities, OSs, and other programs. You should maintain all older versions of software that you have used and retired, such as older versions of Windows and Linux. If a new software version fixes one bug but introduces another, you can use the previous version.

COMPUTER FORENSICS SOFTWARE

Some of the tasks you need to perform while conducting a forensic analysis of digital evidence can be handled by software. The software can be task specific or created as a suite of tools that enable you to perform several tasks at once. Whether you obtain a suite of tools or a task-specific tool, you have the option of selecting a tool that allows you to analyze your digital evidence through the command line or in a GUI. The following sections address both command-line and GUI tools and offer some examples.

Command-line Forensic Tools

As mentioned in Chapter 1, computers used several OSs before MS-DOS dominated the market, although computer forensics was not a major concern at the time. After people began to use PCs, they eventually figured out how to use them for illegal and destructive purposes and to commit crimes and civil infractions. And thus the race began: Software developers began to release computer forensics tools to help private and public sectors determine what was happening on these digital tools (computers). The first tools that analyzed and extracted data from floppy disks and hard disks were MS-DOS tools for IBM PC file systems.

One of the first MS-DOS tools used for a computer investigation was Norton DiskEdit. As needs evolved, programs specifically designed for computer forensics were developed for DOS, Windows, Apple, NetWare, and UNIX systems. Some of these early programs could extract data from file slack and free space; others were capable only of retrieving deleted files. Current programs are more robust and can search for specific words or characters, perform a keyword search, calculate hash values, recover deleted items, perform physical and logical analyses, and much more.

One advantage of using command-line MS-DOS tools for an investigation is that they require few system resources because they're designed to run in minimal configurations. In fact, most tools fit on a bootable floppy disk. Conducting an initial inquiry or a complete investigation with a floppy disk can save time and effort. Most tools also produce a text report that fits on the forensic boot floppy disk. In addition, some command-line DOS tools prompt you for a new disk if one fills up.

Command-line MS-DOS tools are limited in some ways; typically, they can't search archive files, such as Zip (.zip) files or cabinet (.cab) files. They often work only on Microsoft FAT file systems, although one MS-DOS tool, NTFS DOS from SysInternals (*www.sysinternals. com/ntw2k/freeware/ntfsdos.shtml*), can extract data from NTFS systems.

Some command-line forensic tools are created specifically for DOS/Windows platforms; others are created for the Macintosh and UNIX/Linux platforms. Because there are a number of different versions of UNIX and Linux, these platforms are referred to as *nix platforms. For DOS/Windows platforms, a number of companies, such as NTI, MaresWare, Ds2dump from DataLifter, and ByteBack, are well recognized for their work in the command line for the field of forensics. UNIX/Linux tools are covered in more detail in the following section.

As software continues to evolve and investigators develop new needs, vendors will address those needs. As such, the tools listed in this chapter are in *no* way a complete list of tools available for the DOS/Windows or *nix platforms.

Some tools that are readily available in the command line are often overlooked. For example, in Windows 2000 and XP, the Dir command shows you the owner of a file if you have multiple users on the system or network. Try it by following these steps:

1. Click **Start**, **Run**, and type **cmd** to open a command-line shell.

2. Type **cd ** to take you back to the root directory.

3. Type **dir /q > C:\Fileowner.txt**.

4. Using any text editor, open C:\Fileowner.txt to see your results.

UNIX/Linux Command-line Forensic Tools

The *nix platforms have long been the primary command-line interface OSs. Historically, the *nix platforms have not been accepted overwhelmingly as the OS of choice for end users. However, with the recent development of GUIs being shipped with the *nix platforms, they are becoming more popular with home and corporate end users.

This newfound popularity and the staggering number of versions available gives investigators a challenge: learning the *nix command line and investigating the *nix environment. As you're probably aware, the *nix and DOS/Windows environments are significantly different in many ways. In Chapter 12, you learn about several tools available in the *nix environment for forensic analysis. Some of these *nix platform tools are SMART from ASR Data, The Coroner's Toolkit (TCT), and the TCT utilities Autopsy and SleuthKit.

GUI Forensic Tools

Several software vendors have recently introduced computing investigation tools that work in Windows. Command-line DOS tools require a strong understanding of MS-DOS and the various file systems. Because GUI forensic tools don't require the same level of knowledge, they can simplify computer forensics investigations. These GUI tools have also simplified training for beginning examiners in computer forensics. However, you should continue to learn about and use command-line forensic tools because one GUI tool might find critical evidence, whereas another might miss it.

Most GUI tools are put together into suites of tools. For example, the two largest GUI tool providers in today's market, AccessData and Guidance Software, offer tools that perform most of the tasks listed previously in this chapter. As with all software, each suite has its strengths and weaknesses and continues to improve with each release and update.

GUI tools have several advantages, such as ease of use, the capability to perform multiple tasks, and no requirement to learn older OSs. Their disadvantages range from excessive resource requirements (such as needing large amounts of RAM) and producing inconsistent results because of the type of OS used, such as Windows XP Professional or Home Edition. Another concern with using GUI tools is that they create investigator dependencies on using only one tool. In some situations, GUI tools won't work and a command-line tool is required.

4

COMPUTER HARDWARE TOOLS

This section discusses computer hardware that provides computer analysis capabilities for computing investigators. Again, technology changes rapidly, and your choices in hardware affect your choices in software. Hardware manufacturers have designed most computer components to last about 18 months between failures. Hardware is hardware; whether it's for a rack-mounted server or a forensic workstation, eventually it fails. For this reason, you should schedule equipment replacements for your computer hardware periodically—ideally every 18 months if you use the hardware full-time. Most computer forensics operations use a workstation 24 hours a day for a week or longer between complete shutdowns.

You should plan your hardware needs carefully, especially if you're dealing with budget limitations. Include in your planning the amount of time you expect the forensic workstation to be running, how often you expect hardware failures, consultant and vendor fees to support the hardware when it does fail, and how often to anticipate replacing the forensic workstation. The longer you expect the forensic workstation to be running, the more you need to anticipate physical equipment failure and the expense of replacement equipment.

Computer Investigation Workstations

Many computer vendors currently offer a wide range of forensic workstations that you can tailor to meet your specific investigation needs. The more diverse your investigation environment, the more options you need. In general, forensic workstations can be divided into the following categories:

- *Stationary workstation*—A tower with several bays and many peripheral devices
- *Portable workstation*—A laptop computer with a built-in LCD monitor and almost as many bays and peripherals as a stationary workstation
- *Lightweight workstation*—Usually a laptop computer built into a carrying case with a small selection of peripheral options

When considering options to add to a basic workstation, keep in mind that PCs have limitations on how many peripherals they can handle. The more peripherals you add, the more potential problems you might encounter, especially if you're using an older version of Windows 9x. You must learn to balance what you actually need with what your system can handle.

If you're operating a computer forensics lab for a police agency, you need as many options as possible to handle any investigation. If possible, use two or three configurations of PCs to handle diverse investigations. You should also keep a hardware library in addition to your software library. In the private corporate environment, however, consider streamlining your workstation to meet the needs of only the types of systems used in your business.

Building Your Own Workstation

To decide whether you want to build your own workstation, first ask "How much do I have to spend?" Building a forensic workstation is not as difficult as it sounds, but it can quickly become expensive if you aren't careful. If you have the time and skill to build your own forensic workstation, you can customize it to your exact needs and save money, although you might have trouble finding support for problems that develop. For example, peripheral devices might conflict with one another, or components might fail. If you build your own forensic workstation, you should be able to support it from a hardware standpoint.

To build your own forensic workstation, you need to identify what you intend to analyze. If you're analyzing SPARC disks from workstations in a corporate network, for example, you need to include a SPARC drive with a write-protector on your forensic workstation.

If you decide that building a forensic workstation is outside the realm of your skills, several vendors offer hardware specific to computer forensics. You can choose from a full work-station, such as the F.R.E.D unit, or a simple drive-imaging station, such as FIRE IDE. Having a vendor-supplied workstation has its advantages. If you aren't skilled in computer hardware, having vendor support can save you time and frustration when you encounter hardware problems. Of course, you can always mix and match to get the capabilities you need for your forensic workstation.

If you don't have the skills to build and support a PC, you might want to consider taking an A+ Certification course at a college campus near you.

NOTE

Using a Write-Blocker

In recent years, manufacturers have developed hardware and software methods, called write-blockers, for preventing data writes to a disk drive. The first item you should consider for a forensic workstation is a **write-blocker**. Write-blockers can be software or hardware and are used to protect evidence disks by preventing you from writing any data to the evidence disk. Software and hardware write-blockers perform the same function, but in a different fashion.

Software-enabled blockers, such as PDBlock from Digital Intelligence, typically run in a shell mode such as DOS. If you use PDBlock, it helps to know that it changes Interrupt 13 of the workstation's BIOS that prevents any writing to the specified drive. If you attempt to write data to the blocked drive, it signals an alarm advising that no writes have occurred.

Earlier, you learned about checking the software's capability to perform on different OSs; PDBlock is a tool that can be run only from a true DOS mode, not a Windows MS-DOS shell.

With hardware write-blockers, you can connect your evidence disk drive to your workstation and start the OS as usual. Hardware write-blockers are ideal for GUI forensic tools. They prevent any attempt from Windows or Linux to write data to the blocked disk. Hardware write-blockers act as a bridge between the suspect's disk drive and the forensic workstation.

In the Windows environment, when a write-blocker is installed on an attached disk drive, the drive appears as any other attached disk. You can navigate to the blocked drive with any Windows application, such as Windows Explorer to view files, or Word to read files. When you copy data to the blocked drive or write updates to a file with Word, Windows shows that the data copy is successful. However, the write-blocker actually discards the written data—that is, data is written to null. When you restart the workstation and examine the blocked disk, you won't see the data or files you previously copied to it.

Many vendors have developed write-blocking devices that connect to a computer through FireWire, USB 2.0, and SCSI controllers. Most of these write-blockers enable you to remove and reconnect disk drives without having to shut down your workstation, saving you time while processing the evidence disk. For more information on write-blocker specification, go to *www.cftt.nist.gov* and *www.ojp.usdoj.gov/nij/sciencetech/cftt.htm*.

The following are some vendors that provide write-blocking devices:

- *www.digitalintelligence.com*
- *www.forensicpc.com*
- *www.guidancesoftware.com/products/accessprosuites.shtm*
- *www.voomtech.com*
- *www.mykeytech.com*
- *www.wiebetech.com*
- *www.paraben-forensics.com/lockdown.html*

Recommendations for a Forensic Workstation

Before you purchase or build your forensic workstation, determine where your data acquisitions will take place. If you acquire data in the field, consider streamlining the tools you use. With the newer FireWire and USB 2.0 write-blocking devices, you can easily acquire data with Digital Intelligence FireChief and a laptop computer. If you want to further reduce the hardware you carry, consider using a product such as the WiebeTech Forensic DriveDock with its regular DriveDock FireWire bridge.

When choosing a computer as a stationary or lightweight forensic workstation, you want a full tower to allow for expansion devices, such as a 2.5-inch drive converter to analyze a laptop hard drive on a 3.5-inch IDE write-protected drive controller. You want as much memory and processor power as your budget allows, as well as a library of varying sizes of hard drives. In addition, consider a 400-watt or better power supply with battery backup, extra power and data cables, a SCSI drive card, external FireWire and USB ports, an ergonomic keyboard and mouse, and a good video card with at least a 17-inch monitor. If you plan to conduct many investigations, a high-end video card and monitor are recommended.

As with anything else in technology, what your forensic workstation includes is often a matter of preference. Whatever vendor you choose, make sure the devices you include perform the functions you expect to need as an investigator.

Validating and Testing Forensic Software

Now that you have selected some tools to use, you need to make sure the evidence you recover and analyze with your computer forensics software can be admitted in court. To do this, you must test and validate the software. The following sections discuss validation tools available at the time of this writing and how to develop your own validation protocols.

Using National Institute of Standards and Technology (NIST) Tools

The **National Institute of Standards and Technology (NIST)** publishes articles, provides tools, and creates procedures for testing and validating computer forensics software. This software should be verified to enhance computer forensics evidence admissibility in judicial proceedings. NIST is sponsoring a project called **Computer Forensics Tool Testing (CFTT)** to manage the research on computer forensics tools. For additional information on the testing project at NIST, visit *www.cftt.nist.gov*.

NIST has created a general approach for testing computer forensics tools. These general testing criteria are included in the article "General Test Methodology for Computer Forensic Tools," (version 1.9, November 7, 2001), available at *www.cftt.nist.gov/testdocs.html*. The article addresses "the lack of standards or specifications that describe what forensics tools should do and the need for these tools to survive the scrutiny of a judicial process."

The criteria listed in the NIST article are based on standard testing methods and ISO 17025 criteria for testing items for which no standards exist. Your lab must meet the following criteria and keep accurate records so that when new software and hardware become available, the standards are in place for your lab:

- *Establish categories for computer forensics tools*—Group computer forensics software according to categories specified by expert users, such as forensic tools designed specifically to retrieve and trace e-mail.

- *Identify computer forensics category requirements*—For each group, describe the technical features or functions a computer forensics tool in that category must have.

- *Develop test assertions*—Based on the requirements, create tests that prove or disprove the tool's capability to meet the requirements. For example, a data recovery tool should be able to retrieve data from RAM slack.

- *Identify test cases*—Find or create types of cases to investigate with the forensic tool. Identify information to retrieve from a sample disk or other media. For example, use the image of a closed case file created with a trusted forensic tool to test a new tool in the same category and see whether it produces the same results.

4

- *Establish a test method*—Considering the purpose and design of the tool, specify how to test the forensic tool and the instructions that ship with the product.

- *Report test results*—Describe the test results in a report that complies with ISO 17025, which requires that test reports must be accurate, clear, unambiguous, and objective.

Another standards document, ISO 5725, demands accuracy for all aspects of the testing process, meaning that the results must be repeatable and reproducible. "Repeatable results" means that if you work in the same lab on the same machine, you generate the same results. "Reproducible results" means that if you're in a different lab and working on a different machine, the tool still retrieves the same information.

NIST has also developed several tools that evaluate disk drive-imaging tools. The following tools are posted on the CFTT Web site at *www.cftt.nist.gov/disk_imaging.htm* in the FS-TST10.zip file, which contains the **Forensic Software Testing Support Tools (FS-TST)** for testing the imaging capability of a computer forensics tool. The CFTT states that the following testing programs written in Borland C++ 4.5 can be run in MS-DOS 6.3:

- *DISKWIPE*—Initializes the test disk drive to a predefined value for the test

- *BADDISK*—Simulates a bad sector on a disk drive by replacing Interrupt 13

- *BADX13*—Creates a bad sector on an extended BIOS disk drive; sectors are listed in logical block addressing (LBA) format

- *CORRUPT*—Corrupts one bit in a specified file to see if it is detected by the forensics tool

- *ADJCMP*—Compares sector by sector two drives that are not the same size; that is, it adjusts and compares sectors for drives that have different geometries

- *DISKCMP*—Compares two disk drives to determine whether they are actually identical when copied with a forensic imaging tool

- *PARTCMP*—Produces an SHA-1 hash for an entire partition

- *DISKHASH*—Produces an SHA-1 hash for an entire disk drive

- *SECHASH*—Produces an SHA-1 hash for a specified sector

- *LOGCASE*—Logs the case information into a file

- *LOGSETUP*—Provides setup information about a source test disk's configuration

- *PARTAB*—Prints the partition table of the test drive

- *DISKCHG*—Alters data on a drive to determine whether it's detected by the forensic tool being tested
- *SECCMP*—Compares sectors to each other to help validate a data copy
- *SECCOPY*—Allows you to copy a specific sector

Another program created by NIST is the **National Software Reference Library (NSRL)** project. The goal of the NSRL project is to collect all known hash values for commercial software applications and OS files. The primary hash NSRL uses is SHA-1, which is used to generate a known set of digital signatures called the Reference Data Set (RDS). SHA-1 provides a much higher degree of accuracy than any other hashing method, such as MD5 or CRC-32.

The purpose of the NSRL project is to reduce the number of known files included in the forensic examination of a disk drive, leaving only the unknown files. Identifying known good files, such as OS files or application programs, makes it possible to significantly reduce the number of files you need to inspect as possible evidence. You can also use the RDS to identify known bad files, including illegal images such as child pornography or computer viruses. By using this feature on a suspect's hard disk, you can quickly identify and locate known bad files.

The Validation Protocols

After retrieving and examining evidence data with one tool, you should verify your results by performing the same tasks with other similar forensic software. Although this step might seem unnecessary, you might be called to the witness stand and asked "How did you verify your results?" To satisfy the need for verification, you need at least two tools to validate software or hardware upgrades. After you use one forensic analysis tool to retrieve disk data, you use another to see whether you retrieve the same information. The analysis tool you use to compare results should be well tested. You'll perform a tool validation exercise in the Hands-on Projects at the end of this chapter.

It is important that you, as an investigator, are confident in a tool's capability to produce consistent and accurate findings during the analysis. Having some understanding of how the tool works is equally important, as you might not have vendor support in a courtroom.

One way to compare your results and verify your new tool is by using a disk editor, such as Norton DiskEdit, Hex Workshop, or WinHex. A disk editor allows you to view data on a disk in its Raw format. Disk editors typically show files, file headers, file slack, RAM slack, and any other data on the physical disk. Although disk editors aren't known for their flashy interfaces, they are reliable and capable of going to sectors on the digital evidence to verify your findings.

NOTE

Although a disk editor gives you the most flexibility in testing, it might have trouble examining the contents of a compressed file, such as a Zip file or a Microsoft Outlook PST file.

If you decide to use a GUI computer forensics tool, such as FTK or EnCase, follow the recommended steps in the following sections to validate your findings.

Computer Forensics Examination Protocol

1. First, perform the investigation on the digital evidence with one GUI tool.

2. Then perform the same investigation using a disk editor, such as WinHex or Hex Workshop, to verify that the GUI tool is seeing same digital evidence in the same places on the test or suspect drive's bit-stream image.

3. If a file is recovered, obtain the hash value from the GUI and with the disk editor, and then compare the results to verify whether the file has the same value.

Many investigators in both the public and private sectors use FTK and EnCase as their choice of "flagship" forensic software suites, but they don't rely on them solely; investigators' software libraries often include any number of other forensic utilities to supplement the capabilities of FTK or EnCase.

Computer Forensics Tool Upgrade Protocol

In addition to verifying your results by using two disk-analysis tools, you should also test all new version releases and OS patches and upgrades to make sure they are reliable and don't corrupt your evidence data. New version releases and OS upgrades and patches can affect the way your forensic tools perform. If you determine that a patch or upgrade is not reliable, don't use it on your forensic workstation until the issue has been addressed and fixed. If you do have a problem, such as not being able to read old image files with the new release or the disk editor generates errors after you apply the latest service pack, you can file an error report with the forensic application vendor. In most cases, the vendor then addresses the problem and (you hope) provides a new patch, which then prompts another round of validation testing.

One of the best ways to test patches and upgrades is to build a test hard disk to store data in unused space that has been allocated for a file, also known as file slack. You can then use a forensic software tool to retrieve it. If you can retrieve the data with the forensic tool and verify your findings with a second tool, you know the tool is reliable.

As computer forensics tools continue to evolve, you should check the Web for new editions, updates, patches, and validation tests for your tools. Whether it's hardware or software, always validate what the tool is doing as opposed to what it's supposed to be doing. Be confident about your forensic toolbox, and remember to always ask "Why does (or doesn't) this tool work the way it's supposed to?

Chapter Summary

- As part of setting up a computer forensics lab, create a business plan to get the best hardware and software solution for your computing investigation needs.

- The five functions required for all computer forensics tools are acquisition, validation and discrimination, extraction, reconstruction, and reporting.

- Maintaining a computer forensics lab involves creating a software library for older versions of forensic utilities, OSs, and application programs. You should maintain all older versions of software you have used and retired, such as older versions of Windows and Linux.

- Many computer forensics tools run in MS-DOS, including those that find file slack and free space, recover data, and search by keyword. Most of these tools run only in MS-DOS, not a DOS shell. They are also designed to run in minimal configurations and can fit on a bootable floppy disk. Norton DiskEdit and WinHex are MS-DOS tools that enable you to find file slack and unallocated space on a drive.

- Hardware required for computer forensics includes workstations and blockers, such as write-blockers, needed to prevent contamination of evidence. Before you purchase or build your own forensic workstation, consider where you acquire data, which determines the type of hardware configuration you need.

- Computer forensics tools that run in a Windows command-prompt window include DriveSpy and Image. Computing investigation tools that run in Windows and other GUI environments don't require the same level of computing expertise as MS-DOS tools and can simplify training and investigations. These GUI tools have also simplified training for beginning examiners in computer forensics.

- Before upgrading to a new version of a computer forensics tool, you need to run validation testing on the new version. The National Institute of Standards and Technology (NIST) has standard guidelines for verifying forensic software.

Key Terms

brute-force attack — The process of trying every combination of characters—letters, numbers, and special characters typically found on a keyboard—to find a matching password or passphrase value for an encrypted file.

Computer Forensics Tool Testing (CFTT) — A project created by the National Institute of Standards and Technology to manage research on computer forensics tools.

erasable programmable read-only memory (EPROM) — A memory chip for a hardware device that can be reprogrammed with new instructions.

firmware — The software program that's loaded into a memory chip, such as an EPROM.

Forensic Software Testing Support Tools (FS-TST) — A collection of programs that analyze the capability of disk-imaging tools.

keyword search — Finding files or other information by supplying characters, words, or phrases to a search tool.

National Institute of Justice (NIJ) — The research, development, and evaluation agency of the U.S. Department of Justice dedicated to researching crime control and justice issues.

National Institute of Standards and Technology (NIST) — A unit of the U.S. Commerce Department formerly known as the National Bureau of Standards; NIST promotes and maintains measurement standards.

password dictionary — A collection of words or phrases that might be passwords for an encrypted file. Password recovery programs can use a password dictionary to compare potential passwords to an encrypted file's password or passphrase hash values.

write-blocker — A hardware device or software program that prevents a computer from recording data on an evidence disk. Software write-blocker programs typically alter Interrupt 13 write functions to a disk drive in a PC's BIOS. Hardware write-blockers are usually bridging devices located between a disk drive and the computer.

REVIEW QUESTIONS

1. What are the five basic functions of computer forensics tools?

2. A disk's partition can be copied only by using a command-line acquisition tool. True or False?

3. What two types of software acquisitions are typically available for computer forensics software?

4. When performing remote acquisition of a suspect's disk drive, what is a significant feature for this type of data collecting?

5. Hashing, filtering, and file header analysis make up which function of computer forensics tools?

   a. validation and discrimination

   b. acquisition

   c. extraction

   d. reporting

6. The Linux dd command is a command-line type function. True or False?

7. When upgrading to a new software version, you should:

   a. uninstall the previous version

   b. talk to the manufacturer

   c. test and validate the new version

   d. none of the above

8. When determining which tool to use in your lab, what should be your most important consideration?

   a. finding out which one is the most popular

   b. determining what your lab needs

   c. determining which product is cheaper

   d. talking to the vendor

9. Data cannot be written to the disk if run from a DOS shell. True or False?

10. The purpose of using hashing such as MD5 or SHA-1 is to validate the integrity of data. True or False?

11. The NIST has established a standard way to test forensic tools. True or False?

12. Many of the newer GUI-based tools:

    a. can be run from a floppy disk

    b. produce consistent results

    c. use a lot of system resources

    d. none of the above

13. Building your own forensic workstation is more expensive than purchasing one. True or False?

14. Several forensic tools can perform keyword searches. True or False?

15. Most image tools:

    a. perform the same function as a backup

    b. create a sector-by-sector copy of a drive

    c. can help in the retrieval of lost data

    d. b and c

16. The standards for testing are based on which criteria?

    a. U.S. Title 18

    b. ISO 5725

    c. ISO 17025

    d. all of the above

17. Files created by WinZip can be extracted by the _____ tool.

18. List four subfunctions required for reconstructing disk drives.

19. When validating the results of a forensic analysis, you should do which of the following?

    a. Calculate the hash value using two different tools.

    b. Use a different tool to compare the results of evidence found.

c. Repeat the steps used to obtain the digital evidence, using the same tool, and recalculate the hash value to verify the results.

d. Do both a and b.

e. Do both b and c.

f. Do both a and c.

g. Do none of the above.

20. NIST testing procedures are valid only for government agencies. True or False?

HANDS-ON PROJECTS

Project 4-1

In this project, you create and delete files on a floppy disk, and then use AccessData FTK to analyze the disk. In Project 4-2, you erase this floppy disk to ensure that it contains no data by using the SecureClean product. To download and install SecureClean, follow these steps:

1. Use Windows Explorer or My Computer to create a folder named **Projects** in the Chap04 folder in your work folder.

2. Start your Web browser, type **www.whitecanyon.com/secureclean.php** in the Address text box, and then press **Enter**.

3. Click the **try demo** link, scroll down if necessary, and click the **download** link for SecureClean. In the File Download dialog box, click **Save**.

4. Navigate to the **Chap04\Projects** folder in your work folder, and then click the **Save** button to save Secureclean.exe on your hard disk.

5. Close your Web browser. If the Download complete dialog box opens, click **Close**.

6. Navigate to the **Chap04\Projects** folder in your work folder, and then double-click **Secureclean.exe**.

7. When the Installation dialog box opens, click **Next**. Click **Yes** to accept the license agreement, and then click **Next** to accept the default destination folder. Click **Next** to accept the default location for the program files, and then click **Next** to accept the default Start menu folder. SecureClean is installed on your computer.

8. In the InstallShield Wizard Complete dialog box, click **Finish**.

9. When the "What would you like to try first" dialog box opens, click **Cancel** to close the SecureClean program. Then close all open windows.

   Now you're ready to use Microsoft Word and Excel to create and delete files on a floppy disk and use FTK to analyze the disk. Follow these steps:

10. Label a blank, formatted floppy disk as **Chapter 4 – Project 1**.

11. Start a new document in Microsoft Word and type **This is to test deleting files and then wiping them**. Save the file to the floppy disk as **Test file 1.doc**. Close Word.

12. Start Microsoft Excel. In a blank workbook, type a few numbers, and then save the workbook as **Test file 2.xls** on the floppy disk. Close Excel.

13. Use Windows Explorer or My Computer to delete both files from the floppy disk.

14. Start AccessData FTK, and start a new case. Type your name as the investigator's name, use **25** as the case number, **C4Project1** as the case name, and the **Chap04\Projects** folder in your work folder as the case path. Click **Next** until you reach the Add Evidence dialog box.

15. Click the **Add Evidence** button, click the **Local Drive** option button, and then click **Continue**.

16. In the Select Local Drive dialog box, make sure that drive A: and Logical Analysis are selected, and then click **OK**.

17. When the warning message box appears, read the message. Then click **Yes** to continue adding evidence.

18. When the Evidence Information dialog box opens, click **OK**. Click **Next**, accept the default folder, and then click **Finish**. FTK processes the data on the floppy disk.

19. Click the **Deleted Files** button in the Overview tab to display the files that were deleted from the floppy disk, including the two test files you created and deleted. The FTK window might also display temporary files that were created.

20. Click any file in the lower pane to view its contents in the upper-right preview window.

21. Close all open windows.

HANDS-ON PROJECTS

Project 4-2

Now you're ready to use SecureClean to thoroughly remove all traces of data from the floppy disk. To wipe the floppy disk, follow these steps:

1. To start SecureClean, click **Start**, **Programs**, **WhiteCanyon**, **SecureClean 4**, **Clean My Computer**.

2. When the Protected Recycle Bins warning message appears, click **Ok** to continue.

3. In the SecureClean window, click the **Try It Free** button, and then click **Continue**.

4. In the Drive List section, click the check boxes to remove the checkmarks, and then click the **(A:)** check box. Make sure SecureClean is the only open window, and then click **Deep Clean**.

5. When you receive the message to check the hard drive for errors, click **Ok** to continue.

6. Click the **Start Clean Now** button.

7. You see a warning message stating that the data will no longer be recoverable. Click **Ok** to continue.

8. When SecureClean finishes cleaning the floppy disk, click **Ok** to close the program.

9. Start AccessData FTK, and start a new case. Type your name as the investigator's name, use **26** as the case number, **C4Proj2b** as the case name, and the **Chap04\Projects** folder in your work folder as the case path. Click **Next** until you reach the Add Evidence dialog box.

10. Click the **Add Evidence** button, click the **Local Drive** option button, and then click **Continue**. The Select Local Drive dialog box opens.

11. Make sure that drive A: and Logical Analysis are selected, and then click **Ok**. Another warning message appears alerting you about using live evidence. Click **Yes** to continue.

12. The Evidence Information dialog box opens. Click **Ok** to accept the default settings. Click **Next** to accept the default folder, and then click **Finish**.

13. Note that the floppy disk now contains no files. The FTK window shows only the root folder, slack/free space, and perhaps an unknown file type. Click the **Unknown Type** button to see the contents of slack space. If you used SecureClean without deleting any files on the disk, the FTK window shows file names with hexadecimal values of all zeros. If a SecureClean document appears in the FTK window, the contents are reported as "Nothing to view, document is empty." In the Slack/Free Space area, the disk free, FAT1, and FAT2 show all zeros, indicating that the disk contains no data.

14. Close FTK.

Project 4-3

In this project, you create a test disk by planting evidence in the file slack. Then you use FTK and DriveSpy to verify that the disk contains evidence. Feel free to use a hard disk, if one is available and you have the cabling and power cord to hook one up to your machine. However, this lab assumes you're using a floppy disk. To create a test disk for file slack, follow these steps:

1. Label a floppy disk as **Chapter 4 – Project 3**. *Warning:* This disk should contain data you no longer need.

2. Perform an unconditional format from the DOS prompt by typing **format a: /u** or by opening Windows Explorer, right-clicking the floppy disk icon, clicking **Format**, clicking to clear the **Quick Format** check box, if necessary, and then clicking **Start**. You can also use SecureClean as described in Project 4-2 to wipe the disk. (If you're using Windows 98, you need to click the **Full** option to remove the quick formatting.)

3. Start a new document in Microsoft Word and type **Testing for string Namibia**. Save the file as **C4Prj03a.doc** on the floppy disk.

4. Start a new Word document and type **Testing for string XYZX**. Save the file as **C4Prj03b.doc** on the floppy disk. Close Word.

   Now you can document the files you stored in disk slack on a sheet of paper. You also need Hex Workshop to complete the following steps. To document the files, follow these steps:

5. Start Hex Workshop. On a sheet of paper, create a chart that has two columns. Label the columns **Item** and **Sector**.

6. In Hex Workshop, click **Disk**, **Open Drive** on the menu. Make sure the floppy disk drive is selected, and then click **OK**.

7. Click **File**, **Open** from the menu. Navigate to the floppy disk, if necessary, and then double-click **C4Prj03a.doc**. Scroll down until you see "Testing for string Namibia."

8. Click the **Drive A:** tab. Click at the beginning of the right column. Click **Edit**, **Find** from the menu. In the Find dialog box, make sure Text String is selected in the Type text box. Type **Namibia** in the Value text box, click the **Either** option button, and then click **OK**. (If Hex Workshop does not find "Namibia" the first time, repeat this step.)

9. In the Item column on your chart, write **C4Prj03a.doc**. In the Sector column on your chart, write the sector number containing the search text, as shown on the Hex Workshop title bar.

10. Scroll to the bottom of the sector. Type **Murder She Wrote**, and then click the **Save** button on the toolbar. (*Note*: If you are asked to enable the Insert mode, click **OK**, press **Insert**, click to enable the **Disable notification message** check box, and click **OK**, if necessary.)

11. Click the **C4Prj03a.doc** tab. Click **Edit**, **Find** on the menu, type **Murder** in the Value text box, and then click **OK**. Hex Workshop cannot find this text in C4Prj03a. doc. Click **Edit**, **Find** on the menu, and then click **OK** to verify that Hex Workshop does not find "Murder" in the document. Close the file by clicking the lower **Close** button in the upper-right corner of your window.

12. Click **File**, **Open** from the menu. Double-click the **C4Prj03b.doc** file on the floppy disk. Scroll down until you see the "Testing for string XYZX" text you entered earlier. (You might need to use the Find command more than once to find the "XYZX" text.)

13. Click the **Drive A:** tab, if necessary. Click at the beginning of the right column. Click **Edit**, **Find** from the menu, and type **XYZX** as the value you want to find. Click **OK**. On your chart, write down **C4Prj03b.doc** as the file name under Item, and under Sector, note the sector number containing the search text, as shown on the title bar.

14. In the Drive A: tab, type **I Spy** near the end of the disk, in the disk slack space, and then click the **Save** button.

15. Verify that "I Spy" does not appear as part of the file by clicking the **C4Prj03b.doc** tab and searching for this string twice. Close the C4Prj03b.doc file.

In a forensic lab, you would want to generate the disk's MD5 hash value with a tool such as md5sum, and generate a copy by using a tool such as Image.

NOTE

4

HANDS-ON PROJECTS

Project 4-4

Use these steps to verify your results from Project 4-3 with AccessData FTK:

1. Start AccessData FTK, and start a new case. Type your name as the investigator's name, use **27** as the case number, **C4Project2** as the case name, and the **Chap04\Projects** folder in your work folder as the case path. Click **Next** until you reach the Add Evidence dialog box.

2. Click the **Add Evidence** button, click the **Local Drive** option button, and then click **Continue**.

3. In the Select Local Drive dialog box, make sure drive A: and Logical Analysis are selected, and then click **OK**. (Click **Yes** in the warning message box to continue working.)

4. When the Evidence Information dialog box opens, click **OK**. Click **Next**, accept the default folder, and then click **Finish**. FTK processes the files on the floppy disk, and then indicates the evidence items contained on the disk.

5. Click the **Search** tab. Click **Tools, Analysis Tools** from the menu, click to select the **Full Text Indexing** check box, if necessary, and then click **OK**.

6. In the Search Term text box, type **Namibia** and then click **Add**. Type **XYZX** and then click **Add**. Type **Murder** and then click **Add**. Finally, type **I Spy** and then click **Add**. The Search Items list indicates how many matches (hits) FTK finds on the disk for each keyword.

If you're working on a Windows 9x machine and the number of hits for Murder and Spy is listed as zero, try the disk on a Windows 2000 or XP machine to see what results you get.

NOTE

7. Click the **Overview** tab, click **Slack/Free Space**, and then scroll the right pane to see "I Spy."

8. Click the **Search** tab and then click the **Live Search** tab. In the Search Term text box, type **I Spy** and make sure ANSI and Unicode are selected. Click the **Search** button, click to select the **All files** option button if necessary, and click **OK**. When the search is complete, click **View Results**. A "Search Performed" message and the date are displayed in the upper-right corner of the window.

9. Click the expand (+) buttons to find the results of the search, which appears as "1 Hit." In the middle pane, scroll until you find "I Spy."

10. Repeat Steps 6 through 9 for "Murder."

11. The right pane of the FTK window displays details about the data FTK found on the floppy disk that match youyr search criteria. Click each occurence and scroll to the right to see what other information FTK supplies, such as the file's MD5 hash value.

12. Write down the file name and sector information for each item found. Note that FTK finds more than one occurrence of each word on the disk. Below the chart on your sheet of paper, explain why the words appear more than once.

13. Close all open windows.

HANDS-ON PROJECTS

Project 4-5

In this project, you're searching for an excerpt from Walt Whitman's poem "Passage to India":

Sail Forth—steer for the deep waters only

Reckless O Soul, exploring. I with thee and thou with me

For we are bound where mariner has not yet dared to go

And we shall risk the ship, ourselves and all

You need to work with a Windows 9x computer and a Windows 2000 or XP computer to complete this project. To find a hidden poem on a disk that shows no files in Windows Explorer, follow these steps:

1. If necessary, copy the **C4Prj03.img** file from the **Chap04\Projects** folder in your data files to the Chap04\Projects folder in your work folder.

2. Insert a blank, formatted floppy disk in the floppy drive of the Windows 9x computer. To run Toolpath.bat, open a command-prompt window, change to the **Tools** folder in your work folder, type **toolpath**, and press **Enter**.

3. Navigate to the **Chap04\Projects** folder in your work folder. Type **image C4Prj03.img a:** and press **Enter**. Close the command-prompt window.

4. Remove the floppy disk, and move to a Windows 2000 or XP machine. Then start AccessData FTK.

5. Insert the floppy disk you used in the previous steps. In FTK, start a new case. Type your name as the investigator's name, **28** as the case number, **Walt Whitman** as the case name, and the **Chap04\Projects** folder in your work folder as the case path. Click **Next** until you reach the Add Evidence dialog box.

6. Click the **Add Evidence** button, click the **Local Drive** option button, and then click **Continue**.

7. In the Select Local Drive dialog box, make sure drive A: and Logical Analysis are selected, and then click **OK**. (Click **Yes** in the warning message box to continue.)

8. When the Evidence Information dialog box opens, click **OK**. Click **Next**, accept the default folder, and then click **Finish**. FTK processes the files on the floppy disk. Click the **Total File Items** button to display the file items it found, including items in the slack/free space.

4

9. Click **Tools**, **Analysis Tools** from the menu, click to select the **Full Text Indexing** check box if necessary, and then click **OK**.

10. Click the **Search** tab. In the Search Term text box, type an uncommon word that you know is in the poem, such as "bound," and then click **Add**. Click the keyword in the Search Items list, and then click **View Item Results**. Click **OK** in the Filter Search Hits dialog box.

11. Record the data that FTK finds, and then close FTK.

Now you can verify your results with DriveSpy by following these steps:

12. Remove the floppy disk, and return to the Windows 9x computer. Make sure you have removed the Read-only attribute from the DriveSpy.ini file. Use Notepad to edit the DriveSpy.ini file in the Tools folder of your work folder by adding the following lines to the end of the file:

[Search Walt]

100:"bound"

100:"Destiny"

13. Add one other unusual word in the poem, and then save the file and close Notepad.

14. Open a command-prompt window, and navigate to the **Tools** folder of your work folder. Then type **drivespy** to start DriveSpy. Insert the floppy disk in the floppy drive.

15. At the SYS prompt, type **da** and press **Enter**. Then type **p1** and press **Enter**.

16. Type **search walt** and press **Enter**. When asked if you want to disable PAGE mode, type **n**. After a few moments, DriveSpy displays its results. Record the data that DriveSpy finds.

17. Write a one-page report explaining the differences in the results you found using FTK and DriveSpy. Note which one was easier to use and which one you prefer.

18. Close all open windows.

Project 4-6

HANDS-ON PROJECTS

In this project, you plant evidence in three places on a test disk so that you can test for disk slack, and then find the information with FTK. Follow these steps to create a test disk:

1. Label a floppy disk **Chapter 4 – Project 6**.

2. Perform an unconditional format from the DOS prompt by typing **format a: /u** or by opening Windows Explorer, right-clicking the floppy disk icon, clicking **Format**, and then clicking **OK**.

NOTE

You can also use SecureClean as described in Project 4-2 to wipe the disk.

3. Start Microsoft Word, and type **Testing for string Japan** in a new document. Save the file as **C4Prj06a.doc** on the floppy disk.

4. Start a new Word document and type **Testing for string Alaska**. Save the file as **C4Prj06b.doc** on the floppy disk. Close Word.

   Now you can document the files you stored in disk slack on a sheet of paper. You need Hex Workshop to document the files using the following steps:

5. Start Hex Workshop. On a piece of paper, create a chart with two columns. Label the columns **Item** and **Sector**.

6. In Hex Workshop, click **Disk**, **Open Drive** from the menu. Make sure the floppy disk drive is selected, and then click **OK**.

7. Click **File**, **Open** from the menu. Navigate to the floppy disk, if necessary, and then double-click **C4Prj06a.doc**. Scroll down until you see "Testing for string Japan."

8. Click **Edit**, **Find** from the menu. In the Find dialog box, make sure Text String is selected in the Type text box. Type **Japan** in the Value text box, and then click **OK**. If necessary, repeat this step to find the text.

9. On your chart under Item, write **C4Prj06a.doc**. In the Sector column on your chart, write the sector number containing the search text, as shown on the Hex Workshop title bar.

10. Click the **Drive A:** tab. Click **Edit**, **Find** from the menu, and then type **Alaska** as the value you want to find. Click **OK**. If necessary, repeat this step to find the search text. On your chart under Item, write **C4Prj06b.doc**. In the Sector column on your chart, write the sector number containing the search text, as shown on the Hex Workshop title bar.

11. If necessary, press **Insert**, and then click **Disk**, **Next Sector** from the menu until you find an empty sector that shows only zeros in the middle column of the window. Type **Gunsmoke** in this sector. Record the sector number and the word in your chart. Then click the **Save** button on the toolbar to save the file.

12. Use the same technique to find another empty sector. Then type **Bonanza** in this sector. Save the file, and record the sector in your chart.

13. Close all open windows.

In an actual lab situation, you would generate the MD5 hash value of the disk and generate a copy using a tool such as Image. Next, you verify your results with AccessData FTK by following these steps:

14. Start AccessData FTK, and start a new case. Type your name as the investigator's name, **29** as the case number, your work folder as the case path, and **C4Project6** as the case name. Click **Next** until you reach the Add Evidence dialog box.

15. Click the **Add Evidence** button, click the **Local Drive** option button, and then click **Continue**.

16. In the Select Local Drive dialog box, make sure drive A: and Logical Analysis are selected, and then click **OK**. If you see a warning message box, click **Yes** to continue.

17. When the Evidence Information dialog box opens, click **OK**. Click **Next**, accept the default folder, and then click **Finish**. FTK processes the files on the floppy disk, and then indicates that the disk contains two documents.

18. Click the **Search** tab. Click **Tools**, **Analysis Tools** from the menu, click to select the **Full Text Indexing** check box, if necessary, and then click **OK**.

19. In the Search Term text box, type **Japan** and then click **Add**. Type **Alaska** and then click **Add**. Type **Gunsmoke** and then click **Add**. Finally, type **Bonanza** and then click **Add**.

If you're working on a Windows 9x machine and the number of hits for Gunsmoke and Bonanza is listed as zero, try the disk on a Windows 2000 or XP machine to see what results you get. FTK should locate the files.

NOTE

20. Click each item FTK finds, click the **View Item Results** button, and then click **OK**. The right pane displays details about the data FTK found on the floppy disk that match your search criteria. Click each occurrence and scroll to the right to see what other information FTK supplies, such as the file's MD5 hash value.

21. Write the file name and sector information for each item found. Note any discrepancies between the different versions of Windows.

CASE PROJECTS

CASE PROJECTS

Case Project 4-1

For the arson running case project, the insurance company gives you an image that was created with EnCase. Given the assets you decided on in Chapter 3, describe the tools you'll use to evaluate and analyze the image.

Case Project 4-2

For the kidnapping running case project, you need to image the laptop. Select which forensic tool will be most effective, and decide whether you want to use more than one tool to create the image. Write a brief paper outlining your choice of tools.

Case Project 4-3

Research and report on the CRC-32 and MD5 hash work that Brian Deering has done to identify people who transmit child pornography. Write a one- to two-page paper describing the tools he has made available to investigators to thwart this growing problem.

Case Project 4-4

Research the two most popular GUI tools, Guidance Software's EnCase and Access Data's Forensic Toolkit, and compare their features to other products, such as ProDiscover (*www.techpathways.com*) and Ontracks EasyRecover Professional (*www.ontrack.com/easyrecoveryprofessional*). Create a chart that outlines each tool's current capabilities, and write a one- to two-page report on the feature set you found to be most beneficial for your lab.

Case Project 4-5

Research the forensic tools available for Mac OS and Linux. Are tools similar to Hex Workshop available for these operating systems? Download the forensic tools. Based on their documentation, how easy would it be to verify these tools? Select at least two tools, and write a one- to two-page paper describing what you would do, based on what you have learned in this chapter.

Case Project 4-6

You need to establish a procedure for your corporation on how to verify a new forensic software package. Write two to three pages outlining the procedure you'll use in your lab.

CHAPTER 5

PROCESSING CRIME AND INCIDENT SCENES

After reading this chapter and completing the exercises, you will be able to:

- ◆ Collect evidence in private-sector incident scenes
- ◆ Process law enforcement crime scenes
- ◆ Prepare for a search
- ◆ Secure a computer incident or crime scene
- ◆ Seize digital evidence at the scene
- ◆ Review a case using three different computer forensics tools

---

In this chapter, you learn how to process a computer investigation scene. Because this chapter discusses investigation needs only for computing systems, you should supplement your training by studying police science or U.S. Department of Justice (DoJ) procedures to understand field-of-evidence recovery tasks.

This chapter describes the differences between the needs and concerns of a business (private entity) and a law enforcement (public entity) organization, and then discusses incident-scene processing for both corporate investigators and law enforcement investigators. Private-sector security officers often begin investigating corporate computer crimes and then coordinate with law enforcement to complete the investigation. Law enforcement investigators should, therefore, understand how to process incident scenes and take a leadership role in these technical investigations. Because public agencies usually don't have the funding to continuously train sworn officers in the latest advances in computing systems, they must learn to work with private-sector investigators, whose employers can often afford to maintain their investigators' computing skills in technologies such as advanced databases or Web-based applications. Law enforcement investigators should, therefore, learn how to manage private computer examiners when processing a computing investigation.

This chapter also discusses the Fourth Amendment and how it relates to corporate and law enforcement computing investigations in the United States. In particular, this chapter explains how to apply standard crime-scene practices to corporate and law enforcement computing investigations. You learn how to apply the rules of evidence, which are defined in Chapter 6, to the crime scene. Recall from Chapter 3 that a corporate investigator must secure and document evidence from a computer abuse case as carefully as a police detective does for a homicide case.

COLLECTING EVIDENCE IN PRIVATE-SECTOR INCIDENT SCENES

Private-sector organizations include businesses and government agencies that aren't involved in law enforcement. In the United States, these agencies must comply with state public disclosure and federal Freedom of Information Act (FOIA) laws and make the documents they find and create available as public records. State public disclosure laws define state public records as open and available for inspection. For example, divorces recorded in a public office, such as a courthouse, become matters of public record unless a judge orders the documents sealed. Anyone can request a copy of a public divorce decree. Figure 5-1 shows an excerpt of a public disclosure law for the state of Idaho.

State public disclosure laws apply to state records, but the FOIA allows citizens to request copies of public documents created by federal agencies. The FOIA was originally enacted in the 1960s, and several subsequent amendments have broadened its laws. Some Web sites now provide copies of publicly accessible records for a fee.

A special category of private-sector businesses includes ISPs and other communication companies. ISPs can investigate computer abuse committed by their employees, but not by customers. ISPs must preserve customer privacy, especially when dealing with e-mail. However, newer federal regulations related to the Homeland Security Act and the Patriot Act have redefined how ISPs and large corporate Internet users operate and maintain their records. ISPs and other communication companies now can investigate customers' activities that are deemed to create an emergency situation. An emergency situation under the Patriot Act is the *immediate risk of death or personal injury*, such as finding a bomb threat in an e-mail message.

Investigating and controlling computer incident scenes in the corporate environment is much easier than in the criminal environment. In the private sector, the incident scene is often a workplace, such as a contained office or manufacturing area, where a policy violation is being investigated. Everything from the computers used to violate a company policy to the surrounding facility is under a controlled authority—that is, company management. Typically, businesses have inventory databases of computing hardware and software. For investigators, having access to the company's computing asset database helps identify the types of compute forensics tools needed to analyze a policy violation. Knowing what applications are on the suspected computers helps investigators determine the best way to conduct the computer forensics analysis. For example, most companies use a single Web browser, such as

9-338. PUBLIC RECORDS -- RIGHT TO EXAMINE.

(1) Every person has a right to examine and take a copy of any public record of this state and there is a presumption that all public records in Idaho are open at all reasonable times for inspection except as otherwise expressly provided by statute.

(2) The right to copy public records shall include the right to make photographs or photographic or other copies while the records are in the possession of the custodian of the records using equipment provided by the public agency or independent public body corporate and politic or using equipment designated by the custodian.

(4) The custodian shall make no inquiry of any person who applies for a public record, except to verify the identity of a person requesting a record in accordance with section 9-342, Idaho Code, to ensure that the requested record or information will not be used for purposes of a mailing or telephone list prohibited by section 9-348, Idaho Code, or as otherwise provided by law. The person may be required to make a written request and provide their name, a mailing address and telephone number. [The custodian shall make no inquiry of any person who applies for a public record, except that the person may be required to make a written request and provide a mailing address and telephone number, and except as required for purposes of protecting personal information from disclosure under chapter 2, title 49, Idaho Code, and federal law.]

(5) The custodian shall not review, examine or scrutinize any copy, photograph or memoranda in the possession of any such person and shall extend to the person all reasonable comfort and facility for the full exercise of the right granted under this act.

Figure 5-1   Idaho public disclosure law

Microsoft Internet Explorer, Netscape Navigator, or Konqueror. Knowing which browser a suspect used helps you develop standard examination procedures to identify data downloaded to the suspect's workstation.

However, if a company does not publish a policy stating that it reserves the right to inspect computing assets at will or display a warning banner, employees have an expectation of privacy (as explained in Chapter 1). When a suspected employee is being investigated, this expected privacy prevents the employer from legally conducting an intrusive investigation. A well-defined corporate policy states that an employer has the right to examine, inspect, or access any company-owned computing assets. If a company issues a policy statement to all employees, the employer can investigate computing assets at will without any privacy right restrictions. As a standard practice, companies should use both warning banners and policy statements. For example, if an incident is escalated to a criminal complaint, prosecutors prefer showing juries warning banners rather than a policy manual. A warning banner leaves a much stronger impression on a jury.

A corporate policy statement about computing assets lets corporate investigators perform covert surveillance with little or no cause to investigate employees suspected of improper use of company computing assets. An employer can freely initiate any inquiry necessary to protect the company or organization. Being able to access company computing systems without a warrant is an advantage for corporate investigators. Law enforcement investigators cannot do the same without sufficient reason for a warrant.

In addition to making sure that a company has a policy statement on the right to inspect company computers, corporate investigators should know under what circumstances they can examine an employee's computer. Every business or organization must have a well-defined process that describes when an investigation can be initiated. At a minimum, most corporate policies require that employers have a "reasonable suspicion" that a law or policy is being violated. For example, if a policy states that employees may not use company computers for outside business and a supervisor notices a change in work behavior, that change could indicate that an employee is using an office computer to conduct another business and is generally enough to warrant an investigation.

If a corporate investigator finds that an employee is committing or has committed a crime, the employer can file a criminal complaint with the police. Some businesses, such as banks, have a regulatory requirement to report crimes. The employer must turn over all evidence to the police for prosecution, according to the silver platter doctrine discussed in Chapter 1. If this same evidence had been collected by a sworn law enforcement officer, it would require a warrant, which would be difficult to obtain without sufficient probable cause. In the next section, you learn more about probable cause and how it applies to a criminal investigation.

Employers are usually interested in enforcing company policy, not seeking out and prosecuting employees. The only reason an employer approves a computer investigation is to identify employees who are abusing or misusing company assets. Corporate investigators are, therefore, primarily concerned with protecting company assets. Finding evidence of a criminal act during an abuse investigation escalates the investigation from an internal civil matter to an external criminal complaint (see Figure 5-2).

While cooperating with law enforcement officers, corporate investigators should avoid becoming an agent of law enforcement, which can happen when an investigation becomes a criminal complaint without the proper safeguards required under the Fourth Amendment. Being an agent of law enforcement can expose corporate investigators to civil liability. To avoid becoming an agent of law enforcement, keep all documentation of evidence collected

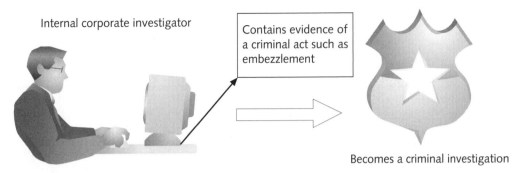

Figure 5-2 Internal civil matter becoming a criminal complaint

to investigate an internal company rules violation. Later in this chapter, you learn more about affidavits and how to apply them to an internal investigation in the private sector.

If you discover evidence of a crime during a company policy investigation, first determine whether the incident meets the elements of criminal law. You might have to consult with your corporate attorney to determine whether the situation is a potential crime. Next, inform management of the incident; they might have other concerns, such as protecting competitively sensitive business data that might be included with the criminal evidence (referred to as *commingled data*). In this case, coordinate with management and the corporate attorney to determine the best way to protect commingled data. After you submit evidence containing sensitive information to the police, it becomes public record. Public record laws include exceptions for protecting sensitive corporate information; ultimately, however, a judge decides what to protect.

After you discover illegal activity in a company and document and report the crime, stop your investigation to make sure you don't become an agent of law enforcement and investigate an employee without safeguards required by the Fourth Amendment. If the information you supply is specific enough to meet the criteria for a search warrant, the police are responsible for obtaining a warrant that requests any new evidence. If you follow police instructions to gather additional evidence after you have reported the crime, you run the risk of becoming an agent of law enforcement. Instead, consult with your corporate attorney for direction on how to respond to a police request for information. The police and prosecutor should issue a subpoena for any additional new evidence, which minimizes your exposure to potential civil liability.

One example of a company rules violation involves employees observing another employee accessing pornographic Web sites. If your organization's policy requires you to determine whether any evidence supports this accusation, you could start by extracting log file data from the proxy server and conducting a forensic examination of the subject's computer. Organizations use a **proxy server** to connect their local area network (LAN) to the Internet. Suppose that during your examination, you find adult and child pornography. Further examination of the subject's hard disk reveals that the employee has been collecting child pornography in separate folders on his workstation's hard disk. In the United States, possessing child pornography is a crime under federal and state criminal statutes.

You survey the remaining content of the subject's disk and find that he's a lead engineer for the team developing your company's latest high-tech bicycle. He has placed the child pornography images in a subfolder where the bicycle plans are stored. By doing so, he has commingled contraband with company's competitively sensitive design plans for the new high-tech bicycle. Your discovery poses two problems about how to deal with this contraband evidence. First, you must report the crime to the police. Many states require reporting evidence of sexual exploitation of children. The second problem is that you must also protect sensitive company information. Letting the high-tech bicycle information become part of the criminal evidence might make it public record, and the design work will then be available to competitors. Your first step is to notify your corporate attorney to get directions on how to deal with the commingled contraband data and sensitive design plans.

Your next step is to work with the corporate attorney to write an affidavit affirming your findings. The attorney should indicate in the affidavit that the evidence is commingled with company secrets and that releasing the information will be detrimental to the company's financial health. When the affidavit is completed, you sign it before a notary, and then deliver the affidavit and the recovered evidence with log files to the police, where you make a criminal complaint. At the same time, the corporate attorney goes to court and requests that all evidence recovered from the hard disk that's not related to the complaint and is a company trade secret be protected from public viewing. You and the corporate attorney have reported the crime and taken steps to protect the sensitive data.

Now suppose that the police detective assigned to the case calls you. In the evidence you have turned over to the police, the detective notices that the suspect is collecting most of his contraband from e-mail attachments. The prosecutor instructed the detective to ask you to collect more evidence to determine whether the suspect is transmitting contraband pictures to other potential suspects. In this case, you should immediately inform the police detective that collecting more evidence might make you an agent of law enforcement. Before collecting any additional information, consult with your corporate attorney or wait until you receive a subpoena or other court order.

Processing Law Enforcement Crime Scenes

To process a crime scene properly, you must be familiar with criminal rules of search and seizure. You should also understand how a search warrant works and what to do when you process one.

For all criminal investigations in the United States, the Fourth Amendment limits how governments search and seize evidence. A law enforcement officer may search for and seize criminal evidence only with **probable cause**, which is facts or circumstances that would lead a reasonable person to believe a crime has been committed or is about to be committed. Probable cause requires meeting the following criteria:

- A specific crime was committed or is about to be committed.

- Evidence of the specific crime exists.

- The place to be searched includes evidence of the specific crime.

With probable cause, a police officer can obtain a search warrant from a judge that authorizes a search and seizure of specific evidence related to the criminal complaint. The judge must be neutral and detached from the complaint and must determine whether there is sufficient probable cause to issue a warrant. Furthermore, a witness under oath or affirmation must assert that a particular location contains specific evidence of criminal activity.

Recall from Chapter 1 that part of the Fourth Amendment states that only warrants "particularly describing the place to be searched, and the persons or things to be seized" can be issued. Note how this excerpt uses the word "particularly." The courts have determined that this phrase means a warrant can only authorize a search of a specific place for a specific thing. Without *specific* evidence and the description of a particular location, a warrant might be weak and create problems later during prosecution. For example, stating that the evidence is in a house located on Elm Avenue between Broadway and Main Street is too general because a dozen houses might be located on both sides of Elm Avenue between Broadway and Main Street. Instead, provide specific information, for example, the exact address: 123 Elm Avenue. Most courts have allowed more generality for computer evidence. For example, you can state that you want to seize a "computer" rather than a "Dell Optiplex GXA." Figure 5-3 shows sample search warrant language for computer evidence that the state of Maryland makes available for computer crime investigators (see *http://ccu.mdsp.org*).

Although several court cases have allowed latitude when searching and seizing computer evidence, making your warrant as specific as possible to avoid challenges from defense attorneys is a good practice. Often a warrant is written and issued in haste because of the nature of the investigation. Law enforcement officers might not have the time to research the correct language for stating the nature of the complaint to meet the requirements of probable cause. However, because a judge can exclude evidence obtained from a poorly worded warrant, you should review these issues with your local prosecutor before investigating a case.

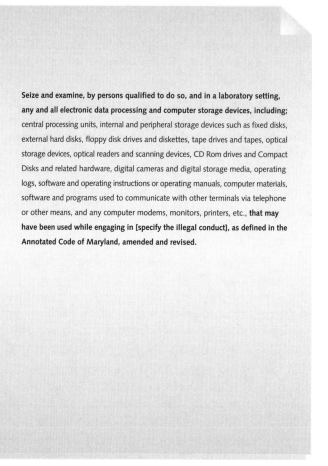

Seize and examine, by persons qualified to do so, and in a laboratory setting, any and all electronic data processing and computer storage devices, including; central processing units, internal and peripheral storage devices such as fixed disks, external hard disks, floppy disk drives and diskettes, tape drives and tapes, optical storage devices, optical readers and scanning devices, CD Rom drives and Compact Disks and related hardware, digital cameras and digital storage media, operating logs, software and operating instructions or operating manuals, computer materials, software and programs used to communicate with other terminals via telephone or other means, and any computer modems, monitors, printers, etc., **that may have been used while engaging in [specify the illegal conduct], as defined in the Annotated Code of Maryland, amended and revised.**

Figure 5-3   Sample search warrant wording for computer evidence

Understanding Concepts and Terms Used in Warrants

You should be familiar with warrant terminology that governs the type of evidence that can be seized. Many computing investigations involve large amounts of data you must sort through to find evidence. Unrelated information (referred to as **innocent information**) is often included with the evidence you're trying to recover. This unrelated information might be personal and private records of innocent people or sensitive information, such as the design plans for a high-tech bicycle. When you find a mix of information, judges often issue a **limiting phrase** to the warrant, which allows the police to separate innocent information from evidence. The warrant must list which items can be seized.

When approaching or investigating a crime scene, you might find evidence related to the crime but not in the location the warrant specifies. You might also find evidence of another unrelated crime. In these situations, the evidence related or unrelated to the crime you're investigating is subject to the **plain view doctrine**, defined in the sixth edition of *Black's Law Dictionary* as follows:

"In search and seizure context, objects falling in plain view of an officer who has the right to be in position to have that view are subject to seizure without a warrant and may be introduced in evidence. *Harris v. U.S.,* 390 U.S. 234, 236, 88 S.Ct. 992, 993, 19 L.Ed.2d 1069. Under 'plain view doctrine,' warrantless seizure of incriminating evidence may be permitted when police are lawfully searching a specified area if it can be established that police had prior justification for intrusion into the area searched, that police inadvertently came across item seized and that it was immediately apparent to the police that the item seized was evidence. *Washington v. Chrisman,* 455 U.S. 1, 5, 102 S.Ct. 812, 816, 70 L.Ed2d 778. However, the plain view doctrine may not be used to extend a general exploratory search from one object to another until something incriminating at last emerges. *Coolidge v. New Hampshire,* 403 U.S. 443, 466, 91 S.Ct. 2022, 2038, 29 L.Ed2d 564."

With few exceptions, warrants require that officers knock and announce their identity when executing a warrant. Exceptions to this rule include situations in which officers expect the suspect to destroy evidence or encounter a suspect who is armed and dangerous. In most computing investigations, destruction of evidence is an important concern. When creating a warrant, the judge should be informed of the potential loss of evidence if you must "knock and announce." Evidence can also be seized as part of an inventory search of a suspect's residence.

PREPARING FOR A SEARCH

Preparing for a computer search and seizure is probably the most important step in computing investigations. The better you prepare, the smoother your investigation will be. The following sections discuss the tasks you should complete before you search for evidence. To perform these tasks, you might need to find answers from the victim (the complainant) and an informant, who could be a police detective assigned to the case, a law enforcement witness, or a manager or co-worker of the **person of interest** to the investigation.

Identifying the Nature of the Case

Recall from Chapter 2 that when you're assigned a computing investigation case, you start by identifying the nature of the case, including whether it involves the private or public sector. For example, a corporate investigation might involve an employee abusing his Internet privileges by excessively surfing the Web or an employee who has filed an equal employment opportunity (EEO) or ethics complaint. Serious cases might involve an employee abusing company computing assets to acquire or deliver contraband. Law enforcement cases could range from a check fraud ring to a homicide. The nature of the case dictates how you proceed and what types of assets or resources you need to apply in the investigation.

Identifying the Type of Computing System

Next, determine the type of computing systems involved in the investigation. For law enforcement, this step might be difficult because the crime scene isn't controlled. You might not know what kinds of computers were used to commit a crime or how or where they were used. In this case, you must draw on your skills, creativity, and sources of knowledge, such as the Uniform Crime Report discussed in Chapter 3, to deal with the unknown.

If you can identify the computing system, determine the size of the disk drive on the suspect's computer and how many computers you have to process at the scene. Also determine which OSs and specific hardware might be involved and whether the evidence is located on a Microsoft, Linux, UNIX, Macintosh, or mainframe computer. For corporate investigators, configuration management records (discussed in Chapter 3) make this step easy to perform. Consultants to the private sector or law enforcement officers might have to investigate more thoroughly to determine these details.

Determining Whether You Can Seize a Computer

The ideal situation for all incident or crime scenes is seizing the computers and taking them to your lab for further processing. However, the type of case and location of the evidence determine whether you can remove computers from the scene. Law enforcement investigators need a warrant to remove computers from a crime scene and transport them to a lab. If removing the computers will irreparably harm a business, the computers should not be taken off site.

If you aren't allowed to take the computers to your lab, determine the resources you need to acquire the digital evidence. Consider which tools can speed data acquisition. With the use of large disk drives, such as a 200 GB drive, acquisition times can increase to several hours. In Chapter 9, you examine data acquisition software and learn which tools meet specific needs for acquiring disk images.

Obtaining a Detailed Description of the Location

The more information you have about the location of a computer crime, the more efficiently you can gather evidence from a crime scene. Environmental and safety issues are your primary concerns when you're working at the scene to gather information about an incident or a crime. Before arriving at an incident or crime scene, identify potential hazards to your safety as well as that of other examiners.

Some computer cases involve dangerous settings, such as a drug bust of a methamphetamine lab or terrorist attack using biological, chemical, or nuclear contaminants. For these types of investigations, you must rely on the skills of **hazardous material (HAZMAT)** teams to recover evidence from the scene. The recovery process might include decontaminating computing components needed for the investigation, if possible. If the decontamination procedure might destroy electronic evidence, a HAZMAT specialist or an investigator in HAZMAT gear should make a bit-stream image copy of a suspect's hard disk. If you have to rely on a HAZMAT specialist to acquire data, coach the specialist on how to connect cables between the computer and hard disks and how to run the software. In this case, you must be exact and articulate in your instructions. Ambiguous or incorrect instructions could destroy that vital evidence. Ideally, a computer forensics investigator trained in dealing with HAZMAT environments should acquire the disk images. However, not all organizations have funds available for this training.

Whether you or a HAZMAT technician is the one acquiring a bit-stream image copy, you should keep some guidelines in mind. Before acquiring the data, a HAZMAT technician might suggest that you put the target disk drive into a special HAZMAT bag, leaving the IDE and power cable out of the bag but providing an air-tight seal around the cable to prevent any contaminants from entering the bag and the target drive. When the data acquisition is completed, power down the computer and then cut the IDE and power cables from the target hard disk. The HAZMAT technician can then decontaminate the bag. When dealing with extreme conditions such as biological or chemical hazardous contaminants, often you need to sacrifice equipment, such as IDE cables and 12-volt power cables, to accomplish a task.

In addition, if the temperature in the contaminated room is higher than 80 degrees, you should take measures to prevent the disk from overheating to prevent damage. Consider cooling the target drive by using sealed ice packs or double-wrapped bags of ice so that moisture doesn't leak out and damage the drive. In extreme conditions, consider the risks the conditions pose to the evidence and your equipment. You'll need to brainstorm for solutions to overcome these problems.

Determining Who Is in Charge

Corporate computing investigations usually require only one person to respond to an incident or crime scene. Processing evidence involves acquiring a bit-stream data image of a subject's disk drive. In law enforcement, however, many investigations require additional staff to collect all evidence quickly. For large-scale investigations, a crime or incident scene leader should be designated. Anyone assigned to a large-scale investigation scene should cooperate with the designated leader to ensure that the team addresses all details when collecting evidence.

Using Additional Technical Expertise

After you collect evidence data, determine whether you need specialized help to process the incident or crime scene. For example, suppose you're assigned to process a crime scene at a data center running Microsoft Windows servers with several RAID disk drives and high-end UNIX servers. If you are the leader of this investigation, you must identify the additional skills needed to process the crime scene, such as enlisting help with a high-end OS. Other concerns are how to acquire data from the RAID servers and how much data you can acquire. RAID servers typically run several terabytes of data, and standard bit-stream imaging tools might not be able to handle such large data sets.

When working with high-end computing facilities, identify the applications the suspect uses, such as Oracle databases. In this case, you might need to recruit an Oracle specialist or site support staff to help extract data for the investigation. Locating the right person can prove to be an even bigger challenge than conducting the investigation.

If you do need to recruit a specialist who is not an investigator, develop a training program to educate the specialist in proper investigative techniques. This advice also applies to specialists you plan to supervise during the search and seizure tasks. When dealing with computer evidence, an untrained specialist can easily and unintentionally destroy evidence, no matter how careful you are in providing instructions and monitoring his or her activities.

Determining the Tools You Need

After you have obtained as much information as possible about the incident or crime scene, you can start listing what you'll need at the scene. Being overprepared is better than being underprepared, especially when you determine that you can't transfer the computer to your lab for processing.

To manage your tools, consider creating an initial-response field kit and an extensive-response field kit. Using the right kit makes processing an incident or crime scene much easier and minimizes how much you have to carry from your vehicle to the computers.

Your **initial-response field kit** should be lightweight and easy to transport. With this kit, you can arrive at a scene, acquire the data you need, and return to the lab as quickly as possible. Figure 5-4 shows some of the items you might need, and Table 5-1 lists all the tools you might need in an initial-response field kit.

Table 5-1   Tools in an Initial-Response Field Kit

Number Needed	Tools
1	Small computer tool kit
1	Large-capacity disk drive
1	IDE ribbon cable, 36 inches or longer (ATA-33 or ATA-100)
1	Forensic boot floppy disk containing your preferred acquisition utility
1	Laptop IDE 40- to 44-pin adapter
1	Laptop personal computer (PC)
1	FireWire or USB dual write-protect external bay IDE disk drive box
1	Flashlight
1	Digital camera or photographic camera with film and flash
10	Evidence log forms
1	Notebook or dictation recorder
10	Computer evidence bags (antistatic bags)
20	Evidence labels, tape, and tags
1	Permanent ink marking pen
10	Floppy disks

5

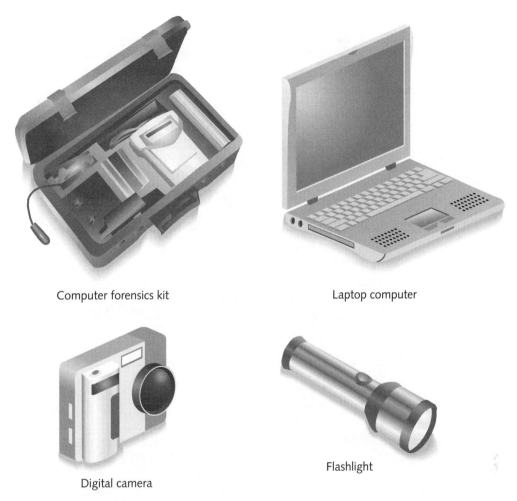

Computer forensics kit   Laptop computer

Digital camera

Flashlight

Figure 5-4   Items in an initial-response field kit

An **extensive-response field kit** should include all the tools you can afford to take to the field. When you arrive at the scene, you should extract only those items you need to acquire evidence. Doing so protects your equipment and minimizes how many items you have to keep track of at the scene. Table 5-2 lists all the tools you might need in an extensive-response field kit, including a digital linear tape (DLT) drive and cartridge, which you can use to store digital evidence. DLT drives and cartridges are examined in more detail in Chapter 6.

Table 5-2   Tools in an Extensive-Response Field Kit

Number Needed	Tools
Varies	Assorted technical manuals ranging from (OS) references to forensic analysis guides
1	Initial-response field kit
1	Portable PC with SCSI card for DLT tape drive or suspect's SCSI drive
1	DLT or Super-DLT portable tape drive
10	DLT or Super-DLT tape cartridges
1	DLT or Super-DLT tape cleaning cartridge
2	Electrical power strips
1	Additional hand tools, including bolt cutters, pry bar, and hacksaw
1	Gloves (leather) and disposable latex gloves (assorted sizes)
1	Hand truck and luggage cart
10	Large garbage bags and large cardboard boxes with packaging tape
1	Rubber bands of assorted sizes
1	Magnifying glass
1	Ream of printer paper
1	Small brush for cleaning dust from suspect's interior CPU cabinet
1	Iomega 250 MB Zip drive
1	Iomega 750 MB Zip drive
1	Iomega 2 GB Jaz drive
10	Iomega 100 MB Zip cartridges
10	Iomega 250 MB Zip cartridges
10	Iomega 750 MB Zip cartridges
10	Iomega 1 GB Jaz cartridges
10	Iomega 2 GB Jaz cartridges
5	Additional assorted hard disk drives for data acquisition

When deciding what items to include in initial-response and extensive-response field kits, you need to analyze your specific needs in your region or organization. Refer to Tables 5-1 and 5-2 for guidelines.

Preparing the Investigation Team

Before you initiate the search and seizure of digital evidence at an incident or crime scene, you must review all the available facts, plans, and objectives with the investigation team you have assembled. The goal of scene processing is to successfully collect and secure digital evidence from the incident or crime scene. The better prepared you are, the fewer problems you encounter when you carry out the plan to collect data.

Keep in mind that digital evidence is volatile. Develop the skills to quickly assess the facts, make your plan, gather the needed resources, and collect data from the incident or crime scene. In some computing investigations, responding slowly might result in the loss of important evidence for the case.

SECURING A COMPUTER INCIDENT OR CRIME SCENE

Investigators secure an incident or crime scene to preserve the evidence and to keep information about the incident or crime confidential. Information made public could easily jeopardize the investigation. If you're in charge of securing a computer incident or crime scene, use yellow barrier tape to prevent bystanders from accidentally entering the scene. Use legal authority, such as police officers or security guards, to prevent others from entering the scene. Legal authority for the corporate incident scene includes trespassing violations; for a crime scene, legal authority includes obstructing justice or failing to comply with a police officer. Access to the scene should be restricted to only those people who have a specific reason to visit the scene. The reason for the standard practice of securing an incident or crime scene is to expand the area of control beyond the actual scene's immediate area. In this way, you avoid overlooking an area that might be part of the scene. Shrinking the scene's perimeter is easier than expanding it.

For major crime scenes, computer investigators aren't usually responsible for defining a scene's security perimeter. These cases involve other specialists and detectives who are collecting physical evidence and recording the scene. For incidents primarily involving computers, computers can be a crime scene within a crime scene. In other words, the computer is a crime scene that contains evidence to be processed. The evidence is virtual data in the computer, but the courts consider it physical evidence. Computers can also contain actual physical evidence, such as DNA evidence on computer keyboards. Crime labs can use special vacuums to extract DNA residue from a keyboard to compare with other DNA samples. In a major crime scene, law enforcement usually retains the computer keyboard.

Evidence is commonly lost or corrupted through **professional curiosity**, which involves police officers and other professionals who aren't part of the crime scene processing team. They just have a compelling interest in seeing what happened. Inevitably, their presence contaminates the scene directly or indirectly. Keep in mind that even those authorized and trained to search crime scenes can inadvertently alter the scene or evidence.

For example, during one homicide investigation, the lead police detective obtained a good latent fingerprint from the crime scene. After he collected the print, he compared it with the victim's fingerprints and those of others who knew the victim. He could not find a fingerprint that matched the latent fingerprint from the scene. The detective suspected he had the murderer's fingerprint and kept it with him for several years until his police department purchased an **Automated Fingerprint Identification Systems (AFIS)** computer. During acceptance testing, the software vendor processed sample fingerprints to see how quickly and accurately the system could match fingerprints in the database. The detective demanded that the acceptance test team run the fingerprint he found at the homicide scene. The detective believed the suspect's fingerprints were in the AFIS database. The acceptance test team complied with the detective's demand. Within minutes, AFIS made a near perfect match of the latent fingerprint. The fingerprint from the old homicide belonged to the detective.

Always remember that professional curiosity can destroy or corrupt evidence, including digital evidence. When working at an incident or crime scene, be aware of what you're doing and what you have touched, either physically or virtually. A police detective can take elimination prints of everyone who had access to the crime scene to identify the fingerprints of known people; computer evidence does not have an equivalent elimination process. You must protect all digital evidence, so make sure that no one begins to examine a suspect's computer before you can preserve and capture a bit-stream image copy of the hard disk. Starting a computer without a forensic boot floppy disk alters important data, such as the date and time stamps of last accessed files. Altering these values destroys vital information on a suspect's or victim's computer.

SEIZING DIGITAL EVIDENCE AT THE SCENE

With proper search warrants, law enforcement can seize all computing systems and associated peripherals. In corporate investigations, however, you might not have authority to seize computers. In civil litigation cases, often corporate investigators have the authority only to make a bit-stream image copy of the suspect disk drive. Rarely does a corporate investigator have the authority to seize all computers.

When seizing computer evidence in criminal investigations, follow the U.S. DoJ standards for seizing digital data (as described in Chapter 6, or see *www.usdoj.gov/criminal/cybercrime/searching.html*). Civil investigations must follow the same rules of evidence as for a criminal investigation, although a company's policy violation doesn't typically require as many detailed procedures or documentation. Generally, a civil computer investigation usually involves less work and equipment than a criminal investigation does for processing an incident or crime scene. For example, suppose you must recover an e-mail message from a plaintiff's or defendant's computer. Initiating a crime scene to recover an e-mail message only introduces conflict for you and the attorneys. For most civil cases, an attorney presents a demand for discovery with specific directions on what you can and cannot do. If you have any questions, doubts, or concerns, consult with your attorney for additional guidance.

Processing a Major Incident or Crime Scene

The following guidelines offer suggestions on how to process an incident or crime scene. As you gain experience in performing searches and seizures, you can add to or modify these guidelines to meet the needs of your specific case. Use your own judgment to determine what steps to take when processing a civil or criminal investigation. For any difficult issues, seek out the opinions of your legal counsel or other technical experts.

Keep a journal to document your activities. Include the date and time you arrive on the scene, the people you encounter, and notes on every significant task you perform. Routinely update the journal as you process the scene.

To secure the scene, use whatever is practical to make sure that only authorized people can access the area. As mentioned earlier, you should secure more area of the scene than necessary. Make sure nothing in this area, including computer evidence, moves until you have had time to record it.

Be professional and courteous to any curious onlookers, but don't offer information about the investigation or incident. Refer journalists to a public information officer or your organization's public relations manager.

Remove anyone who is not investigating the scene unless he or she must help process the scene. For example, the local computing administrator might need to help you collect and recover data.

Take video recordings of the computer area. Start by recording an overall view of the scene, and then record the details with close-up shots, including the back of all computers. Before recording the back of each computer, place numbered or lettered labels on each cable to help identify which cable is connected to which plug if you need to reassemble everything at the lab. Record the area around the computer, including the floor and ceiling, and all access points to the computer, such as doors and windows. Be sure to look under any tables or desks for anything taped to the underside of a table or desk drawer or on the floor out of view. If the area has ceiling panels—false ceiling tiles—remove them and record that area, too. Slowly pan or zoom the camera to prevent blurring in the video image. Always maintain a written camera log for all shots you take.

When you finish videotaping or photographing the scene, sketch the incident or crime scene. Make your sketch a rough draft with notes on objects' dimensions and the distances between fixed objects. For example, a note might read "The suspect's computer is on the south wall, three meters from the southeast corner of the room." When you prepare the report, you can make a clean, detailed drawing from your sketch, preferably using a computer drawing program so that the sketch is in electronic form.

Because computer data is volatile, check the state of each computer at the scene as soon as possible. Determine whether the computer you're investigating is powered on or off. If it is off, proceed with the data acquisition. If it is on, it's your judgment call on what to do next. Standard computer forensics practice has been to kill the computer's power to make sure the suspect computer's data doesn't become corrupt through covert malicious means. There are many urban legends about criminals placing self-destruct mechanisms—both hardware- and software-enabled devices—in computers. Many years ago, a common trick of criminals was altering the Microsoft DOS program Command.com. The criminal would change the directory command (Dir) to the delete-tree (Deltree) command. When an investigator examined the suspect computer's content and entered the Dir command, he would inadvertently start the Deltree command, which deletes all files and folders and their content. More advanced computer criminals have been known to create similar command-altering methods that overwrite a disk drive's content.

As a general rule, pulling the power cord from the suspect's CPU box is a good practice, but again, this is a judgment call because of recent trends in computer crimes. More computing investigations now revolve around network- and Internet-related cases, which rely heavily on log file data. Certain files, such as the Event log and Security log in Windows XP, might lose essential network activity records if the power is terminated without a proper shutdown. These log records are becoming more important to solving cases and identifying suspects in network and Internet investigations.

If you're working on a network or Internet investigation and the computer is on, save data in any current applications as safely as possible and record all active windows or shell sessions. Do not examine folders or network connections or press any keys unless doing so is necessary for the investigation. For systems that are powered on and operating, photograph the screens. If windows are open but minimized, it's safe to expand them so that you can photograph them individually. As a precaution, write down the content of each window verbatim. Do not cut electrical power to a running system unless it's an older Windows 9x or MS-DOS system.

As you're processing the data copying of a live suspect computer, make notes of everything you do. You need these notes to explain your actions in your formal report to prosecutors and other attorneys. When you're done recording the screen content of a suspect computer, save the content of each window to external media. For example, if one window shows a Word or Excel file, save the file to a floppy disk. Keep in mind that the suspect might have changed the file since last using the Save command. If another window is a Web browser, take a screenshot of that page or save the Web page to a floppy disk. If a large database file is open but won't fit on a floppy disk, determine how to save the file so that it doesn't overwrite existing data on the suspect computer's hard disk. If the suspect computer has an Iomega Zip or Jaz drive, use the appropriate media to save the data. If the suspect computer has an active connection to a network server with enough storage, you can save the large file to a folder on the server. To do so, you need the cooperation of the computing support administrator to help direct you to the correct server and folder for storing the file.

If you can't save an open application to an external media device, save the open application to the suspect drive using a new name. Changing the file name avoids overwriting an existing file that might not have been updated already. This method isn't ideal and should be done only in extreme emergency conditions. Remember that your goal is always to preserve as much evidence as possible.

After you have saved all active files on the suspect computer, you can close all applications. If an application prompts you to save before closing, don't save the files. When all applications are closed, perform an orderly shutdown. If you're not familiar with the correct shutdown method for the computer you are examining, consult someone who has expertise in this procedure.

After you record the scene and shut down the system, bag and tag the evidence. If the nature of the case doesn't permit you to seize the computer, create a bit-stream image copy of the hard disk, which you learn to do in Chapter 9.

During the data acquisition phase or immediately after you have collected the evidence, look for information related to the investigation. Look for such items as passwords, passphrases, personal identification numbers (PINs), and Swiss bank account numbers. This information might be in plain view, in a drawer, or in a trash can. When at the scene, collect as much personal information as possible about the suspect or victim. Collect all information related to the facts about the crime or incident, particularly anything that connects the suspect to the victim.

To complete your analysis and processing of an incident or crime scene, collect all documentation and media relevant to the investigation, including the following material:

- Hardware, including peripheral devices
- Software, including operating system and application programs
- All media, such as backup tapes and disks
- All documentation, manuals, printouts, and handwritten notes

Processing Data Centers with an Array of RAIDs

Computer investigators sometimes perform forensic analysis on RAID systems or disk farms, which are rooms filled with extremely large disk systems (usually RAID systems) and are typical of large business data centers, such as the Department of Motor Vehicles (DMV), banks, insurance companies, and ISPs. Performing disk analysis on RAID systems is beyond the scope of this book, but one technique for extracting evidence from large systems is called **sparse evidence file recovery**. This technique extracts only data related to evidence for your case from allocated files. Doing so minimizes how much data you need to analyze. A drawback to this technique is that it doesn't recover residual data in free or slack space. If you have a computer forensics tool that accesses the unallocated space on a RAID system, work with the tool on a test system first to make sure it doesn't corrupt the RAID computer.

Using a Technical Advisor at an Incident or Crime Scene

When working with advanced technologies, recruit a technical advisor who can help you list the tools you need to process the incident or crime scene. For large data centers, the technical advisor is the person guiding you about where to locate data and helping you extract log records or actual evidence from large RAID servers. In law enforcement cases, the technical advisor can help create the search warrant by itemizing what you need for the warrant. When creating a search warrant with the assistance of a technical advisor, you should list his or her name in the warrant. At the scene, the technical advisor can help direct other investigators as necessary to collect evidence properly. Technical advisors have the following responsibilities:

- Know all aspects of the system being seized and searched.

- Direct investigators on how to handle sensitive media and systems to prevent damage.

- Help ensure security of the scene.

- Help document the planning strategy for the search and seizure.

- Conduct ad hoc training for investigators on the technologies being seized and searched.

- Document activities during the search and seizure.

- Help conduct the search and seizure.

Sample Civil Investigation

Most cases in the corporate environment are considered **low-level investigations**, or noncriminal cases. This doesn't mean corporate computing investigations are less important, but that they require less effort than a major criminal case. The example of a low-level civil investigation in this section is an e-mail investigation that resulted in a lawsuit between two businesses. An investigation of this nature requires examining only one or more e-mail messages, not a complete disk forensic analysis.

Mr. Jones at Company A claims to have received an order for $200,000 in widgets from the purchasing manager, Mr. Smith, at Company B. Company A manufactures the widgets and notifies Company B that they are ready for shipment. Mr. Smith at Company B replies that they didn't order any widgets and won't pay for them. Company A locates an e-mail requesting the widgets that appears to be from Mr. Smith and informs Company B about the e-mail. Company B tells Company A that the e-mail did not originate from them and that they won't pay for the widgets.

Company A files a lawsuit against Company B based on the widget order in Mr. Smith's e-mail. The lawyers for Company A contact the lawyers for Company B and discuss the lawsuit. The lawyers for Company A make discovery demands to have a computer forensics analysis performed on Mr. Smith's computer in hopes of finding the original message that caused the problem. At the same time, Company B's lawyers demand discovery on Mr. Jones's computer because they believe the e-mail is a fake.

As a computing investigator and forensics examiner, you receive a call from your boss directing you to fulfill the discovery demands from Company B's lawyers to locate and determine whether the e-mail message on Mr. Jones's computer is real or fake. Because this is an e-mail investigation, not a major crime such as a homicide involving computers, you are dispatched to Company A. When you get there, you find Mr. Jones's computer powered on and running Microsoft Outlook. You are authorized under the discovery order to recover only Mr. Jones's Outlook e-mail folder, the PST file. You aren't authorized to do anything else. You would take the following steps in this scenario:

1. Close the Outlook program on Mr. Jones's computer.

2. Use Windows Explorer to locate the Outlook PST file containing his business e-mail. You might need to use the Windows Search feature to find files ending in .pst.

3. Determine how large the PST file is and connect the appropriate media device, such as a USB Zip drive, to Mr. Jones's computer.

4. Copy the PST file to your external USB drive.

5. Remove your USB drive with the disk cartridge.

6. Fill out your evidence form, stating where on Mr. Jones's disk you located the PST file, along with the date and time you performed this task.

7. Leave Company A and return to your computer forensics lab. Place the Zip disk into your evidence safe.

For most civil incident scenes, you collect only specific items that have been determined germane by lawyers or the Human Resource Department.

Another activity common in the corporate computing environment is performing **covert surveillance** of employees who are abusing their computing and network privileges. The use of covert surveillance of employees must be well defined in company policy before it can be carried out. If a company doesn't have a policy that informs employees they have no privacy rights when using company computers, no surveillance can be conducted without exposing the company to civil or even criminal liability. If no policy exists, the company must create a policy and notify all employees about the new rules. Your legal department should create policy language appropriate for your state or country. The legal department also defines the rights and authority the company has in conducting surveillance of employees according to provincial, state, or country privacy laws.

For covert surveillance, you set up monitoring tools that record a suspect's activity in real time. Real-time surveillance requires **sniffing** data transmissions between a suspect's computer and a network server. Sniffing software allows network administrators and others to determine what data is being transmitted over the network. Other data-collecting tools (called key-logger programs—Spector and WinWhatWhere, for example) are screen capture programs that collect most or all screens and keystrokes on a suspect's computer. Most of these tools run on Windows and usually collect data through remote network connections. The tools are hidden or disguised as other programs from Windows Task Manager and process logs.

Another covert surveillance product is Guidance Software's EnCase Enterprise Edition. The EnCase Enterprise Edition, also known as EEE, is a centrally located server with specialized software that can activate servlets over a network to remote workstations. Computing investigators can perform forensic examinations in real time through this remote connection to a suspect computer.

Sample Criminal Investigation

Crime scenes involving computers range from fraud cases to homicides. Because high-quality printers are now available, one of the most common computer-related crimes is check fraud. Many check fraud cases also involve making and selling false ID cards, such as driver's licenses.

In one recent case, the police received a tip that a check-forging operation was active in an apartment building. After the detective contacted a reliable informant, he had enough information for a search warrant and asked the patrol division to assist him in serving the warrant. When the detective entered the suspect's apartment and conducted a preliminary search, he found a network of six high-end computer workstations with cables connected to devices in the adjacent apartment through a hole in the wall (see Figure 5-5). Unfortunately, the warrant specified a search of only one apartment.

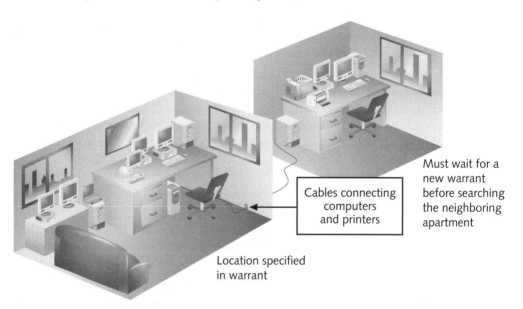

Cables connecting computers and printers

Must wait for a new warrant before searching the neighboring apartment

Location specified in warrant

Figure 5-5   Search warrant limits

The detective contacted the deputy prosecutor, who instructed him to stand guard at both apartments until she could have a judge issue an additional warrant for the neighboring apartment. When he received the second search warrant, the detective entered the adjoining apartment and continued his search, finding more computers, high-quality color laser printers, checks, and stolen blank state driver's licenses. The outcome of the investigation revealed that the perpetrators were three enterprising high school students who were selling fake IDs to fellow students. The check fraud scheme was a new sideline they were developing to improve their personal cash flow.

REVIEWING A CASE

Chapter 2 introduced the tasks for planning your investigation, some of which are repeated in the following list. In this section, you apply each task to your investigation to create a preparation plan for searching an incident or crime scene. These are the general tasks you perform in any computer forensics case:

- Identify the case requirements.

- Plan your investigation.

- Conduct the investigation.

- Complete the case report.

- Critique the case.

5

Suppose you're investigating a case that begins when Steve Billings, a manager of a small business, notices something unusual with two employees. Ten days ago, Martha Heiser, a shipping clerk, began a one-week emergency leave from the company without informing anyone where she was going or how to contact her. Steve is concerned because she should have returned from her leave three days ago.

A supervisor in the Accounts Payable Department, George Montgomery, has also been missing from work for the past five days. Until now, George has been punctual and dedicated to his work, informing Steve about any personal activities that might cause him to be away from the office. Steve talks to other employees, but no one knows why George and Martha are not at work.

To learn where Martha might be, Steve searches the surface of Martha's desk and notices travel brochures for European tours. Steve also looks around George's office and finds notes about a Swiss supplier Steve once used and a floppy disk with the former supplier's name on the label. Steve inserts the disk into his computer's floppy disk drive, opens an MS-DOS prompt, types `a:`, presses Enter, types `dir`, and presses Enter to find the information shown in Figure 5-6.

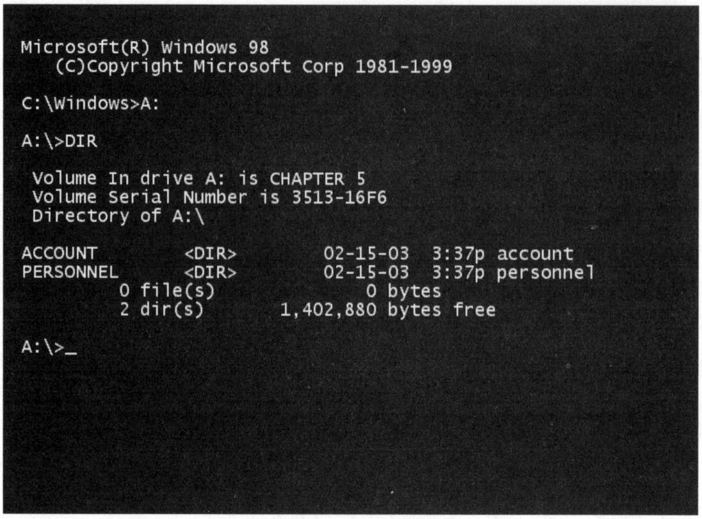

```
Microsoft(R) Windows 98
   (C)Copyright Microsoft Corp 1981-1999

C:\Windows>A:

A:\>DIR

 Volume In drive A: is CHAPTER 5
 Volume Serial Number is 3513-16F6
 Directory of A:\

ACCOUNT        <DIR>         02-15-03  3:37p account
PERSONNEL      <DIR>         02-15-03  3:37p personnel
         0 file(s)                 0 bytes
         2 dir(s)         1,402,880 bytes free

A:\>_
```

Figure 5-6   Contents of George's disk

Steve suspects the disk contains more information, and he calls you, the computing investigator for his company. He describes Martha and George's absence from the company and asks you to examine the floppy disk to see whether it identifies their whereabouts.

Identifying the Case Requirements

Before you analyze the floppy disk, answer the following basic questions to start your investigation:

- *What is the nature of the case?* Two people are missing or overdue at work.

- *What are their names?* George Montgomery and Martha Heiser.

- *What do they do?* George is a supervisor in the Accounts Payable Department, and Martha is a shipping clerk.

- *What is the operating system of the suspect computer?* Microsoft Windows 98.

- *What type of media needs to be examined?* One floppy disk.

- *What is the suspect computer's configuration, such as type, CPU speed, and hard disk size?* A Pentium IV 3.2 GHz processor, 120 GB Western Digital disk.

Planning Your Investigation

To find information about George and Martha's whereabouts, list what you can assume or already know about the case:

- George and Martha's absences might or might not be related.

- George's computer might contain information explaining their absence.

- No one else has used George's computer since he disappeared.

You need to make an image of George's computer and attempt to retrieve evidence related to the case. The following sections discuss three tools you can use to examine the content of the floppy disk: Digital Intelligence DriveSpy, AccessData FTK (demo version), and X-Ways Forensics (also known as WinHex Forensic Edition).

DriveSpy

In the following steps, you use DriveSpy to extract and analyze the image of a floppy disk. Note that in an actual case, you would acquire and analyze the image of a floppy, Zip, or hard disk.

TIP

If you did not install DriveSpy in Chapter 2, follow the instructions in that chapter to install DriveSpy and Image and to create Toolpath.bat.

Now you're ready to create an image of the suspect disk and then extract evidence. You should work on a Windows 98 computer with Microsoft Office installed. You need a blank, formatted floppy disk to complete these steps. Follow these steps to create an image of the suspect disk using DriveSpy:

1. Boot your forensic workstation to DOS. From the command prompt, change to the Tools folder in your work folder, and run Toolpath.bat.

2. In your work folder, create a **Chap05** folder. In the Chap05 folder, create a **Chapter** folder. Navigate to the Chap05\Chapter folder and copy **C5InChap.img** from your student data files to the Chap05\Chapter folder.

3. To prepare for the retrieval, create additional subfolders in the Chap05\Chapter folder called **Files**, **Deleted**, **Slack**, **Free**, and **Hidden**. Create a blank text file in MS-DOS Edit and save it as **hfiles.txt** in the Hidden subfolder.

4. Label a blank, formatted floppy disk **Chapter 5 In Chapter** and insert it in the floppy disk drive. At the prompt, type **image C5InChap.img a:** and press **Enter** to create an image of George's disk on your floppy disk. Image displays the Checksum Verified number, which is the MD5 hash value, to confirm that the C5InChap.img file is identical to the original disk, as shown in Figure 5-7.

```
A:\>C:

C:\>CD \TOOLS

C:\Tools>TOOLPATH.BAT

C:\Tools>SET PATH=C:\WINDOWS;C:\WINDOWS\COMMAND;C:\TOOLS

C:\Tools>CD \

C:\>CD CHAP05\CHAPTER

C:\Chap05\Chapter>IMAGE C5InChap.img A:

IMAGE V1.30: Copyright 1999. Digital Intelligence. Inc
             All Rights Reserved

This copy of IMAGE Licensed to:    Joe Friday
Writing Cylinder:    79 of 79
Checksum Verified:    1F81505C8B5102EBE4EB8A2F1F4628C8

C:\Chap05\Chapter>_
```

Figure 5-7   Using Image to validate data integrity

NOTE

The Checksum Verified number that Image displays is a unique value of the restored floppy disk—something like a fingerprint. This specific number is the MD5 hash value for the re-created floppy. When re-creating the floppy from the Image save-set, the MD5 hash number (usually displayed in hexadecimal form) should always be the same. If not, it's an indicator that the data on the re-created floppy or the Image save-set is corrupted and can't be considered a reliable copy. In Chapter 6, you learn more about MD5 and how it's used to validate data integrity.

Now you can start DriveSpy and use it to recover files and analyze the evidence disk.

NOTE

In the following steps, you should be working from your work folder. So, for example, in a command such as copy *.* C:\Chap05\Chapter\Files, insert your work folder name at the beginning of the path name, after the C:\.

1. Start DriveSpy by typing **drivespy** at the command prompt and pressing **Enter**.

2. At the SYS prompt, type **drive a** and press **Enter** to examine the floppy disk. At the DA prompt, type **part 1** and press **Enter** to switch to Partition mode.

3. At the DAP1 prompt, type **copy *.* C:\Chap05\Chapter\Files /s** and press **Enter** to recover any files stored on the disk. If you're prompted to disable Page mode, type **y** for yes.

4. In this case, seven files are copied. To recover deleted files from the evidence disk, type **unerase *.* C:\Chap05\Chapter\Deleted /s** and press **Enter**. If prompted to disable Page mode, type **y** for yes.

5. To recover the free space, type **savefree C:\Chap05\Chapter\Free\free** and press **Enter**.

6. To save the RAM slack and file slack, type **saveslack C:\Chap05\Chapter\Slack\slack** and press **Enter** (see Figure 5-8).

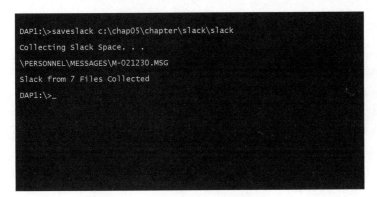

```
DAP1:\>saveslack c:\chap05\chapter\slack\slack
Collecting Slack Space. . .
\PERSONNEL\MESSAGES\M-021230.MSG
Slack from 7 Files Collected
DAP1:\>_
```

Figure 5-8   Using the SaveSlack command

7. Finally, you need to look for hidden files. Type **dbexport *.* C:\Chap05\Chapter\Hidden\hfiles.txt /h/s** and press **Enter**. Then type **a** to append the data to the already existing file.

8. Type **exit** to close DriveSpy, and then close the command-prompt window.

9. Boot your workstation to Windows and use Windows Explorer and WordPad to examine the output created from this DriveSpy session. While examining the recovered data, take note of the file names and contents to determine what might have happened to George and Martha.

You can now meet with Steve and present your findings, including evidence that George and Martha embezzled money and are now in Zurich.

Access Data Forensic Toolkit (FTK)

In the following steps, you use AccessData FTK to extract and analyze the image of a floppy bit-stream image file. In Chapter 9, you learn more on how to acquire a bit-stream image backup of a disk with FTK and other tools.

NOTE

The following steps are designed for FTK Demo. If you have not installed FTK, download FTK Demo from *www.accessdata.com* and install it on your workstation. This exercise can also be performed with a licensed version of FTK. If you have a licensed version of FTK, install the KFF utility and review the licensed version user manual. The licensed version of FTK has many more features that aren't available in the demo version.

To obtain an image of the suspect disk using FTK and to prepare FTK for evidence analysis, follow these steps:

1. If you have already created a Chap05 folder, skip this step. If not, from Windows in your work folder, use Windows Explorer to create a **Chap05** folder. In the Chap05 folder, create a **Chapter** folder. Navigate to the Chap05\Chapter folder and copy **C5InChap.1** from your student data files to the Chap05\Chapter folder.

2. To start FTK, click **Start**, **Programs**, **AccessData**, **Forensic Toolkit**, **Forensic Toolkit**.

3. When a message box about this evaluation version of FTK opens, click **OK** to start the program.

4. In the AccessData FTK Startup dialog box, click the **Start a new case** option button, and then click **OK**.

5. In the New Case dialog box, fill in the case information shown in Figure 5-9, and then click **Next**.

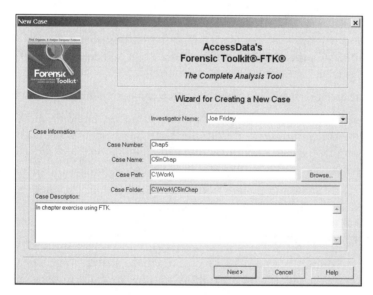

Figure 5-9 The New Case dialog box

6. In the Case Log Options dialog box, click **Next**.

7. In the Evidence Processing Options dialog box, click **Next**.

8. In the Refine Case - Default dialog box, click the **Include All Items** button (see Figure 5-10), and then click **Next**.

9. In the Refine Index - Default dialog box (see Figure 5-11), click **Next**.

10. In the Add Evidence dialog box, click the **Add Evidence to Case** option button.

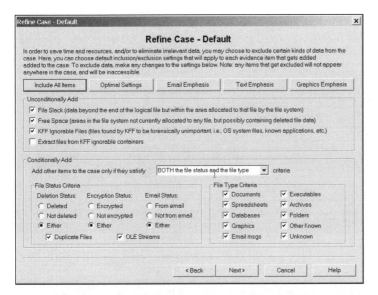

Figure 5-10   The Refine Case - Default dialog box

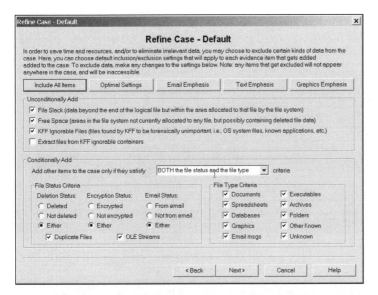

Figure 5-11   The Refine Index - Default dialog box

11. In the Add Evidence to Case dialog box, click the **Acquired Image of Drive** option button, and then click **Continue**.

12. In the Open dialog box, navigate to and click the *work folder***Chap05****Chapter** folder, where you have copied the file C5InChap.1, and then click **Open**.

13. In the Evidence Information dialog box, enter the additional information shown in Figure 5-12, and then click **OK**.

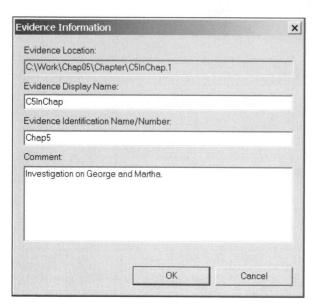

Figure 5-12   The Evidence Information dialog box

14. In the Add Evidence to Case dialog box, shown in Figure 5-13, click **Next**.

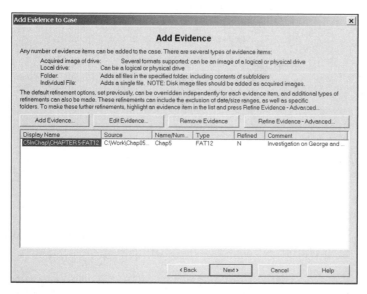

Figure 5-13   The Add Evidence to Case dialog box with image file listed

15. In the Case Summary dialog box (see Figure 5-14), click **Finish** to initiate the analysis. FTK then performs several steps of cataloging data and indexing every word in the C5InChap.1 image save-set. The cataloging process organizes and lists each file in its own section for follow-up analysis (see Figure 5-15). The indexing feature creates a database of every word in the image save-set with its exact location, providing instant lookup for any keywords of interest to the investigation.

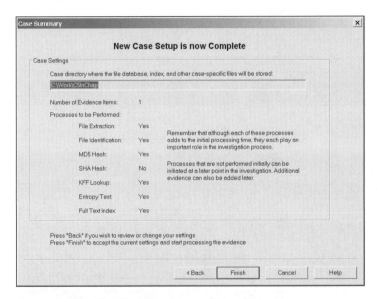

Figure 5-14   The Case Summary dialog box

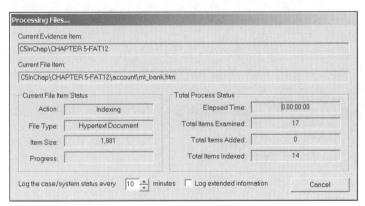

Figure 5-15   The Processing Files dialog box

When FTK finishes the cataloging and indexing task, the FTK window opens to the Overview tab (shown in Figure 5-16), ready for your analysis. To analyze an image with FTK, follow these steps:

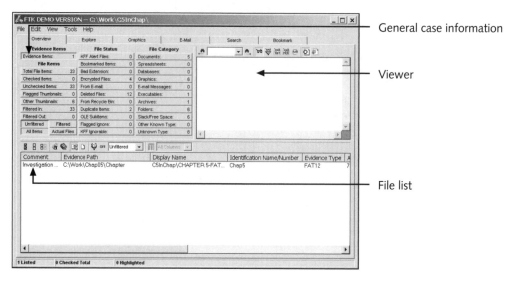

Figure 5-16   The FTK Overview tab

Labels pointing to the figure:
- General case information
- Viewer
- File list

1. In the FTK window, click the **Explore** tab. In the pane at the upper left (the tree view), click to expand the folder tree, and then click the **List all descendants** check box.

NOTE

When you're navigating between the Explorer, Graphic, and E-Mail tabs in the FTK window, only the directories are displayed. If you click a directory in the upper-left pane, the directory's contents are displayed in the lower pane. The List all descendants option enables you to view all files, regardless of which directory they're in, and you can scroll through all files at once.

2. Navigate through each file in the lower pane by clicking the file names one at a time. The upper-right pane displays any text data contained in the files. Read through the text that's displayed to see what information is contained on this disk.

3. When you have located a file containing information you think is important, click the check box next to the file name in the lower pane (see Figure 5-17). Continue searching for additional information, and select additional files of interest as you find them.

4. After you have selected all files of interest, click **Tools, Create Bookmark** from the menu. In the Create New Bookmark dialog box, type a bookmark name and any comments. Then click the **All checked items** button, the **Include in report** check box, and the **Export files** check box, as shown in Figure 5-18. Click **OK**.

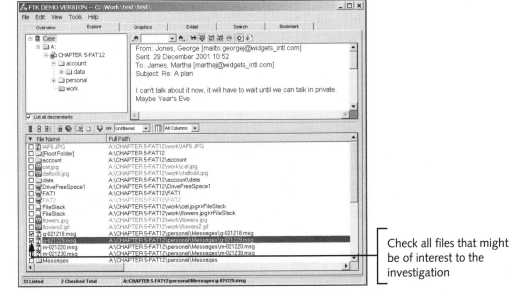

Check all files that might
be of interest to the
investigation

Figure 5-17   Selecting files of interest

NOTE

The purpose of bookmarks in FTK is to provide a way to copy information of
evidence value to a report.

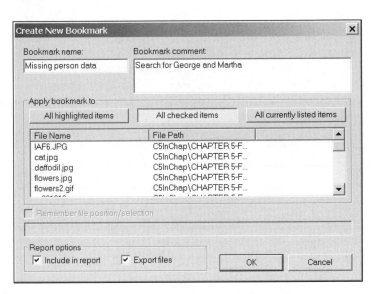

Figure 5-18   The Create New Bookmark dialog box

5. After you have bookmarked key files containing possible evidence, click **File**, **Report Wizard** from the FTK menu. In the Case Information dialog box, enter the information shown in Figure 5-19, and then click **Next**.

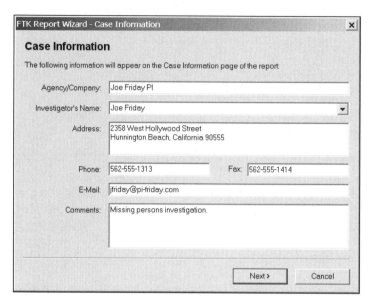

Figure 5-19   The Case Information dialog box

6. In the Bookmarks - A window, click **Next**. Continue clicking **Next** through the remaining report wizard windows until you reach the Report Location window, and then click **Finish**.

7. Step 6 completes the process of extracting data of interest to the investigation. When the Report Wizard displays a prompt asking if you would like to view the report, click **Yes** to see the report in your default Web browser. Click the various links to view the report's content. When you're done, close FTK by clicking **File**, **Exit** from the menu.

X-Ways Forensics

In the following steps, you use X-Ways Forensics to extract and analyze the image of a floppy disk. X-Ways Forensics is a GUI-based computer forensics application that runs on Windows 9x, Me, NT 4.0, 2000, and XP. Like FTK, X-Ways Forensics can read a disk drive directly and can read a bit-stream image backup from two different formats. In Chapter 9, you learn more on how to acquire a bit-stream image backup of a disk with X-Ways Forensics and other tools. To obtain an image of the suspect disk and load a forensic image into X-Ways Forensics, follow these steps:

NOTE The following steps are for the licensed version of X-Ways Forensics. For more information, go to *www.x-ways.net/forensics*. At the time of this writing, X-Ways Technology AG does not provide a demo version of X-Ways Forensics. If you don't have a licensed version, simply follow along by reading the steps and examining the figures.

1. If you have not created Chapter 5 folders in your work folder, create a **Chap05** folder. In the Chap05 folder, create a **Chapter** folder. Navigate to the Chap05\Chapter folder and copy **C5InChap.E01** from your student data files to the Chap05\Chapter folder.

2. To start X-Ways Forensics, click **Start**, **Programs**, **X-Ways Forensics**. The main window is shown in Figure 5-20.

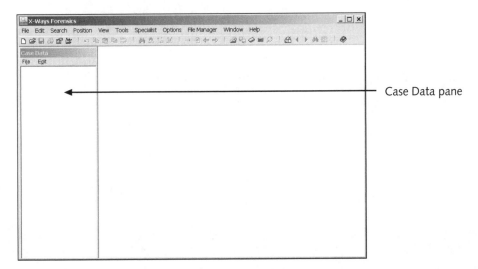

Case Data pane

Figure 5-20   The X-Ways Forensics main window

3. In the Case Data pane shown in Figure 5-20, click **File**, **Create New Case** from the menu. When the Case Data dialog box appears, type the case information in the Description pane, as shown Figure 5-21, and then click **OK**.

4. In the Case Data pane of the X-Ways Forensics main window, click **File**, **Add Image** from the menu. In the Open Files dialog box, navigate to the *work folder***Chap05****Chapter** folder, click the **C5InChap.E01** file, and click **Open**.

5. Next, in the Source of Evidence dialog box, click **OK**. If the file list isn't displayed in the upper pane of the X-Ways Forensics main window, click the **Access** check box (see Figure 5-22).

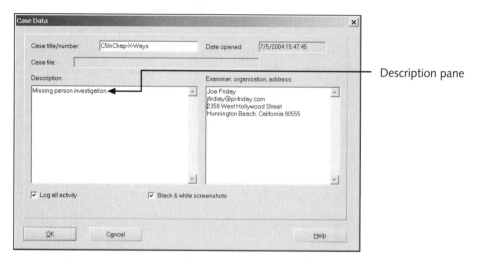

Figure 5-21 Entering a case description

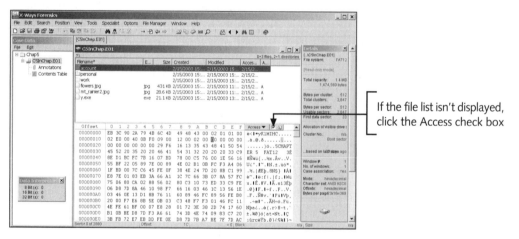

Figure 5-22 The X-Ways Forensics main window after an image has been loaded

Next, you see how to define the path for your output and how to analyze and extract data from the image:

1. Click **Options**, **General** from the menu. In the General Options dialog box (see Figure 5-23), click the **ellipse (...)** button under Folder for temporary files, navigate to your **Chap05\Chapter** folder, and then click **OK** in the Select Folder dialog box. Click **OK** again to close the General Options dialog box.

You might need to restart X-Ways Forensics to implement the new path. When restarted, X-Ways Forensics reloads your case automatically.

NOTE

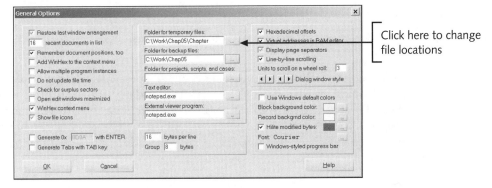

Click here to change file locations

5

Figure 5-23   The General Options dialog box

2. To define what data to extract, click **Tools**, **Disk Tools** from the X-Ways Forensics menu. Click **File Recovery by Name**. When the File Recovery from dialog box opens, click **OK** to accept the default values. Finally, click **OK** in the X-Ways Forensics dialog box stating that 28 files and 0 directories were recovered.

The File Recovery from dialog box contains a scroll arrow button (with left and right arrows), a check box for using the disk partition's allocation table, a check box for intercepting invalid file names, and an Ouput folder ellipse button.

NOTE

3. To define the path for extracting data, in the File Recovery from dialog box, click the **Output folder ellipse (...)** button (see Figure 5-24), navigate to and click the **Chap05\Chapter** folder, and then click **OK**.

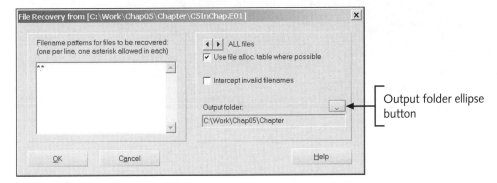

Output folder ellipse button

Figure 5-24   The File Recovery from dialog box

4. In the File Recovery from dialog box, click **OK** to recover all allocated and deleted files. Deleted files are located in unallocated space and are recovered through this process. When the recovery is completed, click **OK**.

To view extracted files, use Windows Explorer and open the recovered files with an application of your choosing. First, use these steps to create a listing of all known data:

1. Click **Specialist**, **Create Drive Contents Table** from the X-Way Forensics menu.

2. In the Create Drive Contents Table dialog box, click to select the **Files, Directories, Existing, Not existent, Particularly thorough file system data structure search, File header signature search in unallocated clusters**, and **Directory browser** check boxes. Click to clear the **Open file in MS Excel** check box (see Figure 5-25) to create a tab-delimited text file, and then click **OK**.

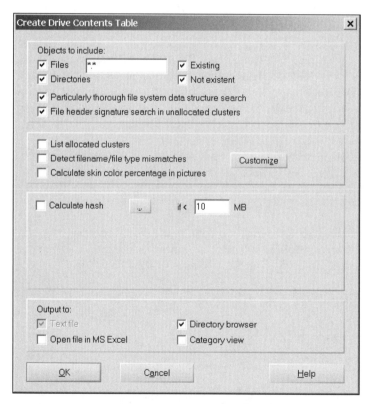

Figure 5-25   The Create Drive Contents Table dialog box

3. In the File Header Search on dialog box, click **OK**.

4. In the Save File As dialog box, navigate to and click your **Chap05\Chapter** folder, and click **Save**.

Next, follow these steps to view graphics files and create a report:

1. Click the **Access** list arrow, and then click **Gallery View** in the list of options.

2. To examine the content of each folder, double-click the folder in the file list at the top (see Figure 5-26).

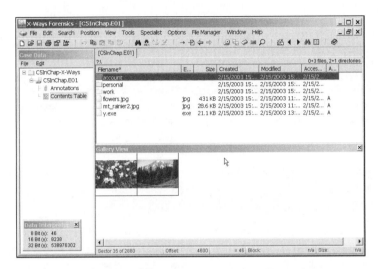

Figure 5-26   Using Gallery View in X-Ways Forensics

3. In the Case Data pane, click **File**, **Create Report** from the menu, and then click **OK** in the X-Ways Forensics dialog box. X-Ways loads the report into your default Web browser. This report lists all the actions taken for this forensic examination.

4. When you're finished reviewing the report, click **File**, **Exit** from the menu to close X-Ways Forensics, and then close your Web browser.

CHAPTER SUMMARY

❑ In the private sector, an incident scene is often a place of work, such as a contained office or manufacturing area. Because everything from the computers used to violate a company policy to the surrounding facility is under a controlled authority, it's easier to investigate and control the scene than in a criminal environment.

❑ Companies should publish policies stating that they reserve the right to inspect computing assets at will; otherwise, the employees' expectation of privacy prevents an employer from legally conducting an intrusive investigation. A well-defined corporate policy states that an employer has the right to examine, inspect, or access any company-owned computing asset. If the policy statement is issued to all employees, the employer can investigate computing assets at will without any privacy right restrictions.

❏ Proper procedure needs to be followed even in private-sector investigations because civil litigations can easily become criminal investigations. As a corporate investigator, you must ensure that sensitive company information doesn't become commingled with criminal evidence.

❏ If an internal corporate case is turned over to law enforcement because of criminal activity, the corporate investigator must avoid becoming an agent of law enforcement because when that happens, affidavits and search warrants are needed.

❏ Criminal cases require a properly executed and well-defined search warrant. A specific crime and specific location must be spelled out in the warrant. For all criminal investigations in the United States, the Fourth Amendment specifies that a law enforcement officer may search for and seize criminal evidence only with probable cause, which is facts or circumstances that would lead a reasonable person to believe a crime has been committed or is about to be committed.

❏ The plain view doctrine applies when evidentiary items that aren't specified in a warrant or under probable cause are in plain view.

❏ When preparing for a case, you need to describe the nature of the case, identify the type of operating system (OS), determine whether you can seize the computer, and obtain a description of the location.

❏ When dealing with a hazardous material (HAZMAT) situation, you might need to have someone else obtain the evidence or obtain HAZMAT certification.

❏ Always take pictures or use a video camera to document the scene. Then methodically record what exists at the scene. Prevent professional curiosity from contaminating evidence by limiting who enters the scene.

❏ As you collect digital evidence, guard against physically destroying or contaminating it. Take precautions to prevent static electricity discharge to electronic devices. If possible, bag or box digital evidence and any hardware you collect from the incident or crime scene. As you collect the hardware, sketch the equipment, including exact markings of where components were located. Tag and number each cable, port, and other connection and record its number and description in a log.

❏ To analyze computer forensics data, learn to use more than one vendor tool. Different vendors offer varying methods for recovering data from magnetic media. Digital Intelligence DriveSpy is a DOS-based tool for recovering data from Microsoft FAT file systems. AccessData FTK is a Windows GUI tool for recovering data from FAT, NTFS, and Ext2 file systems. FTK has a unique method of cataloging and indexing data that speeds up the examination process. The X-Ways Forensics tool from X-Ways Software Technology AG is an alternate Windows GUI program that can analyze FAT and NTFS file systems.

KEY TERMS

Automated Fingerprint Identification Systems (AFIS) — A computerized system for identifying fingerprints that is connected to a central database for identifying criminal suspects and reviewing thousands of fingerprint samples at high speed.

covert surveillance — Observing people or places without being detected, often using electronic equipment such as video cameras or key and screen capture programs.

extensive-response field kit — A portable kit designed to process several computers and a variety of operating systems at a crime or incident scene involving computers. This kit should contain two or more different types of software or hardware computer forensics tools, such as extra disk drives and magnetic tape drives.

hazardous material (HAZMAT) — Chemical, biological, or radiological substances that can cause harm to people.

innocent information — Data that does not contribute to evidence of a crime or violation.

initial-response field kit — A portable kit containing only the minimum tools needed to perform disk acquisitions and preliminary forensic analysis in the field.

limiting phrase — A phrase in a search warrant that limits the scope of a search for evidence.

low-level investigations — Corporate cases that require less effort than does a major criminal case.

person of interest — Someone who might be a suspect or someone with additional knowledge that can provide enough evidence for probable cause for a search warrant or arrest.

plain view doctrine — When conducting a search and seizure, objects in plain view of a law enforcement officer who has the right to be in position to have that view are subject to seizure without a warrant and may be introduced as evidence.

probable cause — Indication that a crime has been committed, evidence of the specific crime exists, and the evidence for the specific crime exists at the place to be searched.

professional curiosity — The motivation for law enforcement and other professional personnel to examine an incident or crime scene to see what happened.

proxy server — A server computer that connects a local area network (LAN) to the Internet.

sniffing — Detecting data transmissions to and from a suspect's computer and a network server to determine the type of data being transmitted over a network.

sparse evidence file recovery — Creating files from separate large portions of data to streamline data analysis.

Review Questions

1. Corporate investigations are typically easier than law enforcement investigations because _____ .

   a. the users have standard corporate equipment and software

   b. the investigator does not have to get a warrant

   c. the investigator has to get a warrant

   d. the users can load whatever they want on their machines

2. If a company publishes a policy stating that it reserves the right to inspect computing assets at will, a corporate investigator can conduct surveillance on an employee with little cause. True or False?

3. If you discover a criminal act while investigating a corporate policy abuse, it becomes a law enforcement investigation and should be referred to law enforcement. True or False?

4. As a corporate investigator, you can become an agent of law enforcement when _____ . (Choose all that apply.)

   a. You begin to take orders from a police detective without a warrant or subpoena.

   b. Your internal investigation has concluded and you have filed a criminal complaint and turned over the criminal evidence to law enforcement.

   c. Your internal investigation begins.

   d. none of the above

5. Probable cause is not needed for a criminal investigation. True or False?

6. If a suspect computer is located in an area that might have toxic chemicals, you must do which of the following? (Choose all that apply.)

   a. Coordinate with the HAZMAT team.

   b. Determine a way to obtain the suspect computer.

   c. Assume the suspect machine is contaminated.

   d. Do not enter alone.

7. To what does the plain view doctrine apply?

8. If you have to call in specialists, expect _____ . (Choose all that apply.)

   a. to train them in proper evidence handling and crime-scene processing

   b. that they will not be familiar with crime-scene protocol

   c. that they know their field

   d. none of the above

9. List three items that should be in an initial-response field kit.

10. When you arrive at the scene, why should you extract only those items you need to acquire evidence?

11. Computer peripherals or attachments can contain DNA evidence. True or False?

12. If a suspect computer is running Windows 98, which of the following can you safely perform?

    a. browsing open applications safely

    b. disconnecting power

    c. either of the above

    d. none of the above

13. Describe what should be videotaped or sketched at a computer crime scene.

14. Data sniffing might be necessary in _____ cases.

15. A search warrant allows you to search the specified location within a 100-yard radius. True or False?

16. You do not need to use an evidence bag when working with evidence collected at a drug lab. True or False?

17. Small companies rarely need investigators. True or False?

18. If a company doesn't distribute a computing use policy stating an employer's rights to freely inspect, employees have an expectation of privacy. True or False?

19. You have been called to the scene of a fatal car crash where a laptop computer is still running. What type of field kit should you take with you?

20. You should always answer questions from onlookers at a crime scene. True or False?

HANDS-ON PROJECTS

HANDS-ON PROJECTS

Project 5-1

You are at the scene of a drug lab that had been producing highly toxic and illegal drugs. There are two computers in the house, but only the HAZMAT people are allowed in. The HAZMAT specialist must retrieve the disk images for you. Write two to three pages of numbered steps that instruct this untrained specialist exactly what he should do to acquire a forensic disk copy.

HANDS-ON PROJECTS

Project 5-2

You are investigating an internal policy violation when you find an e-mail message relating to a serious assault for which a police report will need to be filed. What should you do? Write a two-page paper specifying who in your company you need to talk to first and what evidence has to be turned over to the police.

Project 5-3

You are at a crime scene, which is the home of a suspected drug dealer. You find a computer turned on with three applications running. An online session is also open through a Digital Subscriber Line (DSL) connection. Write a one- to two-page paper outlining what you should do to properly document the crime scene, collect your evidence, and start packaging the evidence.

Project 5-4

Your supervisor asked you to create a spreadsheet that compares the different commercially available computer forensic products for field use. Using your preferred Internet search engine, search for products specifically designed for mobile operations, such as the Digital Intelligence F.R.E.D.D.I.E. unit. For your research, use search keywords such as "computer forensics hardware" to see how many vendors you can find. Create a spreadsheet listing the manufacturer, the product, its cost, and a list of features. Next, write a one-page report stating which vendor provides the best product for mobile computer forensics field work.

CASE PROJECTS

Case Project 5-1

In the arson case, because the insurance company gave you the image, what information do you need about the crime scenes and how the digital evidence was acquired?

Case Project 5-2

For the kidnapping case, what additional evidence could you look for at the victim's home or school to obtain clues about her whereabouts?

Case Project 5-3

Thomas Brown is the primary suspect in a murder investigation. You are a detective for the local police. Thomas works at a large local firm and is reported to have two computers at work in addition to one at home. What do you need to do and what obstacles can you expect to run into while obtaining the evidence you need on this case? Write a two- to three-page report stating what you would do if the company had its own Computer Forensics and Investigations Department and what you would do if the company did not.

Case Project 5-4

A murder in a downtown office building has been widely publicized. You are a police detective and receive a phone call from a computer forensics investigator, Gary Owens, who says he has information that might relate to the murder case. Gary says he ran across a few files while investigating a policy violation at a company in the same office building. Considering the silver platter doctrine, what procedures might you, as a public official, have to follow? Write a one-page paper detailing what you might do.

Case Project 5-5

Your spouse works at a middle school and reports rumors of a teacher, Zane Wilkens, molesting some students and taking illicit pictures of them. Zane allegedly views these pictures in his office. Your spouse wants you to take a disk image of Zane's computer disk and find out if the rumors are true. Write a one- to two-page paper detailing how you would tell your spouse to proceed. Also, explain why walking into Zane's office to acquire a disk image would not preserve integrity of the evidence.

Case Project 5-6

As a computing investigator for your local sheriff's department, you have been asked to respond with a detective to a local school that received a bomb threat from an anonymous e-mail message. The detective has already obtained information from a subpoena sent to the last known ISP where the anonymous e-mail came from, advising that the message was sent from a residence in the school's neighborhood. The detective informs you that the school principal also stated that the school's Web server had been defaced by an unknown hacker. The detective has just obtained a warrant for the search and seizure of a computer at the residence identified by the ISP. Prepare a rapid response plan to ensure the preservation of computer evidence at the suspected residence when the warrant is executed.

6

DIGITAL EVIDENCE CONTROLS

> **After reading this chapter and completing the exercises, you will be able to:**
>
> ♦ Identify digital evidence
> ♦ Secure digital evidence at an incident scene
> ♦ Catalog digital evidence
> ♦ Store digital evidence
> ♦ Obtain a digital hash

This chapter explains how to systematically handle digital evidence so that you don't inadvertently alter or lose data. Even if you are collecting evidence for different types of cases, you must handle all evidence the same way. You should apply the same security controls to evidence for a civil lawsuit as evidence obtained in support of investigating a major crime, such as a murder. The same rules of evidence govern the evidence presented in civil and criminal cases. These rules are similar in English-speaking countries because they have a common ancestor in English common law (judge-made law), dating back to the late Middle Ages.

IDENTIFYING DIGITAL EVIDENCE

Digital evidence can be any information stored or transmitted in digital form. Because you cannot see or touch digital data directly, it is difficult to explain and describe it. Is digital evidence real or virtual? Does data on a disk or other storage medium physically exist, or does it merely represent real information? U.S. courts accept digital evidence as physical evidence, which means that digital data is a tangible object, such as a weapon, paper document, or visible injury, that's related to a criminal or civil incident. Groups such as the **Scientific Working Group on Digital Evidence (SWGDE)** and the **International Organization on Computer Evidence (IOCE)** set standards for recovering, preserving, and examining digital evidence.

For more information about digital evidence, visit *www.ojp.usdoj.gov/nij/ pubs-sum/187736.htm* to download the document "Electronic Crime Scene Investigation: A Guide for First Responders," which provides guidelines for law enforcement and other responders who protect an electronic crime scene and search for, collect, and preserve electronic evidence.

Following are the general tasks investigators perform when working with digital evidence:

- Identify digital information or artifacts that can be used as evidence.
- Collect, preserve, and document the evidence.
- Analyze, identify, and organize the evidence.
- Rebuild evidence or repeat a situation to verify that the results can be reproduced reliably.

Collecting computers and processing a criminal or incident scene must be done systematically. If practical, to minimize confusion, reduce the risk of losing evidence, and avoid damaging evidence, if practical, only one person should collect and catalog digital evidence at a crime scene or lab. If too much evidence or too many systems exist for one person to collect and process all the evidence, all examiners must follow the same established operating procedures, and a lead or managing examiner should control the collection and cataloging of evidence. You should also use standardized forms (discussed later in "Documenting Evidence") for tracking evidence to ensure that you consistently handle evidence in a safe, secure manner.

Understanding Evidence Rules

Consistent practices generally help verify your work and enhance your credibility as a professional. You must handle all evidence consistently. Apply the same security and accountability controls for evidence in a civil lawsuit as for evidence in a major crime to comply with your state's rules of evidence or with the Federal Rules of Evidence. Also keep in mind that evidence admitted in a criminal case can be used in a civil suit, and vice versa. For example, suppose someone is charged with murder and acquitted at the criminal trial because the jury is not convinced beyond a reasonable doubt of the person's guilt. If enough evidence shows that the accused's negligence contributed to a wrongful death, the victim's relatives can use the evidence in a civil lawsuit to recover damages.

As part of your professional growth, keep current on the latest rulings and directives related to collecting, processing, storing, and admitting digital evidence. The following sections discuss some key concepts of digital evidence. You can find additional information at the U.S. Department of Justice Web site (*www.usdoj.gov*) and by using a search engine such as Google to search for "electronic," "best evidence rule," "hearsay," or other relevant expressions to find the latest postings. Be sure to consult with your prosecuting attorney, crown attorney, corporate general counsel, or the attorney who retained you to learn more about how to manage evidence for your investigation.

In Chapters 2 and 5, you learned how to make a bit-stream image copy of an evidence disk. Physical evidentiary data you discover from your forensic examination falls under your state's rules of evidence or Federal Rules of Evidence. However, electronic evidence is unlike other physical evidence because it can be changed more easily. The only way to detect these changes is to compare the original data with a duplicate. Furthermore, distinguishing a duplicate and the original electronically is impossible, so digital evidence requires special legal consideration.

Most federal courts have interpreted computer records as hearsay evidence. Hearsay is secondhand or indirect evidence, such as an overheard conversation or any statements made out of court and not under oath, including letters, diaries, and notes. Because it can't be proved that the contents of these conversations or documents are true, they aren't admissible in court at trial, unless they fall under one of several exceptions to the hearsay rule. The business-record exception allows "records of regularly conducted activity," such as regular business memos, reports, records, or data compilations. Business records are authenticated by verifying that they were created "at or near the time by, or from information transmitted by, a person with knowledge..." and are admissible "if the record was kept in the course of a regularly conducted business activity, and it was the regular practice of that business activity to make the record" (Federal Rules of Evidence, 803(6); see Section V, "Evidence," in *Searching and Seizing Computers and Obtaining Electronic Evidence in Criminal Investigations*, *www.usdoj.gov/criminal/cybercrime/s&smanual2002.htm*).

Generally, computer records are considered admissible if they qualify as a business record. Computer records are usually divided into **computer-generated records** and **computer-stored records**. Computer-generated records are data the system maintains for itself, such as system log files and proxy server logs. They are output generated from a computer process or algorithm, not usually data a person creates. Computer-stored records, however, are electronic data that a person creates and saves on a computer, such as a spreadsheet or word processor document. Some records combine computer-generated and computer-stored evidence, such as a spreadsheet containing mathematical operations (computer-generated records) generated from a person's input (computer-stored records).

Computer records must be shown to be authentic and trustworthy to be admitted into court. Computer-generated records are considered authentic if the program that created the output is functioning properly. These records are usually considered exceptions to the hearsay rule. For computer-stored records to be admitted into court, they must also satisfy an exception to the hearsay rule, usually the business-record exception, so they must be authentic records of regularly conducted business activity. To show that computer-stored records are authentic, the person offering the records (the "offeror"—the plaintiff, or defense) must demonstrate that a person created the data and the data is reliable and trustworthy—in other words, that it wasn't altered when it was acquired or afterward.

Collecting evidence according to the proper steps of evidence control helps ensure that the computer evidence is authentic, as does using established computer forensics software tools. Courts have consistently ruled that computer forensics investigators don't have to be subject matter experts on the tools they use. In other words, if you have to testify about your role in acquiring, preserving, and analyzing evidence, you don't have to know the inner workings of the tools you use, although you should understand their purpose and operation. For example, MD5 and SHA-1 software tools involve complex mathematical formulas. During a cross-examination, an opposing attorney might ask you to describe how these forensic tools work. You can safely testify that you don't know how the formula works, but you do know how to use the tools that implement the formula. In *United States v. Salgado*, 250 F.3d 438, 453 (6th Cir. 2001), the court stated, "It is not necessary that the computer programmer testify in order to authenticate computer-generated records." In other words, the witness must have firsthand knowledge only of the facts relevant to the case. Therefore, you should know how to describe the steps in using the MD5 function in DriveSpy, for example, not how the MD5 hash algorithm works.

When attorneys challenge digital evidence, often they raise the issue of whether computer-generated records were altered or damaged after they were created. Attorneys might also question the authenticity of the computer-generated records by challenging the program or utility that created them. To date, courts have been skeptical of unsupported claims about digital evidence. Asserting that the data changed without specific evidence to show otherwise is not sufficient grounds to discredit the digital evidence's authenticity. Most federal courts that evaluate digital evidence from computer-generated records assume that the records contain hearsay. Federal courts then apply the business-records exception to hearsay as it applies to digital evidence.

As mentioned earlier, one test to prove that computer-stored records are authentic is to demonstrate that a specific person created the records. Establishing who created the digital evidence you recover from your investigation can be difficult because records recovered from slack space or unallocated disk space usually don't identify the author. The same is true for other records, such as anonymous e-mail messages or Internet Relay Chat (IRC) text messages. To establish authorship of the digital evidence in these cases, attorneys can apply circumstantial evidence, which requires finding other clues associated with the suspect's computer or location. The circumstantial evidence might be that the computer has a password consistent with the password the suspect used on other systems, that a witness saw the suspect at the computer at the time the offense occurred, or that additional trace evidence associates the suspect with the computer at the time of the incident.

In addition, computer-stored records must be proved authentic, which is the most difficult requirement to prove when trying to qualify as an exception to the hearsay rule. The process of establishing the trustworthiness of digital evidence originated with written documents and the best evidence rule, which states that to prove the content of a written document, recording, or photograph, ordinarily the original writing, recording, or photograph is required (see Federal Rules of Evidence, 1002). In other words, an original copy of a document is preferred to a duplicate version. The best evidence, then, is the document created and saved on a computer hard disk.

Agents and prosecutors occasionally express concern that a printout of a computer-stored electronic file might not qualify as an original document, according to the best evidence rule. In its most fundamental form, the original file is a collection of 0s and 1s; in contrast, the printout is the result of manipulating the file through a complicated series of electronic and mechanical processes (Federal Rules of Evidence, 803(6); see *Searching and Seizing from Computers and Obtaining Electronic Evidence in Criminal Investigations*, p. 152). To address this concern about original evidence, the Federal Rules of Evidence state: "[I]f data are stored in a computer or similar device, any printout or other output readable by sight, shown to reflect the data accurately, is an 'original'." Instead of producing hard disks in court, attorneys can submit printed copies of files as evidence.

In addition, the Federal Rules of Evidence, 1001(4), allow duplicates instead of originals when the duplicate is "produced by the same impression as the original. . . by mechanical or electronic re-recording. . . or by other equivalent techniques which accurately reproduce the original." Therefore, as long as bit-stream copies of data are properly made and maintained, the copies can be admitted in court, although they aren't considered best evidence. The copied evidence can be a reliable working copy, but it's not considered original.

Courts understand that the original evidence might not be available. For example, you could successfully make one bit-stream copy of the evidence drive, but lose access to the original drive because it has a head crash when you attempt to make a second backup bit-stream copy. Your first successful bit-stream copy then becomes secondary evidence. The attorney needs to be able to explain to a judge that circumstances beyond the examiner's control resulted in loss of the original evidence. Mishaps with evidence happen routinely in all aspects of evidence recovery.

Another example is an investigation that involves a network server. Removing the server from the network to acquire evidence data on the disk could cause harm to a business or its owner, who might be an innocent bystander to a crime or civil wrong. For example, Steve Jackson Games was a business that was the innocent party; evidence of criminal activity had been stored in the form of e-mail on the company computers. Secret Service agents seized all the computers at Steve Jackson Games and effectively put them out of business. SJG sued the Secret Service, which was found liable for damages under the Privacy Protection Act and

Title II of the Electronic Communications Privacy Act. See *Steve Jackson Games v. United States Secret Service and United States of America*, 36 F.3d 457 (USCA 5, 1994).

In this situation, you might not have the authority to create a bit-stream copy or remove the original disk drive. Instead, make your best effort to acquire the digital evidence with a less intrusive or disruptive method. In this context, the recovered materials become the best evidence because of the circumstances.

In summary, computer-generated data, such a system log or the results of a mathematical formula in a spreadsheet, is not hearsay. Computer-stored records that a person generates are subject to rules governing hearsay evidence, however. To qualify as a business-record exception to the hearsay rule, a person must have created the computer-stored records, and the records must be original. The Federal Rules of Evidence treat printouts of digital files and bit-stream image copies as original evidence.

SECURING DIGITAL EVIDENCE AT AN INCIDENT SCENE

The evidence you acquire at an incident scene depends on the nature of the case and the alleged crime or violation. For a criminal case involving a drug dealer's computer, for example, you need to take the entire computer along with any peripherals and media in the area, including floppy disks, CDs, DVDs, printers, and scanners. Seizing peripherals and other media ensures that you leave no necessary components of the system behind; often, it is difficult to predict what components might be critical to the system's operation. On the other hand, if you're investigating an employee, you might need only the hard drive.

Before you obtain digital evidence, ask your supervisor or senior forensic examiner in your organization the following questions:

- Do you need to take the entire computer, all peripherals, and media in the immediate area? Do you need to protect the computer or media while transporting it to your lab? For example, should you place a floppy disk in the floppy disk drive to protect the drive heads?

- Is the computer powered on when you arrive to take control of the digital evidence? (This question is discussed in more detail later in this chapter.)

- Is the suspect you're investigating in the immediate area of the computer? Is it possible that the suspect damaged or destroyed the computer and its media? Will you have to separate the suspect from the computer?

For example, suppose a company employee, Edward Braun, is suspected of using the company computer at his desk to write a book. You suspect that Edward is saving personal files on the company computer's hard disk. Using imaging software, such as Norton Ghost from Symantec, you can copy the hard disk onto another drive, install the duplicate hard drive in the computer, and take the original drive to your forensics lab for examination. This procedure doesn't create a bit-for-bit copy, but you are creating a working copy for continued business operations and taking the original for examination.

Because Edward's supervisors don't want him to know he's being investigated, you must work with the drive when he's not at his desk and is not expected to return. Because most people notice when something is out of order on their desks, before you begin working with Edward's computer, you should photograph the scene, measure the height of his chair, and record the position of sticky notes, pens, and other items on his desk that you must move before you can remove the hard drive. After you create an image of his hard drive and substitute the copy, return Edward's belongings to their original location.

TIP   Standard items to pack when you arrive at a scene include a digital camera, sketchpad, pencils, tape, gloves, a variety of screwdrivers, evidence bags, needle-nose pliers, and bolt cutters.

When handling digital evidence on a powered-on computer, first photograph the screen contents and save active data to removable media. Don't try to create disk images yet; first preserve the data by performing an orderly shutdown on Windows 2000, XP, UNIX, and Linux computers. On Windows 9x machines, turning off the power typically preserves the data on the drive. Every shutdown process has inherent risks to data; to avoid data (evidence) loss, you or your supervisor might have to exercise judgment to determine the best shutdown procedure.

Record the crime or incident scene using still and video cameras. Make sure you take close-ups of all cable connections. Some devices look like a normal hookup to the keyboard, but actually record every keystroke. Dongle devices are also used with some software as part of the licensing agreement. Computer owners who suspect that someone will investigate their computers might set the computer to delete the hard disk's contents by modifying a common command such as Dir. On older DOS systems, you can change command names. For example, a knowledgeable person can change Dir to have it run another internal command or an external batch file, which could be used to produce catastrophic results, especially if you're in the middle of an investigation.

Electronic media is sensitive and easily damaged, altered, or destroyed, so you must take care when obtaining, transporting, and copying digital evidence. In addition to photographing the scene and the computer, remember the media protection measures discussed in Chapter 2 under "Securing Your Evidence."

CATALOGING DIGITAL EVIDENCE

After you determine that an incident scene has digital evidence to collect, you visit the scene. First you need to catalog or document the evidence you find at the scene. Your goal is to preserve evidence integrity; that means you must avoid modifying the evidence as you collect and catalog it. Keep in mind the rules of evidence discussed in the previous section.

First, locate the computing components you need to examine and collect. If the computer is turned off, observe the following guidelines to catalog digital evidence and preserve its integrity:

1. Identify the type of computer you're working with, such as a Windows PC or laptop, a UNIX workstation, or a Macintosh. Do not turn on a suspect computer if it's turned off because some OSs overwrite files as a standard part of their boot process.

2. Use a digital camera to photograph all cable connections, and then label the cables with evidence tags. Photograph or videotape the scene and create a detailed diagram, noting where items are located.

3. Assign one person, if possible, to collect and log all evidence. Minimize the number of people handling evidence to ensure its integrity.

4. Tag all the evidence you collect with the current date and time, serial numbers or unique features, make and model, and the name of the person who collected it.

5. Maintain two separate logs of collected evidence to use as a backup checklist to verify everything you have collected.

6. Maintain constant control of the collected evidence and the crime or incident scene.

If the suspect computer is turned on when you go to collect the digital evidence, you need to perform the following additional steps:

1. If practical, copy any application data displayed on the screen, such as text or a spreadsheet document. Save this RAM data to removable media, such as a floppy disk, Zip, or Jaz disk, using the Save As command. If this isn't possible, take a close-up photograph of the screen. Then close the application without saving data.

2. After you copy the RAM data, you can safely shut down the computer. Use the manufacturer's recommended shutdown method. If you aren't familiar with the method, find someone who is.

3. To access the suspect system, use another OS to examine the hard disk data. On Intel computers, use a specially configured boot disk, which you learned how to create in Chapter 2. For UNIX workstations, remove the drive and inspect the hard drive using another UNIX or Linux system.

4. Acquire the suspect drive with bit-streaming imaging tools.

5. Verify the integrity of your bit-stream image copy of the original disk.

For example, suppose you have been assigned to collect evidence at the home of a suspected drug dealer. When you visit the crime scene, you notice a laptop and a desktop in the front room. The computers appear to be networked together with a network cable. First, review the search warrant and make sure you have the proper authority to conduct a search or seizure. Then take photos to re-create the hardware's physical configuration, sketch the precise locations of cables between the computers, and make a note that the machines are running. You can also use the photos you take at this time to prove the equipment's condition in case it must be returned to the suspect. Next, if the cabling is complicated, tag the cables so that you can re-create the system configuration reliably. Then check the computer setup for anything unusual.

Record the RAM data on both machines on your removable media, and then systematically shut down the computers. Record the item number for each cable and tag each cable with the same number. Finally, disassemble the computers and components, bag and label them, and prepare them for transport.

Lab Evidence Considerations

After you collect digital evidence at the crime or incident scene, you transport it to a forensics lab, which should be a controlled environment that ensures the security and integrity of your digital evidence. In any investigative work, be sure to record your activities and findings as you work. To do so, you can maintain a journal to record the steps you take as you process the evidence. Your goal is to be able to reproduce the same results when you or another investigator repeat the steps you took to collect the evidence.

If you get different results when you repeat the steps, the credibility of your evidence becomes questionable. At best, the evidence's value is compromised; at worse, the evidence will be disqualified. Because of the nature of electronic components, failures do occur. For example, you might not be able to repeat a data recovery because of a hardware failure, such as a disk drive head crash. Be sure to report all facts and events as they occur.

Besides verifying your work, a journal serves as a reference that documents the methods you used to process digital evidence. You and others can use it for training and guidance on other investigations.

Processing and Handling Digital Evidence

When in the lab, you must maintain the integrity of the digital evidence as you do when collecting it in the field. Your first task is to preserve the disk data. If you have a suspect computer that hasn't been copied with a bit-stream imaging tool, you must create a copy. When you do, be sure to make the suspect drive read-only (typically by using a write-blocking device), and document this step. If the disk has been copied with a bit-stream imaging tool, you must preserve the image files. With most bit-stream imaging tools, you can create smaller, compressed volume sets to make archiving your data much easier.

In Chapter 5, you learned how to use bit-stream imaging tools, and in Chapter 2, you examined the steps for preserving your digital evidence as applied to chain-of-custody controls. You use the following steps to create bit-stream image files:

1. Copy all bit-stream image files to a large disk drive. Most forensics labs have several machines set up with disk-imaging software and multiple hard drives

that can be exchanged as needed for your cases. You can use these resources to copy image files to large disk drives.

2. Start your forensics tool to analyze the evidence.

3. Run an MD5 hash check on the bit-stream image files to get a digital signature. At the end of this chapter, you see how to compare the MD5 hash to make sure the evidence has not changed.

4. When you finish copying bit-stream image files to the larger disk, secure the original media in an evidence locker. Don't work with the original media; it should be stored in a locker that has an evidence custody form. Be sure to fill out the form and date it.

STORING DIGITAL EVIDENCE

When securing digital evidence, consider how and on what type of media to save it and what type of storage device is recommended to secure it. The media you use to store digital evidence usually depends on how long you need to keep the evidence. If you investigate criminal matters, store the evidence as long as you can. The ideal media on which to store digital data are CD-Rs or DVDs. These media have long lives, but copying data to them takes a long time. Today's larger disk drives demand more storage capacity; 100 GB disk drives are common, and DVDs can only store up to 17 GB of data.

You can also use magnetic tape to preserve evidence data. The popular **4-mm DAT** magnetic tapes store about 4 GB of data, but like CD-Rs, they are slow to read and write data. The 4-mm DAT is the least robust media currently available. If you're using these tapes, test your data by copying the contents from the tape back to a disk drive. Then verify that the data is good by accessing it with your computer forensics tools or with an MD5 hash comparison of the original data set and the newly restored data set.

If a 30-year life span for data storage is acceptable for your digital evidence, the older DLT magnetic tape cartridge systems are a good choice. Figure 6-1 shows a 4-mm DAT drive and tape and a DLT tape drive.

4-mm DAT drive and tape

DLT tape drive

Figure 6-1 4-mm DAT and DLT tape drives

DLT systems have been used with mainframe computers for several decades and are reliable data-archiving systems. Depending on the size of the DLT cartridge, one cartridge can store up to 80 GB of data in compressed mode. Speed of data transfer from your hard disk drive to a DLT tape is also faster than transferring data to a CD-R or DVD.

The only major drawback to a DLT drive and tapes is cost. A drive can cost from $400 to $800, and each tape is about $40. However, with the current large disk drives, the DLT system does offer significant labor savings over other systems.

Recently, manufacturers such as Quantum Corp. have introduced a high-speed, high-capacity tape cartridge drive system called Super Digital Linear Tape (Super-DLT or SLDT). These systems are specifically designed for large RAID data backups. Smaller external Super-DLT drives can connect to a workstation through a SCSI card.

However, don't rely on one media storage method to preserve your evidence—be sure to make two copies of every bit-stream copy of your data to prevent data loss. Also, if practical, use different forensic imaging tools to create the two separate bit-stream images. For example, you can make one bit-stream copy by using the Linux dd command, and then use DriveSpy's SavePart or SaveSect bit-stream imaging commands to create the second bit-stream copy.

Evidence Retention and Media Storage Needs

You must maintain the chain of custody of your digital evidence so that it's accepted in court or by arbitration. Restrict access to your lab and your evidence storage area. When your lab is open for operations, authorized personnel must keep these areas under constant supervision. When your lab is closed, at least two security staff should protect all evidence storage cabinets and lab facilities.

As a good security practice, your lab should have a sign-in roster for all visitors. For evidence storage containers, most labs use a manual log system that an authorized technician maintains when a container is opened and closed. These logs should be maintained for a period based on legal requirements; consider the statute of limitations, maximum sentence, and expiration of appeal periods in setting retention periods. Make the logs available for inspection by management. A log file for each piece of evidence (your evidence custody form) should contain an entry for every person who has handled the evidence (see Figure 6-2).

If you're supporting a law enforcement agency, you might need to retain your evidence forever, depending on the level of the crime. Check with your local prosecuting attorney's office or state laws to ensure that you're in compliance. For the private sector or corporate environment, check with your company's legal department (the general counsel). This department has the responsibility for setting your organization's standards for evidence retention. Cases involving child pornography are the exception. The evidence must be turned over to law enforcement. This material is contraband and must not be stored by any person or organization other than a law enforcement agency.

Item description:				
Item tag number:				
Person	Date logged out	Time logged out	Date logged in	Time logged in

Figure 6-2 Sample log file

Documenting Evidence

To document your evidence, create or use an evidence custody form, as shown in Chapter 2. Because of the constant changes in technologies and methods for acquiring data, update your evidence custody form to ensure that it addresses these changes. An evidence custody form serves the following functions:

- Identifies the evidence
- Identifies who has handled the evidence
- Lists the dates and times the evidence was handled

After you have established these items, you can add other pieces of information to your form, such as a section that lists the MD5 hash values. Include any detailed information you might need to reference.

Evidence bags also include labels or evidence forms you can use to document your evidence. Commercial companies offer a variety of sizes and styles of paper and plastic evidence bags. Be sure to write on the bag when it's empty, not when it contains digital evidence. Note that for evidence items that are electronic components, you should use antistatic bags.

Create an evidence custody form that you can modify as you progress from one investigation to another. Keep an electronic copy of your form and make adjustments and additions as needed.

6

OBTAINING A DIGITAL HASH

To maintain data integrity, various methods of obtaining a unique identity for file data have been developed. One of the first methods was the **Cyclic Redundancy Check (CRC)**, which uses a mathematical algorithm to determine whether a file's contents have changed. The most recent version is the CRC-32. The most common algorithm used today for computing investigations and forensics is the MD5. Like the CRC, the MD5 is a mathematical formula that translates a file into a unique hexadecimal code value, or a hash value. If a bit or byte in the file changes, it alters the **digital hash**, a unique value that identifies a file. Before you process or analyze a file, you can use a software tool to produce a digital signature of the file. After you process the file, you produce another digital hash. If it's the same as the original hash, you can verify the integrity of your digital evidence with mathematical proof that the file didn't change.

The newest digital signature method is the Secure Hash Algorithm (SHA), developed by the **National Institute of Standards and Technology (NIST)**. SHA is slowly replacing MD5 and CRC-32, although MD5 is still widely used. For more information on SHA, see *csrc.nist.gov/publications/fips/fips180-2/fips180-2.pdf*.

Using a hashing program such as MD5 provides a digital hash (also called a "digital fingerprint"), which is a unique identity code of a file or an entire disk. Digital hashes vary. Most forensic computing hash needs can be satisfied with a **non-keyed hash set**, which is a unique hash number generated by a software tool, such as DriveSpy's MD5 command. The advantage of this type of hash is that it can identify known files, such as executable programs or viruses, that hide themselves by changing their names. For example, many people who view or transmit pornographic material change the file names and extensions to obscure the nature of the contents. However, even if a file's name and extension change, the hash value doesn't.

The alternative to a non-keyed hash is a **keyed hash set**, which is created by an encryption utility's secret key. You could use the secret key to create a unique hash value (a digital fingerprint or hash) for a file. Although a keyed hash set cannot identify files as non-keyed hash methods can, it can produce a unique fingerprint hash set for your digital evidence.

You can use the MD5 command in DriveSpy to obtain the unique digital signature of a file and an entire disk. In the following steps, you use a floppy disk, although you often work with hard disks in actual investigations. In this exercise you work at the command line, but you can apply the same principles to a GUI environment.

First you create a test file and then generate an MD5 hash value for it. Then you change the file and produce another MD5 value, this time noting the change in the hash signature. You need a blank, formatted floppy disk and a Windows 98 computer to complete the following steps:

1. Power on your forensic workstation, booting it to Windows.

2. Write **Chapter 6** on the label of a blank, formatted floppy disk and insert it into the A: drive.

3. Next, click **Start**, **Programs**, **Accessories**, **Notepad**.

4. In Notepad, type **This is a test to see how an MD5 digital hash works**.

5. Click **File**, **Save As** from the menu. In the **File name** text box, type **InChap06.txt**. Click **3½ Floppy (A:)** in the Save in list box, and then click **Save**, as shown in Figure 6-3.

Figure 6-3 Creating a file in Notepad

6. Close Notepad.

Next, use DriveSpy to generate an MD5 hash value for the file you just created:

1. Make sure you're working at the DOS prompt. Change to your hard disk drive, such as C:, by typing **cd c\:** and pressing **Enter**. Type **cd*work folder*** and press **Enter**. (Replace *work folder* with the name of your work folder.)

2. Create a Chap06 folder in your work folder by typing **md Chap06** and pressing **Enter**. Change to this directory by typing **cd Chap06**. Then type **md Chapter** and press **Enter** to create a Chapter folder in the Chap06 folder.

3. To run Toolpath.bat so that DriveSpy is available from any directory, at the prompt type ***work folder*\\tools\\toolpath.bat** and press **Enter**.

4. Change to drive A: by typing **a:** and pressing **Enter**.

5. At the DOS prompt, start DriveSpy by typing **drivespy** and pressing **Enter**.

6. At the SYS prompt, type **output c:*work folder*\\Chap06\\Chapter\\InChplog.txt**, and then press **Enter** to send the output to a log file, as shown in Figure 6-4.

```
SYS>output c:\work\Chap06\Chapter\InChplog.txt

File Opened: c:\work\Chap06\Chapter\InChplog.txt
ECHO to c:\work\Chap06\InChplog.txt: Tue Aug 03 21:41:43 2004

SYS>|
```

Figure 6-4   Sending output to a log file

7. At the SYS prompt, type **drive a** and press **Enter** to access the floppy disk's Drive mode, as shown in Figure 6-5.

8. At the DA prompt, type **part 1** and press **Enter** to access the drive's Partition mode, as shown in Figure 6-6.

NOTE

In Figure 6-6, DriveSpy lists the disk's partition configuration. In this example, it's a FAT12 floppy disk with 2880 sectors. Partition mode also shows where the boot sector and root directory are located and where the data begins.

```
DRIVE Mode Selected.

Drive A Partition Summary:

     PRI  Part  Part                Boot          Start        End
Num  EXT  Code  Type      HID       Code  ACT     Sector       Sector    Size (Mb)
---  ---  ----  --------  ---       ----  ---     ----------   ----------  ----------
  1  PRI  0x01  FAT12               0x80   *           0          2879           1

DA>
```

Figure 6-5   Drive mode view in DriveSpy

```
PARTITION Mode Selected.

Partition 1: Primary, (Active), FAT12 (0x01)
Defined in Partition Table at Absolute Sector: 0 (Entry Number 1)

Sectors/Cluster:       1
Total Sectors:         2880
Total Clusters:        2847
Raw Capacity:          1 Mb
Formatted Capacity:    1 Mb

                  |  Start    End    |
                  |  Sector   Sector |
----------------  | --------  ------ |
Partition         |     0      2879  |
Boot Sector       |     0         0  |
FAT1              |     1         9  |
FAT2              |    10        18  |
Root Dir          |    19        32  |
Data Area         |    33      2879  |

DAP1:\>
```

Figure 6-6   Partition mode view in DriveSpy

9. At the DAP1 prompt, type **dir** and press **Enter** to view the data on the disk, as shown in Figure 6-7. The Dir command lists the date the file was created and the last time it was accessed.

10. At the DAP1 prompt, type **md5 InChap06.txt** and press **Enter** to produce the MD5 hash value. Figure 6-8 shows the hash value, or checksum, for the file.

NOTE   Your MD5 hash results might vary from this figure. In addition, DriveSpy works only under MS-DOS 6.22 or Windows 95, 98, or Me. In Windows 2000 or XP, it doesn't work correctly and produces errors.

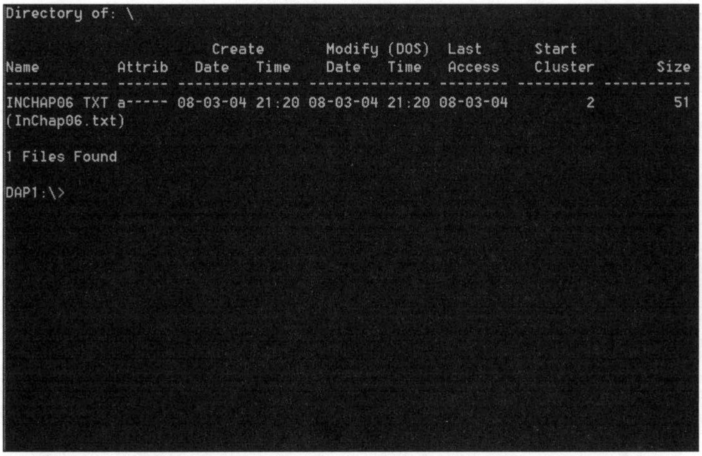

```
Directory of: \

                         Create        Modify (DOS) Last      Start
Name           Attrib    Date   Time   Date   Time  Access    Cluster        Size
-----------    ------    ------ ----   ------ ----  ------    -------      ------
INCHAP06 TXT   a-----    08-03-04 21:20 08-03-04 21:20 08-03-04           2            51
(InChap06.txt)

1 Files Found

DAP1:\>
```

Figure 6-7   Results of the Dir command

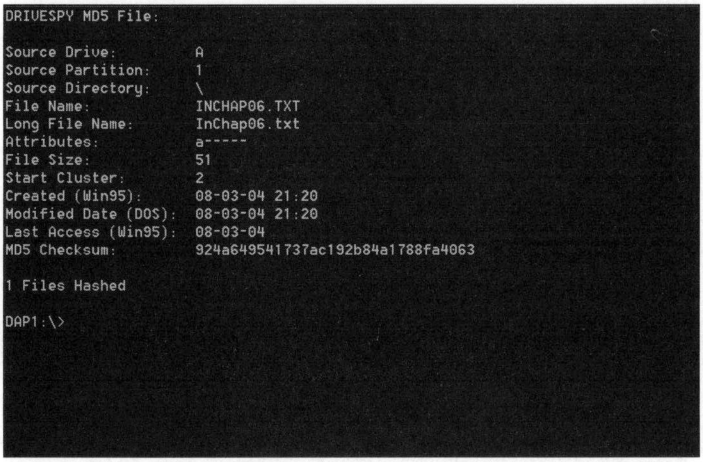

```
DRIVESPY MD5 File:

Source Drive:            A
Source Partition:        1
Source Directory:        \
File Name:               INCHAP06.TXT
Long File Name:          InChap06.txt
Attributes:              a-----
File Size:               51
Start Cluster:           2
Created (Win95):         08-03-04 21:20
Modified Date (DOS):     08-03-04 21:20
Last Access (Win95):     08-03-04
MD5 Checksum:            924a649541737ac192b84a1788fa4063

1 Files Hashed

DAP1:\>
```

Figure 6-8   MD5 hash value for InChap06.txt

11. To be thorough and to verify that the disk contents don't change, you can also generate an MD5 hash value for the disk. At the DAP1 prompt, type **drive a** and press **Enter**. At the DA prompt, type **md5** and press **Enter**. Note that it takes several minutes to generate the hash value of a floppy disk. The results are shown in Figure 6-9. You can also run an MD5 hash for the disk from the DAP1 prompt.

12. To exit DriveSpy, type **exit** and press **Enter**.

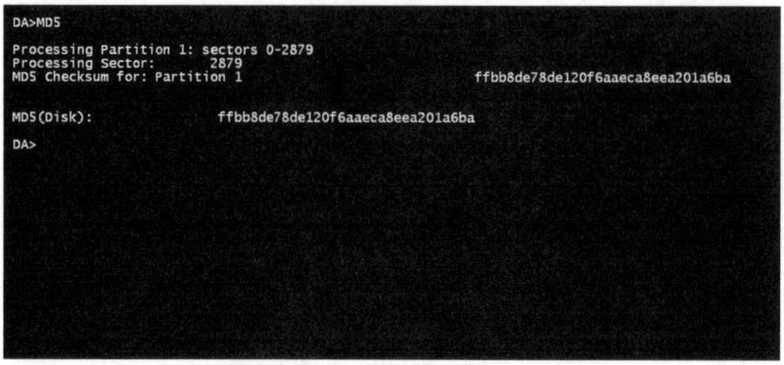

```
DA>MD5
Processing Partition 1: sectors 0-2879
Processing Sector:         2879
MD5 Checksum for: Partition 1                          ffbb8de78de120f6aaeca8eea201a6ba

MD5(Disk):                    ffbb8de78de120f6aaeca8eea201a6ba

DA>
```

Figure 6-9 MD5 hash value for the floppy disk

CHAPTER SUMMARY

❑ Digital evidence is anything stored or transmitted on electronic or optical media. It is extremely fragile and easily altered.

❑ To work with digital evidence, start by identifying digital information or artifacts that can be used as evidence. Collect, preserve, document, analyze, identify, and organize the evidence. Then rebuild evidence or repeat a situation to verify that you can obtain the same results every time.

❑ You must consistently handle all evidence the same way every time you handle it. Apply the same security and accountability controls for evidence in a civil lawsuit as for evidence obtained at a major crime scene to comply with your state's rules of evidence or with the Federal Rules of Evidence.

❑ After you determine that an incident scene has digital evidence to collect, you visit the scene. First you need to catalog or document the evidence you find. Your goal is to preserve evidence integrity, which means you must not modify the evidence as you collect and catalog it. An incident scene should be photographed and sketched, and then each item labeled and put in an evidence bag if possible.

❑ Selecting a media for storing digital evidence usually depends on how long you need to keep the evidence. The ideal storage media are CD-Rs or DVDs. You can also use magnetic tape, such as 4-mm DAT and DLT magnetic tapes, to preserve evidence data.

❑ Digital evidence needs to be copied by using bit-stream imaging to make sure sector-by-sector mapping takes place.

❑ Digital signatures should be used to make sure no changes have been made to the file or storage device. The current standards are CRC-32, MD5 hash, and SHA-1.

KEY TERMS

4-mm DAT — Magnetic tapes that store about 4 GB of data, but like CD-Rs, are slow to read and write data.

computer-generated records — Data generated by the computer, such as system log files or proxy server logs.

computer-stored records — Digital files generated by a person, such as electronic spreadsheets.

Cyclic Redundancy Check (CRC) — A mathematical algorithm that translates a file into a unique hexadecimal code value.

digital hash — A unique value that identifies a file.

International Organization on Computer Evidence (IOCE) — A group that sets standards for recovering, preserving, and examining digital evidence.

keyed hash set — A value created by an encryption utility's secret key.

National Institute of Standards and Technology (NIST) — One of the governing bodies responsible for setting standards for various industries in the United States.

non-keyed hash set — A hash set used to identify files or viruses.

Scientific Working Group on Digital Evidence (SWGDE) — A group that sets standards for recovering, preserving, and examining digital evidence.

6

REVIEW QUESTIONS

1. The laws of most English-speaking countries are derived from:

    a. the Iroquois Nation

    b. the Koran

    c. the British Parliament

    d. none of the above

2. Evidence from a civil suit would never be used in a criminal case. True or False?

3. Typically, how many people are assigned to collect evidence at an incident scene?

    a. one

    b. two

    c. doesn't matter

    d. at least four

4. How should you secure and move a computer case that contains a floppy disk drive?

    a. Move it as is.

    b. Insert a blank disk to protect the heads.

    c. Check with the supervisor to determine the best course in each situation.

    d. Do none of the above.

5. If you find a Windows 2000 computer turned on at an incident scene, what should you do?

6. List two ways to record an incident scene.

7. Why should you note all cable connections for a computer you want to seize as evidence?

   a. to know what outside connections exist

   b. in case other devices are connected

   c. to know what peripheral devices exist

   d. all of the above

8. You should make at least how many bit-stream copies of a suspect drive?

   a. one

   b. two

   c. three

   d. doesn't matter

9. On a Linux system, which of the following commands do you use to create a bit-stream image?

   a. image

   b. dd

   c. ii

   d. SaveSect

10. Two of the older hash algorithms are _____ and _____ .

11. A non-keyed hash uses an encryption tool. True or False?

12. When a file is altered, its MD5 hash value changes. True or False?

13. Weather conditions should be considered when securing or transporting evidence. True or False?

14. Which of the following characteristics should a computer forensics lab have? (Choose all that apply.)

    a. isolation

    b. restricted access

    c. controlled environment

    d. an entry log

15. List three items you should keep in your evidence recovery bag.

HANDS-ON PROJECTS

Project 6-1

In this project, you create your own file, save it, and generate an MD5 hash value. Then you change the contents of the file, generate another MD5 hash value, and compare it to the previous hash value. You need a blank, formatted floppy disk and a Windows 98 computer for this project. To generate an MD5 hash value:

1. Insert a blank, formatted floppy disk in the floppy disk drive. In Windows, start Notepad and type **The rain in Spain falls mainly on the plains.** Save the file as **C6Proj01.txt** on the floppy disk, and then close Notepad.

2. Open a command-prompt window on your computer. Go to the Tools folder of your work folder and then type **Toolpath.bat** to make DriveSpy available from any directory.

3. Start DriveSpy by typing **drivespy** and pressing Enter. At the SYS prompt, type **output c:*work folder*\Chap06\Projects\C6Pr1log.txt**. Then type **drive a** and press **Enter** to see a partition summary for the A: drive.

4. At the DA prompt, type **part 1** to switch to Partition mode and then press **Enter** to see a summary of partition information on the floppy disk.

5. At the DAP1 prompt, type **md5 C6Proj01.txt** and press **Enter** to obtain the hash value of the text file you saved (C6Proj01.txt).

6. Capture the command-prompt window by pressing **Alt+Print Screen**. Start a word processor such as Microsoft Word or WordPad, and then press **Ctrl+V** to paste the image of the command-prompt window into the document. Save the file as **Proj01Screens.doc** in the Chap06\Projects folder in your work folder. (Create the Projects subfolder as you save the file, if necessary.)

7. Exit DriveSpy by typing **exit**, but leave the command-prompt window open.

8. To modify the text file you created, start Notepad and open **C6Proj01.txt** on the A: drive. Change "Spain" to **Maine**. Save the file with the same name, and then close Notepad.

9. Start DriveSpy again, and display partition information on the floppy disk (see Steps 3 and 4). At the DAP1 prompt, type **md5 C6Proj01.txt** and press **Enter** to produce an MD5 hash value for this file. Capture the command-prompt window and paste it into the **Proj01Screens.doc** as you did in Step 6. Compare the hash values in the two versions of the file—they should be different.

10. Save and print **Proj01Screens.doc** for your instructor, exit DriveSpy, and then close all open windows.

6

Project 6-2

In this project, you create a file in Microsoft Excel and generate a hash signature for it. Then you change the file name and extension and generate a new hash signature to determine whether changing the file name and extension changes the hash value. You need a floppy disk and a Windows 98 computer for this project. To generate hash signatures:

1. Insert a floppy disk in the floppy disk drive, if necessary. Start Microsoft Excel (or another spreadsheet program) and type **1234** in a new worksheet. Save the file as **C6Proj02.xls** on the floppy disk. Close Excel.

2. Open a command-prompt window. If necessary, go to the Tools folder of your work folder and then type **toolpath.bat** to make DriveSpy available from any directory.

3. Start DriveSpy by typing **drivespy** and pressing **Enter**.

4. At the SYS prompt, type **drive a** and press **Enter** to see a summary of drive A: in the command-prompt window.

5. At the DA prompt, type **part 1** to switch to Partition mode and then press **Enter** to see a summary of partition information on the floppy disk.

6. At the DAP1 prompt, type **dir** and then press **Enter** to view the files on the floppy disk.

7. At the DAP1 prompt, type **md5 C6Proj02.xls** and press **Enter**. The MD5 hash value for C6Proj02.xls is displayed.

8. Capture the command-prompt window by pressing **Alt+Print Screen**. Start a word processor, such as Microsoft Word or WordPad, and then press **Ctrl+V** to paste the image of the command-prompt window into the document. Save the file as **Proj02Screens.doc** in the Chap06\Projects folder in your work folder.

9. Exit DriveSpy by typing **exit** and pressing **Enter**.

10. In Windows Explorer or My Computer, navigate to the A: drive. Change the file name of C6Proj02.xls to **C6Proj2b.txt**. If a message box opens asking you to confirm the name change, click **Yes**.

11. Start DriveSpy again, and display partition information on the floppy disk (see Steps 3 to 5). At the DAP1 prompt, type **md5 C6Proj2b.txt** and press **Enter** to produce an MD5 hash value for this file. Capture the command-prompt window and paste it into the **Proj02Screens.doc**, as you did in Step 8. Compare the hash values in the two versions of the spreadsheet file and explain the results.

12. Save and print **Proj02Screens.doc** for your instructor, exit DriveSpy, and then close all open windows.

HANDS-ON PROJECTS

Project 6-3

In this project, you download a graphics file and generate a hash signature for it. Then you change the file name and generate a new hash signature to determine whether using a different file name changes the hash value. You need a floppy disk for this project. To produce a hash value on a graphics file, follow these steps:

1. Insert a floppy disk into the floppy disk drive. Start a Web browser such as Internet Explorer, and use a search engine such as Google to find GIF files. Find a site that offers free downloads. Right-click a graphics image, and then save the file as **C6Proj03.gif** on your floppy disk.

2. Open a command-prompt window. If necessary, go to the Tools folder of your work folder and then type **toolpath.bat** to make DriveSpy available from any directory.

3. Start DriveSpy by typing **drivespy** and pressing **Enter**.

4. At the SYS prompt, type **drive a** and press **Enter** to see a summary of drive A: in the command-prompt window.

5. At the DA prompt, type **part 1** to switch to Partition mode and then press **Enter** to see a summary of partition information on the floppy disk.

6. At the DAP1 prompt, type **dir** and then press **Enter** to view the files on the floppy disk.

7. At the DAP1 prompt, type **md5 C6Proj03.gif** and press **Enter**. The MD5 hash value for C6Proj03.gif appears.

8. Capture the command-prompt window by pressing **Alt+Print Screen**. Start a word processor such as Microsoft Word or WordPad, and then press **Ctrl+V** to paste the image of the command-prompt window into the document. Save the file as **Proj03Screens.doc** in the Chap06\Projects folder in your work folder.

9. Exit DriveSpy by typing **exit** and pressing **Enter**.

10. In Windows Explorer or My Computer, navigate to drive A:. Change the file name of C6Proj03.gif to **C6Proj3b.txt**. If a message appears asking you to confirm the name change, click **Yes**.

11. Start DriveSpy again, and display partition information on the floppy disk (see Steps 3 to 5). At the DAP1 prompt, type **md5 C6Proj3b.txt** and press **Enter** to produce an MD5 hash value for this file. Capture the command-prompt window and paste it into the **Proj03Screens.doc** as you did in Step 8. Compare the hash values in the two versions of the graphics file, and explain the results.

12. Save and print **Proj03Screens.doc** for your instructor, exit DriveSpy, and then close all open windows.

6

Project 6-4

In this project, you generate the hash value of a disk, change one file, and note that the hash value has changed. If one file on a disk has changed, the hash value of the disk changes. To change a file and compare its hash value, follow these steps:

1. In the floppy disk drive, insert a floppy disk containing files, such as the ones you used for previous projects in this chapter. Open a command-prompt window.

2. If necessary, go to the Tools folder of your work folder and then type **toolpath.bat** to make DriveSpy available from any directory.

3. Start DriveSpy by typing **drivespy** and pressing **Enter**.

4. At the SYS prompt, type **drive a** and press **Enter**.

5. At the DA prompt, type **md5** and then press **Enter**. The MD5 hash value for the disk is displayed.

6. Capture the command-prompt window, and paste the screen image into a document named **Proj04Screens.doc** in the Chap06\Projects folder in your work folder.

7. Exit DriveSpy by typing **exit** and pressing **Enter**.

8. Use Windows Explorer or My Computer to open a file on the floppy disk. Make a minor change such as deleting a letter, and then save the file.

9. Start DriveSpy again by repeating Steps 2 and 3. Then type **drive a** and press **Enter**.

10. Type **md5** and press **Enter** to generate an MD5 hash value for the floppy disk.

11. Capture the command-prompt window and paste it into the **Proj04Screens.doc** file. Compare the hash values in the two versions of the graphics file, and explain the results.

12. Save and print **Proj04Screens.doc** for your instructor, exit DriveSpy, and then close all open windows.

Project 6-5

Visit the Scientific Working Group for Digital Evidence (SWGDE) Web site at *http://ncfs. org/swgde/index.html* and examine the group's standards. Make a list of 10 pertinent items the site lists for digital evidence. Write a one- to two-page paper outlining the similarities and differences you note between SWGDE's requirements and those covered in this book.

Project 6-6

Write a procedure your lab must follow when dealing with files you suspect have been altered to hide information. You need to generate a numbered list of procedures that's one to two pages long.

CASE PROJECTS

Case Project 6-1

Describe how you received and secured evidence about the arson case from the insurance company. Create an evidence custody form showing that your firm received the image. What additional steps should you take to preserve the evidence?

Case Project 6-2

From the images you acquired of the kidnap victim's laptop, generate an MD5 hash and, if possible (based on your resources), an SHA-1 hash of the image. Explain the importance of obtaining this data at the beginning.

Case Project 6-3

You are hired to go through the office computing systems of an employee suspected of embezzling funds from the firm. What steps do you need to take? Write a one-page paper outlining the procedures you need to follow to make sure the evidence holds up in court.

Case Project 6-4

A suspected child molester has been turned in to the police by his girlfriend. You have to collect his computer equipment from his current residence. Write a one- to two-page paper outlining the steps you need to take to obtain evidence, including what to do in case he has changed the file names of pictures on his disk.

Case Project 6-5

Create your own evidence custody form. Make sure you include all the elements listed in this chapter.

6

7

WORKING WITH WINDOWS AND DOS SYSTEMS

After reading this chapter and completing the exercises, you will be able to:

- ◆ Understand file systems
- ◆ Explore Microsoft file structures
- ◆ Examine New Technology File System (NTFS) disks
- ◆ Understand the Windows Registry
- ◆ Understand Microsoft boot tasks
- ◆ Understand MS-DOS startup tasks

Chapters 7 and 8 provide an overview of computer data and disk drives. This chapter reviews how data is stored and managed on Microsoft operating systems (OSs). To become proficient in recovering data for computer investigations, you should understand file systems and their associated OSs, including legacy OSs (MS-DOS, Windows 9x, and Windows Me, for example) and current OSs, including Windows 2000 and XP. In this chapter, you examine the tasks each OS performs when it starts so that you can avoid altering evidence when you examine data on a disk. Chapter 8 discusses Macintosh and Linux file systems and covers hardware devices such as SCSI, IDE disks, CDs, and CD-RWs.

UNDERSTANDING FILE SYSTEMS

To effectively investigate computer evidence, you must understand how the most popular OSs work and how they store files. In addition to reading this section on file systems, you should also review any book that has the Computer Technology Industry Association (CompTIA) A+ certification for more information on hardware and firmware startup tasks and operations.

A **file system** gives an OS a road map to data on a disk. The type of file system an OS uses determines how data is stored on the disk. A file system is usually directly related to an OS, although some vendors grandfather in prior OSs so that newer ones can read them. For example, disk drives configured in the older Linux Ext2fs and Ext3fs file systems can be accessed with most of the current Linux releases.

No matter which platform you use, you need to understand how to access and modify system settings when necessary. When you need to access a suspect's computer to acquire or inspect data related to your investigation, you should be familiar with the computer's platform. This book examines Windows and DOS PCs in detail; Chapter 8 covers information on Macintosh and Linux. For other computer systems, consult system administrators and vendor-specific manuals.

Understanding the Boot Sequence

To ensure that you don't contaminate or alter data on a suspect's computer, you must understand how to access and modify a PC's Complementary Metal Oxide Semiconductor (CMOS) and BIOS. A computer stores system configuration and date and time information in the CMOS when power to the system is off. The BIOS contains programs that perform input and output at the hardware level. To avoid altering evidence data on a Windows/DOS PC, you need to access CMOS and BIOS settings.

To avoid altering data on the hard disk, you must make sure that when the subject's computer starts, it boots to a floppy drive or CD. Booting to a hard disk overwrites and changes evidentiary data. To do this, you need to access the CMOS setup by monitoring the subject's computer during the initial **bootstrap process** to identify the correct key or keys to use. The bootstrap is contained in ROM and tells the computer how to proceed. As the computer starts, the screen usually displays the key or keys, such as the Delete key, you press to open the CMOS setup screen. You can also try unhooking the keyboard to force the system to tell you what keys to use.

The key you press to access CMOS depends on the computer's BIOS. The popular BIOS manufacturers Award and AMI use the Delete key to access CMOS; other manufacturers use Ctrl+Alt+Insert, Ctrl+A, Ctrl+S, Ctrl+F1, F2, and F10. Figure 7-1 shows a typical CMOS setup screen.

On the CMOS setup screen, check the computer's boot sequence. If necessary, change the boot sequence so that the OS accesses drive A: before any other boot device. Each BIOS

CMOS setup for BIOS features

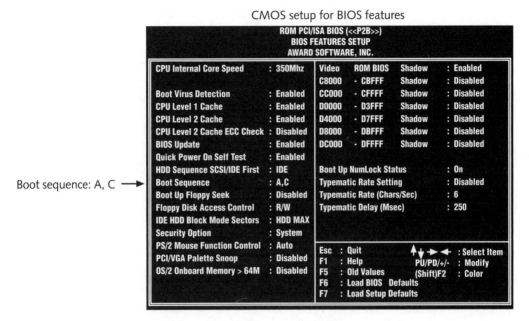

Boot sequence: A, C ──▶

Figure 7-1 Typical CMOS setup screen

vendor's screen is different. For example, in Figure 7-1, you press Tab to move to the appropriate line and then use the arrow keys to change the boot sequence. If necessary, refer to the BIOS vendor's documentation or Web site for instructions on changing the boot sequence.

Understanding Disk Drives

You should be familiar with disk drives and how data is organized on a disk so that you can find data effectively. Disk drives are made up of one or more platters coated with magnetic material, and data is stored on the platters in a particular way. Following is a list of the elements of a disk and the terms for describing disk data structure:

- *Geometry*—The **geometry** reflects the drive's internal organization.
- *Head*—The **head** is the device that reads and writes data to the drive.
- *Tracks*—**Tracks** are individual circles on a disk platter where data is located.
- *Cylinders*—A **cylinder** is a column of tracks on two or more disk platters.
- *Sectors*—A **sector** is an individual section on a track, usually made up of 512 bytes.

Figure 7-2 illustrates a drive's major components. Understanding these parts of a disk drive becomes more important as you progress through the study of computing investigations and forensics.

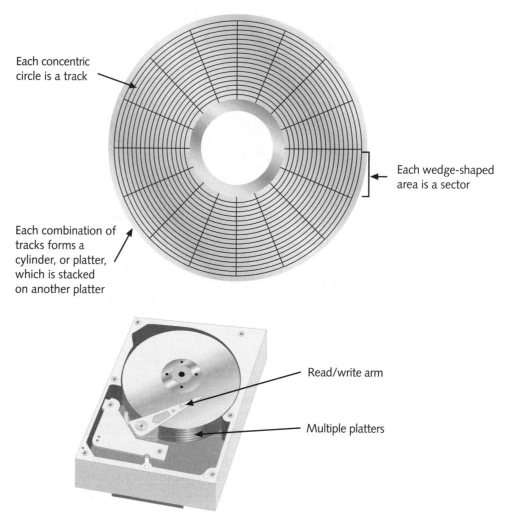

Each concentric circle is a track

Each wedge-shaped area is a sector

Each combination of tracks forms a cylinder, or platter, which is stacked on another platter

Read/write arm

Multiple platters

Figure 7-2   Disk drive structure

A typical disk drive stores 512 bytes per sector. The manufacturer engineers the disk to have a certain number of sectors per track. To determine the number of bytes on a disk, you multiply the number of cylinders (platters) by the number of heads (actually tracks) and by the number of sectors (groups of 512 or more bytes), as shown in Figure 7-3. The hard disk drive industry refers to this calculation as a cylinder, head, and sector (CHS) calculation.

Tracks also follow a numbering scheme starting from zero (0), which is the first value in computing. If a disk lists 79 tracks, you actually have 80 tracks, from 0 to 79.

Other disk properties, such as **zoned bit recording (ZBR)**, **track density**, **areal density**, and **head and cylinder skew**, are handled at the disk drive's hardware or firmware level.

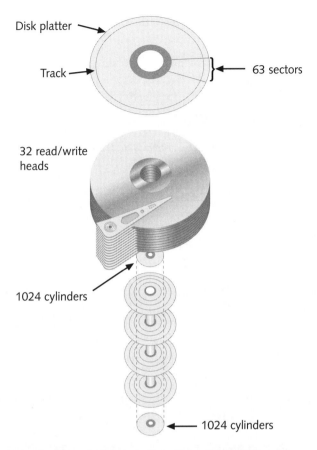

1024 cylinders x 32 heads x 63 sectors = 2,064,384 sectors

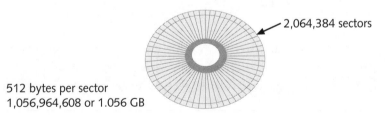

512 bytes per sector
1,056,964,608 or 1.056 GB

Figure 7-3 CHS calculation

ZBR is how most manufacturers deal with a platter's inner tracks being physically smaller than the outer tracks. Grouping the tracks by zones ensures that all the tracks are the same size.

Track density addresses the space between each track. As with old vinyl records, the smaller the space between each track, the more tracks you can place on the platter. On older disks, the space was wider, which allowed the heads to wander, making it possible for specialists to retrieve data from previous writes to a platter.

Areal density refers to the number of bits in one square inch of a platter. Note that this number includes the unused space between tracks. Head and cylinder skew are used to improve disk performance. As the read-write head moves from one track to another, starting sectors are offset to minimize lag time.

For more details on disk drives, visit *www.storagereview.com*.

TIP

Exploring Microsoft File Structures

Because most PCs use Microsoft software products, you should understand Microsoft file systems so that you know how Windows and DOS computers store files. In particular, you need to understand clusters, the File Allocation Table (FAT), and the New Technology File System (NTFS). The method an OS uses to store data determines where data can be hidden. When you examine a computer for forensic evidence, you need to explore these hiding places to determine whether they contain files or parts of files that might be evidence of a crime or policy violation.

In Microsoft file structures, sectors are grouped to form **clusters**, which are storage allocation units of 512, 1024, 2048, 4096, or more bytes. Clusters combine to make larger blocks of data that work as one larger storage unit. Combining sectors minimizes the overhead of writing or reading files to a disk. The OS groups one or more sectors into a cluster. The number of sectors in a cluster varies according to the disk size. For example, a double-sided, 3½-inch floppy disk has one sector per cluster; a hard disk has four or more sectors per cluster.

Clusters are numbered sequentially starting at 2 because the first sector of all disks contains a system area, the boot record, and a file structure database. The OS assigns these cluster numbers, which are referred to as **logical addresses**. Sector numbers, however, are referred to as **physical addresses** because they reside at the hardware or firmware level.

Disk Partitions

Many hard disks are partitioned, or divided, into two or more sections. A **partition** is a logical drive. For example, an 8 GB hard disk might contain four partitions or logical drives. FAT16 does not recognize disks larger than 2 MB, so these disks have to be partitioned into smaller sections for the FAT to recognize the additional space. Someone who wants to hide data on a hard disk can create hidden partitions or voids—large unused gaps between partitions on a disk drive. For example, partitions containing unused space (the voids) can be created between the primary partition and the first logical partition. This unused space between partitions is called the **partition gap**. If data is hidden in a partition gap, a disk editor utility could also be used to alter information in the disk's partition table. Doing so removes all references to the hidden partition, concealing it from the computer's OS. Another technique is to hide incriminating digital evidence at the end of a disk by declaring a smaller number of bytes than the actual drive size. With disk-editing tools, however, you can access these hidden or vacant areas of the disk.

One way to examine a partition's physical level is to use a disk editor, such as Norton DiskEdit, WinHex, or Hex Workshop. These tools enable you to view file headers and other critical parts of a file. Both tasks involve analyzing the key hexadecimal codes the OS uses to identify and maintain the file system. Table 7-1 lists the hexadecimal codes in a partition table and identifies the file system structure.

7

Table 7-1   Hexadecimal Codes in the Partition Table

Hexadecimal Code	File System
01h	DOS 12-bit FAT
04h	DOS 16-bit FAT for partitions smaller than 32 MB
05h	Extended partition
06h	DOS 16-bit FAT for partitions larger than 32 MB
07h	NTFS
0Bh	DOS 32-bit FAT
0Ch	DOS 32-bit FAT for Interrupt 13 support

In some instances, you might need to identify the OS on an unknown disk. You can use Norton DiskEdit, WinHex, or Hex Workshop for this task. The following steps show you how to use Hex Workshop:

1. If necessary, install Hex Workshop. Check with your instructor about where you should install it on your computer.

2. To download the trial version, use your browser to go to *www.hexworkshop.com* and follow the download instructions. Follow the online instructions to install and start Hex Workshop.

3. Insert a floppy disk in the floppy drive.

4. In Hex Workshop, click **Disk, Open Drive** from the menu to see a list of your logical drives. Click your **C:** drive (or whichever drive is your working drive), and click **OK**. Figure 7-4 shows a typical Hex Workshop window for a hard disk. If you're working on a Windows 98 machine, the upper-right pane of the Hex Workshop window shows "MSWIN4." If you're on an NTFS machine, that pane reads ".R.NTFS."

5. Click **Disk, Open Drive** again, but this time, select the floppy disk, and then click **OK**.

In addition to identifying the OS, tools such as Hex Workshop can identify file types. Computers use file headers to identify file types with or without an extension. In the

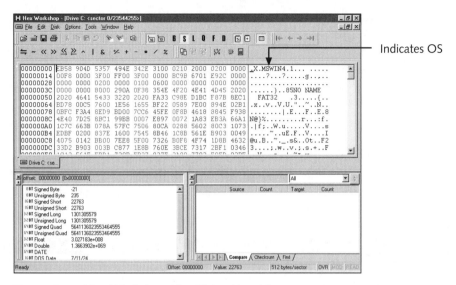

Indicates OS

Figure 7-4 Hex Workshop identifying the OS

following steps, you use Hex Workshop to identify file types. Before performing the steps, use Windows Explorer or My Computer to find a folder on your system containing a bitmap (.bmp) file and a folder containing a Word document (.doc). To use Hex Workshop to identify file types, follow these steps:

1. To open a bitmap file on your computer, click **File**, **Open** from the Hex Workshop menu. Navigate to a folder containing a bitmap (.bmp) file, and then double-click the .bmp file. This process should be the same on any OS.

2. As shown in Figure 7-5, the upper-right corner of the Hex Workshop window identifies the file type for the graphic. For .bmp files, it shows "BM6," "BM," or "BMF." The center section of the window shows "424D," which also indicates a .bmp file.

3. To open a Word document, click **File**, **Open** from the menu. Navigate to a folder containing a Word document (.doc) file, and then double-click the .doc file. As shown in Figure 7-6, the first line contains a row of zeros followed by "D0CF 11E0 A1B1 1AE1," which identifies the file as a Microsoft Office document. The same file header is displayed for an Excel or a PowerPoint file. It does not apply to Access databases.

4. Close Hex Workshop.

In the Hands-on Projects, you apply these techniques to other file types.

Master Boot Record

On Windows and DOS computer systems, the boot disk contains a file called the **Master Boot Record (MBR)**, which stores information about the partitions on a disk and their

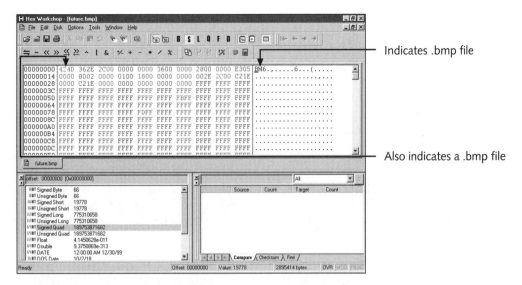

Indicates .bmp file

Also indicates a .bmp file

Figure 7-5   Hex Workshop indicating a .bmp file with "BM6"

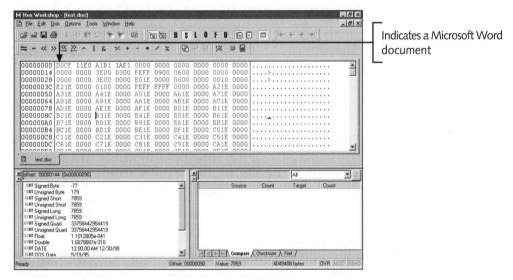

Indicates a Microsoft Word document

Figure 7-6   Hex Workshop indicating a Microsoft Office file

locations, size, and other critical items. Several software products can replace the MBR. You can use third-party boot utilities, such as PartitionMagic, to install two or more OSs on a single disk. Because these boot utilities can interfere with some computer forensics data acquisition tools, however, you need several different data acquisition tools. You can't rely on any one vendor product for computer forensics tasks.

Examining FAT Disks

The **File Allocation Table (FAT)** is the file structure database that Microsoft originally designed for floppy disks. FAT is used on file systems before Windows NT and 2000. The FAT database contains file names, directory names, date and time stamps, the starting cluster number, and attributes (archive, hidden, system, and read-only) of files on a disk. PCs use the FAT to organize files on a disk so that the OS can find the files it needs. The FAT is typically written to a disk's outermost track.

There are three versions of FAT—FAT12, FAT16, and FAT32—and a variation called Virtual File Allocation Table (VFAT). Microsoft developed VFAT to handle long file names when it released the first version of Windows 95 and Windows for Workgroups. The FAT version used in Microsoft DOS 6.22 had a limitation of eight characters for file names and three characters for extensions. The following list briefly discusses the evolution of FAT versions:

- *FAT12*—This version is used specifically for floppy disks, so it has a limited amount of storage space. It was originally designed for MS-DOS 1.0, the first Microsoft OS, which was used for floppy disk drives and drives up to 16 MB.

- *FAT16*—To handle large disks, Microsoft developed FAT16, which is still used on older Microsoft OSs such as MS-DOS 3.0 through 6.22, Windows 95 (first release), and Windows NT 3.5 and 4.0. FAT16 supports disk partitions with a maximum storage capacity of 2 GB.

- *FAT32*—When disk technology improved and disks larger than 2 GB were created, Microsoft developed FAT32, which is used on Microsoft OSs such as Windows 95 (second release), 98, Me, 2000, and XP. FAT32 can access up to 2 terabytes of disk storage. One disk can have multiple partitions in FAT16, FAT32, or NTFS.

Cluster sizes vary according to the size of the hard disk and the file system. Table 7-2 describes the number of sectors and bytes assigned to a cluster on FAT16 and FAT32 disks according to hard disk size.

Table 7-2   Sectors and Bytes per Cluster

Drive Size	Number of Sectors	FAT16	FAT32
256–511 MB	16	8 KB	4 KB
512 MB–1 GB	32	16 KB	4 KB
1–2 GB	64	32 KB	4 KB
2–8 GB	8	N/A	4 KB
8–16 GB	16	N/A	8 KB
16–32 GB	32	N/A	16 KB
More than 32 GB	64	N/A	32 KB

Microsoft OSs allocate disk space for files by clusters. This practice results in **drive slack**, composed of the unused space in a cluster between the end of an active file and the end of the cluster. Drive slack includes **RAM slack** and **file slack**. For example, suppose you create a large text document containing 5000 characters—that is, 5000 bytes of data. If you save this file on a FAT16 1.6 GB disk, a Microsoft OS automatically reserves one cluster for your 5000-byte file.

For a 1.6 GB disk, the OS allocates about 32,000 bytes, or 64 sectors (512 bytes per sector), for your file. The unused space, 27,000 bytes, is the file slack space (see Figure 7-7). RAM slack is created in the unused space on a sector. The file in the previous example used up 10 sectors, or 5120 bytes, so 120 bytes of a sector is not used; however, DOS must write in full 512-byte chunks of data (sectors). The data to fill the 120-byte void is pulled from RAM and placed in the area between the end of the file (EOF) and the end of the last sector used by the active file in the cluster. Any information in the RAM at that point, such as logon IDs or passwords, is placed in RAM slack when you save a file. File fragments and passwords are often found in these areas.

NOTE

You see RAM slack primarily on older systems. You don't run into it as often on newer systems.

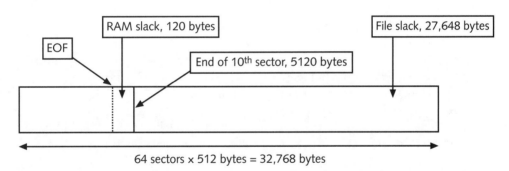

Figure 7-7   File slack space

An unintentional side effect of FAT16 having large clusters was that it reduced fragmentation as cluster size increased. The OS added your extra data to the end of the file and allowed the file to expand to this assigned cluster until it consumed the remaining reserved 27,000 bytes of space. At the same time, this increased cluster size resulted in inefficient use of disk space. This inefficient allocation of sectors to clusters is why, when nearly full FAT16 drives were converted to FAT32, users discovered they had a lot of extra free disk space because the files wasted less space.

When you run out of room for an allocated cluster, the OS allocates another cluster for your file, which creates more slack space on the disk. As files grow and require more disk space, assigned clusters are chained together. Typically, chained clusters are contiguous (next to one another) on the disk. However, as some files are created and then deleted, and other files are expanded, the chain can be broken or fragmented. By using a tool such as Norton DiskEdit, you can view the cluster-chaining sequence and see how FAT addresses link clusters to one another (see Figure 7-8).

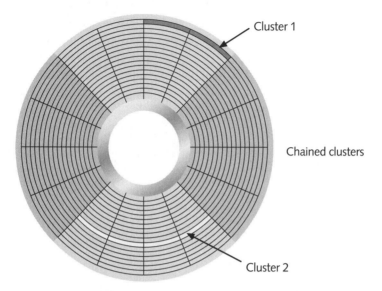

Figure 7-8   Chained clusters as a result of increasing file size

One tool that lists the order of cluster assignments for a file is DriveSpy's **Chain FAT Entry (CFE)** command, shown in Figure 7-9. DriveSpy shows each cluster assignment as a whole. In this view, you can see that this file is fragmented—the starting cluster is 368, and then it jumps to 5556. On the third line, you can see that it jumps from 399 to 370 and then to 376. This figure also shows the **end-of-file (EOF) marker** of 0x0FFFFFFF. This code is typically used with FAT file systems to show where the file ends.

Figure 7-9   DriveSpy CFE command

Figure 7-10 shows the same FAT32 cluster assignment in Norton DiskEdit. FAT32 systems list the volume number along with other file information. In this figure, the primary master disk drive is represented as [0]. The numbers to the right of each [0] define the content of the FAT32 cluster assignment. That is, the number listed to the immediate right of each [0] is the next cluster to which the file is written.

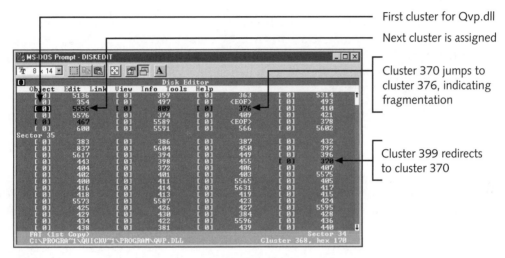

Figure 7-10   FAT32 cluster assignment in Norton DiskEdit

When the OS stores data in a FAT file system, it assigns a starting cluster position to a file. Data for the file is written to the first sector of the first assigned cluster. When the file runs out of room in this first assigned cluster, FAT assigns the next available cluster to the file. If the next available cluster isn't contiguous to the current cluster, the file becomes fragmented. Within the FAT for each cluster on the **volume** (the partitioned disk), the OS writes the next assigned cluster, which is the number to the right of [0] in the FAT cluster assignment. Think of clusters as buckets that can hold a specific number of bytes. When a cluster (or bucket) fills up, the OS allocates another cluster (bucket) to collect the extra data.

In Norton DiskEdit, you select a file and then the associated clusters are highlighted. In Figure 7-10, the status bar at the bottom shows that you're currently on cluster 368, which is the starting cluster for the file. The cluster listed to the right of that [0] is 5556 (not shown in this screenshot). You can see another example of how fragmented this file is by looking at cluster 399, which lists 370 as the next cluster (pointed out in Figure 7-10).

On rare occasions, such as a system failure or sabotage, these cluster chains can break. If they do, data can be lost because it becomes disassociated with the previous chained cluster. FAT looks forward for the next cluster assignment, but doesn't provide pointers to the previous cluster. Rebuilding these broken chains can be difficult.

Many recent disk forensics tools have automated much of the file rebuilding process. These improved features make it easier to recover lost data.

TIP

Deleting FAT Files

When a file is deleted in Windows Explorer or with the MS-DOS Delete command, the OS inserts a HEX E5 (0xE5), which many hex-editing programs reflect as the lowercase Greek letter sigma (σ) in the first letter position of the file name in the FAT database. The sigma symbol instructs the OS that the file is no longer available and that a new file can be written to the same cluster location.

In Microsoft OSs, when a file is deleted, the only modifications made are that the directory entry is marked as a deleted file, with the HEX E5 character replacing the first letter of the file name, and the FAT chain for that file is set to zero. The data in the file remains on the disk drive. The area of the disk where the deleted file resides becomes **unallocated disk space** (also called "free disk space"). The unallocated disk space is now available to receive new data from either new files or other files needing more space as they grow. Most forensic tools recover any data still residing in this area.

Examining NTFS Disks

The **New Technology File System (NTFS)** was introduced when Microsoft created Windows NT. NTFS is the primary file system for Windows XP. Each generation of Windows NT, 2000, and XP has included minor changes in NTFS configuration and features. The NTFS design was partially based on, and incorporated many features from, Microsoft's project for IBM with the OS/2 operating system; in this OS, the file system was called **High Performance File System (HPFS)**. When Microsoft created Windows NT, it provided backward compatibility so that NT could read OS/2 HPFS disk drives. Since the release of Windows 2000 and XP, this backward compatibility is no longer available.

To be an effective computing investigator and forensic examiner, you should maintain a library of old OSs and application software. Also keep older hardware that's in good operating condition. You might need old software and hardware to do your analysis because some forensic tasks can't be performed with modern tools on older OSs and hardware.

TIP

NTFS offers significant improvements over the older FAT file systems. NTFS provides much more information about a file, including security features, file ownership, and other file attributes. NTFS also gives you more control over files and folders (directories) than the older FAT file systems.

NTFS was Microsoft's move toward a journaling file system. The system keeps track of transactions such as file deletion or saving. This journaling feature is helpful because it records the transaction before the system carries it out. That way, in a power failure or other interruption, the system can complete the transaction or go back to the last good setting.

In NTFS, everything written to the disk is considered a file. On an NTFS disk, the first data set is the **Partition Boot Sector**, which starts at sector [0] of the disk and can expand to 16 sectors. Immediately after the Partition Boot Sector is the **Master File Table (MFT)**. The MFT, similar to the FAT in earlier Microsoft OSs, is the first file on the disk. An MFT file is created at the same time a disk partition is formatted as an NTFS volume. The MFT usually consumes about 12.5% of the disk when it's created. As data is added, the MFT can expand to take up 50% of the disk. (The MFT is covered in more detail in the next section, "NTFS System Files.")

One of the most significant advantages of NTFS over FAT is that it results in much less file slack space. Compare the cluster sizes in Table 7-3 to Table 7-2, which showed FAT cluster sizes.

Table 7-3   Cluster Sizes in an NTFS Disk

Drive Size	Sectors per Cluster	Cluster Size
0–512 MB	1	512 bytes
512 MB–1 GB	2	1024 bytes
1–2 GB	4	2048 bytes
2–4 GB	8	4096 bytes
4–8 GB	16	8192 bytes
8–16 GB	32	16,384 bytes
16–32 GB	64	32,768 bytes
More than 32 GB	128	65,539 bytes

The clusters are smaller for the smaller disk drives. This feature saves more space on all disks using NTFS.

NTFS also uses **Unicode**, an international data format. Unlike the **American Standard Code for Information Interchange (ASCII)** 8-bit configuration, Unicode uses an 8-bit, a 16-bit, or a 32-bit configuration. These configurations are known as **UTF-8 (Unicode Transformation Format)**, UTF-16, and UTF-32, respectively. For Western-language alphabetic characters, UTF-8 is identical to ASCII (see *www.unicode.org/versions* for more details). Knowing this feature of Unicode comes in handy when you perform keyword searches for evidence on a disk drive. (This feature is discussed in more detail in Chapter 10.) Because NTFS offers many more features than FAT, more utilities are used to manage it.

NTFS System Files

Because everything on an NTFS disk is a file, the first file, the MFT, contains information about all files located on the disk, including the system files the OS uses. In the MFT, the first 15 records are reserved for system files. Records within the MFT are referred to as **meta-data**. Table 7-4 lists the first 15 meta-data records you find in the MFT.

Table 7-4 Meta-data Records in the MFT

File name	System File	Record Position	Description
$Mft	MFT	0	Base file record for each folder on the NTFS volume; other record positions in the MFT are allocated if more space is needed.
$MftMirr	MFT 2	1	The first four records of the MFT are saved in this position. If a single sector fails in the first MFT, the records can be restored, allowing for recovery of the MFT.
$LogFile	Log file	2	Previous transactions are stored here to allow for recovery after a system failure has occurred in the NTFS volume.
$Volume	Volume	3	Information specific to the volume, such as label and version, is stored here.
$AttrDef	Attribute definitions	4	A table listing the attribute names, numbers, and definitions.
$	Root file name index	5	This is the root folder on the NTFS volume.
$Bitmap	Boot sector	6	A map of the NTFS volume showing which clusters are in use and which are available.
$Boot	Boot sector	7	Used to mount the NTFS volume during the bootstrap process. Additional code is listed here if this is the boot drive for the system.
$BadClus	Bad cluster file	8	For clusters that have unrecoverable errors, an entry of the cluster location is made to this file.
$Secure	Security file	9	The unique security descriptors for the volume are listed in this file. This is where the access control list (ACL) is maintained for all files and folders on the NTFS volume.
$Upcase	Upcase table	10	This converts all lowercase characters to uppercase Unicode characters for the NTFS volume.
$Extend	NTFS extension file	11	Various optional extensions are listed here, such as quotas, object identifiers, and reparse point data.
		12-15	Reserved for future use.

NTFS Attributes

When Microsoft introduced NTFS, the way its OS stores data on disks changed significantly. In NTFS, all files and folders have file attributes. Individual elements of a file, such as its name, security information, and even the data, are considered file attributes. Each attribute has a unique **attribute type code**; for more detail, visit *www.microsoft.com*.

NTFS attributes fall into two categories: **resident attributes** and **nonresident attributes**. Attributes stored in the MFT are referred to as resident attributes. The MFT consists of records that are approximately 1024 bytes. Small items, such as file name, creation date, modified dates, privileges, and so forth, are stored here. If a file is less than 750 to 800 bytes, it can also be stored as a resident attribute. Anything larger is stored as a nonresident attribute. In Windows 2000 and XP, all file and folder data is stored in the MFT. If more room is needed for file growth, the MFT assigns an **inode** to the file attribute. An inode links attribute records to other attribute records within the MFT. Table 7-5 shows the fields (attributes) in each record of the MFT.

7

TIP

Linking data with inodes originated with UNIX. The inode linking used in an MFT works differently from UNIX or Linux inodes (discussed in Chapter 8). The MFT inodes link records only within the MFT—that is, to resident attributes.

Table 7-5   Attributes in the MFT for Windows 2000 and XP

Attribute Type	Purpose
Standard information	Time stamp data and link (inode) count information is listed here.
Attribute list	Attributes that do not fit within the MFT (nonresident attributes) are listed here along with their locations.
File name	The long and short names for the file are contained here. Up to 255 Unicode bytes are available for long file names. For POSIX requirements, additional names or hard links can also be listed here.
Security descriptor	Ownership and who has access rights to the file or folder are listed here.
Data	File data is stored here. Multiple data attributes are allowed for each file. When more space is needed for additional data, an inode is assigned to link to a new MFT attribute record.
Object ID	The volume-unique file identifier is listed here. Not all files need this unique identifier.
Logged tool stream	This field is used by the Encrypted File System service that was implemented in Windows 2000 and XP.
Reparse point	This field is used for volume mount points and for Installable File System (IFS) filter drivers. For the IFS, it marks specific files used by drivers.
Index root	Implemented for use of folders and indexes.
Index allocation	Implemented for use of folders and indexes.
Bitmap	Implemented for use of folders and indexes.

Table 7-5 Attributes in the MFT for Windows 2000 and XP (continued)

Attribute Type	Purpose
Volume information	Used by the $Volume system file. The volume version number is listed here.
Volume name	Used by the $Volume system file. The volume version label is listed here.

If a file is extremely large, such as a large database file, the MFT assigns the data to a nonresident attribute area of the disk. The file entry has links from the MFT to areas outside the MFT in the unallocated space of the disk volume.

Data is linked to nonresident attributes by directly accessing cluster positions on the disk volume. That is, when a disk is created as an NTFS file structure, the OS assigns logical clusters to the entire disk's partition. These assigned clusters are called **logical cluster numbers (LCNs)**. LCNs become the addresses that allow the MFT to read and write data to the disk's nonresident attribute area.

When data is written to nonresident attribute disk space, an LCN address is assigned to the MFT file (record) entry. This file entry is given a **virtual cluster number (VCN)** for every LCN used to store data for each file in a nonresident disk. A VCN is associated with the LCN for files that extend into the nonresident attribute disk space (see Figure 7-11).

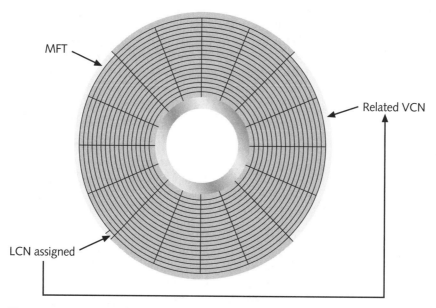

Figure 7-11 MFT relationship with VCNs and LCNs

The first VCN used for each file that extends into the nonresident attribute area of a disk volume starts at zero (0). The numbering of the LCN also starts at zero (0), which is the beginning area of the disk partition (the volume).

NTFS Data Streams

Of particular interest in NTFS are **multiple data streams**. Data can be appended to existing files when you're examining a disk. Data streams can obscure valuable evidentiary data, either intentionally or by coincidence.

In NTFS, a data stream becomes an additional data attribute of a file and allows the file to be associated with different applications. As a result, it remains one data unit. You can also store information about a file in a data stream. In its resource documentation Web page, Microsoft states: "For example, a graphics program can store a thumbnail image of a bitmap in a named data stream within the NTFS file containing the image." From a Windows NT, 2000, or XP DOS shell, you can create a data stream by using the following command. Note that the data stream is defined in the MFT by the colon between the file extension and the data stream label.

```
C:\echo text_message > myfile.txt:stream1
```

To display the content of a data stream, use the following MS-DOS command:

```
C:\more < myfile.txt:stream1
```

NOTE

Be aware that if you save a file with data streams attached to a FAT volume, the data streams aren't transferred.

If you perform a keyword search and retrieve a file associated with a keyword, you might not be able to open the data stream. A data stream isn't displayed when you open a file in a text editor. The only way you can tell whether a file has a data stream attached is by examining the MFT entry for that file. If you see a colon with a name following it in the MFT, that's a data stream file.

NTFS Compressed Files

To improve data storage on disk drives, NTFS provides compression similar to FAT DriveSpace 3, a Windows 98 compression utility. Under NTFS, individual files, folders, or entire volumes can be compressed. With FAT16, you can compress only a volume. When you're running a Windows XP, 2000, or NT system, the compressed data is displayed normally when you access it through Windows Explorer or through applications such as Microsoft Word.

During an investigation, typically you work from a bit-stream image copy of a compressed disk, folder, or file. Your forensic workstation OS might be able to see the compressed data only as an unusual binary file. If you do encounter and identify compressed data, you need to uncompress the data or use a computer forensics tool that can uncompress it automatically. Only a few advanced computer forensic tools can uncompress and examine compressed data.

NTFS Encrypted File System (EFS)

When Microsoft introduced Windows 2000, it added built-in encryption to NTFS, referred to as **Encrypted File System (EFS)**. EFS implements a **public key** and **private key** method of encrypting files, folders, or disk volumes (partitions). Only the owner or user who encrypted the data can access encrypted files. The owner holds the private key, and the OS holds the public key. (Encryption is covered in more detail later in this chapter.)

When a Windows XP or 2000 user implements EFS, a **recovery certificate** is generated and sent to the local Windows XP or 2000 administrator's account. The purpose of the recovery certificate is to provide a mechanism that recovers encrypted files under EFS if there's a problem with the user's original private key. The recovery key is stored in one of two places. When the user of a networked workstation initiates EFS, the recovery key is sent to the local domain server's administrator account. If the workstation is standalone, the recovery key is sent to the workstation's administrator account.

Users can apply EFS to files stored on their local workstations or on a remote server. Windows XP and 2000 automatically decrypt the data when the user or an application initiated by the user accesses an EFS file, folder, or disk volume.

Future plans for EFS include allowing the user to grant other users access to his or her EFS data. If a user copies a file encrypted with EFS to a folder that isn't encrypted, the copied data is saved in unencrypted format.

EFS Recovery Key Agent

The Recovery Key Agent implements the recovery certificate, which is in the Windows XP or 2000 administrator account. Windows XP or 2000 administrators can recover a key in two ways: through Windows or from an MS-DOS command prompt. These three functions are available when using the MS-DOS command prompt:

- Cipher
- Copy
- Efsrecvr

For specific information on how to use these commands, enter the question mark switch after each command, as shown in the following list. With the exception of the Copy command, these switches work only on NTFS systems. Encrypted files aren't part of FAT12, FAT16, or FAT32 OSs.

- cipher /?
- copy /?
- efsrecvr /?

TIP

If you copy an encrypted file from an NTFS disk to a floppy disk, it's automatically unencrypted.

To recover an encrypted EFS file, a user can e-mail it or copy the file to the administrator. The administrator can then run the Recovery Key Agent function to restore the file. For additional information, review the appropriate Microsoft Windows Resource Kit documentation (*www.microsoft.com/windows/reskits/default.asp*) for the latest procedures on how to recover EFS certificates.

Deleting NTFS Files

7

Typically, you use Windows Explorer to delete files from a disk. When a file is deleted from Windows XP, 2000, or NT, the OS renames the deleted file and moves it to the Recycle Bin. Another method of deleting files is using the Del (delete) command from the MS-DOS shell prompt. This method doesn't rename and move the file to the Recycle Bin, but eliminates it from the MFT listing in the same way the FAT does.

When you delete a file by using Windows Explorer, you can restore the deleted file from the Recycle Bin. To do this, the OS takes the following steps when you delete a file or a folder in Windows Explorer:

1. Windows changes the file name and moves the file to a subdirectory with a unique identity in the Recycle Bin.

2. Windows stores information about the original path and file name in the **Info2 file**, which is the control file for the Recycle Bin. It contains ASCII data, Unicode data, and the date and time of the deletion for each file or folder.

NTFS files deleted in an MS-DOS shell function in a similar way as FAT files. The following steps also apply when a user empties a Recycle Bin. When a file is deleted in an MS-DOS shell, the OS performs the following tasks:

1. The associated clusters are designated to be free; that is, they are marked as available for new data.

2. The $Bitmap file attribute of the MFT is updated to reflect the deletion of the file, showing that this space is available.

3. The file attribute record for the file in the MFT is marked as being available.

4. Any inodes and VFN/LCN cluster locations linked to nonresident data are removed from the MFT.

5. A run list is maintained in the MFT of all cluster locations on the disk's nonresident attribute area. When the list of links is deleted, any reference to the links is lost.

NTFS is more efficient than FAT for reclaiming deleted space. Deleted files are overwritten more quickly.

TIP

UNDERSTANDING THE WINDOWS REGISTRY

When Microsoft created Windows 95, it consolidated initialization (.ini) files into the **Registry**, a database that stores hardware and software configuration information, user preferences (including user name and passwords), and setup information. The Registry has been updated since its inception and is still used in Windows XP.

For investigative purposes, the Registry can contain valuable evidence. You can use the Regedit (Registry Editor) program for Windows 9x systems and Regedt32 for Windows 2000 and XP. For more information on how to use Regedit and Regedt32, see the Microsoft Windows Resource Kit documentation for the appropriate OS. You can find the information at *www.microsoft.com/windows/reskits/default.asp* or order the manual with a CD from Microsoft Press. In general, you can use the Edit, Find menu command in the Registry Editor to locate entries that might contain trace evidence, such as information identifying the last person to log on to the computer, which is usually stored in the user account information. Windows 9x systems do not reliably record a user's logon information, but you can find other related user information, such as network logon data, by searching for all occurrences of "username" or application licenses.

You can also use the Registry to determine the most recently accessed files and peripheral devices. In addition, all installed programs deposit information in the Registry. The list includes items such as Internet sites accessed, recent files, and even chat rooms accessed.

As a computing investigator and forensic examiner, you should explore the Registry of all Windows systems. On a live system—meaning one that's currently running—be careful not to alter any Registry setting because doing so could corrupt the system, possibly making it unbootable.

Although several commercial products are available, AccessData has released the FTK Registry Viewer that enables you to access the Registry.

NOTE

Windows 9x Registry

In Windows 95 and 98, the Registry is contained in two binary files, System.dat and User.dat, which are located in the Windows folder in the root directory. System.dat contains confidential user information, installed programs, and system settings.

The User.dat file contains desktop configurations and the most recently used files. The default user information is in the Windows directory, but you can find other users in the

C:\Windows\Profiles*user* directory. In Windows 9x, the Registry is composed of hives that contain keys. Your primary keys (also known as hives) are HKEY_CURRENT_USER and HKEY_LOCAL_MACHINE. The two hives generate HKEY_USERS, HKEY_CURRENT_CONFIG, and HKEY_CLASSES_ROOT.

Although you can examine the Registry in a variety of ways, one of the easiest is loading the forensic image of a Windows 9x machine into AccessData's FTK and then clicking File, Registry Viewer. This method enables you to view all the hives, including the Protected Storage area, which contains confidential user information. Note that if you're using the demo version of Registry Viewer, this feature is disabled.

Windows 2000 and XP Registry

For Windows 2000 and XP, Registry information is contained in the \Winnt\ System32\Config and \Windows\System32\Config folders, respectively. The System, SAM, Security, Software, and NTUser.dat files are the ones you need to examine a drive.

As with Windows 9x machines, you can retrieve the Registry from the forensic image by opening the image in FTK and then clicking File, Registry Viewer. On a live system, you can retrieve the Registry by using FTK Imager and then examining the data. To practice retrieving the Registry, log onto a Windows 2000 or XP machine and follow these steps:

1. To create two new users in XP, click **Start**, **Control Panel**, **User Accounts**. Simply follow the wizard that opens to create the accounts in either OS. Name them **User1** and **User2**, and give them both the password of **password**. (*Note*: If you're in Windows 2000, click **Start**, **Settings**, **Control Panel**, and then double-click **Users and Passwords**.)

2. Log off your current user account, which is probably Administrator. Then log on and off both of the two new user accounts.

3. Log back on to your original account.

4. Next, you need to create a copy of your Registry. Start FTK Imager by double-clicking the icon.

5. Click **File**, **Open Evidence Item** from the menu. Make sure the Logical Drive option button is selected, and then click **Next**. Select the drive you're on and click **Finish**. (*Note*: These applications are updated about every six months, so the steps might not be exactly the same as written here.)

6. Expand the folder view in the left pane so that you can access the Windows or Winnt folder. Then expand the **System32** folder. Right-click the **Config** folder, and click **Export Files**.

7. In the dialog box that opens, click the **Desktop** icon, and then click **OK**. When the Export Results dialog box opens, click **OK**. Close FTK Imager.

7

8. Start AccessData Registry Viewer. If it's not on your desktop, access it through the Start button.

9. Click **File**, **Open** from the menu. Navigate to your desktop. Click the **Config** folder, and click **Open**. Click **SAM**, which contains user information, and then click **Open**.

10. Maximize your window. Expand the SAM tree on the left side of the window, as shown in Figure 7-12. You want to see the Account and Users subfolders.

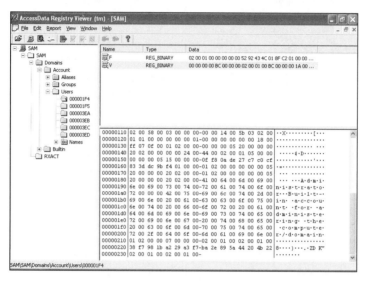

Figure 7-12   Registry Viewer with the SAM file open

11. Expand the **Users** subfolder, and click the first user folder listed. Typically, unless changes have been made, it's the built-in Administrator account.

12. In the upper-right pane, click the entry that has the Name value "V." In the lower-right pane, scroll all the way to the bottom. (If the lower pane isn't visible, expand it by dragging.) You should see the user account name and any comments entered at the time of creation.

13. Repeat Steps 11 and 12 for other users.

14. Close Registry Viewer. Leave the Config folder on your desktop for other exercises.

An extensive amount of information is stored in the Registry. The preceding exercise is merely an example. In one of the Hands-on Projects at the end of this chapter, you attempt to retrieve users' passwords. With the Registry data, you can ascertain when users went online, when they accessed a printer or an external device, and many other events. A lot of the information is beyond the scope of a beginner's text, so you are encouraged to expand your knowledge by attending as many training sessions or classes as are available to you.

UNDERSTANDING MICROSOFT BOOT TASKS

You should have a good understanding of what happens to disk data at startup. In some investigations, you must preserve the data on the disk as the perpetrator of a crime or security incident last used it. Any access to a computer system after it was used for illicit reasons alters your disk evidence.

Recall from Chapter 6 that altering disk data on a suspect computer lessens its evidentiary quality considerably. In some instances, improperly accessing a suspect computer could cause it to completely lose its worthiness as evidence, thus making the digital evidence useless for any litigation.

The following sections review the files that are activated when a Windows machine starts up. Knowing what happens when your computer starts helps you know what to look for when you examine a disk drive.

Windows XP, 2000, and NT Startup

Although Windows NT is significantly different from Windows 95 and 98, the startup methodology for the NT OSs—NT, 2000, and XP—is about the same. There are some minor differences in how specific system start files function, but they basically accomplish the same orderly startup.

All NTFS computers perform the following steps when the computer is turned on:

1. Power-on self test (POST)
2. Initial startup
3. Boot loader
4. Hardware detection and configuration
5. Kernel loading
6. User logon

Windows XP uses the files discussed in the following section to start up. These files can be located on the system partition or the boot partition.

Startup Files for Windows XP

The **NT Loader (NTLDR)** file loads the OS. NTLDR is located in the root folder of the system partition. When the system is powered on, NTLDR reads the Boot.ini file, which displays a boot menu. After you have selected the mode to boot to, Boot.ini runs Ntoskrnl.exe and reads Bootvid.dll, Hal.dll, and the startup device drivers.

Boot.ini specifies the Windows XP path installation. The Boot.ini file, located in the root folder of the system partition, contains options for selecting the Windows version.

If a system has multiple booting OSs using older systems such as Windows 9x or DOS, NTLDR reads the **BootSect.dos** file, which contains the address, or boot sector location, of each OS. The BootSect.dos file is a hidden file located in the root folder of the system partition.

The **NTDetect.com** file is located in the root folder of the system partition. When the boot selection is made, the NTLDR runs NTDetect.com, a 16-bit real-mode program. This real-mode program queries the system for basic device and configuration data, and then passes its findings to NTLDR. This program identifies components and values on the computer system, such as the following:

- CMOS time and date value
- Buses attached to the motherboard, such as Industry Standard Architecture (ISA) or Peripheral Component Interconnect (PCI)
- Disk drives connected to the system
- Mouse input devices connected to the system
- Parallel ports connected to the system

NTBootdd.sys is the device driver that allows access to SCSI or ATA drives that aren't related to the BIOS. Controllers that do not use Interrupt 13 (INT-13) use this file. This program runs in privileged processor mode with direct access to hardware and system data. The NTBootdd.sys file is located in the root folder of the system partition. On some workstations, a SCSI disk drive is used as the primary boot disk. The function of the NTBootdd.sys file is to provide a method for the OS to directly communicate with the SCSI disk.

Ntoskrnl.exe is the Windows XP OS kernel. It is located in the *%system-root%*\ Windows\System32 folder.

Hal.dll is the Hardware Abstraction Layer dynamic link library. The HAL allows the OS kernel to communicate with the computer's hardware. It is located in the *%system-root%*\ Windows\System32 folder.

At startup, data and instruction code are moved in and out of the **PageFile.sys** file to optimize the amount of physical RAM available.

The Registry key HKEY_LOCAL_MACHINE\SYSTEM contains information the OS requires to start system services and devices. This system Registry file is located in the *%system-root%*\Windows\System32\Config\System folder.

Device drivers contain instructions for the OS for hardware devices, such as the keyboard, mouse, and video card, and are stored in the *%system-root%*\Windows\System32\Drivers folder.

TIP

To identify the specific path for *%system-root%* at a DOS prompt, type the Set command and then press Enter, with no additional switches or parameters. The Set command, when run alone, displays all current *%system-root%* paths.

Windows XP System Files

Next, you need to examine the core OS files that Windows XP, 2000, and NT use, usually located in *%system-root%*\Windows\System32 or *%system-root%*\Winnt\System32. Table 7-6 describes the essential files Windows XP uses. Although a few of these files are repeats of previous table entries, you should be aware of their key roles.

Table 7-6 Windows XP System Files

File name	Description
Ntoskrnl.exe	The XP executable and kernel
Ntkrnlpa.exe	The physical address support program for accessing more than 4 GB of physical memory (RAM)
Hal.dll	The Hardware Abstraction Layer (described earlier)
Win32k.sys	The kernel-mode portion of the subsystem for Win32
Ntdll.dll	System service dispatch stubs to the executable functions and internal support functions
Kernel32.dll	Core Win32 subsystem DLL file
Advapi32.dll	Core Win32 subsystem DLL file
User32.dll	Core Win32 subsystem DLL file
Gdi32.dll	Core Win32 subsystem DLL file

Contamination Concerns for XP

When you start a Windows XP or older NTFS workstation, several files are immediately accessed. When any of these or other related OS files are accessed at startup, the last access date and time stamp for the files changes to the present time. This change destroys any potential evidence that might be needed to show when a Windows XP workstation was last used. For this reason, you should have a strong working knowledge of the boot process so that you understand what occurs during a system startup.

Windows 9x and Me Startup

Windows 9x OSs have similar boot processes. Windows Me is also similar, with one important exception: You cannot boot to a true MS-DOS mode. When conducting a computing investigation and forensic examination, being able to boot to MS-DOS is much preferred, especially if you're running a later version of Windows 95 OEM SR2 (version 4.00.1111) or a newer one in which the MS-DOS boot mode can read and write to a FAT32 disk.

Windows 9x OSs have two modes: **DOS protected-mode interface (DPMI)** and **protected-mode GUI**. Many current computer forensics tools use the DPMI mode and work only in MS-DOS mode. They must be run from MS-DOS, not an MS-DOS shell from Windows, because certain disk drive accesses used by these MS-DOS tools conflict with the GUI.

The system files used by Windows 9x have their origin in MS-DOS 6.22. The **Io.sys** file communicates between a computer's BIOS, hardware, and the OS kernel. During the boot phase of a Windows 9x system, Io.sys monitors the keyboard for an F8 keystroke. If F8 is entered during the startup process, Io.sys loads the Windows Startup menu. The options on the Windows Startup menu range from booting to Windows normally to running in Safe mode to perform maintenance.

Option 5 listed in the Windows Startup menu (see Figure 7-13) is "Command prompt only." By selecting this option, you can go directly into a Windows 9x version of MS-DOS.

Microsoft Windows 98 Startup Menu

1. Normal
2. Logged (\BOOTLOG.TXT)
3. Safe mode
4. Step-by-step confirmation
5. Command prompt only
6. Save mode command prompt only

Enter a choice: 1

Figure 7-13   Windows 9x startup options

You need to be familiar with MS-DOS 6.22 or Windows 9x MS-DOS. **Msdos.sys** is a hidden text file containing startup options for Windows 9x. In MS-DOS 6.22, the Msdos.sys file is the actual OS kernel. In Windows 9x, Msdos.sys has a different role; it has replaced the Autoexec.bat and Config.sys files in MS-DOS 6.22. The Msdos.sys file is usually located in the root directory of the C: drive.

The **Command.com** file provides a prompt when booting to MS-DOS mode (DPMI). You can run a limited number of MS-DOS commands built into Command.com, called the internal MS-DOS commands, which are described in the following list:

- Dir—List directories.

- Cd (Chdir)—Change directory location.

- Cls—Clear the screen of all output.

- Date—Display the CMOS calendar value.

- Copy—Copy a file from one location to another.

- Del (Erase)—Erase a file.

- Md (Mkdir)—Create a subdirectory.

- Path—Define where to find other commands and programs.

- Prompt—Define what your MS-DOS prompt looks like.

- Rd (Rmdir)—Erase a directory or folder.

- Set—Define or remove environmental variables.

- Time—Display the CMOS clock value.

- Type—List the content of a text file on screen.

- Ver—Get the MS-DOS version number in which you're working.

- Vol—Display the volume label of the disk drive.

As described earlier, system files in Windows 9x and Me that contain valuable information can easily be altered during startup, destroying their evidentiary value.

UNDERSTANDING MS-DOS STARTUP TASKS

Similar to Windows 9x, MS-DOS uses three files when booting: Io.sys, Msdos.sys, and Command.com. Two other files are then used to configure MS-DOS at startup: Config.sys and Autoexec.bat. MS-DOS 6.22 boot files use the same names for the first three files.However, there are some important differences between these files and those in Windows 9x.

Io.sys is the first file loaded after the ROM bootstrap loader finds the disk drive. Io.sys then resides in RAM and provides the basic input and output service for all MS-DOS functions.

Msdos.sys is the second program to load into RAM immediately after Io.sys. This original Msdos.sys file is the actual kernel for MS-DOS, and not a text file like the Windows 9x and Me Msdos.sys files. After Msdos.sys finishes setting up the DOS services, it looks for the Config.sys file to configure the device drivers and other settings. Msdos.sys then loads Command.com, which contains the same internal DOS commands in MS_DOS 6.22 as in Windows 9x. As the loading of Command.com nears completion, Msdos.sys looks for and loads Autoexec.bat.

Config.sys is a text file containing commands typically run only at system startup. These unique commands enhance the computer's DOS configuration.

Autoexec.bat is an automatically executed batch file containing customized settings for MS-DOS. In this batch file, you can define the default path and set environmental variables, such as temporary directories.

MS-DOS accesses and resets the last access dates and times on files when powered up. In Chapter 2, you created a boot floppy disk that prevents you from changing data on a suspect's hard disk.

Other Disk Operating Systems

Years ago, there were several other microcomputer OSs, such as Control Program for Microprocessors (CP/M), Digital Research Disk Operating System (DR-DOS), and Personal Computer Disk Operating System (PC-DOS). Of these OSs, only DR-DOS is still commercially available. As mentioned in Chapter 1, you might encounter an old computer that uses one of these OSs. If you do, you need to call upon your talents and those of your network of experts to research, explore, and test these old OSs. This section describes the unique features and facts for each OS.

In the 1970s, Digital Research created the first nonspecific microcomputer OS, CP/M. Computers using CP/M originally had 8-inch floppy disk drives and did not support hard disk drives. The CPU was the Z-80 from Zilog, which could access up to 64 KB of RAM. The file system was unique to CP/M. In the early 1980s, IBM provided an expansion card with a built-in Z-80 CPU that allowed users to process the many applications available for CP/M at that time.

After Microsoft developed MS-DOS, Digital Research created DR-DOS to compete against MS-DOS. In 1988 DR-DOS was the final OS Digital Research produced; it used FAT12 and FAT16 file systems. DR-DOS has a richer command environment than MS-DOS. DR-DOS is now primarily sold as an embedded OS for out-of-the-box ROM or Flash ROM systems.

When IBM created the first PC using the Intel 8088 processor, it needed an OS. In the early 1980s, IBM contracted with Microsoft, then a startup company. In 1981, Microsoft purchased a program called 86-DOS from a small company called Seattle Computing. 86-DOS could run on the Intel 8088 16-bit processor and was a modification of Digital Research's CP/M. Microsoft then supplied 86-DOS to IBM for use on its PCs, and IBM called it PC-DOS.

PC-DOS works much like MS-DOS. IBM maintained upgrades to PC-DOS until Microsoft released Windows 95. The OS files in PC-DOS are slightly different from MS-DOS. For example, Io.sys is called Ibmio.sys, and Msdos.sys is called Ibmdos.sys. PC-DOS uses FAT12 and FAT16 file systems, so accessing data from PC-DOS is no different than working with MS-DOS.

DOS Commands and Batch Files

After Microsoft introduced Windows 95, the use of MS-DOS commands and batch files has steadily declined. However, some MS-DOS commands are still used, so you can apply them to batch files for your computing administrative functions.

Batch files can control the quality of your work because they repeat the same series of commands every time with no mistakes. They are ideal for investigations with important tasks that might become repetitive when you must sort through large quantities of data.

MS-DOS has several commands you can combine into a single batch file, which then work like a single command. A simple batch file could copy a file from one folder to another folder or disk, and then compare the original file to the newly copied file. The MS-DOS commands to use for this batch file are Copy, Fc (for File Compare), and Echo. Copy copies a file from a source to a target. You use Fc to verify that the file was copied properly. The Echo command turns the screen output on or off. Figure 7-14 shows the batch file you're about to create. Cpverify.bat copies the Whatsnew.txt file to the Temp folder, and then verifies that the file was copied to that folder. To create this file, use the following steps on a Windows 98 machine:

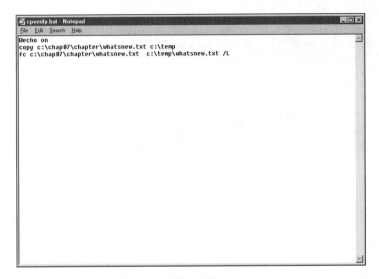

Figure 7-14   The batch file Cpverify.bat

1. If necessary, create a folder named **Temp** in the root directory.

2. Open Notepad and type **This is a test**.

3. Save the file as **Whatsnew.txt** in the C:\Chap07\Chapter folder. (If necessary, go to your work folder that contains the chapter files.)

4. Create a file in Notepad by clicking **File**, **New** from the menu.

5. Type **@echo on** and press **Enter**.

6. Type **copy C:\Chap07\Chapter\Whatsnew.txt C:\Temp** and press **Enter**.

7. Type **fc C:\Chap07\Chapter\Whatsnew.txt C:\Temp\Whatsnew.txt /L** and press **Enter**.

8. Save the file as **Cpverify.bat** in the C:\Chap07\Chapter folder.

9. Close Notepad.

10. Open a command prompt window.

11. Navigate to the folder where you stored Cpverify.bat.

12. To run the batch file, type **cpverify** and press **Enter** (see Figure 7-15).

13. Exit the command prompt window.

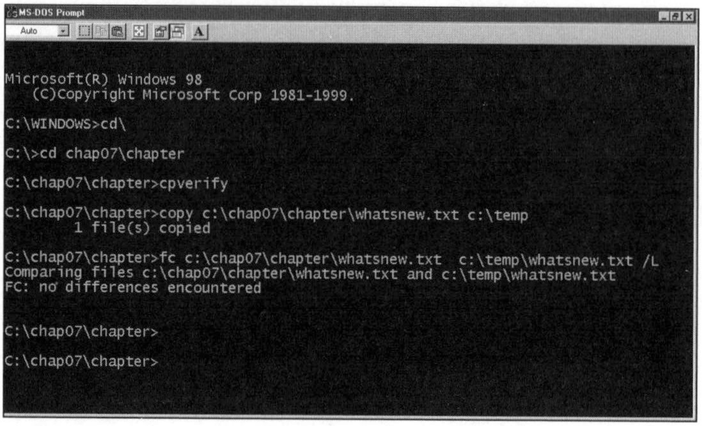

Figure 7-15 Results of Cpverify.bat

MS-DOS provides functions such as parameter passing and conditional execution commands. Parameter passing is used quite frequently in batch files, as you'll see later in this section. The commands unique for batch files are listed in Table 7-7. These commands are a mix of internal and external MS-DOS commands.

Table 7-7 DOS Batch Commands

Batch Command	Function
@	Suppresses the display of commands on the screen.
Call	Initiates another batch file. When it completes the called batch file, it returns control to the original batch file, such as Call Batch1.
Choice	Stops the batch file and waits for input from the keyboard. The keystroke input is then interrupted with the If Errorlevel command.
Echo	Turns on or off the display of commands on the screen as they run—for example, Echo On or Echo Off.
For..In..Do	Repeats a command or group of commands in a For-Next loop.
Goto	Jumps to a predefined label in the batch file. Labels are defined by any name value that's not already defined as an MS-DOS command and ends with a colon—Loop:, for example.
If	Allows for a conditional execution of a command. If true, the command is executed; if false, it is skipped.

Table 7-7   DOS Batch Commands (continued)

Batch Command	Function
Pause	Halts the batch job execution, displays a message, and waits for any key to be pressed before continuing the batch file execution.
Rem	Allows you to insert comments in the batch file. All text to the right of the Rem command is ignored.
Shift	For parameters that are passed within a batch file. Moves all the parameters one parameter to the left.

You can pass up to 10 command parameters from the command line to the batch file. Parameters in MS-DOS batch files are numeric values preceded by a percent sign, which tells the batch file that a parameter value is expected. The number indicates which parameter is passed. In Cpverify.bat, you could change the fixed file values to parameters to pass. The following is the original batch file:

```
@echo on
copy C:\Chap07\Chapter\Whatsnew.txt C:\Temp
fc C:\Chap07\Chapter\Whatsnew.txt C:\Temp\Whatsnew.txt /L
```

The following is the parameter-passing batch file:

```
@echo on
copy %1 %2
fc %1 %2 /L
```

When you run this new batch file, you enter the path and file names at the prompt. To modify Cpverify.bat, follow these steps:

1. Open a new text file in Notepad.

2. Type **Testing versatility of batch files**.

3. Save the file as **testing.txt** in the **C:\Chap07\Chapter** folder in your work folder.

4. Open **Cpverify.bat** in Notepad.

5. Delete the second line, type **copy %1 %2**, and then press **Enter**.

6. Delete the third line, type **fc %1 %2 /L**, and then press **Enter**.

7. Save the file with the same name and in the same location, and then close Notepad.

8. Open a command prompt window.

9. Use the **cd** command to access the **C:\Chap07\Chapter** folder in your work folder.

10. Type **Cpverify Testing.txt C:\Temp\Testing.txt**, and then press **Enter**.

Cpverify.bat copies the Testing.txt file to the Temp folder, and then displays a message indicating that the original and copied files are the same. The advantage of using parameters is that you don't have to update your batch file every time you want to repeat a specific group of tasks.

NOTE

MS-DOS has many more commands, switches, and functions. It's highly recommended that you learn more about these commands as you progress through your training as a computing investigator and forensic examiner.

CHAPTER SUMMARY

- Microsoft used FAT12 and FAT16 on older operating systems, such as MS-DOS, Windows 3.x, and Windows 9x. The maximum partition size is 2 GB. Newer systems use FAT32. FAT12 is now used almost exclusively on floppy disks.

- The Registry in older Windows OSs keeps a record of attached hardware, user preferences, network information, and installed software. Buried deep in the Registry is information such as passwords contained in two binary files: System.dat and User.dat.

- To find a hard disk's capacity, use the cylinders, heads, and sectors (CHS) calculation. To find a disk's byte capacity, multiply the number of heads, cylinders, and sectors.

- Sectors are grouped into clusters and clusters are chained. This is done because the OS can track only a given number of allocation units (65,536 in FAT16 and 4,294,967,296 in FAT32). Clusters are logical addresses.

- The New Technology File System (NTFS) is more versatile because it uses the Master File Table (MFT) to track information such as security items, the first 750 bytes of data, long and short file names, and a list of nonresident attributes.

- File slack, random access memory (RAM) slack, and drive slack are all areas in which valuable information, such as downloaded files, swap files, passwords, and logon IDs, can reside on a drive.

- To be an effective computer forensics investigator, you need to maintain a library of older operating systems and applications.

- NTFS uses Unicode to store information. Unicode is an international code and uses a 16-bit configuration instead of the 8-bit configuration that ASCII and other older representation codes use.

- Hexadecimal codes supply information about files and OSs. You can determine the file type by using tools such as WinHex and Hex Workshop.

- NTFS uses inodes to link file attribute records to other file attribute records. Attributes fall into two categories—resident and nonresident attributes.

- NTFS can compress individual files, folders, or entire partitions. FAT16 can compress only entire volumes.

KEY TERMS

American Standard Code for Information Interchange (ASCII) — A coding scheme using seven or eight bits that assigns numeric values to up to 256 characters, including letters, numerals, punctuation marks, control characters, and other symbols.

areal density — The number of bits per square inch of a platter.

attribute type code — In NTFS, the code assigned to file attributes such as the file name and security information.

Autoexec.bat — An automatically executed batch file containing customized settings for MS-DOS, including the default path and environmental variables, such as temporary directories.

bootstrap process — Information contained in ROM that the computer accesses during its startup process; this information tells the computer how to access the OS and hard drive.

Boot.ini — Specifies the Windows path installation along with a variety of other startup options.

BootSect.dos — If the machine has a multiple booting system, NTLDR reads BootSect. dos, which is a hidden file, to determine the address of the sector location of each OS. *See also* NT Loader (NTLDR).

Chain FAT Entry (CFE) — A DriveSpy command that displays all the clusters in a chain that start at a specified cluster.

clusters — Storage allocation units composed of sectors. Clusters are 512, 1024, 2048, or 4096 bytes long.

Command.com — Provides a prompt when booting to MS-DOS mode.

Config.sys — A text file containing commands typically run only at system startup to enhance the computer's DOS configuration.

cylinder — The intersection of tracks on two or more disk platters.

device driver — Contains instructions for the OS for hardware devices, such as the keyboard, mouse, and video card.

DOS protected-mode interface (DPMI) — Used by many computer forensics tools that don't operate in the Windows environment. It allows DOS programs to access extended memory while protecting the system. (See *www.windowsitlibrary.com/Content/175/09/5.html* for more details.)

drive slack — Any information that had been on the storage device previously. It can contain deleted files, deleted e-mail, or file fragments. Both file slack and RAM slack constitute drive slack. *See also* file slack and RAM slack.

Encrypted File System (EFS) — A combination of symmetric key and public/private key encryption first used in Windows 2000 on NTFS-formatted disks. The file is encrypted with a symmetric key, and then a public/private key is used to encrypt the symmetric key. (See *www.serverwatch.com/tutorials/article.php/2106831* for more details.)

end-of-file (EOF) marker — The code 0x0FFFFFFF is typically used with FAT file systems to show where the file ends.

7

File Allocation Table (FAT) — The original Microsoft file structure. It's written to the outermost track of a disk and contains information about each file stored on the drive. The variations are FAT12, FAT16, and FAT32.

file slack — The slack space created when a file is saved. If the allocated space is larger than the file, the remaining space is slack and can contain passwords, logon IDs, and deleted e-mail.

file system — Gives an OS a road map to data on a disk.

geometry — The internal organization of a drive.

Hal.dll — The Hardware Abstraction Layer dynamic link library tells the OS kernel how to interface with the hardware.

head and cylinder skew — A method manufacturers use to minimize lag time. The starting sectors of tracks are slightly offset from each other to move the read-write head.

head — The device that reads and writes data to a disk platter.

High Performance File System (HPFS) — The file system IBM uses for its OS/2 operating system.

Info2 file — In Windows NT, 2000, and XP, the control file for the Recycle Bin.

inode — Links attribute records to other attribute records within the MFT.

Io.sys — This MS-DOS file communicates between a computer's BIOS and hardware and with MS-DOS code.

logical address — When files are saved, they are assigned to clusters. The OS numbers these clusters starting at 2. The cluster number defines the logical address.

logical cluster number (LCN) — Used by the NTFS Master File Table (MFT), it refers to a specific physical location on the drive. *See also* virtual cluster number (VCN).

Master Boot Record (MBR) — On Windows and DOS computer systems, this boot disk file contains information about the files on a disk and their locations, size, and other critical items.

Master File Table (MFT) — Used by NTFS to track files. It contains information about access rights, date and time stamps, system attributes, and parts files.

meta-data — In NTFS, this term refers to information stored in the MFT.

Msdos.sys — A hidden text file containing startup options for Windows 9x. Note that in MS_DOS 6.22 and earlier, it was not a text file, but an actual OS executable.

multiple data streams — Ways in which data can be appended to a file (intentionally or not). In NTFS, data streams become an additional data attribute of a file.

New Technology File System (NTFS) — Created by Microsoft to replace FAT. NTFS uses security features, allows for smaller cluster sizes, and uses Unicode, which makes it a much more versatile system. NTFS is used mainly on newer OSs, such as Windows 2000, 2003, and XP.

nonresident attributes — When referring to the NTFS MFT, all data that's stored in a location separate from the MFT.

NTBootdd.sys — A device driver that allows access to SCSI or ATA drives that aren't referred to in the BIOS.

NTDetect.com — A command file that identifies hardware components during bootup and sends the information to NTLDR.

NT Loader (NTLDR) — A program that loads Windows NT. It's located in the root folder of the system partition. *See also* Bootsect.dos.

Ntoskrnl.exe — The kernel for the Windows XP.

PageFile.sys — At startup, data and instruction code are moved in and out of PageFile.sys to optimize the amount of physical memory (RAM) available during startup.

partition — A logical drive on a disk. It can be the entire disk or a fraction thereof.

Partition Boot Sector — The first data set of an NTFS disk. It starts at sector [0] of the disk drive and can expand up to 16 sectors.

partition gap — Partitions created with unused space or voids between the primary partition and the first logical partition.

physical address — The actual sector in which a file is located. Sectors reside at the hardware and firmware level.

private key — In encryption, the key used to decrypt the file.

protected-mode GUI — Provides the same items for Windows that Config.sys provided for DOS. It loads all the device drivers. (See *www.windowsitlibrary.com/Content/175/09/5.html* for more details.)

public key — In encryption, the key used to encrypt a file; it's held by a certificate authority, such as a global registry, network server, or company such as VeriSign.

RAM slack — The slack space in the last sector of a file. Any data currently residing in RAM at the time the file is saved can appear in this area, whether the information was saved or not. It can contain logon IDs, passwords, and phone numbers for dial-ups.

recovery certificate — A method NTFS uses so that a network administrator can recover encrypted files if the file's user/creator loses his or her private key encryption code.

Registry — In Windows, the Registry contains information about hardware, network connections, user preferences, installed software, and other critical information. Use Regedit or Regedt32 from the Run dialog box to access the Registry.

resident attributes — When referring to the MFT, all attributes stored in the NTFS MFT. *See also* Master File Table (MFT) and New Technology File System (NTFS).

sector — An individual section on a track, typically made up of 512 bytes.

Set command — When used at the command line with no switches or attributes, this command displays all current system-root paths.

track density — The space between tracks on a disk. The smaller the space between tracks, the more tracks on a disk. Older drives with wider track densities allowed wandering.

tracks — The individual concentric circles on a disk platter.

unallocated disk space — All data area on the disk that does not contain an active file. The data in this area includes but is not limited to deleted files.

Unicode — A character code representation that's replacing ASCII. It's capable of representing more than 64,000 characters and non-European-based languages.

UTF-8 (Unicode Transformation Format) — One of three formats Unicode uses to translate the many languages of the world for digital representation.

virtual cluster number (VCN) — When a file is saved in the NTFS, it's assigned both a logical cluster number and a virtual cluster number. The logical cluster number is a physical location; the virtual cluster number consists of chained clusters. *See also* logical cluster number (LCN).

volume — Any storage media, such as a floppy disk, a partition on a hard drive, the entire drive, or several drives. On Intel systems, a volume is any partitioned disk.

zoned bit recording — How most manufacturers deal with a platter's inner tracks being physically smaller than the outer tracks. Grouping the tracks by zones ensures that the most storage space is used. Inner tracks contain fewer sectors than the outer tracks.

REVIEW QUESTIONS

1. In DOS and Windows 9.x, Io.sys is the first file loaded after the ROM bootstrap loader finds the disk. True or False?

2. Sectors typically contain how many bytes?

   a. 256

   b. 512

   c. 1024

   d. 2048

3. What does CHS stand for?

4. Zoned bit recording is how manufacturers ensure that the outer tracks store as much data as possible. True or False?

5. Areal density refers to:

   a. the amount of data per disk

   b. the amount of data per partition

   c. the amount of data per square inch

   d. the amount of data per platter

6. Clusters in Windows always begin numbering at what number?

7. What is the ratio of sectors per cluster in a 3½-inch floppy disk?

   a. 1:1

   b. 2:1

   c. 4:1

   d. 8:1

8. List three things contained in the FAT.

9. Windows 2000 can be configured to access which of these file formats? (Choose all that apply.)

   a. FAT12

   b. FAT16

   c. FAT32

   d. NTFS

10. In a FAT32 system, a 123 KB file uses how many sectors?

11. What is the space on a drive called when a file is deleted? (Choose all that apply.)

   a. disk space

   b. unallocated space

   c. drive space

   d. free space

12. List two features that NTFS provides that FAT does not.

13. What does MFT stand for?

14. In NTFS, files smaller than 750 bytes are stored in the MFT. True or False?

15. RAM slack can contain passwords. True or False?

16. A virtual cluster consists of what kind of clusters?

17. The Windows Registry in Windows 9x consists of what two files?

18. On what OS is HPFS found?

19. Device drivers are used to do what?

20. In an MS-DOS batch file, what does the statement COPY %1 %2 require the user to do?

HANDS-ON PROJECTS

HANDS-ON
PROJECTS

Project 7-1

In this project, you compare two files created in different versions of Microsoft Word to determine whether the files are different at the hexadecimal level. Keep a journal log of what you find. Use a Windows 2000 or XP computer for this project. Follow these steps to compare two files created in different versions of Word:

1. Start Microsoft Word on a Windows 2000 or XP machine the way you usually do.

2. In your C:*work folder*\Chap07 folder, create a new folder called **Projects**.

3. In a new document, type **This is a test**.

4. Click **File**, **Save** from the menu.

5. In the Save as dialog box, make sure the Save as type option is set to Word Document (*.doc), and then save the file as **Mywordnew.doc** in the C:*work folder*\\Chap07\\Projects folder.

6. Click **File**, **Save As** from the menu. In the Save As dialog box, change the Save as type option to **Word 6.0/95 (*.doc)** if you have Word 2002 or earlier; otherwise, use **Word 97–2003 & 6.0/95 – RTF**, and then save the file as **Myword95.doc** in the C:*work folder*\\Chap07\\Projects folder.

7. Close Word and start Hex Workshop.

8. Click **File**, **Open** from the menu. In the Open dialog box, navigate to the C:*work folder*\\Chap07\\Projects folder, and then double-click **Mywordnew.doc**.

9. Starting from the left, notice the first section and middle sections of the window. It should show eight zeros in the first pane, followed by D0CF 11E0 A1B1 1AE1 in the middle pane.

10. Check the length of the file by clicking **File**, **Print Preview** from the menu. Note that the file is lengthy. Close the Print Preview window. Print the first page of the file by clicking **File**, **Print** from the menu, clicking the **Pages** option button, and setting the range to print from **1** to **1**. Then click **OK**.

11. Click **File**, **Close** from the menu to close Mywordnew.doc in Hex Workshop.

12. In Hex Workshop, click **File**, **Open** from the menu. In the Open dialog box, navigate to the C:*work folder*\\Chap07\\Projects folder, and then double-click **Myword95.doc**.

13. Examine the screen, and then print the first page of the file as described in Step 10.

14. Close Myword95.doc in Hex Workshop.

15. Compare the two printouts. There should be no difference if you're using Word 2002 or earlier. If you're using Word 2003, you might have different results.

**HANDS-ON
PROJECTS**

Project 7-2

Based on the steps in the chapter, you create a batch file that formats a disk for you and prompts you for the disk you want. Use a Windows 9x computer for this project. To create a batch file, follow these steps:

1. Start Notepad.

2. In a new Notepad document, type **@echo off** and press **Enter**.

3. Type **format %1** and press **Enter**.

4. Save the file as **Myformat.bat** in the C:*work folder*\\Chap07\\Projects folder. Close Notepad.

5. In the floppy disk drive, insert a floppy disk containing data you no longer need.

6. Open a command prompt window.

7. Use the **cd** command to switch to the C:*work folder*\Chap07\Projects folder.

8. Type **myformat a:** at the prompt and press **Enter**. When prompted for a volume label, press **Enter**. When prompted to format another, press **n** and then press **Enter**.

9. After the format is completed, type **exit** at the prompt and then press **Enter**.

HANDS-ON PROJECTS

Project 7-3

This project uses DriveSpy to determine the capacity and geometry of all physical drives on your system. You also examine the partition tables and partitions of a drive. To determine the capacity and geometry of connected drives, follow these steps:

1. In Chapter 2, you installed DriveSpy on a Windows 98 machine. Access the command prompt and use the cd command to view the contents of the Tools folder in your work folder. To start DriveSpy, type **drivespy** and press **Enter**.

2. To keep track of what you do, create an output file at the SYS> prompt by typing **output C:*work folder*\Chap07\Projects\C7prj03.txt** and pressing **Enter**. Substitute your drive letter, if necessary. (Note that if you used file names longer than eight characters, you need to use the DOS abbreviation.)

3. At the SYS> prompt, type **drives** and press **Enter**. The physical drives connected to your machine are listed in the DriveSpy window.

4. Type **drive 0** and press **Enter** to access the drive level.

5. At the D0> prompt, type **drives** and press **Enter**. The physical drives connected to your computer are again listed in the DriveSpy window.

6. Examine the partition level by typing **part 1**. At the D0P1> prompt, type **drives** and press **Enter**. Note that this is one of the few commands that operates at all levels of the disk.

7. At the D0P1> prompt, type **tables** and press **Enter**. The partition tables of the drive you're currently accessing are listed in the DriveSpy window.

8. Type **q** to exit DriveSpy.

9. Restart DriveSpy by typing **drivespy** and pressing **Enter**. At the SYS> prompt, type **output C:*work folder*\Chap07\Projects\C7prj03.txt** and press **Enter**. When prompted to append data to the current file, type **a** for append.

10. At the SYS> prompt, type **drive 0** and press **Enter**.

11. Type **parts** and press **Enter**. Information appears about all partitions on a disk, including the boundary of the partitions, size, and type.

12. Exit DriveSpy. Use Notepad to print the output file.

7

HANDS-ON PROJECTS

Project 7-4

In this project, you use Hex Workshop to become familiar with different file types. You can use any Windows computer, including Windows 98, 2000, or XP, on which Hex Workshop is loaded. To use Hex Workshop to view file types, follow these steps:

1. On your hard disk, locate or create Microsoft Excel (.xls), Microsoft Word (.doc), .gif, .jpg, and .avi files.

2. Start Hex Workshop.

3. For each file, click **File**, **Open** from the menu to open the file.

4. Click **File**, **Print** from the menu to print the acquired information. You might want to check Print Preview first to ascertain how many pages the file contains before you begin to print. Only the first page is needed.

5. On each printout, circle the item that identifies the file type. Do this for all five file types.

6. Close Hex Workshop.

HANDS-ON PROJECTS

Project 7-5

In this project, you can use a Windows 2000 or XP machine. Your machine can be formatted as NTFS or FAT32. If you followed the exercise in the chapter, you can use the Config folder created earlier and begin at Step 8. Otherwise, begin with the first step:

1. To create two new users, click **Start**, **Control Panel**, **User Accounts**. Simply follow the wizard that opens to create the accounts on either operating system. Name them **User1** and **User2**, and give them both the password of **password**.

2. Log off your current user account, which is probably Administrator. Then log on and off both new user accounts.

3. Log back on to your original account.

4. Next, you need to create a copy of your Registry. Start FTK Imager by double-clicking the icon.

5. Click **File**, **Open Evidence Item** from the menu. Click the **Logical Drive** option button, and click **Next**. Click the drive or partition you're currently on, and click **Finish**.

6. Expand the folder view in the left pane so that you can access the Windows or Winnt folder. Then expand the **System32** folder. Right-click the **Config** folder and click **Export Files**.

7. In the dialog box that opens, click the **Desktop** icon to send the **Config** folder to your desktop. Close FTK Imager.

8. Start AccessData's Password Recovery Toolkit (PRTK). If it's not on your desktop, click **Start**, **Programs** (**All Programs** in XP), **AccessData**, **Password Recovery Toolkit**.

9. In the Simple Start dialog box that opens, select the first option, which is selecting one or multiple files in a single directory and recovering the passwords. Click **OK**. If the Simple Start dialog box has been disabled on your system, click **Analyze**, **Select Files**.

10. Navigate to the Config folder, click the **SAM** file, and then click **Add**. PRTK immediately begins attempting to recover the passwords. Click the **Stop** button in the Recovery Properties dialog box that's open.

11. Notice the number of users listed on your machine. If you have an XP machine, you might note that Microsoft Technical Support has user accounts built in to make accessing your machine easier when you call for assistance.

12. Close PRTK.

HANDS-ON PROJECTS

Project 7-6

In this project, you examine the FAT and clusters of a drive. Make sure you're working on a noncritical drive of a Windows 98 machine. To examine clusters, follow these steps:

1. Access the command prompt and start DriveSpy.

2. At the SYS> prompt, type **output C:*work folder*\Chap07\Projects\C7prj06.txt** and press **Enter**. This creates an output file in the Chap07\Projects folder in your work folder. (Note that if you used file names longer than eight characters, you need to use the DOS abbreviation.)

3. Type **drive 0** and press **Enter** to access Drive mode, and then type **part 1** and press **Enter** to access Partition mode.

4. At the D0P1> prompt, you should see information indicating the number of clusters on the disk. Record this number.

5. To get the FAT entry for a specific cluster, type **gfe *cluster number***. Substitute any number between 0 and the total number of clusters you wrote down in Step 4, and then press **Enter**.

6. Next, type **cfe *cluster number*** and then press **Enter**. This gives you the chain of clusters that originate at a specific cluster. Typically, you would have already used a tool such as Norton DiskEdit to tell you what clusters were chained.

7. Finally, you can find out which clusters are assigned to a specific file. If you are in a DOS shell, use the Windows desktop to find the name of a file you can use for testing. Return to the DOS shell and type **cde *filename*** (*filename* is the test file).

8. Exit DriveSpy.

9. To examine the output file, type **edit C:*work folder*\\Chap07\\Projects\\C7prj06.txt** at the MS-DOS prompt, and press **Enter**. (Replace the drive letter, if necessary.) Scroll through the output file and locate the cluster link listing for the test file you selected. If necessary, close all open windows.

CASE PROJECTS

Case Project 7-1

For the arson running case project, decide whether you're going to work from the image or restore it to a drive. Next, determine the file system type: FAT32, NTFS, and so forth. Next, determine whether any files used EFS or another encryption method. Write a short paper on your findings, and if any encryption methods were used, include a discussion of what forensic tools you could use to open those files.

Case Project 7-2

For the kidnapping running case project, use FTK or another tool to determine which files have bad extensions. Next, use a hex editor to examine the file headers and determine what type of files they really are. Write a short paper describing how these procedures might help you solve the case.

Case Project 7-3

A client who is a Windows user calls and says that the amount of space that should be on the drive isn't showing up in the partitions she has defined. What is the most likely cause of the missing or unrecognized space?

Case Project 7-4

An employee suspects that his password has been compromised. He changed it two days ago, yet it seems someone has used it again. What might be going on?

MACINTOSH AND LINUX BOOT PROCESSES AND FILE SYSTEMS

After reading this chapter and completing the exercises, you will be able to:

♦ Understand Macintosh file structures

♦ Explore Macintosh boot tasks

♦ Examine UNIX and Linux disk structures

♦ Understand UNIX and Linux boot processes

♦ Examine CD data structures

♦ Understand other disk structures

In Chapter 7, you explored the Microsoft OSs, including DOS and Windows, and the Microsoft file systems. Because computer forensics investigators must understand how most OSs store and manage data, this chapter continues that exploration by examining the Linux and Macintosh OSs. Chapters 7 and 8 provide a foundation for you to build from as you become more knowledgeable about current and legacy OSs and their associated file systems. It's also critical for you to understand that you can use a different OS to forensically analyze another OS.

In addition to Linux and Macintosh OSs, this chapter discusses media and hardware such as CDs, IDE hard drives, SCSI hard drives, and the RAID configuration. These devices store data in particular ways, which you should understand so that you can retrieve evidence data as needed.

UNDERSTANDING THE MACINTOSH FILE STRUCTURE

The current Macintosh OS is Mac OS X version 10.3, known as Panther. Apple expects to release Tiger Mac OS X version 10.4 in 2005. Macintosh OS X is built on a core called Darwin, which consists of a **Berkeley Software Distribution (BSD) UNIX** application layer built on top of a Mach microkernel. This section primarily addresses older Macintosh OS 9 file systems. The Macintosh is a popular computer for schools and graphics professionals, and Apple's innovations continue to make it popular in the PC market. As a result, computer forensics investigators must be familiar with the Mac OS file and disk structure.

Macintosh uses the **Hierarchical File System (HFS)**, in which files are stored in directories, or folders, that can be nested in other folders. With Mac OS 8.1, Apple introduced the Mac OS **Extended Format (HFS+)**, which continues to be used with Mac OS X. The primary difference between HFS and HFS+ is that HFS was limited to 65,536 blocks per volume, and HFS+ raised this number to more than 4 billion. Consequently, HFS+ supports smaller file sizes on larger volumes, resulting in more efficient disk usage. Mac OS X also supports the Unix File System (UFS), which is not covered in this book. The **File Manager** utility handles reading, writing, and storing data to physical media. It also collects data to maintain the HFS and manipulates files, folders, and other items. The **Finder** is another Macintosh tool that works with the OS to keep track of files and maintain users' desktops.

In the older Mac OS, a file consists of two parts: a **data fork** and a **resource fork**. As shown in Figure 8-1, each fork contains the following information vital to each file:

- Resource map
- Resource header information for each file
- Window locations
- Icons

The data fork typically contains data that the user creates, such as text or spreadsheets. Applications, such as Microsoft Word or Excel also read and write to the data fork. When you are working with an application file, the resource fork contains additional information, such as the menu, dialog boxes, icons, executable code, and controls. In the Mac OS, the resource or data fork can be empty. Because File Manager is in charge of reading and writing to files, it can access both forks.

Understanding Volumes

A volume is any storage medium used to store files. A volume can be all or part of the storage media for hard disks; however, in the Mac OS, a volume on a floppy disk is always the entire floppy. With larger disks, the user or administrator defines a volume. Multiple clients can be on a volume, as shown in Figure 8-2.

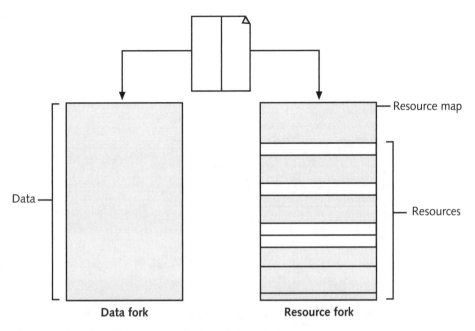

Figure 8-1   Mac OS resource fork and data fork

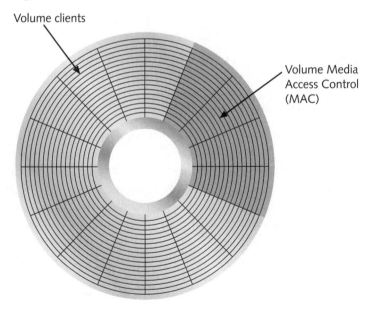

Figure 8-2   Multiple volumes on a disk

Volumes have **allocation blocks** and **logical blocks**. A logical block is a collection of data that cannot exceed 512 bytes. When you save a file, File Manager assigns the file to an allocation block, which is a group of consecutive logical blocks. On a floppy disk, an allocation block is usually one logical block. As the volumes increase in size, one allocation block might be composed of three or more logical blocks. Figure 8-3 illustrates the relationship between these two blocks.

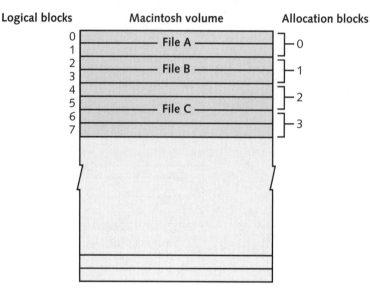

Figure 8-3 Logical and allocation block structures

File Manager can access a maximum of 65,535 allocation blocks per volume. If a file fork contains information, it always occupies one allocation block. For example, if a data fork only contains 11 bytes of data, it occupies one allocation block, or 512 bytes, on a floppy disk. That leaves more than 500 bytes empty in that fork.

The Macintosh file system has two descriptors for the end of file (EOF)—the **logical EOF** and the **physical EOF**. The logical EOF is the number of bytes that contain data. The physical EOF is the number of allocation blocks for that file, as shown in Figure 8-4.

Macintosh reduces file fragmentation by using **clumps**, which are groups of contiguous allocation blocks. As a file increases in size, it occupies more of the clump. By adding more clumps to larger files, volume fragmentation is kept to a minimum.

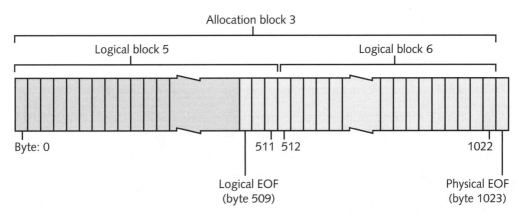

Figure 8-4   Logical EOF and physical EOF

EXPLORING MACINTOSH BOOT TASKS

Macintosh computers don't use the same type of BIOS firmware commonly found in PC-based systems. Instead, they use **Open Firmware**, which is a processor- and system-independent boot firmware (part of the boot ROM in most Power PC–based Macintosh systems). Open Firmware controls the microprocessor after hardware initialization and diagnostics are performed but before control is passed to the OS. It's responsible for building the device tree, probing for IO devices, and loading the OS kernel from the disk.

You must understand the Open Firmware process to be able to control boot device selection when booting a Macintosh system. This applies whether you are using a dedicated Macintosh forensics system to examine a suspect disk or are forced to boot a suspect system by using removable media.

For older Macintosh OSs, the first two logical blocks on each volume (or disk) are the boot blocks, which contain information about system startup. The startup block contains information about the system configuration. Optional executable code for the system file can also be placed within the boot blocks. Typically, system startup instructions are stored in the HFS system file, not the boot blocks.

Older Macintosh OSs use a **Master Directory Block (MDB)**, also known as a **Volume Information Block (VIB)**. All information about the volume is stored in the MDB and written to the MDB when the volume is first initialized. A copy of the MDB is also written to the next to last block on the volume. This copy is updated whenever the extents overflow file or the catalog increases in size. File Manager uses the **extents overflow file** to store any information not in the MDB or **Volume Control Block (VCB)**. The **catalog** is used to maintain relationships between files and directories on a volume. Whenever the system has to mount a volume, it creates a new VCB. When the volume is unmounted (no longer needed by the user), the VCB is removed. (See *http://developer.apple.com/techpubs/mac/ Files/Files-100.html* for more details.) The purpose of the copied MDB is to support disk utility functions. When the OS mounts the volume, some information from the MDB is written to a VCB, which is stored in system memory and used by File Manager.

A system application called **Volume Bitmap** tracks each block on a volume to determine which blocks are in use and which ones are available to receive data. Volume Bitmap has information about the blocks' usage but not about their content.

File Manager stores file-mapping information in two locations: the extents overflow file and the file's catalog entry. Volume Bitmap's size depends on the amount of allocated blocks for the volume.

The Mac OS 9 file system uses a B*-tree file system for File Manager. **B*-tree** organizes the directory hierarchy and file block mapping for File Manager. In the B*-tree, files are nodes (records or objects) containing file data. Each node is 512 bytes long. The nodes that contain actual file data are called **leaf nodes**; they are the bottom level of a B*-tree file and store data for individual files. The B*-tree also has the following nodes that handle file information:

- The **header node** stores information about the B*-tree file.
- The **index node** stores link information to the previous node and the next node.
- The **map node** stores a node descriptor and a map record.

Using Macintosh Forensic Software

Macintosh has maintained its hold on a specific share of the market, so depending on your corporation, you may or may not run across this OS in your investigations. It's a good idea to be familiar with the software available for Macintosh or have someone in your networking arsenal who is.

For Mac OSs earlier than Mac OS X, you have a couple of tools to choose from. Expert Witness, originally from ASRData and now owned by Guidance Software, was developed specifically for the Macintosh. Black Bag Technologies (*www.blackbagtech.com*) has developed forensic software for the Macintosh in recent years. It deals specifically with the files that Macintosh hides from the user. One of the features, PhantomSearch, looks only for hidden files that experienced users can utilize to hide information.

For Mac OS X and later, almost any forensics tool that can be used with a UNIX or Linux computer can be used to examine a Macintosh volume. As mentioned earlier, you simply need to be aware of the differences, compared to a PC's boot process.

Examining UNIX and Linux Disk Structures

In addition to Windows and Macintosh OSs, contemporary computers and networks use UNIX and Linux. Many flavors of UNIX are on the market, including System V variants, such as System 7, SGI IRIX, Sun Solaris, IBM AIX, and HP-UX, as well as BSD variants, such as FreeBSD, OpenBSD, and NetBSD. Linux is also available in many distributions, such as Caldera, Red Hat, SuSe, Mandrake, and Debian. All Linux references in this text are to Red Hat Linux/Fedora because of its popularity and ease of use. Linux is probably the most consistent UNIX-like OS available today because the Linux kernel is regulated under the **GNU General Public License (GPL)** agreement. The GPL states that anyone may use, modify, and redistribute software developed under the GPL. It furthermore stipulates that software distributed under the GPL must have its source code made publicly available, and that any works derived from GPL code must also be licensed under the GPL. BSD variations are released under the BSD license, which is similar to the GPL but makes no requirements on those who produce derivative works, save that the original copyright remain attached.

GPL and BSD variations are examples of open-source software. Open-source software is enjoying wide popularity because it's freely available, can be modified to suit the user's needs, and has a reputation for stability and security. This renowned stability and security derives from the software's open-source nature. Because anyone can view the source code and make revisions and contributions, bugs are found and fixed quickly. It does, however, require a higher level of skill from users.

Table 8-1 lists several system files from popular UNIX OSs. They are some of the files you need to examine when dealing with a UNIX or Linux partition. These files can yield information about users and some of their activity.

Table 8-1   UNIX System Files

OS	System Files	Purpose
AIX	/etc/exports	Configuration file
	/etc/filesystems	File system table of devices and mount points
	/etc/utmp	Current user's logon information
	/var/adm/wtmp /etc/security/lastlog	Logon and logoff history information User's last logon information
	/var/adm/sulog	Substitute user attempt information
	/etc/group	Group memberships for the local system
	/var/log/syslog	System messages log
	/etc/security/passwd	Master password file for the local system
	/etc/security/ failedlogin	Failed logon attempt information
HP-UX	/etc/utmp /etc/utmpx	Current user's logon information
	/var/adm/wtmp /var/adm/wtmpx	Logon and logoff history informationLogon and logoff history information
	/var/adm/btmp	Failed logon attempt information
	/etc/fstab	File system table of devices and mount points
	/etc/checklist	File system table information (version 9.x)
	/etc/exports	Configuration files
	/etc/passwd	Master password file for the local system
	/etc/group	Group memberships for the local system
	/var/adm/syslog.log	System messages log

Table 8-1   UNIX System Files (continued)

OS	System Files	Purpose
	Syslog	System log files
	/var/adm/sulog	Substitute user attempt information
IRIX	/var/adm/syslog	System log files
	/etc/exports	Configuration files
	/etc/fstab	File system table of devices and mount points
	/var/adm/btmp	Failed logon information
	/var/adm/lastlog /var/adm/wtmp /var/adm/wtmpx	User's last logon information Logon and logoff history information Logon and logoff history information
	/var/adm/sulog	Substitute user attempt information
	/etc/shadow	Master password file for the local system
	/etc/group	Group memberships for the local system
	/var/adm/utmp /var/adm/utmpx	Current user's logon information
Linux	/etc/exports	Configuration files
	/etc/fstab	File system table of devices and mount points
	/var/log/lastlog /var/log/wtmp	User's last logon Logon and logoff history information
	/var/run/utmp	Current user's logon information
	/var/log/messages	System messages log
	/etc/shadow	Master password file for the local system
	/etc/group	Group memberships for the local system
Solaris	/etc/passwd	Account information for local system
	/etc/group	Group information for local system
	/var/adm/sulog	Switch user log data
	/var/adm/utmp	Logon information
	/var/adm/wtmp /var/adm/wtmpx /var/adm/lastlog	Logon history information
	/var/adm/loginlog	Failed logon information
	/var/adm/messages	System log files
	/etc/vfstab	Static file system information
	/etc/dfs/dfstab /etc/vfstab	Configuration files

In the following steps, you use standard Linux commands to find information about your Linux system:

1. Start your Linux computer and open a terminal window, if necessary. If your computer starts at a graphical desktop, click the **Red Hat or Fedora** icon on your desktop, point to **System Tools**, and then click **Terminal**.

2. To find the name of your computer and the Linux kernel revision number it uses, type **uname –a** and press **Enter**. Record or capture a screen image of the results.

TIP

To capture a screen image in Linux, use the GIMP graphics program. In Linux Red Hat 9, click the Red Hat icon on the desktop, point to Graphics, and then click The GIMP. Close all windows and palettes except the main GIMP window, if necessary. Click File on the menu bar, point to Acquire, and then click Screen Shot. Click the Single Window option button, if necessary, to capture a window, and then click OK. Click the window you want to capture. To save the image, right-click the captured image, point to File, and then click Save As.

3. Type **ls –l** and then press **Enter** to list the files in the current directory. Write down the name of one file in the directory.

4. To determine the access time of a file (the last time a command was executed on the file), type **ls –ul** *filename* (*filename* is the name of the file you wrote down in Step 3), and then press **Enter**. Record or capture a screen image of the results.

5. Type **netstat –s** at the Linux command prompt, and then press **Enter** to see a list of protocol information your computer uses to communicate with other systems connected to your Linux computer.

The standard Linux file system is called the **Second Extended File System (Ext2fs)**, which can support disks as large as 4 TB and files as large as 2 GB. Ext3fs is a journaling version of Ext2fs that reduces file recovery time after a crash. Of the file structures you have studied so far, Linux is most closely related to Macintosh. (The most recent versions of Mac OS are built on BSD UNIX.) Linux, however, is unique in that it uses **inodes**, or information nodes, that contain descriptive information about each file or directory. (See "Understanding Inodes," later in this chapter, for more in-depth information.) Specifically, an inode is a pointer to other inodes or blocks. When the last pointer to a file is deleted, the file is effectively deleted. Instead of copying a file to every directory in which it is listed, by using inodes, Linux can store the file in one location and create pointers to that file in other locations, as shown in Figure 8-5. For example, suppose you need to access the MyDatabase file when you're working in the Clients, Accounting, and General_Documents directories. Instead of making individual copies of MyDatabase in each directory, you create the file once in one directory, and then create pointers to MyDatabase from the other two directories. The data blocks shown in this figure are discussed in the following paragraphs.

Each inode keeps an internal link count. When that number becomes 0, Linux deletes the file. To find deleted files during a forensic investigation, you search for inodes that contain some data and have a link count of 0.

The Linux file structure is made up of meta-data and data. Meta-data includes items such as the user ID (UID), group ID (GID), size, and permissions for each file. An inode contains the modification, access, and creation (MAC) times, not a file name. Inodes have a number

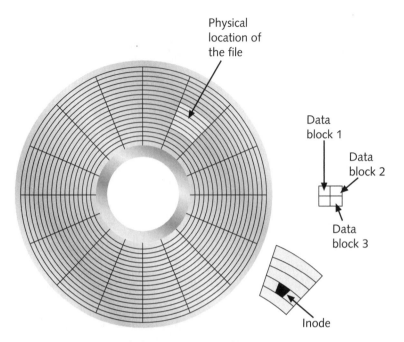

Figure 8-5   Using inodes to represent files

that's linked with the file name in the directory called *file_name*. To keep track of files and data, Linux pairs the inode number with the file name. The data portion of the Linux file structure contains the file's contents.

UNIX and Linux Overview

In UNIX and Linux, everything is a file, including disk drives, the monitor for a workstation, any connected tape drives, a network interface, system memory, directories, and actual files. All UNIX files are defined as objects, which means that a file, like an object in an object-oriented programming language, has properties and methods (actions such as writing, deleting, and reading) that can be performed on the file.

UNIX consists of four components that define the file system: boot block, superblock, inode, and data block. A block is a disk allocation unit that ranges from 512 bytes and up. The bootstrap code is located in the boot block. A UNIX or Linux computer has only one boot block, which is located on the main hard disk. The superblock contains vital information about the system and is considered part of the meta-data. The superblock indicates the disk geometry, available space, and the location of the first inode and keeps track of all the inodes. Linux keeps multiple copies of the superblock in various locations on the disk to prevent losing such vital information.

The superblock manages the UNIX or Linux file system, including configuration information about the file system, such as the block size for the disk drive, file system names, blocks reserved for the inodes, free inode list, free block starting chain, volume name, and inodes for last update time and backup time.

Inode blocks are the first data after the superblock on a UNIX or Linux file system. An inode is assigned to every file allocation unit. As files or directories are created or deleted, inodes are also created or deleted. The link between the inodes associated with files and directories controls access to those files or directories.

The final component in the UNIX and Linux file system is a **data block**, which is where directories and files are stored on a disk drive. This location is directly linked to the inodes. As in Microsoft file system structures, the Linux file system on a PC has 512-byte sectors. Typically, a data block consists of 4096 or 8192 bytes with clusters of hard disk sectors. Figure 8-6 shows that when you save a file, the data blocks are clustered and a unique inode is assigned.

8

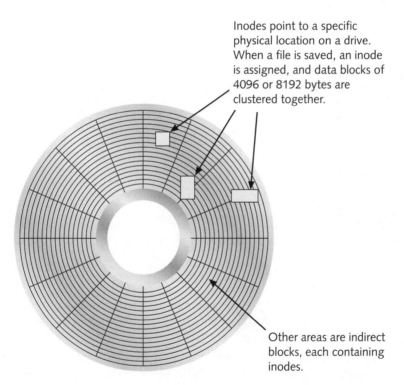

Inodes point to a specific physical location on a drive. When a file is saved, an inode is assigned, and data blocks of 4096 or 8192 bytes are clustered together.

Other areas are indirect blocks, each containing inodes.

Figure 8-6   Clustering sectors and blocks to save a file in Linux

As with other OSs, the size of a data block determines how much of the disk space is wasted. The larger the data block, the higher the likelihood of fragments. If you create a 512 KB database, 19 data blocks of 8192 bytes are clustered to save the file, and 3648 bytes are left empty but allocated. In addition to keeping track of the file size, the inode keeps track of the number of blocks assigned to the file.

When manufactured, all disks have more storage capacity than the manufacturer states. For example, a 20 GB disk might actually have 20.5 GB of free space because disks always have bad sectors despite the most careful procedures. DOS and Windows don't keep track of bad sectors, but Linux does in an inode called the **bad block inode**. The root inode is inode 2, and the bad block inode is inode 1. Some forensic tools ignore inode 1 and fail to recover valuable data for cases. Someone trying to mislead a computer forensics investigation can access the bad block inode in Linux and list good sectors in it, and then hide information in these supposedly "bad" sectors.

To find the bad blocks on your Linux computer, you can use the `badblocks` command, although you must log on with a system administrator account to do so. Linux also includes two other commands that provide bad block information—the `mke2fs` and `E2fsck/` commands. The `badblocks` command can destroy valuable data when you run it, but the `mke2fs` and `e2fsck` commands include safeguards that prevent them from overwriting important information.

In the following steps, you check a floppy disk for bad blocks. You need a blank floppy disk or one containing data you no longer need.

1. Boot your Linux computer to a graphical desktop. Insert a floppy disk in the floppy drive, but don't mount it. If your system is set to mount disks automatically, click the **Red Hat** icon on your desktop, point to **System Tools**, and then click **Disk Management**. Make sure the floppy drive is selected, and then click the **Unmount** button.

2. To open a terminal window, click the **Red Hat** icon on your desktop, point to **System Tools**, and then click **Terminal**.

3. To perform this step and the next one, you need /sbin in your path, or you need to be in that directory. At the command prompt, type **mke2fs -c /dev/fd0** and press **Enter**. Note that /dev/fd0 specifies the location of the first floppy drive on the system. If you're using a different floppy drive, such as fd1, use that location instead. Linux reads and displays disk information, including any bad blocks. After the command prompt appears, record or capture a screen image of the results. (*Note*: Depending on your current location, you might need to type **./mke2fs –c /dev/fd0** and make a similar correction in Step 4).

4. To compare the results of the `mke2fs` and `e2fsck` commands, type **e2fsck –c /dev/fd0** and press **Enter**. (Replace "fd0" with your floppy drive, if necessary.) Linux again reads and displays disk information, including any bad blocks. After the command prompt appears, record or capture a screen image of the results.

5. To find information about the `badblocks` command, type **man badblocks** and then press **Enter**. The first manual page for the `badblocks` command is displayed. Press **Page Down** to see additional pages. Record or capture a screen image of each page.

You can display information about files and directories by using the Linux ls (list) command. The ls command has options for determining the type of information to display. Figure 8-7 shows some of the information you can display with the ls command and the -l option, which you type as ls -l.

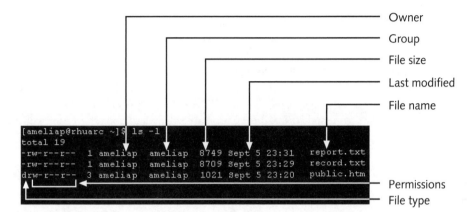

Figure 8-7   Information about an inode

In the following steps, you use the ls command and some of its options. You need to use a computer with Red Hat or Fedora Linux installed.

1. Start your Linux computer and open a terminal window, if necessary. If your computer starts at a graphical desktop, click the **Red Hat** icon on your desktop, point to **System Tools**, and then click **Terminal**.

2. Navigate to your home directory, if necessary. For example, type **cd /home/*username*** (*username* is the name of your home directory). Be sure to insert a space after the cd command. Then press **Enter**.

3. At the command prompt, type **ls –A** and press **Enter**. (Be sure to insert a space after the ls command.) The ls command with the -A option lists all files, including hidden ones, but not the current or parent directories. Write down the files and directories listed.

4. At the command prompt, type **ls –a** and press **Enter**. Linux commands are case sensitive, so the ls command with the -a option lists all files, including hidden ones and their parent and current directories. Record the results and compare them to the results from Step 3.

5. To find the inode number for the files in the current directory, type **ls –i** and press **Enter**. What do you notice about the numbering scheme? Record the results. (*Note*: If you're using a fresh install that has not been used previously, this step might not produce any results.)

6. To find detailed information about the files in the current directory, including size, permission, and modification time, type **ls –l** and press **Enter**. Record the results, and write down the differences and similarities you observed for these commands.

To provide more information about a file or directory, UNIX and Linux file systems implement a **continuation inode**, which has more room for higher-level features for files and directories. The continuation inode for a file or directory contains information such as the mode and file type, the quantity of links in the file or directory, the file's or directory's access control list (ACL), the least and most significant bytes of the ACL UID and GID, and the file or directory status flag. The status flag field of an inode contains unique information about how Linux handles a file or directory. It's a bit containing information that defines permissions, usually expressed in octal format. Table 8-2 describes the code values.

Table 8-2   Code Values for an Inode

Code Values	Description
4000	UID on execution—set
2000	GID on execution—set
1000	Sticky bit—set
0400	Read by owner—allowed
0200	Write by owner—allowed
0100	Execution/search by owner—allowed
0040	Read by group—allowed
0020	Write by group—allowed
0010	Execution/search by group—allowed
0004	Read by others—allowed
0002	Write by others—allowed
0001	Execution/search by others—allowed

Understanding Inodes

Inodes provide a mechanism for linking data stored in data blocks. A block is the smallest amount of data that can be allocated in a UNIX or Linux file system. The size of the block depends on how the disk volume was initiated. Block sizes can range from 512 bytes and up. Many Linux implementations assign 1024 bytes per block.

The Linux Ext2fs and Ext3fs file systems are improvements over the original Ext file system from the first Linux release. One significant improvement in Ext3fs is that it adds linking information to each inode. In Ext3fs, if one inode becomes corrupt, data can be recovered more easily than in Ext2fs. In Ext3fs, each inode has additional information that links the other inodes in a chain of inodes.

When a file or directory is created on a UNIX or Linux file system, an inode is assigned. An assigned inode contains the following information about a file or directory:

- The mode and type of the file or directory
- The number of links to a file or directory
- The UID and GID of the file's or directory's owner
- The number of bytes contained in the file or directory
- The file's or directory's last access time and last modified time
- The inode's last file status change time
- The block address for the file data
- The indirect, double-indirect, and the triple-indirect block addresses for the file data
- Current usage status of the inode
- The number of actual blocks assigned to a file
- File generation number and version number
- The continuation inodes link

This first inode has 13 pointers. Pointers 1 through 10 link directly to data storage blocks in the disk's data block area. Each pointer contains a block address indicating where data is stored on the disk. These pointers are direct pointers because each pointer is associated with one block of data storage.

As a file grows, the OS provides up to three layers of additional inode pointers. The pointers in the first layer or group are called **indirect pointers**. The pointers in the second layer are called **double-indirect pointers**, and the pointers in the last or third layer are called **triple-indirect pointers**.

To expand storage allocation, the OS initiates the original inode's 11th pointer, which links to 128 pointers inodes. Each of these pointers links directly to 128 individual blocks located in the data block area of the disk drive. If all 10 pointers in the original inode are consumed with file data, the 11th pointer links to another 128 pointers. The first pointer in this indirect group of inodes points to the 11th block. The last block of these 128 inodes is block 138.

NOTE

The term "indirect inodes" refers to the 11th pointer in the originating inode, which points to another group of inode pointers. That is, it's indirectly linked to the original inode.

If more storage is needed, the 12th pointer position of the original inode is used to link another 128 inode pointers. From each of these 128 pointers, another 128 pointers are created. This second level of inode pointers are then linked directly to blocks in the data block area of a disk drive. The first block pointed to for this double-indirect pointer is block 139.

If more storage is needed, the 13th pointer links to 128 pointer inodes, each of which points to another 128 pointers; and each second layer of pointers points to a third layer of 128 pointers. At this triple-indirect pointer level, data storage blocks are linked. Figure 8-8 shows how data is linked with inodes in a Linux file system.

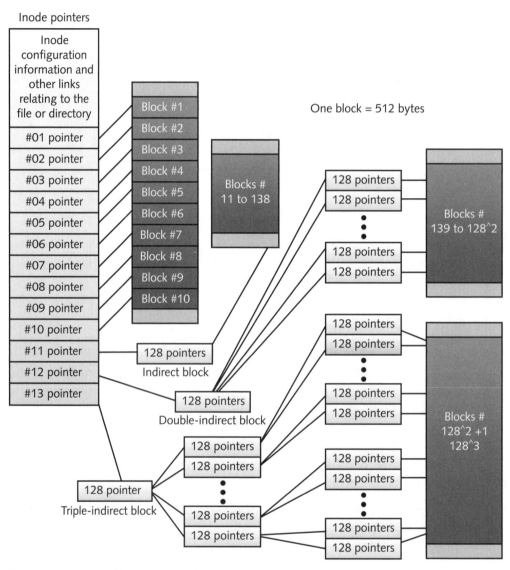

Figure 8-8   Linux file system inode pointers

To work with files and directories, you work at the Linux command line using a particular shell, which is a command-line interpreter that provides an interface for entering commands and viewing their results. Table 8-3 lists useful commands for most UNIX and Linux shells, including switches that are unique to a UNIX version.

TIP

For more information on UNIX and Linux commands and their options, use the `man` command, which displays pages from the online manual. For example, to learn more about the `ls` command, type `man ls` at the Linux command prompt.

Table 8-3   UNIX and Linux Shell Commands

Shell Command	Associated Switches	Purpose
cat *file* more *file*		Displays the contents of a file (similar to the MS-DOS Type command)
dd	Refer to man pages for available switches	Copies a disk drive by blocks, which is the same as creating a bit-stream copy of a disk drive
df bdf (HP-UX)	-k (Solaris)	Displays partition information for local or NFS mounted partitions
find	Refer to man pages for available switches	Locates files matching a specific attribute, such as name, last modification time, or owner
netstat	-a	Identifies other systems that are connected via the network to a UNIX or Linux system
ps	ax (BSD) -ef (Sys V)	Displays the status of OS processes
uname	-a	Displays the name of the system

8

UNDERSTANDING UNIX AND LINUX BOOT PROCESSES

As a computer forensics investigator, you'll probably need to acquire digital evidence from a UNIX or Linux system that can't be shut down, such as a Web server or file server, so you must understand the boot processes for UNIX and Linux to identify potential problems. When you turn on the power to a UNIX workstation, instruction code located in firmware on the system's CPU loads into RAM. This firmware is called memory-resident code because it's located in ROM.

As soon as the memory-resident code is loaded into RAM, the instruction code checks the hardware. Typically, the code first tests all components, such as RAM chips, to verify that they are available and capable of running. Then it probes the bus, looking for a device containing the boot program, such as a hard disk, floppy disk, or CD. When it locates the boot device, it starts reading the boot program into memory. The boot program, in turn, reads the kernel into memory. When the kernel is loaded, the boot program transfers control of the boot process to the kernel.

The first task of the kernel is to identify all devices. It then configures the identified devices and starts the system and associated processes. After the kernel becomes operational, the system is usually booted to single-user mode, in which only one user can log on. Single-user mode is usually an optional feature that allows users to access other modes, such as maintenance mode. If a user bypasses single-user mode, the kernel runs system startup scripts that are specific to the workstation and then runs in multiuser mode. Users can then log on to the workstation.

As the kernel finishes loading, it identifies the root directory, the system swap file, and dump files. It also sets the hostname and time zone, runs consistency checks on the file system, mounts all partitions, starts network service daemons, sets up the NIC, and establishes user and system accounting and quotas.

 Review the documentation of the UNIX system you're examining for more information on the boot process.

NOTE

Understanding Linux Loader and GRUB

Linux Loader (LILO) is an older Linux utility that initiates the boot process, which usually runs from the disk's MBR. LILO is a boot manager that allows you to start Linux or other OSs, including Windows. If a system has two or more OSs located on different disk partitions, LILO can be set up to start any one of them. For example, you might have Windows 2000 on one partition and Linux on another. When you turn on the computer, LILO displays a list of available OSs and asks which one you want to load.

LILO uses a configuration file named Lilo.conf located in the /Etc directory. This file is a script containing the location of the boot device, the kernel image file (such as Vmlinux), and a delay timer that specifies how much time you have to select the OS you want to use.

Grand Unified Boot Loader (GRUB) is more powerful than LILO. It, too, resides in the MBR and enables you to load a variety of OSs. GRUB can load any kernel onto a partition with minimal headaches. Erich Boleyn created GRUB in 1995 to deal with multiboot processes and a variety of OSs. GRUB works from the command line or can be menu driven. For more details, see *www.gnu.org/software/grub/manual*.

UNIX and Linux Drives and Partition Schemes

UNIX and Linux view disk drives and their associated partitions in ways that are significantly different from MS-DOS and Windows. For example, in Windows XP, the primary master disk that contains the first boot partition is typically listed as the C: drive. In UNIX and Linux, disks and partitions within each disk are labeled as paths, with each path starting at the root (/) directory. For IDE disk drives, the primary master controller disk is defined as /dev/hda. The first partition on the primary master disk is defined as /dev/hda1; this device is equivalent to drive C: in Windows or MS-DOS. If other partitions are located on the primary master disk, their numbered values are incremented; for example, the second partition on the primary master disk is /dev/hda2. If a disk has a third partition, it is /dev/hda3, and so on.

Disk drives that are connected to the primary slave or secondary master or slave controller are defined as /dev/hdb. Any additional disk drives are incremented alphabetically. For example, if a third disk drive is mounted, it is listed as /dev/hdc, and so on.

If a SCSI controller is installed on a UNIX or Linux workstation, it has a designation similar to that of IDE disk drives and partitions. The first drive connected to the SCSI controller is identified as /dev/sda. The first partition for this drive is listed as /dev/sda1. Any additional partitions, such as a second partition, are incremented by one; for example, the second partition on a SCSI disk drive is /dev/sda2.

EXAMINING CD DATA STRUCTURES

CDs and DVDs have rapidly become the preferred way to store large amounts of data. Many people now use CD and DVD burners to transfer digital information from a hard disk to a CD or DVD. As a computer forensics investigator, you might need to retrieve evidence from CDs and DVDs; these optical media store information in a manner different from magnetic media. To create a CD, a laser burns flat areas (lands) on the top side of the CD (the side without the label). Lower areas not burned by the laser are called pits. The transitions from lands to pits have the binary value of 1, or on. Where there's no transition, the location has a binary value of 0, or off. Figure 8-9 illustrates the basic structure of a CD.

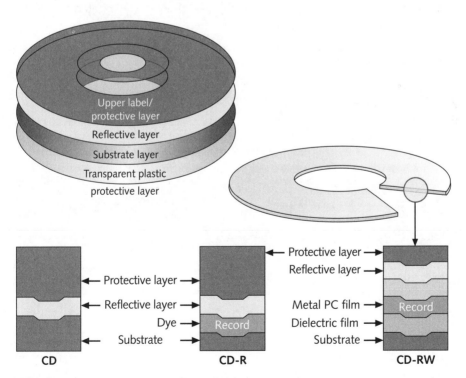

Figure 8-9   Physical makeup of a CD

The **International Organization of Standardization (ISO)** has established standards for CDs, including ISO 9660 for a CD, CD-R, and CD-RW and ISO 13346 for DVDs. ISO 9660 has an extension standard called Joliet, which allows for long file names under Microsoft Windows 9x, NT, 2000, and XP. Under ISO 13346 for DVDs, the Micro-UDF (M-UDF) function has been added to allow for long file names.

A variety of products have been developed to make CDs more versatile. The writeable CD-R has a dye layer substance that changes when a laser heats it. The heat from the dye causes a change in the CD's reflective ability. This change in reflectivity is what changes the values of 1s and 0s.

Rewriteable CD-RW disks use a medium that changes appearance depending on the temperature the laser applies. This medium is called a **phase change alloy** (also known as a Metal PC layer) that changes from **amorphic** (meaning noncrystalline) to crystalline. The amorphic condition is achieved when the laser heats the Metal PC layer to 600° Celsius. When the laser cools it to 200° Celsius, the Metal PC layer becomes crystalline. Each change either reflects or deflects light, which signals that a bit is set to 0 or 1.

On the surface of a CD, data is configured into three regions: the lead-in area, the program area, and the lead-out area. The lead-in area contains the table of contents in the subcode Q-channel. Subcode channels are additional data channels that provide start and end markers for tracks, time codes for each frame, the table of contents in the lead-in area, and graphic codes. Up to 99 tracks are available for the table of contents. The lead-in also synchronizes the CD as it's spinning.

The program area of the CD stores data. As with the lead-in area, up to 99 tracks are available for this area. The lead-out area is the end-of-CD marker for the storage area. Figure 8-10 shows a CD's logical layout.

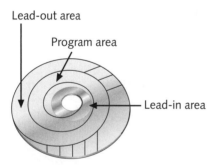

Figure 8-10   Logical layout of a CD

A unit of storage on a CD is called a frame, which includes a synchronized pattern, a control and display symbol, and eight error correction symbols. Each frame contains 24 17-bit symbols, and frames are then combined into blocks that form a sector. A block on a CD is 2352 bytes for music CDs (also called CD-DAs) or 2048 bytes for data CDs. CD players that are slower than or equal to 12X use a **constant linear velocity (CLV)** method for reading discs, usually music CDs. Newer CD players that are 12X or faster read discs by using a **constant angular velocity (CAV)** system.

Unlike CDs, DVD disk file structures use a Universal Disk Format (UDF) called Micro-UDF (M-UDF). For backward compatibility, some DVDs have integrated ISO 9660 to allow for compatibility with current OSs.

UNDERSTANDING OTHER DISK STRUCTURES

This section covers media and hardware devices that you might encounter as part of an investigation, including SCSI disks, IDE/EIDE disks, and RAID configurations. Although some of these devices were popular in the early days of computing, they have been upgraded to deal with high-end or high-speed devices. You should be familiar with the purpose of each device, its basic operation, and the problems it poses during a forensic investigation.

Examining SCSI Disks

Small computer system interface (SCSI) is an input/output standard protocol device. SCSI allows a computer to access devices such as hard disk drives, tape drives, scanners, CD-ROM drives, and printers. Its original purpose was to provide a common bus communication device for all computer vendors. When Shugart Systems created SCSI in 1979, it was designed to work with many of the leading computer manufacturers. As SCSI evolved, it became a standard for PCs, Macintosh, and many UNIX workstations. Older Macintosh systems such as the Mac SE shipped with only a SCSI port.

When you examine and process evidence on a computer system, you need to inventory all connected devices to make sure you collect all possible magnetic media that can help you determine what you need to investigate. During this inventory, you should identify whether the computer uses a SCSI device. If so, determine whether it's an internal SCSI device, such as a hard disk drive, or an external device, such as a scanner or tape drive. If the computer is using external media devices, such as a tape drive with tapes, or removable disk drives, such as a Jaz drive, examine the content of these devices as part of your investigation. Determine whether you have the right SCSI card, cables, adapters, and terminators to examine a suspect's SCSI drive. You also need the correct software drivers that allow your OS to communicate with the SCSI device.

The **Advanced SCSI Programming Interface (ASPI)** provides several software drivers that allow communication between the OS and the SCSI component. Currently, Windows XP, 2000, Me, and 9x have integrated ASPI drivers, which make adding a SCSI card to a Windows workstation easy. The Windows 98 Config.sys file typically contains ASPI drivers that allow you to read a CD from an emergency boot disk or a Windows 98 startup disk. However, to access a SCSI device from MS-DOS, you must configure MS-DOS to install the correct SCSI driver. Most manuals or textbooks covering A+ certification from CompTIA contain information on how to do this.

When applying a SCSI device to your forensic workstation, you might have to change the port number on the hard disk, for example, to make sure duplicate port numbers aren't assigned to other devices. If you're using a SCSI UltraWide card, such as the Adaptec 29160, port 7 is usually reserved for the SCSI card itself. Verifying which ports are used for your SCSI system is a good practice to adopt.

One characteristic of a SCSI device is proper termination. A SCSI terminator is a resistor that's connected to the end of the SCSI cable or device. Newer SCSI devices typically use an integrated self-terminator. Some newer SCSI cards, such as the Adaptec 29160, self-correct and allow for access to a SCSI driver. It might, however, take several seconds for the device to adjust.

One problem with older SCSI disk drives is identifying which jumper group terminates and assigns a port number. Use Web search engines to find specification sheets that list this information for different types of SCSI drives.

Examining IDE/EIDE Devices

Most forensic disk examinations involve EIDE disk drives. You might, however, encounter the older IDE disk drive versions. When accessing these types of drives on your forensic workstation, you should know how the drives work.

All Advanced Technology Attachment (ATA) drives from ATA-33 through ATA-133 IDE and EIDE disk drives use the standard 40-pin ribbon or shielded cable. ATA-66, ATA-100, and ATA-133 can use the newer 40-pin/80-wire cable. These newer cables provide considerably faster data transfer rates.

If you're examining a pre-ATA-33 IDE disk drive, it might not work correctly or be accessible to your workstation, although PCs are usually backward compatible with older IDE drives. When you must access an older IDE disk drive, you might need to locate an older Pentium I or 486 PC and rely on your technical skills and those of other experts to investigate the disk.

For more information about ATA disk drive architecture and future developments, consult the Web pages of T13 (*www.t13.org*). T13, a committee of the International Committee for Information Technology Standards (*www.incits.org*), is the current authority on ATA standards.

The CMOS on current PCs uses logical block addressing (LBA) and enhanced cylinder, head, and sector (CHS) configurations. When you connect an ATA-33 or newer disk drive to a PC, the CMOS automatically identifies the proper setting of the disk, which is convenient when you're installing hard disks on your workstation. However, this automatic identification feature can pose problems during an investigation. If you need to make a duplicate copy of a pre-ATA-33 256 MB disk drive, for example, you need the CHS configuration for the drive. Suppose you have a spare 4.0 GB drive that you plan to use to store a copy of the 256 MB disk. When you connect the two drives and power on your workstation, you enter CMOS and manually set CMOS to match the same CHS as the 256 MB disk drive. When you restart your workstation and access CMOS, you find that the CHS you applied did not take effect. To solve this problem, use a disk-imaging tool such as NTI SafeBack, Columbia Data Products SnapCopy, or Guidance Software EnCase. These tools force the correct CHS configuration onto the target disk drive so that you can copy evidence data correctly.

Another solution is to obtain a 486 PC. The CMOS and BIOS used in the 486 don't automatically adjust the CHS of newer ATA disk drives, but do allow you to set the CHS manually. However, one disadvantage of using a 486 PC is that the IDE ATA controller doesn't recognize disk drives larger than 8.4 GB. If you need to manually configure the CHS of a disk drive larger than 8.4 GB, you can explore other alternatives. One solution is to acquire an Enhanced Industry Standard Architecture (EISA) card that's engineered to connect to an IEEE 1394 FireWire device. Several vendors make EIDE disk drive bays that connect to FireWire, and one vendor in Taiwan produces an EISA FireWire card.

Another option when you're using a 486 PC is to acquire an older ISA SCSI card and an A-Card IDE adapter card. A-Card, a Taiwan manufacturer, sells SCSI-to-IDE adapter cards for various SCSI models. A-Card sells one card designed for UltraWide SCSI that prevents any write accesses to the connected IDE disk drive. One of many good sources for A-Cards is Microland USA (*www.microlandusa.com*). For the adapter card that prevents data from being written on a disk, locate the model card AEC7720WP that's listed with a write-blocker feature. (Note that when you're searching for these products, enter the product number in a search engine, because some might not be listed on their main site.) With an EISA FireWire card, a FireWire-to-EIDE interface, or a SCSI card with an IDE A-Card adapter, you can manually change the CHS on any EIDE disk drive from a 486 PC.

Examining the IDE Host Protected Area

In 1998, T13 created a new standard for ATA disk drives (ATA or ATAPI-5 AT; ATAPI stands for Attachment with Packet Interface-5). This new standard provides a reserved and protected area of an IDE disk drive, which is out of view of the OS. This feature is called Protected Area Run Time Interface Extension Service (PARTIES). Many disk manufacturers also refer to it as Host Protected Area (HPA) in their documentation.

Service technicians use this protected area to store data created by diagnostic and restore programs. Using the protected area eliminates the need for a CD disaster recovery disk. Accessing the protected area might require a password and always requires special commands that can be run only from the computer's BIOS level. A disk partition utility such as Fdisk can't see a protected area of a disk because it's accessible only at the BIOS level, not the OS level.

One commercially available tool that creates and writes data to a protected area is Area 51 from StorageSoft, Inc. With Area 51, you can create a protected area with the ATA-4 specification. This protected area is referred to as a BIOS Engineering Extension Record (BEER) data structure. Another product called BIOS, XBIOS Direct Access Reporter

(BXDR) from Sanderson Forensics in England (*www.sandersonforensics.co.uk*) can count the sectors on a disk drive. This tool can also access the protected area of a disk drive.

Exploring Hidden Partitions

You can use disk-editing tools to disable disk partitions, which hides them from view of the OS. Disabling partitions can hide evidence that could be vital to your investigation. You can manually reinstate a hidden partition by correcting the modified bit settings in the disk partition table.

Because the hard disk you're investigating might have a hidden partition, use bit-streaming imaging tools that can access unpartitioned areas of a disk drive. This potential problem is covered in Chapter 10.

Understanding RAID

Redundant array of independent (formerly "inexpensive") **disks (RAID)** is a computer configuration involving two or more disks. Originally, RAID was developed as a data-redundancy measure to minimize data loss caused by a disk drive failure. As technology improved, RAID also provided larger data storage capabilities.

Several levels of RAID can be implemented through software or special hardware controllers. For Microsoft Windows XP, 2000, and NT servers and workstations, RAID 0 or 1 is available. For a high-end data-processing environment, RAID 5 is common and is often based in special RAID towers. These high-end RAID systems often have their own integrated controllers that connect to high-end servers or mainframes. These types of RAIDs provide redundancy and high-speed data access and can make many small disks appear as one very large disk drive.

Other variations of RAID besides 0, 1, and 5 are specific to their vendor or application.

TIP

RAID 0 provides rapid access and increased data storage (see Figure 8-11). In RAID 0, two or more disk drives become one large volume, so the computer views the disks as a single disk. The tracks of data on this mode of storage cross over to each drive. The logical addressing scheme makes it appear that each track of data is continuous throughout all disk drives. That is, if you have two disks configured as a RAID 0, track one starts on the first physical disk and continues to the second physical disk. When viewed from a booted OS such as Windows XP, the two disk drives appear as one large disk drive. The advantage of RAID 0 is speed and increased data storage capability. Its biggest disadvantage is lack of redundancy; if a disk fails, data is not continuously available.

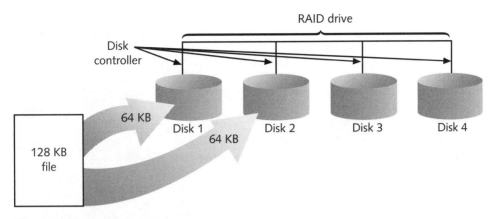

Figure 8-11   RAID 0: Striping

RAID 1 is made up of two disk drives for each volume and is designed for data recovery in the event of a disk drive failure. The content of the two disks in RAID 1 are identical. When data is written to a volume, the OS writes the data twice—once to each drive at the same time. If one drive fails, the OS switches to the other disk drive. Figure 8-12 shows a RAID 1 drive.

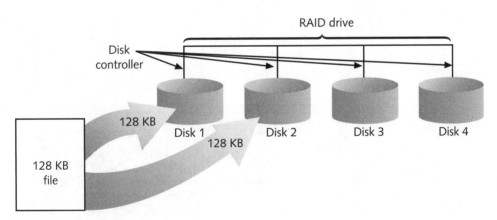

Figure 8-12   RAID 1

RAID 1 ensures that data is not lost and helps prevent computer downtime. The only disadvantage of RAID 1 is the extra cost of purchasing disk drives that support this type of RAID.

Like RAID 1, RAID 2 provides rapid access and increased data storage by configuring two or more disk drives as one large volume. The difference with RAID 2 is that data is written to disk on a bit level. An error-correcting code (ECC) is used to verify whether the write is successful. RAID 2, therefore, has better data integrity checking than RAID 0. Because of the bit-level writes and the ECC, however, RAID 2 is slower than RAID 0. Figure 8-13 shows a RAID 2 volume.

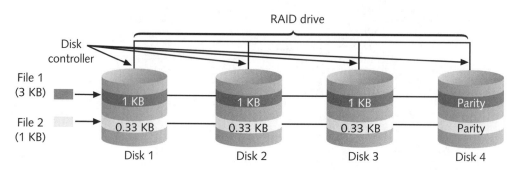

Figure 8-13   RAID 2: Striping (bit level)

RAID 3 uses data striping and dedicated parity and requires at least three disk drives. Similar to RAID 0, RAID 3 stripes tracks across all disk drives that make up one volume. RAID 3 also implements dedicated parity of the data. Dedicated parity provides recovery in the event of corrupt data. Dedicated parity is stored on one disk drive in the RAID 3 array of disk drives. RAID 4 uses data striping and dedicated parity (block writing) similarly to RAID 3, except data is written in blocks rather than bytes.

RAID 5 is similar to RAIDs 0 and 3 in that it uses distributed data and distributed parity and stripes data tracks across all disks within the RAID array. But unlike RAID 3, RAID 5 places parity recovery data on each drive. If a disk in a RAID array has a data failure, the parity on the other disk drives automatically rebuilds the corrupt data when the failed drive is replaced. Figure 8-14 shows RAID 5.

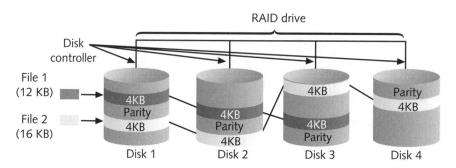

Figure 8-14   RAID 5: Block-level striping with distributed parity

In RAID 6, distributed data and distributed parity (double parity) function the same way as RAID 5, except it has redundant parity on each disk drive within the RAID array. The advantage of RAID 6 over RAID 5 is that it recovers any two disk drives that fail because of the additional parity stored on each disk.

RAID 10, or mirrored striping, is also known as RAID 1+0 and is a combination of RAID 1 and RAID 0. It provides fast access and redundancy of data storage. RAID 15, or mirrored striping with parity, is also known as RAID 1+5 and is a combination of RAID 1 and

RAID 5. It provides the most robust data recovery capability and speed of access of all RAID configurations and is also more costly.

Windows 2000, NT, and XP support RAID 0, 1, and 5. See *www.webopedia. com* for more details.

TIP

Investigating RAID Disks

When you examine a RAID computing system, you need extra storage to copy all the data. If you're attempting to create a bit-stream image of a large amount of data, such as a terabyte, try retrieving data in smaller chunks. In many instances, you might have to resort to **sparse recovery**, meaning you copy only the files or directories that the user in question has accessed in accordance with the charges or allegations against him or her.

You might not be able to create bit-stream image backups for very large RAID server configurations. In these special cases, consult with vendor engineers to determine how to best capture data from a RAID array. RTools and EnCase, for example, can retrieve data from RAID devices.

CHAPTER SUMMARY

- □ The Macintosh OS uses the Hierarchical File System (HFS), in which files are stored in folders that can be nested in other folders. The File Manager utility handles reading, writing, and storing data to physical media. It also collects data to maintain the HFS and is used to manipulate files, folders, and other items. The Finder utility works with the OS to keep track of files and maintain users' desktops.

- □ In the Mac OS, a file consists of two parts: a data fork and a resource fork. The resource fork contains a resource map and resource header information for each file, window locations, and icons. The data fork typically contains data the user creates, such as text or spreadsheets. Application programs also read and write to the data fork. When you're working with an application file, the resource fork contains additional information, such as the menu, dialog boxes, icons, executable code, and controls.

- □ A volume is any storage media used to store files. In the Mac OS, although a volume can be all or part of the storage media for hard disks, a volume on a floppy disk is always the entire floppy. For larger disks, the user or administrator defines a volume.

- □ Volumes have allocation blocks and logical blocks. A logical block is a collection of data that cannot exceed 512 bytes. An allocation block is a group of consecutive logical blocks. When you save a file, File Manager assigns the file to an allocation block. On a floppy disk, an allocation block is often one logical block. As volumes increase in size, one allocation block can be composed of three or more logical blocks.

8

❏ For older Macintosh OSs, the first two logical blocks on each volume (or disk) are the boot blocks, which contain information about system startup. The startup block contains information about system configuration. Optional executable code for the system file can also be placed within the boot blocks. Typically, system startup instructions are stored in the HFS system file rather than the boot blocks.

❏ The Linux Second Extended File System (Ext2fs) uses inodes. When the internal link count reaches 0, a file is considered to be deleted. The superblock on a Linux system keeps track of the geometry and available space on a disk, along with the list of inodes. Ext3fs is a journaling version of Ext2fs that reduces file recovery time after a crash.

❏ The Linux file structure is made up of meta-data and data. Meta-data includes items such as the user ID (UID), group ID (GID), size, and permissions for each file. An inode contains the modification/access/creation (MAC) times, not a file name. What they have instead is an inode number that is linked with the file name in the directory called *file_name*. Pairing of the inode number with the file name is how Linux keeps track of files and data. The data portion of the Linux file structure contains the contents of the file.

❏ CDs and DVDs are optical media used to store large amounts of data. They adhere to standards defined by ISO 9660 and ISO 13346, respectively. A unit of storage is called a frame, which contains 24 17-bit symbols.

❏ SCSI connectors are used for a variety of peripheral devices. They offer unique challenges to a forensic investigation, such as finding the correct device drivers and interfaces.

❏ IDE/EIDE drives are some of the physical drives you might run across in your investigations. You need to keep older drives in your lab in case you need to restore items from IDE drives.

❏ RAID is used to effectively store material that many people might need to access. It makes data recovery faster and more efficient.

Key Terms

Advanced SCSI Programming Interface (ASPI) — Provides several software drivers that allow for communication between the OS and the SCSI component.

allocation blocks — The number of logical blocks assembled in the Macintosh file system when a file is saved.

amorphic — A condition achieved when a laser heats the Metal PC layer to 600° Celsius.

bad block inode — In the Linux file system, the inode that tracks the bad sectors on a drive.

B*-tree — A file system used by the Mac OS that consists of nodes, which are objects, and leaf nodes, which contain data.

Berkeley Software Distribution (BSD) UNIX — A variation of UNIX created at the University of California, Berkeley.

catalog — An area the Macintosh file system uses to maintain the relationships between files and directories on a volume.

clump — In the Macintosh file system, a contiguous allocation block. Clumps are used to keep file fragmentation to a minimum.

constant angular velocity (CAV) — CD players that are 12X or faster use this system to read CDs.

constant linear velocity (CLV) — CD players slower than or equal to 12X use this method to read CDs.

continuation inode — Contains information such as the mode and file type, the quantity of links in the file or directory, the file's or directory's access control list (ACL), the least and most significant bytes of the ACL UID and GID, and the file or directory status flag.

data block — In the Linux file system, a cluster of hard disk sectors, normally 4096 or 8192 bytes.

data fork — The part of the Macintosh file structure that contains a file's actual data.

double-indirect pointers — The pointers in the second layer or group of an OS.

extents overflow file — Used by Macintosh File Manager when the list of a file's contiguous blocks becomes too long. The list's overflow is placed in the extents overflow file. Any file extents not in the MDB or VCB are contained here.

Extended Format (HFS+) — Used by Mac OS 8.1 and higher, the primary difference between HFS and HFS+ is that HFS was limited to 65,536 blocks per volume, and HFS+ raised this number to more than four billion. HFS+ supports smaller file sizes on larger volumes, resulting in more efficient disk usage.

File Manager — In the Macintosh file system, this utility handles reading, writing, and storing data to physical media. It also collects data to maintain the HFS and is used to manipulate files, folders, and volumes.

Finder — Works as part of the Macintosh OS to keep track of files and maintain the user's desktop.

GNU General Public License (GPL) — An agreement that defines Linux as open-source software, meaning that anyone can use, change, and distribute the software without owing royalties or licensing fees to another party.

header node — Stores information about the B*-tree file in the Macintosh file system.

Hierarchical File System (HFS) — The system the Mac OS uses to store files, consisting of folders and subfolders, which can be nested.

index node — Stores link information to the previous and next node in the Macintosh file system.

indirect pointers — The pointers in the first layer or group of an OS.

inode — A key part of the Linux file system that contains UIDs, GIDs, modification times, access times, creation times, and file locations.

International Organization of Standardization (ISO) — An organization set up by the United Nations to ensure compatibility in a variety of fields, including engineering, electricity, and computers. The acronym is the Greek word for equal.

leaf nodes — The bottom-level nodes of the B*-tree system that contain data in the Macintosh file system.

logical blocks — In the Macintosh file system, a collection of data that cannot exceed 512 bytes. They are assembled in allocation blocks to store files.

logical EOF — In the Macintosh file system, the number of bytes that contain data.

map node — Stores the node descriptor and a map record in the Macintosh file system.

Master Directory Block (MDB) — On older Macintosh systems, the location where all volume information is stored. A copy of the MDB is kept in the next-to-last block on the volume.

Open Firmware — The platform-independent boot firmware used on Macintosh systems to gather information, control devices, and load the OS.

phase change alloy — The Metal PC layer of a CD-RW that allows it to be written to several times.

physical EOF — In the Macintosh file system, the number of allocation blocks assigned to the file.

redundant array of independent disks (RAID) — A configuration of two or more hard drives with redundant storage features so that if one drive fails, the other drives can take over.

resource fork — The part of the Macintosh file system that contains the resource map, header information for the file, window locations, executable code, and icons.

Second Extended File System (Ext2fs) — The file system most used by Linux today.

small computer system interface (SCSI) — An input/output standard protocol device.

sparse recovery — Recovering data only from files accessed by the user because of large volumes.

triple-indirect pointers — The pointers in the third layer or group of an OS.

Volume Bitmap — A system application used to track blocks that are in use and blocks that are available.

Volume Control Block (VCB) — Contains information from the MDB and is used by File Manager in the Macintosh file system.

Volume Information Block (VIB) — Another name for the Master Directory Block. *See* Master Directory Block (MDB).

REVIEW QUESTIONS

1. The data fork of the older Macintosh systems contains executable code. True or False?

2. In the Macintosh file system, the entire floppy is a volume. True or False?

3. The physical EOF for a file is:

   a. where the file actually ends

   b. where the end of the allocation block is located

   c. either of the above

   d. neither of the above

4. The B*-tree file system is used by which Mac OS?

5. A General Public License Agreement allows you to:

   a. use software without paying anyone

   b. alter software without paying anyone

   c. sell software without paying anyone

   d. all of the above

6. Name two Linux file systems.

7. Linux keeps only one copy of the superblock. True or False?

8. What does the superblock in Linux define? (Choose all that apply.)

   a. file system names

   b. disk geometry

   c. location of the first inode

   d. available space

9. The bad block inode can be used to hide data. True or False?

10. The Linux OS provides up to _____ layers of direct and indirect pointers.

11. In Linux, _____ initiates the boot process.

12. CD-RWs use a changeable media called _____ .

13. Older Macintosh operating systems have only what type of port?

14. You might encounter problems when connecting an old IDE disk. True or False?

15. The Macintosh uses a(n) _____ , which consists of folders and subfolders.

16. On the older Macintosh systems, the two parts of a file are the _____ and the _____ .

17. On the Macintosh, a logical block is _____ bytes long.

18. Inodes in Linux are:

   a. folders

   b. file names

   c. pointers

   d. none of the above

19. The superblock is located on only one area of the drive. True or False?

20. ISO 9660 pertains to _____ .

HANDS-ON PROJECTS

Because you use forensics tools and other software in later chapters to analyze the contents of disks using a variety of OSs, the Hands-on Projects in this chapter provide opportunities for research and hands-on work.

Project 8-1

On the Internet, research how Macintosh keeps track of deleted files. Determine whether Mac OS can restore files even after the Trash has been emptied. Write a short report explaining how Mac OS handles deleted files. Specify which version of Mac OS you're discussing.

Project 8-2

Recall that you can use software tools such as Hex Workshop to view file headers and other critical parts of a file by analyzing the key hexadecimal codes the OS uses to identify and maintain the file system. For example, the hex code 07h in a file header indicates that the file was saved on an NTFS disk. Linux and UNIX use the Hexdump command to produce the hexadecimal representation of a file in much the same way Hex Workshop does. In this project, you use the hexdump command to find a file's hexadecimal value. To do the steps in this project, you need to work at a computer running Red Hat Linux.

1. Boot your Linux computer. Copy the student data files Hex_test.txt and Hexdump. format to the **/home/*username*/Chap08/Projects** folder (create this folder, if necessary) on your Linux computer.

2. Open a terminal window, if necessary. If your computer starts at a graphical desktop, click the **Red Hat** icon in the lower-left corner of the desktop, point to **System Tools**, and then click **Terminal**.

3. Use the cd command to change to the /Chap08/Projects directory. For example, if you stored the /Chap08/Projects folder in your home directory, and you're currently working in your home directory, type **cd /chap08/projects** and then press **Enter**.

4. Verify that the current directory contains the Hexdump.format and Hex_test.txt files. At the command prompt, type **ls** and then press **Enter**. If the list of files does not include Hexdump.format and Hex_test.txt, change to the appropriate directory.

5. To view the contents of the Hexdump.format file, type **cat hexdump.format** and press **Enter**.

6. To display the hexadecimal representation of the Hex_test.txt file, type **hexdump –f hexdump.format hex_test.txt** and press **Enter**. The hexadecimal representation of the Hex_test.txt file appears on the left of the screen, and explanatory text appears on the right. Record or capture a screen image of the results.

7. To display the hexadecimal information in a different format, type **xxd hex_test.txt** and press **Enter**. Record or capture a screen image of the results.

8. Use the online manual by typing **man hexdump** and pressing **Enter**. Note the options you can use with the hexdump command. Then press **q** to exit the manual pages and return to the command prompt. Close the terminal window.

9. On the Internet, use a search engine to find information on hexadecimal representation in Linux. Based on what you find, write a short report explaining why the results of the hexdump command are different from the results of the xxd command and why both representations are valid.

Project 8-3

On the Internet or in your library, research why Apple decided to change to the BSD UNIX format for its file structure. Write a one- to two-page paper outlining the reasons for the change and the pros and cons of this decision.

8

Project 8-4

On the Internet or in your library, research information available for computer forensics investigations on a RAID system. List the available software and write a short report describing the tasks the forensic software can perform.

Project 8-5

Several forensic vendors use the UNIX/Linux dd command to create bit-stream copies. In this project, you use this command on a Linux partition. To perform the steps in this project, you need to work at a Linux computer, such as one running Red Hat Linux. To research the Linux dd command, follow these steps:

1. At the Linux command prompt, type **man dd** and press **Enter**. Record or capture a screen image of the results. Close the terminal window, if necessary.

2. Access the Internet and find at least three ways of using the dd command.

3. Write a brief report explaining the following:

   □ The number and type of options for using the dd command

   □ The options you found on the Web that weren't listed when you used the man command

   □ New uses you discovered for the dd command

Project 8-6

Use the Internet to research how to install a SCSI hard disk on a Linux system. Write a one- to two-page procedure describing how to install a SCSI disk as the second disk on a Linux system. If possible, obtain a SCSI drive and apply what you discovered.

CASE PROJECTS

Case Project 8-1

You receive a computer system from the officer who tagged and bagged the evidence at a crime scene in a suspect's home. You examine the computer and discover that it uses a SCSI hard disk on a Windows system. How will you continue the investigation? Write a one- to two-page outline of your options for accessing a SCSI drive.

Case Project 8-2

Crestin Real Estate uses a four-disk RAID system. Each disk is 20 GB. Crestin Real Estate also uses a Linux server with two Macintosh computers connected to the server. Crestin asks you to investigate a case of possible fraud, in which someone logged on to the Crestin system using multiple user IDs. What are the obstacles to finding the information you need for this case? Write a one- to two-page outline listing the people you need to talk to at Crestin Real Estate and how you plan to proceed in the investigation.

Case Project 8-3

A user at a local ISP, which uses Linux servers exclusively, is sending e-mail messages with possible physical and sexual harassment content. The ISP contacted you to retrieve information about the case. What approach should you take for the case? Write a two-page report outlining the procedures you need to follow.

9

DATA ACQUISITION

**After reading this chapter and completing the
exercises, you will be able to:**

◆ Determine the best acquisition method

◆ Plan data-recovery contingencies

◆ Use MS-DOS acquisition tools

◆ Use GUI acquisition tools

◆ Use X-Ways Replica and other tools for data acquisition

◆ Recover data from PDAs

In this chapter, you learn how to acquire digital evidence from disk drives. Your goal when acquiring data is to preserve the digital evidence. You usually have only one chance to create a reliable copy of disk evidence with a data-acquisition tool. Although these tools are generally dependable, you should still take steps to make sure you obtain a verifiable bit-stream copy of the evidence. Because all software tools can fail, however, you must learn how to use other tools and methods besides your standard tools. In this chapter, you work with these data-acquisition tools: DriveSpy (an MS-DOS tool from Digital Intelligence), Forensic Toolkit (FTK) Explorer (a GUI tool from AccessData), and X-Ways Replica (X-Ways Software Technology AG). Other data-acquisition tools are described in the last section of this chapter. You can accomplish most digital evidence acquisitions for your investigations with a combination of the tools covered in this chapter.

DETERMINING THE BEST ACQUISITION METHOD

You can acquire digital evidence from disk drives in three ways: creating a bit-stream disk-to-image file, making a bit-stream disk-to-disk copy, or creating a sparse data copy of a folder or file.

Creating a bit-stream disk-to-image file is the most common data-acquisition method and offers the most flexibility for your investigation. Using this method, you can make one or many duplicate copies of a suspect's disk drive. In other words, you can replicate the original disk bit-for-bit on another disk. In addition to re-creating the original disk, you can use other forensic analysis tools, such as EnCase, FTK, SMART, Sleuth Kit, X-Ways Forensics, and iLook, to read the most common types of bit-stream image files you create. These programs read the image file as though it were the original disk, so you don't have to rebuild the bit-stream image file on a target disk drive. This feature saves you time and disk resources. Because some of these tools automatically adjust the target drive's geometry to match the original drive, you do not need an investigation disk that's identical to the original suspect disk.

In some cases, however, you can't make a bit-stream disk-to-image file because of hardware or software errors or incompatibilities. In these situations, you might have to create a disk-to-disk bit-stream image copy of the suspect's disk drive to acquire data. Although several bit-streaming programs can copy data exactly from one disk to another, only a few can adjust the target disk's geometry cylinder, head, and track configuration so that the copied data matches the original suspect drive. These disk-to-disk imaging tools include SafeBack, SnapCopy, and Norton Ghost 2002 or later. All these tools must run in MS-DOS. See the vendors' manuals for instructions on using these tools for bit-stream disk-to-disk copying.

When performing a bit-stream disk-to-disk copy of a suspect's disk drive, collecting evidence from a large disk drive can take several hours. If your time is limited, consider using the sparse data copy method, which lets you create exact copies of files or folders. Use this method only when you don't need to examine the entire disk drive, such as when you want to acquire a Microsoft Outlook Express PST or OST mail file or are working with a RAID server. If you have to recover data from a RAID server with several terabytes of data storage, the sparse method might be the only way you can acquire the evidence. Many data-recovery experts believe that the sparse data copy method will become the preferred method as data storage continues to grow.

To determine which data acquisition method to use for an investigation, consider the size of the source disk drive; whether you can retain the source disk drive as evidence or must return it to the owner, how much time you have for the data acquisition, and where the evidence is located.

If the source disk is very large, such as 200 GB or more, make sure you have a target disk that can store a bit-stream image file of the large disk. If you don't have a target disk of the right size, review alternatives for reducing the size of the data to create a verifiable copy of the suspect drive. Older Microsoft disk compression tools, such as DoubleSpace or DriveSpace, eliminate only slack disk space between files. Other compression methods use an **algorithm** to reduce file size. Data acquisition and compression tools use **lossless compression**, which does not discard data when it compresses files, or **lossy compression**, which can lose data but not perceptible quality when a file is restored. Both compression methods are discussed in more detail in Chapter 11. Many bit-stream imaging tools use lossless data compression to save disk space. The advantage of using lossless compression when making a bit-stream image file is that your target disk drive doesn't have to be as large as the suspect's disk drive. For example, suppose you need to make a bit-stream image of a Western Digital Drivezilla 120 GB suspect disk. By using the compression option available in several acquisition tools, you might be able to create the image on an 80 GB disk. On a typical target disk, you can compress files to reduce the size of the original disk by about 50%. However, if the suspect disk already contains compressed data, such as several large Zip files, the bit-stream image tool cannot compress the data any further.

For computer forensics data acquisition, using a lossless compression method is acceptable, but lossy compression is not. WinZip and PKZip are lossless compression tools and restore compressed data to its original form. That is, after you decompress data, these tools do not alter data when they reconstruct it. If you run an MD5 hash on a file before and after you compress it with WinZip, both versions have the same MD5 hash value. However, if the compressed file becomes corrupt because of a hardware or software error, the MD5 hash value is different. When you compress data, you should run a Cyclic Redundancy Check (CRC-32), an MD5, or an SHA-1 or better hash on the original data to compare the decompressed output to the compressed image file and make sure the data hasn't changed. As an added precaution to ensure that no changes to the data have occurred, perform two separate hashes on the evidence with different algorithms. For example, obtain an MD5 *and* an SHA-1 hash. This procedure isn't mandatory; however, it's a good precaution to establish that nothing has changed during the processing of data.

Therefore, when working with large disks, consider using a data acquisition tool that can compress the original drive into a bit-stream image file, such as EnCase or SafeBack. You could also use a DLT or Super-DLT (SDLT) tape drive to save large volumes of data quickly.

If you cannot retain the original evidence disk drive and must return it to the owner, as in a discovery demand for a civil litigation, determine how to acquire the data as quickly and reliably as possible. Make sure you have a good copy because most discovery demands provide only one chance to capture data. Use a forensics tool you know is reliable.

If you can't take a computer off-line for several hours, determine the best way to copy the evidence drive as quickly as possible, whether by creating an image of the entire drive or by using the sparse data copy method. You might also need to develop or rely on your personal negotiation skills to persuade a hostile party to give you more time to copy a drive. The better negotiator you are, the better your chances of obtaining a good image copy of the evidence.

9

Planning Data Recovery Contingencies

Because you're working with electronic data, you need to take precautions to protect your bit-stream digital evidence. You should also make contingency plans in case software or hardware doesn't work or you encounter a failure during an acquisition. The most common and time-consuming technique for preserving evidence is creating a duplicate copy of your evidence image file. Many computer investigators do not make duplicate copies of their evidence because they don't have enough time or resources to make a second bit-stream image copy of the evidence. However, if the first copy of your evidence doesn't work correctly, having a duplicate is worth the effort and resources. Be sure you take whatever steps are necessary to minimize the risk of failure in your investigation.

As a standard practice, make at least two bit-stream image copies of the digital evidence you collect. If you have more than one bit-streaming tool, such as EnCase and SafeBack, use both to obtain the two copies. If you have only one tool, such as DriveSpy, consider making one copy using the disk-to-disk method and another copy using the disk-to-image file method. The more critical the investigation is, the more you need two copies of the evidence. Remember that Murphy's Law applies to computer forensics, too: If anything can go wrong, it will.

Many acquisition tools do not copy data residing in a host protected area of a disk drive. (Refer to Chapter 8 for a discussion of host protected areas.) For these situations, consider using a hardware acquisition tool that can access the drive at the BIOS level, such as Image MaSSter Solo, which can copy the host protected area of a disk drive.

Another area of concern is the environment where the evidence is located. In Chapter 5, you learned to consider possible hazardous materials (HAZMAT) risks or threats when processing an incident or crime scene. In addition to addressing HAZMAT concerns, answer the following questions:

- Does the evidence location have adequate electrical power?
- Is there enough light at the evidence location, or do you have to bring floodlights, flashlights, or other kinds of lighting?
- Is the temperature of the evidence location too warm, too cold, or too humid?

Using MS-DOS Acquisition Tools

The original software tools developed for computing investigations and forensics were created for MS-DOS. Many of these tools are still commercially available and are easy to use. Because they fit on a forensic boot floppy disk, they require fewer resources to make a bit-stream disk-to-image file or disk-to-disk copy of the evidence. Computer forensics examiners should know how to use DOS tools, such as DriveSpy and its commands. This section focuses on DriveSpy, although other DOS data-acquisition tools are similar.

DriveSpy has two types of commands that enable you to save digital evidence from a source disk and write to a target disk: data-preservation commands and data-manipulation commands. Each type has special applications for acquiring and re-creating digital evidence. Before you learn more about DriveSpy data-acquisition commands, you should understand how DriveSpy refers to and accesses sector ranges.

Understanding How DriveSpy Accesses Sector Ranges

DriveSpy provides two methods of accessing disk sectors. The first method defines the absolute starting sector followed by a comma and the total number of sectors to read on a drive. For example, if the starting sector is 1000 on the primary master drive (drive 0) of the computer and you want to copy the next 100 sectors, DriveSpy uses the following format:

```
0:1000,100
```

When you specify that you want to copy sectors `0:1000,100`, DriveSpy copies from absolute sector 1000 to absolute sector 1099 because sector 1000 is the first sector, and sector 1099 is 100 sectors after that. DriveSpy uses this format for designating disk sectors with the CopySect, WriteSect, SaveSect, and Wipe commands, which are explored later in this chapter. The CopySect, WriteSect, and SaveSect commands work similarly to the UNIX or Linux dd command.

The second way of specifying sectors is to list the absolute starting and ending sectors. Note that an **absolute sector** starts at the beginning of a disk; a **relative sector** starts at the beginning of the current partition. The concept is similar to absolute and relative cell referencing in a spreadsheet. To designate a start and end sector value, you include a hyphen between the sector values. For example, if the starting sector is 1000 on the primary master drive (drive 0) of the computer and you need to copy through absolute sector 1100 (the next 101 sectors), this is the format:

```
0:1000-1100
```

With some DriveSpy commands, you can direct data from a specified sector range to another sector, which can be on the same disk or a different disk. For example, if you're recovering data from a damaged part of a disk, you can transfer the data to a good part of the disk. To designate the target location, you list the drive number followed by a colon and the starting absolute sector number. For example, to copy data from absolute sectors 1000–1099 on the primary master drive to absolute sectors 2000–2099 on a secondary drive, use this CopySect command:

```
CopySect 0:1000,100 1:2000,100
```

If you're working in the DriveSpy Partition mode, the DriveSpy screen shows a logical sector number and an absolute sector number. Be sure to use the absolute sector number. In the following steps, you use DriveSpy to examine absolute and logical sectors. Use a Windows 98 computer, boot into DOS, and then follow these steps:

1. From the DOS command prompt, navigate to the **Tools** folder of your work folder.

2. At the command prompt, type **drivespy** and press **Enter** to start DriveSpy.

3. At the SYS prompt, type **d0** and press **Enter** to access your hard disk.

4. Note the numbers for the start and end sectors of the disk and select a number between them, such as 2344.

5. At the D0 prompt, type **sector 2344** and press **Enter**. A sector map appears, as shown in Figure 9-1.

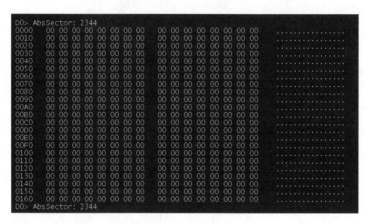

Figure 9-1 A sector map in Drive mode

6. Press **Esc** to return to the D0 prompt.

7. Type **p1** and press **Enter** to use Partition mode.

8. At the D0P1 prompt, type **sector 2344** and press **Enter**. (Replace 2344 with the sector number you used in Steps 4 and 5, if necessary.) A map of sector 2344 in Partition 1 appears, as shown in Figure 9-2.

DriveSpy displays a relative sector (RelSector) and an absolute sector (AbsSector).

NOTE

9. Press **Esc** to return to the D0P1 prompt, and then type **exit** and press **Enter** to exit DriveSpy.

Compare the sector numbers in the two figures. Notice that in Figure 9-1, the absolute sector is 2344; in Figure 9-2, the relative sector is 2344. Also note that the absolute sector in Figure 9-2 is not the same as the one in Figure 9-1.

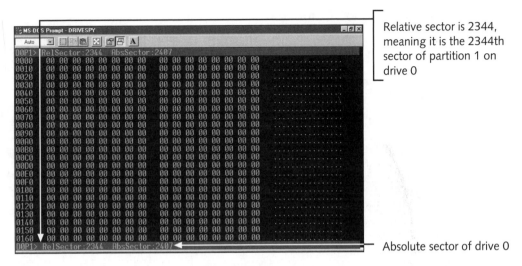

Relative sector is 2344, meaning it is the 2344th sector of partition 1 on drive 0

Absolute sector of drive 0

9

Figure 9-2   A sector map in Partition mode

Using DriveSpy Data-Preservation Commands

You can preserve and re-create digital evidence with the DriveSpy SavePart and WritePart commands. These two commands restore only FAT16 or FAT32 disk partitions. When restoring a FAT16 saved partition, use a partition utility such as FDisk to partition the target drive as a FAT16. For a FAT32 saved partition, use a partition utility to partition the target drive as a FAT32.

The SavePart command acquires an entire partition allocated on a disk, regardless of the file system. In other words, the SavePart command acquires an image of a non-DOS partition, such as an NTFS or a Linux partition. The WritePart command re-creates the saved partition file in its original form.

Restoring a non-DOS partition to a DOS partition re-creates the data, although the partition's format isn't exactly the same as the original non-DOS partition. The partition contains the data, but appears to be a DOS FAT file system partition that has unreadable file and directory structures.

NOTE

The CopySect command, used to copy an absolute sector range from one disk to another, is limited when trying to match source and target disks. To make an exact copy of a suspect's disk drive, you need a disk of the identical make, model, and size. CopySect does not adjust the geometry of the target disk drive to match the original source drive. Instead, use the SavePart and WritePart commands to duplicate partitions for FAT16 and FAT32 disks. For all other file systems, see "Using the SaveSect Command" and "Using the WriteSect Command" later in this chapter.

Using the SavePart Command

Use the SavePart command in DriveSpy's Partition mode to create an image file of a specified disk partition of a suspect's drive. For example, the following command sends an image of the current partition to the Chap09.img file in the Chap09\Chapter folder:

```
SavePart \Chap09\Chapter\Chap09.img
```

DriveSpy uses lossless data compression to reduce the size of the saved image file. It then saves every sector of the disk partition in the image file you specify. You can redirect the image file's output to another disk to preserve the image file. If the target disk for the image file is too small for the entire image, DriveSpy automatically requests another disk. For example, if you have a 40 GB suspect disk and two 20 GB target disks connected to your forensic workstation, you can use the SavePart command to write data to the first 20 GB disk. When space runs out on the first disk, DriveSpy asks for another disk. You can then specify the drive and folder path to redirect the image file output to the second 20 GB disk.

You can also use the SavePart command to save image data to removable media, such as a 2 GB Jaz disk. SavePart creates image volumes on removable disks, requesting additional disks as necessary. After saving a partition, DriveSpy generates an MD5 hash and stores it in the image file. When the image is restored, the MD5 hash is verified.

In the following steps, you use DriveSpy to save a partition. Normally, you use the SavePart command on a hard disk that has multiple partitions. However, because performing a SavePart command on a large partition can take several hours, in this exercise you examine your hard disk and save a partition from a floppy disk. You need a floppy disk that contains a few files to complete these steps. The following steps must be performed in Windows 98 DOS:

1. If necessary, create the **Chap09** folder in your work folder and the **Chapter** subfolder in the Chap09 folder. Then change to the **Chap09\Chapter** folder in your work folder and run **Toolpath.bat**.

2. At the command prompt, type **drivespy** and press **Enter** to start DriveSpy.

3. At the SYS prompt, type **output Chap9rp1.txt** and then press **Enter** to create an output file to record your actions and results.

4. At the SYS prompt, type **drives** and then press **Enter** to list all the drives connected to your investigation workstation. Figure 9-3 shows a system with one hard drive. The drives and partitions on your system might be different.

NOTE

The computer used in Figure 9-3 has an older 11 GB drive that doesn't show the logical block addressing (LBA). Newer disks show the LBA along with the CHS values. Your computer forensics tool can interpret these older drives in the same way it interprets newer drives.

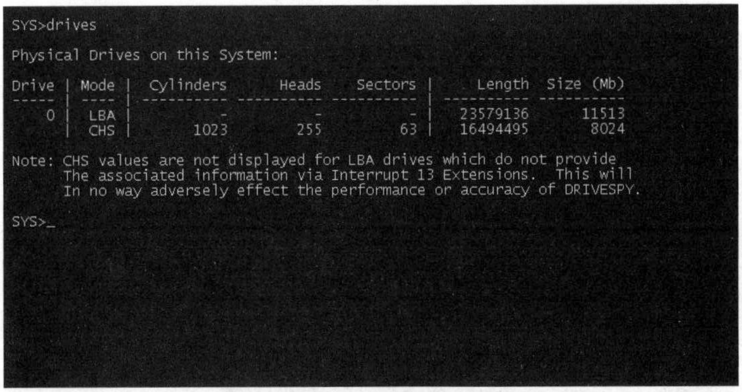

```
SYS>drives
Physical Drives on this System:

Drive | Mode | Cylinders    Heads     Sectors |   Length  Size (Mb)
----- | ---- | ----------  --------  --------- | ---------  ---------
    0 | LBA  |      -          -          -    | 23579136     11513
      | CHS  |    1023        255         63   | 16494495      8024

Note: CHS values are not displayed for LBA drives which do not provide
      The associated information via Interrupt 13 Extensions.  This will
      In no way adversely effect the performance or accuracy of DRIVESPY.

SYS>_
```

Figure 9-3 Listing the drives on your system

5. At the SYS prompt, type **d0** and then press **Enter** to select the disk drive containing the partition you want to copy, such as drive 0. The partitions on drive 0 appear on the screen, as shown in Figure 9-4.

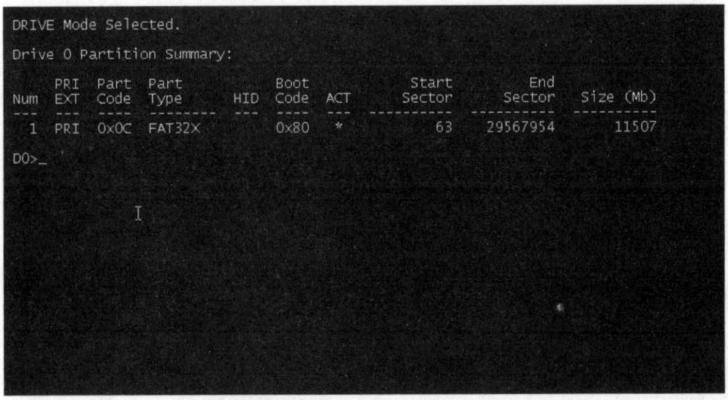

```
DRIVE Mode Selected.
Drive 0 Partition Summary:

      PRI  Part  Part              Boot            Start        End
Num   EXT  Code  Type      HID     Code  ACT       Sector      Sector    Size (Mb)
---   ---  ----  --------  ---     ----  ---      ----------  ----------  ----------
  1   PRI  0x0C  FAT32X            0x80   *             63    29567954       11507

D0>_
```

Figure 9-4 Listing the partitions on a drive

6. At the D0 prompt, type **part 1** and then press **Enter** to select the partition you want to save, such as partition 1. The contents of partition 1, including sectors, appear on the screen, as shown in Figure 9-5.

7. Although you normally use the SavePart command at this point to save the contents of the current hard disk partition, here you switch to a floppy disk and acquire its partition to save time. Insert a floppy disk containing a few files into the floppy disk drive. At the D0P1 prompt, type **drive a** and press **Enter** to access the floppy disk.

8. At the DA prompt, type **part 1** and press **Enter** to access the partition level.

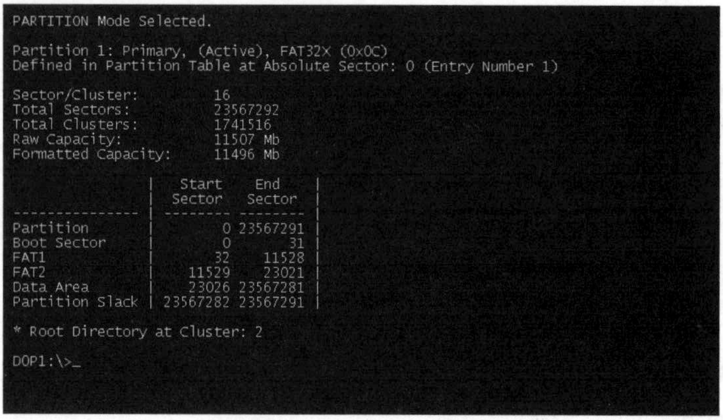

```
PARTITION Mode Selected.

Partition 1: Primary, (Active), FAT32X (0x0C)
Defined in Partition Table at Absolute Sector: 0 (Entry Number 1)

Sector/Cluster:         16
Total Sectors:          23567292
Total Clusters:         1741516
Raw Capacity:           11507 Mb
Formatted Capacity:     11496 Mb

                    |  Start    End   |
                    | Sector   Sector |
--------------- | -------- -------- |
Partition       |       0 23567291 |
Boot Sector     |       0       31 |
FAT1            |      32    11528 |
FAT2            |   11529    23021 |
Data Area       |   23026 23567281 |
Partition Slack | 23567282 23567291 |

* Root Directory at Cluster: 2

DOP1:\>_
```

Figure 9-5   Listing the contents of a partition

9. At the DAP1 prompt, type **savepart C:*work folder*\Chap09\Chapter\
   Case_9sp.ima** and press **Enter** to copy the partition on the floppy disk to an
   image file named Case_9sp.ima on your hard disk. (Replace the drive letter
   and *work folder* with the drive letter and work folder you're using.)

   DriveSpy creates the image file, listing details about the partition and displaying
   a progress indicator. Depending on the size of the disk, it might take a few
   minutes or several hours to create the image file. When finished, DriveSpy
   generates an MD5 hash value, as shown in Figure 9-6.

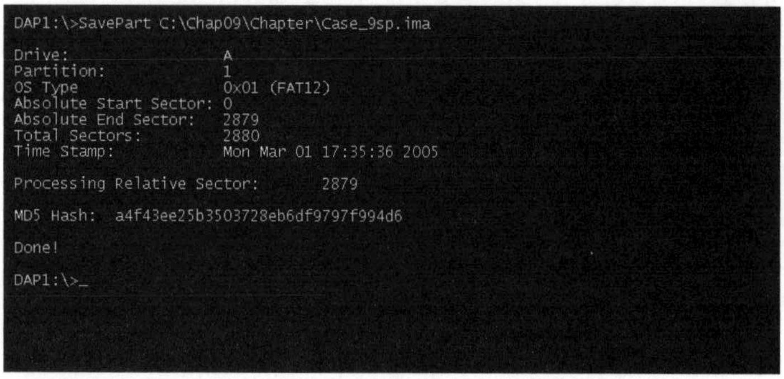

```
DAP1:\>SavePart C:\Chap09\Chapter\Case_9sp.ima

Drive:                  A
Partition:              1
OS Type                 0x01 (FAT12)
Absolute Start Sector:  0
Absolute End Sector:    2879
Total Sectors:          2880
Time Stamp:             Mon Mar 01 17:35:36 2005

Processing Relative Sector:      2879

MD5 Hash:  a4f43ee25b3503728eb6df9797f994d6

Done!

DAP1:\>_
```

Figure 9-6   Using SavePart to create an image file

10. At the DAP1 prompt, type **exit** and then press **Enter** to close DriveSpy.

Drives with multiple partitions have a gap between each partition. This gap, also referred to
as a partition gap, is the space between the end of one partition and the start of another. For
example, suppose one disk has three partitions. The first partition, partition 1, ends on
absolute sector 8610839, as shown in Figure 9-7. Partition 2 starts on absolute sector
8610903 and ends on absolute sector 17221679. Partition 3 starts on absolute sector
17221743 and ends on absolute sector 39070079. Each partition ends on one sector and the

next partition starts 64 sectors later. On this system, 64 sectors between each partition are not used by the file system.

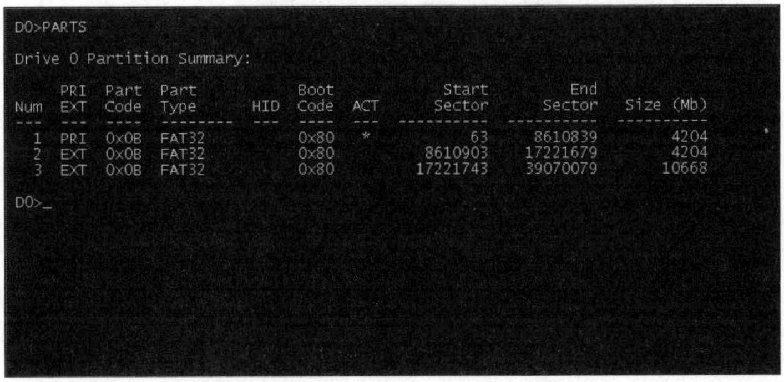

Figure 9-7   Partition table

You cannot use the SavePart command to inspect or extract data from partition gaps, although you can use other DriveSpy commands to do so. You learn how to use these other DriveSpy commands later in this chapter.

In the early days of computer crime, criminals attempting to hide data used these partition gaps to store incriminating evidence. In Chapter 10, you learn how to deal with these situations when processing evidence.

Using the WritePart Command

The counterpart to the SavePart command is WritePart, which you use in DriveSpy's Partition mode to re-create the saved partition image file created with the SavePart command. For example, the following command restores the Case_9sp.ima image file to the Case_9 folder on the D: drive:

```
WritePart D:\Case_9\Case_9sp.ima
```

The WritePart command decompresses the SavePart image file and writes it to a specified disk drive. WritePart checks the target drive and writes to that drive only if it's equal to or larger than the original disk. When WritePart creates the partition on the target drive, it changes the partition number to match the source drive. If the image file spans more than one volume (disk), DriveSpy prompts you in the same manner as the SavePart command for the location of the next image volume.

In the following exercise, you restore the Case_9sp.ima file you created with the SavePart command. If you were doing this on an actual hard disk with multiple partitions, you would have to be extremely careful that you were working on the correct drive and the correct partition. Note that you cannot use the WritePart command with Windows running. Reboot to an MS-DOS prompt, if necessary. The following exercise demonstrates how to use the WritePart command with a floppy disk, but typically, you use WritePart for a hard disk partition.

To perform the following steps, you can use a blank floppy disk. However, because the WritePart command was developed for use on a hard disk, your system might lock if you do use a floppy disk. If your system locks during the following steps, create a small hard disk partition that's larger than the floppy disk, and then restore the image to that partition. Use a partition tool such as FDisk, Partition Magic, or Norton Gdisk to create a 1.5 MB partition, for example. Then substitute all references to drive A: (or DA) in the following steps with the newly created drive and partition, such as D1P1. To restore the Case_9sp.ima image file, follow these steps:

1. At an MS-DOS prompt (not in a command prompt window), navigate to the **C:***work folder***\\Tools** folder, type **toolpath.bat**, and then press **Enter**. Then type **cd C:***work folder***\\Chap09\\Chapter** and press **Enter** to navigate to the Chap09\\Chapter folder in your work folder. (Replace the drive letter and *work folder* with the ones you're using, if necessary.)

2. At the command prompt, type **drivespy** and press **Enter** to start DriveSpy.

3. At the SYS prompt, type **output Chap9rp2.txt** and press **Enter** to create an output file.

4. At the SYS prompt, type **drive a** and press **Enter** to access the floppy drive. (If you're using a hard disk partition, use the partition number, as in **drive 1**.) At the DA prompt, type **part 1** and press **Enter** to access the partition level of the floppy disk.

5. At the DAP1 prompt, type **writepart Case_9sp.ima** and press **Enter** to restore the image file you created in the Chap09\\Chapter folder in your work folder to a floppy disk. When a warning appears, type **y** to continue. DriveSpy takes a few minutes to restore the image file. Together, Figures 9-8 and 9-9 show the output file of the WritePart command.

6. At the DAP1 prompt, type **exit** and then press **Enter** to close DriveSpy. Reboot your machine to Windows.

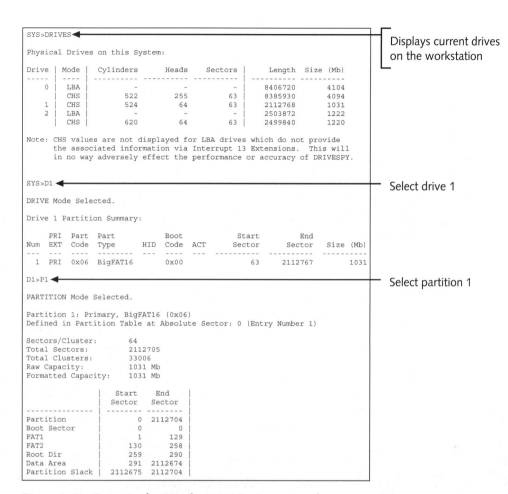

```
SYS>DRIVES◄─────────────────────────────────────────────┐
                                                          ├─ Displays current drives
Physical Drives on this System:                           ┘  on the workstation

Drive │ Mode │ Cylinders    Heads     Sectors │   Length  Size (Mb)
───── │ ──── │ ──────────  ──────── ────────── │ ────────── ──────────
    0 │ LBA  │      -          -          -    │  8406720    4104
      │ CHS  │    522        255         63    │  8385930    4094
    1 │ CHS  │    524         64         63    │  2112768    1031
    2 │ LBA  │      -          -          -    │  2503872    1222
      │ CHS  │    620         64         63    │  2499840    1220

Note: CHS values are not displayed for LBA drives which do not provide
      the associated information via Interrupt 13 Extensions.  This will
      in no way adversely effect the performance or accuracy of DRIVESPY.


SYS>D1 ◄──────────────────────────────────────────────────── Select drive 1

DRIVE Mode Selected.

Drive 1 Partition Summary:

     PRI  Part  Part            Boot              Start       End
Num  EXT  Code  Type      HID   Code   ACT       Sector      Sector    Size (Mb)
---  ---  ----  --------  ---   ----   ---     ----------  ----------  ----------
  1  PRI  0x06  BigFAT16         0x00                  63     2112767        1031

D1>P1 ◄─────────────────────────────────────────────────── Select partition 1

PARTITION Mode Selected.

Partition 1: Primary, BigFAT16 (0x06)
Defined in Partition Table at Absolute Sector: 0 (Entry Number 1)

Sectors/Cluster:      64
Total Sectors:        2112705
Total Clusters:       33006
Raw Capacity:         1031 Mb
Formatted Capacity:   1031 Mb

                 │  Start     End   │
                 │ Sector   Sector  │
--------------   │ -------- ------- │
Partition        │      0   2112704 │
Boot Sector      │      0         0 │
FAT1             │      1       129 │
FAT2             │    130       258 │
Root Dir         │    259       290 │
Data Area        │    291   2112674 │
Partition Slack  │ 2112675  2112704 │
```

Figure 9-8   Output of using the WritePart command

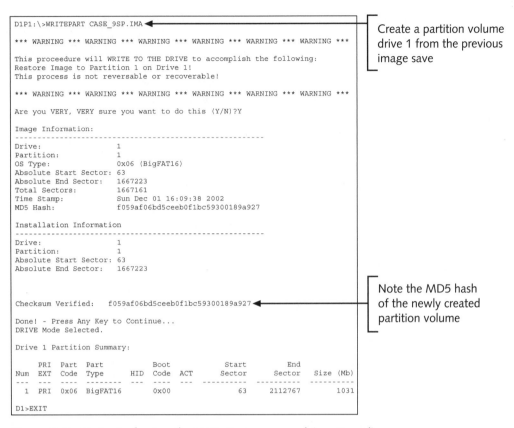

Create a partition volume drive 1 from the previous image save

Note the MD5 hash of the newly created partition volume

```
D1P1:\>WRITEPART CASE_9SP.IMA

*** WARNING *** WARNING *** WARNING *** WARNING *** WARNING *** WARNING ***

This proceedure will WRITE TO THE DRIVE to accomplish the following:
Restore Image to Partition 1 on Drive 1!
This process is not reversable or recoverable!

*** WARNING *** WARNING *** WARNING *** WARNING *** WARNING *** WARNING ***

Are you VERY, VERY sure you want to do this (Y/N)?Y

Image Information:
---------------------------------------------------------
Drive:                  1
Partition:              1
OS Type:                0x06 (BigFAT16)
Absolute Start Sector:  63
Absolute End Sector:    1667223
Total Sectors:          1667161
Time Stamp:             Sun Dec 01 16:09:38 2002
MD5 Hash:               f059af06bd5ceeb0f1bc59300189a927

Installation Information
---------------------------------------------------------
Drive:                  1
Partition:              1
Absolute Start Sector:  63
Absolute End Sector:    1667223


Checksum Verified:   f059af06bd5ceeb0f1bc59300189a927

Done! - Press Any Key to Continue...
DRIVE Mode Selected.

Drive 1 Partition Summary:

      PRI  Part  Part                Boot            Start       End
 Num  EXT  Code  Type      HID       Code  ACT       Sector      Sector    Size (Mb)
 ---  ---  ----  --------  ---       ----  ---       ----------  --------- ----------
   1  PRI  0x06  BigFAT16            0x00                    63    2112767       1031

D1>EXIT
```

Figure 9-9   Output of using the WritePart command (continued)

Using DriveSpy Data-Manipulation Commands

DriveSpy has two additional sector-copying commands that help you collect and preserve data: SaveSect and WriteSect. With these two commands, you can isolate specific areas of a disk and preserve them for later examination. The exercises covering these commands in the following sections assume you have three additional disk drives, each one larger than 230 MB, connected to your workstation. However, the steps can be performed with one additional disk drive connected to your workstation. If you have only one additional disk drive, change drive 3 (d3) to drive 1 (d1) for the steps in the exercises covering the SaveSect and WriteSect commands.

Using the SaveSect Command

The SaveSect command copies specific sectors on a disk to a file. It copies the sectors as a bit-stream image so that the file is an exact duplicate of the original sectors. Because the created file is not compressed, it's called a "flat file." In Chapter 10, you examine the contents of flat files with a variety of evidence-recovery tools. You can also use SaveSect to collect sector data that might be located in partition gaps. If a partition is hidden or deleted, use this command to copy the entire hidden section or deleted partition to a flat file.

You can use the SaveSect command in DriveSpy's Drive and Partition modes; you list only the source sector values, and you specify a file as the target. For example, the following command saves sectors 40000 to 49999 to a file named Part_gap.dat:

```
SaveSect 1:40000-49999 C:\Chap09\Chapter\Part_gap.dat
```

To save a sector in DriveSpy, follow these steps in Windows 98 DOS:

1. From the DOS command prompt, navigate to the **Tools** folder of your work folder. At the command prompt, type **drivespy** and press **Enter** to start DriveSpy.

2. At the SYS prompt, type **output C:*work folder*\Chap09\Chapter\ Chap9rp4.txt** and press **Enter** to create an output file to record your actions and results. (Replace the drive letter and *work folder* name, if necessary.)

3. At the SYS prompt, type **drives** and press **Enter** to determine which drive to copy.

4. At the SYS prompt, type **d3** (or **d1** if using only one extra drive) and press **Enter** to access the drive you want to copy. Substitute the number for your drive as necessary.

5. At the D3 prompt, type **p1** and press **Enter** to select the partition that contains the sectors you want to copy. (Note that typing "p1" is the same as typing "part 1.")

6. At the D3P1 prompt, type **savesect 3:0–415232 C:*work folder*\Chap09\ Chapter\Case_9s.dat** and press **Enter** to copy sectors 0 to 415232 to a data file named Case_9s.dat. (Replace the drive letter and *work folder* name, if necessary.) See Figure 9-10. (*Note*: If you're using only one extra drive, use the following command for drive 1: **savesect 1:0–415232 C:*work folder*\ Chap09\Chapter\Case_9s.dat**).

7. At the D3P1 prompt, type **exit** and then press **Enter** to close DriveSpy.

9

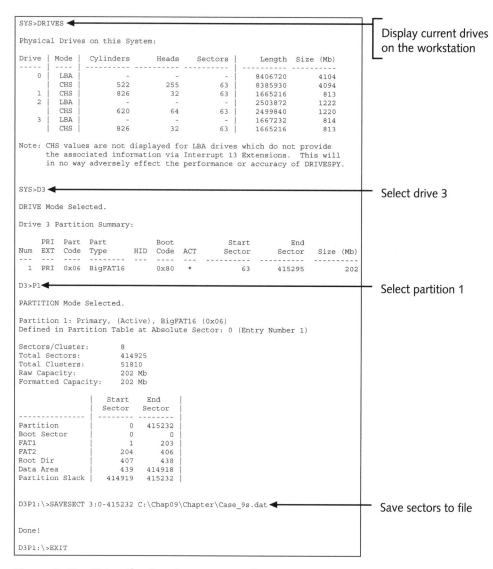

```
SYS>DRIVES ◄────────────────────────────────────────┐        Display current drives
                                                     │        on the workstation
Physical Drives on this System:

Drive │ Mode │ Cylinders   Heads    Sectors │   Length   Size (Mb)
----- │ ---- │ ---------- --------- --------- │ ---------- ----------
    0 │ LBA  │     -          -         -    │  8406720    4104
      │ CHS  │    522        255        63   │  8385930    4094
    1 │ CHS  │    826         32        63   │  1665216     813
    2 │ LBA  │     -          -         -    │  2503872    1222
      │ CHS  │    620         64        63   │  2499840    1220
    3 │ LBA  │     -          -         -    │  1667232     814
      │ CHS  │    826         32        63   │  1665216     813

Note: CHS values are not displayed for LBA drives which do not provide
      the associated information via Interrupt 13 Extensions.  This will
      in no way adversely effect the performance or accuracy of DRIVESPY.


SYS>D3 ◄───────────────────────────────────────────────────     Select drive 3

DRIVE Mode Selected.

Drive 3 Partition Summary:

      PRI  Part Part                Boot            Start        End
Num   EXT  Code Type       HID      Code  ACT      Sector     Sector    Size (Mb)
---   ---  ---- --------   ---      ----  ---    ---------- ----------  ----------
  1   PRI  0x06 BigFAT16            0x80   *           63     415295         202

D3>P1 ◄──────────────────────────────────────────────────       Select partition 1

PARTITION Mode Selected.

Partition 1: Primary, (Active), BigFAT16 (0x06)
Defined in Partition Table at Absolute Sector: 0 (Entry Number 1)

Sectors/Cluster:        8
Total Sectors:      414925
Total Clusters:      51810
Raw Capacity:       202 Mb
Formatted Capacity: 202 Mb

                 │ Start     End    │
                 │ Sector   Sector  │
---------------  │ --------  ------- │
Partition        │      0    415232 │
Boot Sector      │      0         0 │
FAT1             │      1       203 │
FAT2             │    204       406 │
Root Dir         │    407       438 │
Data Area        │    439    414918 │
Partition Slack  │ 414919    415232 │


D3P1:\>SAVESECT 3:0-415232 C:\Chap09\Chapter\Case_9s.dat ◄───────  Save sectors to file


Done!

D3P1:\>EXIT
```

Figure 9-10   Using the SaveSect command

Using the WriteSect Command

With the WriteSect command, you can re-create the data acquired through the SaveSect command. You use the WriteSect command in DriveSpy's Drive or Partition mode to re-create an absolute sector range from a SaveSect file to a target disk drive. For example, the following command writes a flat file named Part_gap.dat starting at absolute sector 10000 on drive 2:

```
WriteSect C:\Chap09\Chapter\Part_gap.dat 2:10000
```

The disadvantage of using the WriteSect command is that if you aren't careful, you can easily overwrite data on a target disk. Always review commands to verify where you are sending data. If you're using only one extra drive, change d3 to d1 as described in the previous exercise on the SaveSect command. To write a sector data file in DriveSpy, follow these steps:

1. From a DOS command prompt, navigate to the **Tools** folder of your work folder. At the command prompt, type **drivespy** and press **Enter** to start DriveSpy.

2. At the SYS prompt, type **output C:*work folder*\Chap09\Chapter\ Chap9rp5.txt** and press **Enter** to record the commands you use and their results in an output file. (Replace the drive letter and *work folder* name, if necessary.)

3. At the SYS prompt, type **drives** and press **Enter** to list the drives the system recognizes. Select the drive to which you want to copy data, and verify that it does not contain any vital data.

4. At the SYS prompt, type **d3** and press **Enter** to access the drive you want. Substitute the number for your drive as necessary.

5. At the D3 prompt, type **writesect C: *work folder*\Chap09\Chapter\ Case_9s.dat 3:0** and press **Enter** to start transferring data to absolute sector 0 on drive 3 (see Figure 9-11). Substitute drive and folder names as necessary. (*Note*: If you're using only one extra drive, use the following command for drive 1: **writesect C: *work folder*\Chap09\Chapter\Case_9s.dat 1:0**).

6. Type **y** when a warning appears.

7. At the D3 prompt, type **exit** and then press **Enter** to close DriveSpy.

Like the SavePart command, SaveSect can save an entire disk drive to a data file. The SaveSect and WriteSect commands are useful if you need to acquire a disk image from a non-Microsoft FAT file system. For example, you can use the SavePart and WritePart commands on a Linux Ext2fs disk. Make sure the target drive where you plan to save the SavePart output file is larger than the source drive.

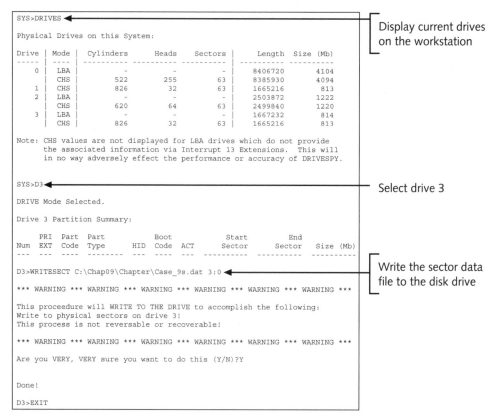

```
SYS>DRIVES

Physical Drives on this System:

Drive | Mode | Cylinders   Heads    Sectors  |   Length  Size (Mb)
----- | ---- | ---------- ---------- ---------- | ---------- ----------
    0 | LBA  |         -         -          -  |  8406720       4104
      | CHS  |       522       255         63  |  8385930       4094
    1 | CHS  |       826        32         63  |  1665216        813
    2 | LBA  |         -         -          -  |  2503872       1222
      | CHS  |       620        64         63  |  2499840       1220
    3 | LBA  |         -         -          -  |  1667232        814
      | CHS  |       826        32         63  |  1665216        813

Note: CHS values are not displayed for LBA drives which do not provide
      the associated information via Interrupt 13 Extensions.  This will
      in no way adversely effect the performance or accuracy of DRIVESPY.


SYS>D3

DRIVE Mode Selected.

Drive 3 Partition Summary:

       PRI  Part  Part                 Boot                Start        End
Num    EXT  Code  Type       HID       Code   ACT         Sector     Sector    Size (Mb)
---    ---  ----  --------   ---        ----   ---         ----------  ----------  ----------

D3>WRITESECT C:\Chap09\Chapter\Case_9s.dat 3:0

*** WARNING *** WARNING *** WARNING *** WARNING *** WARNING *** WARNING ***

This proceedure will WRITE TO THE DRIVE to accomplish the following:
Write to physical sectors on drive 3!
This process is not reversable or recoverable!

*** WARNING *** WARNING *** WARNING *** WARNING *** WARNING *** WARNING ***

Are you VERY, VERY sure you want to do this (Y/N)?Y


Done!

D3>EXIT
```

Display current drives on the workstation

Select drive 3

Write the sector data file to the disk drive

Figure 9-11   Using the WriteSect command

USING WINDOWS ACQUISITION TOOLS

Many computer forensics software vendors have developed data-acquisition tools that you can run in Windows. These tools make acquiring evidence from a suspect's disk more convenient, especially when you use the tools with hot-swappable devices that use USB-2 or FireWire to connect hard disks to your workstation.

However, Windows data-acquisition tools do have some drawbacks. Because Windows can easily contaminate your evidence drive, you must protect it with a well-tested hardware write-blocking hardware device. (Chapter 4 contains information about using write-blocking devices.) Another drawback is that Windows tools cannot acquire data from the host protected area on a disk. If you know or suspect that the evidence disk drive contains evidence in the host protected area, use an MS-DOS tool, such as X-Ways Replica, to acquire the disk.

AccessData FTK Imager

FTK Imager is a typical data-acquisition program for Windows that's included with a licensed copy of the AccessData Forensic Toolkit. FTK Imager, like most Windows data-acquisition tools, requires that you use a device such as a USB or parallel port dongle for licensing. Learning how FTK Imager acquires data can help you understand how other Windows acquisition tools work. If you're using only the demonstration version of FTK you downloaded from the AccessData Web site, you do not have a copy of FTK Imager. In that case, read the steps and examine the figures, but don't perform the steps in this section.

FTK Imager is designed to view evidence disks and bit-stream disk-to-image files created with other forensic software, such as EnCase, SafeBack, and SMART. FTK Imager has a window similar to Windows Explorer with an additional pane that shows the contents of the selected file (see Figure 9-12).

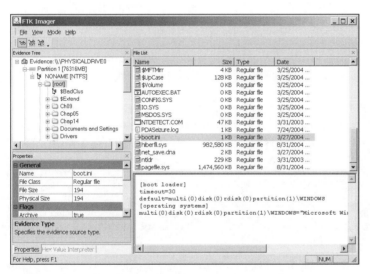

Figure 9-12   The FTK Imager main window

FTK Imager can make bit-stream disk-to-image copies of evidence disks and enables you to acquire the evidence disk from a logical partition level or a physical drive level. You can also define the size of each bit-stream image file volume, allowing you to segment the image you save into one or many volumes. For example, you can specify that each volume segment is 100 MB if you plan to store the volumes on 100 MB Zip disks, or you can specify the volume segments as 650 MB so that you can record the volumes on CD-Rs.

Because FTK Imager is designed to run on versions of Windows from 9x through XP, the evidence disk from which you're acquiring data must have a hardware write-blocking device between your investigation workstation and the evidence drive. This device ensures that you don't contaminate your evidence while using a Windows program. Any USB, FireWire, or SCSI write-blocker protects your evidence when using FTK Imager.

Like all Windows tools, FTK Imager cannot acquire the host protected area of an evidence drive. Recall from Chapter 8 that you should compare actual sectors displayed in a disk editor to the computer's BIOS settings. In other words, if the disk drive's specifications indicate that it has 11,000,000 sectors and the BIOS displays 9,000,000, a host protected area of 2,000,000 sectors might be assigned to the drive. If you suspect an evidence drive has a host protected area, you must use an advanced MS-DOS tool, such as Replica, SafeBack, or SnapBack, to include a disk's host protected area in the data acquisition. With MS-DOS tools, you might have to define the exact sector count to make sure you include more than what the BIOS shows as the number of known sectors on the drive. Review specific vendor product manuals to determine how to account for a drive's host protected area.

The following exercise shows you how to use FTK Imager to make a forensic bit-stream disk-to-image file. The FTK Imager Image command makes a bit-stream image file of a suspect's disk drive or partition volume. To perform this acquisition, you need a write-blocking device (such as Digital Intelligence FireChief or WeibeTech Forensic DriveDock), the suspect disk drive, and a target disk drive to receive the acquisition. FireChief is a FireWire device that allows you to connect disk drives while your workstation is running, a process called hot-swapping. When you connect the disk drives, Windows makes the drive accessible.

 If you don't have a licensed copy of FTK, you should read, but not perform, the following steps. In addition, if you don't have access to a hardware write-blocker, such as Digital Intelligence FireChief, you can still try the exercise, but **NOTE** start at Step 4.

To prepare for a data acquisition and then acquire an evidence disk with FTK Imager, follow these steps:

1. Boot a forensic workstation to Windows using an installed write-blocker, such as Digital Intelligence FireChief.

2. Connect the evidence disk to a write-blocking device or the FireChief write-block bay.

3. Connect the target disk to the FireChief writeable bay.

4. Click **Start**, **Programs** (**All Programs** in Windows XP), **AccessData**, **Forensic Toolkit**, **FTK Imager** to start FTK Imager.

5. Click **File**, **Create Disk Image** from the menu to open the Select Source dialog box.

6. In the Select Source dialog box, click the **Physical Drive** option button (see Figure 9-13), and then click **Next**. In the Drive Selection drop-down list, select the suspect drive, and then click **Finish**.

7. In the Create Image dialog box, click **Add**. Next, in the Select Image Type dialog box (see Figure 9-14), click the **Raw (dd)** button, and then click **Next**.

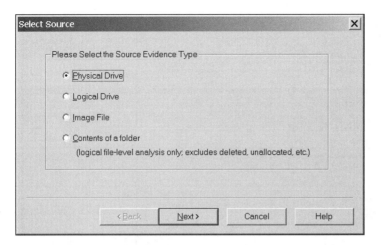

Figure 9-13   The Select Source dialog box

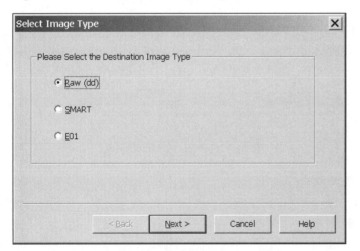

Figure 9-14   The Select Image Type dialog box

8. In the Select Image Destination dialog box, click **Browse** and navigate to the location for the image file. Figure 9-15 shows the location fields filled in. Then click **Finish**.

9. Next, in the Create Image dialog box, click **Start**.

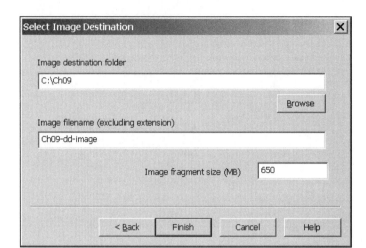

Figure 9-15   Selecting where to save the image file

> 10. When FTK Imager is finished, the screen in Figure 9-16 is displayed, inform-
> ing you whether the image save was successful or whether there were any
> errors or problems. Click **Close**, and then click **Finish** to exit FTK Imager.

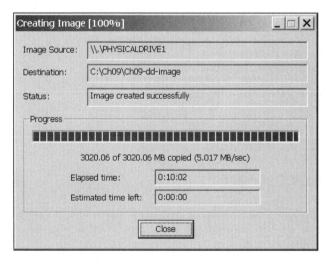

Figure 9-16   A completed image save with FTK Imager

Using X-Ways Replica

X-Ways Software Technology AG, the creator of WinHex, has created a MS-DOS program called Replica. Replica is a compact bit-streaming application program that's small enough to load onto a forensic bootable floppy disk. Replica produces a dd-like bit-stream image of a disk drive. Similar to the UNIX/Linux dd command, Replica has several options allowing you to acquire an entire disk drive or specific sectors. Replica copies data from one drive to image segment files or from one disk to another disk.

One of the most important features of Replica is its capability to identify and access the host protected area of a disk drive. Replica is included with the purchase of X-Ways Forensics or X-Ways Evidor. For more information on X-Ways Software Technology AG computer forensics products, see *www.sf-soft.de*.

Using Replica

9

To use Replica, create a forensic boot floppy as described in Chapter 2, or load it onto your forensic workstation. To run Replica, you must be in MS-DOS. Replica doesn't run in a Windows DOS shell because it needs to access the computer's BIOS. When Replica starts, it first checks the computer's BIOS to see whether Host Protected Area (HPA) is implemented. If HPA is on, Replica asks if you would like to turn it off. If you answer yes, it turns off HPA and then instructs you to restart the computer. When the computer reboots to MS-DOS, HPA is opened, which allows all sectors of the disk drive to be copied. Follow these steps to turn off HPA and then acquire a bit-stream image of a disk drive:

1. At the DOS prompt, type **replica** and press **Enter**.

2. If you're prompted to eliminate the HPA, type **y** for yes, and then restart the computer and restart Replica.

3. In the Select the source screen, enter the number of the disk drive to copy (for example, 2).

4. In the Select the partition screen, enter the number of the partition or enter **0** to copy an entire disk.

5. Next, in the Select the DESTINATION screen, enter the number corresponding to the type of acquisition to make; for example, enter **0** to create an image file.

6. In the next screen, type the name of the image file, including the full path, and press **Enter**.

NOTE Replica image file-naming conventions allow you to leave the extension blank or type a number or letter value. Replica automatically increments the extension name for each new volume segment created.

7. At the segment split prompt, type the size for each volume segment, for example, 650.

8. In the Ready to clone screen, type **y** for yes to create a Replica log file to record any errors or other related information for the acquisition.

9. At the hash prompt, type **m** (for MD5) and press **Enter** to record the MD5 value of the suspect disk drive (see Figure 9-17).

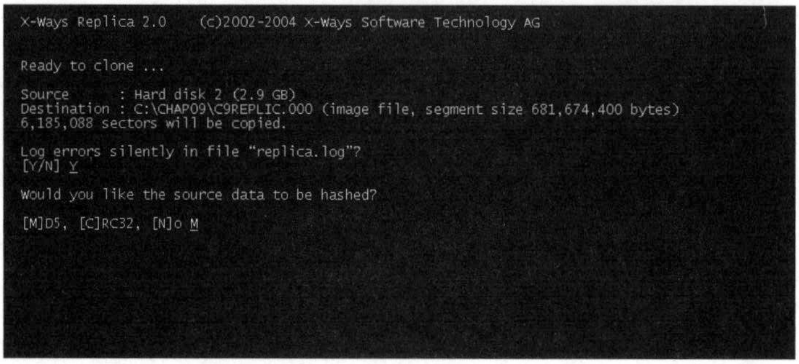

Figure 9-17 Selecting the type of hashing

10. In the Proceed screen, type **y** for yes and press **Enter** to initiate the acquisition.

The screen shown in Figure 9-18 is displayed when Replica finishes copying all sectors into the image file.

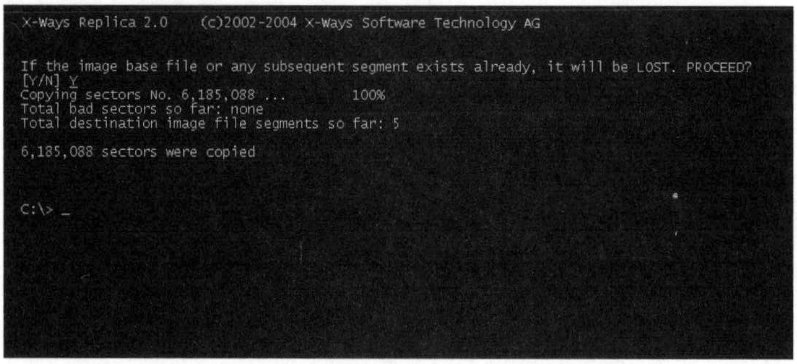

Figure 9-18 The completed cloning of the disk

PDA DATA ACQUISITIONS

PDAs can store, send, and receive data from various devices. Some vendors have begun integrating PDAs into cell phones. Because PDAs can store data, they have become an important source of evidence for computing investigators.

Many people who use a PDA typically copy (synch) the data to their computers. When conducting an investigation that involves PDAs, try to determine whether the suspect or subject regularly synchs his or her PDA to a host computer. Under ideal circumstances, creating a duplicate host PC that's associated with the PDA is preferable. The duplicate host PC can be used to download and examine the PDA's content.

If you can't determine whether the suspect PDA is regularly synched to a host computer, you need a specialty PDA forensic examination program. Paraben Forensic Tools (*www.paraben-forensics.com*) offers products for forensic examinations of PDAs and cell phones. Paraben's PDA Seizure and Cell Seizure programs can download PDA and cell phone data. Similar to other GUI-based computer forensics tools, PDA Seizure and Cell Seizure have easy-to-use interactive screens (see Figure 9-19 for an example) that you can use to download and examine data collected from PDAs and cell phones.

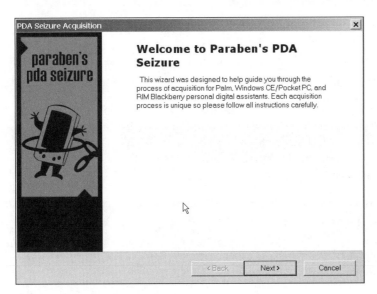

Figure 9-19   Paraben PDA Seizure

Because of the variety of PDA designs among different vendors, you might need to test these devices to get them to download data. PDA Seizure typically uses a PDA's debug and hot-synch modes to acquire data. Paraben Forensic recommends reading the user manual for the PDA you're examining to learn how to put the device into debug mode. As part of an investigation involving a PDA or cell phone, be sure to seize all cables and power supplies associated with the suspect's PDA or cell phone.

For example, an acquisition from a Palm Zire with a USB connection requires the following preliminary items and steps to acquire data:

- A Palm Zire with the correct Zire USB-to-USB mini cable
- The demo version of Paraben PDA Seizure (downloaded from *www.paraben-forensics.com/pda.html* and installed on your workstation)
- If available, the section of the Palm Zire user manual that describes how to do a soft reset of the PDA
- A paper clip unfolded at one end so that the open end protrudes outward

To prepare a Palm Zire for acquisition, follow these steps:

1. From your investigation workstation, start PDA Seizure.
2. Connect the Zire to the USB cable attached to the investigation workstation.
3. On the Zire, press and hold the scroll-down button
4. Continuing to hold the scroll-down button, insert the unfolded end of a paper clip into the reset hole on the back of the Zire. When the scroll-down clicking noise stops, remove the paper clip.
5. Continue to hold the scroll-down button for 10 full seconds after removing the paper clip from the reset hole.
6. After 10 seconds, release the scroll-down button. The date and time should appear on the screen. If they don't, repeat Steps 3 through 5.

NOTE Your PDA might have different features that require slightly different methods to download data to PDA Seizure. The download wizard in PDA Seizure might not have the specific instructions to acquire data from your PDA. In this case, you need to consult the PDA's user manual to determine how to put it into debug or console mode.

These instructions are specific to Palm Zire PDAs for PDA Seizure. Follow these steps to download the Zire's data to the investigation workstation:

NOTE If you don't have a Palm Zire, you can follow along by reading the steps.

1. Select **Tools, Acquire Image** from the PDA Seizure menu.
2. In the Acquire Image Wizard, follow the prompts and instructions until you come to the Palm Console Mode Wizard.
3. In this window, activate the **Zire Hot-sync** button using the stylus to initiate the download.

4. In the last window of the Acquire Image Wizard, click **Finish** to complete the download.

5. In the PDA Seizure window, shown in Figure 9-20, you can click the **Search** tab to enter keywords of interest to your investigation.

Figure 9-20   The PDA Seizure window after data has been downloaded

General Considerations for PDA Investigations

The following are some general procedures to consider when investigating PDA or cell phone devices. To seize a PDA and associated PC, follow this procedure:

1. First seize the PDA and the host computer with PDA caddy and cables.

2. Make sure to collect all documentation—the user manual and associated software—on how to use the PDA.

3. Obtain the power supply for the suspect PDA device; recharge the batteries as soon as possible and leave it plugged into the PDA to ensure it has enough battery power.

4. Before processing the PDA, perform a standard bit-stream image and a non-forensic backup copy (for example, Norton Ghost) of the original host PC.

5. Try to obtain or locate any passwords used on the PDA device.

NOTE

The most difficult task when acquiring and examining PDAs is obtaining the password for the device. If a suspect is not cooperative, consult with the PDA vendor, encryption experts, or LISTSERV sources for additional methods on how to access protected data for the specific PDA you're examining.

Re-create the Host Computer

To collect all evidence from a PDA and suspect host computer, you need to create a working host computer. Then, to conduct your examination, download the PDA data to the reconstructed host computer. Perform the following general steps to reconstruct and examine a host computer with the PDA data:

1. Reconstruct a working host construct by installing the PDA's caddy or cables, along with any required peripheral card.

2. Install the nonforensic backup copy, such as Norton Ghost, to the new host computer. Make sure it boots to the same configuration as the suspect's (original) host PC.

NOTE

If you have Guidance Software's EnCase or NTI's SafeBack, you can re-create the host computer from either of these bit-stream image copies. This eliminates the need to use a standard backup utility, such as Norton Ghost.

3. Install the specific PDA software associated with the seized PDA.

4. Next, read the user manual for the PDA to determine the procedure for downloading its data to the host computer, and then download the data per the manual's directions.

5. Using the PDA-specific software on the re-created workstation (see Figure 9-21 for an example), examine all its contents for related evidence.

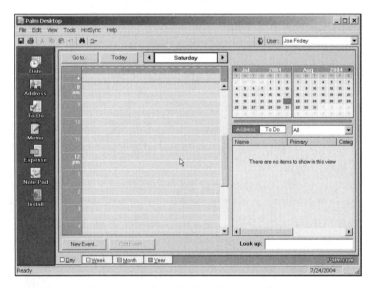

Figure 9-21   Example of a Palm Desktop application

Using Other Forensics-Acquisition Tools

In addition to DriveSpy, FTK Imager, and Replica, you can use other data-acquisition tools that are commercially available, including SnapBack DatArrest from Columbia Data Products and SafeBack from NTI. The cost of these tools ranges from $600 to $2500. Prices on some tools are discounted for law enforcement officers working in the field of computer forensics. Contact the vendors for specifics on law enforcement discounts.

Exploring SnapBack DatArrest

SnapBack DatArrest from Columbia Data Products (sold separately or with AccessData FTK) is an old, reliable MS-DOS forensic data-acquisition tool that can perform a bit-stream data copy of an evidence drive in three ways: disk to SCSI drive (magnetic tape or Jaz disk), disk to network drive, and disk to disk. Each method is a separate program that fits on a forensic boot floppy disk. SnapBack DatArrest provides network drivers so you can boot from a forensic boot floppy disk and access a remote network server disk. You can then save a data acquisition image directly to a remote networked server drive.

You can restore image files created on a network drive or removable media to a new target drive for follow-up examination and analysis. SnapCopy is a disk-to-disk utility that adjusts the target drive geometry to match the original suspect's disk drive. SnapCopy is the only automated disk-to-disk tool that allows you to copy data to a slightly smaller target drive than the original suspect's drive.

Exploring SafeBack

SafeBack, another reliable MS-DOS data-acquisition tool, is small enough to fit on to a forensic boot floppy disk. SafeBack performs an SHA-256 calculation for each sector copied to ensure data integrity. During the data acquisition, SafeBack creates a log file of all the transactions it performs. The log file includes a comment field where you can identify the investigation and the data you collect. SafeBack does the following:

- Creates disk-to-image files
- Copies from a source disk to an image on a tape drive
- Copies from a source disk to a target disk (disk-to-disk copy), adjusting the target drive's geometry to match the source drive
- Copies from a source disk to a target disk using a parallel port laplink cable
- Copies a partition to an image file
- Compresses acquired files to reduce the number of volume segments

9

SafeBack provides the following four programs:

- Master.exe, the main SafeBack utility program

- Remote.exe, for connecting two computers and transferring data with a parallel port laplink cable

- Restpart.exe, for restoring a partition that is saved separately from the entire suspect's disk

- Taspi.exe, for connecting SCSI devices for your data acquisition

AccessData FTK and iLook can read SafeBack image files.

Exploring EnCase

EnCase is a Windows forensics tool from Guidance Software that you can use to create a forensic boot floppy disk (see Figure 9-22 for an example of its interface). EnCase loads a program called En.exe on the floppy disk; En.exe a reliable forensic data-acquisition tool that compresses data to reduce the amount of storage space required for the volume segments. In fact, the En.exe program has one of the best compression algorithms of the data-acquisition tools.

NOTE   You explore EnCase in more detail in Chapter 10.

You must use EnCase to restore images created with En.exe. You can acquire data disk-to-disk, disk to network server drive, or through the parallel port with a laplink cable to another computer's disk drive. EnCase, FTK, and iLook can read EnCase image files.

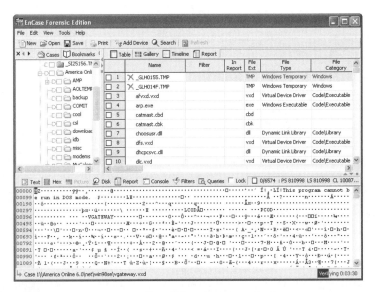

Figure 9-22 An example of the EnCase interface

CHAPTER SUMMARY

- You can acquire digital evidence from disk drives in three ways: creating a bit-stream disk-to-image file, making a bit-stream disk-to-disk copy, or creating a sparse data copy of a specific folder path or file.

- Several tools on the market allow you to restore disks that are larger or smaller than the suspect source drive.

- Lossless compression is an acceptable method for computer forensics because it does not alter the data in any way. Lossy compression alters the data and is not acceptable.

- Because you're dealing with electronic data, you need to protect your bit-stream digital evidence and make contingency plans in case software or hardware doesn't work or you encounter a failure during an acquisition. The most common and time-consuming technique for preserving evidence is creating a duplicate copy of your evidence image file. Also, make sure you perform at least two data acquisitions using different methods.

- The partition gap is an area where information can be stored. DriveSpy's SavePart command can retrieve this information.

- Some command-line tools can be dangerous, such as the CopySect command. It doesn't notify you that it's about to overwrite critical information. You must keep a careful log of what sectors you are writing to and from.

- Windows data acquisition tools add convenience and ease of use to a forensic investigation. They also enable you to use hot-swappable devices such as Zip and Jaz drives. However, you must write-protect your evidence and access the host protected area of a disk.

- In addition to DriveSpy, FTK Imager, and Replica, you can use other data-acquisition tools that are commercially available, including SnapBack DatArrest from Columbia Data Products and SafeBack from NTI.

- Many high-tech investigations now involve the search and seizure of PDA and cell phone devices. Typically, examining these devices requires specialized software programs to extract the data. Many of these devices must be switched to debug mode so that data from them can be transferred to a forensic workstation for analysis.

KEY TERMS

absolute sector — The actual count of each sector of data, starting at the very beginning of the disk drive. Absolute sector 0 (zero) is typically the same location as the Master Boot Record (MBR) of a disk drive. The Sector command in DriveSpy's Drive mode displays the absolute sector values of the disk drive.

algorithm — A short mathematical procedure or procedural steps used to solve a problem.

lossless compression — A compression method in which no data is lost. With this type of compression, a large file can be compressed to take up less space, and then decompressed without any loss of information.

lossy compression — A compression technique that can lose data but not perceptible quality when a file is restored. Files that use lossy compression include JPEG and MPEG.

relative sector — The actual count of each sector of data on a partition. Relative sector 0 (zero) starts at the very beginning of the disk partition. The Sector command in DriveSpy's Partition mode displays the relative sector values of the disk partition.

REVIEW QUESTIONS

1. EnCase, FTK, SMART, and iLook treat the image file as though it were the original disk. True or False?

2. A tool that uses _____ compression maintains the MD5 hash value of the file when it's uncompressed.

3. List two tools that use lossless compression.

4. List two disk-to-disk imaging tools that run in DOS.

5. When dealing with an extremely large drive of 2 TB or more, which of the three data-acquisition methods should you use?

6. Whenever possible, you should make a duplicate copy of the evidence. True or False?

7. You are using DriveSpy and want to copy 150 sectors; the starting sector is 1709 on the primary master hard drive. Which of the following formats correctly specifies these sectors? (Choose all that apply.)

   a. 0:1000, 150

   b. 0:1709, 150

   c. 1:1709, 150

   d. 0:1709-1858

8. The logical sector number and absolute sector number refer to the same data on a disk. True or False?

9. In DriveSpy, which command can you use to store an image on removable media?

   a. CopyDisk

   b. WritePart

   c. SavePart

   d. Output

10. Which DriveSpy command can acquire specific sectors on a disk drive?

    a. CopyDisk

    b. SaveSect

    c. SavePart

    d. WritePart

11. WriteSect can overwrite areas of the target disk without warning. True or False?

12. When using a Windows data-acquisition tool, what are two drawbacks you should keep in mind?

13. Like all Windows tools, FTK Imager cannot acquire data in the host protected area of an evidence drive. True or False?

14. When seizing a PDA to answer a civil lawsuit discovery demand, what do you need to collect before processing the device to extract the digital evidence?

15. Using WinZip or PKZip is acceptable for reducing the size of digital evidence for storage needs. True or False?

16. SnapBack DatArrest provides network drivers so that you can save a data acquisition image directly to a remote networked server drive. True or False?

17. List three ways data you can acquire data from a disk drive for forensic examination.

18. Identify one strength of the En.exe program.

HANDS-ON PROJECTS

Project 9-1

In this project, you create files and compare their MD5 hash values before and after compression. First, you download the IrfanView image viewer, if necessary, and then use it to save an uncompressed graphics file as a compressed file. Then you save the compressed file as an uncompressed file and compare MD5 hash values for each file.

1. On your Internet-accessible workstation, visit the shareware Web site CNet Central (*www.download.com/IrfanView/3000-2192_4-10311994.html* or *www.irfanview.de*) and download IrfanView. Click the **Downloads** link in the Cnet home page, and then type **IrfanView** in the Search text box.

2. Install the program on your workstation in the location your instructor specifies.

3. Start Paint and draw a rectangle. Save the file as **Shape1.bmp** in the Chap09\Projects folder in the work folder on your system. (If necessary, create a Projects folder.) Close Paint.

4. Start IrfanView and open Shape1.bmp. Click **File**, **Save as** from the menu, click **GIF** in the Save as type list box, and save the file as **Shape1.gif** in the Chap09\Projects folder in the work folder on your system. Close Shape1.bmp by opening the newly created Shape1.gif file.

5. Save Shape1.gif as **Shape2.bmp** in the Chap09\Projects folder in the work folder on your system. Close IrfanView.

6. Start DriveSpy, switch to Partition mode, and generate an MD5 hash for both .bmp files and the .gif file.

7. Compare the values and write one page explaining why the hash values are the same or different.

Project 9-2

In this project, you learn how to recover data from a deleted partition. Before you begin, you must prepare a hard disk with three separate partitions. After you complete the drive's configuration, you recover and analyze deleted partitions. You need the following items to complete this project:

- Forensic workstation with MS-DOS, Windows 9x, DriveSpy, and FTK Demo or Licensed version installed

- Disk partition utility, such as FDisk (included with DOS), Gdisk, or Partition Magic

- Spare IDE hard disk larger than 25 MB

- Spare IDE cable and 12-volt power extension cable

- Student data files for Chapter 9 Hands-on Projects

To build the sample evidence disk, follow these steps:

1. On your forensic workstation, use Windows Explorer to create a folder named **Chap09\Projects**.

2. Next, copy **C9-2_P1.sav**, **C9-2_P2.sav**, and **C9-2_P3.sav** from the Chap09\Projects folder in your student data files to the Chap09\Projects folder in the work folder on your workstation.

3. Shut down your workstation. With the power off, connect the spare hard disk with the correct jumper setting, such as single drive or cable. Select the forensic workstation's secondary host adapter channel.

4. Power on the forensic workstation and access the system's BIOS. Activate the newly connected secondary IDE host adapter channel to make the spare disk accessible.

5. Reboot the forensic workstation to DOS. From DOS, run FDisk or your favorite partition utility on the newly installed hard drive and create partitions with the following sizes:

   ❏ Primary partition: 5 MB

   ❏ Extended partition: 20 MB or more

   ❏ First logical partition: 1 MB

   ❏ Second logical partition: 5 MB

NOTE Depending on your drive's geometry and the nature of FAT, the actual sizes of each partition might be slightly larger than the values you entered. This should not cause a problem because the sizes are adjusted when you restore data to each partition.

6. Exit FDisk or your partition utility and boot the forensic workstation to DOS.

To install the first sample partition, follow these steps:

1. At the DOS command prompt, navigate to the **Tools** folder of your work folder, type **toolpath.bat**, and then press **Enter**.

2. Change to the **Chap09\Projects** folder in your work folder.

3. At the DOS command prompt, type **drivespy** and press **Enter** to start DriveSpy.

4. At the SYS prompt, type **output C:\Chap09\Projects\C9-2P0.log** and press **Enter** to create an output log.

5. At the SYS prompt, type **d1** and press **Enter** to navigate to the newly partitioned disk.

6. At the D1 prompt, type **p1** and press **Enter** to navigate to the first partition on the disk.

7. At the D1P1 prompt, type **writepart C:\Chap09\Project\C9-2_P1.sav** and press **Enter**. Then press **y** to continue the data copy.

8. When DriveSpy prompts you to redirect output to the next data save-set, press **Ctrl+C** to end the program.

Because the WritePart command assumes you're saving to smaller media, such as a floppy disk, it requests additional media. You press Ctrl+C to end this task, close DriveSpy, and return to the DOS prompt. To continue restoring the second partition, you need to restart DriveSpy. To install the second partition, P2, follow these steps:

1. Make sure you're working in the Chap09\Projects folder in your work folder. At the DOS command prompt, type **drivespy** and press **Enter** to start DriveSpy.

2. At the SYS prompt, type **d1** and press **Enter** to navigate to the newly partitioned disk.

3. At the D1 prompt, type **p2** and press **Enter** to navigate to the second partition on the disk.

4. At the D1P2 prompt, type **writepart C:\Chap09\Projects\C9-2_P2.sav** and press **Enter**. Then press **y** to continue the data copy.

5. When DriveSpy prompts you to redirect output to the next data save-set, press **Ctrl+C** to end the program.

To install the third partition, P3, follow these steps:

1. Make sure you are working in the Chap09\Projects folder in your work folder. At the DOS command prompt, type **drivespy** and press **Enter** to start DriveSpy.

2. At the SYS prompt, type **d1** and press **Enter** to navigate to the newly partitioned disk.

3. At the D1 prompt, type **p3** and press **Enter** to navigate to the third partition on the disk.

4. At the D1P3 prompt, type **writepart C:\Chap09\Projects\C9-2_P3.sav** and press **Enter**. Then press **y** to continue the data copy.

5. When DriveSpy prompts you to redirect output to the next data save-set, press **Ctrl+C** to end the program.

This completes the first preparation of re-creating the sample drive. The next section requires you to delete the second partition with FDisk or your favorite partition utility. The following steps provide instructions for using FDisk, a built-in DOS program, to delete the second partition:

1. At the DOS command prompt, type **fdisk** and press **Enter**. Be sure to enable large disk support.

2. On the FDisk main menu, select option **5. Change current fixed disk drive**, select the sample disk, which should be **2**, and press **Enter**.

3. On the FDisk main menu, select option **3. Delete partition or Logical DOS Drive**, and press **Enter**.

4. On the FDisk Delete menu, select option **3. Delete Logical DOS Drive(s) in the Extended DOS Partition**, and press **Enter**.

5. Select the 1 MB logical partition by typing the associated drive letter in the prompt box and pressing **Enter**.

6. Leave the label name box blank and press **Enter**. Then type **y** and press **Enter** to confirm the deletion.

7. Exit FDisk and shut down the workstation.

This completes the preparation of the sample disk. Next, you process the evidence and recover the deleted partition. First, use these steps to create a work folder and navigate to the sample disk:

1. Boot the forensic workstation to DOS, navigate to the Tools folder in your work folder, type **toolpath.bat**, and then press **Enter**.

2. At the command prompt, navigate to the **Chap09\Projects** folder in your work folder.

3. At the command prompt, type **md C9-2rcvr** and press **Enter** to create a folder named C9-2rcvr in the Chap09\Projects folder.

4. Type **cd C9-2rcvr** and press **Enter**.

5. At the command prompt, type **drivespy** and press **Enter** to start DriveSpy.

6. At the SYS prompt, type **output C9-2rcvr.log** and press **Enter** to create an output log.

7. At the SYS prompt, type **d1** and press **Enter** to navigate to the sample disk.

After you navigate to the sample disk, DriveSpy displays the partition table with only two partitions. Note the ending sector number of the first partition and the starting sector number of the next partition.

The DriveSpy partition table shows that the last sector number for the first partition is 12095 and the first sector number of the next partition is 16191. Your sector numbers might vary. (You can use the Parts command to list the starting and ending sectors for all the partitions.) There are 4095 sectors not accounted for in this table. More than 4000 sectors lie between the end of partition 1 and the start of partition 2. It is this area that might contain a deleted partition. To recover data from this unaccounted for area of a disk, you use the DriveSpy SaveSect command, which copies all sectors that you define to a data file. You can then analyze this data file with a variety of tools, such as FTK and Data Lifter. To copy a deleted partition with the SaveSect command, follow these steps:

1. At the DriveSpy D1 prompt, type **SaveSect 12096-16190 C9-2rcvr.1** and press **Enter**. DriveSpy copies the deleted partition to a file named C9-2rcvr.1.

2. At the D1 prompt, type **exit** and press **Enter** to close DriveSpy.

In Step 1, you specified the first sector immediately after the last sector of partition 1 as the starting sector to copy. The very last sector to copy is one sector less then the starting sector of partition 2.

This completes the acquisition steps for the partition recovery task. Next, you extract, or carve, data from raw sector copy data. You'll use FTK to analyze and extract any evidence from this data set. The SaveSect command is useful for creating raw uncompressed data save-sets of a disk drive. Some computer forensics tools that can read SaveSect data save-sets are FTK, FTK Imager, Data Lifter, and iLook.

When you copied deleted partitions, you were instructed to create a save-set called C9-2rcvr.1. FTK is designed to automatically load raw data files such as those created with the SaveSect command. FTK can read save-set file extensions such as .e01, 001, and .1, and searches for any additional file extensions for the same file name with incrementing numeric extension values. If you create two or more save-sets, such as C9-2rcvr.1, C9-2rcvr.2, and C9-2rcvr.3, FTK loads all three save-set files.

Start FTK and use the Startup Wizard to start a new case for your save-set C9-2rcvr.1. Determine which files have been allocated and which files have been deleted. Write a short report of your findings. After FTK has completed its analysis, try to determine what the deleted partition contains. (*Hint*: It is something that originated in Greenland. Try to determine its native name. Research your evidence results on the Internet, if necessary.)

Project 9-3

In Project 9-2, you restored a disk with three partitions and analyzed the missing second partition. For this project, you can use either DriveSpy or FTK to analyze partitions 1 and 3 on that restored disk. Use the steps and explanations in Project 9-2 to complete this project. Try to determine which files are allocated and which files have been deleted on the restored disk. Write a two-page report outlining the files on the partitions and the files that were deleted.

Project 9-4

In this project, you work with an example of a Linux Ext2fs formatted disk partition. The purpose of this project is to familiarize you with the Linux file system by using DriveSpy and FTK. To prepare for this project, you need the following items:

❑ Forensic workstation with Windows 9x or later and FTK

❑ Spare disk space over 70 MB on your analysis hard disk

❑ Data file C9-4Lxsc.exe

To prepare the files, follow these steps:

1. Copy **C9-4Lxsc.exe** from the Chap09\Projects folder in your student data files to the Chap09\Projects folder in your work folder on your hard disk.

2. In Windows Explorer, double-click **C9-4Lxsc.exe** to extract C9-4Lxsc.sav, which is a file created by the DriveSpy SaveSect command. C9-4Lxsc.sav is a bit-stream copy of a small Linux partition that can be analyzed by FTK, iLook, and EnCase version 4 or later.

In the following steps, you use FTK Demo version to analyze the C9-4Lxsc.sav file. FTK Demo reads up to 5000 records, and then stops analyzing any additional records. You need to read only the first 5000 records of the Linux partition in C9-4Lxsc.sav to complete this project.

UNIX and Linux password files are typically located in the file /Etc/Passwd. The field layout for the Passwd file is as follows:

◻ account_name

◻ password_hash

◻ user_number

◻ group_number

◻ GECOS information

◻ Home directory

◻ Login script shell

For example, the root account might look like this:

```
root:Z2an19ifF903V:100:100:Joe Friday:/root:/bin/bash
```

To use FTK to analyze a bit-stream image file, follow these steps:

1. Start FTK. Start a new case, and complete the New Case Wizard to initialize the case. As a standard practice, it's a good idea to use descriptive information when filling in the case information fields.

2. Click each tab in the FTK window to examine the contents of the Linux partition.

3. Click the **Explore** tab, and then click to enable the **List all descendants** check box. Examine the contents of the folder shown in the Explore tab.

4. Click the **Search** tab, and then click the **Live Search** tab.

5. In the Search Term text box, type **root:** and then click the **Insert Item** button. Be sure the ASCII and Unicode check boxes are selected under Item Type. Then click **Search**, verify that the **All files** option button is selected, and click **OK**.

6. Click the **View Results** button when the search is finished. Click to expand the **Search Performed** items at the upper right. Scroll the upper-right pane to try to locate the password file for this Linux partition.

9

Project 9-5

In this project, you create a nonworking Linux partition so that you can examine it with DriveSpy. Because DriveSpy is designed to read data from FAT file systems, you cannot identify files and folders. However, you can search for keywords in Drive mode when examining non-FAT file system disks. You need the following items for this project:

❏ MS-DOS or Windows 9x forensic workstation with DriveSpy installed

❏ Disk partition utility, such as FDisk or Partition Magic (FDisk is included with DOS)

❏ A project disk, which is a spare hard disk larger than 48 MB, and a work folder on a disk with at least 55 MB

❏ Spare IDE cable and 12-volt power extension cable

❏ Data file C9-4Lxsc.exe stored in the Chap09\Projects folder in your work folder

To prepare the project disk, follow these steps:

1. Connect the project disk to the secondary IDE host adapter channel of a forensic workstation that is powered off.

2. Boot the forensic workstation and run FDisk or your preferred partition tool to create a 48 MB primary partition.

3. Restart the forensic workstation.

You do not need to format the project disk. The WriteSect command in DriveSpy runs from Drive mode, not Partition mode.

Next, you create a working nonbootable Linux partition that allows you to use DriveSpy to perform keyword searches. See Project 9-4 for instructions on copying and creating the Linux bit-stream file C9-4Lxsc.exe. Follow these steps to create a Linux partition:

1. Boot the forensic workstation to DOS.

2. At the command prompt, navigate to the **Tools** folder in your work folder, type **toolpath.bat**, and then press **Enter**.

3. Navigate to the folder where you stored C9-4Lxsc.sav, such as the Chap09\Projects folder in your work folder.

4. At the command prompt, type **drivespy** and press **Enter**.

5. At the SYS prompt, type **d1** and press **Enter**.

6. At the D1 prompt, **writesect C9-4lxsc.sav 63-94751** and press **Enter**. Then press **y** to continue.

7. At the D1 prompt, type **exit** and press **Enter**.

The WriteSect command physically writes data to the target disk. It does not reconfigure the target drive to the configuration of a fully functional Linux disk. All data collected by the

SaveSect command on the original Linux partition is written to the target drive. This allows you to perform a forensic examination on the Linux partition. Be sure to save the restored Linux partition.

After you have created the nonbootable Linux partition, you can use DriveSpy to examine it. First, follow these steps to update Drivespy.ini with the following keyword under a new search label:

1. Start Notepad and then open **Drivespy.ini** from the Tools folder in your work folder.

2. Scroll to the end of the file and press **Enter** to insert a new line, if necessary.

3. Type **[Search C9-5]** and then press **Enter**.

4. Type **100:root:** and then press **Enter** to specify that you want to search for data that exactly matches root:.

5. Save Drivespy.ini and then close Notepad.

After you update Drivespy.ini, you can use DriveSpy to perform the search on the Linux partition:

1. Start DriveSpy. At the SYS prompt, type **d1** and press **Enter**.

2. At the D1 prompt, type **output linux.log** and press **Enter**.

3. At the D1 prompt, type **search C9-5** and press **Enter**.

4. After DriveSpy completes the search, type **exit** and then press **Enter**.

Using a text editor such as DOS Edit, (or rebooting to Windows to use Notepad or WordPad), examine the output file Linux.log to try to locate the password file. On UNIX and Linux systems, the password file contains the user account name followed by a colon and then a hash value. This hash value is typically the password for that user account.

Finding the password file on a UNIX or Linux hard disk is handy for investigation purposes. By locating the password file and the associated hash value for the super user account root, you can use a disk editor, such as Hex Workshop, WinHex, or Norton DiskEdit, to overwrite the existing password with null (all zero) values over the password hash. Locating the correct password file can take a lot of effort because systems often contain old versions of password files. When the disk is reconnected to the UNIX or Linux system and booted, at the password prompt for the root account, press **Enter** to access the system.

CASE PROJECTS

CASE
PROJECTS

Case Project 9-1

Based on your evaluation of the arson running case example, you have been directed by the insurance company attorney to convert the EnCase image of the suspect drive to a Raw (dd) format image. The attorney has informed you that the converted image file must be sent to another investigator in another state to perform additional analysis unrelated to your work. Write a brief description of how you can convert this image from an EnCase format to a dd format using a tool such as FTK Imager.

Case Project 9-2

Now that you have examined the collected evidence in the kidnapping running case example, you need to perform a forensic bit-stream image copy of the laptop's disk drive. You should perform two different image copies of this drive. If available, use two different bit-stream image tools to make two separate copies of the laptop drive. Write a report on what tool or tools you used for this imaging task. Include in the report all procedures, evidence controls, and steps you have taken to perform this task.

Case Project 9-3

At a murder scene, you have started a bit-stream image copy. You are in the back bedroom of the house, and a small fire has started in the kitchen. If the fire cannot be extinguished, you have only a few minutes to acquire data from a 10 GB hard disk. Write one to two pages outlining your options for preserving the data.

Case Project 9-4

You need to acquire an image of a disk on a computer that can't be removed from the scene, and you discover that it's a Linux computer. What are your options for acquiring the disk image? Write a brief paper specifying the hardware and software you would use to acquire an image.

Case Project 9-5

A bank has hired your firm to investigate employee fraud. The bank uses four 20 TB machines on a local area network (LAN). You can talk to the network administrator, who is familiar with where the data is stored. What approach must you take, and what diplomacy do you need to use? Write one to two pages outlining the problems you expect to encounter and how to rectify them. Be sure to address customer privacy issues.

Case Project 9-6

You are investigating a case involving a 2 GB disk drive that you need to copy at the scene. Write one to two pages describing three options you have to accurately copy the disk. Be sure to address your software and media choices.

10

COMPUTER FORENSICS ANALYSIS

> **After reading this chapter and completing the exercises, you will be able to:**
>
> ◆ Understand computer forensics analysis
> ◆ Use DriveSpy to analyze computer data
> ◆ Use AccessData's Forensic Toolkit (FTK)
> ◆ Use EnCase to analyze computer data
> ◆ Perform a computer forensics analysis
> ◆ Address data-hiding techniques

This chapter explains how to apply your computer forensics skills and techniques to a computing investigation. You learn how to refine the organization of an investigation and use data analysis tools and practices to process digital evidence. The first section of this chapter explains the basic concepts of processing data to recover digital evidence. The second section describes how to use utilities such as Digital Intelligence's DriveSpy, AccessData's Forensic Toolkit (FTK), and Guidance Software's EnCase to analyze recovered evidence. You also learn how to systematically investigate specific operating systems and discover where data is often intentionally hidden.

In Chapter 14, you learn how to assemble the data you found and analyzed, and then present it in court or to a board of inquiry as a technical expert or an expert witness.

UNDERSTANDING COMPUTER FORENSICS ANALYSIS

Examining and analyzing digital evidence depends on the nature of the investigation and the amount of data you have to process. For most law-enforcement-related computing investigations, the investigator is limited to working with data defined in the search warrant. A private-sector investigator can be limited when working under the direction of a court order for discovery. If the corporate investigator is dealing with company policy, he or she might be looking only for specific items. The goal in any investigation often involves locating and recovering one or two items, which simplifies and speeds processing.

In the corporate environment, however, especially if the case involves litigation, the company attorney often directs the investigator to recover as much information as possible. Satisfying this demand becomes a major undertaking involving many hours and days of tedious work. These types of investigations can involve **scope creep**, where every piece of new evidence prompts the attorney to demand that you examine other areas to recover more evidence, widening the scope of the investigation. Scope creep increases the time and resources needed to extract, analyze, and present all the evidence.

Recent criminal investigations have required more detailed examination of evidence just before trial to help prosecutors fend off attacks from defense attorneys. Defense attorneys typically have the right of full discovery of the digital evidence being used against their clients. However, new evidence found while complying with the defense request for full discovery often isn't revealed to the prosecution. Its purpose is only to help the defense attorney better defend the accused. The defense request for full discovery applies only to criminal cases in the United States; civil cases are handled differently.

Refining the Investigation Plan

Recall from Chapter 2 that you begin any computer forensics case by creating an investigation plan that defines the investigation's goal and scope, the materials needed, and the tasks to perform. The investigation's scope is determined by the nature of the case. For example, in criminal cases requiring a search warrant or civil litigation cases requiring a subpoena, you can recover only data that's specified in the search warrant or subpoena. Other cases, such as employee abuse investigations for a corporation, might not specify limitations in recovering data. When a supervisor or an attorney requests that you recover and analyze digital data, refine the investigation plan by determining the elements of the case described in the following list. If refining the plan raises concerns about the case, such as not having enough resources to complete the investigation on time, inform your management or attorney of the problem.

- Determine the scope of the investigation.
- Estimate the number of hours it will take to complete the case.
- Determine whether you should collect only what's relevant to the investigation if you are investigating a large system with a lot of data (sparse evidence file recovery, as described in Chapter 5).

- Determine whether you must investigate further if you find more clues than anticipated (scope creep).

- Determine whether you have adequate resources to complete the investigation.

- Establish the deadline for completing the investigation.

After you refine the description of the investigation and acquire the disk you need to analyze, you're ready to search for evidence on the disk. In general, you perform the following tasks systematically:

- Examine file and folder (or directory) date and time stamps.

- Locate and extract all log files.

- Locate and recover any temporary print spool files.

- Locate and recover any encrypted or archived (for example, zipped or cabinet) files.

- Perform a keyword search on all data within the digital evidence.

- Examine Windows shortcut, Internet, Recycle Bin, and Registry files.

As computer hardware, OSs, and software applications evolve, review the latest releases of hardware and software to determine how they store data. Determine whether they use new methods to store data and whether current forensic tools can access the data.

You also need to determine the suspect's motive—namely, why the suspect is doing what he or she is doing. In addition, you need to ascertain how the suspect is accomplishing the crime. In much the same way a criminal profiler acts, you as a forensics investigator need to determine what to look for in each case. Profilers look for patterns in a suspect's actions, whether it's a murderer or a serial rapist. Forensic investigators have to perform a similar task using digital evidence.

10

USING DRIVESPY TO ANALYZE COMPUTER DATA

In previous chapters, you have used DriveSpy to find digital data. In this chapter, you examine other features of DriveSpy. Before you learn these additional features, download a copy of the DriveSpy user manual from *www.digitalintelligence.com/support.php*.

To use DriveSpy, you need DriveSpy.exe, DriveSpy.ini, and the help file, DriveSpy.hlp, which should be stored in the Tools folder of your work folder from your Chapter 2 installation of DriveSpy. The DriveSpy.ini file is a simple text file that specifies licensing, file, and search features. You customize DriveSpy.ini by modifying its settings to suit a particular disk forensic examination.

The DriveSpy.ini file is divided into four sections: License, File Headers, File Groups, and Search. Comment fields begin with a semicolon and describe each section and function. The **[License]** section contains the following information, as shown in Figure 10-1:

- Owner's name (the licensee)
- Organization's name
- E-mail address of the owner
- Level of functionality of the DriveSpy release
- Number of licenses issued to the owner
- Notes and comments
- Expiration date for the license
- License key, a 12-digit hexadecimal number

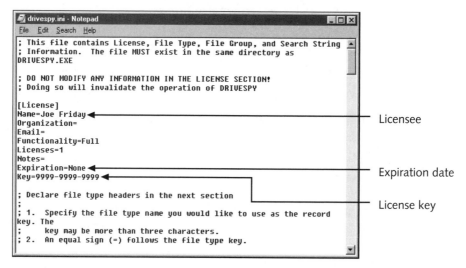

Figure 10-1   The [License] section of DriveSpy.ini

NOTE   The key that comes with your textbook allows you to contact Digital Intelligence for a 120-day license. When the .ini file for DriveSpy and Image is e-mailed to you, do *not* change the [License] section.

The **[File Headers]** section contains the hexadecimal number values for many known file types. These hexadecimal numbers are the header data contained in the first several bytes of all specialized data files, such as Microsoft Word documents or Excel spreadsheets and any associated templates. The file header uniquely identifies the file type.

You can use the file header information in DriveSpy to search for specific files that might have had their extensions changed. If someone changes an Excel file named FootballBets.xls to Report.wpt, DriveSpy can identify Report.wpt as an Excel file by reading the hexadecimal values in the file header. Forensics tools look at the file header in addition to the extension listed. Most can also tell you when the two conflict. FTK and EnCase use these same headers to identify files.

For example, suppose you are hired for a case in which law enforcement seized a computer during a raid on an illegal gambling operation. The suspect knows he has a high-risk operation that's subject to a police investigation and raid, so he probably hides or changes files containing gambling evidence. The detective handling this case informs you that the suspect has a temporary employment service called Acme Personnel Quick Help.

You are instructed to perform a forensic analysis on the suspect's computer and look for specific evidence of the bookmaking operation. You create a bit-stream image copy of the original evidence drive, as described in Chapters 2, 4, and 9. Then you shut down your investigation workstation and secure the original evidence disk drive. Now you're ready to start your disk examination.

Your first task is to examine and locate all known files in the folders on the duplicated evidence disk drive. You use DriveSpy to list all allocated files. (You learn how to do this with the Dir /s /a command in the "DriveSpy Scripts" section later in this chapter.) You note that Microsoft Office is installed on the evidence drive, but don't find any Excel (.xls) files. After talking to the detective, you find out that the suspect used Excel and might have saved Excel files on the C: partition. You can use information in the DriveSpy.ini [File Headers] section to search for a specific file type. One way to hide data is to change the extension of a sensitive or an incriminating file. In the "Addressing Data-hiding Techniques" section later in this chapter, you learn about other techniques for hiding evidence.

To search for files of a particular type, you can use DriveSpy to read the header section of a specific group of files or all files on an evidence disk drive. DriveSpy uses the information listed in the beginning of the [File Headers] section of DriveSpy.ini, shown in Figure 10-2.

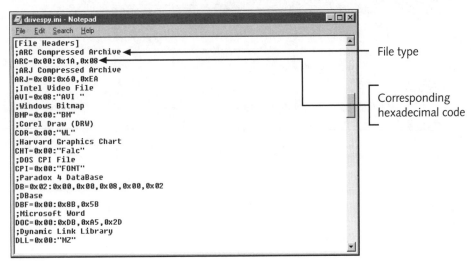

Figure 10-2   The [File Headers] section of DriveSpy.ini

TIP Digital Intelligence routinely updates the [File Headers] section as new file types are created. You can download the latest [File Headers] and [File Groups] information from the Digital Intelligence Web site at *www.digitalintelligence. com/support.php*.

In the [File Headers] section, the file type is specified in a comment field—a line beginning with a semicolon. The line after the file type is the corresponding header value. This is the header for Microsoft Excel:

```
XLS=0x00:0xD0,0xCF,0x11,0xE0,0xA1,0xB1,0x1A,0xE1,0x00,0x00
```

The 0x before each value is the **designator** that tells DriveSpy the next value is a hexadecimal number. Without the 0x, DriveSpy treats the value as a decimal number or ASCII character value. Therefore, the first 10 bytes of an Excel file are the hexadecimal values D0, CF, 11, E0, A1, B1, 1A, E1, 00, and 00.

Also, note that the first hexadecimal number (0x00) is followed by a colon. This first hexadecimal number is called the **offset**, which is the first byte where the actual header starts. In an Excel file, the offset starts at the first byte position of zero (0x00). Other types of files use different offsets. For example, in an .avi file, the header starts at byte eight from the beginning byte (0) of the file. Figure 10-3 shows an .avi file open in Hex Workshop.

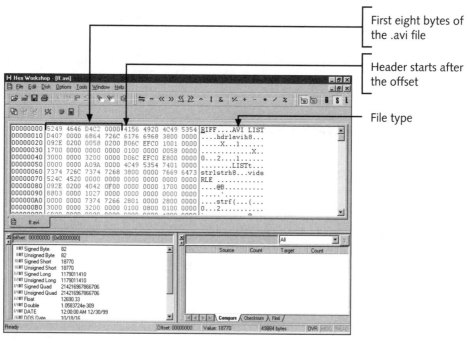

Figure 10-3   Offset of an .avi file

Based on the information in the [File Headers] section of DriveSpy.ini, you can search for any file with the Excel spreadsheet header value of 0xD0, 0xCF, 0x11, 0xE0, 0xA1, 0xB1, 0x1A, 0xE1, 0x00, or 0x00 and an offset of 0x00. You used this search technique in Chapter 7.

You can also add your own file headers to the DriveSpy.ini file. If you encounter a special file, use a tool such as Hex Workshop, WinHex, or Norton DiskEdit to find the file header and offset values. Examine several files with the same extension so that you can determine whether this file type has a common offset. Then add the file header and offset information to DriveSpy.ini in the [File Headers] section.

The **[File Groups]** section is a convenient place to consolidate similar file types under one group heading. For example, the Graphics file group in DriveSpy.ini lists the extensions of the graphics file types defined in the [File Headers] section, as shown in Figure 10-4.

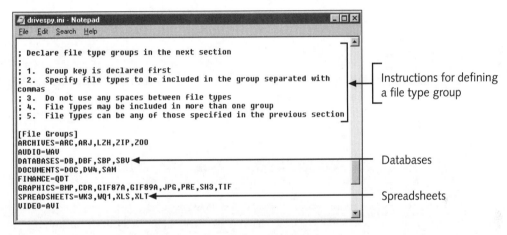

Figure 10-4   The [File Groups] section of DriveSpy.ini

For a particular file group, you can list file types of interest to the investigation, and then search for several header types at one time.

Returning to the example of the gambling suspect, you could look for all known spreadsheets in addition to Excel spreadsheets, such as Quattro Pro, Lotus 123, Quicken, Superbase 4, or all-in-one products such as Microsoft Works, OpenOffice, and StarOffice. An important exception to this recommendation is when you are analyzing a disk under the authority of a search warrant that limits your search to certain types of files. For example, if the warrant explicitly states that you can recover only Excel files, you cannot look for other spreadsheet formats such as Quattro Pro. If the warrant allows you to recover spreadsheet files, you can search for all spreadsheet formats. Consult with the investigator or prosecutor in charge of the case for guidance.

If necessary, you can define your own file groups. For example, suppose you are investigating an intellectual property case involving Microsoft Word documents, Harvard Graphics images, TIFF graphic files, and Waveform Audio files. First find the label names for each of these file types in the [File Headers] section of DriveSpy.ini.

- Microsoft Word: DOC
- Harvard Graphics 3.0: SH3
- Harvard Graphics Show File: SHW
- TIFF file: TIF
- Waveform Audio: WAV

For example, "Microsoft Word" is the name of the DOC file type. To create a new group for your intellectual property investigation, insert the following text in the DriveSpy.ini [File Groups] section:

INTEL_PROP=DOC,SH3,SHW,TIF,WAV

Note you can give the file group any unique name. Use descriptive, meaningful names that specify the case number and suspect name to clarify the purpose of the file group. Do not use short cryptic labels.

The **[Search]** section in DriveSpy.ini (see Figure 10-5) can include one or many keywords. You can create your own search group and keywords for DriveSpy and for other applications, such as EnCase. The [Search] section is the one that computer forensics investigators use most often.

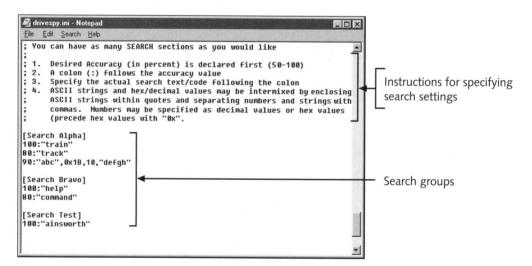

Figure 10-5 The [Search] section of DriveSpy.ini

To improve the data search, you can define the level of accuracy for the search from 50% to 100%. The accuracy is defined by entering the percentage value with a colon between the percentage number and the keyword. For example, if you want to search for the word "bookmaking," you enter 100: "bookmaking". Because the search is not case sensitive, DriveSpy searches the specified evidence disk or data set for text that exactly matches "bookmaking" except for the case. For example, it would find Bookmaking, BOOKMAK-ING, and bookmaking.

If you think the evidence disk might contain misspelled words, you can lower the accuracy of comparison. For example, if you set the accuracy to 50% by entering 50: "bookmaking" in the [Search] section of DriveSpy.ini, DriveSpy finds any word containing at least 5 letters that match any of the 10 letters in "bookmaking," such as "bookkmaking" and "bookmake-ing," which are possible misspellings of bookmaking.

However, a 50% search can produce **false-positive hits**, which means the search finds matches that don't apply to the case. In this example, any sequential combination of 10 letters produces a successful match. False-positive hits include bookie, maker, lookie, booking, kmake, bokzmake7, and so on. Later in the chapter, you see that other forensic tools have features that account for these items. To minimize false-positive hits, increase the percentage value. It's best to start high at 100% and decrement 10% at a time to minimize the number of matches found.

DriveSpy interprets keywords enclosed by quotation marks, such as "bookmaking", as literal keywords. That is, when quotation marks are used, DriveSpy searches for those values exactly. You can search for any character you can type on a keyboard, such as `1a2b[}\` or `^&87 2%20`.

One character you can't search for literally is the quotation mark because DriveSpy interprets it as the start and end of the literal string and produces errors if you use it in a search. Instead, you can use the hexadecimal value (a decimal value can be used, but is not recommended) of a quotation mark. You can find hexadecimal equivalents of characters in an ASCII chart or in Hex Workshop—click Help, Contents from the menu, select the Index tab, if necessary, and then click ASCII Character Set and Display. The hexadecimal value for a quotation mark is 22, and the decimal value is 34. To search for quotation marks, use 0x22 in the search text where you expect quotation marks to appear.

For example, suppose you want to search for "place bets by Friday", including the quotation marks. You could enter `100:0x22,"place bets by Friday",34` in the [Search] section of the DriveSpy.ini file. This line starts with 100 to specify that DriveSpy search for text that exactly matches the keyword after the colon. Following the colon is the 0x22 value, which is the hexadecimal equivalent of a quotation mark. A comma then separates the hexadecimal value from the literal "place bets by Friday" followed by another comma. The last value, 34, is the ASCII decimal equivalent of a quotation mark. You can use hexadecimal or decimal values in the [Search] section.

Another way to search for specific values, such as uppercase letters, requires listing all ASCII uppercase hexadecimal values. For example, to search for the word BOOKMAKING, use the following search string:

```
100:0x42,0x4F,0x4F,0x4B,0x4D,0x41,0x4B,0x49,0x4E,0x47
```

To search for the capitalized word Bookmaking, use the following hexadecimal value, as shown in Figure 10-6:

`0x42,0x6F,0x6F,0x6B,0x6D,0x61,0x6B,0x69,0x6E,0x67`

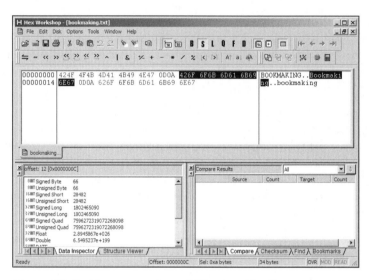

Figure 10-6   Hex conversion of "Bookmaking"

When you have finished updating DriveSpy.ini, save it in the same location as the DriveSpy. exe and DriveSpy.hlp files. As a standard practice, before you change DriveSpy.ini, you should make a backup copy of this file and store it in a safe location.

DriveSpy Command Switches

DriveSpy provides several switches, or parameters, to make its shell commands flexible. Most of these switches are similar to DOS command switches. Appendix B contains a list of the most commonly used switches for DriveSpy. Note that the wildcards commonly used in DOS and Windows, such as the asterisk (*) and the question mark (?), are also used in DriveSpy.

DriveSpy Keyword Searching

You use the DriveSpy Search command to search a drive at the physical level (Drive mode) or the logical level (Partition mode). You can also use Search to analyze specific files and folders by specifying one or more keywords the files are likely to contain. To record results from the search, create an output file by using the Output command before using the Search command. You can then examine the results of the search thoroughly. (If you don't create an output file, the search results scroll off the screen and you can't see the results.) Always use the Output command to create a log of your work.

The Search command has a variety of switches for specifying which files or folders to search. Refer to Appendix B for more details on Search command switches. Before using the Search command, update the DriveSpy.ini file by adding the keywords you want to use to search the evidence drive.

The Search command is extremely reliable in locating keywords in a formatted file. In Drive mode, Search can analyze other file systems, such as NTFS, HFS, and UNIX/Linux, and search the partition gap areas of a disk drive. In Partition mode, you can streamline Search to search specific files and folders. The only disadvantage to the Search command is that it cannot analyze archive files, such as .zip files, or encrypted files.

DriveSpy Scripts

With DriveSpy, you can use the Script command to run predefined commands. The Script command runs a script file that lists DriveSpy shell commands. A script is a plaintext file containing the commands you want to run. Consider using a script file to ensure consistent processing of an investigation that might involve more than one disk media, such as several hard disks. By using scripts, you ensure that you haven't left out any important commands or steps that you need to perform for each disk. Script commands are similar to the old DOS batch files.

To use the Script command, specify the name of the script and the associated path, as in the following example:

```
script C:\Chap10\Chapter\Scr_File.scr
```

You can then run the Script command from the DriveSpy System, Drive, or Partition prompts.

To create a script file, use a text editor such as Notepad to enter the commands you want to run in their proper syntax. As in a DOS batch file, you enter each command line by line, and DriveSpy runs the commands in the order in which they are listed. The following is an example of a simple script file:

```
output C:\Chap10\Chapter\Case_10.log
page off
drive a
part 1
dbexport C:\Chap10\Chapter\CaseDBexp.txt
dir *.xls /s /A
Search Spreadsheets
copy *.* /S /T:xls C:\Chap10\Case_10\XLS_File
quit
```

This script performs the following functions:

- Records in a log file the output of the commands

- Turns off Page mode

- Switches to drive A: and then Partition 1

- Exports a detailed list of all files
- Lists the .xls files in the partition
- Searches for spreadsheets as specified in the [Search] section of DriveSpy.ini
- Copies the spreadsheets to the XLS_File folder
- Exits DriveSpy

If necessary, you can run other scripts from any script. That is, you can nest script calls from one script to another script file. When the called script file completes its commands, it returns control to the previous script. For example, suppose you need to create two file listings of all Microsoft Excel files on a disk. The output for both files should be stored in different folders for further analysis. One folder contains all allocated (files not deleted) Excel files. The other folder contains all deleted Excel files. You can create a nested script file to automate these tasks.

To list all the Excel files on the suspect's disk, use the Dbexport command to write the recovered Excel files in descending order to a folder, as in C:\Chap10\Chapter\Case_10\Xls_File. Then write the deleted Excel files in ascending order to C:\Chap10\Chapter\Case_10\Xls_Del. To do this, you can create three separate script files. The first script runs the initialization commands for your investigation. The next two scripts contain the additional command to extract the Excel files. To create the main script file, follow these steps:

1. If necessary, create a **Chap10\Chapter** folder in your work folder.

2. Start Notepad.

3. Type the following DriveSpy commands, substituting the appropriate drive for C: and adding any necessary references to your work folder:

```
output C:\Chap10\Chapter\Case_10\Case_10.log
Page off
Drive 1
Part 1
Dbexport C:\Chap10\Chapter\Case_10\Dbexp_10.txt
Script C:\Chap10\Chapter\Case_10\Scr_file.scr
Script C:\Chap10\Chapter\Case_10\Scr_del.scr
Quit
```

4. Save this script file as **Scr_main.scr** in the Chap10\Chapter folder.

NOTE   The DriveSpy manual specifies using .scr for script files. However, Windows might associate .scr files with a Windows program, making it awkward to manually edit the file in Windows. If necessary, you can use a different extension, such as .txt or .spt, for DriveSpy scripts to minimize conflicts.

Now that you have completed the main script for your investigation, you can create the two other scripts that are called from the main script:

1. Start a new document in Notepad.

2. Type the following command, substituting the appropriate drive for C and adding your work folder, if necessary:

```
copy *.xls /S /-O C:\Chap10\Chapter\Case_10\Xls_file
```

3. If necessary, create a subfolder called **Case_10** in the Chapter subfolder of the Chap10 folder. Save this Notepad file as **Scr_file.scr** in the Chap10\Chapter\Case_10 folder.

4. Start a new document and then type the following command (adding your work folder, if needed):

```
unerase *.xls /S /O C:\Chap10\Chapter\Case_10\Xls_del
```

5. Save this file as **Scr_del.scr** in the Chap10\Chapter\Case_10 folder.

6. Close Notepad.

NOTE

As a standard practice, consider building a library of several scripts to not only keep track of what you have done, but also to reuse during other investigations. Other applications, such EnCase, can also create a variety of scripts for your convenience.

10

DriveSpy Data Integrity Tools

This section examines three commands you have already used in the text: Wipe, MD5, and Dbexport. These commands ensure the integrity of disk media in a variety of ways.

Use the Wipe command to overwrite possibly sensitive data from a disk or data that could corrupt any output data to the disk. You can overwrite data on a specific sector, partition, or drive or eliminate data from unallocated space, such as file slack space, unallocated free space on a logical partition, or the master boot record. You can use Wipe in Drive mode or Partition mode. Appendix B lists common switches for the Wipe command.

Because Wipe can remove all the data from a disk, including your system disk, carefully check the switches and specified drives before pressing Enter to run the Wipe command.

Another data integrity feature that DriveSpy provides is an RFC-compliant MD5 hash function. Use the MD5 command to collect the MD5 hash signatures for any data on a disk. You use an MD5 hash signature to verify that the file has not changed; in other words, it serves as a fingerprint for the file. You can obtain the hash value of specific files, a partition, or an entire disk. MD5 operates at the Drive or Partition level.

You can use the following switches (described in more detail in Appendix B) with the MD5 command:

- /S—Examines all subdirectories recursively

- /A—Hashes files with specific attributes

- /O—Sorts output

- /T—Hashes files of a specified type
- /G—Hashes files in a specified group

To hash an entire drive or partition, depending on the current mode, use the following command:

```
MD5
```

To hash all files in a partition, use the following command:

```
MD5 *.* /S
```

To hash a specific file, use the following command:

```
MD5 filename.ext
```

When you use the MD5 command in Partition mode for FAT file system disks, MD5 lists the boot sector, first FAT, second FAT, root directory, and then the data area of the partition. In Drive mode, MD5 provides one hash signature value for the entire physical disk, whether the disk uses a FAT file system or not.

The third data integrity DriveSpy command is Dbexport, which creates a text file of all specified data in the selected file or disk. Dbexport also lists all deleted files in addition to current allocated files on a disk drive. The Dbexport output file contains the following fields:

- File path
- File name
- File extension
- File long name
- File size
- Starting cluster position on the partition
- File archive switch setting
- Directory switch setting
- Volume switch setting
- System switch setting
- Hidden switch setting
- Read-only switch setting
- Erased pseudo-attribute setting
- File date values
- Creation date
- Modification date

- Last access date
- MD5 file hash signature (/MD5 switch must be used)
- Header values of each file (/HDR switch must be used)

You can import the text file that Dbexport produces into most spreadsheet or database programs, such as Excel or Access.

You can use Dbexport only in DriveSpy Partition mode with switches that are similar to the ones used with the MD5 function. They are explained in detail in the vendor documentation and in Appendix B. The unique switch is /HDR, which lists the first 12 bytes for each file.

To list all files in a partition, use the following command:

```
Dbexport
```

To list all Excel files in the current default directory, use the following command:

```
Dbexport *.xls
```

To list all Excel files in the current directory and all subdirectories with an MD5 hash signature for each file, use the following command:

```
Dbexport *.XLS /S /MD5
```

DriveSpy Residual Data Collection Tools

Deleted files on a Microsoft FAT file system disk become residual data, which resides in unallocated or slack space of the partition. DriveSpy provides the SaveSlack and SaveFree commands to copy this residual data and save it in a file you can analyze. You have used these commands several times in this book already.

The SaveSlack command allows you to copy all slack space from individual files or all files on a partition. The destination file must have an 8.3 file name because it's created from a DOS program. Because the file contains formatted and unformatted binary data, .dat is an appropriate extension. To copy all file slack space on the current partition to an output file named Slack_10.dat in the Chap10\Chapter\Case_10 folder on drive C:, use the following command:

```
SaveSlack C:\Chap10\Chapter\Case_10\Slack_10.dat
```

To save all file slack space for all Excel files in the current default directory to a file named Xls_slk.dat in the Chap10\Chapter\Case_10 folder on drive C:, use the following command. (The /S switch indicates that SaveSlack should retrieve data from slack space in all subdirectories.)

```
SaveSlack *.xls C:\Chap10\Chapter\Case_10\Xls_slk.dat /S
```

You can use SaveSlack only in DriveSpy Partition mode. The switches are described in detail in Appendix B and in the vendor documentation. The two unique items are /RAM, which saves only the RAM slack of files, and /FILE, which saves only the disk slack area of files.

10

The SaveSlack command is one of the few tools that enables you to separate RAM slack from disk slack in different data files.

Similar to the SaveSlack command, the SaveFree command collects all unallocated disk space on a partition. It works only in Partition mode and does not have any switches. To save data in the unallocated space on the current partition to a file named Free_10.dat in the Chap10\Chapter\Case_10 folder on drive C:, use the following command:

```
SaveFree C:\Chap10\Chapter\Case_10\Free_10.dat
```

The advantage of using this command is that it collects all unallocated space from a disk partition and saves it to a data file for follow-up analysis. You can examine deleted files and even RAM slack from this data.

Other Useful DriveSpy Command Tools

In addition to the Wipe, MD5, and Dbexport data-integrity commands and the SaveSlack and SaveFree residual data-collection commands, DriveSpy includes several other useful commands, including FAT interrogation commands and navigation and viewing tools.

The **Get FAT Entry (GFE)** command displays the FAT entry for a specified cluster and works only in DriveSpy Partition mode. The primary advantage of the GFE command is that it provides the next cluster link for a specified FAT entry, which helps you rebuild fragmented deleted files. For example, if you locate data of evidence value for your investigation in an unallocated cluster, you can check the FAT to see where the next link is located. Using the GFE command with the cluster number of the evidence fragment, you can determine the location of the next cluster associated with the first fragment of evidence. By using this command for unallocated disk space, you can piece together the remaining fragmented clusters of a deleted file.

You must supply the cluster number of the FAT entry you want to display. For example, the following command displays the FAT entry for cluster 230:

```
GFE 230
```

The disadvantage of using the GFE command is that it returns only the next higher numbered cluster location. Because of the limitations of FAT, it doesn't locate the beginning cluster.

The Chain FAT Entry (CFE) command displays all clusters after a cluster you specify. Use the CFE command to list all known FAT entries on all cluster positions for residual file data in unallocated disk space. Like GFE, the CFE command works only in Partition mode of the disk, and you have to designate the starting cluster. For example, the following command lists all FAT cluster links starting with the cluster number you have specified until it runs out of FAT links:

```
CFE 230
```

The CFE command only works forward from the cluster number you provide. It doesn't list previous cluster positions of a deleted file.

Like the CFE command, **Chain Directory Entry (CDE)** displays all directory cluster positions and works only in Partition mode. You must specify the directory you're searching. For example, the following command displays directory cluster positions in MyDocuments:

```
CDE MyDocuments
```

The Trace Directory Cluster (TDC) command helps you rebuild a directory on a disk partition. It supplies the name of the directory that resides in the specified cluster position. You can use the TDC command only in Partition mode. For example, to determine the directory in cluster 1111, use the following command:

```
TDC 1111
```

The Cluster command displays a specified cluster in a hexadecimal view, letting you quickly examine a specified cluster area of a partition. You can use the Cluster command only in Partition mode.

The Boot command enables you to examine the boot sector area of a disk partition and displays the boot sector statistics for the specified partition. You can use the Boot command only in Partition mode.

The PartMap command provides a sector map of a partition, listing the starting and ending sector positions of each component of the partition. You can use the PartMap command only in Partition mode.

The Tables command produces a sector map of a partition, listing each partition table for all partitions on a disk drive. You can use the Tables command in Drive and Partition modes.

USING OTHER DIGITAL INTELLIGENCE COMPUTER FORENSICS TOOLS

In addition to DriveSpy, Digital Intelligence offers other tools for performing computer forensics functions. These tools are compact enough to fit on a forensic boot floppy disk and are sold individually. They are not included with your 120-day license, but are described here for your reference. For more information on any of these programs, visit *www. digitalintelligence.com*.

Using PDBlock and PDWipe

The **PDBlock** program, designed to prevent data from being written on a disk drive, can be used only in a true MS-DOS environment. Running PDBlock from a Windows DOS shell causes unpredictable errors. PDBlock works at the BIOS level by turning off the write capability of Interrupt 13. It's designed to work with all IDE, EIDE, and some SCSI disk drives. Make sure you test PDBlock and any other write-blocker utility before you use it for investigation data acquisitions.

The **PDWipe** program is designed to overwrite hard disk drives, cleaning all data from the drive. You use PDWipe to overwrite all sectors of a disk, which means you must then repartition and format the disk to make it usable. PDWipe is used in a computer forensics investigation to sanitize a disk used in a previous investigation. Most forensic tools come with software or physical write-blockers and wipe tools. A variety of shareware and freeware tools meet the U.S. Department of Defense wipe criteria, which means the media must be wiped at least three to seven times to prevent possible retrieval of sensitive information. These tools comply with the Department of Defense 5220.22-M disk-sanitizing standard.

USING ACCESSDATA'S FORENSIC TOOLKIT

Throughout this book, you have used various features of FTK; this section emphasizes a few of the commonly used features. Using a command-line tool such as DriveSpy allows you to understand what a GUI tool such as FTK does for you at the touch of a button. Demo copies of FTK are available at *www.accessdata.com*. If you have not downloaded the product before this chapter, be sure to download and install the latest release of the FTK demo and the Known File Filter (KFF).

FTK can perform forensic analysis on the following file systems:

- Microsoft FAT12, FAT16, and FAT32
- Microsoft NTFS (for Windows NT, 2000, and XP)
- Linux Ext2fs and Ext3fs

FTK offers flexibility in analyzing data from several sources, including bit-stream imaging files from other vendors. It can also read entire evidence drives or subsets of data on specific evidence drives, allowing you to consolidate large volumes of data from many sources when processing a computer forensics analysis. For example, you might have several workstations and servers where suspects might have stored incriminating evidence. With FTK, you can store everything from bit-stream image files to recovered server folders on one investigation drive.

FTK analyzes the following bit-stream image file types:

- EnCase image files
- Linux or UNIX dd image files
- New Technologies, Inc. (NTI) SafeBack image files
- FTK Imager dd image files
- DriveSpy's SaveSect output files

AccessData has a separate program called the **Known File Filter (KFF)**, which integrates only with FTK. KFF filters known application software files from view, such as MSWord. exe, and identifies known illegal images, such as child pornography. KFF compares known file hash digital signatures to files on your evidence disk drive or bit-stream image file to see whether it contains contraband images. Periodically, AccessData updates the known digital signatures and posts an updated KFF. There is also a national database (*www.nsrl.nist.gov*) containing the updated hashes.

FTK also produces a case log file, where you can maintain a detailed log of all activities during your examination. All transactions, such as keyword searches or data extractions, are recorded in the log file for the current case. This log is also handy for reporting errors to AccessData. At times, however, you might not want the log feature turned on. Make sure you're aware of the implications before you begin. Many times during an investigation, you follow a lead or gut reaction instead of being systematic. If opposing attorneys were to see such log files, they might question your technique. It's better to find the items, and then perform a systematic search with the log file feature turned on. This approach isn't meant to conceal evidence, but to show that the results are consistently reproducible. (In Chapter 14, you learn more about attorney work product and discoverable evidence.)

FTK provides two options for searching for keywords. One option is an indexed search (described in Chapter 5). Indexing catalogs all words on the evidence disk so that FTK can find them quickly. This option returns rapid search results, although it does have some shortcomings. For example, in an indexed search, you can't search for hexadecimal string values. Also, depending on how the data is stored on the evidence disk drive, indexing might not catalog every word. In addition, indexing an evidence disk or bit-stream image file takes several hours to complete. Running this feature is best done overnight.

The other option, which overcomes the shortcomings of an indexed search, is the live search, which you have performed in previous chapters. You can use this option to search for alphanumeric and hexadecimal values on the evidence disk. This feature also accesses and compares all data on the evidence drive or bit-stream image file.

Figure 10-7 shows the number of hits in a live search in FTK from an image generated from a suspected arsonist's laptop. Figure 10-8 shows the actual hits. As you examine each hit, you can right-click to add it to your bookmarks, which adds the result to your final report.

Figure 10-7   FTK showing the progress of a live search

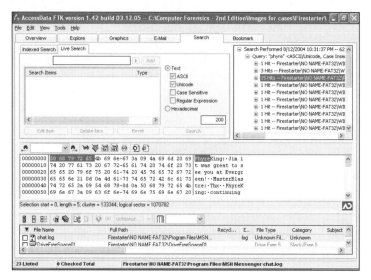

Figure 10-8 Viewing live search results in FTK

Much like the percentage search parameters you can use in DriveSpy, FTK enables you to search with several different features. The first is stemming, which allows you to look for words with extensions such as "ing," "ed," and so forth. It also searches for similar-sounding words, synonyms, and fuzzy representations. In an FTK query, a fuzzy search for "raise" would also find "raize," for example. So you find results that are close, but not exact.

In many cases, you are looking only for files that were accessed or changed during a certain time period. You can use this feature while in indexed search mode. Simply click the Options button and make your selections, as shown in Figure 10-9.

During the data-analysis processing, FTK opens compressed file systems, including Microsoft cabinet (.cab) files, Microsoft personal e-mail folders (.pst or .ost), and .zip files. FTK indexes any compressed data files it can open.

You can generate FTK reports with the FTK Report Wizard. To generate a report, you first need to **bookmark** specific findings of evidence during an examination. FTK and other computer forensics programs use bookmarks to tag and document discovered digital evidence. As you are analyzing an evidence disk, you designate a bookmark when you find data you want to note, such as evidence relevant to your investigation. To tag an item, simply right-click and select Bookmark. Or highlight an item, click Tools, Add Bookmark, fill in a descriptive name for the bookmark (see Figure 10-10), and click OK.

When you are using the FTK Report Wizard, you can select the bookmarked data you want to include in a report. FTK then integrates all the specified bookmarks and related case information in an HTML document. Each bookmark appears as a hyperlink in the HTML document, allowing the reader to view the report in a browser. The FTK Report Wizard

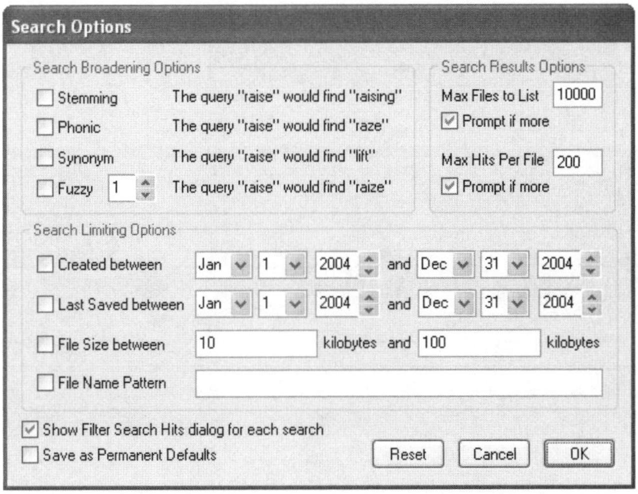

Figure 10-9   Selecting search options in FTK

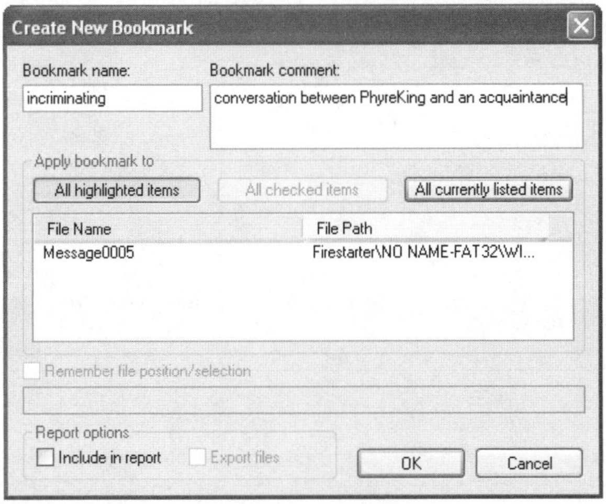

Figure 10-10   Creating a bookmark

also allows you to insert external documents, such as a Microsoft Word report, into the HTML file. Before printing an FTK report, you might need to use Adobe Acrobat or a conversion program to convert the HTML code to a PDF file.

A password recovery program available from AccessData is the Password Recovery Toolkit (PRTK), which is designed to accept possible password lists from many sources, allowing investigators to open password-protected files. You can create a password list in many ways, including generating a password list with FTK, as shown in Figure 10-11, or creating a text file of passwords yourself, as shown in Figure 10-12. You can download a free demo version of PRTK from the AccessData Web site at *www.accessdata.com*.

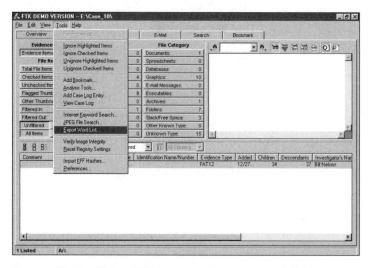

Figure 10-11   Using FTK to generate a password list

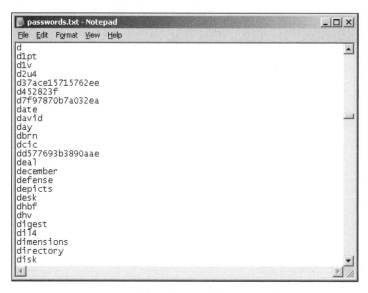

Figure 10-12   A partial list of possible passwords

FTK identifies known encrypted files and those that seem to be encrypted. For example, a simple encrypted file is a password-protected WinZip file or PGP file. If you are in the Overview tab of FTK and click the Encrypted Files button under the File Status column, FTK lists all files that appear to be encrypted. For password-protected WinZip or PGP files, if you select them in the bottom pane, FTK shows you the files contained in the zipped files. Your next step is to export the files by right-clicking and making the appropriate selection.

Figure 10-13 shows a .zip file selected and the file it contains. You can use a shortcut by clicking all files that need to be exported in the lower pane. Then right-click and select Export Files. At the top of the Export Files dialog box, make sure you have selected the All checked files option button (see Figure 10-14). You can then import these files into PRTK and attempt to crack them.

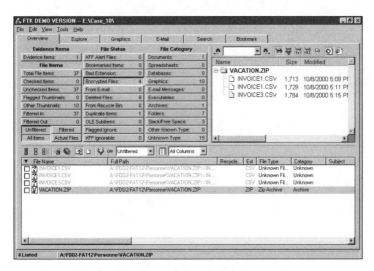

Figure 10-13   FTK displaying encrypted files

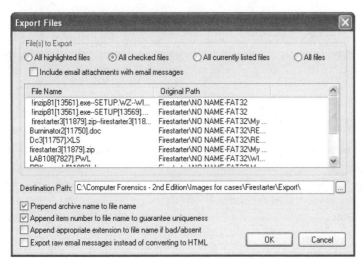

Figure 10-14   Exporting encrypted files

Be aware that the new WinZip9.0 password-protected files are virtually impossible to crack. You need to search on the suspect's machine to ascertain what version of WinZip was used. Take a moment in Windows Explorer to navigate to the area where AccessData is located (typically Program Files, AccessData). Select the Dictionaries folder and look at the wide variety you can choose (see Figure 10-15). Better yet, you can create your own dictionary based on the case, and PRTK allows you to create a biographical profile of a suspect to attempt to create passwords from that information.

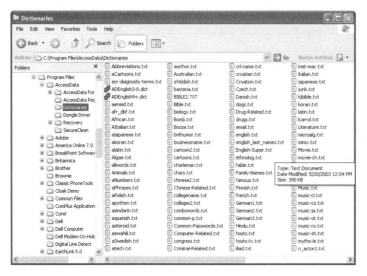

Figure 10-15   Dictionaries available for PRTK

Be aware that the more RAM on your machine for password cracking, the better because password cracking is memory intensive. In addition, keep in mind that you can add multiple images in FTK. Many times, you acquire a desktop, a laptop, *and* a PDA during an investigation. To make your task simpler, you can add all these images to the same case.

USING GUIDANCE SOFTWARE'S ENCASE

EnCase is a forensic software tool that has been around for many years and is widely used by law enforcement. It has a lot of powerful features that you can put to good use. The Enterprise Edition allows you to access hard drives remotely over a network. Imagine the cost savings when you suspect an employee of wrongdoing, but your investigator is in New York City and the suspect works in the company offices in Hong Kong. Although going to Hong Kong would be a great trip, being able to remotely image that person's hard drive over the network from NYC and perform your forensic examination saves a lot of time.

For data acquisition, you have a few choices. With a licensed copy of EnCase, you can create a boot floppy disk. The steps are quite simple. Before beginning, you must go to the download area of Guidance Software's Web site and get Bootfloppy.E01. (Try downloading the file at *www.guidancesoftware.com\support\downloads\packets\bootfloppy.EO1*, but note that this link might change in the future.) While you are there, notice there's also an ISO image for a boot CD that you can download. If you don't have a licensed version of EnCase, you can follow along with the steps and figures.

1. Click **Tools**, **Create Boot Disk**.

2. Click **Next** until you reach the screen shown in Figure 10-16 to select the location of the boot floppy image.

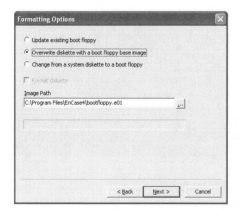

Figure 10-16 Selecting formatting options and a path location for a boot floppy disk

3. Continue following the wizard. If it asks for En.exe, simply navigate to the folder where EnCase is installed to retrieve the file. If necessary, click **Finish** to complete the process.

NOTE

More detailed instructions can be found in the vendor documentation.

The forensics boot floppy has a built-in software write-blocker that protects the suspect drive from contamination. The CD boot disk has similar features. Be aware that these features are for acquisition only.

After a forensic copy has been created, you need to start a new case and then add the drive image. Start EnCase and then follow these steps to begin using the features of EnCase:

1. Click **File**, **New** to open the Case Options dialog box (see Figure 10-17).

2. Fill in a specific case name and investigator. You need to click the ... (ellipses) button to specify the locations for exported files and for any temporary files for each case, as shown in Figure 10-17. When you're done, click **Finish**.

3. To add the drive image, click **File**, **Add Device**.

4. In the Add Device dialog box, click the **Add Evidence Files** button. Select the file location of your forensic image, as shown in Figure 10-18, and then click **Open**.

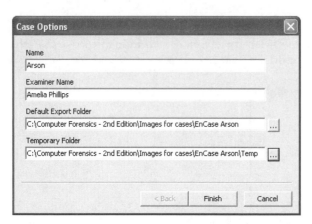

Figure 10-17 The Case Options dialog box in EnCase

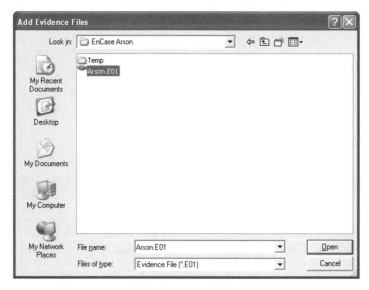

Figure 10-18 The Add Evidence Files dialog box

5. Continue to click **Next** until you see the Finish button. It might take a few minutes for the file to load and for EnCase to validate the image.

The image is now loaded. Typically, the EnCase layout has two panes at the top and one at the bottom. You can alter this layout by clicking the greater than, less than, or pause buttons on the center divider.

EnCase also has a built-in search feature. To perform a search, follow these steps:

1. Click **View**, **Keywords**.

2. Right-click the **Keywords** icon in the left pane, and click **New Folder**. The insertion point should be next to the new folder. Name it whatever category you like, such as Drug Related, Arson, Espionage, and so on.

3. Right-click the new folder, and click **Add Keyword List**. Add the keywords related to the case, and then click **OK**. Now you can click the selection boxes to the left of each keyword you want to search on.

4. Click the **Search** button on the toolbar, and in the Search dialog box, click **Selected keywords only** (see Figure 10-19). Click **Start** to begin the search.

Figure 10-19   The Search dialog box

As with most forensic GUI tools, EnCase allows you to select the type of files you want to view. For the running arson case project you've been working with, for example, select the My Documents folder and then select the Pleasure folder underneath it in the pane on the left. In the pane on the right, click the Gallery button. You can then scroll through the pictures, as shown in Figure 10-20.

You can also select a variety of options from the View menu, including Bookmarks, File Signatures, Hash Sets, Security Ids, Keywords, and more. These options simplify much of what you have to do. For example, if you choose View, File Types and then select the Mail option, you get the view shown in Figure 10-21. Notice the different e-mail types you can use for a search.

Figure 10-20   EnCase in Gallery view

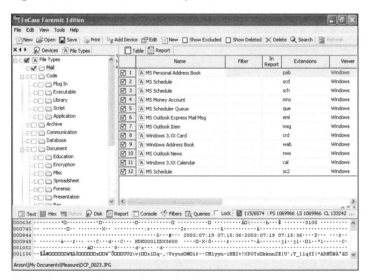

Figure 10-21   Mail options in EnCase

Another helpful feature is the timeline. If you click the Timeline button in the pane on the right, you can see at a glance when items were created, deleted, or modified (see Figure 10-22). In addition, by clicking the Options button at the top, you can change the color coding to your liking.

You can also bookmark items in EnCase. In Gallery view, for example, you simply select or deselect the checkmark above each graphics thumbnail, and then press Ctrl+B or click Edit, Bookmark Files from the menu. This action adds all the selected files to the bookmark area. Click View, Bookmarks from the menu to see all the bookmarked items. Next, click the Report button in the pane on the right to see a view similar to Figure 10-23.

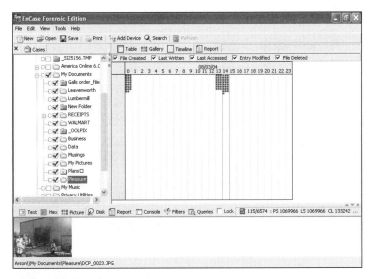

Figure 10-22   EnCase in Timeline view

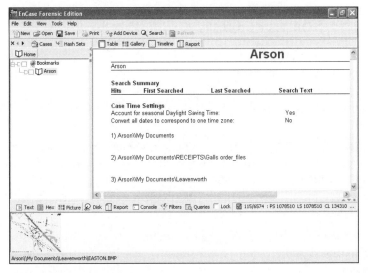

Figure 10-23   EnCase Report feature

EnCase also has a powerful scripting feature. To see the sample scripts that are available, click View, Scripts. Figure 10-24 shows a script used for a Linux machine to find certain types of system files. The pane on the left shows the variety of OSs and file types you can search with a script. To learn more about scripting, you can read the Guidance Software documentation or take an EnCase training course.

Throughout this book, you have been introduced to a variety of forensic software tools. The key point to keep in mind is that each one has its strengths and weaknesses. Having more than one tool in your forensics arsenal is strongly recommended, and you should regularly test new products and new versions of existing tools.

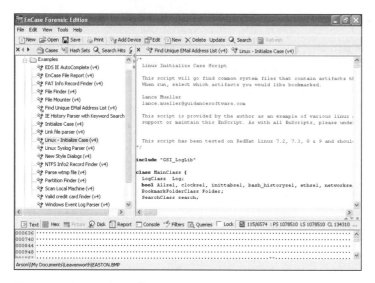

Figure 10-24 A sample EnCase script

Approaching Computer Forensics Cases

When approaching a new case, you need to be sure you know exactly what the case requires. This section describes a few basic cases and an approach to each. Nothing is cast in concrete; these descriptions are guidelines only. In computer forensics, you are the electronic gumshoe. Many times, you simply have to follow leads that you uncover from both physical and electronic evidence.

For example, say that a man is accused of viewing child pornography during a certain time frame. The time frame limits what information you should search for. Then you search for temporary Internet files and graphics. Unless necessary or you happen to notice something else, your case does not require you to search for anything else. This approach saves you time and your client money.

An employee suspected of industrial espionage can require the most work. A small camera might need to be set up to monitor his or her physical activities in the office. You might need to plant a software or hardware key logger, and you need to engage the services of the network administrator to monitor Internet and network activities. In this situation, you might want to remotely image the employee's drive and then use FTK Registry Viewer to determine what peripheral devices have been accessed.

Gathering evidence for a case of harassing e-mail depends on whether it's an internal corporate investigation or a public/civil suit. An internal investigation tends to be much easier. You can get the network logs and the e-mail server backups fairly easily. For a man accusing a woman of cyberstalking, however, you need to contact the ISP and the e-mail service. Some companies, such as AOL, have a system set up to handle these situations, but others do not. Be aware that many companies do not keep e-mail for longer than 90 days and many keep it only two weeks.

Profiling people by using the Web sites they access and viewing the types of files on their machines is quite easy. Try to develop a "feel" for the type of perpetrator or suspect you're dealing with, based on the content of the drive image. Check the logs of ICQ, Yahoo! Instant Messenger, and other chat programs. Each application has a way to access the logs; you can do a search on Google or the chat program's Web site to find this information. Create keyword lists based on common words you see the person using. Always ask "Why would they use this particular method?"

PERFORMING A COMPUTER FORENSICS ANALYSIS

As a standard practice, you should use the following basic steps for all computer forensics investigations. For more information on basic processes and recommendations, visit the International Association of Computer Investigative Specialists (IACIS) Web site at *www. cops.org*.

10

1. Before starting an investigation, use only recently wiped media (disks) for the target drive that have been reformatted and inspected for computer viruses. For example, use Digital Intelligence PDWipe, the DriveSpy Wipe command, or AccessData's SecureClean tool to clean all data from the target disk drive you plan to use.

2. Inventory the hardware on the suspect's computer and note the condition of the computer when seized. Document all physical hardware components as part of your evidence-acquisition process.

3. On a PC, remove the original disk drive, and then check the date and time values in the system's CMOS.

4. Record how you acquired data from the original disk—note, for example, that you performed a bit-stream image copy or a disk-to-disk bit-stream copy. The tool you use should also create an MD5 or SHA-1 hash for validation of the image.

5. When examining the forensic bit-stream image copy of the disk's contents, process the data methodically and logically.

6. List all directories (folders) and files on the copied bit-stream image or disk. For example, use the DriveSpy Dbexport command with a switch appropriate to the needs of the investigation.

7. If possible, examine the contents of all data files in all directories, starting at the root directory level of the volume partition.

8. For all encrypted files that might be related to the investigation, make your best effort to recover the contents of each file. For example, use password recovery tools, such as AccessData's PRTK or NTI's Password Recovery.

9. Create a document that lists the directories and files on the evidence drive. Note where specific evidence is found, indicating the relationship to the investigation.

10. Identify the function of every executable (binary or .exe) file that does not match known hash values. For example, after you perform a hash search that shows no listing for a specific executable file, examine the file to see what it does and how it works.

11. Always maintain control of all evidence and findings, and document everything as you progress through your examination.

Setting Up Your Forensic Workstation

Chapter 3 discussed setting up an investigator's lab. This chapter extends that discussion by explaining how to set up your forensic workstation in your lab. Before you can start an investigation, your forensic workstation must be configured correctly and ready to process the investigation. The following lists provide general descriptions of the minimum components and software to install on your forensic workstation. Adjust these lists to your specific investigation needs. You need the following computer hardware for your forensic workstation:

- PC with color monitor, keyboard, mouse, and CD-RW drive

- Cables and tools, including IDE ribbon cables (preferably 36 inches), extra 12-volt power extenders and splitters, assorted tools such as screwdrivers, an IDE 40-to-44-pin adapter bridge for notebook computer drives, and an optional SCSI card with cables

- One or more spare target drives to collect and analyze evidence

You also need the following software installed on your forensic workstation:

- Windows 9x or later installed on the C: drive and a forensic boot floppy disk. If you're using Windows 9x, configure the Msdos.sys file to allow you to boot to an MS-DOS prompt or to Windows. (Refer to Chapter 2 for specific instructions.)

- Bit-stream acquisition tool such as DriveSpy (you can use the SavePart, SaveSect, and CopySect commands). You can also use programs such as EnCase's En.exe DOS, Ontrack's CaptureIt, FTK Explorer, or Linux dd to acquire data.

- A computer forensics analysis tool, such as DriveSpy, FTK, or EnCase, and a write-blocker utility.

Besides the specified hardware and software, you also need the following types of media and other equipment:

- CD-Rs

- Floppy disks

- Evidence forms and labels

- Antistatic wrist strap and pad

Install all necessary and available hardware and software components before you start your forensic analysis to ensure that you do not overlook a necessary step or file. Add any other hardware components that can contribute to your investigation, such as Zip drives or Jaz drives. You also want to make sure that the forensic workstation is isolated from your network and from the Internet. Remember to test each component, both hardware and software, before applying it to an actual investigation. Become familiar with all the tools before the actual disk examination.

Performing Forensic Analysis on Microsoft File Systems

When analyzing digital evidence on Microsoft file systems, use the following general steps, adapting them as necessary to suit the needs of your investigation:

1. Before connecting a disk-to-disk bit-stream copied evidence disk to the investigation workstation, run an antivirus program to scan all forensic workstation disk drives for viruses.

2. After connecting the disk-to-disk bit-stream copied evidence disk, run an antivirus program again on all disks, including the copied evidence drive.

NOTE

You should run an antivirus utility for copied suspect disks, not on bit-stream image files, such as EnCase, **dd**, and SaveSect save-set volumes.

3. For the copied suspect disk, examine all boot files located in the root directory for the primary boot drive. Determine whether a boot manager utility is installed, and then identify all separate boot volumes.

4. Recover all deleted files and save them to a specified location on an investigation work drive. For example, create a subfolder on the investigation workstation to store all recovered data. Use the DriveSpy Unerase command with the appropriate switches to do so.

5. Recover all file slack and unallocated (free) space to an investigation subfolder. For example, use the DriveSpy SaveSlack and SaveFree commands with the appropriate switches.

FAT Disk Forensic Analysis

When analyzing a FAT disk, your first step is to make a bit-stream image copy of the evidence disk. Preserve the evidence disk by creating image volumes that can be stored on CDs. Then re-create the original evidence volume from the CDs to an evidence disk that you use for the forensic analysis. Determine whether to copy the entire drive or each partition volume separately. If your target disk is not identical to the evidence disk, copy each partition with the DriveSpy SavePart command, for example. If your target disk is identical to the evidence disk, you can use the DriveSpy CopySect command. The following steps, which outline how to acquire evidence from a FAT disk, are just an example, not an exercise:

1. Prepare the investigation target drive as outlined in the preceding steps.

2. In DOS, create a case folder (such as the Chap10\Chapter folder you create for this chapter's exercises) for storing your evidence. For a live investigation, you might use a folder name that reflects the case number, such as Case_10-2. If the target disk is drive E:, for example, and you are working at the DOS command line, you would type **md e:*work folder*\Chap10\Chapter** and then press **Enter**. This is the main folder for storing your evidence.

3. You would then change to the Chap10\Chapter directory by typing **cd e:*work folder*\Chap10\Chapter** and pressing **Enter**. Then use the DOS md command to create the following subfolders in your Chapter folder: unerase, allocate, image, residual, ssheets, dbase, and so forth.

NOTE   The name of the SSheets folder changes depending on the kinds of files you are seeking. For example, if you are searching for graphics files, you could name this folder Graphics.

4. Connect the suspect evidence disk and target (investigation) disk to the investigation workstation. If a hardware write-blocker is available, use it on the suspect disk.

5. Boot the investigation workstation to DOS using the forensic boot floppy disk or Windows 9x DOS mode. If no hardware write-blocker is installed, use a software write-blocker, such as Digital Intelligence PDBlock.

6. Run a data acquisition tool such as DriveSpy (using the SavePart command) or FTK Explorer on the suspect disk drive. If you're using the DriveSpy Save-Part and WritePart commands, create a partition on the target evidence drive that's the same size as on the original evidence drive.

7. When you are finished, archive the bit-stream image data to a CD-R or other media, such as tape or Jaz cartridges.

8. Secure the evidence drive and any archive media in an appropriate evidence storage container, maintaining correct evidence controls.

After you have completed the acquisition steps of the computer evidence, you can process and analyze the data.

Processing and Analyzing Computer Evidence

This step requires attention to detail. Keep the processing and analysis of your investigation free from any intentional or unintentional interference to maintain the integrity of your findings. To process digital evidence from a computer, you must extract all relevant data from the acquired evidence. In this section, you learn how to examine an entire disk. Remember to tailor your processing and analysis to the specific needs of the investigation, such as one governed by a search warrant specifying that you can locate and recover only Excel spreadsheets. If you find a Quicken file, for example, you cannot recover it because of the warrant's restrictions. However, in civil litigation cases, the attorney you're working for might direct you to recover everything.

The following steps are recommendations; how you apply each step depends on the investigation. Each computer forensics examination should include most, if not all, of these tasks, which use DriveSpy. You can also use other tools such as FTK or EnCase; refer to their user guides for instructions. To prepare to use DriveSpy, you use the following steps. This is an example, not an exercise.

1. If the evidence disk was saved with the DriveSpy SavePart command, restore all partitions of the original evidence drive to a target drive. Reboot the investigation workstation after you have restored each partition to make the newly created partition on the target drive visible to the operating system.

2. Boot the investigation workstation to DOS (MS-DOS 6.22 or Windows 9x DOS mode).

3. If available, run PDBlock on the target evidence drive. For example, type **PDBlock 1** (the 1 assumes the target evidence drive is the second drive on your forensics machine) and press **Enter**. This command write-blocks the second drive on the machine.

4. At the DOS prompt, change to the investigation work drive where you previously created the folders. For example, to change to the C:\Chap10\ Chapter folder in your work folder on the investigation drive (drive E:), type **E:** and press **Enter** to change to the E: drive, and then type **cd** *work folder***Chap10****Chapter** and press **Enter**.

5. Using a text editor such as DOS Edit or Windows Notepad, update the DriveSpy.ini search keyword values. (In Windows Explorer, first make sure the read-only attribute is not selected in the Properties dialog box for the DriveSpy.ini file.) For example, if you stored DriveSpy.ini in a special folder on the C: drive called Tools, you can use the DOS Edit utility by typing **edit C:***work folder***Tools****DriveSpy.ini**, and then pressing **Enter**. The DriveSpy. ini file opens so that you can edit it. At the end of the DriveSpy.ini file, type lines similar to the following, substituting search terms relevant to your case:

```
[Search Case10_1]
100:"invoice"
100:"Bank"
100:"swiss"
```

6. Save and exit DriveSpy.ini.

After updating the DriveSpy.ini file and creating the necessary folders, your next task is to recover the evidence from the target evidence drive. The following steps assume that the evidence drive is the second hard disk on your system:

10

1. At the DOS prompt, change to the Tools folder on your drive, and then run **Toolpath.bat**.

2. On your primary disk, create a subfolder to the C:\Chap10\Chapter folder called Case10_1. This subfolder should be located on your primary disk, not the evidence disk.

3. Navigate to C:*work folder*\Chap10\Chapter\Case10_1, type **DriveSpy**, and then press **Enter** to start DriveSpy.

4. At the SYS prompt, create an output file to record your actions and findings by typing **output Case10_1.log**, and then pressing **Enter**.

5. At the SYS prompt, type **drive 1** and then press **Enter** to examine the partition on the target drive. At the D1 prompt, type **part 1** and press **Enter**.

NOTE

If the target evidence disk has more than one partition, repeat Steps 1 to 3 to recover all evidence. Use your preferred disk partition utility, such as FDisk, Gdisk, or Partition Magic.

The next task is to establish an integrity baseline for the evidence. To do this, use the Dbexport command with the MD5 switch to create an output file that provides a record of all file data on the evidence disk. You can run Dbexport again at the end of the examination to compare the final output to the first Dbexport listing and ensure that no data on the evidence drive has been altered. To create an evidence integrity baseline, follow these steps:

1. At the D1P1 prompt, type **dbexport Dbexp_10.Txt /MD5 /Hdr /S** and press **Enter**.

2. To create a baseline for the first and second FAT, boot sector, root directory, and combined data area of the partition, run the MD5 command from Partition mode by typing **MD5** at the D1P1 prompt and pressing **Enter**.

NOTE

Running MD5 with no switches or parameters produces a hash value for all major sections of a disk partition.

After creating a data integrity baseline, collect all recoverable deleted files and residual data from the target evidence disk. In the following steps, you do so using the DriveSpy Copy, Unerase, SaveSlack, and SaveFree commands:

1. At the D1P1 prompt, type **copy *.* /S E:*work folder*\Chap10\Chapter\Case10_1\Allocate** and then press **Enter** to copy all allocated data from the target evidence partition to the Allocate folder. Type **y** to disable Page mode.

2. At the D1P1 prompt, type **copy *.* /S /T:xls E:*work folder*\Chap10\Chapter\Case10_1\SSheets** and then press **Enter** to recover only specific

allocated file types, such as Microsoft Excel spreadsheets, and store them in the SSheets folder. Type **y** to disable Page mode.

3. At the D1P1 prompt, type **unerase *.* /S E:*work folder*\Chap10\\Chapter\Case10_1\Unerase** and then press **Enter** to recover all deleted files with the Unerase command and store them in the Unerase folder. Then type **y** to disable Page mode.

4. At the D1P1 prompt, type **unerase *.* /S /T:xls E:*work folder*\Chap10\\Chapter\Case10_1\SSheets** and then press **Enter** to recover only specific deleted files, such as Microsoft Excel spreadsheets, and store them in the SSheets folder. Type **y** to disable Page mode.

5. At the D1P1 prompt, type **saveslack E:*work folder*\Chap10\Chapter\\Case10_1\Residual\Slack_10.dat** and then press **Enter** to use the SaveSlack command to collect all residual data located in file slack space and store it in a file named Slack_10.dat in the Residual folder. Type **y** to disable Page mode.

6. At the D1P1 prompt, type **savefree E:*work folder*\Chap10\Chapter\\Case10_1\Residual\Free_10.dat** and then press **Enter** to use the SaveFree command to collect all residual data located in unallocated disk space and store it in a file named Free_10.dat in the Residual folder. Type **y** to disable Page mode.

10

Your responsibility is to collect as much information about the case as possible (within the bounds of the search warrant or subpoena). The more information you have, the better you can identify keywords that might help you locate evidence. In the next example, you apply the DriveSpy Search command to the investigation. The Search command searches only for words you have listed in the DriveSpy.ini file. To run keyword searches with DriveSpy, follow these steps:

1. At the D1P1 prompt, type **search case10_1** and then press **Enter** to start searching for the keywords you entered earlier. Type **y** to disable Page mode.

2. At the D1P1 prompt, change from Partition mode to Drive mode by typing **d1** and then pressing **Enter**. Data might reside on the partition gap, which does not show up on the logical level.

3. At the D1 prompt, type **search case10_1** and press **Enter** to run the search pattern again.

4. At the D1 prompt, type **quit** and then press **Enter** to exit DriveSpy.

Some considerations when analyzing MS-DOS and Windows 9x OSs are the use of older compression utilities such as DriveSpace or DoubleSpace. If you encounter partition volumes compressed with DriveSpace or DoubleSpace, you must reconstruct the evidence partition on a target investigation drive. After you have duplicated the original evidence drive, you must reboot your forensic workstation with the target evidence drive so that you can access the compressed partition.

NOTE   DriveSpace and DoubleSpace partition volumes compress disks by eliminating file slack space, so these volumes do not have file slack space.

Other ways to acquire data with DriveSpy range from searching for unique file headers to recovering residual fragments of partially overwritten files. By using the Search command to find hexadecimal values and the GFE, CFE, CDE, and TDC commands, you can piece together partial or whole file fragments.

After you have collected all the data you need, analyze its content to find evidence related to your investigation. Analyzing digital evidence is the most time-consuming and sometimes difficult investigation task. Recent GUI tools, such as FTK, EnCase, FacTracker, and ProDiscover DFT, make analysis faster than DOS tools, such as DriveSpy. No matter which tool you use, learn how to maximize its capabilities to make the analysis task successful.

For example, suppose you need to recover Microsoft Word documents located in unallocated free space of a suspect's disk drive. With DriveSpy, you can recover specific deleted Word files by searching for unique keywords those files are likely to contain. If the keywords appear in unallocated space, you can use the SaveSect command to extract the sectors to a data or text file. Suppose you're looking for Word documents containing the phrase "pay off" and the name "Joe." You can create a [Search] section in DriveSpy.ini with the following keywords:

```
[Search CASE10_1A]
100:"pay off"
100:"Joe"
```

In DriveSpy Partition mode, you can then run a logical search by typing `Search Case10_1a` at the D1P1 prompt. To restrict the search to only .doc files, you can type `Search *.doc Case10_1a` at the D1P1 prompt. Similarly, to conduct a physical (Drive mode) search, type `Search Case10_1a` at the D1 prompt. In Drive mode, DriveSpy searches the entire drive, including data areas within and between partitions. You can use Drive mode to search non-FAT drives, such as NTFS, Linux Ext2fs and Ext3fs, and UNIX drives.

When you locate the keyword from a logical (Partition mode) search in unallocated space, use the Cluster command to examine it for evidentiary value. For physical searches, use the Sector command to examine it for evidentiary value. You can then use the SaveSect command to extract the evidence to an external data file. You need to find the starting absolute sector number where the evidence is located to use the SaveSect command. Estimate how many sectors to copy by examining the clusters following the initial cluster for each keyword found. In Cluster or Sector view, scroll through the data area to determine where the data ends. When you have located the possible ending cluster area, note the absolute sector number. To recover unallocated evidence data, follow these steps:

1. In DriveSpy, locate the cluster position from the keyword search results. For example, Figure 10-25 indicates that the name Joe first appears at cluster position 1307.

2. At the D1P1 prompt, type **cluster 1307** and then press **Enter**. You're simply using the Cluster command with the cluster position (see Figure 10-25).

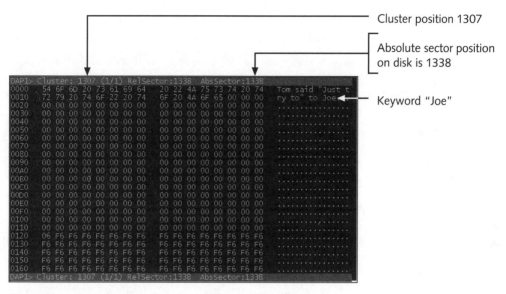

Cluster position 1307

Absolute sector position on disk is 1338

Keyword "Joe"

Figure 10-25 Location of Joe at cluster position 1307

3. Note that the absolute sector value (AbsSector) of cluster 1307 is absolute sector 1338.

4. Press **Page Down** to scroll to the end of the cluster listing, and look for the last absolute sector value, or the ending absolute sector, which is also 1338 because this is a short file.

5. Press **Esc** to exit Cluster view and return to the DriveSpy shell prompt. Now you can use the SaveSect command to extract the data from unallocated disk space and save it in a text file. Recall from Chapter 9 that with the SaveSect command, you specify the starting sector and then the number of sectors to read.

6. At the D1P1 prompt, type **savesect 1 1338,1 E:*work folder*\Chap10\ Chapter\Kw_Joe.Txt** and then press **Enter**.

In an actual investigation, you would repeat these steps until you have completed the evidence recovery. Next, you must sort through the evidence to determine what's of value to the case. Consider the following guidelines as you examine the evidence:

- Create separate folders to store evidence, such as one folder for spreadsheets and another for e-mail. You can further subdivide these folders into subjects or people of interest.

- For complex investigations, maintain a log, preferably in a database that allows you to collect relevant information and notes of your observations. Create as many fields as necessary to sort the data more easily.

- Periodically review the data you have collected to refresh your knowledge of the facts you gathered.

- Apply deductive reasoning to your findings to help build new leads. Determine new keywords you can use to search for related evidence. Become skilled at building on little pieces of information to create bigger pieces of the investigation puzzle.

- Research data you're not familiar with, such as unknown file types. This data might be evidence that solves the case.

NTFS Forensic Analysis

Performing computer forensics on an NTFS file system is similar to performing computer forensics on FAT file systems. Most computer forensics tools allow you to analyze NTFS disks. Some are easy to use; others can challenge your technical ability and knowledge of NTFS file structures. DOS-based tools include DriveSpy and NTI NTFS suite, and GUI-based tools include FTK, EnCase, Pro Discover DLT, FactFind, and iLook.

NTFS DOS Analysis

The current release of DriveSpy (version 1.64 as of this writing) provides limited analysis capability for NTFS disks. To use DriveSpy, you must access the target evidence NTFS drive in Drive mode (at the physical level). With DriveSpy, you can't directly examine the data structures on an NTFS partition, such as directories and file names, or the dates and times that directories and files were created, modified, and last accessed, as you can with a FAT file system.

On an NTFS disk, you can perform a keyword search in both an ASCII version and a Unicode version of the keyword. (Refer to Chapter 3 for instructions on performing ASCII and Unicode searches.) For example, the following entries in the DriveSpy.ini file search for "Joe" as ASCII text and as Unicode ("J",0x00,"o",0x00,"e",0x00):

```
[Search CASE10_1B]
100:"Joe"
100:"J",0x00,"o",0x00,"e",0x00
```

You use the null (0x00) values between each literal character because Unicode is a 16-bit code, whereas ASCII is only an 8-bit code.

The NTFS analysis tools from NTI are easier to use than DriveSpy when accessing NTFS disks from DOS. The NTFS suite of tools allows you to list the contents of the MFT, and copy specific files from the NTFS drive to a DOS FAT partition. You can also copy file slack space and unallocated space to a data file for additional analysis. DiskSearch NT is a tool in the NTI suite for performing keyword searches on the target evidence disk.

SysInternals (*www.sysinternals.com*) offers an additional product for NTFS investigations called NTFSDOS, which runs on MS-DOS and Windows 9x systems. The freeware version reads NTFS drive partitions from Windows 9x systems. This read-only feature makes it ideal for performing forensic analysis. For NTFS data recovery, an ideal combination of DOS tools is DriveSpy to perform physical level searches and NTFSDOS to examine NTFS file structures.

NTFS GUI Analysis

Using GUI tools such as FTK, EnCase, Pro Discover DFT, FactFind, and iLook makes viewing and locating evidence on NTFS disks much easier than with DOS tools. In particular, the GUI tools show directory and file structures, which speeds up processing time for the analysis.

With a tool such as FTK, you can view an NTFS disk or a variety of bit-stream image files on an NTFS disk partition. FTK provides a viewer similar to Windows Explorer that includes allocated files, deleted files, and unallocated disk space.

UNIX and Linux Forensic Analysis

Most computer forensics tools have been developed for Microsoft file systems. However, to respond to the recent popularity of Linux, several forensic software programs now enable you to examine Ext2fs and Ext3fs Linux file systems. Organizations such as @stake have also contributed to the development of freeware UNIX file system analysis tools. This section introduces you to computer forensics tools you can use with UNIX and Linux file systems, but you should also obtain additional training in UNIX system administration to enhance your ability to analyze data and determine its evidentiary value to an investigation.

Windows Forensics Tools for Analyzing UNIX and Linux Data

Many of the leading GUI computer forensics tools can analyze UNIX and Linux file systems, including EnCase, FTK, and iLook. You don't need advanced UNIX system knowledge to use these tools on a UNIX or Linux file system. You can perform the same forensic analysis that you do with FAT and NTFS file systems.

Figure 10-26 shows an example of a Linux Ext2fs file system in FTK, which configures the directories, files, and unallocated space in the same manner as it does for NTFS or FAT file systems.

Note that the naming conventions used in a Linux or UNIX environment are more cryptic at first glance than DOS and Windows file names. Understanding how UNIX systems work and the purpose of each file and directory helps when investigating these types of systems.

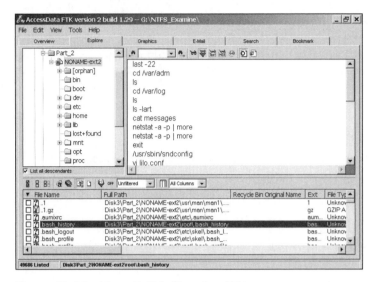

Figure 10-26 Linux Ext2fs file using FTK

UNIX and Linux Forensics Tools

UNIX forensics tools were originally designed to help UNIX system administrators identify hacker activities on systems and network servers. The freeware tools Sleuthkit, Knoppix-STD, Autopsy, and TASK offer analysis capabilities from several UNIX and Linux platforms. These tools have been designed to perform analysis on imaged and live systems. For additional information on these tools and others, visit the following Web sites:

- Freeware UNIX and Linux data analysis: Purdue University, *www.cerias.purdue.edu/homes/carrier/forensics*

- The Coroner's Toolkit (TCT): *www.porcupine.org/forensics/tct.html*

- TASK: *www.atstake.com* (As of this writing, @stake was acquired by Symantec; you might need to do some research to see how software changes take place. Older versions of the software might still be available on other sites.)

Because high-end UNIX and Linux systems are often used as Web servers, investigating these computers involves working with a live system. Depending on the use of a UNIX or Linux server, you might not be able to shut down the computer to perform a data acquisition. For example, UNIX servers are used to provide services as critical as a shuttle launch for NASA. Customers also expect e-commerce sites to be available around the clock. Many of those sites use UNIX servers and cannot be taken off-line.

As a standard practice for all UNIX or Linux systems, your first task is to preserve any data temporarily stored in volatile memory. That is, determine which applications are running, including those running in the background such as batch jobs, and save the active data. Preserving active data often results in evidence that can make your case.

For all UNIX and Linux systems, use the following checklist to help preserve volatile data. This list is ranked in order of importance:

- Running processes
- Network connections
- System memory
- Swap space
- Console messages

UNIX and Linux systems can also have multiple user accounts. To investigate intrusion incidents on these systems, you must examine system log files to help identify which accounts were used to compromise the system. You might need to recover data if skilled hackers have deleted log files to cover their tracks.

If you're working on a live system, always use the redirect output parameter to redirect the results of your analysis work to an external media device, such as a floppy disk. For example, to preserve the output from the UNIX `ps` (process status) command to a text file, first mount the floppy disk by typing `mount /dev/fd0 /mnt/floppy` and pressing Enter, and then save the output of the `ps` command to a text file named Psdata.txt on the floppy disk by typing `ps -aux > /floppy/psdata.txt` and pressing Enter. Keep in mind that deleted files that still have running processes can be recovered from a live system via the /proc directory. It's always a good idea to examine /Etc/Syslog.conf, /Etc/Inetd.conf, and shell history data files.

For intrusion investigations, examine the following data areas on UNIX and Linux systems:

- All running processes
- All network connections
- All deleted files
- File system
- Current status of memory
- Contents of the swap file
- Backup media to compare to the current system
- All background processes

Reconstruct all events to see what happened to a system after it was attacked. Look for discrepancies in time-based components, such as system files, password files, and log files. Examine the files that were created or modified during the period of the incident, and then analyze and hypothesize how the incident occurred. The following list shows the items that need to be examined.

- *System*—Includes registers, peripheral memory, and cache files.
- *Physical memory*—Use the `dd` command to copy the contents of RAM to a file.
- *Network state*—Use the `netstat` command to identify the computer's network accesses and connections.

10

- *Current running processes*—Use the `ps` command to find the names of all current processes.

- *Terminate current processes*—Use the `kill` command to terminate current processes without overwriting current file space.

- *Disk data acquisition*—Run an MD5 or SHA-1 hash on all files and directories. Before shutting down the computer, copy all logs and other system accounting files to external media.

Some useful UNIX commands to use when analyzing disk content are included in Appendix B, which also lists the log and data files to inspect on Solaris, HP-UX, AIX, and IRIX UNIX systems and on Linux systems.

If the system you're investigating has been attacked, determine whether a root kit has been installed on it. A **root kit** is a hacker tool that allows backdoor access to a system. For the latest information on root kits, visit the Computer Emergency Response Team (CERT) Web page at *www.cert.org*.

Macintosh Investigations

Investigating newer Macintosh systems that have implemented the Berkeley Standard Distribution (BSD) UNIX file system are no different from investigating any other type of UNIX or Linux disk. To investigate older Macintosh systems, Mac OS 9 or later, use one of the Windows, UNIX, or Linux forensic tools, such as EnCase, iLook, SMART, or TASK. You use EnCase or iLook on older Macintosh file systems the same way you examine a FAT or NTFS disk partition.

ADDRESSING DATA-HIDING TECHNIQUES

Data hiding involves changing or manipulating a file to conceal information. People can hide data by changing a file extension, setting a file's attribute to hidden, or using encryption to keep the contents secret.

One skill many home computer users developed was programming in the specific computer manufacturer's assembly language. Assembly programming involves cryptic system commands called mnemonics. Listing these commands in a program allows programmers to use a computer's CPU to directly manipulate functions and data. With these skills, some computer users developed programming tools that could change data. They could create a low-level encryption program that shifted binary data, making the altered data unreadable when accessed with a text editor or word processor. They accomplished this by shifting or rearranging bits for each byte within a specified file. To secure a file that might contain sensitive or incriminating information, programmers could run the assembler program (also called a macro) on the file to scramble the bits. To access the file, programmers ran another program to restore the scrambled bits to their original settings.

Some low-level encryption programs are still used today and can make it difficult for an investigator to analyze the data for a suspect disk drive. To examine such a disk, start by identifying as many files as possible to find some you're not familiar with that might lead to new evidence. Training in one or more programming languages such as Visual Basic, Visual C++, or Perl is also helpful.

Hiding Partitions

One way to hide partitions is to create a partition on a disk, and then use a disk editor such as Norton DiskEdit to manually delete any reference to it. To access the deleted partition, users can edit the partition table to re-create the links. When users restart the computer, the hidden partition reappears.

Another way to hide partitions is to use a disk-partitioning utility, such as PartitionMagic, System Commander, or Linux Loader (LILO), which provides a startup menu that allows you to select an OS. The system then ignores other bootable partitions.

To circumvent these techniques, be sure to account for all disk space when examining an evidence disk. Analyze any areas of the disk that contain space you can't account for so that you can determine whether these areas contain additional evidence. For example, in Figure 10-27, DriveSpy lists all the starting and ending sectors for each partition on the drive. Note that Partition 1 ends at sector 205631 and Partition 2 starts at sector 248031. This leaves a 42400-sector gap between these two sectors.

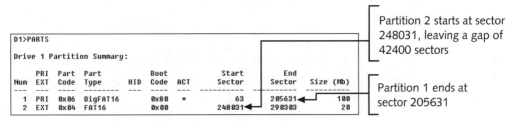

Figure 10-27   DriveSpy showing starting and ending sectors

To access the partition gap area of a disk with DriveSpy, you need to work in Drive mode. To view the content of the data area, set DriveSpy to Drive mode, and then examine and analyze a partition gap area with the Sector, Search, CopySect, and SaveSect commands.

For example, using the DriveSpy SaveSect command, you can copy the contents of the sector gap shown in Figure 10-27 to a data file for further examination. To determine the sector range for the SaveSect command, add one to the ending sector number of Partition 1, and subtract one from the beginning sector number of Partition 2. If the first partition ends at sector 205631, the beginning sector position of the partition gap is 205631 + 1, or 205632. If the second partition starts at sector 248031, the ending sector position of the partition gap is 248031 − 1, or 248030. The partition gap ranges from sector 205632 to sector 248030. To copy the sector gap to a data file, at the DriveSpy D1 prompt, type `SaveSect 205632-248030 E:\`*work folder*`\Chap10\Chapter\Part_gap.dat` and press Enter.

With Hex Workshop you can examine the contents of the partition gap, as shown in Figure 10-28.

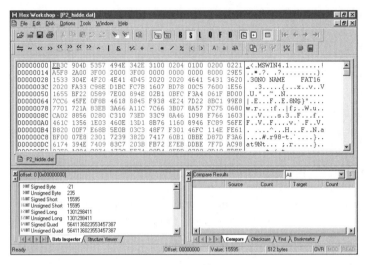

Figure 10-28   Viewing the partition gap with Hex Workshop

To carve (or salvage) data from the recovered partition gap, apply other computer forensics tools such as FTK or WinHex, as shown in Figure 10-29.

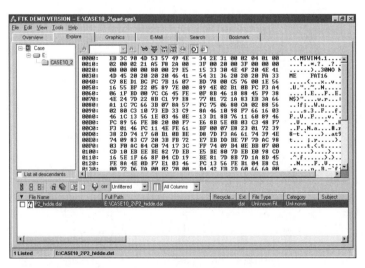

Figure 10-29   Salvaging a partition gap with FTK

Marking Bad Clusters

Another data-hiding technique is placing sensitive or incriminating data in free space on disk partition clusters. This method of hiding data is more common with FAT file systems. By using a disk editor such as Norton DiskEdit, the good clusters can be marked as bad clusters. The OS then considers these clusters as unusable. The only way they can be accessed from the OS is by changing them to good clusters with a disk editor.

To mark a good cluster as bad using Norton Disk Edit, you must update the first FAT table for the specific cluster or clusters you want to mark as bad. Then you type the letter B in the FAT cluster location, as shown in Figure 10-30. To access the alleged bad cluster, you can use any DOS disk editor to write and read data to it.

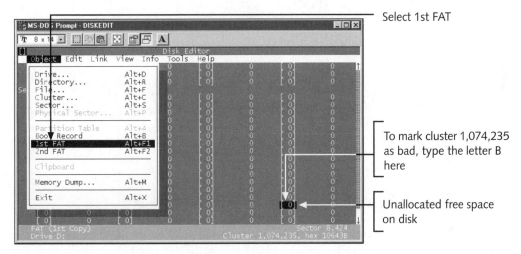

Select 1st FAT

To mark cluster 1,074,235 as bad, type the letter B here

Unallocated free space on disk

Figure 10-30   Marking a good cluster as bad

NOTE

If a FAT partition containing clusters marked as bad is converted to an NTFS partition, the bad clusters remain marked as bad on the NTFS partition. Hence, if data is hidden in these marked bad clusters, the conversion to NTFS does not affect their content. Most GUI tools skip clusters marked as bad for FAT and NTFS file systems.

Bit-shifting

To hide data, you can also shift bit patterns to alter the byte values of data. This technique has been around for many years. By altering the bit pattern, data can be changed from readable code to something that looks like binary executable code. Hex Workshop provides simple switches for altering the bits or byte patterns of specified data and entire files. To shift bits in a text file, follow these steps:

1. In Windows, start Notepad, and then type **TEST FILE. Test file is to see how shifting bits will alter the data in a file.**

2. Save it as **Bit_shift.txt** in the Chap10\Chapter folder in your work folder. Close Notepad.

3. Start Hex Workshop. Click **File**, **Open** from the menu. Navigate to the Chap10\Chapter folder in your work folder, and then double-click **Bit_shift.txt** (see Figure 10-31).

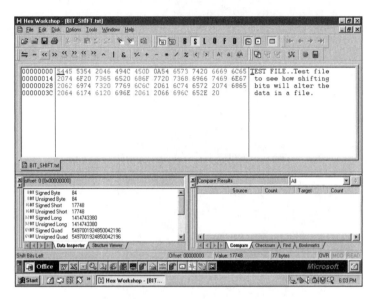

Figure 10-31   Bit_Shift.txt open in Hex Workshop

4. Click the **Shift Left** button (<<) on the Operations toolbar. The Shift Left Operation dialog box opens, as shown in Figure 10-32. You use this dialog box to specify how you want to treat the data, the ordering scheme to use for bytes, and whether you shift the bits for selected text or the entire file.

5. Click **OK** to accept the default settings and shift the bits in Bit_shift.txt to the left.

6. To save the updated file, click **File**, **Save As**. Use the Save As dialog box to save the file as **Bit_shift_left.txt** in the Chap10\Chapter folder in your work folder (see Figure 10-33). Notice the @ symbols at the far right.

7. To return the file to its original configuration, you can shift the bits back to the right by clicking the **Shift Right** button (>>) on the Operations toolbar. Click **OK** to accept the default settings in the Shift Right Operation dialog box. The file appears in its original format, as shown in Figure 10-34.

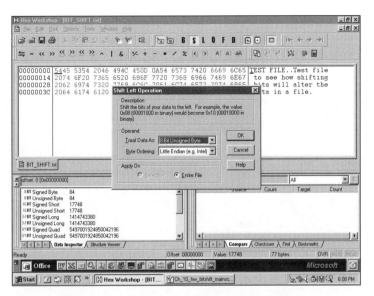

Figure 10-32 The Shift Left Operation dialog box

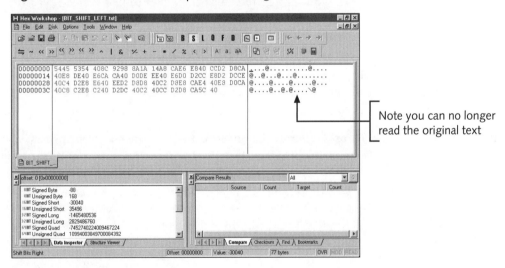

Note you can no longer read the original text

Figure 10-33 Shifting the bits

8. Click **File**, **Save As** from the menu. Use the Save As dialog box to save the file as **Bit_shift_right.txt** in the Chap10\Chapter folder in your work folder.

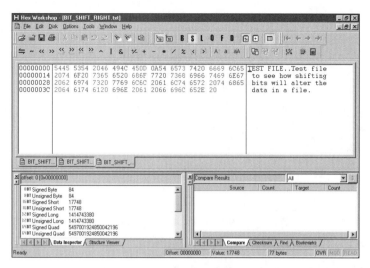

Figure 10-34 Shifting back to the original configuration

Now you can use Hex Workshop to test these three files to find their MD5 hash values to determine whether Bit_shift.txt is different from Bit_shift_right.txt. Note that you can also use DriveSpy to find MD5 hash values. To check the MD5 values in Hex Workshop, follow these steps:

1. With Bit_shift_right.txt open in Hex Workshop, click **File**, **Open** to open **Bit_shift.txt**, and then repeat to open **Bit_shift_left.txt**.

2. Click the **Bit_shift.txt** tab in the upper pane to make it the active file.

3. Click **Tools**, **Generate Checksum** from the menu to open the Generate Checksum dialog box. You use this dialog box to select the type of algorithm you want to use to generate a value, such as an MD5 hash value.

4. In the Select Algorithms list, click **MD5**, and then click **Generate**. The Checksum tab opens in the lower-right pane, displaying the MD5 hash value of Bit_shift.txt. Write down the MD5 hash value displayed for this file for future comparison to other changes to the file.

5. Repeat Steps 2 through 4 for Bit_shift_left.txt and Bit_shift_right.txt.

6. Examine the Checksum window for each file and compare each MD5 hash value for each file.

7. Close Hex Workshop.

Instead of shifting bits, marking bad clusters, and hiding partitions, people who want to hide data can use advanced encryption products, such as PGP or BestCrypt.

Using Steganography

The term steganography comes from the Greek word for "hidden writing." It is defined as the art and science of hiding messages in such a way that only the intended recipient knows the message is there. Many **steganography** tools were created to protect copyrighted material by inserting digital watermarks into a file. When viewing a stenographic file, such as a text document or graphic, the digital watermark is not visible. If you examine a graphics file such as a bitmap (.bmp) file with a disk editor such as Hex Workshop, it is difficult to find a watermark. A nonsteganographic .bmp file is the same size as an identical steganographic .bmp file, and they look the same when you view both files in a graphic viewer utility such as IrfanView. However, if you run a CRC-32, MD5, or SHA-1 hash comparison on both files, you'll find that the hashes are not equal. Chapter 12 discusses a few steganography utilities available for lossy graphics files. These tools insert data into the graphics file, but often alter the original file in size and clarity.

To hide data, people can use steganography programs to insert covert information into a variety of data files. The CNET central downloads area lists several freeware and shareware programs for steganography. If someone wanting to secure a message encrypts a plain text file using a program such as PGP, and inserts the encrypted text into the steganography file, the file becomes extremely difficult to crack. However, most steganography programs can insert only small amounts of data into a file, and usually require a password to restrict accessing the inserted data.

To detect steganography in evidence, you need prior information about the case; otherwise you cannot detect files that might have been used to hide data. During your examination, look for steganography programs such as S-Tools, DPEnvelope, jpgx, and tte. If you locate any of these programs, look for files that might have been used to hide data—specifically graphic files, but even text documents can be used for steganography. To help identify steganography output files, use the following list as a guideline:

1. Locate the modified date and time stamp of the steganography program.

2. If you are using DriveSpy, use the Dbexport command with the MD5 switch and transfer the output into a text file that you can open in a spreadsheet or database program. For example, at the D1P1 prompt, type **dbexport E:*work folder*\Chap10\Chapter\Dbexport.txt /md5** and press **Enter**.

3. In a spreadsheet or database program, sort all files in the Dbexport output file by modified date and time.

4. Generate a list of all files that have a date and time equal to or after the modified date and time of the steganography application.

5. Carefully examine each file in the generated listing.

If you locate files, especially graphics files such as .bmp files, that appear to have been created by the steganography program, attempt to reverse-engineer the file by re-creating known nonsteganographic images in the steganographic image files. This is a trial-and-error process and might not be practical unless the investigation is extremely important. Try building a timeline of possible output files that match the last used date of the steganography utilities. You can build a timeline with tools such as the DriveSpy Dbexport command, FTK, and EnCase.

Examining Encrypted Files

Encrypted files are encoded to prevent unauthorized access and can be difficult to examine for forensic evidence. To decode an encrypted file, users supply a password or passphrase that indicates they are authorized to decrypt the file. Without the passphrase, recovering the contents of encrypted data is difficult. Many commercial encryption programs use a technology called **key escrow**, which is designed to recover encrypted data if users forget their passphrases or if the user key is corrupted after a system data failure. Forensic examiners can use the key escrow to attempt to recover encrypted data. Although some vendors are developing key recovery tools, the amount of resources needed typically requires national institutions to use experts and powerful computer systems to crack encryption schemes. If you do encounter encrypted data in your investigation, make an effort to persuade the suspect or person of interest to reveal the passphrase.

Recovering Passwords

Password recovery is probably the easiest of tasks to perform during a computer forensic analysis. Several vendors have produced password crackers, such as PRTK, Advanced Password Recovery Software Toolkit, and @stake's LC5 (L0phtCrack). These tools crack passwords by guessing the password, which is called a dictionary attack, or performing a brute-force attack. In a dictionary attack, the program generates common words found in the dictionary and tries them as passwords. Some password-cracking programs allow you to import additional unique words that are typically extracted from evidence. Recall that FTK, for example, allows you to export a word list that you can import into the PRTK companion tool.

Brute-force attacks use every possible letter, number, and character found on a keyboard. Eventually, a brute-force attack can crack any password; however, this method is very time and processor intensive. Some passwords are so complex that the time to crack them can be measured in days, weeks, years, decades, and so on. Key sizes of 128 bits to 512 bits make the job of breaking passwords extremely difficult with the current technology available. Development of quantum computing in the future will likely make today's encryption schemes obsolete. Until then, some password schemes will remain unbroken.

Other programs help you build profiles of a suspect to help determine the suspect's password. These programs consider information such as the names of relatives or pets, favorite colors, and schools attended. The principle behind these multiple input programs is that people have a habit of using things they are comfortable with, especially if it requires memorizing something secret like a password.

CHAPTER SUMMARY

◻ When conducting computer forensics analysis, you must guard against scope creep so that you remain focused on the primary job. When looking at a case, you should consider the time needed to perform your analysis, what information is actually relevant, whether you have adequate resources, and whether there is a deadline.

◻ For all operating systems, you need to determine where the digital evidence is most likely stored by examining date and time stamps, log files, temporary spool files, encrypted or archived files, shortcuts, Recycle Bins, and Registry files.

◻ The DriveSpy.ini file contains critical information about your license in the [License] section. You can update the remaining sections as needed for your investigation. For example, in the [Search] section, you can specify one or more keywords likely to be in files you want to examine. Use the [File Headers] section to keep a list of common file headers and their hexadecimal representation for file types such as spreadsheets, word processors, and databases, making it easier to locate files using almost all the popular computer forensics tools. Use the [File Groups] section to specify spreadsheets, graphics, and so forth.

◻ Other useful features of DriveSpy are script files, which are text files containing a sequence of commands as a way to automate repetitive tasks. DriveSpy has other tools that retrieve residual data, such as free space and slack space, and can help retrieve clusters associated with deleted files.

◻ The PDBlock program is designed to prevent data from being written on a disk drive. PDWipe is designed to overwrite all sectors on a disk, cleaning all data from the drive.

◻ FTK is a data analysis tool that allows you to examine image files and directly access a target evidence disk, folder, or specific file.

◻ For any computer forensics investigation, prepare the disks where you store images of your evidence by wiping the disks and inspecting them for computer viruses. Inventory the hardware on the suspect's computer and note the condition of the computer when seized. Remove the original disk drive, and then check the date and time values in the system's CMOS. Record how you acquired data from the original disk. List all folders and files on the copied bit-stream image or disk, and examine the contents of all data files in all folders starting at the root folder of the volume partition. Research the function of every executable file that does not match known hash values. Maintain control of all evidence and findings, and document everything as you progress through your examination.

◻ UNIX and Linux machines are still commonly used as Web servers. You need to collect volatile data, log files, swap files, and a variety of other files when investigating these systems. You might also be required to perform a live system analysis.

◻ Data hiding involves changing or manipulating a file to conceal the file or its contents from anyone other than the owner of the file. For example, bit-shifting allows you to alter files easily. Encryption can be used to protect data, as can passwords. Some tools are available for password cracking.

10

❏ Steganography was created to protect the copyrights of online art. People have since used it to hide data. You can use tools such as DriveSpy MD5 to identify known files containing steganographic data.

KEY TERMS

bookmark — A marker or address that identifies a specific place or location for subsequent retrieval.

Chain Directory Entry (CDE) — A DriveSpy command that displays all directory cluster positions.

designator — The 0x before each value that tells DriveSpy the following value is a hexadecimal number.

false-positive hits — A system incorrectly provides a positive validation when, in fact, it is false.

[File Groups] — The section of DriveSpy.ini where you can list all the extensions or file headers for graphics files or spreadsheets.

[File Headers] — The section of DriveSpy.ini that contains the hexadecimal number values for many known file types. These hexadecimal numbers are the header data contained in the first several bytes of all specialized data files, such as Microsoft Word documents or Excel spreadsheets and any associated templates.

Get FAT Entry (GFE) — A DriveSpy command that displays the FAT entry for a specified cluster.

key escrow — A technology designed to recover encrypted data if users forget their passphrase or if the user key is corrupted after a system failure.

Known File Filter (KFF) — A program database updated periodically by AccessData that contains the hash values of known files, such as MSWord.exe, or illicit items floating on the Web. It's used to quickly identify the files for evidence or eliminate them from the investigation if they are legitimate files.

[License] — The section of the DriveSpy.ini file that contains the product license code and owner's name for DriveSpy.exe.

offset — A value added to a base address to produce a second address.

PDBlock — A program designed to prevent writing to a disk drive.

PDWipe — A program used to overwrite hard disk drives, overwriting all data on the drive.

root kit — A prebuilt package of programs that allows an intruder to install a network sniffer and obtain user IDs and passwords to your most sensitive systems.

scope creep — An unexpected situation or condition that increases the level of work.

[Search] — The section of the DriveSpy.ini file where you can specify what keywords you want to search for in an image file or document.

steganography — A cryptographic technique for embedding information into something else (such as an image or a sound file) for the sole purpose of hiding that information from casual observers.

REVIEW QUESTIONS

1. The offset in a hexadecimal code is:

   a. the 0x at the beginning of the code

   b. the 0x at the end of the code

   c. the first byte after the colon

   d. the 0x00:, which is the first byte where the header starts

2. List four groups of file types you might search for using the DriveSpy Search command.

3. If you were looking for the word "gamble" and thought it might be misspelled, what would you do in DriveSpy?

4. Newer Macintosh systems are based on which of the following operating systems?

   a. DOS

   b. BSD UNIX

   c. System VII

   d. Atari

5. How does DriveSpy specify file headers?

6. You can eliminate known files from an investigation because:

   a. you know they are relevant

   b. you know they are associated with the OS or an application

   c. you know they are not relevant

   d. you know they are associated with the company

7. For which of the following reasons do you wipe a disk?

   a. to ensure the quality of the new forensic evidence

   b. to make sure unwanted data is not retained on a disk

   c. neither of the above

   d. both a and b

8. The SaveSlack command in DriveSpy can be performed only on an entire partition. True or False?

9. For what do you use the SaveFree command in DriveSpy?

10. AccessData's FTK cannot analyze Linux dd files. True or False?

11. The Known File Filter (KFF) is part of FTK's arsenal. True or False?

12. List the two broad categories of computer forensics tools.

13. NTFSDOS is a freeware program that allows a Windows 9x computer to read NTFS partitions. True or False?

10

14. List two computer forensics tools that can be used on UNIX or Linux machines.

15. What is the primary reason you might not be able to shut down a Linux machine involved in an investigation?

16. If you are working on a live system, all output should be directed to:

   a. a workstation

   b. an external disk or storage media

   c. the internal hard disk

   d. the network

17. List three elements of a UNIX or Linux system that contain volatile data.

18. You can use the Linux dd command to copy the contents of RAM to a disk. True or False?

19. For what legal and illegal purposes can you use steganography?

20. Password recovery is now included in all computer forensics tools. True or False?

Hands-on Projects

HANDS-ON PROJECTS

Project 10-1

In this project, you compare the results from DriveSpy's Search tool and AccessData's FTK Index and Live search. To perform a keyword search using DriveSpy, follow these steps:

1. In Windows, open a DOS prompt and run the **Toolpath.bat** file in the Tools folder of your drive. Insert a blank, formatted floppy disk in the floppy disk drive. Change to the Chap10\Projects folder in your work folder, and then type **image C10Prj01. img a:** and press **Enter** to transfer C10Prj01.img from your student data files to the floppy disk.

2. Start Notepad, and then open **DriveSpy.ini**.

3. Type the following text at the bottom of the file:

   ```
   [Search George]
   100:"larva"
   ```

4. Save the file with the same name and location, and then close Notepad.

5. At the command prompt, type **drivespy** and press **Enter** to start DriveSpy, and then type **output george.log** and press **Enter** to create an output log.

6. At the SYS prompt, type **da** and press **Enter**.

7. At the DA prompt, type **search george** and press **Enter** to start the search. Describe the results.

NOTE

You might be prompted to disable Page mode after typing "search george." If so, type y.

8. Exit DriveSpy and close the command prompt window.

   Now you are ready to analyze the same file using FTK. Make sure the floppy disk with the restored C10Prj01.img file is in the floppy disk drive or create a C10Prj01.1 file using FTK Imager before performing these steps.

9. Start FTK. (Click **Start**, point to **Programs** or **All Programs**, point to **AccessData**, point to **Forensic Toolkit**, and then click **Forensic Toolkit**.) Click **Cancel** when the AccessData FTK Startup window opens.

10. Click **File**, **Add Evidence** from the menu to open the Add Evidence dialog box. Click **Next**.

11. In the Evidence Processing Options dialog box, click to clear all check boxes, and then click **Next**.

12. In the Add Evidence to Case dialog box, click **Add Evidence**.

13. Under Type of Evidence to Add to Case, click the **Local Drive** option button, and then click **Continue**.

14. In the Select Local Drive dialog box, click the **Logical Analysis** option button if it's not already selected, click **A: [- FAT]** in the Select a drive list box, and then click **OK**. You might see a dialog box warning you that you're using live evidence; if so, simply click **YES**.

15. In the Evidence Information dialog box, click **OK**. In the Add Evidence to Case dialog box, click **Next**.

16. In the Case Summary dialog box, click **Finish**.

17. After FTK processes the evidence, click **Tools**, **Analysis Tools** from the menu to open the Analysis Tools dialog box. Click to enable the **Full Text Indexing** check box, and then click **OK**.

18. In the FTK main window, click the **Search** tab. In the Search Term text box, type **larva** and then click **Add**. Note the number of hits and files FTK reports finding on the disk.

19. Click the **Live Search** tab. In the Search Term text box, type **larva** and then click **Add**. Click **Search**. When the Filter Search Hits dialog box opens, click **All files**, and then click **OK**. When the live search has finished, click **View Results**.

20. The upper-right pane shows the number of search items found. Click the **+** next to that to begin viewing your results.

10

21. Compare these results to the ones found in the DriveSpy output file George.log. Write a short report describing the similarities and differences between the two tools.

Project 10-2

In this project, you work with a DOS tool that allows you to read data files on an NTFS file system disk drive. You need the following hardware and software to perform this project:

- Windows 9x computer with a SCSI drive and a SCSI controller

- The following Windows 2000 system files must be copied on your Windows 9x workstation before installing NTFSDOS for Windows 98; copy these files to C:\Windows\Commands\. Depending on how your system is set up, it might be C:\Windows or C:\WINNT.

  - **Ntfs.sys** located in the \System32\Drivers folder

  - **Ntoskrnl.exe** located in the \System32 folder

  - **Autochk.exe** located in the \System32 folder

  - **Ntdll.dll** located in the \System32 folder

  - **C_437.nls** located in the \System32 folder

  - **C_1252.nls** located in the \System32 folder

  - **L_intl.nls** located in the \System32 folder

- The freeware version of NTFSDOS (downloaded from *www.sysinternals.com/ntw2k/freeware/ntfswin98.shtml*) for Windows 98 installed on a Windows 95 or 98 O/S

- Source disk drive containing an NTFS boot partition from a Windows 2000 or XP workstation

- Necessary IDE and power cables to connect the NTFS partitioned disk

To install NTFS98ro.exe on your Windows 9x system, follow these steps:

1. Before booting your forensic workstation, connect the NTFS disk to the computer.

2. Use a Web browser to visit *www.sysinternals.com/ntw2k/freeware/ntfswin98.shtml*. At the bottom of the Web page, click the **Download NTFS for Windows 98 (Read-Only) (1.1 MB)** link. Navigate to where you can save downloaded files, such as a Temp folder, and then click **Save**.

3. After you download NTFSDOS for Windows 98, use Windows Explorer to navigate to where you saved NTFS98ro.exe, and then double-click **NTFS98ro.exe** to install it in its default location. When prompted for the NTFS system files, navigate the install program to the C:\Windows\Commands folder.

To access an NTFS drive from MS-DOS (6.22 or Windows 9x), follow these steps:

4. After installing NTFS98ro.exe, open Windows Explorer and navigate to the NTFS disk drive.

5. Using Windows Explorer, navigate to the root (C:\) folder and make note of all files with the following extensions: .com, .ini, .sys, and .bat.

6. Locate the Ntldr file, and then use Windows Explorer to copy it to the Projects folder on your forensic workstation. For example, type **copy E:\Ntldr.*** **C:\Chap10\ Projects** and press **Enter**.

7. Exit Windows Explorer.

HANDS-ON
PROJECTS

Project 10-3

In this project, you compare a FAT drive to an NTFS drive by using FTK. The two student data files listed in the following project requirements don't need to be restored to separate hard disks. These two files are bit-stream images of 40 MB disk partitions that were created by the DriveSpy SaveSect command. FTK can directly read these bit-stream files as image files. To perform this project, you need the following items:

- C10fat16.exe and C10ntfsn.exe, located in the Chap10\Projects folder in your student data files

- 250 MB of free space on your work drive

- A GUI forensics tool such as FTK, iLook, or EnCase version 4 or newer

To use FTK to compare FAT and NTFS disks, follow these steps:

1. Use Windows Explorer to copy C10fat16.exe and C10ntfsn.exe from the Chap10\Projects folder in your data files to the work folder on your forensic workstation.

2. In Windows Explorer, double-click **C10fat16.exe** and then **C10ntfsn.exe** to expand these files to their original sizes.

3. Start FTK and follow the New Case Wizard, entering case names and numbers that are easy to remember.

4. In the Add Evidence to Case dialog box, click **Add Evidence**. Next, click the **Acquired Image of Drive** option button and click **Continue**.

5. In the Open dialog box, navigate to the folder where you copied and uncompressed C10FAT16.exe, click **C10fat16.001**, click **Open**, and then click **OK** in the Evidence Information dialog box.

6. In the Add Evidence to Case dialog box, click **Add Evidence**. Next, click the **Acquired Image of Drive** option button and click **Continue**.

7. In the Open dialog box, navigate to the folder where you copied and uncompressed C10NTFSN.exe, click **C10ntfsn.001**, and then click **Open**.

10

8. In the Evidence Information dialog box, click **OK**, and then click **Next** in the Add Evidence to Case dialog box.

9. In the Case Summary dialog box, click **Finish**.

10. When FTK finishes processing, examine both disks in FTK and list the similarities and differences between the two file system formats.

**HANDS-ON
PROJECTS**

Project 10-4

In this project, you explore steganography and learn how data is inserted and extracted from a steganographic (steg) file. For this project, you need the following files and software:

- An assortment of graphics image files, preferably BMP, JPG, and GIF files.

- An image-viewing utility, such as IrfanView (available for download from *www.irfanview.com*), ThumbsPlus, or Quick View.

- A steganography tool, such as S-Tools. (You can download steganography tools from *www.stegoarchive.com*.) Note that because information on the Web changes constantly and without notice, if you have difficulty locating this or any other Web site, use your favorite Web search engine to search for other sources.

To experiment with steganography, follow these steps:

1. Using your preferred Web search engine, locate and download a steganography utility to a folder on your forensic workstation. For example, in your search engine, type the word steganography and navigate to a Web site that offers a freeware steg program, such as S-Tools, and download the utility. After you download the utility, install it and study any documentation associated with it.

2. Use Notepad to create several short text messages of no more than two sentences and save each text message as an individual file. Save these messages in the C:\Chap10\Projects folder in your work folder.

3. Start the steg program. Go to the Help menu and read how to insert a message into an image file. Following the instructions, insert a message into several graphics. Most steg programs create a new image file from the original image file.

4. Open each image file in a graphics viewer, such as IrfanView, and note that the newly created steg file seems no different from the original image.

5. Using your preferred computer forensics software, analyze the MD5 hash values for the before-and-after images. Also determine whether the after image (the steg image) has any other characteristics different from the original file, such as byte size.

6. Write a brief report about the characteristics of each nonsteg file and steg file: the MD5 hash value, any size differences, any visual character differences from each before-and-after image, and so forth.

Project 10-5

In this project, you use FTK to compare an NTFS drive to a compressed NTFS drive. The two student data files listed in the following project requirements do not have to be restored to separate hard disks. These two files are bit-stream images of 40 MB disk partitions that were created by the DriveSpy SaveSect command. FTK can directly read these bit-stream files as image files. To perform this project, you need the following:

- C10ntfsn.exe and C10ntfsc.exe, located in the Chap10\Projects folder in your student data files

- 250 MB of free space on your work drive

- A GUI forensics tool, such as FTK, iLook, or EnCase version 4 or newer

To use FTK to compare FAT and NTFS disks, follow these steps:

1. In Windows Explorer, copy C10ntfsn.exe and C10ntfsc.exe to the work folder on your forensic workstation, if necessary.

2. In Windows Explorer, double-click **C10ntfsn.exe** and then **C10ntfsc.exe** to expand these files to their original sizes.

3. Start FTK and follow the New Case Wizard.

4. In the Add Evidence to Case dialog box, click **Add Evidence**. Next, click the **Acquired Image of Drive** option button and click **Continue**.

5. In the Open dialog box, navigate to the folder where you copied and uncompressed C10NTFSN.exe, click **C10ntfsn.001**, and then click **Open**. Click **OK**.

6. In the Add Evidence to Case dialog box, click **Add Evidence**. Next, click the **Acquired Image of Drive** option button and click **Continue**.

7. In the Open dialog box, navigate to the folder where you copied and uncompressed C10NTFSC.exe, click **C10ntfsc.001**, and then click **Open**.

8. In the Evidence Information dialog box, click **OK**, and then click **Next** in the Add Evidence to Case dialog box.

9. In the Case Summary dialog box, click **Finish**.

10. When FTK finishes processing, examine both disks in FTK and list any similarities and differences between the two file system formats.

Project 10-6

In this project, you work independently to perform a digital forensics analysis using your preferred computer forensics tool. Your goal in this project is to recover and analyze the data from four different image volumes from four different disk drives. To perform this project, you need the following:

- Your preferred computer forensics tool, such as DriveSpy, FTK, EnCase, or iLook.

- C10ntfsn.exe, C10ntfsc.exe, C10fat16.exe, and C10fat32.exe, located in the Chap10\Projects folder in your student data files.

- 500 MB of disk space.

- Optional target disk drives to perform a WriteSect command of each save-set volume if you plan to use DriveSpy. For all GUI tools, these save-sets load as acquired image files.

NOTE   If you plan to write these save-sets to a target disk, the total number of sectors for each volume is 96327 sectors, starting at absolute sector 63. For example, to use the WriteSect command in Drive mode for the second disk drive connected to your workstation, type d1> writesect C10ntfsn.001 63-96389 and press Enter.

Using a computer forensics tool, perform the following tasks:

- Determine whether there are any identical files in the acquired image files.

- Determine whether any graphics are identical and whether there are any other differences between identical pictures, such as MD5 hash values, byte size, and picture quality.

- Create a report of your findings, noting anything unusual you find and stating what might cause these differences. In addition, note any other data values you find that might create new leads for further investigations.

Project 10-7

HANDS-ON PROJECTS

In this project, you work independently to examine a bit-stream image save-set of an OS/2 High Performance File System (HPFS) acquired image file. You need a blank hard drive and appropriate cables to complete this task.

NOTE   At the time of this writing, no computer forensics tools can read the data structure of an HPFS-formatted disk. However, the previous version of Windows NT 3.5 or older can read HPFS file systems. Performing disk forensics on an HPFS file system requires examining the disk at a physical level, such as using DriveSpy's Drive mode.

Complete the following tasks:

- Write the HPFS save-set file **C10-7hpf.sav** to a target disk.

- The total number of sectors for each volume is 82655 sectors, starting at absolute sector 0. For example, to use the WriteSect command in Drive mode for the second disk drive connected to your workstation, type **d1> writesect C10-7hpf.sav 0-82655** and press **Enter**.

NOTE　The data on the target drive, including the partition format such as FAT16, is overwritten by the data from file C10-7hpf.sav. Any previous data on the disk, such as the partition type, is overwritten with the HPFS file system format. Accessing the disk can be done only from the physical level, such as using DriveSpy's Drive mode.

- After you have rebuilt the HPFS disk using the WriteSect command in DriveSpy, in Drive mode, use the Sector command (for example, Sector 0) and scroll through the contents of the disk. Determine the contents of sectors 63, 500, and 1000.

- Write a short report of your findings from this examination. State in your report how you accessed this file system and what other information you may have found.

CASE PROJECTS

10

Case Project 10-1

For the arson running case project (file name: Arson.E01), create a list of search terms that would apply to the case. Recall that creating search terms for a case is similar to searching with keywords on the Internet. For arson, make a list of terms that relate to explosives, bombs, or fires. Run the search in DriveSpy and in FTK or another GUI tool. Include in your report any findings that would be relevant to the insurance firm.

Case Project 10-2

For the kidnapping running case project (file name: Kidnapping.1), run a search for the missing girl's name and her friend. Also search for the man she met on the Internet. Recall that her name is Amy Capri and the man she met on the Internet is Gary Cleary. Write a report showing what clues you found as to her possible location.

Case Project 10-3

You have several graphics files that were transmitted via e-mail from an unknown source to a suspect in an ongoing investigation. The lead investigator tells you that at least four messages should be embedded in the files. Use your problem-solving and brainstorming skills to determine a procedure to follow. Write a short report outlining what to do.

Case Project 10-4

The disk you're currently investigating contains several password-protected files and other files whose headers do not match the extension. Write a report describing the procedures you need to follow to retrieve the evidence. Identify the mismatched file headers to extensions and discuss techniques you can apply to recover passwords from the protected files.

Case Project 10-5

You are asked to investigate and recover data from an old OS/2 computer. You need to access the hard disk and look for specific data based on a discovery demand from a plaintiff's attorney. Write a one-page report on what you need to access on an OS/2 disk drive and list which data files you can recover from the drive. Then list other methods you can use to recover any unallocated data from an OS/2 disk.

11

RECOVERING IMAGE FILES

After reading this chapter and completing the exercises, you will be able to:

♦ Recognize image files

♦ Understand data compression

♦ Locate and recover image files

♦ Analyze image file headers

♦ Identify copyright issues with graphics

Many computer forensics investigations involve graphics images, especially those downloaded from the Web and circulated via e-mail. To examine and recover image files successfully, you need to understand the basics of computer graphics, including image file characteristics, common image file formats, and compression methods for reducing file size. This chapter begins with brief introductions to computer graphics and data compression, and then explains how to locate and recover image files based on information stored in image file headers. You learn to identify image file fragments, repair damaged file headers, and reconstruct file fragments. In addition, you analyze image file headers, including those from unknown graphics file formats.

This chapter also explores tools you can use to view the images you recover and discusses two computer graphics issues: steganography and copyrights. Steganography involves hiding data, including images, in files. Copyrights determine the ownership of media, such as images downloaded from a Web site.

Recognizing an Image File

An image file contains a graphic, such as a digital photograph, line art, three-dimensional image, or scanned replica of a printed picture. You might have used a graphics program to create or edit an image, such as Microsoft Paint or Adobe Photoshop. A graphics program creates and saves one of three types of image files: bitmap, vector, or metafile. **Bitmap images** are collections of dots, or pixels, that form an image. **Vector images** are mathematical instructions that define lines, curves, text, ovals, and other geometric shapes. **Metafiles** are combinations of bitmap and vector images.

You can use two types of programs to work with image files: graphics editors and image viewers. You use graphics editors to create, modify, and save bitmap, vector, and metafile image files. You use image viewers to open and view image files, but not change their contents. When you use a graphics editor or an image viewer, you can open a file in one of many image file formats, which are indicated by the file extension, such as .bmp, .gif, or .eps. Each format has different qualities, including the amount of color and compression it uses. If you open an image file in a graphics editor that supports multiple file formats, you can save the file in a different file format. However, converting image files this way can change the quality of the image. You convert image files in a Hands-on Project at the end of the chapter to see how conversion can change an image.

Understanding Bitmap and Raster Images

Bitmap images store graphics information as grids of individual **pixels**, short for "picture elements." **Raster images** are also collections of pixels, but store pixels in rows to make the images easy to print. In most cases, printing an image converts, or **rasterizes**, the image to print the pixels line by line instead of processing the complete collection of pixels.

The quality of a bitmap image displayed on a monitor is governed by **screen resolution**, which determines the amount of detail displayed in the image. **Resolution** is related to the density of pixels on your screen and depends on a combination of hardware and software. Monitors can display a range of resolutions; the higher the resolution, the sharper the image. Computers also use a hardware component called a video card that contains a certain amount of memory for displaying images. The more advanced the video card's electronics and the more memory it has, the more detailed instructions it can accept, resulting in higher-quality images.

For example, the monitor and video card on your Windows computer might support an 800 × 600 resolution, which means they display 800 pixels horizontally and 600 pixels vertically. The higher the number of pixels, the smaller the pixels must be to fit into the monitor's area and, therefore, the smaller your pictures appear. Because a bitmap image is defined by pixel size, images displayed at a higher resolution use smaller pixels than images displayed at a lower resolution.

Software also contributes to the quality of displayed images. Software includes drivers, which are coded instructions that set display parameters for the video card. Software also includes the programs you use to create, modify, and view images. Some programs, such as IrfanView, allow you to view many types of images; other programs allow you to view or work with only the image files created by those programs.

Computer graphics professionals can use programs that support high resolutions to achieve more control over the presentation of bitmap images they create and edit. However, bitmap graphics, especially those with low resolution, usually lose quality when you enlarge them.

Another setting that affects image quality is the number of colors the monitor displays. Image files can contain different amounts of color per pixel, but each must support the colors with bits of space. The following list shows the number of bits used per colored pixel:

- 1 bit = 2 colors
- 4 bits = 16 colors
- 8 bits = 256 colors
- 16 bits = 65,536 colors
- 24 bits = 16,777,216 colors

Bitmap and raster image files use as much of the color palette as possible. However, when you save a bitmap or raster image file, the resolution and color might change, depending on the colors in the original file and whether the file format supports those colors.

Understanding Vector Images

Vector files are different from bitmap and raster files; a raster image uses dots and the vector format uses lines. A vector file stores only the mathematics for drawing lines and shapes; a graphics program converts the calculation into an image. Because vector files store mathematical calculations, not images, they are generally smaller than bitmap files, thereby saving disk space. You can also enlarge a vector image without affecting image quality—to make an image twice as large, a graphics program multiplies by two instead of manipulating pixels. CorelDraw, Adobe Illustrator, and other drawing programs create vector files. Although you can save vector graphics in a bitmap file format, you should not save photos, scanned graphics, and other bitmap or raster images in a vector format.

Understanding Metafile Graphics

Metafile image files combine raster and vector graphics and can have the characteristics of both image types. For example, if you scan a photograph (a bitmap image) and then add text or arrows (vector drawings), you create a metafile.

Although metafile images have the features of both bitmap and vector files, they also share the limitations of bitmap and vector files. For example, if you enlarge a metafile image, the area that was created with a raster format loses some resolution, but the vector-formatted area remains sharp and clear.

11

Understanding Image File Formats

Image files are created and saved in a graphics editor, such as Microsoft Paint, Macromedia Freehand, Adobe Photoshop, or the GIMP for Linux. Some graphics editors, such as Paint, work only with bitmap graphics. Others, such as Freehand, work only with vector graphics, and some programs, such as Photoshop, work with both.

Most graphics editors enable you to create and save files in one or more of the **standard image file formats**. Standard bitmap image file formats include the Graphic Interchange Format (.gif), Joint Photographic Experts Group (.jpg or .jpeg), Tagged Image File Format (.tif or .tiff), and Windows Bitmap (.bmp). Standard vector image file formats include Hewlett Packard Graphics Language (.hpgl) and AutoCad (.dxf).

Nonstandard image file formats include less common formats, such as Targa (.tga) and Raster Transfer Language (.rtl); proprietary formats, such as Photoshop (.psd), Illustrator (.ai), and Freehand (.fh9); newer formats, such as Scalable Vector Graphics (.svg); and formats related to old or obsolete technology, such as Paintbrush (.pcx). Because you can open standard image files in most or all graphics programs, they are easier to work with during a computer forensics investigation. If you encounter files in nonstandard formats, you might need to rely on your investigative skills to identify the file as an image file, and then find the right tools for viewing the file.

To determine whether a file is an image file and to find a program for viewing a nonstandard image file, you can search the Web by using a search engine or a dictionary Web site. For example, suppose you find a file with a .tga extension during an investigation. None of the programs on your forensic computer can open the file, and you suspect this file could provide crucial evidence. To uncover the file contents, you must first identify a program that can open the file and let you view it. To find the program used to create the TGA file, follow these steps:

1. Start a Web browser.

2. In the Address text box, type **www.webopedia.com**.

3. In the Search area, type **tga** in the Enter a word for a definition text box, and then press **Enter**. Webopedia then lists pages on its Web site that describe the TGA file format.

4. Click the first **Webopedia: Data Formats and Their File Extensions** link. A page opens listing file formats that begin with "T."

5. Scroll down to .tga and record the description in a text file or on a sheet of paper. Now you can compare this description to one on another dictionary Web site.

6. Click your browser's Address text box, type **whatis.techtarget.com**, and press **Enter**.

7. Scroll to the Fast References section, and click the **Every file format in the world** link.

8. In the Browse File Formats Alphabetically section, click the **T** link. Scroll down to find the TGA file format, and record the descriptions of Targa bitmap files. Also, list the applications that can be used to create and view Targa files.

Understanding Data Compression

Most image file formats, including GIF and JPEG, compress their data to save disk space and to reduce the amount of time it takes to transfer the image from one computer to another. Other formats, such as BMP, rarely compress their data or do so inefficiently. In this case, you can use compression tools to compact data and reduce file size. **Data compression** is the coding of data from a larger form to a smaller form. Image files and most compression tools use one of two data compression schemes: lossless or lossy. You need to understand how compression schemes work to understand what happens when an image is altered.

Reviewing Lossless and Lossy Compression

Lossless and lossy compression schemes were introduced in Chapter 9. As you learned, lossless compression techniques reduce file size without removing data. When you uncompress a file that uses lossless compression, you restore all its information. GIF and Portable Network Graphics (PNG) are image file formats that reduce file size with lossless compression. Lossless compression saves file space by using mathematical formulas to represent the data in a file. These formulas generally use one of two algorithms: Huffman coding or Lempel-Ziv-Welch (LZW) coding. Each algorithm uses a code to represent redundant bits of data. For example, if an image file contains a large area of the color red, instead of having to store 200 bytes all colored red, the algorithm can set one byte to red and then have another byte specify that there are 200 of those bytes. Therefore, only two bytes are used.

Lossy compression is significantly different because it compresses data by permanently discarding bits of information in the file. Some of the discarded bits are redundant, but others are not. When you uncompress an image file that uses lossy compression, you lose information, although most people don't notice the difference unless they print the image on a high-resolution printer or increase the image size. In either case, the removed bits of information reduce image quality. JPEG is one graphics file format that uses lossy compression. If you open a JPEG file in a graphics program, for example, and save it as a JPEG file with a different name, the file automatically uses lossy compression, which reduces image quality. The JPEG format reapplies the lossy file compression, removing more bits of data, when you save an existing file with a new name. If you simply rename a file by using Windows Explorer or the command line, however, the file doesn't lose any more data.

Another form of lossy compression, **vector quantization (VQ)**, uses vectors. VQ uses complex algorithms to determine what data to disregard based on vectors in the image file. In simple terms, VQ discards bits similarly to the way rounding off decimal values discards numbers.

Some popular lossless compression utilities include WinZip, PKZip, and FreeZip. Lzip is a lossy compression utility. You use these compression tools to compact folders and files for data storage and transmission. Remember that the difference between lossless and lossy compression is the way the data is represented *after* it has been uncompressed. Lossless compression produces an exact replica of the original data after it has been uncompressed, whereas lossy compression typically produces an altered replica of the data after it has been uncompressed.

11

LOCATING AND RECOVERING IMAGE FILES

If a computer forensics investigation involves image files, you need to locate and recover all the image files on a drive and determine which ones are pertinent to your case. Because images aren't always stored in standard image file formats, you should examine all files that your computer forensics tools find, even if they are not identified as image files.

Operating systems have tools for recovering image files, but these tools are time consuming to use and their results are difficult to verify. Instead, you can use computer forensics tools dedicated to analyzing image files. As you work with these tools and those included with different OSs, develop standard procedures for your organization and continue to refine them so that other investigators can benefit from your experience. You should also follow standard procedures for each case to produce a thorough analysis.

You can use computer forensics tools to analyze images based on information in the image file. There's more to an image file than meets the eye. Each image file contains a header with instructions for displaying the image; this header information helps you identify the file format. The header is complex and difficult to remember, however; instead of memorizing the header information, you can compare a known good file header with that of a suspected file. For example, if you find an image that you suspect is a JPEG, but can't display the image with a bitmap graphics program, check the file header to verify its contents. You can determine whether the header has been altered by comparing it to another JPEG file header. You could then use the information in the good JPEG file header to supply the instructions for displaying the picture. In other words, you use the good JPEG header information to create a baseline analysis.

Before you can examine an image file header, often you need to reconstruct a fragmented image file. To do so, you need to identify the data patterns the image file uses. If some of the file header has been overwritten with other data, you might also need to repair the damaged header. By rebuilding the image file header, you can then perform a forensic analysis on the image file.

NOTE For a quick reference on image file headers, check out the DriveSpy.ini file for some of the more common headers. This information can come in handy and save you time in the future.

Identifying Image File Fragments

If an image file is fragmented across different areas on a disk, you must first recover all the fragments to re-create the image file. Recovering pieces of a file is called **carving**, also known as **salvaging** outside North America. To carve an image file's data from file slack space and free space, you should be familiar with the data patterns of known image file types. Most computer forensics programs recognize these data patterns to help you identify image file fragments, which is the first step in recovering deleted data. After you recover the pieces of a fragmented image file, you restore the data fragments to continue your examination. You use DriveSpy later in this chapter to carve known data sets from residual data that you recover, and then restore this information to view the image file.

Repairing Damaged Headers

When you're examining recovered data remnants from files in slack or free space, you might find data that appears to be a header for a common image file type. If you locate header data that's partially overwritten, you must reconstruct the header. To do this, you compare the hexadecimal values of known image file formats to the pattern of the file header you found to make it readable again.

Each image file type has a unique file header value. As you become familiar with these common image header values, you can spot residual data from partially overwritten headers in file slack or free space. For example, a JPEG file has a hexadecimal header value of FF D8 FF E0 00 10. Most JPEG files also include the hexadecimal data value 4A 46 49 46 immediately following the preceding data string; this value is represented by the ASCII letters JFIF. If you find a file fragment with JFIF or some of the header values unique to JPEG files, you can identify the file as a JPEG image.

TIP

To learn more about hexadecimal values for well-known image files, open a file that already contains the hex values, such as the Drivespy.ini file, and examine the [File Headers] section.

Suppose you're investigating a possible intellectual property theft by a contract employee of the Exotic Mountain Tour Service (EMTS). EMTS has just finished an expensive marketing and customer service analysis. Based on this analysis, EMTS plans to release advertising for its latest tour service. Unfortunately, EMTS suspects that a contract travel consultant might have given sensitive marketing data to a competitor. An EMTS manager found a floppy disk that the contract travel consultant used. Your task is to determine whether the floppy disk contains proprietary EMTS data, including brochures with images.

As you examine the file slack or free space of the contract consultant's floppy disk, you find the letters FIF. You document that these letters are located at the beginning of cluster 499 on the floppy disk. You know that JPEG file headers always include JFIF, so you suspect that you found a fragment of a JPEG file header. You find several other JPEG files in allocated disk space on the floppy disk, and you also document these files.

Carving Data from Unallocated Space

After you identify fragmented data, you can use a computer forensics program to recover the fragmented file. In this section, you use DriveSpy to locate and carve data from unallocated space, and then use the SaveSect command to save a file as an external file.

To begin the carving task, perform the standard data preservation steps of creating a duplicate bit-stream copy of the original floppy disk (the one the EMTS manager found). In the following steps, you restore the Ch11hdfx.sav file from your student data files to a blank, unformatted floppy disk that serves as the EMTS target investigation floppy disk.

In this example, you use Digital Intelligence's Image utility and then continue with DriveSpy for the next set of steps. To restore a saved image file, follow these steps:

1. Insert an unformatted or clean floppy disk in the floppy drive, open a DOS command prompt window, and navigate to the directory containing Image.exe on your system.

2. Copy the **Ch11hdfx.sav** file from the Chap11\Chapter folder in your student data files to the **Tools** folder in your work folder.

3. At the DOS prompt, type **image Ch11hdfx.sav a:** (changing the drive letter, if necessary), and then press **Enter** to create an image file on the floppy disk.

4. Type **exit** to close the command prompt window.

Now that you've restored the file, you can begin searching for image files. In this example, you're searching for a JPEG file, but before you start, you need to determine whether your tool requires additional configuration. You're using DriveSpy to search the disk, so the additional configuration required in this example is updating the Drivespy.ini file to add a search label for the keyword JFIF so that you can identify JPEG files from the file header. To update the Drivespy.ini file, follow these steps:

1. Start Notepad or another text editor.

2. Click **File**, **Open** from the menu. In the Open dialog box, click **All Files** in the Files of type drop-down list, and navigate to where Drivespy.ini is stored (such as the Tools folder in your work folder). Then double-click **Drivespy.ini** to open it.

3. Scroll to the end of the file and press **Enter**, if necessary, to create a new line. Insert new search text by typing **[Search Chap11]** and pressing **Enter**. Then type **70:"JFIF"** and press **Enter**. (You include quotation marks around JFIF because you're searching for a literal value on the floppy disk.)

4. Save **Drivespy.ini**, and then close Notepad.

Note that you set a sensitivity level of 70 to search for values containing at least three of the four specified letters. This setting lets you locate partially overwritten data, such as JFFF or FIF. If you want a perfect match, you would enter 100:"JFIF". Because the keyword JFIF contains four letters, each letter is 25% of the total. To reduce the acceptable hit rate by 25%, round off the percentage value to 70%. (DriveSpy works only in 10% increments, so always round down.) If DriveSpy finds too many hits, you can decrease the sensitivity level and run the keyword search again to help minimize the number of hits.

After you update the search text in Drivespy.ini, you're ready to use DriveSpy to locate all possible JFIF keywords. If necessary, use Windows Explorer or My Computer to create a Chap11 folder in your work folder and a Chapter folder in the Chap11 folder. To complete the following steps, you need your EMTS investigation floppy disk. To locate JPEG files on a disk, follow these steps:

1. Open a DOS command prompt window, change to the Tools folder in your work folder, and press **Enter**. Type **Toolpath.bat** to run the Toolpath batch file so that you can use DriveSpy from any directory.

2. Navigate to the Chap11\Chapter folder, and then start DriveSpy by typing **drivespy** and pressing **Enter**.

3. At the DriveSpy SYS prompt, type **output Hdr_find.log** and then press **Enter** to create an output log file.

4. Make sure the EMTS target floppy disk is in the floppy drive. At the SYS prompt, type **drive a** (substituting the correct drive letter, if necessary) and then press **Enter**.

5. At the DA prompt, type **part 1** and then press **Enter** to display partition information for the floppy disk.

6. At the DAP1 prompt, type **search Chap11** and then press **Enter** to start the keyword search you specified in the previous set of steps. When a message appears asking whether you want to turn off Page mode, type **y**.

DriveSpy then searches the floppy disk for data matching the search criteria and records this data in Hdr_find.log. Leave DriveSpy open for the next set of steps. Now you can examine the Hdr_find.log output file to identify possible unallocated data sets that contain the full or partial JPEG header values:

1. Start Notepad or another text editor.

2. Click **File**, **Open** from the menu. In the Open dialog box, click **All Files** in the Files of type drop-down list, navigate to the **Chapter11\Chapter** folder in your work folder, and then double-click **Hdr_find.log** to open it.

Note that the log file shows that DriveSpy searched the floppy disk for JFIF and found one piece of data consisting of the letters FIF at beginning cluster position 499, sector 530, with an offset of 6 bytes. The offset is the amount of data between the beginning of sector 530 and the beginning of the text DriveSpy found, or the first letter F. Remember, sectors start counting offsets at zero (0). There are six characters between the beginning of the sector and the first letter F, thereby making F the seventh character in the sector.

Now that you have located the potential JPEG file, you can carve it from the floppy disk. First you must determine which sectors to carve on the disk by examining the contents of the EMTS floppy disk:

1. Close Notepad.

2. At the DAP1 prompt, type **dir** and press **Enter** to list the files on the first partition of the floppy disk (see Figure 11-1). DriveSpy shows that the disk contains four files in allocated space: Sawtooth_1.jpg, Stream_1.jpg, Stream_2.jpg, and East_side_1.jpg. Leave DriveSpy open for the next set of steps.

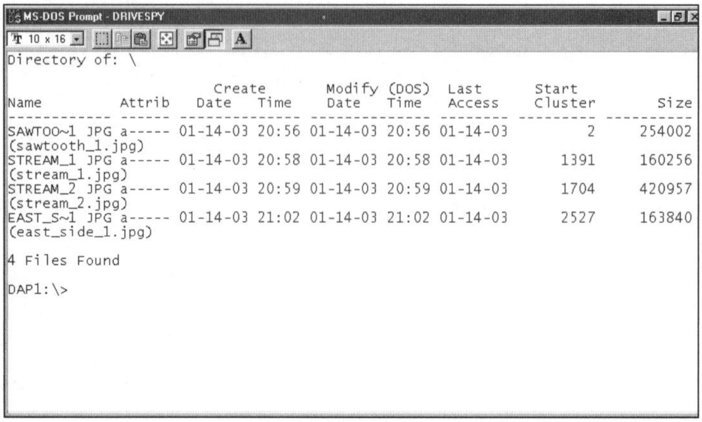

Figure 11-1 Files on the EMTS disk

The results of the keyword search reveal that the EMTS disk might contain a JPEG file starting at cluster 499. As shown in Figure 11-1, the first file listed starts at cluster 2, and the second file starts at cluster 1391. Because you're examining a floppy disk, you know it contains exactly 512 bytes per sector and one sector is assigned for every cluster. The larger the FAT disk, the higher the number of sectors per cluster. If this were a 2 GB disk drive, you would need to calculate how many 512-byte sectors it contained per cluster.

You can calculate the total cluster size by multiplying the number of sectors per cluster. Then you divide the file byte size by the total cluster size and round up the result to the next integer. Table 11-1 shows the number of maximum clusters, cluster size, and maximum volume size for FAT12, FAT16, and FAT32 disks.

Table 11-1 Calculating Total Cluster Size

Attribute	FAT12	FAT16	FAT32
Number of clusters (max)	4086	65,526	~268,435,456
Cluster size used	0.5 KB to 4 KB	2 KB to 32 KB	4 KB to 32 KB
Maximum volume size	16,736,256	2,147,123,200	About 2^{41}

The EMTS disk contains 1389 clusters between the starting position of the first file, Sawtoo~1.jpg, which starts at cluster 2, and the second file, Stream_1.jpg, which starts at cluster 1391. Because Sawtoo~1.jpg is 254,002 bytes long, you can determine its ending position by using the following formula:

```
Ending_cluster = start_cluster + total_clusters - 1
Ending_cluster = 499 + 892 - 1
Ending_cluster = 1390
```

Another method you could use is as follows:

```
(file_byte_size ÷ 512) ÷ number_of_sectors_per_cluster =
total_number_of_clusters_assigned
```

To locate the exact ending cluster position of a file (assuming the file is contiguous), add the total number of clusters assigned to the starting cluster position. To determine each cluster assigned to the starting cluster, use the DriveSpy Cluster Link End (CLE) command to list all forward cluster links. For example, the total number of bytes in the Sawtoo~1.jpg file is 254,002, with 512 bytes per sector and one sector per cluster. You can determine the ending cluster position with the following formula:

$$(254002 \div 512) \div 1 = 496.1$$

Therefore, the Sawtoo~1.jpg file ends at cluster 496, leaving a significant amount of unaccounted-for-data from cluster 497 through cluster 1390. You can determine this because you know that the second file, Stream_1.jpg, starts at cluster 1391. Because the keyword search revealed a potential JPEG header at cluster 499, a deleted JPEG file probably starts at cluster 499 and ends near or on cluster 1390.

TIP
Remember that when a user deletes a file, it's not necessarily completely deleted. In most cases, only the first bit of the first sector is removed, and the area is marked in the FAT or Master File Table (MFT) to indicate that the user can write to the cluster again.

11

To recover the deleted data that's not listed as a deleted file in the FAT, you need to determine the absolute sector starting position for the beginning and ending clusters of the area you're going to carve. You can use DriveSpy and the SaveSect command to find the absolute values. Keep in mind that the SaveSect command interprets only the absolute sector value. If you use the relative sector number, you collect the wrong data. You need to use the absolute sector number to obtain the correct sector values. To determine absolute sectors for carving, follow these steps:

1. At the DAP1 prompt in the DriveSpy window, type **cluster 499** and then press **Enter** to determine the beginning absolute sector number (see Figure 11-2).

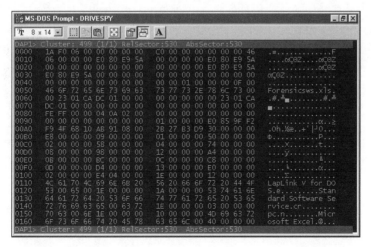

Figure 11-2 Determining the beginning absolute sector number

2. On a separate sheet of paper, record the AbsSector (absolute sector) number, located at the top and bottom of the DriveSpy window. (You should see absolute sector 530.)

3. Press **Esc** to close the cluster view.

4. At the DAP1 prompt, type **cluster 1390** and press **Enter** to determine the ending absolute sector number, which is one less than the next file's cluster starting number. In Figure 11-3, note the AbsSector number at the top and bottom of the DriveSpy window (absolute sector 1421).

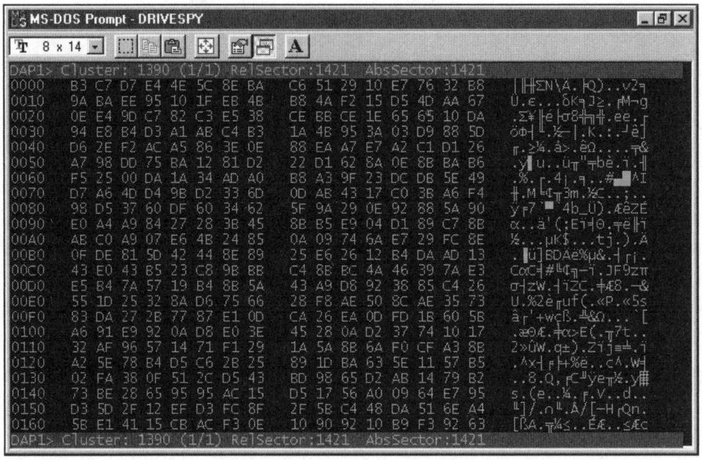

Figure 11-3   Determining the ending absolute sector number

5. Press **Esc** to close the cluster view. Leave DriveSpy open for the next set of steps.

You determined that the beginning absolute sector is 530 and the ending absolute sector number is 1421 for the possible JPEG file. Next you need to isolate, or carve, these sectors and save them in a file by following these steps:

1. At the DAP1 prompt, type **savesect 530-1421 Bad_hdr.jpg** and then press **Enter**. DriveSpy extracts the data in sectors 530 to 1421 and saves it in a file named Bad_hdr.jpg on the floppy disk.

2. At the DAP1 prompt, type **exit** and then press **Enter** to close DriveSpy.

Now that you have carved the potential JPEG file you located with the JFIF keyword search, the next step is to rebuild the JPEG header with the correct hexadecimal values. To perform this task, you use Hex Workshop to manually insert the correct hexadecimal codes. Then you save the repaired file as a new file so that you can test whether the values you placed in the header are the correct values. To test the repaired file, you simply need to see whether you can view the image with an image viewer.

Rebuilding File Headers

Before attempting to edit an image file you recovered, try to open it with an image viewer such as Microsoft Photo Editor. To test whether you can view the image, you can double-click the recovered file in its current location in Windows Explorer. If you can open and view the image, you have successfully recovered the image file. If the image isn't displayed in the image viewer, you must manually inspect and correct the header data values.

If some of the data you recovered from the image file header is corrupt, you might need to recover more pieces of the file before you can view the image, as you'll see in the next section. Because Bad_hdr.jpg is a damaged image file, when you attempt to open it, you might see a message box similar to the one in Figure 11-4.

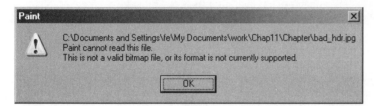

Figure 11-4   Message box indicating a damaged image file

If you can't open an image file in an image viewer, the next step is to examine the file's header data to see whether it matches the header in a good JPEG file. If the header doesn't match, you must manually insert the correct hexadecimal values by using a tool such as Hex Workshop. You can then inspect and correct the hexadecimal values. To inspect a file with Hex Workshop, follow these steps:

1. Start Hex Workshop. Click **File**, **Open** from the menu. Navigate to the **Chap11\Chapter** folder in your work folder, and then double-click **Bad_hdr.jpg** (see Figure 11-5).

2. In the upper-left column of the Hex Workshop window, note that the hexadecimal values starting at the first byte position are all zeros (00000000) and the first seven bytes all contain the number 11. Leave Hex Workshop open for the next set of steps.

The correct hexadecimal characters for a JPEG file are FF D8 FF E0 00 10 4A 46 49 46. The first seven bytes of the Bad_hdr.jpg file are all 11, indicating that this file header data isn't correct for a JPEG file. You must convert the first seven bytes to the correct hexadecimal characters for a JPEG image. To repair the file, continue with the following steps in Hex Workshop:

1. In the pane on the left, click to the left of the first hexadecimal value of 11. Then type **FFD8 FFE0 0010**, which are the correct hexadecimal values for the first six bytes of a JPEG file.

2. In the pane on the right, click to the left of ".FIF" and type **J**, as shown in Figure 11-6.

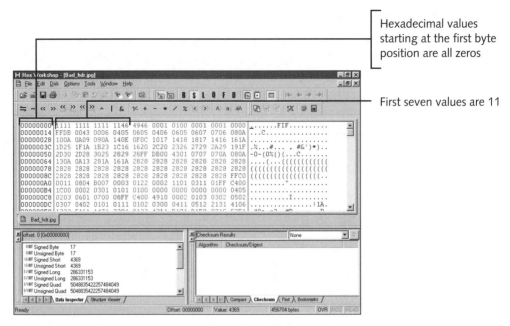

Hexadecimal values starting at the first byte position are all zeros

First seven values are 11

Figure 11-5   Bad_hdr.jpg open in Hex Workshop

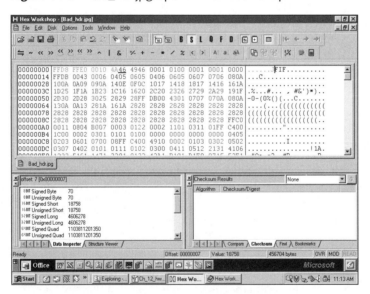

Figure 11-6   Inserting correct hexadecimal values for a JPEG file

TIP

In Hex Workshop, when you type a keyboard character in the pane on the right, the corresponding hexadecimal value appears in the pane on the left. So, for example, when you type the letter J in the right pane, the hexadecimal value 4A appears in the left pane.

3. Click **File**, **Save As** from the menu. In the Save As dialog box, navigate to the **Chap11\Chapter** folder in your work folder, type **Good_hdr.jpg** as the file name, and then click the **Save** button.

4. Close Hex Workshop.

Note that every two hexadecimal values you entered in the previous steps are equivalent to one ASCII character. For example, the uppercase letter "A" has a hexadecimal value of 41, and the lowercase letter "a" has a hexadecimal value of 61. Most disk editors have a reference chart that converts hexadecimal values to ASCII characters. For example, Hex Workshop includes a useful ANSI (ASCII) character set, shown in Figure 11-7.

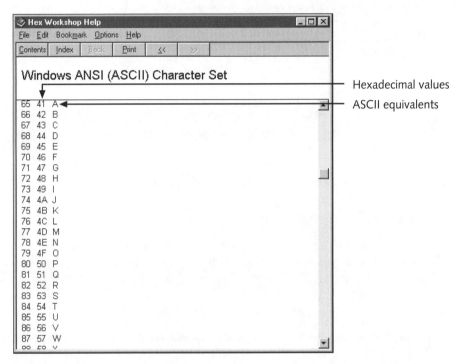

Figure 11-7   ASCII equivalents to hexadecimal values

After you repair an image file header, you can test the updated file by opening it in an image viewer, such as Microsoft Photo Editor, IrfanView, ThumbsPlus, QuickView, or ACDSee. To test the repaired JPEG file, follow these steps:

1. In Windows Explorer, navigate to the Chap11\Chapter folder in your work folder and double-click **Good_hdr.jpg**. The file opens in your default image viewer, such as Microsoft Photo Editor, as shown in Figure 11-8.

2. Now you can view the Good_hdr.jpg file to verify that you successfully carved the file from slack space. Close the image viewer.

Figure 11-8 Good_hdr.jpg open in Microsoft Photo Editor

The process of repairing file headers is not limited to JPEG files. You can apply the same technique to any file for which you can determine the header value, including Microsoft Word, Excel, and PowerPoint documents as well as other image formats. You need to know only the correct header format for the type of file you're attempting to repair.

Reconstructing File Fragments

You might occasionally encounter corrupt data that prevents you from recovering data fragments for files such as image files. Whether the data corruption is accidental or intentional, you need to know how to examine a suspect disk and extract possible data fragments to reconstruct files for evidentiary purposes. In this section, you learn how to identify files that have been intentionally corrupted and recover them with DriveSpy.

In some computer forensics investigations, the suspect has intentionally corrupted cluster links in a disk's FAT. Anyone can use a disk-editing tool, such as Norton DiskEdit, to access the FAT and mark specific clusters as bad by typing the letter "B" at the specific cluster. After you mark a cluster as bad, it appears with a zero value in a disk editor. As Figure 11-9 shows, cluster position 156 has a zero value, indicating that this cluster doesn't link to any other clusters on the disk. The OS ignores clusters marked in this manner and doesn't use them, allowing someone to attempt to hide data by using Norton DiskEdit to mark the clusters as bad.

To locate files of a particular type, such as JPEG image files, you can use the DriveSpy Search command to locate potential JPEG files with a corrupt cluster. If you're searching for other types of files, update the [Search] section in Drivespy.ini to add the specific header string of the file type. In an actual investigation, you usually copy a bit-stream image of the original evidence drive to a target investigation disk. In the following steps, you use a floppy disk. First, create the floppy disk for the following steps:

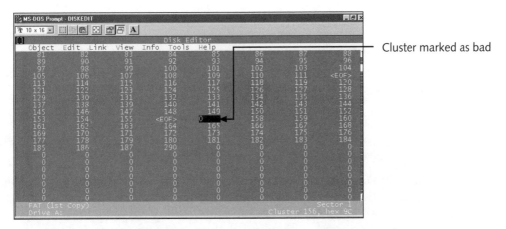

Figure 11-9   Bad cluster appearing as zero in Norton DiskEdit

1. Open a DOS command prompt window. Make sure Ch11Frag.sav is in the Chap11\Chapter folder in your work folder. Insert a floppy disk in the floppy drive.

2. In the command prompt window, navigate to the **Tools** folder in your work folder, and type **Toolpath.bat**.

3. Type **image Ch11Frag.sav a:** (replacing the drive letter, if necessary), and then press **Enter**.

4. To locate potential unallocated files, navigate to the **Chap11\Chapter** folder, and then start DriveSpy by typing **drivespy** and pressing **Enter**.

5. At the SYS prompt, type **output Ch11frag.log** and then press **Enter** to create an output log file.

6. At the SYS prompt, type **drive a** and then press **Enter** to navigate to the floppy drive.

7. At the DA prompt, type **part 1** and then press **Enter**.

8. At the DAP1 prompt, type **search Chap11** and then press **Enter** to search for JPEG files on the floppy disk. Type **y** when prompted to disable Page mode. Exit DriveSpy.

   Now continue with these steps to examine the output file so that you can determine whether DriveSpy identified recoverable files:

9. Start WordPad, and open the log file **Ch11frag.log** in the Chap11\Chapter folder in your work folder.

10. Scan the file to find any occurrences of the letters JFIF. Ch11frag.sav contains five potential JPEG headers.

Some of the data containing three or more of the letters in JFIF might be JPEG headers, but some might not. You need to examine file type characteristics, such as other hexadecimal characters in this data, to determine which ones are actual JPEG headers.

As you examine Ch11frag.log, note that Ch11frag.sav contains five potential JPEG headers at cluster positions 156, 1036, 2835, 448, and 1187. All the clusters are in unallocated disk space. Your next task is to determine whether other file fragments are linked to these clusters, which might be part of the JPEG file. To do so, you can use the DriveSpy Chain FAT Entry (CFE) command. (Refer to Chapter 7 for more information on the CFE command.) To confirm the cluster content, follow these steps:

1. Start DriveSpy. At the DAP1 prompt in DriveSpy, type **cluster 156** and then press **Enter** to examine the data at cluster 156.

NOTE

The header appears corrupt because it doesn't reflect the right header information for a known JPEG file.

2. Press **Page Down** to inspect cluster 156 and the next cluster to determine whether the file continues past cluster 156. Additional data appears, indicating that the corrupted JPEG file extends past cluster 156.

3. Press **Esc** to exit the cluster view and return to the DAP1 prompt.

4. To collect the unallocated file cluster links, at the DAP1 prompt, type **cfe 156** and then press **Enter** to see whether other clusters are linked to cluster 156 (see Figure 11-10). DriveSpy reports the results as 156, 0x000, which indicates that no clusters are linked to cluster 156.

Figure 11-10   Clusters linked to cluster 156

5. At the DAP1 prompt, type **cfe 157** and then press **Enter** to see whether other clusters are linked to cluster 157. Many other clusters are linked to cluster 157, as shown in Figure 11-11, indicating that a number of clusters are used with 157 to create a file.

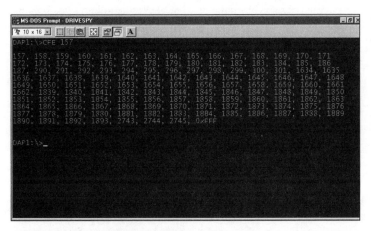

Figure 11-11   Clusters linked to cluster 157

6. At the DAP1 prompt, type **cfe 448** and then press **Enter** to see whether other clusters are linked to cluster 448, which is the next cluster DriveSpy has identified as containing a potential JPEG header. DriveSpy reports the results as 448, 0x000.

7. At the DAP1 prompt, type **cfe 449** and press **Enter**.

8. At the DAP1 prompt, type **cfe 1036** and press **Enter** to see whether other clusters are linked to cluster 1036, which is the next cluster DriveSpy has identified as containing a potential JPEG header. Then type **cfe 1037** and press **Enter**.

9. At the DAP1 prompt, type **cfe 1187** and press **Enter**. Then type **cfe 1188** and press **Enter**.

10. At the DAP1 prompt, type **cfe 2835** and press **Enter** to check the links to the last known cluster. Then type **cfe 2836** and press **Enter**. Note that both clusters 2835 and 2836 have zero values, indicating that they aren't linked to other clusters on the disk. Leave DriveSpy open for the next set of steps.

Using the DriveSpy CFE command, you identified all cluster links associated with the unallocated JPEG file headers except the last cluster, 2835. Note that the cluster 2836 has a zero value, as does cluster 2835, indicating that you have obtained all the pieces of data for your image.

The next task is to determine which specific unallocated cluster might be linked to cluster 2835. To do so, one method is to use the DriveSpy Get FAT Entry (GFE) command to map all possible cluster links. This task takes a lot of time and effort because you must first list all unallocated clusters and then manually run the GFE command on each one to see whether the unallocated cluster links to cluster 2835. A more effective method is to copy all the sectors immediately after a nonlinked cluster until you reach the cluster immediately before the next allocated or deleted file cluster on the disk.

To continue recovering fragmented unallocated files, you can use the DriveSpy SaveSect command. First, you need to create a script file listing all clusters associated with each unallocated file you found with the initial keyword search. To do this, you open the log file you created and copy each group of sectors into another text file. Start by using DriveSpy to determine the absolute sector numbers for each cluster range in the file you want to recover. Figure 11-12 shows the cluster numbers associated with clusters 448 and 449 in a script file.

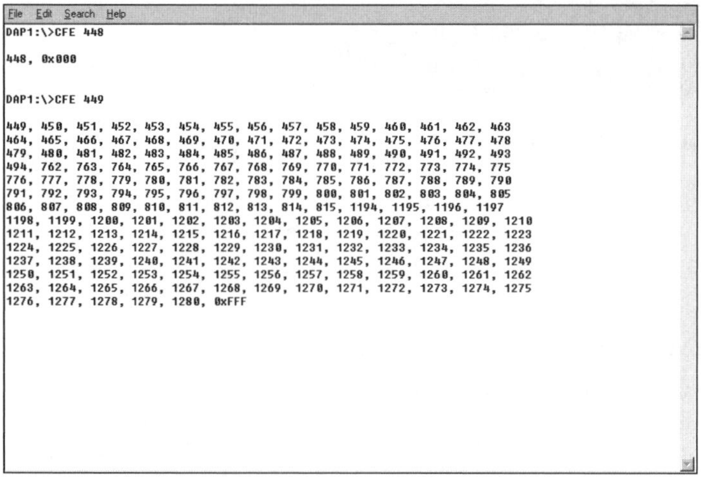

```
 File  Edit  Search  Help
DAP1:\>CFE 448

448, 0x000


DAP1:\>CFE 449

449, 450, 451, 452, 453, 454, 455, 456, 457, 458, 459, 460, 461, 462, 463
464, 465, 466, 467, 468, 469, 470, 471, 472, 473, 474, 475, 476, 477, 478
479, 480, 481, 482, 483, 484, 485, 486, 487, 488, 489, 490, 491, 492, 493
494, 762, 763, 764, 765, 766, 767, 768, 769, 770, 771, 772, 773, 774, 775
776, 777, 778, 779, 780, 781, 782, 783, 784, 785, 786, 787, 788, 789, 790
791, 792, 793, 794, 795, 796, 797, 798, 799, 800, 801, 802, 803, 804, 805
806, 807, 808, 809, 810, 811, 812, 813, 814, 815, 1194, 1195, 1196, 1197
1198, 1199, 1200, 1201, 1202, 1203, 1204, 1205, 1206, 1207, 1208, 1209, 1210
1211, 1212, 1213, 1214, 1215, 1216, 1217, 1218, 1219, 1220, 1221, 1222, 1223
1224, 1225, 1226, 1227, 1228, 1229, 1230, 1231, 1232, 1233, 1234, 1235, 1236
1237, 1238, 1239, 1240, 1241, 1242, 1243, 1244, 1245, 1246, 1247, 1248, 1249
1250, 1251, 1252, 1253, 1254, 1255, 1256, 1257, 1258, 1259, 1260, 1261, 1262
1263, 1264, 1265, 1266, 1267, 1268, 1269, 1270, 1271, 1272, 1273, 1274, 1275
1276, 1277, 1278, 1279, 1280, 0xFFF
```

Figure 11-12 Cluster numbers for clusters 448 and 449

To minimize the number of clusters to look up, group the cluster numbers into contiguous blocks and find the absolute sector numbers of the first and last cluster values in each range. For example, you can look up cluster ranges 449–494, 792–815, and 1194–1180. Follow these steps in DriveSpy to find the starting and ending absolute sector numbers for these cluster ranges:

1. At the DAP1 prompt in the DriveSpy window, type **cluster 448** and press **Enter** to find the absolute sector number of this cluster. As Figure 11-13 shows, the absolute sector number is 479.

Absolute sector number for cluster 448

Figure 11-13   Absolute sector number for cluster 448

2. Press **Esc** to return to the DAP1 prompt, type **cluster 494**, and press **Enter**. As Figure 11-14 shows, the absolute sector number of cluster 494 is 525.

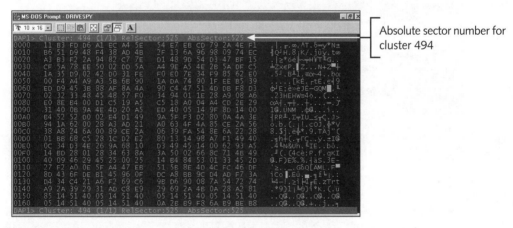

Absolute sector number for cluster 494

Figure 11-14   Absolute sector number for cluster 494

3. Press **Esc** to return to the DAP1 prompt, type **cluster 792**, and press **Enter**. As shown in Figure 11-15, the absolute sector number of cluster 792 is 823.

4. Press **Esc** to return to the DAP1 prompt, type **cluster 815**, and press **Enter**. As Figure 11-16 shows, the absolute sector number of cluster 815 is 846.

5. Press **Esc** to return to the DAP1 prompt, type **cluster 1194**, and press **Enter**. As Figure 11-17 shows, the absolute sector number of cluster 1194 is 1225.

6. Press **Esc** to return to the DAP1 prompt, type **cluster 1280**, and press **Enter**. As Figure 11-18 shows, the absolute sector number of cluster 1280 is 1311.

7. Press **Esc** to return to the DAP1 prompt, and leave DriveSpy open.

Absolute sector number for cluster 792

Figure 11-15   Absolute sector number for cluster 792

Absolute sector number for cluster 815

Figure 11-16   Absolute sector number for cluster 815

The absolute sector numbers are 479–525, 823–846, and 1225–1311. Now you need to use the SaveSect command to build a script file that copies each group of absolute sectors into three individual files. When typing the commands, be sure you don't insert blank lines between the commands or at the end of the script. Blank lines anywhere in the script generate errors in DriveSpy.

1. Start Notepad, and in a new document, type the following SaveSect commands:

```
SaveSect 479-525 C11_448.jpg
SaveSect 823-846 C11_448.jpg
SaveSect 1125-1311 C11_448.jpg
```

2. Save this script as **Ch11svsc.scr** in the Chap11\Chapter folder in your work folder, and then close Notepad.

Figure 11-17   Absolute sector number for cluster 1194

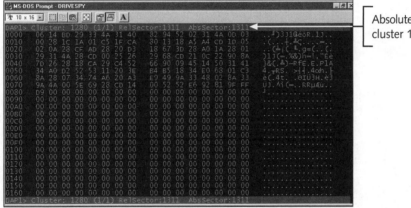

Figure 11-18   Absolute sector number for cluster 1280

NOTE   Because the last keyword search for cluster 2835 revealed no additional links, as an investigator, you would want to copy all sectors (using the SaveSect command) from sector 2835 to the very last sector on the disk, 2848, to capture any residual data that might be left in this portion of unlinked clusters of the drive.

When you run this script, DriveSpy extracts the sectors you specified, and asks if you want to cancel, overwrite, or append the sector groups. You can select the Append option to combine all groups into one file. To extract the sectors containing the JPEG file in unallocated disk space, follow these steps to run the script in DriveSpy:

1. At the DAP1 prompt in the DriveSpy window, type **script Ch11svsc.scr** and press **Enter**.

2. When the (C)ancel, (O)verwrite, or (A)ppend prompt appears, type **A**. This prompt appears twice—type **A** each time.

3. Type **exit** and then press **Enter** to close DriveSpy.

The file you recovered from cluster 448 has a corrupt header. You can use Hex Workshop to insert the correct hexadecimal values to see whether you can read this file, as you did earlier in the "Rebuilding File Headers" section. To rebuild the header in Hex Workshop, follow these steps:

1. Start Hex Workshop. Click **File**, **Open** from the menu. Navigate to the **Chap11\Chapter** folder in your work folder, and then double-click **Ch11_448.jpg**.

2. In the left pane, click to the left of the first hexadecimal value, and then type **FFD8 FFE0 0010**, which are the correct hexadecimal values for the first six bytes of a JPEG file.

3. In the pane on the right, click to the left of "FIF" and type **J** (to replace the "d"). Your Hex Workshop window should be similar to the one in Figure 11-19.

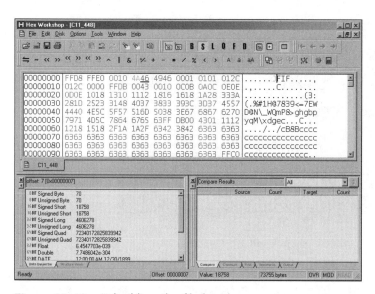

Figure 11-19   Rebuilding the file header

4. Click **File**, **Save** from the menu. Click **Yes** to create a backup.

5. Close Hex Workshop.

Now you can test the file by opening it in an image viewer:

1. Use Windows Explorer to navigate to the Chap11\Chapter folder, and then double-click **Ch11_448.jpg**. The file opens, as shown in Figure 11-20.

2. You won't see a complete image because the file is corrupt beyond repair. Close your image viewer.

Figure 11-20 The corrupted image file

Parts of the recovered image are misaligned because the file is corrupt. Recovering deleted images is not an exact science. Your success in image recovery varies depending on the quality of the media.

Identifying Unknown File Formats

With the continuing changes in technology and computer graphics products, eventually you'll encounter image file formats you're not familiar with. In addition, suspects might use older computer systems with programs that create uncommon or obsolete image file formats. Therefore, you must research both old and new file types. Knowing the purpose of each format and how it stores data is part of the investigation process.

When you examined the Ch11frag.sav floppy disk image, the keyword search found a file with an .xif extension. This file, Zpict0~1.xif, is in the drive's allocated space and appeared when you used the DriveSpy Dir command. Because the file has the letters "pict" as part of its name, it might be an image file, although XIF is not a common image file format. The [File Groups] section of Drivespy.ini doesn't include a reference to this file format.

The Internet is the best source for learning more about file formats and their associated extensions. You have already used the Webopedia site to research the TGA file format. You can also use any popular search engine to search for "file type" or "file format" and find the latest list of Web sites with information on file extensions. If you still can't find a specific file extension, try refining your search by entering the file extension along with the words "file format" in a search engine. To search for information about XIF files, follow these steps:

1. Start your Web browser.

2. In the Address text box, type **www.google.com** and then press **Enter**.

3. Type **xif file format** in the text box, and then press **Enter**. A page of links opens.

4. Click a few links to learn more about the XIF file format.

Xerox Pagis (produced by ScanSoft, Inc., a subsidiary of the Xerox corporation) is a scanning program that produces images in the XIF format. The .xif extension, commonly called XIFF, is derived from the more common TIFF file format with some unique modifications. You might also find that Pagis offers a free viewer utility you can download to display XIFF files. For more information about XIFF files and the Pagis viewer, go to the Xerox Pagis Web sites at *www.scantips.com/pagis1.html*.

The following three popular sites provide information to help analyze file formats. Keep in mind that information on the Web changes frequently; use a search engine to find image file information if you can't access the following Web sites:

- *www.digitek-asi.com/file_formats.html*

- *www.wotsit.org*

- *http://whatis.techtarget.com*

ANALYZING IMAGE FILE HEADERS

You should analyze image file headers when you find new or unique file types that computer forensics tools do not recognize. The simplest way to access a file header is to use a hexadecimal editor, such as Hex Workshop. You can then record the hexadecimal values in the header and use them to define a file type in Drivespy.ini.

For example, suppose you encounter a XIFF file. Because the [File Headers] section of Drivespy.ini does not define this file type, you need know the file's known good header value. Start by comparing a TIFF file header to a XIFF file header to determine whether the header is different or the TIFF file was simply renamed to have a XIFF extension. TIFF is a well-established file format used for transmitting faxes and for printed publications. All TIFF files start at position zero (offset 0 is the first byte of a file) with hexadecimal 49 49 2A. These hexadecimal values translate to ASCII II*. Figure 11-21 shows a TIFF file named Sawtooth_050.tif open in Hex Workshop.

All TIFF files start at position zero

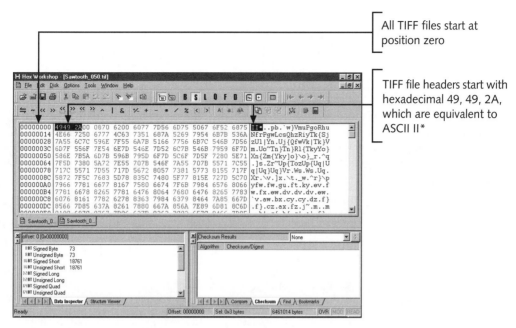

TIFF file headers start with hexadecimal 49, 49, 2A, which are equivalent to ASCII II*

Figure 11-21 A TIFF file open in Hex Workshop

For XIFF files, the first three bytes are the same as a TIFF file, followed by other hexadecimal values that distinguish it from a TIFF file (see Figure 11-22).

XIFF file header

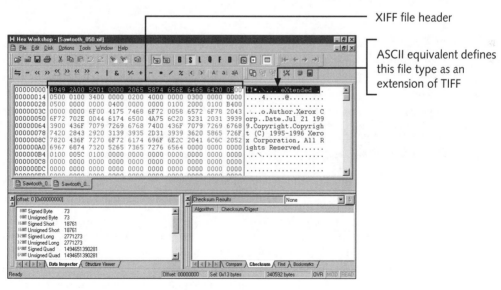

ASCII equivalent defines this file type as an extension of TIFF

Figure 11-22 A XIFF file open in Hex Workshop

As you can see, the XIFF header starts with hexadecimal 49 49 2A and has an offset of four bytes of 5C 01 00 00 20 65 58 74 65 6E 64 65 64 20 03. With this information, you can configure your tool to detect a XIFF file header.

Tools for Viewing Images

Throughout this chapter, you have been learning about recognizing file formats, using compression techniques, salvaging header information, recovering image files, and saving your modifications. After you recover an image file, you can use an image viewer to open and view the graphic. Several hundred image viewers are available that can read many graphics file formats, although no one viewer program can read every file format. Therefore, it is best to have many different viewer programs available for every investigation.

Many popular viewer utilities are freeware or shareware programs, such as ThumbsPlus, ACDSee, Quick View, and IrfanView, that can be used to view a wide range of image file formats. Most GUI computer forensics tools, such as EnCase, FTK, and iLook, include image viewers that display only common image formats, especially GIF and JPEG, which are often involved in Internet-related investigations. However, for unusual file formats, such as RAW, TNA, PCX, PPM, or FSH, integrated viewers often simply identify the data as an image file or might not recognize the data at all. Being unable to view all formats can prevent you from finding critical evidence for your case. Be sure that you analyze, identify, and inspect every unknown file on a disk drive.

NOTE

In some cases, GUI tools allow you to open files with external viewers. EnCase, for example, offers this type of integration.

In the following steps, you download IrfanView from the Web, if necessary. You use this image viewer in the Hands-on Projects at the end of the chapter. If you have already downloaded and installed IrfanView, you simply need to download and install the All_ plugins.exe file. To download and start IrfanView, follow these steps:

1. Start your Web browser.

2. In the Address text box, type **www.irfanview.com** and press **Enter**.

3. In the left column, click the **Download** link. Two download links are listed: one for IrfanView and one for the plug-ins. You need to download both.

4. Click the **TUCOWS Worldwide Network – Download IrfanView** link. Navigate the download process, selecting an operating system and mirror site as needed. If the File Download dialog box opens, click the **Save** button. In the Save As dialog box, navigate to the folder where you store downloaded files, such as a temporary folder. Then click the **Save** button to download Iview395.exe.

5. Return to the IrfanView Web page, and then click the **TUCOWS World-wide Network – Download IrfanView plugins** link. Save the Irfanview_plugins_395.exe file in the same folder as Iview395.exe, and then close your Web browser.

6. Use Windows Explorer to navigate to the folder where you downloaded the IrfanView files. Double-click **Iview395.exe** to start the IrfanView Setup Wizard. Accept the defaults to install the program on your computer.

7. To install the IrfanView plug-ins, double-click **Irfanview_plugins_395.exe**. The IrfanView Plug-ins Setup Wizard starts. Click **Next** and then click **OK** to install the plug-ins.

8. To become familiar with the file formats IrfanView supports, start IrfanView by clicking **Start**, pointing to **Programs** (**All Programs** in Windows XP), pointing to **IrfanView**, and then clicking **IrfanView 3.95**.

9. Click **File**, **Open** from the menu. In the Open dialog box, click the **Files of type** list arrow, and then review the list of image file types. Click a blank area of the Open dialog box to close the list. Then click **Cancel** to close the dialog box.

10. Close IrfanView.

Understanding Steganography in Image Files

When you open some image files in an image viewer, they might not seem to contain information related to your investigation. However, someone might have hidden information inside the image by using a data-hiding technique called steganography. As noted in Chapter 10, steganography uses a host file to cover the contents of the secret message.

Steganography might sound like a relatively new term and technique, but it has been used since ancient times. The term comes from the Greek words *steganos*, which means covered or secret, and *graphie*, which refers to writing. Ancient Greek rulers used steganography to send covert messages to their diplomats and troops via messengers. To protect the privacy of the message, the rulers shaved the heads of their messengers and tattooed the message on their skull. After the hair grew enough to cover the message, the messengers left for their destinations, where they would shave their heads so that others could read the message. This method was a clever way to send and retrieve encrypted information, but it was inefficient because it took a long time for the messenger's hair to grow back. Also, depending on the shape and size of the messenger's head, this method offered only a limited amount of space to write messages. However, it effectively allowed the Greeks to send secret messages until their enemies discovered this early form of steganography and began intercepting the messengers.

TIP

Contemporary steganography is also inefficient because an image file can hide only a certain amount of information before its size and structure changes. However, it does allows someone to send covert information to a recipient unless someone else detects the hidden data.

The two major forms of steganography are insertion and substitution. Insertion places data from the secret file into the host file without displaying the secret data when you view the host file in its associated program. The inserted data is hidden unless you review the data structure. For example, if you create a Web page by using HTML, you can display images and text in a Web browser without revealing the HTML code. Figure 11-23 shows a typical Web page as it was intended to be viewed in a Web browser. This Web page contains hidden text, which is shown in Figure 11-24 along with the source HTML code. To detect hidden inserted text, you need to compare what the file displays and what the file contains. Depending on your skill level, this process can be difficult and time consuming.

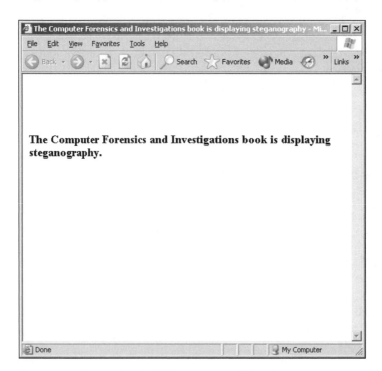

Figure 11-23   A simple Web page in a Web browser

The second type of steganography, substitution, replaces bits of the host file with other bits of data. When using a bitmap image file, for example, you could replace bits used for pixels and their colors with hidden data. To avoid detection, you need to substitute only those bits that result in the least amount of change.

Figure 11-24   HTML code with hidden text

For example, if you use an 8-bit image file, each pixel is represented by eight bits of data. These eight bits contain information about the color each pixel displays on the monitor. The bits are prioritized from left to right, such as 11101100. The first bit on the left is the most significant bit (MSB), and the last bit on the right is the least significant bit (LSB). As the names suggest, changing the MSB affects the pixel display more than changing the LSB does. Furthermore, you can usually change only the last two LSBs in an image without producing a noticeable change in the shade of color the pixel displays. To detect a change to the last two LSBs in an image file, you need to use a **steganalysis** tool, which is software designed to identify steganography techniques.

For example, if your secret message is converted to binary form to equal 01101100 and you want to embed this secret message into a picture, you would alter the last two bits of four pixels. You would break the binary form into sections of two, as in 01 10 11 00 and insert the bits into the last two bits of each pixel, as shown in Table 11-2.

Table 11-2   Bit Breakdown of Secret Message

Original Pixel	Altered Pixel
1010 1010	1010 1001
1001 1101	1001 1110
1111 0000	1111 0011
0011 1111	0011 1100

The sequence of the two bits was used to substitute the last two bits used for the pixel. This bit substitution can't be detected by the human eye, which can see only about six bits of color. Figure 11-25 shows the original picture, a simple line drawing, on the left and the altered image on the right.

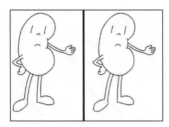

Figure 11-25   Original and altered images

The altered image contains the hidden picture shown in Figure 11-26.

Figure 11-26   Hidden image

Whether using insertion or substitution, image files tend to be the files of choice for steganography because they contain enough bits to manipulate for hiding data. Therefore, you should always inspect image files for steganography evidence, especially if your suspect is technically savvy.

 Steganography can be used with file formats other than image files, such as MPEG and AVI files.

TIP

Finding the hidden data in a steganography file can be extremely difficult. You can use several different steganalysis tools ("steg tools") to detect, decode, and record the hidden data. If you suspect steganography has been used, search the suspect device for evidence of steg tools, such as Stash-IT, Contraband, or S-Tools.

Using Steganalysis Tools

Several steganalysis tools can detect hidden data in image files, even in files that have been renamed to protect their contents. A steganalysis tool must be able to detect variations of the graphics image. If the image file has been renamed, a steganalysis tool can use the file header to identify the file format and indicate whether the file contains an image.

Although steganalysis tools can help identify hidden data, steganography is generally difficult to detect. In fact, if steganography is done correctly, in most cases you can't detect the hidden data unless you can compare the altered file with the original file. Check to see whether the file size, image quality, or file extensions have changed. If so, you might be dealing with a steganography image. As an example of the complexity of detecting steganography, Niels Provos and Peter Honeyman at the University of Michigan conducted a study of more than two million images obtained from eBay auctions. They were unable to report finding a single hidden message.

TIP Steganography and steganalysis tools are changing as rapidly as some OSs. Current steg tools include Stegowatch, Outguess, StegDetect, and S-Tools. For a list of other steganography and steganalysis tools, use a search engine to search for "steganography" or "steganalysis."

Steg tools compare a suspect file to a known good version or a known bad version of the image file. Some recent tools can detect steganography without a known good or bad file. Because the files are binary, these tools make complex mathematical calculations to verify the file's authenticity by checking the file size and palette color. Other tools compare the hash value of a known good or known bad file to the suspect file to determine whether steganography was used on the image file.

You can also use steg tools to determine which sectors of the image hide data. Keep in mind that this investigation task can be time consuming. Your first obstacle is obtaining the original image to compare to the known steganography file. In some cases, you can find the original file on the suspect's computer or can recover it if it was deleted. If the file name has been changed, you might need to view each image file you recover to try to find a match. If you can't find the original file, you can still analyze the suspect file by using a steg tool to detect the hidden data. In the Hands-on Projects at the end of this chapter, you analyze a steganography file.

IDENTIFYING COPYRIGHT ISSUES WITH GRAPHICS

Steganography was originally created to protect copyrighted material by inserting digital watermarks into a file. When working with image files, computer investigators also need to be aware of copyright laws, especially in the corporate environment, to guard against copyright violations.

The U.S. Copyright Office Web site precisely defines how copyright laws pertain to graphics (see *www.copyright.gov* for information on the 1976 Copyright Act). Copyright laws as they pertain to the Internet, however, are not as clear. For example, a server in another country might host a Web site, which could mean that it's regulated by the copyright laws in that country. Because each country has its own copyright laws, enforcement can be difficult. Contrary to what some might believe, there is no international copyright law.

The U.S. Copyright Office Web site identifies what can and cannot be covered in copyright law in the United States:

> *Copyright protects "original works of authorship" that are fixed in a tangible form of expression. The fixation need not be directly perceptible so long as it may be communicated with the aid of a machine or device. Copyrightable works include the following categories:*
>
> 1. *literary works;*
>
> 2. *musical works, including any accompanying words;*
>
> 3. *dramatic works, including any accompanying music;*
>
> 4. *pantomimes and choreographic works;*
>
> 5. *pictorial, graphic, and sculptural works;*
>
> 6. *motion pictures and other audiovisual works;*
>
> 7. *sound recordings;*
>
> 8. *architectural works.*
>
> *These categories should be viewed broadly. For example, computer programs and most "compilations" may be registered as "literary works"; maps and architectural plans may be registered as "pictorial, graphic, and sculptural works."*

Anything that would ordinarily be copyrighted through noncomputer means and is now being created on digital media is considered to be copyrighted as long as the process for obtaining a copyright has been followed.

CHAPTER SUMMARY

❏ An image file contains a graphic, such as a digital photograph, line art, a three-dimensional image, or a scanned replica of a printed picture. A graphics program creates and saves one of three types of image files: bitmap, vector, or metafile. Bitmap images are collections of dots, or pixels, that form an image. Vector images are mathematical instructions that define lines, curves, text, and geometric shapes. Metafiles are combinations of bitmap and vector images.

❏ When you use a graphics editor or image viewer, you can open a file in one of many image file formats indicated by the file extension, such as .bmp, .gif, or .eps. Each format has different qualities, including the amount of color and compression it uses. If you open an image file in a graphics program that supports multiple file formats, you can save the file in a different file format. However, converting image files this way can change image quality.

◻ Bitmap images store graphics information as grids of individual pixels (short for "picture elements"). The quality of a bitmap image displayed on a monitor is governed by screen resolution, which determines the amount of detail displayed in the image. Vector files are different from bitmap and raster files; a raster image uses dots and the vector format uses lines. A vector file stores only the mathematics for drawing lines and shapes; a graphics program converts the calculation into the appropriate image. You can enlarge a vector image without affecting image quality. Metafile image files combine raster and vector graphics and can have the characteristics of both image types.

◻ Most graphics editors let you create and save files in one or more of the standard image file formats, such as Graphic Interchange Format (GIF), Joint Photographic Experts Group (JPEG), Windows Bitmap (BMP), or Encapsulated Postscript (EPS). Nonstandard image file formats include less common formats, such as Targa (TGA) and Raster Transfer Language (RTL); proprietary formats, such as Photoshop (PSD); newer formats, such as Scalable Vector Graphics (SVG); and formats related to old or obsolete technology, such as Paintbrush (PCX).

◻ Most image file formats, including GIF and JPEG, compress their data to save disk space and reduce transmission time from one computer to another. Other formats, such as BMP, rarely compress data or do so inefficiently. In this case, you can use compression tools to compact data and reduce file size. Lossless compression saves file space by using mathematical formulas to represent the data in a file. Lossy compression compresses data by permanently discarding bits of information contained in the file.

◻ If a computer forensics investigation involves image files, you need to locate and recover all the image files on a drive and determine which ones are pertinent to your case. Because images are not always stored in standard image file formats, you should examine all files that your computer forensics tools find, even if they are not identified as image files. An image file contains a header with instructions for displaying the image. Each type of image file has its own header, and examining the header helps you identify the file format. Because the header is complex and difficult to remember, you can compare a known good file header with that of a suspected file.

◻ When you're examining recovered data remnants from files in slack or free space, you might find data that appears to be a header for a common image file type. If you locate header data that's partially overwritten, you must reconstruct the header. To do this, you compare the hexadecimal values of known image file formats to the pattern of the file header you found to make it readable again. After you identify fragmented data, you can use a computer forensics program to recover the fragmented file.

◻ If you can't open an image file in an image viewer, the next step is to examine the file's header data to see whether it matches the header in a good JPEG file. If the header doesn't match, you must manually insert the correct hexadecimal values with a hex editor, such as Hex Workshop. You can then inspect and correct the hexadecimal values within a file.

❏ The Internet is the best source for learning more about file formats and their associated extensions. You can use Webopedia or any popular search engine to search for "file type" or "file format" and find a list of Web sites with information on file extensions.

❏ You should analyze image file headers when you find new or unique file types that computer forensics tools don't recognize. The simplest way to access a file header is to use a hex editor, such as Hex Workshop. You can record the hexadecimal values in the header and then use them to define a file type in Drivespy.ini.

❏ Many popular viewer utilities are freeware or shareware programs, such as ThumbsPlus, ACDSee, QuickView, and IrfanView, that enable you to view a wide range of image file formats. Most GUI forensic tools, such as EnCase, FTK, and iLook, include image viewers that display only common image formats, especially GIF and JPEG.

❏ Steganography is a method for hiding data by using a host file to cover the contents of a secret message. The two major forms of steganography are insertion and substitution. Insertion places data from the secret file into the host file without displaying the hidden data when you view the host file in its associated program. The inserted data is hidden unless you review the data structure. Substitution replaces bits of the host file with other bits of data.

❏ Several steganalysis tools can detect hidden data in image files, even in files that have been renamed to protect their contents. Steganalysis tools must be able to detect variations in a graphics image. If the image file has been renamed, steganalysis tools can use the file header to identify the file format and indicate whether the file contains an image.

KEY TERMS

bitmap image — A representation of a graphics image in a grid-type format.

carving — The process of removing an item from a group of items. *See also* salvaging.

data compression — A complex algorithm used to reduce file size.

metafiles — Combinations of bitmap and vector images.

nonstandard image file format — A less common graphics file format, including proprietary formats, newer formats, formats that most image viewers don't recognize, and formats related to old or obsolete technology.

pixel — A small dot used to create images; the term comes from "picture element."

raster image — A bitmap file that organizes pixels in rows; usually created when a vector image is converted to a bitmap image.

rasterize — To convert a bitmap file to a raster file for printing.

resolution — Density of pixels on the screen.

salvaging — Another term for carving used outside North America; the process of removing an item from a group of items. *See also* carving.

screen resolution — The density of pixels displayed on your monitor.

standard image file format — An image file format that most or all graphics programs can open.

steganalysis — The practice of detecting and decoding steganography.

vector image — An image based on mathematical equations.

vector quantization (VQ) — A form of vector image that uses an algorithm similar to rounding off decimal values to eliminate unnecessary data.

REVIEW QUESTIONS

1. Graphics images stored on a computer cannot be recovered after they are deleted. True or False?

2. When you carve an image file, recovering the image depends on which of the following skills?

    a. recovering the image from a tape backup

    b. recognizing the pattern of the data content

    c. recognizing the pattern of the header content

    d. recognizing the pattern of a corrupt file

3. What type of compression uses a data algorithm that allows the image to be viewed without losing any portion of the image?

4. When investigating images, you should convert images into one standard format. True or False?

5. Images use data compression to accomplish which of the following goals? (Choose all that apply.)

    a. Save space on a hard drive.

    b. Provide a crisp and clear image.

    c. Eliminate redundant data.

    d. Provide data that can be posted on the Internet.

6. Salvaging a file is also known in North America by which of the following terms?

    a. data recovery

    b. scavenging

    c. Recycle Bin

    d. carving

7. JPEG image file headers typically begin with:

    a. FIFO

    b. GFIF

    c. JFIF

    d. JIFF

11

8. Each type of image file has a unique header containing a set of information that distinguishes it from every other type of image file. True or False?

9. Copyright laws do not apply to Web sites. True or False?

10. When viewing a header, you need to include the binary information in the information file of your disk editor to view the image. True or False?

11. When recovering a file with DriveSpy, your first objective is to recover the sector values. True or False?

12. Bitmap (.bmp) files are an example of _____ compression.
    a. WinZip
    b. lossy
    c. Lzip
    d. lossless

13. A JPEG file uses _____ compression.
    a. WinZip
    b. lossy
    c. Lzip
    d. lossless

14. Only four file formats can compress image files. True or False?

15. When you increase your screen resolution, you also enlarge a displayed image. True or False?

16. A JPEG file is an example of a vector graphic. True or False?

17. JPEG and XIFF files:
    a. have identical values for the first three bits of their file headers
    b. have unique values for the first three bits of their file headers
    c. differ from other image files because their headers contain a larger number of bits in the file header
    d. differ from other image files because their headers contain a smaller number of bits in the file header

18. A FAT-formatted drive has 64 sectors per cluster if it's 40 GB or larger. True or False?

19. Steganography is an efficient way of communicating secretly. True or False?

20. Some clues left on a drive that might indicate steganography was used could be:
    a. multiple copies of an image file
    b. image files with the same name but different file sizes
    c. S-Tools and Contraband located in the Programs (or All Programs) list
    d. all of the above

HANDS-ON PROJECTS

To perform the Hands-on Projects in this chapter, copy the Chap11\Projects folder from your student data files to the work folder on your system.

Project 11-1

DriveSpy recovered five possible JPEG file headers from the Ch11frag.sav file. In this chapter, you identified a JPEG header at cluster 448 on your floppy disk, and then carved and recovered the JPEG file. In this project, you carve the other four files from Ch11frag.sav to see how many you can recover.

Using the sets of steps in this chapter as a reference, carve the other files from Ch11frag.sav to see how many you can recover. There are four additional files (156, 1036, 1187, 2835) in various conditions that may or may not be recoverable. Follow these steps to confirm the cluster content, making sure you document your findings as you proceed:

1. Open a DOS command prompt window, change to the **Tools** folder in your work folder, and type **Toolpath.bat**.

2. Navigate to the Chap11\Projects folder, and then start DriveSpy by typing **drivespy** and pressing **Enter**.

3. Make sure the floppy disk containing the files you carved is in the floppy drive. At the SYS prompt, type **drive a** (substituting the drive letter of your floppy drive, if necessary) and press **Enter**.

4. At the DA prompt, type **part 1** and press **Enter** to display partition information for the floppy disk.

5. At the DAP1 prompt, type **cluster *xxx*** (replacing *xxx* with the cluster you want to examine) and press **Enter** to examine the data at that cluster.

6. Press **Page Down** to inspect the cluster and view the next cluster to determine whether the file continues past that cluster.

7. Press **Esc** to exit the cluster view and return to the DAP1 prompt. Leave DriveSpy open for the next set of steps.

   To collect the unallocated file cluster links, follow these steps:

8. At the DAP1 prompt, type **cfe *xxx*** (replacing *xxx* with the cluster you want to find), and press **Enter** to see whether other clusters are linked to this cluster.

9. At the DAP1 prompt, type **cfe *xxx*** (replacing *xxx* with the cluster you found in Step 8), and press **Enter** to see whether other clusters are linked to the next sequential cluster.

10. Repeat Steps 8 and 9 to link all clusters.

11. Document your findings, which you'll use for Project 11-2. When you're finished, close any open windows.

11

Project 11-2

In this project, you salvage an image file.

1. Open a DOS command prompt window, insert a floppy disk, type **image Ch11frag.sav a:**, and press **Enter**. (You must be in the directory containing Ch11frag.sav.)

2. At the DOS prompt, type **scandisk A:\Ch11frag.sav** (type **chkdsk** if you're using Windows 2000 or XP), and press **Enter** to scan the restored image of Ch11frag.sav and check for file errors. ScanDisk identifies several FAT errors in Ch11frag.sav.

   Now you can use IrfanView to try to view the files you carved in Project 11-1. If you have not already downloaded IrfanView, follow the instructions in "Tools for Viewing Images" earlier in this chapter.

3. To start IrfanView, click **Start**, point to **Programs** (**All Programs** in Windows XP), point to **IrfanView**, and then click **IrfanView 3.95**.

4. Click **File**, **Open**. In the Open dialog box, navigate to the floppy drive, and then double-click the **CH11frag.sav** file. Review the image, and then close IrfanView.

   If the image file doesn't appear clearly in IrfanView, it's probably still too fragmented. Repeat Project 11-1 to carve the image again.

5. Close IrfanView.

Project 11-3

In this project, you use IrfanView to open image files and then save them in a compressed graphics format different from the original graphics format. You should note any changes in how the image file is displayed because of the compression change. If you haven't already downloaded IrfanView, follow the instructions in "Tools for Viewing Images" earlier in this chapter. To save image files in various graphics formats, follow these steps:

1. Start IrfanView.

2. Click **File**, **Open** from the menu. In the Open dialog box, navigate to the Chap11\Projects folder in your work folder, and then double-click **Spider.bmp** to open the file.

3. Click **File**, **Save as** from the menu. To save the file as **Spider.jpg**, change the file type to JPG and save the file to the same location.

4. Save Spider.jpg as **Spider2.bmp** in the same location.

5. Open each image file and compare the files side by side. Document any changes you notice.

6. Open **Flower.gif** in the Chap11\Projects folder in your work folder and save it as **Flower.jpg** in the same location.

7. Save Flower.jpg as **Flower2.gif** in the same location.

8. Open each image file, and document any changes you see when comparing the files.

9. Open **Cartoon.bmp** in the Chap11\Projects folder in your work folder and save it as **Cartoon.gif** in the same location.

10. Save Cartoon.gif as **Cartoon2.bmp** in the same location.

11. Open each image file, and document any changes you see when comparing the files.

12. Close IrfanView.

13. In a text file or notebook, describe your conclusions after performing these steps.

HANDS-ON PROJECTS

Project 11-4

In this project, you identify and view a file that has an unknown file format and use the Internet to help you identify the file and the program used to view the file.

1. Use any computer forensics tool to recover one or more images from the Wheels.alb file in the Chap11\Projects folder in your work folder.

2. Start IrfanView and view **Wheels.alb**. You should see an error message identifying Wheels.alb as an unknown file format.

3. Start your Web browser, and use your favorite search engine to search for **alb file format**.

4. Click some of the links to learn more about the ALB file format. Record the program that can be used to view or create the ALB file format.

   Next, you search the Web to find a tool for viewing the file. (*Hint:* You might already have a tool that enables you to view the file.)

5. In the Address text box, type **tucows.com** and press **Enter** to go to the Tucows home page.

6. In the search box, type the name of the ALB viewer you want to download, and then click the link for your viewer. Select your region, select the mirror site for downloading, and then click the **Download** button if the download doesn't start automatically. Save the file to your desktop.

7. After the file has been downloaded to your desktop, double-click the file icon to install the viewer. Accept the defaults for the installation paths and the option to add a desktop icon for the program.

8. Double-click the desktop icon to start the image viewer program.

9. Click **File**, **Open** from the menu. Navigate to the Chap11\Projects folder, and then double-click **Wheels.alb**.

10. Document what you see in the Wheels.alb file.

11

Project 11-5

In this project, you use S-Tools to create a steganography file for hiding an image.

1. Start your Web browser.

2. In the Address text box, type **www.stegoarchive.com** and press **Enter**. Download and install S-Tools version 4. (Follow the downloading steps in Project 11-4 if necessary.)

3. Start S-Tools and Windows Explorer.

4. Drag **Rushmore.bmp** from the Chap11\Projects folder to the Actions window in the S-Tools window.

   Now you can hide text in the Rushmore.bmp image file by dragging a text file to the image.

5. Drag **findme.txt** from the Chap11\Projects folder to the **Rushmore.bmp** image. The Passphrase dialog box opens.

6. Type **FREEDOM** in the Passphrase and Verify passphrase text boxes, and then click **OK**. A hidden data window opens in the S-Tools window.

7. Right-click the hidden data window, and then click **Save as** on the shortcut menu. Save the image as **Steg.bmp** in the Chap11\Projects folder in your work folder.

8. Close the Steg.bmp and Rushmore.bmp windows, but leave S-Tools open for the next project.

Project 11-6

In this project, you reveal the hidden data in an image file by using the following steps in S-Tools:

1. Drag **jazzystage.bmp** from the Chap11\Projects folder in your work folder to the Actions window in the S-Tools window.

2. Right-click the **jazzystage.bmp** window, and then click **Reveal** on the shortcut menu. A security dialog box opens, requesting a passphrase.

3. Type **steg** in the Passphrase and Verify passphrase text boxes.

4. Click the **Encryption algorithm** list arrow, and then click **DES**. Click **OK**. The Revealed Archive dialog box opens, identifying Steg.txt as the hidden file.

5. Right-click **Steg.txt**, and then click **Save as** on the shortcut menu. Save Steg.txt in the Chap11\Projects folder in your work folder.

6. In Windows Explorer, navigate to the Chap11\Projects folder in your work folder, and then double-click **Steg.txt** to open it in a text editor.

7. Document your findings.

8. Close S-Tools and your text editor.

CASE PROJECTS

Case Project 11-1

Continue your analysis of the drive image for your investigation of the arson running case example. Determine whether any incriminating images are contained in the electronic evidence. Include the location of the file when you document any images you believe to be of evidentiary value.

Case Project 11-2

Continue your analysis of the drive image for your investigation of the kidnapping running case example, focusing on the images contained in the electronic evidence. Include the location of the file when you document any images you believe to be of evidentiary value.

Case Project 11-3

You're investigating a case involving an employee who's allegedly sending inappropriate material via e-mail in attachments that have been compressed with a zip utility. As you examine the employee's hard disk, you find a file named Orkty.zip, which you suspect is an image file because it was discovered in an e-mail. When you try to open the file in an image viewer, a message is displayed, indicating that the file is corrupt. Write a two- to three-page report describing how you can recover Orkty.zip for further investigation.

Case Project 11-4

You work for a mid-size corporation known for its inventions and that does a lot of copyright and patent work. You're investigating an employee suspected of selling and distributing animations that were created for your corporation. During your investigation of the suspect's drive, you find some files with an unfamiliar extension of .cde. The network administrator mentions that other .cde files have been sent through an FTP server to another site. List the steps for determining the contents of the .cde files.

Case Project 11-5

You're investigating an employee named Lori Hosier at a nuclear research facility. Lori is suspected of using a high-capacity removable disk to provide designs for nuclear weapons and reactors to the highest bidder. Halon W. Heels, the IT director, tells you that the reactor designs aren't classified but are considered a matter of national security. Halon found one of the suspected disks on Lori's desk and gives it to you. When you examine the disk, you find a file named Retro.11A. List the steps you would take to determine the contents of Retro.11A.

12

NETWORK FORENSICS

After reading this chapter and completing the exercises, you will be able to:

♦ Understand Internet fundamentals

♦ Understand network basics

♦ Acquire data on a Linux computer

♦ Understand network forensics

♦ Understand the use of network tools

♦ Understand the goals of the Honeynet Project

This chapter is meant to serve as an overview of network forensics, not to provide in-depth coverage of this topic. Tracing network forensic information can take long, tedious hours of work, but this field overlaps computer forensics in many areas. It's assumed that you have had an introductory networking class or Net+ equivalent. The information in this chapter should give you an idea of how the two fields of computer and network forensics complement each other.

As a computer forensics investigator, much of what you deal with includes e-mail fraud and e-mail harassment. On the corporate side, an investigation can also include misuse of the company's Internet access for pornography or game playing, for example. Network forensics differs from network security in that it deals with attempting to track down the results of an intrusion or event and the source of an intrusion. Network security, on the other hand, deals with preventing intrusions and taking precautions. This chapter also touches on tools that administrators and hackers alike can use to gain access to other machines on a network.

Understanding Internet Fundamentals

Because e-mail programs typically use some Internet protocols to exchange messages, you need to understand the fundamentals of the Internet to understand how e-mail works. For example, you should be familiar with Internet connection methods, technical rules, and similarities among e-mail applications.

The Internet is a huge collection of networks containing multiple forms of information. To access this information, you need to connect, or log on, to a server that's a member of a network that participates on the Internet. A common way to do so is to use a standard phone modem or a DSL, satellite, or cable link to connect to an **Internet service provider (ISP)**, which offers a service or membership that allows you to access information available on the Internet.

After a connection to your ISP has been established, you can log on to the server by supplying your user name, such as your e-mail address, and your password. If you enter the correct information, the ISP allows you to join its network, which is connected to the Internet. You can then access the Internet by using a Web browser or an e-mail program, for example.

To read your e-mail messages, you use an e-mail program, such as Pine, Eudora, or Outlook. E-mail programs provide a service similar to Web browsers, except they interpret and display e-mail messages. When you use an e-mail program to compose a message, the program encodes the message according to an e-mail standard, such as Multipurpose Internet Mail Extensions (MIME), a type of coding that contains information for sending messages from point to point.

TIP

In addition to MIME, e-mail programs can use another type of coding method called Uuencode. MIME is the enhanced version of coding used for e-mail messages. Although some people attempt to hide information by using Uuencode for e-mail messages, UNIX, DOS, and Windows all have a Uudecode utility that investigators can use to decode the message. Request for Comment (RFC) 2045 and 2046 describe the MIME format in detail.

Internet Protocols

Just like the spoken language, the Internet has standards and rules it must follow to make information available to different programs. Every computer that participates on the Internet must observe a protocol, or set of standards, to communicate with other computers on the Internet. The Internet uses the TCP/IP suite of protocols that addresses specific tasks in the electronic communication process. These protocols include User Datagram Protocol (UDP), File Transfer Protocol (FTP), and a variety of other connection-based and connectionless protocols.

When discussing IP addressing in this book, it's assumed that Internet Protocol version 4 (IPv4) is still in effect. Be aware, however, that IPv6 is already in use in countries such as

China. Each computer that accesses the Internet is assigned an IP address that other computers use to find it. An IP address is 32 bits long and is divided into four groups of eight bits, called octets. At their most basic level, computers interpret data as combinations of 0s and 1s. Each bit is represented with a 0 or 1 for off or on, respectively. Knowing that the bit is either on or off, an IP address would look like 11001011.00110111.00011101.10101010 in binary, which is 203.55.29.170 in dotted decimal form, also known as **dotted quad**.

Because most people don't remember numeric values easily, various servers on the Internet provide the Domain Name Service (DNS), an interpreter service that converts IP addresses into named addresses, such as *www.yahoo.com*, and vice versa. These addresses have different forms, but they all reference the same Web site being hosted on a single machine.

IP addresses are purchased or assigned in blocks. There are different classes of IP ranges. (For a review of these IP classes, consult a Net+ textbook or other networking reference.) For private individuals, their ISP assigns the next available IP address when they dial in. Corporations, on the other hand, might assign IP addresses to specific areas. It's possible to use these addresses to trace attacks and the origin of spam or viruses. Anyone working in network forensics needs to have a firm grasp of IP addressing concepts.

UNDERSTANDING NETWORK BASICS

12

Networks need to be properly hardened in today's world. **Hardening** includes everything from applying the latest patches to **layered network defense strategies**, which hide the most valuable data at the innermost perimeter. Each **network operating system (NOS)** has its own approach to security. You must be familiar with each or have a resource in your collection of experts.

Like the Internet, most networks today use the TCP/IP suite. Several other protocol suites exist, such as IPX/SPX used by older Novell NetWare systems. Keeping everyone on the same suite makes communication between organizations, customers, and clients easier. It also, however, makes it easier for hackers to penetrate a network.

The number of available IP addresses is running out, so in addition to helping secure networks, many organizations are resorting to using **network address translation (NAT)**. NAT uses nonroutable IP addresses, such as those in the series 10.0.0.1 to 10.125.125.125, to assign addresses to nodes on LANs. This way, all an outsider sees is the one IP address of the primary server or router.

Another approach network administrators take is to use DHCP servers. Each machine on a network requests its IP address from the DHCP server every time it starts up. Because not everyone is accessing the network continuously, this method allows the server to see what IP addresses are available.

Testing your network is just as important as testing your server. You need to be up to date on the latest methods used by external intruders trying to enter networks and internal personnel attempting to sabotage networks. In the early and mid-1990s, most network attacks were launched from the inside. The ratio of attacks was around 70% internal and 30% external. Even though the numbers are currently evening out, internal intruders are still a problem.

For example, in a large corporation that hires a lot of contractors, these workers have as much (and sometimes more) privileges on the network as regular employees. Now imagine what happens when a contractor leaves to work for the competition. (Keep in mind that regular employees can do the same.) That person might attempt to transmit proprietary company information or at least access that portion of the network and copy the information. Small companies are just as susceptible, if not more so, to this type of industrial espionage. Most small companies don't even have precautions in place because they typically have fewer than 10 employees.

Acquiring Data on Linux Computers

Because many network forensics tools are UNIX or Linux based, it's a good idea to become familiar with acquiring data from a Linux machine and using Linux commands. Linux is an extremely powerful OS, especially when you're working at the shell command prompt. You can use the built-in dd command to copy data from a disk drive. The options for this command give you flexibility when you're copying data. With the dd command, you can make a bit-stream disk-to-disk file, a disk-to-image file, a block-to-block copy, or a block-to-file copy. (Recall from Chapter 8 that in UNIX and Linux file systems, blocks are the same as sectors in a Microsoft file system.) You can also use the dd command to write directly to a tape drive. You can then use the **gzip** command to compress image files and minimize your storage needs.

The main advantage of using the dd command is that it's freely available as part of Linux. Other advantages are that it copies data from any disk Linux can mount and access. The dd command can make images of Ext2fs, Ext3fs, most UNIX file systems, FAT12, FAT16, FAT32, NTFS, HFS, and HPFS disks. The dd command copies any data on any disk or tape media that Linux can access. Note that AccessData FTK, X-Ways Forensics, Guidance Software's EnCase, SMART, Sleuth Kit used with Autopsy, and iLook can read dd image files. You should know how to use the dd command in case you encounter UNIX and Linux systems that might not be compatible with other MS-DOS or Windows tools.

The following are the disadvantages of using the dd command:

- You need to know advanced UNIX shell scripting and commands.
- You must specify the number of blocks per volume segment to create a volume save-set.
- You might not be able to use the dd command on your PC, depending on the distribution and version of Linux you're using.
- You cannot use the dd command to automatically adjust drive geometry to match the target drive.

To use the dd command as a data acquisition tool for computer forensics, you must build a bootable Linux floppy disk or bootable CD from an ISO image. To do so, you can use several freeware Linux boot packages available from the Internet. Several Linux distributors now provide ISO images that can be downloaded and copied to CDs. These bootable CD versions are standalone—that is, when booted from a CD-ROM drive, they run a memory-resident version of Linux on a PC. These RAM Linux OSs, such as Gnome or KDE, typically provide a GUI with all the associated services and applications of most Linux distributions. Some of the better-known Linux CDs designed for general use are Knoppix, MandrakeMove, Fedora Rescue, and Gentoo Live.

In addition to the general-use Linux CDs, F.I.R.E. and Penguin Sleuth Kit are Linux boot CDs specifically designed for computer forensics analysis. They are primarily intended for network forensics analysis of computers that have been compromised or damaged from a hacker or virus. Both of these Linux distributions are in still in beta testing.

One of the easiest Linux boot utilities to use is Tom's Root Boot Kit, which is loaded on a floppy disk. To download this boot utility for Linux, visit *www.tux.org/pub/distributions/tinylinux/tomsrtbt/start_here.html*. If you plan to use this utility, you should routinely visit this Web site to download the latest updates.

 NOTE   In the next section, you learn how to apply the dd imaging task from a Linux boot floppy. The same techniques shown in the following exercise can apply to many of the Linux ISO CDs mentioned previously.

The following steps describe how to download the utility and then use Windows to create a floppy disk containing Tom's Root Boot Kit. To download a DOS version of Tom's Root Boot Kit, follow these steps:

1. Start a Web browser, type **www.tux.org/pub/distributions/tinylinux/tomsrtbt** in the Address text box, and then press **Enter** to open the Tux.org Web page.

2. Click the most recent version of Tomsrtbt for DOS, such as **tomsrtbt –2.0.103.dos.zip**. If the File Download dialog box opens, click **OK** or **Save** to save the file. If the Unknown File Save dialog box opens, click **Save File**.

3. In the Save As dialog box, navigate to a folder on your system where you usually download files and click **Save**.

4. After the file downloads, close the File Download dialog box, if necessary, and then close your Web browser.

After you download Tom's Root Boot Kit, you need to configure a floppy disk. Tom's Root Boot Kit includes an Install.bat program, which automatically formats a floppy disk and loads the Linux kernel (the core of the Linux OS). WinZip or PKZip must be installed on your system to complete the following steps. To successfully create a Tom's Root Boot Kit, you need a computer running Windows 9x or MS-DOS 6.22 OS. The Install.bat file does not run from a DOS shell in Windows. To prepare and load a boot floppy disk for Tom's Root Boot Kit, follow these steps:

NOTE If you downloaded a version of Tom's Root Boot Kit other than Tomsrtbt-2.0. 103.dos.zip, the installation instructions might be different. For additional information about Tom's Root Boot Kit, visit *www.toms.net/rb*.

1. In Windows Explorer, navigate to the folder where you downloaded the file containing Tom's Boot Root Kit. Double-click the zip file, such as **Tomsrtbt-2.0.103.dos.zip**. Extract the files to a folder containing temporary files, such as C:\Temp. If you're using PKUnzip from a DOS shell to extract the files, as shown in Figure 12-1, type **pkunzip Tomsrt~1** and press **Enter**. (Because you're limited to eight characters for DOS file names, the file Tomsrtbt-2.0.103.dos.zip is shortened to Tomsrt~1.zip.)

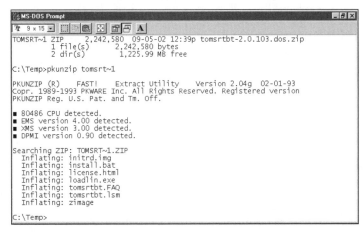

Figure 12-1 Extracting Tom's Root Boot Kit using PKUnzip

2. Reboot your workstation to MS-DOS.

3. Change to the folder where you unzipped Tom's Root Boot Kit, such as C:\Temp.

4. At the DOS prompt, type **install.bat** and then press **Enter**.

5. Follow the prompts as they are displayed on the screen, and insert a floppy disk into the floppy drive. Press **Enter** to continue with the installation.

6. After the message "Try again / do another? y/n?" appears, type **n** and then press **Enter** to exit the installation. Your computer reboots to Tom's Root Boot Kit.

Before you use the Tom's Root Boot Kit floppy disk to acquire data from Linux disks, you should understand how Linux and UNIX label disk drives. Depending on the type of controllers installed on the computer, Linux and UNIX designate drives on an IDE hard disk with the abbreviations shown in Table 12-1.

Table 12-1 Linux Drive Designations on IDE Hard Disks

IDE Disk Drive	Abbreviation
Primary master	hda
Primary slave	hdb
Secondary master	hdc
Secondary slave	hdd

For each drive, the partitions are numbered starting at 1. The first partition for the primary master drive is hda1. The second partition then becomes hda2, and so on. Partition hda1 is equivalent to the C partition in DOS.

Table 12-2 shows the abbreviations Linux and UNIX use to designate drives on a SCSI hard disk.

Table 12-2 Linux Drive Designations on SCSI Hard Disks

SCSI Disk Drive	Abbreviation
First SCSI drive	sda
Second SCSI drive	sdb
Third SCSI drive	sdc

12

Similar to the IDE drives, the partitions on a SCSI hard disk start at 1. The first partition for the first SCSI drive is sda1, the second partition on this drive is sda2, and so on.

To use Tom's Root Boot Kit for a data acquisition, you must boot the PC with the floppy disk. Before starting the PC, connect the source and target disk drives, noting on which controller each drive is located. For example, the suspect's disk might be connected to the primary master IDE controller, and the target drive might be connected to the primary slave IDE controller.

Before you install your target disk drive, make sure that an MS-DOS FAT16 or FAT32 partition has been configured on the target disk drive. The partition must also be formatted so that data can be copied to the target drive. Then follow these steps to boot your PC with Tom's Root Boot Kit floppy disk:

1. If the PC is not already shut down, perform an orderly shutdown. If you're working in Tom's Root Boot Kit, press **Ctrl+Alt+Delete** to shut down the Linux OS.

2. Make sure your source disk is connected to the primary master IDE controller on your forensic workstation. This requires you to remove the original OS disk from your workstation to acquire the suspect disk.

3. Connect the target disk to the next controller, such as the primary slave IDE cable connector.

4. Insert your Tom's Root Boot Kit floppy disk, and power on the PC.

5. As the PC is powering up, access the BIOS to make sure you can boot from the floppy disk drive. Watch for a splash screen or refer to your workstation's motherboard manual to determine what key to press during the bootstrap process to access the BIOS. Change the setting to boot from the floppy disk drive, if necessary.

6. Restart the computer.

7. When the "boot:" prompt appears, press **Enter**.

8. At the login prompt, type **root** (be sure to use all lowercase letters), and then press **Enter**.

9. At the password prompt, type **xxxx** and then press **Enter**.

Now you're ready to initiate the disk acquisition. The dd command has several options or switches for flexibility in copying data. Table 12-3 lists these options.

Table 12-3   dd Command Switches

Switch	Description
if=	Input file name or device, such as a disk drive
of=	Output file name or device, such as a disk drive
bs=	Block size in bytes (optional: bs=1M is one megabyte)
count=	Number of blocks to transfer at a time
seek=	Block position to start the next block segment write location; this switch advances the position to the next location to start writing data
skip=	Block position to start the next block segment read location; this switch advances the position to the next location to start reading data
conv=	Changes data output to a different format, such as ASCII to Extended Binary-Coded Decimal Interchange Code (EBCDIC)

To use the dd command to acquire data from an evidence disk, follow these steps:

1. After you boot the PC with the Linux boot floppy disk, create a mount point for the source hard disk (such as the C: disk). At the shell prompt (#), type **mkdir /mnt/hda1** and then press **Enter**.

2. At the shell prompt (#), create a mount point for the primary slave disk drive (such as the D: disk) by typing **mkdir /mnt/hdb1** and then pressing **Enter**.

3. Mount the primary master disk by typing **mount -t msdos /dev/hda1 /mnt/hda1** and then pressing **Enter**.

4. Mount the primary slave disk by typing **mount -t msdos /dev/hdb1 /mnt/hdb1** and then pressing **Enter**.

5. To create a one-volume dd image file (disk-to-image file), type **dd if=/dev/hda of=/mnt/hdb1/image-file.img** and then press **Enter**.

Linux and UNIX commands don't describe their actions or results unless you specify a switch to use verbose mode. When you use the dd command, the computer might seem to hang as it copies data. Depending on the size of your source drive, copying the data to the target disk might take several hours. If your workstation has a disk LED indicator, check to see whether it's on or flashing. If it isn't on steadily or is flashing, review and repeat the data acquisition steps. Linux is not compatible with all computer hardware, and drives on the Linux boot disk might be able to access only less common or older Intel computers.

To make multiple volumes of a disk with the dd command, you must perform some calculations first. First, you need to determine the number of bytes per volume (that is, a segment), which are the individual volumes that when combined make a copy of the entire source disk. Then you calculate the number of segments you need to create to successfully copy all the blocks on the disk. For example, suppose a disk drive is 4.8 GB and you plan to archive the volume segments to 650 MB CD-Rs. To determine the number of volume segments necessary to collect all blocks on the source drive, you perform the following calculations:

1. Determine how many bytes you want to store on the CD-Rs, such as 600 MB, leaving at least 50 MB free in case the actual size of the final volume segment is larger than 650 MB. This is a common problem when determining a segment's maximum size. You should underestimate the size of a segment volume to ensure that it fits on your target storage or archive media, such as CD-Rs or CD-RWs.

Media sizes advertised by the manufacturer are not what the computer reports. A CD advertised as holding 650 MB of data actually holds only 619.89 MB because of the way all manufacturers calculate disk size. When the computer reports 650 MB of data being exported, there are actually 681,574,400 bytes of data to be written. The manufacturer uses the formula that 1 KB is equal to 1000 bytes, but the computer OS counts 1 KB as 1024 bytes. A hard drive's actual size can be calculated by the information on the label. Remember: Number of cylinders × number of heads × number of sectors × 512 = disk size. Sectors contain 512 bytes, so 1 KB (two sectors) contains 1024 bytes.

2. Divide the number of bytes on the disk by the number of bytes that can be stored on a CD.

3. For disks that produce a remainder, add one extra volume segment to your calculation. For a 10 GB source disk, the calculation is 10,737,418,240 ÷ 619,890,000 = 17.32, meaning you need 17 full volumes and one partial volume, or 18 volume segments.

Instead of typing individual commands with various options at the shell prompt, you can create a Linux script file, similar to a batch file in DOS. Linux reads the script file and performs the commands as specified. Creating a script file is possible only if you are running a fully configured Linux system with a text editor, such as vi. Entering and running each command for every volume segment is difficult and prone to typing errors. Creating a script that lists all dd segment volumes saves time and eliminates mistakes.

To use the dd command, you need to define the input source, the output source, the block size, and the number of blocks to save to each segmented volume. The following script includes commands for creating an image—that is, a volume segment of a 10 GB disk drive that will be divided into 17 segment volumes. Note that each command starts one block after the last block of the previous command line. For example, the first command line reads from block 0 through block 600, which is defined with the count=600 switch. The input file is defined as a disk, such as the entire primary master disk drive, with the if=/dev/hda switch. The output file in this example is defined as a specific target disk, path, and file name with the of=/mnt/hdb1/hda_vol_01 switch. Note that each block is defined as 1 MB in size with the bs=1M switch. With this configuration, each volume is 619,890,000 bytes, which easily fits on a CD-R or CD-RW.

The next command line skips to block 601 and reads from the source drive, /dev/hda, and writes the next volume segment, /mnt/hdb1/hda_vol_02, to the target disk drive. The following commands continue to increment to the next set of 600 blocks on the disk drive:

```
dd if=/dev/hda of=/mnt/hdb1/hda_vol_01 bs=1M count=600
dd if=/dev/hda of=/mnt/hdb1/hda_vol_02 bs=1M count=600 skip=601
dd if=/dev/hda of=/mnt/hdb1/hda_vol_03 bs=1M count=600 skip=1201
.
.
.
dd if=/dev/hda of=/mnt/hdb1/hda_vol_18 bs=1M count=400 skip=10601
```

Note that the last dd command's count=400 value copies the remaining data on the drive.

After you create the volume segments of a source disk using the dd command, you can copy each volume segment to a CD-R or CD-RW. The purpose of this step is to preserve the data as part of evidence retention for your investigation.

If you need to re-create the source disk from the dd volume segments, you need an identical disk drive. The dd command doesn't adjust for disk drive geometry differences because it writes the data to the target drive in the same order it used when reading the data from the original disk drive or a volume segment. The DriveSpy WriteSect command works the same way as the dd command, in that the target drive must have the same geometry as the original source disk. You can copy data acquired from a source drive or image file to a different target drive, but the logical data structures, such as directories, will not link correctly. You'll be able to read the drive only at a physical level rather than at a logical level—the data will be on the target drive, but you won't be able to determine the file name, its path, or any other related data, such as date and time values.

Restoring a dd volume segment requires changing the input (if=) values with the output (of=) values and changing the skip= option to the seek= option. The following is a script for restoring the previous dd command segment:

```
dd if=/mnt/hdb1/hda_vol_01 of=/dev/hda bs=1M count=600
dd if=/mnt/hdb1/hda_vol_02 of=/dev/hda bs=1M count=600 seek=601
dd if=/mnt/hdb1/hda_vol_03 of=/dev/hda bs=1M count=600 seek=1201
.

.

.
dd if=/mnt/hdb1/hda_vol_18 of=/dev/hda bs=1M count=400 seek=10601
```

To make a duplicate copy of a disk drive, you can use the following dd command. (Recall that dd does not adjust the drive geometry.)

```
dd if=/dev/hda of=/dev/hdc
```

If you have a tape drive mounted to the system from which you're acquiring data, use the following dd command to copy the contents of the entire drive:

```
dd if=/dev/hda of=/dev/rst0
```

As a standard practice for all dd imaging or copying, you should run a hash check on the original media to ensure its quality. By using the redirect function in the shell command line, you can store the output from the md5sum or sha1sum commands. Save the hash output file as a validation record of the original evidence.

> On a Linux floppy boot disk, these commands might not be available, but should be available on one of the many CD versions listed previously.

NOTE

To use these commands at the Linux or UNIX shell prompt, type:

```
md5sum /dev/hda > hda_md5_hash.txt
```

or

```
sha1sum /dev/hda > hda_sha1_hash.txt
```

Earlier in this section, you learned how to use the mount command to access disks. In Linux and UNIX, you must also unmount the disks by using the umount (*not* unmount) command to disable the connection between the OS and the disk drive, as in the following command:

```
umount /mnt/hdb1
```

When you have finished your data acquisition from the Linux floppy boot disk, be sure to perform an orderly shutdown with the shutdown command. If you don't shut down properly, open files could be corrupted, which could damage your evidence data. Because of the limited amount of space on a floppy disk, the shutdown command is not available with Tom's Root Boot Kit. To shut down Tom's Root Boot Kit, press Ctrl+Alt+Delete. (Newer versions of Tom's Boot Kit might require simply typing "exit" to log off.) To shut down a Linux computer, you use the following command:

```
shutdown -h 0
```

NOTE   For additional information on Linux forensic processing, see *The Law Enforcement and Forensic Examiner Introduction to Linux, A Beginner's Guide*, by Special Agent Barry J. Grundy, NASA Office of Inspector General, Computer Crimes Division, at *www.ohiohtcia.org/linuxintro-LEFE-2.0.5.pdf*.

UNDERSTANDING NETWORK FORENSICS

Network forensics is the systematic tracking of incoming and outgoing traffic on your network. When intruders break into your network, they are going to leave a trail behind. As any experienced tracker knows, some intruders are harder to trace than others. As mentioned previously, you have to know your network's standard traffic pattern. You need to be able to determine whether you are truly under attack or someone has inadvertently installed an untested patch, for example.

An internal bug in one of your own custom programs could be causing a problem, too, so making sure you're not the cause of any network problems is equally critical. A lot of time and resources can be wasted determining that a bug in your own program or perhaps even an untested open-source program caused the "attack."

Criminal hackers typically find holes in networks and OSs before others and exploit those weaknesses. Ethical hackers work hard to plug the holes and even predict where the next onslaught of network attacks will come from.

Approach to Network Forensics

As mentioned earlier, network forensics is a long, tedious process. Like computer forensics, answers don't just miraculously appear, and unfortunately, the trail can go very cold very quickly in network forensics.

A standard procedure you might use in network forensics is as follows:

- Always use a standard image for the machines on your network. Note that this is not a bit-stream image, but an image that has all the standard applications used in a computer laboratory or office.
- When an intrusion detection/prevention incident takes place, make sure the way in has been closed.
- Acquire the compromised drive(s).
- Make a bit-stream image of the drive(s).
- Compare the image to the original image.

Some graduate students at Highline Community College, Seattle University, and University of Washington, reporting to Dave Dittrich of the University of Washington, used this technique as part of a National Science Foundation (NSF) project. They went one step farther to create a software package that retrieves the bit-stream image of a compromised drive remotely on the network and stores it on the server. The students also created software that compares the compromised image to the original drive image.

In computer forensics, you can work from the image to find most of the deleted or hidden files and partitions. On some occasions, you want to restore the image to a physical drive so that you can run programs that your lab doesn't have licensed copies of. With network forensics, you have to restore the drive to see how these items work. For example, intruders might have transmitted a Trojan horse that gave them access to the system and used a root kit or other program to gain root/administrative access to the system.

The problem you have is that whatever **malware** the attacker used—a Trojan horse program, a virus, a virus–worm combination, or other type of malicious code—is now on whatever machine you restore the disk image to. As a responsible investigator, you must first make sure you're on an isolated system where the drives can be wiped to the Department of Defense (DoD) level or destroyed, and you make sure aren't connected to an essential network. (Recall that the DoD level requires wiping at least three times.)

Network Logs

Network logs record traffic in and out of a network. Network servers, routers, firewalls, and other devices record the activities and events that move through them. A common way of examining network traffic is by running a Tcpdump program. Running a Tcpdump can result in hundreds and thousands of lines of records. A sample dump is shown here:

```
TCP log from 2005-12-16:15:06:33 to 2005-12-16:15:06:34.
Wed Dec 15 15:06:33 2005; TCP; eth0; 1296 bytes; from 204.146.
114.10:1916 to 156.26.62.201:126
Wed Dec 15 15:06:33 2005; TCP; eth0; 625 bytes; from 192.168.114.
30:289 to 188.226.173.122:13
Wed Dec 15 15:06:33 2005; TCP; eth0; 2401 bytes; from 192.168.5.
41:529 to 188.226.173.122:31
Mon Dec 15 15:06:33 2005; TCP; eth0; 1296 bytes; from 206.199.79.
28:1280 to 10.253.170.210:168;first packet
Mon Dec 15 15:06:33 2005; TCP; eth0; 625 bytes; from 192.168.5.
72:1247 to 10.40.199.255:214
Mon Dec 15 15:06:33 2005; TCP; eth0; 2401 bytes; from 192.168.5.
44:290 to 110.150.70.190:26
Mon Dec 15 15:06:33 2005; TCP; eth0; 2401 bytes; from 192.168.5.
119:253 to 192.22.192.204:206;lost data
Mon Dec 15 15:06:33 2005; TCP; eth0; 1296 bytes; from 192.168.5.
95:1646 to 156.26.62.201:12
Mon Dec 15 15:06:33 2005; TCP; eth0; 625 bytes; from 206.199.79.
5:1566 to 6.234.186.83:145
Mon Dec 15 15:06:33 2005; TCP; eth0; 1296 bytes; from 204.146.
114.14:2017 to 183.74.83.174:103
Mon Dec 15 15:06:33 2005; TCP; eth0; 2401 bytes; from 204.146.
114.50:645 to 132.130.65.172:127
```

12

```
Mon Dec 15 15:06:33 2005; TCP; eth0; 2401 bytes; from 192.168.5.
5:1184 to 83.141.167.38:64
Mon Dec 15 15:06:33 2005; TCP; eth0; 81 bytes; from 192.168.5.
117:963 to 203.68.142.136:112
END
```

Using a network analysis tool, you could generate the top 10 Web sites being visited and the top 10 users in your organization. The following sample output gives you an idea of what information you could find:

```
Top 10 External Sites Visited:
     4897 188.226.173.122
     2592 156.26.62.201
     4897 110.150.70.190
     4897 132.130.65.172
     4897 192.22.192.204
     4897 83.141.167.38
     1296 167.253.170.210
     1296 183.74.83.174
      625 6.234.186.83
      789 89.40.199.255


Top 10 Internal Users:
     4897 192.168.5.119
     4897 192.168.5.41
     4897 192.168.5.44
     4897 192.168.5.5
     2401 204.146.114.50
     1296 192.168.5.95
     1296 204.146.114.10
     1296 204.146.114.14
     1296 206.199.79.28
      625 192.168.5.72
```

You must examine the logs to look for a pattern. Several automated software packages, such as Tripwire, can tell you when something suspicious has occurred. In addition to network logs, you should also examine router logs, firewall logs, and logs for other devices set up on your network.

When you're tracing **distributed denial-of-service (DDoS) attacks**, your trace might go through other businesses, not just yours or your ISP's. In DDoS attacks, hundreds or even thousands of machines can be used. These machines are known as **zombies** simply because they have unwittingly become part of the attack.

As with all investigations, you must keep in mind the preservation of evidence and maintaining the chain of evidence. Your investigation might turn up other companies who have been compromised. In much the same way you wouldn't turn over proprietary company information to become public record, other companies appreciate the same protection. In these situations, the best course of action is to contact those companies and enlist their aid in tracking down the intruders, or you should report the incident to the authorities to enlist their aid.

Using Network Tools

A variety of tools are available for network administrators. The ones covered in this chapter are freeware and work on Windows 9x, Windows NT, Windows 200x, and UNIX.

PsTools (*www.sysinternals.com/ntw2k/utilities.shtml*) is a suite of tools created and maintained by Mark Russinovich and Bryce Cogswell. These tools are great for examining Windows products. Figure 12-2 shows the opening page of PsTools.

Figure 12-2   Opening page of PsTools

The following list is just a few examples of the powerful tools available for Windows NT/XP/200x in the PsTools suite:

- RegMon shows all Registry data in real time.

- Process Explorer shows what files, Registry keys, and DLLs are loaded at any given time.

- Handle shows what files are open and which processes are using these files.

These tools give you a lot of power to monitor your network efficiently and thoroughly. For example, an employee couldn't deny that he was running a particular program without permission because you can pull out the records PsTools generates to prove otherwise.

The following list describes some additional tools available in the PsTools suite:

- *PsExec*—Runs processes remotely

- *PsGetSid*—Displays the security identifier (SID) of a computer or a user

- *PsKill*—Kills processes by name or process ID

- *PsList*—Lists detailed information about processes

- *PsLoggedOn*—Displays who's logged on locally

- *PsPasswd*—Allows you to change account passwords

- *PsService*—Enables you to view and control services

- *PsShutdown*—Shuts down and optionally restarts a computer

- *PsSuspend*—Allows you to suspend processes

Although these tools are beneficial for network administrators, imagine what would happen if a rogue user in your organization was able to get administrative rights and start using these tools. In one situation, by using PsShutdown, a student was able to log on to another student's machine and remotely shut it down because the other student had failed to give a default user a password. The situation always comes back to having your system properly locked down. Alternatively, you can use these tools to better monitor your system and shut down machines or processes that could be harmful.

In Chapter 4, you were introduced to R-Tools. Although it's not a computer forensics tools per se, it can be used to obtain bit-stream images over a network. In one case, an employee in Hong Kong was suspected of industrial espionage. The main network investigator, located in New York City, was too busy to fly out. Fortunately, with R-Tools he could remotely image the drive and then use a standard forensic software package to examine the evidence. EnCase Enterprise Edition is capable of the same remote imaging of drives.

UNIX/Linux Tools

One of the more popular Linux tools is Knoppix-STD (*www.knoppix-std.org*). You can download the ISO image and burn it to your CD. In addition to being a boot CD, it has a lot of powerful features for examining drives and accessing network information.

To use this tool, you have to make sure the system you're using can boot from the CD by adjusting the BIOS. Knoppix-STD contains a lot of tools originally put together by Klaus Knopper that are maintained and updated by Knoppix users. For more detailed information, visit *www.knoppix.net*. The CD has tools in a variety of categories, including authentication, encryption, forensics, firewalls, IDs, honeypots, network utilities, password tools, packet sniffers, vulnerability assessment, and wireless tools.

Packet sniffers are devices and/or software placed on a network to monitor traffic. Most network administrators use sniffers for increasing security and tracking bottlenecks. However, hackers can use them to obtain information illegally. On TCP/IP networks, sniffers look at packets, hence the term "packet sniffers." Most network sniffers work at layer 2 or 3 of the OSI model. To understand and determine what's happening on the network, you often have to look at the higher layers, however.

A few of the Knoppix-STD tools include the following:

- *dcfldd*—The U.S. DoD computer forensics lab's version of the dd command

- *memfetch*—Forces a memory dump

- *photorec*—Grabs files from a digital camera

- *snort*—A popular network intrusion detection system that performs packet capture and analysis in real time (*www.snort.org*)

- *oinkmaster*—Helps manage your snort rules so that you can specify what items to ignore as regular traffic and what items should raise alarms

- *john*—The latest version of John the Ripper, which is a password cracker

- *chntpw*—Enables you to reset passwords on a Windows computer, including the Administrator password

- *tcpdump* and *ethereal*—Packet sniffers

With the Knoppix-STD tools on a portable CD, you can examine almost any network machine and get a feel for what's going on. You can also image someone's machine and inspect what items are on the machine without the other person ever being aware that you're examining the machine's contents.

To see how Knoppix works, go to *www.knoppix-std.org* and download the ISO image for the tools. Following the procedure for copying an ISO image, burn it to a CD and label the CD. Although the Knoppix bootable CD works on an NTFS volume, it's easier to access a DOS or FAT32 drive. Go to any PC with Windows 2000, XP, or 98 formatted as a FAT32 volume. It should be on a live network.

12

1. If the machine is on, open the CD drive and leave it open.

2. Reboot the machine and close the drive. Check the BIOS to make sure you can boot from the CD.

3. The CD should automatically start. You might need to specify what resolution you want.

4. When it's fully booted, you see the Knoppix logo in the middle of your screen (see Figure 12-3.)

Figure 12-3   The Knoppix logo

5. Right-click anywhere on the screen. When the menu is displayed, click **XShells**, **Root Aterm**.

6. Type **cd ..** as many times as necessary to access the root. Your prompt should read **root@0[/]**.

7. To access the hard drive, type **mount -t vfat /dev/hda1 /mnt**.

8. To begin examining the files on the hard drive, type **cd /mnt**.

9. Type **ls -l** to get the directory listing.

10. Next, you use a sniffer. Minimize the Aterm window. Right-click anywhere on the screen, and click **Sniffers**, **ethereal**.

11. When the window opens, click **Capture**, **Start**. If the Capture Options dialog box opens, click **OK** to accept the defaults. You should see the Ethereal window and the tracking window, as shown in Figure 12-4.

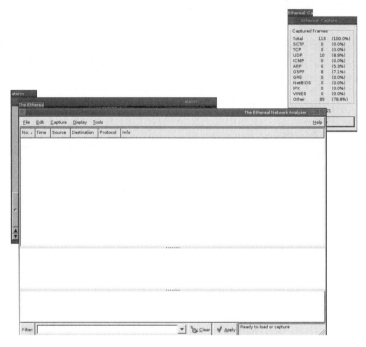

Figure 12-4 Ethereal during a capture in Knoppix

12. After a few minutes, click **Stop**. It takes a few seconds for the program to load. When it's finished, you should see a screen similar to Figure 12-5.

13. Click **File**, **Quit**. Right-click anywhere on the screen, and click **Shutdown**. A message is displayed when Knoppix has been stopped. Remove the CD and close the drive. The system then shuts down.

Another good Linux tool is The Auditor (*www.remote-exploit.org/?page=auditor*), a robust tool that fittingly has a Trojan warrior for a logo. The Auditor is based on Knoppix and contains more than 300 tools, including more than 20 for scanning, 10 for network scanning, tools for brute-force attacks, tools for Bluetooth and wireless networks, and more. It also comes with forensic tools, such as Autopsy and Sleuth Kit.

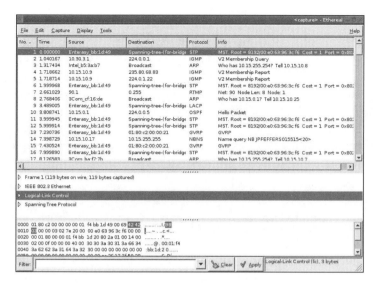

Figure 12-5   Ethereal after a capture in Knoppix

The Auditor is designed to be easy to use for your security needs and is updated frequently. It includes built-in Web browsers, editors, and graphics tools so that you can generate reports. In addition, it contains word lists from many languages with more than 64 million entries.

Network Sniffers

Network sniffers, as mentioned earlier in this chapter, operate on layer 2 or 3 of the OSI model. When using network sniffers, you should be conscious of the difference between capture and analysis tasks. Some network sniffers perform packet captures, some are used for analysis, and some handle both.

Windows has many proprietary tools for network sniffing. Most are capable of capturing and analyzing packets. The problem is that you can't feed their data directly into other tools. Most tools can read anything captured in PCAP format. As a forensics expert, you must choose the tool that best suits your purposes. For example, if your network is being hit with SYN flood attacks, you want to find packets with the SYN flag set. In a SYN flood attack, the attacker keeps asking your server to establish a connection. Although your server can handle thousands of connections, it can handle only a limited number of establishing connections. Several good tools are available in this situation. Tcpdump, Tethereal (the text version of Ethereal), and Snort can be programmed to look in TCP headers to find the SYN flag. You can find a reference for TCP headers at *www.iana.org/assignments/tcp-header-flags*.

Tcpslice is a good tool for breaking down large libpcap (PCAP library) files. When using this tool, you must be aware of the trace timestamps. This information allows you to select specific time periods. Another tool, Tcpreplay, is used to work with applications that cannot read libpcap formats. It literally replays the trace for those applications. Tcpdstat is a tool that works close to real time. It generates libpcap statistics and breaks them down by protocol.

Ngrep can be used to examine e-mail headers or IRC chats. It collects and hashes the data for verification later. Etherape is a way to graphically view network traffic. Another GUI tool, Netdude, deals with large traces and Tcpdump outputs with ease. Richard Bejtlich, author of *The Tao of Network Security Monitoring—Beyond Intrusion Detection* (Addison-Wesley, ISBN 0-321-24677-2), states "Netdude is any forensic analyst's nightmare because it makes it easy to alter almost any aspect of a packet. The best defense is to compute hashes of trace files once they are created."

Argus (*www.qosient.com/argus*) is a session data probe, collector, and analysis tool. This real-time flow monitor can be used for security, accounting, and network management.

Ethereal, which comes with Knoppix-STD and The Auditor, also offers a Windows version, shown in Figure 12-6. Ethereal can be used in a real-time environment to open saved trace files. One of its important features is its capability to rebuild sessions. Select a packet of interest, right-click it, click Tools, and follow TCP Stream. Ethereal then traces back the packets associated with an exploit.

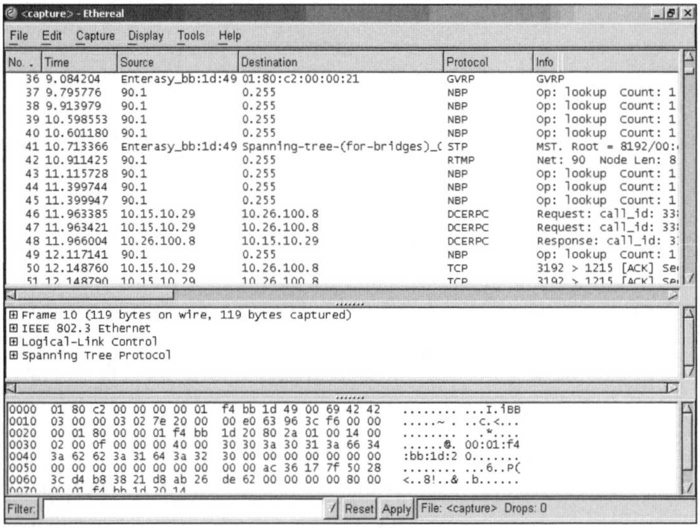

Figure 12-6   Ethereal in a Windows environment

You can find additional information about network forensic tools at many of the ongoing forums available at the sites mentioned in this chapter. If you're interested in learning even more about network forensics, the next section covers the Honeynet Project.

THE HONEYNET PROJECT

The Honeynet Project (*www.honeynet.org*) was developed to make information widely available in an attempt to thwart Internet and network hackers. Many people participate in this worldwide project. The opening Web page for the site is shown in Figure 12-7.

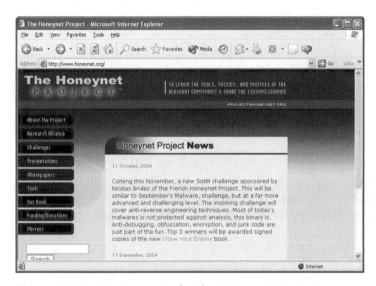

Figure 12-7   Opening page for the Honeynet Project

When the first DDoS attacks began, the major concerns were the high monetary impact and the amount of time it took to track down these attacks. In any corporation, you have to determine the value of the data you're protecting and weigh it against the price of the defense system you plan to install. When an attack strikes, your first response is to stop the attack and prevent it from going further. Then you need to see what defense procedures worked and what additional procedures might be needed. It's critical your staff be trained and informed. The Honeynet Project was set up as a resource to help network administrators deal with these attacks.

The Honeynet Project involves setting up **honeypots** and **honeywalls** at various locations in the world. A honeypot is a computer set up to look like any other machine on your network, but it lures the attacker to it. In this way, you can take the honeypot offline and not affect the running of your network. Honeywalls are appliances, namely computers, set up to "monitor the outbound connections and snort-inline intrusion prevention systems" (see *www.honeynet.org/papers/cdrom/*). They also capture what attackers do without them realizing it. The legality of honeypots has been questioned, however. Currently, they can't be used in court, but the results can certainly be used to determine how culprits are breaking in. The findings are then used to create better safeguards for networks.

The best part of the Honeynet Project is the Honeynet Challenges (*www.honeynet.org/misc/chall.html*). You can attempt to ascertain what an attacker did and then post your results online. After a certain amount of time has passed, the solution is posted along with the comments of others in the project. It's one of the fastest ways to learn what's happening in the world of network intrusions. If you try any of the challenges, make sure you load them on a nonessential machine because they contain live viruses, worms, and Trojans. By attempting to solve the scan of the month, you get a lot of practice in what to look for and how to go about conducting a network forensics evaluation. Figure 12-8 shows the opening page for the Honeynet Challenges. Many people post solutions for each challenge, and as part of your learning, you could try to re-create their solutions.

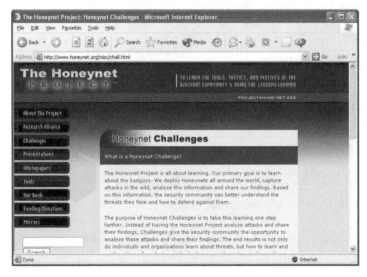

Figure 12-8   The Honeynet Challenges opening page

Chapter Summary

- Network forensics is a specialized field that requires a lot of the time and effort. It deals with tracking down internal and external network intrusions.

- Most people access the Internet via an Internet service provider, which provides a connection to the backbone of the Internet. Internet connections can be dial-up, DSL, cable, or T1 or T3 lines.

- Most networks today use the TCP/IP suite of protocols. For e-mail, some common protocols are MIME, SMTP, POP3, and IMAP.

- Networks must be hardened by using good architecture, NAT, and layered network defense strategies. Organizations should also use intrusion detection and prevention systems.

- Each NOS has its own way of handling security, and you must become familiar with how yours operates.

❏ Tools such as PsTools, Knoppix-STD, and others can be used to monitor what's happening on your network. They can also be used by intruders who obtain administrative rights to attack your network from the inside.

❏ The Honeynet Project is designed to help people learn the latest intrusion techniques that hackers are using.

KEY TERMS

distributed denial-of-service (DDoS) attacks — In these attacks, an Internet attacker uses other online machines, unbeknownst to them, to launch an attack. These machines are known as zombies.

dotted quad — A term used to refer to the IP addressing scheme of Web sites, routers, and similar devices.

gzip — A UNIX/Linux command that compresses image files and minimizes your storage needs.

hardening — A process of ensuring network security, which includes tasks as simple as applying updated OS patches and as complex as using layered network defense strategies.

honeypot — A computer set up to lure an attacker.

honeywall — An intrusion prevention and monitoring system that watches what an attacker does.

Internet service provider (ISP) — A local or national service that provides a connection to the Internet.

layered network defense strategies — An approach to network hardening that places the most valuable data at the innermost perimeter of a network.

malware — Any type of intrusive code that is used to attack a system including viruses, worms, virus-worms, Trojans, and so on.

network address translation (NAT) — Using nonroutable IP addresses on your LAN to hide the number of computers or nodes on your network.

network operating system (NOS) — An OS product used with network servers; includes products such as UNIX, Windows Server 2003, and Novell NetWare.

packet sniffers — Devices and/or software used to examine network traffic. On TCP/IP networks, they examine packets, hence the term.

zombie — A computer used without its knowledge or consent in a DDoS attack.

REVIEW QUESTIONS

1. If you discover during your investigation that another company's machines are being used as part of a DDoS attack, what should you do?

2. What Linux command copies the entire contents of one drive to another drive?

3. What procedures should you follow when you realize that a computer on your network has been compromised?

4. Which of the following is the most common suite of protocols in use today on the Internet?

   a. SPX/IPX

   b. NetBEUI

   c. TCP/IP

   d. none of the above

5. Layered network defense is ineffective against the common attacker. True or False?

6. A DNS server:

   a. finds the domain name for an IP address

   b. assigns IP addresses

   c. handles databases

   d. is used by the administrator to determine who is doing what

7. IPv6 is currently being used in some countries. True or False?

8. Small companies don't have to worry about network intruders or industrial espionage. True or False?

9. Tcpslice allows you to break large trace files into smaller ones. True or False?

10. Criminal hackers typically find the holes in OSs before anyone else. True or False?

11. Of the tools available with PsTools, which one monitors Registry data in real time?

    a. PsList

    b. Handle

    c. RegMon

    d. PsUpTime

12. To unmount a drive in Linux, which of the following commands should you use?

    a. /mnt/hdb1

    b. umount /mount/hdb0

    c. umount /mnt/hdb1

    d. none of the above

13. Honeypots are considered evidence that can be used in court. True or False?

14. In corporations, the most common problems involve:

    a. e-mail harassment

    b. Internet abuse

    c. accessing restricted areas

    d. all of the above

15. Name three types of log files you should examine after a network intrusion.

HANDS-ON PROJECTS

The objective of these Hands-on Projects is to give you practice in using tools that are freely available for network forensics. Most network forensics tools are created by experienced users, not necessarily major vendors that supply extensive documentation.

Project 12-1

If you have not already done so, download the Knoppix-STD image and burn it to a CD. Boot one of your lab machines using the CD. Choose five tools from the menu that look interesting. If you can't figure out how to use them, do an Internet search to look for documentation. Write a short paper describing how to use these tools and how they would be effective in dealing with network intrusion and forensics.

Project 12-2

Download the PsTools suite from *www.sysinternals.com/ntw2k/utilities.shtml*. Work with another student to test the tools on your lab network. Using the instructions that come with the suite, install the software and do the following:

◻ Remotely shut down your partner's machine.

◻ Change the password for your partner's account.

◻ Retrieve your partner's SID.

Project 12-3

Download the documentation for the Honeywall CD. Based on your reading, determine what hardware is needed to attach it to a network. Attempt to write a step-by-step procedure for how you would install it on your network.

Project 12-4

Go to the Honeynet Project Web site (*www.honeynet.org*) and locate the page with the most recently solved challenge. Select three solutions that have been submitted. Compare the results of each. Write a short paper describing these solutions and compare their findings.

Project 12-5

Download Ethereal from *www.ethereal.com*. Load it on a machine connected to a live network. Perform a capture for approximately five minutes, and then save the file. Open FTK Imager and perform a hash value on the file. Reopen Ethereal and examine the trace. What patterns do you see? Are you on a network using NAT, or are routable IP addresses visible? Do any addresses show up more than others?

12

CASE PROJECTS

Case Project 12-1

The FBI has notified you that nodes on your network have been used as zombies in an attack against another Web site. What steps should you take to prevent further exploits? What information do you need from the FBI to assist you in your internal investigation?

Case Project 12-2

Assume you're a network administrator, and you're receiving calls saying that users can't access the company Web site or get responses from e-mail. You discover that your network is under a DDoS attack. What steps should you take to stop the attack and prevent a similar attack in the future?

Case Project 12-3

A user on your network calls to complain that her co-workers are receiving e-mail from her that she didn't send. What type of attack is this? Who do you need to inform to prevent it from spreading?

13

E-MAIL INVESTIGATIONS

After reading this chapter and completing the exercises, you will be able to:

♦ Explore the roles of the client and server in e-mail

♦ Investigate e-mail crimes and violations

♦ Understand e-mail servers

♦ Use specialized e-mail computer forensics tools

This chapter explains how e-mail works and how messages are sent and received via the Internet. It also discusses how you can trace, recover, and analyze e-mail messages by using forensic software tools specifically created for investigating e-mail.

Over the past decade, e-mail has become a primary means of communication, and most computer users have e-mail programs to receive, send, and manage their e-mail messages. These programs, known as e-mail clients, differ in how and where they store and track e-mail messages. Some e-mail clients are installed separately from the OS and, therefore, require their own directories and information files on the local computer. Other e-mail clients take advantage of existing software, such as your Web browser, and install no additional software on the client machine. Throughout this chapter, you see how e-mail programs on the server interact with e-mail programs on the client, and vice versa. You also learn how to recover deleted e-mail from a client machine, regardless of which type of software has been used on the client, and how to trace an e-mail back to the sender.

EXPLORING THE ROLES OF THE CLIENT AND SERVER IN E-MAIL

You can send and receive e-mail in two environments: via the Internet or in a controlled network (LAN, MAN, or WAN). Both environments distribute data, such as e-mail messages, from one central server to many connected client computers, a configuration called **client/server architecture**. The server computer uses a server OS, such as Windows Server 2003, Novell NetWare, or UNIX, and runs an e-mail server program, such as Exchange Server, GroupWise, or Sendmail, to provide e-mail services. Client computers run an OS such as Windows or Linux and use e-mail programs, such as Eudora or Outlook, to contact the e-mail server and send and retrieve e-mail messages (see Figure 13-1).

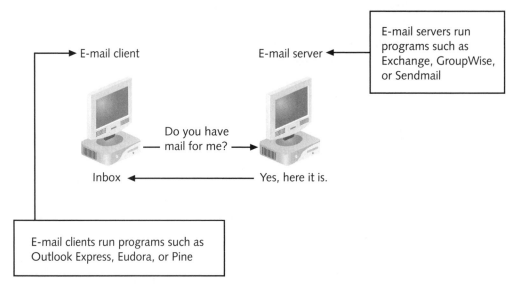

E-mail client

E-mail server

E-mail servers run programs such as Exchange, GroupWise, or Sendmail

Do you have mail for me?

Inbox

Yes, here it is.

E-mail clients run programs such as Outlook Express, Eudora, or Pine

Figure 13-1 E-mail in a client/server architecture

Regardless of the OS or e-mail program, each user accesses his or her e-mail based on permissions granted by the administrator in charge of the e-mail server. These permissions prevent others from accessing your e-mail. To retrieve your messages from the e-mail server, you identify yourself to the server, as you do when you log on to the network. Then the e-mail messages are delivered to your computer.

E-mail services on the Internet and a LAN both use client/server architecture, but they differ in how client accounts are assigned, used, and managed and in how users access their e-mail. Overall, a LAN e-mail system is for the private use of LAN users, and Internet e-mail systems are for public use. On a LAN, the e-mail server is generally part of the local network, and an administrator is dedicated to managing the server and the services it supplies. In most cases, a LAN e-mail system is specific to a company, used only by its employees, and is regulated by its business practices, which usually involve strict security and acceptable use policies. For example, with LAN e-mail, users can't create their own accounts. User names in LAN e-mail addresses tend to follow some type of naming convention. For example, John Smith at Some Company would use *jsmith* as the user name followed by the domain name of the company, *somecompany.com*, to create the e-mail address of *jsmith@somecompany.com*. The network administrator who is responsible for the e-mail server ultimately determines the naming convention used on the network.

TIP

In an e-mail address, everything after the @ symbol represents the domain name. You need to know the domain information when you investigate e-mail to identify who is the point of contact at that domain name.

In contrast, a company that provides public e-mail services, such as AOL, Hotmail, or Juno, owns the e-mail server on an Internet-based e-mail system. They accept everyone who signs up for their service. E-mail companies provide their own servers and administrators. Anyone can receive Internet e-mail services by connecting to the Internet, signing up for an e-mail account, and providing a user name and password. After users sign up, they can access their e-mail from any machine connected to the Internet. In most cases, Internet e-mail users are not required to follow a standardized naming convention for their user names. For example, Jim Shu could be *stinky@juno.com*. The bottom line is that users are allowed to choose their own user names, but not the domain name, for their e-mail addresses, as long as the user name isn't already in use.

For computer investigators, tracing LAN e-mail is easier because the accounts use standard names established by the network or e-mail administrator. For example, *jane.smith @mycompany.com* could be easily recognized as the e-mail address for an employee named Jane Smith. Tracking Internet e-mail users, on the other hand, is more difficult because those user accounts don't always use standard naming schemes, and e-mail administrators aren't familiar with all the user accounts on their servers. For example, identifying the owner of an e-mail account isn't easy with an address such as *itty_bitty@hotmail.com*.

13

INVESTIGATING E-MAIL CRIMES AND VIOLATIONS

Investigating crimes or policy violations involving e-mail is similar to investigating other types of computer abuse and crimes. Your goal is to find out who is behind the crime or policy violation, collect the evidence, and present your findings to build a case for prosecution or arbitration.

Identifying E-mail Crimes and Violations

E-mail crimes and violations depend on the city, state, and sometimes country in which the e-mail originated. For example, in the state of Washington, sending unsolicited e-mail, also known as spam, is illegal. However, in other states, spam is not considered a crime. Consult with an attorney for your organization to determine what specifically constitutes an e-mail crime.

Committing crimes with e-mail is becoming commonplace. More investigators are finding communications that link suspects to a crime or policy violation through e-mail. For example, some people use e-mail when committing crimes such as narcotics trafficking, extortion, sexual harassment, stalking, fraud, child abductions, terrorism, child pornography, and so on. Because e-mail has become a major communications medium, any crime or policy violation can involve e-mail.

Examining E-mail Messages

After you have determined that a crime has been committed using e-mail, first access the victim's computer to recover the evidence. Using the victim's e-mail client, find and copy any potential evidence contained in the e-mail. It might be necessary to log on to the e-mail service and access any files or directories that are protected or encrypted. If you can't actually sit down at the victim's computer to access the offensive e-mails, you have to guide the victim on the phone to open and print a copy of an offending message, including the header, as you will do in the following section. The header of the e-mail message contains unique identifying numbers, such as the IP address of the server that sent the message. This information helps you trace the e-mail to the suspect.

TIP   Before you work with a victim on the phone, create written procedures for opening and printing an e-mail header and message text using a variety of e-mail programs, according to your state, county, or company's laws or policies. These steps help you give consistent instructions and can be helpful when training new forensic investigators.

In some cases, you might have to recover e-mail after a suspect has deleted it and tried to hide it from you. You see how to recover those messages later in this chapter. For now, you continue working with a victim's computer as a cyber-detective.

Copying an E-mail Message

Before you start an e-mail investigation, you need to copy and print the e-mail message involved in a crime or policy violation. You might want to forward the message as an attachment to another e-mail address as well, depending on your department's guidelines.

The following steps explain how to use Microsoft Outlook, included with the Microsoft Office suite, to copy an e-mail message. (*Note*: Depending on the version of Outlook you use, the steps might vary slightly.) You use a similar procedure to copy messages in other e-mail programs, such as Outlook Express and Eudora. If Microsoft Outlook or Outlook Express is installed on your computer, perform the following steps and copy any e-mail message in your Inbox folder to a floppy disk:

1. Insert a formatted floppy disk into the floppy drive (the A: drive, for example). Use Windows Explorer or My Computer to open a window showing the floppy disk icon.

2. Start Outlook, if necessary, by clicking **Start**, pointing to **Programs** (**All Programs** in Windows XP), and then clicking **Microsoft Outlook**. The Outlook window opens.

3. Make sure the Folder List is open, as shown in Figure 13-2, and click the folder containing the message you want to copy. For example, click the **Inbox** folder. A list of messages in that folder appears in the right pane of the Outlook window.

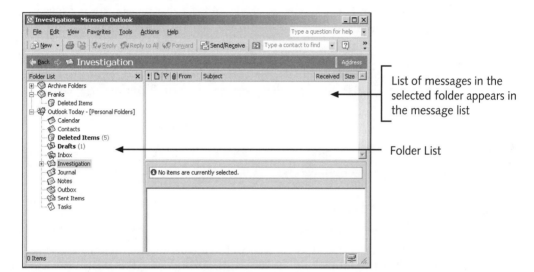

List of messages in the selected folder appears in the message list

Folder List

Figure 13-2   The Folder List in Outlook

4. Resize the Outlook window so that you can see the message you want to copy and the icon for the floppy disk.

5. Drag the message from the Outlook window to the floppy disk icon.

TIP Instead of dragging, you can also click a message in the Inbox, and then click File, Save As. In the Save As dialog box, click the Save in list arrow and navigate to the disk or folder where you want to copy the message, making sure you select the .msg format if you want to make a duplicate of the message. (For Outlook Express, you select the .eml format.) If you select the .txt format, you get only the contents of the message. After you have selected a storage location and format, click the Save button.

With many GUI e-mail programs, you can copy an e-mail message by dragging the message to a storage medium, such as a folder or disk, or by using a Save dialog box to save the message in a different location. For e-mail programs that you run from the command line (such as Pine used with UNIX), however, open the message, and then use the option to copy the e-mail message, usually located at the bottom of the screen. After you copy an e-mail message, work only with the copy, not the original version of the message. You do this to eliminate the chances of changing or altering the original evidence by mistake.

Printing an E-mail Message

After you acquire a copy of e-mail evidence, you should print it to include in your report. The following steps explain how to print an e-mail in Outlook or Outlook Express. If you're using a different e-mail program, read but do not perform the following steps:

1. Use Windows Explorer or My Computer to navigate to the location where you stored a copy of the e-mail message, such as a floppy disk.

2. Double-click the message you want to print. The message opens in an e-mail program, such as Outlook.

3. Click **File**, **Print** from the menu to open the Print dialog box.

4. Change print settings, if necessary, in the Print dialog box, and then click the **Print** (or **OK**, depending on your e-mail client) button.

If you're using Pine or another command-line e-mail client, open the e-mail message and select the print option at the bottom of the screen.

Viewing E-mail Headers

After you copy and print an e-mail message, use the e-mail program that created the message to find the e-mail header. This section includes instructions for viewing an e-mail header in a variety of different e-mail clients, including Windows GUI clients, such as Microsoft Outlook, Outlook Express, and Eudora; Pine, a command-line e-mail client used with UNIX; common Web-based e-mail providers, such as AOL, Hotmail, and Yahoo!; and an unusual Web-based client called WebTV. After you open e-mail headers, copy and paste them into a text document so that you can read them with a text editor such as Notepad or Pico (used with UNIX). You examine the headers in the next section.

Whether you're working in a computer lab or elsewhere, installing and becoming familiar with as many e-mail clients as possible is beneficial. Often more than one e-mail program is installed on a single computer, and you need to find out which ones your suspect is using. The following steps assume you know how to open the Outlook e-mail program:

1. Create a Chap13 folder with a Chapter subfolder in your work folder.

2. Start Outlook as you usually do, and then select the original of the message you copied in the previous section.

3. Right-click the message, and then click **Options** to open the Message Options dialog box. The Internet headers text box at the bottom of the dialog box contains the message header, as shown in Figure 13-3.

4. Drag to select all the message header text, and then press **Ctrl+C** to copy the text to the Clipboard.

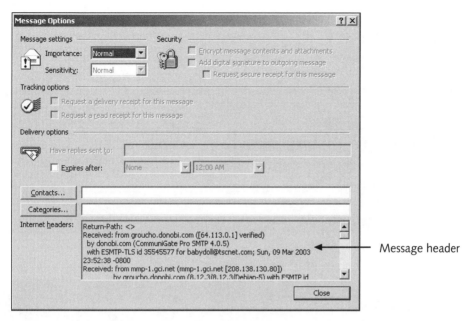

Figure 13-3   Microsoft Outlook e-mail header

5. Start a text editor, such as Notepad, and then press **Ctrl+V** in a new document window to paste the message header text.

6. Save the message header document as **Outlook Header.txt** in the
   Chap13\Chapter folder in your work folder. Then close Outlook Header.txt.

7. Close Outlook.

To retrieve an Outlook Express e-mail header, follow these steps:

1. Start Outlook Express as you usually do, and then display the message you
   want to examine in the Outlook window.

2. Right-click the message, and then click **Properties** to open a dialog box
   showing general information about the message.

3. Click the **Details** tab to display the header for the e-mail message (see
   Figure 13-4).

4. To see a detailed version of the header, click the **Message Source** button (see
   Figure 13-5).

5. Drag to select all the message header text, and then press **Ctrl+C** to copy the
   text to the Clipboard.

6. Start a text editor, such as Notepad, and then press **Ctrl+V** in a new document window to paste the message header text.

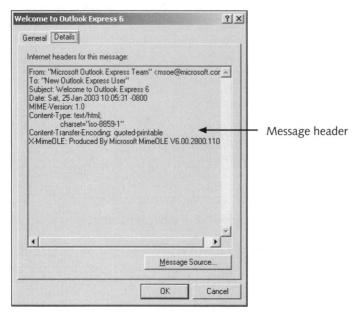

Figure 13-4 Outlook Express e-mail header

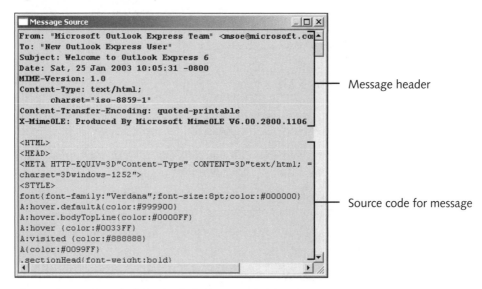

Figure 13-5 Detailed Outlook Express e-mail header

7. Save the message header document as **Outlook Express Header.txt** in the Chap13\Chapter folder in your work folder.

8. Close all open windows and dialog boxes, and then close Outlook Express.

To retrieve an e-mail header in Eudora, follow these steps:

1. Start Eudora as you usually do, and open the Inbox.

2. Double-click the e-mail message to open it.

3. Click the **BLAH BLAH BLAH** button on the toolbar above the message. The e-mail header appears, as shown in Figure 13-6.

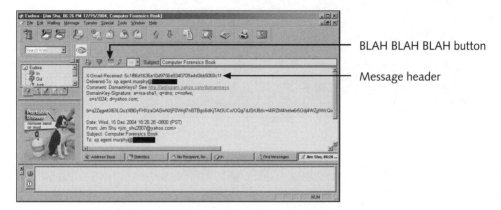

Figure 13-6   Eudora e-mail header

4. Drag to select all the message header text, and then press **Ctrl+C** to copy the text to the Clipboard. Start a text editor, such as Notepad, and then press **Ctrl+V** in a new document window to paste the message header text.

5. Save the message header document as **Eudora Header.txt** in the Chap13\Chapter folder in your work folder. Then close Eudora Header.txt.

6. Close Eudora.

The previous steps used a GUI to help you find the header information. Now you see how to find this same information with e-mail software provided at the command prompt using UNIX. Follow these steps to retrieve e-mail headers using Pine for UNIX:

1. Start Pine by typing **pine** at the command prompt and then pressing **Enter**. The Pine e-mail screen appears with the available options shown at the bottom.

2. Type **s** to display the setup options.

3. Type **c** to configure the e-mail configuration options.

4. Scroll the list of options, and then use the arrow keys to highlight the **[ ] enable-full-header** option. Then type **x** to select the option.

5. Type **e** to exit configuration mode.

6. When asked if you want to save or commit the changes, type **y**. You return to the Pine main options.

7. Use the arrow keys to select an e-mail message and then select **O** in the options at the bottom of the screen (see Figure 13-7).

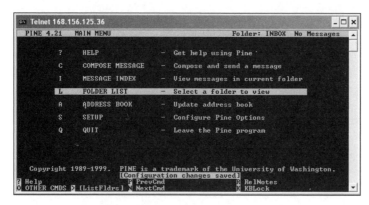

Figure 13-7   Pine e-mail options

8. Type **h** to open the e-mail header for this message (see Figure 13-8).

Message header

Figure 13-8   Pine e-mail header

9. Type **q** to exit Pine (and **y** to confirm, if necessary).

These steps also work with (ELM), another command-line e-mail program for UNIX and Linux. For older UNIX applications, such as mail or mailx, you can print the e-mail headers by using the `print` command. When the e-mail message is open, type an uppercase P to use the `print` command. You can also save the e-mail message into a directory and use the command `type saved e-mail >> printer` (*saved e-mail* is the name of the saved e-mail message and *printer* is the name of the printer). For example, if you had an e-mail message called Nightmare and a printer called MyPrinter, you could print this e-mail message by typing the following at the command prompt:

```
type Nightmare >> MyPrinter
```

AOL, Hotmail, Juno, and Yahoo! are popular Internet e-mail service providers. With an Internet e-mail service, you can use any computer connected to the Internet to send and receive e-mail, making these messages more difficult to trace. To view AOL e-mail headers, follow these steps:

1. Start AOL as you usually do.

2. Double-click the e-mail message to open it.

3. Click the **Details** link below the subject line. The header appears, as shown in Figure 13-9.

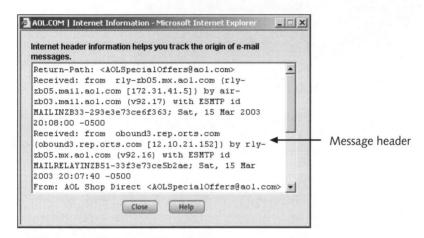

Figure 13-9 shows:

```
AOL.COM | Internet Information - Microsoft Internet Explorer    _ □ ×

Internet header information helps you track the origin of e-mail
messages.

Return-Path: <AOLSpecialOffers@aol.com>
Received: from  rly-zb05.mx.aol.com (rly-
zb05.mail.aol.com [172.31.41.5]) by air-
zb03.mail.aol.com (v92.17) with ESMTP id
MAILINZB33-293e3e73ce6f363; Sat, 15 Mar 2003
20:08:00 -0500
Received: from  obound3.rep.orts.com
(obound3.rep.orts.com [12.10.21.152]) by rly-      ◄──── Message header
zb05.mx.aol.com (v92.16) with ESMTP id
MAILRELAYINZB51-33f3e73ce5b2ae; Sat, 15 Mar
2003 20:07:40 -0500
From: AOL Shop Direct <AOLSpecialOffers@aol.com>

        Close       Help
```

Figure 13-9   AOL e-mail header

4. Drag to select all the message header text, and then press **Ctrl+C** to copy the text to the Clipboard. Start a text editor, such as Notepad, and then press **Ctrl+V** in a new document window to paste the message header text.

5. Save the message header document as **AOL Header.txt** in the Chap13\ Chapter folder in your work folder.

6. Close AOL.

Follow these steps to view e-mail headers in Hotmail:

1. Start Hotmail as you usually do.

2. Click the e-mail message to open it.

3. Click **Options**, **Preferences** from the menu. (In MSN/Hotmail 8, click **Options**, **Mail Display Settings**.)

13

4. Click **Advanced Headers**. (In MSN/Hotmail 8, click the **Advanced** option in Message Headers.) The header appears in the Hotmail window, similar to what's shown in Figure 13-10.

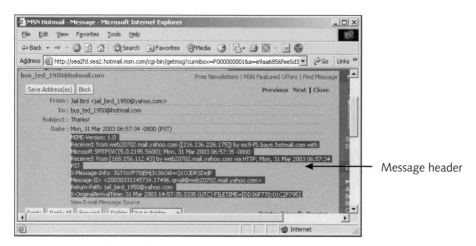

Figure 13-10 Hotmail e-mail headers option

5. Drag to select all the message header text, and then press **Ctrl+C** to copy the text to the Clipboard. Start a text editor, such as Notepad, and then press **Ctrl+V** in a new document window to paste the message header text.

6. Save the message header document as **Hotmail Header.txt** in the Chap13\Chapter folder in your work folder.

7. Close Hotmail.

To view e-mail headers in early versions of Juno, follow these steps:

1. Start Juno as you usually do.

2. Double-click a message to open it.

3. Click **File**, **Save as** from the menu. In the File name text box, type **Juno Email Header**.

4. In the Save as type drop-down list box, click **Text**.

5. Navigate to the Chap13\Chapter folder in your work folder, and then click the **Save** button.

6. Use My Computer or Windows Explorer to go to the Chap13\Chapter folder in your work folder.

7. Double-click **Juno Email Header.txt** to open it in Notepad. The e-mail header appears, as shown in Figure 13-11.

8. Close Notepad, and then close Juno.

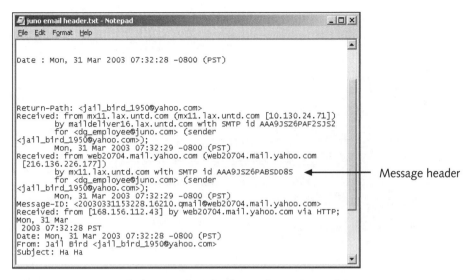

Figure 13-11   E-mail message header for early versions of Juno

To view an e-mail header in a more recent version of Juno, follow these steps:

NOTE

If you don't have a Juno e-mail account, you can set up a free account through the Juno Web site at *www.juno.com*.

1. Open Juno as you normally do.

2. If your version of Juno opened in your last working e-mail directory, click the **Go to E-mail** tab at the top.

3. Click **Options**.

4. Click to select **Show Headers** under Preferences. (Some versions might require selecting Reading Messages under Preferences and clicking to select the **Show full message header** check box.)

5. Click **Save**.

6. Scroll back to the top, if necessary, and click the **Inbox** tab.

7. Open a message and the header appears, as shown in Figure 13-12.

Follow these steps to view e-mail headers in Yahoo!:

1. Log on to your Yahoo! mail account.

2. Click the **Mail Options** link. The Mail Options window opens.

3. Click the **General Preferences** link, and then click **Show All headers on incoming messages**.

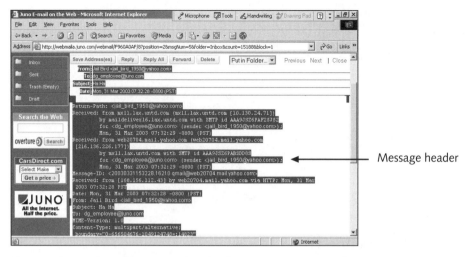

Figure 13-12   E-mail message header for recent versions of Juno

4. Click the **Save** button to put your new settings into effect. Any e-mail messages you open will include the header. (Figure 13-13 later in this chapter shows a sample Yahoo! e-mail header.)

5. Drag to select all the message header text, and then press **Ctrl+C** to copy the text to the Clipboard. Start a text editor, such as Notepad, and then press **Ctrl+V** in a new document window to paste the message header text.

6. Save the message header document as **Yahoo Header.txt** in the Chap13\Chapter folder in your work folder.

7. Close Yahoo!

WebTV (now called MSN TV) is a specialized TV with computer-like accessories. This combination allows you to use the Internet and e-mail and view messages and Web pages on your TV. To view the headers of a WebTV e-mail message, you must forward a copy of the message to yourself, enter a special symbol in the Subject line, and then send the message to another e-mail address. If you don't have WebTV, read but do not perform the following steps:

1. Start WebTV as you usually do.

2. Open the e-mail message by using the arrow keys to highlight the e-mail message and then pressing **Enter** or **Return**.

3. Scroll down with the arrow keys if necessary, click the **Forward** button on the e-mail toolbar, and then press **Enter** or **Return** to forward a copy of the message.

4. In the To text box, type your e-mail address to send the message to yourself.

5. In the message area, press **Enter** or **Return** three or four times to insert a few blank lines.

6. Hold down the **Alt** key, type **1234**, and then release the **Alt** key to insert a unique symbol or character, such as a square or 123¢, in the message.

7. Drag to select the square symbol or other unique character, and then press **Ctrl+C** to copy the symbol to the Clipboard.

8. Click in the Subject text box, and then press **Ctrl+V** to paste the symbol.

9. Click **Send** and then press **Enter** or **Return** to send the e-mail to your e-mail account.

10. Start your e-mail program, if necessary, and open the message you just sent to yourself. The message includes the header text.

11. Drag to select all the message header text, and then press **Ctrl+C** to copy the text to the Clipboard. Start a text editor, such as Notepad, and then press **Ctrl+V** in a new document window to paste the message header text.

12. Save the message header document as **WebTV Header.txt** in the Chap13\Chapter folder in your work folder, if possible.

13. Close your e-mail program and WebTV.

All the e-mail clients reviewed in this section supply the same information in the e-mail header. Keep in mind that not all e-mail clients are included here, and as new e-mail clients and versions emerge, they will have different options for retrieving e-mail headers. In most cases, however, you can find information about displaying message headers in the program's Help files.

Examining E-mail Headers

In the previous steps, you used Microsoft Outlook to open and save the header for an e-mail message. Now you can open the header you saved and examine it to gather information about the e-mail message. You can use the e-mail header to gather supporting evidence and ultimately track the suspect to the e-mail's originating location. The primary piece of information you're looking for is the originating e-mail's domain address or an IP address. Other helpful pieces of information in the header include the date and time the message was sent, the file names of any attachments, and the unique message number for the message, if it's supplied. To open and examine an e-mail header, follow these steps:

1. Use My Computer or Windows Explorer to navigate to the Chap13\Chapter folder in your work folder.

2. Double-click a file containing message header text, such as **Outlook Header.txt**. The message header opens in Notepad.

Figure 13-13 shows a sample message header copied from a fictitious Yahoo! e-mail message. (The e-mail addresses are not real addresses.) Line numbers have been added for reference.

13

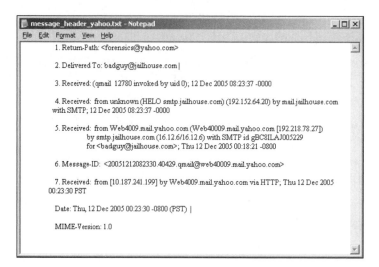

Figure 13-13, which shows the e-mail header in a Notepad window:

```
message_header_yahoo.txt - Notepad                        _|□|×|
File  Edit  Format  View  Help
        1. Return-Path: <forensics@yahoo.com>

        2. Delivered To: badguy@jailhouse.com|

        3. Received: (qmail 12780 invoked by uid 0); 12 Dec 2005 08:23:37 -0000

        4. Received: from unknown (HELO smtp.jailhouse.com) (192.152.64.20) by mail.jailhouse.com
        with SMTP; 12 Dec 2005 08:23:37 -0000

        5. Received: from Web4009.mail.yahoo.com (Web40009.mail.yahoo.com [192.218.78.27])
                by smtp.jailhouse.com (16.12.6/16.12.6) with SMTP id gBC8ILAJ005229
                for <badguy@jailhouse.com>; Thu 12 Dec 2005 00:18:21 -0800

        6. Message-ID: <20051212082330.40429.qmail@web40009.mail.yahoo.com>

        7. Received: from [10.187.241.199] by Web4009.mail.yahoo.com via HTTP; Thu 12 Dec 2005
        00:23:30 PST

        Date: Thu, 12 Dec 2005 00:23:30 -0800 (PST) |

        MIME-Version: 1.0
```

Figure 13-13 A sample e-mail header with line numbers added

The message header shown in Figure 13-13 provides a lot of information. Lines 1 to 5 identify from where your e-mail server received the message. Line 1 shows the return path, or the e-mail address an e-mail program would use to send a reply. Do *not* rely on the return path to show the source account of the e-mail message, however. It is easy to fake, or spoof, an e-mail address in the Return-Path line, usually indicated as the "Reply to" field in an e-mail.

Line 2 identifies the recipient's e-mail address. When you are investigating e-mail involved in a crime or company policy violation, you should verify this address by confirming it with the e-mail service provider. Request a bill or a log to make sure the account name identified in Line 2 is being used by the victim. (Check with your attorney general's office to determine the type of documentation you need.)

Line 3 indicates the type of e-mail service that sent the e-mail, such as qmail (UNIX e-mail), and includes an identifying number, such as 12780. Later, you match this number to one on the appropriate e-mail log. For the message shown in Figure 13-13, after you have located the UNIX e-mail server physical location, you open the e-mail log for that UNIX e-mail server and match the identification numbers.

Line 4 identifies the IP address of the e-mail server that sent the e-mail message, such as 192.152.64.20. Line 4 also identifies the name of the server sending the e-mail message: in this case, *smtp.jailhouse.com*.

TIP

A good indicator of a spoofed e-mail address is if the Received from server (shown in Line 4) and the Return-Path server (shown in Line 1) are different.

Line 5 contains the name of the e-mail server (or list of e-mail servers) that sent or passed the e-mail message to the victim's e-mail server.

Lines 6 and 7 provide information important for e-mail investigators. Line 6 shows a unique message number that the sending e-mail server assigned to the message. In Figure 13-13, it's 20051212082330.40429. You can use this number to track the e-mail on the originating e-mail server through the e-mail logs. Line 7 identifies the IP address of the server sending the e-mail and lists the date and time the offending e-mail was sent. For example, 10.187.241.199 is the IP address of the sending server Web40009.mail.yahoo.com, and Thu 12 Dec 2005 00:23:30 PST is the date the message was sent. Line 7 might also identify the e-mail as being sent through an HTTP client, as it does in Figure 13-13.

The e-mail message header shown in Figure 13-13 does not include a Line 8, which usually identifies any attachment included with the e-mail. The attachment can be any type of file, from a program to a picture. If a message includes an attachment, investigate it as a supporting piece of evidence. If you are working with the victim, in most cases, the attachment is still attached to the e-mail. If you are investigating a suspect's machine, remember to work with the copied version and start searching for the attached file by using the Search or Find feature of the computer's OS (or a computer forensics tool) to determine whether the file was saved and still exists on the hard disk. In most cases, if you supply the name of the attachment, you can find it on the computer. If you do not find the attachment on the hard disk, use the tools and skills you have learned in this book to recover the missing attachment. After you find the file, copy it to a working directory to prevent any accidental changes to the original data.

13

If you are investigating an e-mail that has an attachment with an unfamiliar file extension, such as .mdf, you can use the Internet to research the file to find out what program creates a file of this type. Visit *www.whatis.com* to check file extensions and match the file to a program.

TIP

When searching a suspect's computer, you should use computer forensics tools to look for specific files. Using these tools allows a more thorough search of the machine, based on the file header rather than the file extension.

Examining Additional E-mail Files

E-mail programs either save e-mail messages on the client computer or leave them on the server. The storage of e-mail files depends on the settings on the client and server computers. On the client computer, you could save all your e-mail in a separate folder for recordkeeping purposes. For example, in Microsoft Outlook, you can save sent, drafted, deleted, and received e-mails in a file with a file extension of .pst, or you can save off-line files in a file with a file extension of .ost.

If you're using Microsoft Outlook as your e-mail program, you can attach a personal e-mail file (.pst) or an off-line e-mail file (.ost) to your Outlook program. You can then read the e-mail messages in these files without logging on to the user's e-mail account. Each e-mail program lets you open a certain type of data file that contains a collection of e-mails. In the previous example, this collection of e-mails is contained in the .pst file. In Hands-on Project 13-4, you open and examine a .pst file in Outlook.

Each e-mail program also maintains an electronic personal address book for the user. A suspect's personal address book can contain valuable information to link criminal e-mail abuse to other participants as well as the suspect's physical address and his or her involvement in a crime. In Hands-on Project 13-6, you open and examine a personal address book in Outlook.

After seeing how Microsoft Outlook operates, UNIX e-mail might seem a little easier. In UNIX, e-mail is handled on a per-user basis. However, UNIX allows the administrator to create groups for e-mail distributions. As a member of a group, you get all the messages for that group. A UNIX e-mail server allows the members of an e-mail group to view the same messages. If the UNIX administrator adds you to the same group the suspect is a member of, you can read the suspect's e-mail messages without logging on as the suspect.

When an online e-mail program uses a Web browser to connect to the e-mail server, as with AOL, Hotmail, and Yahoo!, the e-mail messages are Web pages. Like any other Web page, these e-mail messages leave files on the computer that include information about the message. These files are stored in different folders, including History, Cookies, Cache, Temp, Temporary Internet Files, and any folders created by the client computer for e-mail programs such as AOL. Scan the folder lists or use computer forensics tools to find the folders used for the e-mail program.

After you have found these folders, you can view and open them and the files they contain, which often provides valuable information for your investigation. The files in these directories are usually helpful when you have seized a suspect's drive. When you are working on the victim's machine, these files help you document offensive material.

For some of these files, you need to download a program to read the data. For example, you might need to download a cookie reader to read cookies, which Web sites use to track users' activity. You can, however, pick out key phrases and words without using a specialized reader.

Tracing an E-mail Message

After you have read the suspect e-mail, determined that a crime or policy violation has been committed, checked for and opened any attached files, and opened the e-mail header to record the IP address from the originating source, you can track down the source of the e-mail abuse.

For example, if you're investigating the source of the e-mail message shown in Figure 13-13, you can look up the Web site *www.jailhouse.com* on the Internet to find out who is responsible for that domain name. If the point of contact or responsible party is not listed on the Web site or the domain name does not have a Web site, you need to use a registry site, such as those in the following list, to determine the point of contact for that domain name:

- *www.arin.net*—Use the American Registry for Internet Numbers (ARIN) to map an IP address to a domain name and to find the point of contact for the domain name.

- *www.internic.com*—Like *www.arin.net*, you use *www.internic.com* to find the IP address of a domain name and the point of contact for the domain name.

- *www.freeality.com*—A comprehensive Web site that has options for searching for a suspect, including by e-mail address, phone numbers, and names.

- *www.google.com*—A general search engine you can use to search for information on the Web and additional postings on discussion boards.

Using one of these Web sites, you can find the suspect's full e-mail address, such as *badguy@jailhouse.com*, and all the suspect's contact information. Keep in mind that the suspect might have posted false information. Make sure you verify your findings by checking the network logs against the e-mail addresses, as described in the next section.

Using Network Logs Related to E-mail

After you identify the contact people at the domain names in the header, confirming the e-mail's route might be necessary. To verify the path with the header information, you need to use the device log that identifies the e-mail as having taken the path. The networking devices to focus on are **routers**, which pass network traffic on the Internet. Network administrators maintain a log of the traffic handled by their routers. In general, a log is a text file that tracks the events that happen on that device. The log files for a router can track all inbound and outbound traffic on its ports. Routers have rules to allow or disallow traffic onto their network based on the destination address. In most cases, a router is set up to track all traffic that flows through its ports. The network administrator that manages routers can supply the log files you need. Review the router logs on behalf of your victim's offending e-mail, looking for the identifying message ID number, as in line 3 in Figure 13-13.

Network administrators often maintain logs for firewalls, devices that filter Internet traffic; these logs can help verify whether the e-mail message passed through that device. Firewalls such as WatchGuard, CISCO Pix, and Checkpoint maintain log files that track Internet traffic destined for other networks or for the network the firewall is protecting. When the network administrator provides firewall log files, you can open them in a text editor, such as Notepad in Windows or vi in UNIX. Figure 13-14 shows a typical log file for a WatchGuard Firebox II. Although Figure 13-14 shows the log file open in Notepad, some devices use special programs to read log files.

13

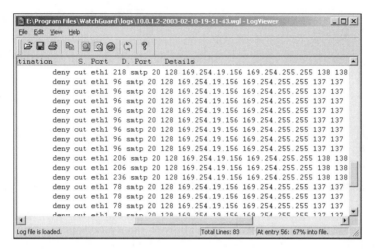

Figure 13-14   A firewall log

UNDERSTANDING E-MAIL SERVERS

E-mail servers perform tasks that keep logs you can examine and use in your investigation. An e-mail server is a computer running a server OS that's loaded with a software package that uses e-mail protocols for its services. As a computer forensics investigator, you can't know everything about all e-mail servers. Your focus is not to learn how a particular e-mail server works, but how to retrieve information about e-mail messages for an investigation. In most cases, you must work closely with the network administrator or the e-mail administrator. (In some instances, they are the same person.) Administrators are usually willing to help you find the data or files you need and might even offer new ways to find this information. If you can't work with an administrator, conduct research on the Internet or use the computer forensics tools discussed later in this chapter to investigate the e-mail server software and OS being used.

To investigate e-mail abuse, you should know how an e-mail server records and handles the e-mail it receives. Some e-mail servers are databases that store multiple users' e-mails, and others use a flat file system. All e-mail servers can maintain a log of all e-mails that are processed. Some e-mail servers are set up to log e-mail transactions by default. Others provide an option for logging, but must be configured to do so. Most e-mail administrators log system operations and message traffic on their e-mail servers to recover e-mail messages in case of a disaster, to make sure the firewall and e-mail filters are working properly, and to enforce company policy. However, the e-mail administrator can turn off logging or use circular logging, which allocates space for a log file on the server, and then starts overwriting from the beginning when logging reaches the end of the time frame or the specified log size. Circular logging saves valuable server space. However, you cannot recover a log after it's overwritten. For example, on Monday the e-mail server records e-mail traffic in a file named Mon.log. For the next six days, the e-mail server uses a log for each day, such as Tues.log, Wed.log, and so forth. On Sunday at midnight, the e-mail server starts recording e-mail traffic information in Mon.log, overwriting the information logged the previous Monday. The only way to access the log file information is from a backup file, which many e-mail administrators create before a log file is overwritten.

As shown in Figure 13-15, e-mail logs generally identify the e-mail messages an account received, the IP address from which they were sent, the time and date the e-mail server received them, the time and date the client computer accessed the e-mail, the IP addresses, the contents of the e-mail, system-specific information, and any other information the e-mail administrator wants to track. These e-mail logs are usually formatted in plain text and can be read by using a basic text editor, such as Notepad or vi.

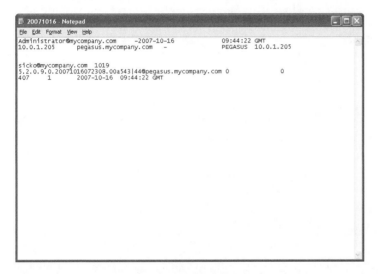

Figure 13-15   An e-mail server log file

In most cases, administrators set e-mail servers to continuous logging mode. The administrator can also log all the e-mail information in the same file, or use one log file to record, for example, date and time information, the size of the e-mail, and the IP address. These separate log files are extremely useful when you have an e-mail header from the client machine that has a date and time stamp and an IP address, and you want to filter or sort the log files to narrow your search.

After you have identified the source of the offending e-mail, contact the network or e-mail administrator of the suspect's network as soon as possible. Some e-mail providers, especially Internet e-mail providers, do not keep their logs for a long time, and their logs might contain key information for your investigation.

In addition to logging e-mail traffic, e-mail servers help your investigations by maintaining a copy of a client's e-mail, even if the user has deleted messages from the Inbox. Some e-mail servers don't completely delete an e-mail message from the server until the system is backed up. Even if the suspect deletes the e-mail, in some cases the e-mail administrator can recover the e-mail without restoring the entire e-mail system. With other systems, however, the e-mail administrator must recover the entire e-mail server to retrieve one deleted message.

This process is similar to the deletion of files on a hard drive; the file is marked for deletion, but it's not truly deleted until another piece of data is written in the same place. E-mail servers wait to overwrite the area until the server has been backed up. If you have a date and time stamp for an e-mail message, the e-mail administrator should be able to recover the message from backup media if the message is no longer available on the e-mail server.

Examining UNIX E-mail Server Logs

The UNIX OS, which has been used for more than 30 years, has several different versions and spin-offs. UNIX supports different e-mail servers, including mail, mailx, qmail, Pine, and Sendmail, to name just a few. This section focuses on the log and configuration files that the Sendmail e-mail server creates by default. Other UNIX e-mail servers produce similar log files in similar locations.

The files that provide helpful information to an e-mail investigation are log files and configuration files. Sendmail creates a number of files on the server to track and maintain the e-mail service. The first one to be aware of is /Etc/Sendmail.cf, which contains configuration information for Sendmail, allowing the investigator to determine where the log files reside.

Sendmail uses the Sendmail.cf file as an instruction page. Sendmail refers to the Sendmail.cf file to find out what to do with an e-mail message after it's received. For example, if a server receives an e-mail from an unsolicited site, a line in the Sendmail.cf file can tell the Sendmail server to discard the unwanted e-mail.

Similar to the Sendmail.cf file, the Syslogd file includes e-mail logging instructions—it specifies how and which events Sendmail should log. Viewing the Syslogd file allows you to determine how Sendmail is set up to log e-mail events. The Syslogd configuration file can be located in /Etc/Syslog.conf and contains three bits of information: the event, the priority level of concern, and the action taken when it was logged. By examining this log, you can see what happened to an e-mail message when it was logged. By default, Sendmail can display an event message, log the event message to a log file, or send an event message to a remote log host. Figure 13-16 shows a typical Syslog.conf file. Note that the lines beginning with pound signs (#) are comments describing the purpose of the commands.

The Syslog.conf file simply specifies where to save different types of e-mail log files. The first log file it configures is /Var/Log/Maillog. This log file usually contains **Simple Mail Transport Protocol (SMTP)** communications used between servers. Figure 13-17 shows a sample of a log monitoring SMTP.

As shown in Figure 13-17, the IP addresses (10.0.1.1) and the date and time stamp (May 21 10:10:34) identified in the mail log are important information in an e-mail investigation. Use the IP address and date and time stamp to compare with the e-mail header of the message the victim received to confirm the originator of the e-mail.

The Maillog file also contains information about **Post Office Protocol version 3 (POP3)** events. Figure 13-18 shows the first two lines of a POP3 event. The POP3 event information

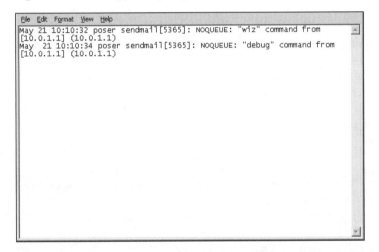

Figure 13-16   A typical Syslog.conf file

```
File  Edit  Format  View  Help
May 21 10:10:32 poser sendmail[5365]: NOQUEUE: "wiz" command from
[10.0.1.1] (10.0.1.1)
May  21 10:10:34 poser sendmail[5365]: NOQUEUE: "debug" command from
[10.0.1.1] (10.0.1.1)
```

Figure 13-17   A sample mail log with SMTP information

also includes an IP address and a date and time stamp to make your comparisons against the
e-mail message the victim received.

Typically, UNIX installations are set to store logs such as Maillog in the /Var/Log directory.
However, an administrator can change the log location, especially when an e-mail service
specifies a different location. If you're examining a UNIX computer and do not find the
e-mail logs in /Var/Log, you can find log files by using the `find` or `locate` command. For
example, type `locate *.log` at the UNIX command prompt.

Note that UNIX and Linux use the forward slash (/) in file paths, and Windows
uses the backslash (\) in file paths.

TIP

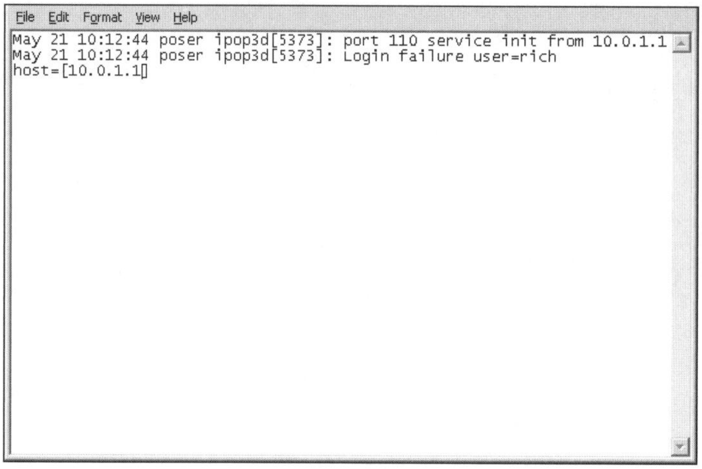

File Edit Format View Help
```
May 21 10:12:44 poser ipop3d[5373]: port 110 service init from 10.0.1.1
May 21 10:12:44 poser ipop3d[5373]: Login failure user=rich
host=[10.0.1.1]
```

Figure 13-18   A sample mail log with POP3 information

If you need further assistance on where a file is created by default, you can use the UNIX manual pages for the type of e-mail service running on the machine. Be aware that a new directory is created on the client computer when a user logs on for the first time and runs Pine or Elm (UNIX e-mail programs). The directory is created in /Home/Username/Mail. If the server has been configured to deliver e-mail messages to client machines and has not been configured to maintain copies of e-mails on the server, the only copy of the e-mail is on the client computer in the user's mail folder.

If the UNIX e-mail server is set to store all messages on the server, you can access e-mail messages by requesting that the UNIX administrator create e-mail groups and add you to the same group as the suspect. UNIX e-mail servers do not usually use groups to prevent users from accidentally viewing e-mail that doesn't belong to them. However, e-mail groups can be useful for investigative purposes with the appropriate warrants.

Examining Microsoft E-mail Server Logs

Microsoft Exchange Server, generally called Exchange, is the Microsoft version of an e-mail server. Exchange uses a database, as do many other e-mail servers, and is based on the Microsoft Extensible Storage Engine (ESE), which uses several files in different combinations to provide e-mail service. The files most useful to a computer forensics investigator are .edb and .stm database files, checkpoint files, and temporary files.

In older versions of Exchange, .edb files were the only database files associated with Exchange; newer versions of Exchange Server use both the .edb file and the .stm database files. An .edb file is responsible for messages formatted with the Messaging Application Programming Interface (MAPI), a newer format used with e-mail, and the .stm database file is responsible for messages that aren't formatted with MAPI properties. These two files constitute the Information Store, a storage area for e-mail messages.

As a database server, Exchange logs information about changes to its data, also called transactions, in a transaction log. To prevent loss of data from the last backup, a checkpoint file or marker is inserted in the transaction log to mark the last point at which the database was written to disk. These files allow the e-mail administrator to recover lost or deleted e-mail messages in the event of a disaster, such as a power failure. Exchange also creates .tmp, or temporary, files when it's busy converting binary data to readable text. Again, Exchange uses these files to prevent data loss.

Like UNIX e-mail servers, Exchange maintains logs to track e-mail communication. For example, RES#.logs (reserved log files), such as res1.log, track information about database overflow. They are used to make sure the database can keep up with the changing environment without losing data.

Microsoft Exchange servers can also maintain a log called Tracking.log that tracks e-mail messages. If the Message Tracking feature has been turned on and the e-mail administrator selects verbose (detailed) logging, as shown in Figure 13-19, you can see the contents of the message.

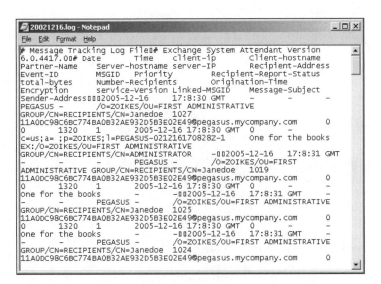

Figure 13-19   A message tracking log in verbose mode

With this option selected, you can see the date and time stamp, IP address of the sending computer, and the contents or body of the e-mail message. Outside of special computer forensics tools, the message tracking log shown in verbose mode provides the most information about e-mail messages sent and received in Exchange.

Another log used for troubleshooting and investigating the Exchange environment is the troubleshooting log. You can read this troubleshooting log, also known as the diagnostic log, by using Windows Event Viewer, shown in Figure 13-20, which is available through Administrative Tools. Each event logged has an ID number with a severity level.

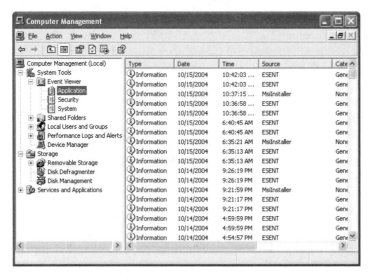

Figure 13-20   Event Viewer

To examine the details about an e-mail event, double-click the event to open its Event Properties dialog box, shown in Figure 13-21. This dialog box provides date and time information, for example, that might be useful if you suspect the e-mail server has been tampered with to alter its contents.

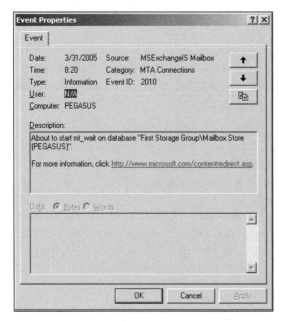

Figure 13-21   The Event Properties dialog box

Examining Novell GroupWise E-mail Logs

Novell NetWare is another network operating system that offers e-mail services. The Novell e-mail server software is called **GroupWise**, which uses a set of databases as do Microsoft Exchange and UNIX Sendmail. GroupWise has up to 25 databases for user e-mails. Each database is stored in the Ofuser directory object (NetWare refers to all entries in its structure, including directories and users, as "objects") and is referenced by a user name followed by the unique identifier and a .db file extension, such as JimShu020307.db.

TIP

In addition to the 25 databases GroupWise has for user e-mails, it uses another database called Ngwdfr.db for delayed or deferred e-mail delivery. By default, this database is stored in the Ofmsg directory object. This is similar to how Microsoft Exchange Server uses the TMP directory.

GroupWise shares resources with the e-mail server databases, as do Microsoft and UNIX e-mail servers. GroupWise gives the first folder to be shared at the post office or on the e-mail server the file name PU020101.db, regardless of who shares the folder. GroupWise then names the next folder to be shared by changing the file name to the next sequential number, PU020102.db, and so on, increasing by one for each folder name. These files contain information such as user files that have been shared for other users to view.

These files are important if the user has shared an address book on the GroupWise server. In this case, if the user who created the PU*xxxxxxx*.db files shares those files, they are available for searching on the server. If the user has decided not to share an address book, the data is stored in a file called User.db. In either case, you can view the user's personal address book by using one of these two files.

GroupWise mailboxes make recovering data easy. GroupWise has two ways of organizing the mailboxes on the server. The first is with permanent index files identified with an .idx file extension. These files are updated and renamed at the end of every day. The GroupWise server uses these index files to keep the mailboxes in order. Microsoft and UNIX can also sort mailboxes in order, but they do not use a specific index file to do so.

The second organizing method involves the GroupWise QuickFinder action. The incremental indexing files are used to maintain changes to the e-mail server temporarily throughout the day. Then QuickFinder writes any changes to the IDX file at scheduled times of the day.

The GroupWise folder and file structure can be complex because it uses the Novell directory structure. As such, GroupWise has a number of files scattered within the post office directory, but maintains centralized control of the e-mail service and associated files by using a specialized database called Guardian, Ngwguard.db. The Guardian database is a directory of every database in the GroupWise environment. As its name suggests, the Guardian database tracks changes in the GroupWise environment and protects the database against all processes that want to change the GroupWise databases. The Guardian database must clear these processes before they change a GroupWise database. Although the Guardian database

13

protects the e-mail server data, it is also considered a single point of failure. If it's erased or becomes corrupt, you must recover the database from a backup and begin your forensic investigation again. The Guardian database does include some built-in safeguards against data loss. The Ngwguard.fbk, Ngwguard.rfl, and Ngwguard.db files contain backup copies and log files from the Guardian database. They prevent the total loss of the Guardian database and make it possible to track changes without affecting the server's performance.

Similar to other e-mail servers, GroupWise generates log files. The GroupWise logs are maintained in a standard log format in the GW\volz*.log directory. Use these logs to match the e-mail header with the IP address of a suspect.

USING SPECIALIZED E-MAIL FORENSICS TOOLS

For many e-mail investigations, you can rely on e-mail message files, e-mail headers, and e-mail server log files to investigate e-mail crimes. However, if you can't find an e-mail administrator willing to participate in the investigation, or you encounter a highly customized e-mail environment, you can use data recovery tools and forensic tools specially designed to recover e-mail files.

As technology has progressed for the use of e-mail and other services, so too have the tools for recovering information lost or deleted from a hard drive. In previous chapters, you reviewed many tools available for data recovery, such as AccessData's Forensic Toolkit (FTK) and EnCase. You can also use these tools in the investigation and recovery of e-mail files. Other tools are specifically built for e-mail recovery, including recovering deleted attachments from the hard drive. These tools include, but are not limited to, FINALeMAIL, Sawmill-GroupWise, DBXtract, MailBag Assistant, Paraben, EnCase, FTK, and Audimation.

When you use one of these third-party programs to search a machine for a .db file, for example, you can find where the administrator stores .db files for the e-mail server. To find log files, use *.log as the search criteria. You're likely to find at least two logs specific to e-mail—one listing logged events for messages and the other listing logged events for accounts accessing the e-mail.

FTK, EnCase, and other computer forensics tools enable you to find e-mail database files, personal e-mail files, off-line storage files, and log files. Some tools allow you to view messages and other files with a special viewer; others require you to use a text editor to compare information such as the date and time stamp, user name, domain name, and message contents to determine whether this information matches what was found on the victim's machine.

One advantage of using data-recovery tools is that you don't need to know how the e-mail server or e-mail client operates to extract data from these computers. Data recovery tools do the work for you and allow you to view the evidence on the machine.

After you compare e-mail logs with the e-mail messages, verify the e-mail account, message ID, IP address, and date and time stamp, and determine that there's enough evidence for a warrant, you can obtain and serve your warrant for the suspect and his or her computer equipment. When serving your warrant and collecting the suspect's computer, remember to follow the evidence-handling rules and control measures your agency or organization uses, as described in previous chapters.

TIP   When requesting a search warrant, consider whether you are looking for more than one topic area. If you intend to investigate different crimes, make sure to include probable cause for each crime so that you can obtain a single warrant. The warrant should then cover all areas of interest. At times, your investigation might require obtaining a second warrant after executing the first warrant. For example, if you're investigating a drive for evidence of harassment and, during the execution of the first warrant, you come across e-mail that suggests your suspect is also distributing narcotics over the Internet, you need a second warrant to address the narcotics issue.

After all the evidence has been bagged and tagged, you need to begin copying it to another source for further investigation. As you are copying evidence data, document everything you're doing. For example, if you create a bit-stream image of the evidence, document the procedure and tool you use. You're then ready to proceed with the forensic data acquisition and analysis, as you learned in Chapter 9.

For example, with the FINALeMAIL tool, you can scan e-mail database files on the suspect's Windows computer and locate any e-mail messages the suspect has deleted—these are message that do not have data location information associated with them—and restore the messages to their original state. When you run FINALeMAIL, you can search the computer for lost or deleted e-mail messages and for other files associated with e-mail. Figure 13-22 shows two e-mail databases that FINALeMAIL found—one database for Outlook Express and one for Eudora.

To examine the Eudora Mail database, select it in the left pane, and then double-click Out.mbx in the right pane to open the Recover E-mail File dialog box. As shown in Figure 13-22, there are five Jane Doe messages and five administrator messages. By double-clicking the message you want to view, you can see the contents of the message, as shown in Figure 13-23. In this case, the subject line and the body of the e-mail message are the same.

13

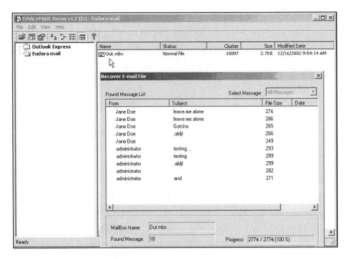

Figure 13-22 FINALeMAIL e-mail search results

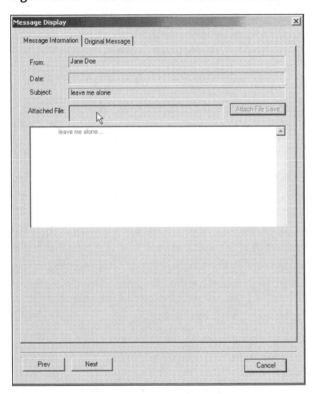

Figure 13-23 FINALeMAIL message contents

FINALeMAIL is not as flashy as other tools, but it's quick, fairly easy to use, and affordably priced. It enables you to see whether any attachments were sent with the e-mail and lets you view them if necessary.

Another tool to consider is FTK, an all-purpose program used for file discoveries. It's not task or file specific and indexes drives for faster data retrieval, allowing you to investigate the drive more thoroughly. As with FINALeMAIL, FTK can filter or find files that are specific to e-mail clients and servers. In FTK, you can configure these filters by simply supplying the information in the search parameters.

Other tools available for investigating e-mail servers include EnCase, a general data recovery tool; Sawmill, which reads logs generated by NetWare's GroupWise e-mail server; DBXtract for Microsoft .dbx files; and The Coroner's Toolkit, a UNIX toolset that can help recover e-mail messages from a UNIX e-mail server. These tools have features similar to the ones discussed for FINALeMAIL and FTK.

CHAPTER SUMMARY

□ You can send and receive e-mail via the Internet or a local area network (LAN). Both environments distribute data, such as e-mail messages, from one central server to many connected client computers, a configuration called client/server architecture. The server computer uses a server OS to provide e-mail service. Client computers run an OS, such as Windows or Linux, and use e-mail programs to contact the e-mail server and send and retrieve e-mail messages.

□ Investigating crimes or policy violations involving e-mail is similar to investigating other types of computer abuse and crimes. Your goal is to find out who is behind the crime, collect the evidence, and build a case.

□ After you have determined that a crime has been committed using e-mail, first access the victim's computer to recover the evidence contained in the e-mail. If possible, physically access the victim's computer, and then use the e-mail program on that computer to find a copy of an offending e-mail message the victim received.

□ Before you start an e-mail investigation, you need to copy and print the e-mail message involved in a crime or policy violation. You might want to forward the message to another e-mail address as well, depending on your department's guidelines.

□ After you copy and print an e-mail message, use the e-mail program that created the message to find the e-mail header. You can use the e-mail header to gather supporting evidence and ultimately track the suspect to the e-mail's originating location by finding the originating e-mail's domain address or IP address. Also helpful are the date and time the message was sent, the file names of any attachments, and the unique message number for the message, if it's supplied. When you find the originating e-mail address, you can track the message to a suspect by doing reverse lookups.

13

❏ To investigate e-mail abuse, you should know how an e-mail server records and handles the e-mail it receives. Some e-mail servers are databases that store multiple users' e-mails; others are a flat file system. All e-mail servers can maintain a log of all e-mails that are processed. Some e-mail servers are set up to log e-mail transactions by default. Others provide the option for logging but must be configured to do so.

❏ For many e-mail investigations, you can rely on e-mail message files, e-mail headers, and e-mail server log files to investigate e-mail crimes. However, if you can't find an e-mail administrator willing to participate in the investigation, or you encounter a highly customized e-mail environment, you can use data recovery tools and computer forensics tools specifically designed to recover e-mail files.

KEY TERMS

client/server architecture — A network architecture in which each computer or process on the network is either a client or a server. Clients are the systems that request services from the server. A server has systems that process the request from clients.

GroupWise — The Novell e-mail server software, a database server similar to Microsoft Exchange and UNIX Sendmail.

Post Office Protocol version 3 (POP3) — A protocol used to retrieve e-mail messages from an e-mail server.

router — A network device that connects a number of local area networks together.

Simple Mail Transfer Protocol (SMTP) — A protocol used for sending e-mail messages between servers.

REVIEW QUESTIONS

1. E-mail is always stored on the server instead of on the client. True or False?

2. E-mail can be used when the following crimes or policy violations are committed:

    a. phishing scams

    b. credit card fraud

    c. murder

    d. corporate espionage

    e. extortion

    f. all of the above

3. In Microsoft Outlook, you can save multiple e-mail messages in a single file. True or False?

4. It's easier to locate an Internet e-mail user than a LAN e-mail user. True or False?

5. When investigating a potential e-mail crime, what is your first step in the investigation?

    a. Determine whether a crime was actually committed.

    b. Recover the evidence.

    c. Trace the IP address to its origin.

    d. Write a report.

6. When searching a victim's computer for a crime committed with a specific e-mail message, which of the following provides the information for determining the originator of the offensive e-mail?

    a. e-mail header

    b. user name and password

    c. firewall log

    d. all of the above

7. UNIX, NetWare, and Microsoft e-mail servers create specialized databases for every user using the e-mail service. True or False?

8. Which of the following is a current encoding standard of e-mail?

    a. SMTP

    b. MIME

    c. Outlook

    d. Pine

9. All e-mail headers contain the same types of information. True or False?

10. When you access your e-mail, what type of computer architecture are you using?

    a. workgroup

    b. domain

    c. client/server

    d. none of the above

11. To identify the person responsible for an Internet domain name, you can use the Traceroute command. True or False?

12. What is your first step in the investigation of an e-mail crime?

    a. Obtain the e-mail header.

    b. Classify the violation.

    c. Copy the e-mail.

    d. Find the attachments.

13. E-mail servers do not keep records of e-mail. True or False?

14. E-mail servers are the only computing devices that can be used to track e-mail. True or False?

13

15. What information is *not* contained in an e-mail header? (Choose all that apply.)

    a. street addresses

    b. Internet addresses

    c. domain name

    d. contents of the message

    e. type of e-mail server used to send the e-mail

16. What are the files of interest when you're investigating an e-mail server?

    a. .dbf database files

    b. .emx e-mail files

    c. .log log files

    d. .slf server log files

17. Internet e-mail accessed with a Web browser leaves files in temporary folders. True or False?

18. When confronted with an e-mail server that no longer contains a log with the date information you need for your investigation, and the client has deleted the e-mail, what should you do?

    a. Run the Traceroute command and obtain the information from other networking sources.

    b. Restore the e-mail server from a backup of the e-mail server.

    c. Check the current database files for an existing copy of the offending e-mail.

    d. Do nothing. After it's deleted, the file is no longer recoverable.

19. All e-mail clients allow you to view e-mail headers. True or False?

20. To analyze e-mail evidence, an investigator must be aware of an e-mail server's internal operations. True or False?

HANDS-ON PROJECTS

Project 13-1

In this project, you use Outlook Express and work with a lab partner to send and examine e-mail messages:

1. In Outlook Express, click the **Create Mail** button on the toolbar to open a new message window.

2. In the To text box, type your lab partner's e-mail address. In the Subject text box, type **E-mail Investigation**.

3. In the message area, type **This message is an e-mail under investigation**.

4. Click the **Attach** button on the toolbar to add an attachment. The Insert Attachment dialog box opens.

5. Click the **Look in** list arrow, and then navigate to the Chap13\Projects folder in the student data files. (If necessary, create a Projects folder.) Then double-click **Biscoccti1.xif**. The Biscoccti1.xif file appears in the Attach text box of the E-mail Investigation message, as shown in Figure 13-24.

Figure 13-24   E-mail message with attachment

6. Click the **Send** button to send the e-mail message and attachment to your lab partner.

7. After your lab partner sends you a message, click the **Send/Recv** button on the toolbar. Then double-click the e-mail message your lab partner sent you to open the message.

8. Right-click the **Biscoccti1.xif** e-mail attachment, and then click **Save As** on the shortcut menu. The Save Attachment As dialog box opens.

TIP

By default, the newer Outlook Express versions prevent you from viewing attachments. If you receive a message indicating that Outlook Express removed Biscoccti1.xif as an unsafe attachment, click Tools, Options, click the Security tab, click to clear the "Do not allow attachments to be saved or opened that could potentially be a virus" check box, and then click OK.

9. Click the **Save in** list arrow, and then navigate to the Chap13\Projects folder in your work folder. Save the e-mail attachment as **Biscoccti1.xif** in this folder, replacing the original, if necessary.

10. Click **File**, **Properties** from the menu to open the E-mail Investigation dialog box. Click the **Details** tab to view the message header.

11. Copy the text in the Internet headers for this message text box to a Notepad document named **Header.txt** and save it in the Chap13\Projects folder in your work folder.

12. Write down the IP address, domain names, date and time stamps, and any attachments found in the Header.txt file.

13. Close all open windows.

Project 13-2

In this project, you investigate an unknown file type using resources available on the Web:

1. Connect to the Internet, if necessary, and start your Web browser.

2. In the Address text box, type **www.google.com** and then press **Enter**.

3. In the Search text box, type **xif** and then click the **Search** button.

4. Click the link with a definition of the .xif file extension, and copy the definition to a text document named **XIF definition.txt**. Save this document in the Chap13\Projects folder.

5. Using the Google Web page, locate an application that allows you to read the .xif file.

6. When you finish reviewing the results, close any open windows and log off.

Project 13-3

In this project, you find the personal e-mail file and personal address book by using the Windows search feature:

1. Click **Start**, **Find**, or **Search** (depending on which Windows version you're using).

2. In Windows XP, click **All files and folders**, navigate to **My Computer**, and then type ***.pst** in the text box for search parameters. Click the **Search** button.

3. Write down the name of the file you find and where it's located.

4. Repeat Steps 1 to 3, but search for ***.ost** instead of *.pst.

5. Repeat Steps 1 to 3, but search for ***.pab** instead of *.pst.

NOTE   You might find more than one .pst, .ost, or .pab file, or you might find none. If you don't find any files, you can copy the Jim_shu's.pst file from your Chapter 13 student data files to use in the following projects.

Project 13-4

In this project, you view the files you found in Project 13-3:

1. Start Outlook Express as you usually do.

2. Click **Local Folders** in the left pane, if necessary.

3. Click **File**, point to **New**, and then click **Folder** to open the Create Folder dialog box.

4. In the Folder name text box, type **E-mail Investigation**. Then click **OK**.

5. Click **E-mail Investigation** to select it.

6. Click **File**, point to **Import**, and then click **Messages** to open the Outlook Express Import dialog box.

7. Scroll to select **Personal Folder File**. (You might need to select the type of application you're importing from first—Microsoft Outlook, in this case—then select the Personal Folder File or .pst file.) Then click **Next**.

8. Click the **Browse** button near the top of the window.

9. Refer to the information you wrote down in Project 13-3, and navigate to the folder where your .pst file is stored. Click the .pst file you want to view, and then click **Next**.

10. Click the **Use Current Folder** option to import the file to the E-mail Investigation folder. Then click **Finish**.

11. Click to expand the contents of your **E-mail Investigation** folder. You should see the files contained in the .pst file.

12. Delete all the e-mail messages, and then close all open windows.

Project 13-5

In this project, you examine a personal address book:

1. Start Outlook as you usually do, if necessary.

2. Click **File**, **Import and Export** from the menu.

3. Click **Import from another program or file**, and then click **Next**.

4. In the top pane, scroll down to click **Personal Address Book**, and then click **Next**.

5. Click the **Browse** button. Refer to the information you wrote down in Project 13-3, and navigate to the folder where your .pab file is stored. Click the .pab file, and then click **OK**. Click **Next** to continue, and then click **Finish**.

6. Click the **Address Book** button. Click the **Show Names From the** list arrow, and then click the new personal address book. The contents of the address book are listed in the window.

7. Close Outlook.

13

Project 13-6

In this project, you use the demo version of AccessData FTK to recover deleted e-mail and attachments:

1. Click **Start**, point to **Programs** or **All Programs**, point to **AccessData**, point to **Forensic Toolkit**, and then click **Forensic Toolkit**.

2. When the KFF Hash Library dialog box opens, click **OK**. When the trial version message appears, click **OK**.

3. Click the **Start a new case** option, and then click **OK**. Enter the following information, and then click **Next**:

   ❑ **Investigator Name: Your own name**

   ❑ **Case Number: 2005-09-1A**

   ❑ **Case Name: E-mail Investigation**

   ❑ **Case Path: C:**work folder**\\Chap13**

   ❑ **Case Folder: E-mail Investigation**

4. Accept the default settings in the Case Log Options dialog box by clicking **Next**.

5. Accept the default settings in the Processes to Perform dialog box by clicking **Next**.

6. Near the top of the Refine Case - Default dialog box, click the **E-mail Emphasis** button, and then click **Next**.

7. Accept the default settings in the Refine Index dialog box by clicking **Next**.

8. Click **Add Evidence**. In the Add Evidence to Case dialog box, select the local drive where e-mail programs are installed on your computer, and then click **Continue**.

9. Select the local drive (such as C:), click **OK** twice, and then click **Next**.

10. In the New Case Setup is now Complete dialog box, click **Finish**. FTK builds a new case file for this investigation.

11. After FTK has finished the indexing process, click the **E-mail** button in the General tab.

12. Review the e-mail messages that FTK recovered, and then close all open windows.

CASE PROJECTS

Case Project 13-1

For the arson running case example, use the tools from this chapter and the Firestarter image from the data files to determine whether there's any e-mail evidence supporting a case of arson. Write a brief report on your findings.

Case Project 13-2

For the kidnapping running case example, use the tools from this chapter and the Kidnapping image from the data files to determine whether there's any e-mail evidence supporting a case of kidnapping. Write a brief report on your findings.

Case Project 13-3

You receive a call from a high school student named Marco who claims he has just received an e-mail from another student threatening to commit suicide. Marco is not sure from where the student wrote and sent the e-mail. Write a brief report on how you should proceed.

Case Project 13-4

A mother calls you to report that her 15-year-old daughter has run away from home. The mother has access to her daughter's e-mail account and says that her daughter has a number of e-mail messages in her Inbox suggesting that she has run away to be with a 35-year-old woman. Write a brief report on how you should proceed.

Case Project 13-5

The Research and Development Department of a large manufacturing firm contacts you to conduct an e-mail investigation, claiming that an employee is violating International Traffic in Arms Regulations (ITAR) by sending out missile-guidance specifics to a party outside the continental United States. Write a brief report on how you should proceed.

13

Case Project 13-6

Billy Williams at the local city hall contacts your shift supervisor, Mike Mackenzie, with a complaint of sexual harassment using the city's e-mail system. You are assigned to find the suspect and build a case to terminate the city employee. When interviewing the victim, Billy, you discover that he was involved with the suspect, Mary Jane, but ended the relationship against Mary Jane's wishes. Both he and the suspect still work for the city. Billy has kept a series of offending e-mail messages and offers it for your review. When you interview Mary Jane, she denies any wrongdoing and claims she is being set up. After your investigation, you confirm that she is being set up—the alleged victim is actually the one sending the offensive e-mail. Write a brief report on how your investigation would prove Mary Jane's innocence.

14

BECOMING AN EXPERT WITNESS AND REPORTING RESULTS OF INVESTIGATIONS

After reading this chapter and completing the exercises, you will be able to:

♦ Understand the importance of reports

♦ Understand guidelines for writing reports

♦ Generate report findings with forensic software tools

♦ Prepare for testimony

♦ Prepare for testifying in court

♦ Prepare for depositions

This chapter explains the rules of evidence and procedure as they apply to reports and disclosure requirements. You examine the Federal Rules of Evidence (FRE) and the Federal Rules of Civil Procedure (FRCP) applicable in U.S. federal courts and learn how they parallel comparable rules in most states. You also learn how to write and document a report in anticipation of testimony. You learn about the types of testimonial opportunities—trial, deposition, or hearing—and that you might be called on to testify as a technical or scientific witness or an expert witness. Computer forensics examiners need to be prepared to avoid problems when giving testimony.

Understanding the Importance of Reports

You write a report to communicate the results of your computer forensics examination or investigation. A report presents evidence as testimony in court, at an administrative hearing, or as an affidavit. Besides presenting facts, reports can communicate expert opinion.

For civil cases, including those involving computer forensics investigations, U.S. district courts require that expert witnesses submit written reports; state courts are also starting to require reports from expert witnesses, although the details of report requirements vary. Therefore, if you're a computer forensics examiner involved in a civil case, you must write a report explaining your investigation and findings. Specifically, Rule 26, FRCP, requires that parties who anticipate calling an expert witness to testify must provide a copy of the expert's written report that includes all opinions, the basis for the opinions, and the information that was considered in coming to the opinions. The report must also include related exhibits, such as photographs or diagrams, and the witness's curriculum vitae listing all publications the witness contributed to during the preceding 10 years. (These publications do not have to be relevant to the case.)

In addition to opinions and exhibits, the written report must specify the fees paid for the expert's services and list all other civil or criminal cases in which the expert has testified, in trial and deposition as an expert, for the preceding four years. This includes all instances of trial or deposition expert testimony, without regard to outcome, but not cases in which the expert acted as a consulting expert and did not provide expert testimony, or cases in which he or she testified as a **lay witness** (a witness testifying to personally observed facts).

Although the requirements for information on the list are not specific, you should keep a copy of any deposition notice or subpoena for reference. Either document has the following information:

- Style of the case (for example, *John Smith, Plaintiff v. Paul Jones, Defendant*)
- Jurisdiction
- Date
- Cause number (court case file number)

There are no requirements to include the details of testimony, although later you should summarize key points of your testimony for future reference and keep a copy of the transcript of your testimony, if it's available.

As an expert witness, you should be aware that lawyers use services called **deposition banks** (libraries), where they can deposit and withdraw examples of expert witnesses' previous testimony. Some of these services have hundreds of thousands of depositions on file and might have several deposition examples for expert witnesses who testify regularly. After a case is resolved, a lawyer sends copies of the opposing expert witnesses' depositions to the bank for deposit. In preparation for a trial, when the opposing party has identified an expert witness, the attorney might request copies of this witness's previous testimony. Lawyers might also request transcripts of previous testimony by their own potential experts to ensure that the experts haven't previously testified to a contrary position.

Limiting the Report to Specifics

You can now submit documents electronically in many courts; the standard format in federal courts is Portable Document Format (PDF). Do not file a report directly with the court unless an attorney or the court has directed you to do so.

The client (who might be an attorney, a detective, or an investigator) should define the investigation's goal or mission. All reports to the client should start by stating this mission or goal, which is usually to find information on a specific subject, recover certain significant documents, or recover certain types of files or files with certain dates and times. Clearly defining the goals reduces the amount of time and cost of the examination and is especially important with the increasing size of hard drives and networks. Hard drives now routinely exceed 100 GB, and networks can encompass terabytes of data, thousands of systems, hundreds of servers, and applications spanning several states or countries.

Types of Reports

Before you begin writing, identify your audience and the purpose of the report. If the audience has little technical knowledge, you might have to dedicate part of your report to educating the audience on technical issues. You can do this with a set of several stock paragraphs that you keep on hand for the purpose of education, and polish and improve them over time.

An **examination plan** is a document that lets you know what questions to expect when you are testifying (see a sample in Figure 14-1). The attorney prepares the examination plan and uses it to guide you in your testimony. You can propose changes, such as those involving clarification, definition, or substantive information the attorney didn't identify. For example, if the attorney misuses an expression or a term in the examination plan, that could indicate other nonexperts won't understand it. Examination time should then be used to address definition of the expression if it has relevance to the testimony. If the expression is not part of relevant testimony, drop it from the examination plan. The changes aren't normally extensive because the attorney structures the examination from your reports. You are still operating under a time constraint for presenting your report, but the constraint is ultimately controlled by the judge. The examination plan allows the attorney to document that testimony has been elicited for each point on which you have relevant knowledge. There are multiple sources for questions: the attorney who hired you and the opposing counsel. (Your retaining attorney should anticipate the paths of cross-examination, incorporate them into the examination plan, and determine how to minimize their effect through preemption or redirection.) There might be more than one opposing attorney, especially if there's more than one opposing party, and in many jurisdictions, the jury may submit written questions. (Each jury-proposed question is subject to evaluation against the same rules of evidence as questions posed by the attorneys).

Do not include anything in the examination plan that you wouldn't want the jury to see. If opposing counsel asks about the examination plan, acknowledge that you have one. A possible course of action is for retaining counsel to ask to have the plan admitted into

14

evidence. If asked on cross-examination whether you have a script, you can reply "No, I have reviewed an examination plan," or something similar. If asked whether you rehearsed, you can answer "No. I have, however, prepared to testify."

WITNESS EXAMINATION PLAN

WITNESS:_Karen Stolz_____/Factors:_____Expert and Treating for P.

Direct Examination - Expected Testimony   Objection/Rule/

Testimony on CV

Identity and Address Iowa Bureau of Criminal Investigation

Position (Current) Computer Forensic Examiner

Undergraduate   Iowa State University summa cum laude 1990 BS Computer Engineering

Summer Internship 1989 Des Moines Police Department

Neurology residency, University of Massachusetts MC 86-89

Chief resident in neurology, UM MC 88-89____explain neurology

Fellowship in Electroencephalography and Clinical Neurophysiology, UWMC-Seattle 89-90

Fellowship in Sleep Disorders Medicine, Univ. Michigan MC. 90-91

Academic Appointments

Lecturer, Dept of Computer Science, University of Iowa 1998-Current

Instructor, Iowa Police Academy, 1999-Current

Professional Society Certifications

P.E.   1999

CISSP 2001

Membership

American Society for Industrial Security

Publications

       Journal of the Iowa State Bar Association, May 1999,   "Computer Forensics on Raid Servers-Testifying to a Reasonable Certainty"

How many systems have you conducted forensic examination on?

What is your relationship to the Plaintiff?   Retained by his attorney to examine the hard drive of his computer for all financial records. I have never actually met or talked with Mr. Smith.

How long did it take you conduct this examination?

What types of files were you looking for?   Why those file types?   Where did you find those file types?

What condition were the files in?

What is your opinion as to the cause of that condition?

Can you say for a reasonable certainty that the financial data files were deleted intentionally? Yes.

Are you able to state to a reasonable certainty who deleted the financial data files? Yes.

What is your fee for examining the hard drive, preparing a report and testifying?

Cross Examination - Expected Testimony

How many times have you worked for Mr. Sawyer as an expert witness? I've had 16 contracts as consulting expert or expert witness.

Have you ever previously testified that overwrite utilities are not 100% reliable? Yes, but that was in 1994 and utilities are so far as I can tell 100% reliable today.

Figure 14-1   A sample examination plan

A verbal report is less structured than a written report. Typically, it takes place in an attorney's office where the attorney requests your consultant's report. As an expert hired as a trial consultant, you'll use this verbal report form often. Furthermore, others cannot force the attorney to release a verbal report; it cannot be mishandled or inadvertently released. This report is preliminary and addresses areas of investigation yet to be completed, such as the following:

- Tests that have not been concluded
- Interrogatories

- Document production

- Depositions

Mention to the person to whom you're presenting the report that your factual statement and opinion are still tentative and subject to change as more information comes in.

A written report is frequently an affidavit or a declaration. Because this type of report is sworn to under oath (and penalty of perjury or comparable false swearing statute), it demands attention to detail, carefully limiting what you write, and thorough documentation and support of what you write.

When writing a report, use a natural language style. Describe yourself in the first person, not the third person; for example, don't call yourself "Your Affiant" when "I" is appropriate and clearly more natural. Remember, somebody (probably a judge) will read your report or affidavit. Keep the reader interested in what you have to say. Pay attention to word usage, grammar, and spelling, especially because you're using formal writing for this report. Your report should also include your curriculum vitae or refer to it.

One function a report provides is a basis for an affidavit. That is, a report's findings can be used as a means to justify an affidavit to collect more evidence. An affidavit can be used to support issuing an arrest warrant or a search warrant and can be used at a probable cause hearing, as evidence in a grand jury hearing, or at civil motion hearings.

In civil cases, federal courts, as a matter of rule, require that all technical, scientific, or expert witnesses provide a report before trial. See FRCP 26 (a) (2), FRE 702, 703, and 705, and the rule stated in *Daubert v. Merrell Dow Pharmaceuticals, Inc.*, 509 U.S. 579, which is that the testimony is based on sufficient facts or data, the testimony is the product of reliable principles and methods, and the witness has applied the principles and methods reliably to the facts of the case. This rule is followed in more than half the states. The remaining states generally follow the rule established in *Frye v. United States*, 293 F. 1013 (D.C. Cir. 1923), which states that testimony is inadmissible unless it is "...testimony deduced from a well-recognized scientific principle or discovery, the thing from which the deduction is made must be sufficiently established to have gained general acceptance in the particular field in which it belongs." To minimize your exposure of being deposed, avoid producing a written report for as long as you can. If you must produce the informal or preliminary report in written form, understand that actions or statements you don't make are as important as what you do and say.

14

Written preliminary reports are **high-risk documents** that opposing counsel could receive in **discovery** if you become a disclosed expert witness. A high-risk document in this context refers to a written report that addresses subjects relevant to the case; you might be examined over the written report. If the written report states a contrary or more equivocal position than you take in your final report or testimony, you should expect opposing counsel to try to discredit your testimony by using the written report. It's simply better if there's no written report to provide. Just as you should use certain important words in a report, you should avoid using other words, especially in the written report or preliminary report. For example, do not use the words "preliminary copy," "draft copy," "working draft," or similar words. This language offers an opening for opposing counsel, making it appear that the attorney who retained you contributed to what should be your independent professional judgment. Do not produce a written report and later destroy it before a final resolution of the case or any discovery issue related to the report. Destroying the report could be considered destroying or concealing evidence; among lawyers, this is called **spoliation**, and it could subject your retaining party or attorney to monetary or evidentiary sanctions.

Instead, include the same information you would supply in an informal verbal report. First, restate the assignment to confirm between you and the retaining attorney that the work you have done is properly focused. Next, summarize what has been accomplished. Identify the systems you have examined, what tools you have used, and what you have seen. State evidence preservation or protection processes you have implemented. (See Chapters 6 and 9 for more information about these processes.) The following list shows additional items to include in your report:

- Summarize your billing to date and estimate costs to complete the effort.
- Identify the tentative conclusion (rather than the preliminary conclusion).
- Identify areas of further investigation and obtain confirmation from the attorney on the scope of your examination.

Guidelines for Writing Reports

The long-preferred method for expressing an opinion has been to frame a hypothetical question based on available factual evidence. This method is less favored today but still has validity, even if it's not formally used. You can construct a hypothetical question to guide and support your opinion. State the facts necessary to the question, but don't include any unnecessary facts unless they are alternative facts that allow the opinion to remain the same—that is, if one set of facts is not supported and the other is supported. An expert opinion is governed by FRE, Rule 705, and the corresponding rule in many states. Rule 705 relates to expert testimony; for more information, visit *www.law.cornell.edu/rules/fre/rules.htm#Rule705*.

The following text from a court transcript illustrates an exchange between an attorney and a computer forensics expert. Note that the word "presented" is used in this transcript; it means that the attorney handed the expert something while asking a question.

> **Mr. Stiubhard**: *Mr. Noriki, presented with a hard drive of 40 MB, an attached Maxtor manufacturer's data sheet that indicated it was manufactured in May 2002, previous testimony by a detective that the notebook computer in which this drive was found was manufactured by Dell Computer Corporation in June 2002 and purchased by the owner in June 2002. Based on those facts testified to, do you have an opinion whether this is original equipment on this system?*
>
> **Mr. Noriki**: *Yes.*
>
> **Mr. Stiubhard**: *Mr. Noriki, what is your opinion on whether this hypothetical hard drive would be the original equipment with the system?*

> **Mr. Noriki**: *Based on facts you have provided, it is my professional opinion that the hard drive would . . . .*

Hypothetical questions can be abused and made so complex that the finder of fact (the expert) might not be able to remember enough of the question's fact pattern to evaluate the answer. Another abuse of the hypothetical question is that it effectively allows attorneys to recite their favored facts to the jury repeatedly and in the order and with the emphasis they want to apply.

The law previously required that an expert who does not have personal knowledge about the system or the occurrence must give his or her opinions by response to hypothetical questions, which ask the expert witness to express an opinion based on hypothetical facts without specifically referring to a particular system or situation. In this regard, you as a forensic investigator (that is, an expert witness) differ fundamentally from an ordinary witness. You didn't see or hear the incident in dispute, but give evidence as an opinion based on professional knowledge and experience, even if you might never have seen the system, data, or scene. Although the rules of evidence have relaxed requirements on the formal structure and requirements of an expert rendering an opinion, it's helpful to privately structure a hypothetical question, whether it's asked in court or stated in a report. This ensures that you as a witness are basing your opinion on facts expected to be supported by evidence. Evaluate every fact you're relying on to form your opinion. If a fact could be changed or not used, and your opinion wouldn't change, it's not relevant to your opinion and should be excluded from your hypothetical question.

As an expert witness, you may testify to an opinion, or conclusion, if four basic conditions are met:

- The opinion, inferences, or conclusions depend on special knowledge, skill, or training not within the ordinary experience of lay witnesses or jurors.

- The witness must be shown to be qualified as a true expert in the field of expertise (which is why the curriculum vitae is important).

- The witness must testify to a reasonable degree of certainty (probability) regarding his or her opinion, inference, or conclusion.

- Generally, expert witnesses must first describe the data (facts) on which their opinion, inference, or conclusion is based, or they must testify in response to a hypothetical question that sets forth the underlying evidence.

Report Structure

The structure of a report should include all the sections shown in the following list, although the order varies depending on organizational guides or case requirements:

- Abstract
- Summary
- Table of contents
- Body of report

- Conclusion

- Reference

- Glossary

- Acknowledgements

- Appendixes

Adjust the sections shown in this list to suit the report's purpose. Each section has a particular role. The section title tells the reader at first glance what you're discussing, so make sure it conveys the essential point of the report. For example, the body of the report might have a title of "Investigation Findings ABC Bicycle, Inc.: Intellectual Property Theft."

If the report is long and complex, you should provide an abstract. More people read the abstract than the entire report, so writing one for your report is important. The abstract, or summary and table of contents, give readers an overview of the report and a list of section titles so that they can see the points included and decide what they need to review. An abstract simply condenses the report into miniature form to concentrate on the essential information. The abstract should be one or two paragraphs totaling about 150 to 200 words. Remember that the abstract should not be a mere recital of the subject covered; it should describe the examination or investigation and present the report's main ideas in a summarized form. Informative abstracts do not duplicate references or tables of results. As with any research paper, write the abstract last.

The body consists of the introduction and component sections. The introduction should state the purpose of the report and show that you are aware of its terms of reference. You should also state any methods used and any limitations and indicate how the report is structured. It's important to justify why you are writing the report, so make sure you answer the question "What is the problem?" You should also give the reader a map of what you are delivering. Introduce the problem, moving from the broader issues to your specific problem, finishing the section with the precise aims of the paper (key questions). Craft this introduction carefully, setting up the processes you used to develop the information in logical order. Refer to *relevant* facts, ideas, and theories as well as related research by other authors. For the component sections, organize them logically under headings to reflect how you classify information and to ensure that your information remains relevant to the investigation.

Two other main parts of your report are the conclusion and supporting materials (references and appendixes). The conclusion starts by referring to the report's purpose, states the main points, draws conclusions, and possibly renders an opinion. References and appendixes list the material to which your work refers. Follow guidelines on format for presenting references. Use a style manual as a reference, such as *Gregg Reference Manual: A Manual of Style, Grammar, Usage, and Formatting*; *The Chicago Manual of Style: The Essential Guide for Writers, Editors, and Publishers*; or the style manual from the Modern Language Association (MLA). Appendixes provide additional resource material not included in the text.

Writing Reports Clearly

To produce clear, concise reports, you should critique and assess the quality of your writing. Consider the following criteria:

- *Communicative quality*—Is it easy to read?

- *Ideas and organization*—Is the information relevant and clearly organized?

- *Grammar and vocabulary*—Is the language simple and direct so that the meaning is clear and the text is not repetitive? However, key technical terms should be used consistently; you shouldn't try to use variety for those terms. Using different words for the same thing might raise questions.

- *Punctuation and spelling*—Are they accurate and consistent?

Good scientific/technical/expert reports share many of the qualities of other kinds of writing. To write is to think, so a report that lays out ideas in a logical order facilitates logical thinking. Make each sentence follow from the previous one, building an argument piece by piece. Group related ideas and sentences into paragraphs, and group paragraphs into sections. Create a flow from the beginning of the report to the end. The report should be grammatically sound, use correct spelling, and be free of writing errors. Avoid jargon, slang, or colloquial terms. If technical terms must be used, define them in ordinary language (or refer readers to the glossary section of your report). Defining acronyms and any abbreviations not used as standard measurement units is particularly important. If there's any possibility of misinterpreting an abbreviation, define it or use the full expression. For example, m. or M. is routinely used in scientific/technical writing as an abbreviation for "meter," but nontechnical readers (especially in the United States) might assume it's an abbreviation for "mile." Most lawyers (and judges) and jurors are not technically trained.

Considering Writing Style

Style means the tone of language you use to address the reader. Be sure to avoid repetition and vague language. Repeat only what's necessary, such as key words or technical terms.

Be precise and be specific. Avoid generalizing, as in "There was a problem, so we...." Instead, state the problem specifically and describe what you or others did to solve the problem. Avoid presenting too many details and personal observations. Although it's acceptable and appealing to use "I" or "we" in a report, too many sentences with "I" and "we" become repetitive.

Most of the report describes what you did, so it should be in past tense, but use present or future tense as appropriate. Use active rather than passive voice to avoid boring writing and contorted phrases. For example, "the software recovered the following data" is more direct and, therefore, more interesting to read than "the following data was recovered by the software."

14

A final caution in writing style: Project objectivity. You must communicate calm, detached observations in your report. Don't become emotionally involved in the investigation. Don't think in terms of catching somebody or proving something; do not develop an agenda, other than finding the truth. Always try to identify the flaws in your thinking or examination; it's better to identify the flaws than to allow opposing counsel to do it for you at an embarrassing moment. It's not your job to win the case. Don't become an advocate for anything other than the truth and your honest objective opinion.

Designing the Layout and Presentation of Reports

Layout and presentation involve matters ranging from clear title and section headings to accurate spelling and punctuation. As mentioned, think of your readers and how to make the report appealing to them. Be sure to edit and check your text.

A numbering structure is part of the layout. An author usually chooses one of the following two layout systems: decimal numbering or legal-sequential numbering. After you choose a system, be sure to follow it consistently throughout the report.

A report using the decimal numbering system divides material into sections, as shown in the following example. With the decimal system, readers can scan the headings and understand how one part of the report relates to the other.

1.0 Introduction
       1.1 Nature of incident
              1.1.1 Victim
2.0 First Incident
       2.1 Witness 1
              2.1.1 Witness testimony
3.0 Location of Evidence
       3.1 Seizure of Evidence
              3.1.1 Transportation of Evidence
4.0 Analysis of Evidence
       4.1 Chain of Evidence
              4.1.1 Extraction of Data
5.0 Conclusion
       5.1 Results
              5.1.1 Expert Opinion

An alternative is to use legal-sequential numbering, as in the following example:

I. Introduction
> 1. Nature of the Incident
> 2. The Victim
> 3. Witnesses to the Crime
> 4. Location of Evidence

II. Examination
> 5. Chain of Evidence
> 6. Extraction of Evidence
> 7. Analysis of Evidence

This system is frequently used in pleadings. Each Roman numeral represents a major aspect of the report, and each Arabic number is a significant piece of supporting information. The system of legal-sequential organization is meaningful to lawyers but might not be as effective with nonlawyers. Generally, this system doesn't give readers as strong a set of visual cues about the organization and relative importance of information in the report.

Including Signposts

Apart from structure, layout, and presentation, your main tool in writing reports is your language. Choose language that gives your reader signposts to what you're trying to communicate. A signpost draws readers' attention to a point or shows them the sequence of a process. It assists readers in scanning the text quickly by highlighting the main points and the logical development of information. For example, the first substantive section of your report could start with "This is the report of findings from the forensic examination of computer SN 123456."

Within the first section, the steps could be introduced with "The first step in this examination was," "The second step in this examination was," and so on. In these examples, "first" and "second" are signposts that show the sequence of information or tasks.

When you want to evaluate something, you might include a signpost such as "The problem with this is..." To show that you're drawing a conclusion, introduce the point with "This means that" or "The result shows that..."

Providing Supporting Material

Use material such as figures, tables, data, and equations to help tell the story as it unfolds. Refer to this material directly in the text and integrate the points they make into your writing. Number figures and tables sequentially as they're introduced (for example, Figure 1, Figure 2, and so forth with another sequence for Table 1, Table 2, and so on).

14

Captions should supply descriptive information, not be just a simple title. In charts, label all axes and include units. Insert a figure or table after the paragraph in which it's first mentioned, or gather all supporting material together after the reference section (before any appendixes).

Formatting Consistently

Within the report, the exact format of items is less important than being consistent in applying formatting. For example, if you indent paragraphs, be sure to indent them all. Use fonts consistently, and use a consistent style of headings throughout (for example, major headings in bold with initial capitals, minor headings in italics, and so forth). Write "%" or "percent" but do not use both. In other words, establish a template and stick to it.

Explaining Methods

Explain how you studied the problem, which should follow logically from the purpose of the report. Depending on the kind of data, this section might contain subsections on examination procedures, materials or equipment, data collection and sources, and analytical or statistical techniques. Supply enough detail for readers to understand what you did.

Data Collection

Data collection is a critical portion of the report. Without good data recording in a laboratory notebook or record, completing a report beyond this point is futile. If your data collection process becomes the subject of discovery or examination, presenting data in a well-organized manner is important. Using tables, if practical, allows readers to easily follow any data manipulations. Tables should be clearly labeled as to their content and numbered for ease of referral in the discussion section.

Including Calculations

In most cases, an investigator or forensic software performs some hashing calculations in the forensic examination of a computer. If you use any hashing, be sure to give the common name, such as "Message Digest 5 (MD5) hash." Generally, you don't need to give examples of each type of hash if you're using standard tools; you explain generally what they do, and you cite the authority or policy you rely on for using the tool.

Providing for Uncertainty and Error Analysis

In computer forensics, many results can be absolutely true if stated conservatively, but might be a guess if you overreach. Therefore, the statement of limitations of knowledge and uncertainty is necessary to protect your credibility. For example, if you know that the date and time stamp for a file from a PC's Windows OS indicates that it was created at a certain time, you need to state that a PC clock could easily be reset. In addition, you should state that there's no absolute assurance that a file's date and time stamp is a reflection of its creation, but that there might be other reliable indicators related to that date and time stamp, such as date and time stamps of other files, creation date and time stamps for directories, creation order of certain files, and information in automatic backups.

Explaining Results and Conclusions

Explain your actual findings, using subheadings to divide the section into logical parts with the text addressing the report objective. Link your writing to figures and tables as you present the results. For each, describe and interpret what you see. If you have many similar figures, select representative examples for brevity and put the rest in an appendix. Mention any uncertainty in observation. Make comments on the results as they're presented, but save broader generalizations and conclusions for later. Answer the question "What did I find out?"

Discuss the importance of what you found in light of the overall report objectives. Take a step back from the details and synthesize what has (and has not) been learned about the problem and what it all means. Describe what you actually found, not what you hoped to find. Begin with specific comments and expand to more general issues.

This discussion section is often combined with the results or conclusion section. Decide whether understanding and clarity are improved if you include some discussion as you cover the results. The conclusion should restate the objective, aims, and key questions and summarize your findings with clear, concise statements. Keep the conclusion section brief and to the point.

Providing References

Within the text, cite references by author and year unless instructed otherwise. In the reference section, list alphabetically only the people and publications you cite in the report. (If none are cited, omit the section.) Give enough detail so that someone else could actually track down the information. List all authors in your publications. Follow a standard format, such as the ones shown in the following examples, and note the distinctions in different reference formats for italics, capitalization, volume and page numbers, publisher address, and other style concerns.

The Harvard (author-date) system is the one typically used in the sciences and social sciences and promoted in professional writing and communications. All examples in this section are based on the generally accepted author-date system of referencing.

When you write a report, you must cite references to all material you have used as sources for the content of your work. These citations must be made wherever and whenever you quote, paraphrase, or summarize someone else's opinions, theories, or data in the text of your report. References can be to any source, from books, periodicals, newspapers, Web sites, and reports to personal communications and interviews. A list of references, in alphabetical order based on authors' surnames, should be attached to your report.

The titles of books, journals, and other major works are set in italics (or can be underlined when handwritten). The titles of articles and smaller works found within a larger work are surrounded by quotation marks.

14

For citations in your text, the author's surname and initials, year of publication for the material cited, and page numbers, if required, should be listed. Page numbers of your references are necessary only if you quote or paraphrase particular passages or provide lists or figures from the sources, as in the following examples:

- Personal (unpublished) communications:

  Cited in the text only, as in "... x is recoverable using tool A (Koenick, F., pers. comm.)."

- Lecture notes:

  Stiubhard, C. K. "The Curriculum Vitae." May 1, 2000 lecture for CIS 411/511, CTIN and City University, 2000.

- Web site:

  Law Office of Christopher K. Stiubhard. Internet: *www.stiubhardlaw.com*, 2003.

- Single-author journal paper:

  O'Herlighy, T. A., S.J. "Development of Relationships on the Internet." *Journal of the Advocate* 7, 130142, 2001.

- Multiple-author journal paper:

  Noriki, H. W., C. K. Stiubhard, and M. D. Clay. "Investigation of Counterfeiting of Spare Parts—A Statistical Analysis." *The Frontline Journal of Aviation* 8, 150152, 2002.

- Book:

  Clark, Franklin and Diliberto, Ken. *Investigating Computer Crime*, CRC Press, New York, 1996.

- Government/technical report:

  "The Examination of Computers." Report XYZ-001, United States Department of Justice, 2000.

- Chapter in an edited volume:

  Pellegrino, A. "Investigation of the Automated Backup Copies of Microsoft Application Files." In Noriki, H. W., Pellegrino, A., Stiubhard, C. K., Koenick, F. eds., *Computer Forensics*. Learning Technology, Springfield, MA, 2003.

Including Appendixes

If necessary, one or more appendixes containing material such as raw data, figures not used in the body of the report, and anticipated exhibits can be included. Arrange appendixes in the order referred to in the report. They are considered additional material and might not be examined by the reader at all. Some portions of the appendixes might be considered optional, but others are required. For example, exhibits are required under FRCP, Rule 26, as is the curriculum vitae (unless bona fides are integrated into the report).

Report Formats

Whether you are working for a law firm, computer forensics firm, a research laboratory, or a law enforcement agency, these organizations have established formats for reports. Be sure to get samples from them before beginning your report.

GENERATING REPORT FINDINGS WITH FORENSIC SOFTWARE TOOLS

With many computer forensics software tools, such as FTK Explorer, DriveSpy, iLook, or EnCase, log files and reports are generated when performing an analysis. These reports and logs are typically in plaintext format, a word processor format, or HTML format. In this section, you learn how to integrate a computer forensics log file tool or report generator into your official investigation report. It's this final product that you present to your customer, attorney, or client.

As an example of a report from a computing investigation, you reexamine a case from Chapter 5, where you processed and analyzed a floppy disk by using DriveSpy and then tracked down George Montgomery and Martha Heiser. If necessary, refer to Chapter 5 for specifics of this investigation and instructions on how to re-create the bit-stream image of the floppy disk.

After you have created the bit-stream image as described in Chapter 5, you'll use FTK to examine the data again to create a report with the FTK Report Wizard. In the following steps, you re-create the floppy disk by using the Image utility, as described in Chapter 5:

14

1. Access a command prompt. Change to the **Tools** folder in your work folder and run **Toolpath.bat**.

2. In your work folder, create a **Chap14** folder. In the Chap14 folder, create a **Chapter** folder. Navigate to the Chap14\Chapter folder and copy **C5InChap.img** from your Chapter 5 student data files to the Chap14\Chapter folder.

3. Label a blank, formatted floppy disk **Chapter 14 In Chapter** and insert it in the floppy drive. At the prompt, type **image C5InChap.img a:** and press **Enter** to create an image of George's disk on your floppy disk. Image displays the checksum value to verify that the C5InChap.img file is identical to the original disk. Close the command prompt window.

Using FTK Demo Version

If you have not already done so, download a copy of FTK Demo from *www.accessdata.com*.

NOTE

The following exercise should be run in Microsoft Windows XP or later. Using Windows 95 or 98 will produce slightly different results in how the recovered data is displayed in FTK. For example, in Windows XP, several files are automatically carved from the disk's free space. In Windows 98, only the data from these files is displayed as recovered slack and free space.

The following steps guide you through the analysis and report creation process in FTK:

1. Write-protect the floppy disk by moving the write-protect tab to the closed position and place the disk in the floppy (A:) drive.

2. To start FTK, click **Start**, point to **Programs** or **All Programs**, point to **AccessData**, point to **Forensic Toolkit**, and then click **Forensic Toolkit**.

3. When the Demo warning banner appears, click **OK**.

4. In the AccessData FTK Startup dialog box, click **Start a new case**, and then click **OK**.

5. In the New Case dialog box, fill out the information for the investigator's name, case number, and case name. Click the **Browse** button, navigate to and click the **C:** drive of your computer, and then click **OK**. (*Note*: FTK automatically creates a folder at the root level of your C: drive.)

6. In the Case Description text box, type a brief description of the investigation, and then click **Next**.

After you have completed the new case information, you need to enter other case specifications before you can start the forensic analysis:

1. In the Case Log Options dialog box, click **Next**.

2. In the Processes to Perform dialog box, click **Next**.

3. In the Refine Case - Default dialog box, click **Next**.

4. In the Refine Index - Default dialog box, click **Next**.

5. In the Add Evidence dialog box, click the **Add Evidence** button.

6. In the Add Evidence to Case dialog box, click the **Local Drive** option button (see Figure 14-2), and then click **Continue**.

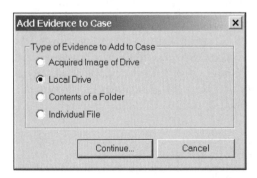

Figure 14-2 The Add Evidence to Case dialog box

7. In the Select Local Drive dialog box, make sure the A: drive option and the Logical Analysis option button are selected, and then click **OK**. When the Warning dialog box appears, click **Yes** to continue to the next step.

8. In the Evidence Information dialog box, enter additional comments about this case, and then click **OK**.

9. In the Add Evidence dialog box, click **Next**.

10. In the New Case Setup is now Complete dialog box, verify the specifications. If they are incorrect, click the **Back** button to update the specifications. If they are correct, click **Finish**.

When the FTK Processing Files window is displayed, FTK starts analyzing data on the investigation floppy disk. When the analysis is complete, the main FTK window opens, showing all data sets found from this examination.

Analyzing with FTK

When the processing has finished, locate and extract data from the floppy disk, using FTK to process the investigation. For example, to collect pictures for the report with FTK, follow these steps:

1. In the main FTK window, click the **Graphics** tab, and then click the **List all descendants** check box.

2. Click the **cat picture** in the upper pane, and then click the check box in the lower pane for the **cat.jpg** file.

3. Click the **mountain picture** in the upper pane, shown in Figure 14-3, and then click the check box in the lower pane for the **mt_rainier2.jpg** file.

Figure 14-3 Viewing mt_rainier2.jpg

To locate encrypted files with FTK, follow these steps:

1. Click the **Overview** tab, click the **Encrypted Files** button, and then click to select the **X.ZIP** file in the lower pane.

2. Click the check box next to file **X.ZIP**.

3. Right-click **X.ZIP** and then click **Export File** on the shortcut menu.

4. Click to clear all check boxes at the bottom of the Export Files dialog box (see Figure 14-4).

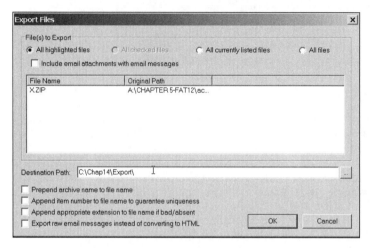

Figure 14-4   The Export Files dialog box

5. In the Export Files dialog box, click **OK**, and then click **OK** in the Export Files message box.

Next, you search for any occurrences of specific keywords related to this investigation. To start searching for the names George and Martha, you need to access the Search tab in FTK and run an indexed search by following these steps:

1. Click the **Search** tab.

2. In the Search Term text box, type **George** and then click **Add**.

3. In the Search Term text box, type **Martha** and then click **Add**.

4. Click **View Cumulative Results**, and then click **OK** in the Filter Search Hits dialog box.

5. In the upper-right window, click the plus sign to expand the search results.

6. Click all the check boxes in the lower pane (or simply click **Check all files in current list**), as shown in Figure 14-5.

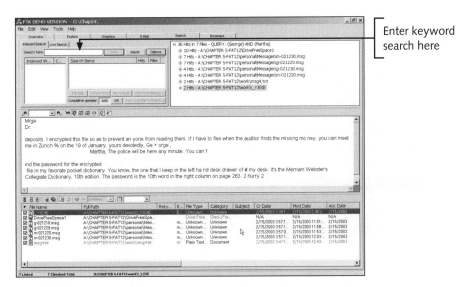

Enter keyword search here

Figure 14-5   Indexed search results

In the results of the indexed search, examine all text message contents. From this examination, you should find references to Zurich and money. To continue the investigation, follow these steps to do a live search for the keyword "Account":

1. In the Search window, click the **Live Search** tab.

2. In the Search Term text box, type the keyword **Account** and then click **Add**. Click **Search**, and then click **OK** in the Filter Search Hits dialog box.

3. When the search is finished, click **View Results** in the Live Search Progress dialog box.

4. In the upper-right pane (see Figure 14-6), click all **plus signs** to expand the search results.

5. Read the contents of these search results to find additional information that might support the investigation.

6. Click all **check boxes** that haven't been selected in the lower pane.

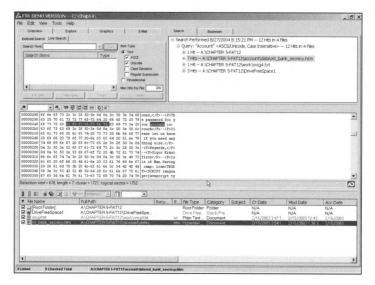

Figure 14-6 Live search results

Next, you learn how to bookmark the data you have selected for your report. To bookmark investigation findings, follow these steps:

1. In the Search window, right-click any file that has been selected in the lower pane, and then click **Create Bookmark**.

2. In the Create New Bookmark dialog box, type **Ch14_search_results** in the Bookmark name text box. Click the **All checked items** button, and then click to select the **Include in report** and **Export files** check boxes.

3. In the Bookmark comment section, type any comments that describe this particular bookmark (see Figure 14-7), and then click **OK**.

After you have bookmarked specific data of interest to the investigation, you can generate a report of your findings. The FTK Report Wizard has a feature that allows you to insert other documents into the final FTK report. Later in this section, you learn how to add these other documents, including your narrative report, to the FTK HTML report. Any Web browser can read the HTML report that FTK creates.

The next step is to write a narrative report of what you found on the floppy disk. This narrative should follow the recommendations previously discussed in this chapter for your report's contents. To review your findings for this investigation, follow these recommended steps in FTK:

1. Click the **Overview** tab and then click the **Checked Items** button.

2. In the lower pane, click the first file **!_Y.EXE**.

3. In the upper-right pane, scroll down and read the contents of the bookmark, and make note of its contents for your report.

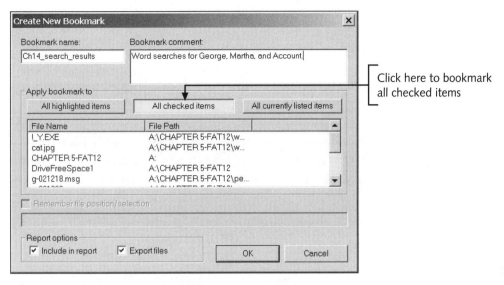

Figure 14-7 Completing the bookmark information

4. To locate a specific keyword within the data set displayed in the upper-right pane, type a keyword value in the Search text box.

5. Repeat Steps 2 and 3 and examine each file. Note the password in the mt_bank_secrecy.htm file, shown in Figure 14-8.

14

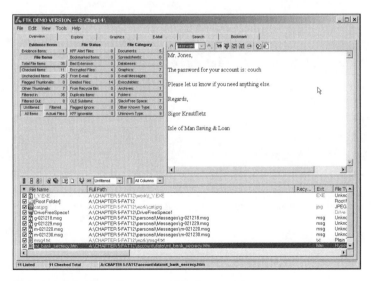

Figure 14-8 Locating a specific keyword

6. To get a full view of a graphics file, first click the **Graphics** button under the File Category column in the upper-left pane and select a graphics file in the lower pane.

7. To view binary files, click the **Encrypted Files** button under the File Status column in the upper-left pane, click **X.ZIP**, then click the **HEX** icon above the upper-right pane.

To review your findings, note what facts you discovered from this analysis. In the first file, you found several text messages that seem to be correspondence between Martha Heiser and George Montgomery, and you discovered key elements that require further examination. Of specific interest are these words:

- Encrypted this file
- Flee when the auditor finds the missing money
- Meet me in Zurich
- Merriam Webster's Collegiate Dictionary

The next step is to analyze the disk to look for additional clues. For example, some new words to search for possible clues might be vacation, password, and bank. Collect as many new words of interest as possible, and run additional searches to see if you can find new clues. Note that a data set of interest is the mt_bank_secrecy.htm file, which seems to be an HTML file containing a message. Of interest for this data set is the reference to a password for an account at Isle of Man Savings and Loan:

```
Mr. Jones,

The password for your account is: couch

Please let us know if you need anything else.

Regards,

Sigor Krautfletz

Isle of Man Savings and Loan
```

The last data set of interest for this case is the X.zip file containing three files that have the same name of "Swiss" but different extensions. You exported this file earlier with FTK. FTK creates a subfolder named Export, where it automatically copies exported data for your forensics examination.

Using WinZip or PKUnzip, attempt to extract the content of X.zip for your follow-up examination. If an error occurs when extracting this file, you might have forgotten to clear the "Prepend archive name to file name" and "Append item number to file name to guarantee uniqueness" check boxes in the Export Files dialog box. If you do encounter an error, open FTK and export X.zip again with all check boxes cleared.

The X.zip file is a password-protected PKZip file. During your examination, you found a reference to the password "couch" for a bank account. Try that password to see whether it successfully opens this compressed archive file.

After you have successfully unzipped the password-protected X.zip file, you can continue your examination and inspect the content of all three extracted files. Depending on the spreadsheet application you have available, open one of the three files to view its contents. Figure 14-9 shows the contents of the Swiss.xls file.

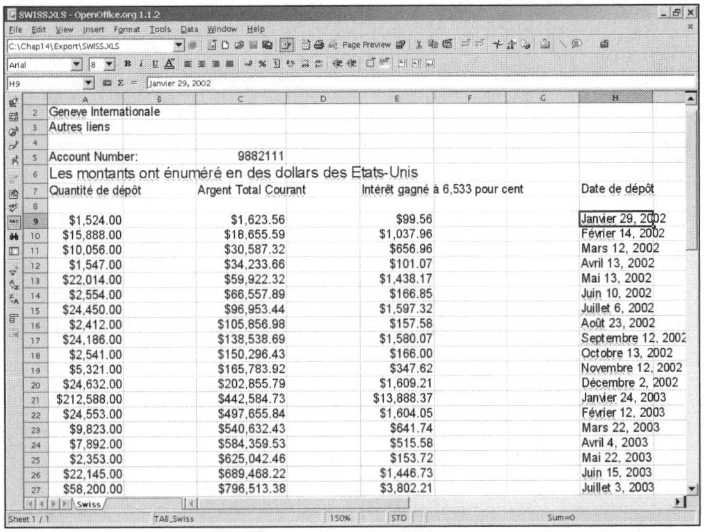

2	Geneve Internationale			
3	Autres liens			
4				
5	Account Number:	9882111		
6	Les montants ont énuméré en des dollars des Etats-Unis			
7	Quantité de dépôt	Argent Total Courant	Intérêt gagné à 6,533 pour cent	Date de dépôt
8				
9	$1,524.00	$1,623.56	$99.56	Janvier 29, 2002
10	$15,888.00	$18,655.59	$1,037.96	Février 14, 2002
11	$10,056.00	$30,587.32	$656.96	Mars 12, 2002
12	$1,547.00	$34,233.66	$101.07	Avril 13, 2002
13	$22,014.00	$59,922.32	$1,438.17	Mai 13, 2002
14	$2,554.00	$66,557.89	$166.85	Juin 10, 2002
15	$24,450.00	$96,953.44	$1,597.32	Juillet 6, 2002
16	$2,412.00	$105,856.98	$157.58	Août 23, 2002
17	$24,186.00	$138,538.69	$1,580.07	Septembre 12, 2002
18	$2,541.00	$150,296.43	$166.00	Octobre 13, 2002
19	$5,321.00	$165,783.92	$347.62	Novembre 12, 2002
20	$24,632.00	$202,855.79	$1,609.21	Décembre 2, 2002
21	$212,588.00	$442,584.73	$13,888.37	Janvier 24, 2003
22	$24,553.00	$497,655.84	$1,604.05	Février 12, 2003
23	$9,823.00	$540,632.43	$641.74	Mars 22, 2003
24	$7,892.00	$584,359.53	$515.58	Avril 4, 2003
25	$2,353.00	$625,042.46	$153.72	Mai 22, 2003
26	$22,145.00	$689,468.22	$1,446.73	Juin 15, 2003
27	$58,200.00	$796,513.38	$3,802.21	Juillet 3, 2003

Figure 14-9 Contents of the Swiss.xls file

This file is a spreadsheet that appears to contain deposit entries from January 2002 through December 2004. Note also that the language appears to be French and the bank name is Geneve Internationale.

Now that you have completed your examination, minimize FTK and start your word processor to write a brief narrative of your findings. An example of this narrative might be as follows:

> *On January 10, 2005, I examined a floppy disk drive for Widgets International. This examination was predicated on information that management of Widgets International was concerned about the whereabouts of two employees who had been absent from work for more than two days. Management provided no additional information about the circumstances of the missing employees.*
>
> *The Widgets International Security Department supplied the following information about their concerns. The missing employees are George Montgomery and Martha Heiser. Mr. Montgomery works in the Accounts Payable Department. Ms. Heiser is the executive secretary for Mr. Thompson, senior vice president of marketing for Widgets International.*

14

After receiving the floppy disk from Mr. Wilson Smith of Widgets International's Security Department, I immediately made a duplicate bit-stream image copy of the floppy by using the Digital Intelligence Image program. When the image copy was completed, I returned it to Mr. Smith for his retention.

Following the creation of the bit-stream image copy of the floppy disk, I created a working copy of the saved image file. I examined the content of the floppy disk by using AccessData Forensics Toolkit (FTK) to determine what the disk contained.

With FTK, I located several text messages that appeared to be e-mail correspondence between George Montgomery and Martha Heiser. The date and time stamps of these messages show activity in December 2001. I could not determine whether the computer used to record these messages had the correct time and dates on its internal clock.

Further examination of the message contents revealed that George Montgomery might have had financial problems. Later messages revealed that he had resolved his financial dilemma but did not state how. Additional messages indicate that George Montgomery was concerned about the police arresting him because of undisclosed activity.

While examining the disk for other facts, I found a hidden password-protected zip file and a Web-based e-mail message from an offshore bank, Isle of Man Savings and Loan, that contained a password. The password in this message is "couch."

I extracted the X.zip file with FTK and was successful in extracting all its contents by using the same password from the Web e-mail message mt_bank_secrecy.htm. The X.zip file contained three files that appear to be different formats of the same spreadsheet. The spreadsheet content shows what appear to be deposits to a Swiss bank, Geneve International. The dates in these spreadsheets appear to be French.

The date and time stamps for the mt_bank_secrecy.htm file show that the file was created on February 15, 2003, but the last entry of deposit transaction shows December 2004. The discrepancies of this date and time value along with the date and time stamps for the e-mail messages indicate that the computer used to generate these files might not be running correctly. Because of this, the accuracy of when these files were created cannot be verified.

For additional information on data recovered for this examination, see the FTK report in HTML format.

After completing this narrative report, save it to the C:\Chap14\Export folder with the name Chap_14_narrative.rtf. Next, use the following steps to run FTK Report Wizard so that you can integrate all components, such as evidence and report files, into the final HTML document:

1. Maximize FTK. In the FTK main window, click **File**, **Report Wizard** from the menu. The Report Wizard starts and opens to the FTK Report Wizard – Case Information dialog box.

2. Enter the appropriate report header information about the case, and then click **Next**.

3. In the FTK Report Wizard – Bookmarks – A dialog box, click **Next** to accept the default options.

4. In the FTK Report Wizard – Bookmarks – B dialog box, click **Next** to accept the default options.

5. In the FTK Report Wizard – Graphic Thumbnails dialog box, click the **Export full-size graphics and link them to the thumbnails** check box, and then click **Next**.

6. In the FTK Report Wizard – List by File Path dialog box, click the **Include a list by file path section in the report**, **Include in the report**, and **Export to the report** check boxes, and then click **Next**.

7. In the FTK Report Wizard – List File Properties – A dialog box, click **Next** to accept the default options.

8. In the FTK Report Wizard – Supplementary Files dialog box, click **Add Files** and navigate to the Chap14\Export folder in your work folder.

9. In the Open dialog box, hold down the **Ctrl** key, click the **Chap_14 _narrative.rtf** and **Swiss.xls** files, and then click **Open**.

10. In the FTK Report Wizard – Supplementary Files dialog box, click **Next**.

11. In the FTK Report Wizard – Report Location dialog box, click **Finish**.

12. When the wizard finishes processing, click **Yes** to view the report in your Web browser. Close FTK and your Web browser when you have completed inspecting your report.

NOTE

To reexamine the report later, from Windows Explorer navigate to the C:\Chap14\Report folder and double-click the Index.html file.

Forming an Expert Opinion

This section offers an example of how to provide an expert opinion—in this case, on whether a disk contains files from a Windows 95 or later OS. For this exercise, you need to review FAT12, FAT16, and FAT32 file systems in Chapter 7. You can also refer to the "Overview of FAT Directory Structures" section in Appendix B for additional information on FAT directory structures. Specifically, you need to learn how to identify the differences in older MS-DOS systems versus newer OSs, such as Windows XP.

14

Determining the Origin of a Floppy Disk

In this exercise, you determine whether a floppy disk was created from an MS-DOS 6.22 OS or a Windows 95 or later OS. You need the following items:

- C14-ea.ima from your student data files
- Digital Intelligence Image utility
- Digital Intelligence DriveSpy, FTK, or your preferred computer forensics tool

To create the floppy disk, follow these steps:

1. In Windows, use Windows Explorer or My Computer to copy **C14-ea.ima** from the Chap14\Chapter folder in the student data files to the Chap14\Chapter folder in your work folder.

2. Open a command prompt window or boot your computer to MS-DOS.

3. At the DOS command prompt, navigate to the **Tools** folder in your work folder, type **Toolpath**, and press **Enter**.

4. Change to the Chap14\Chapter folder in your work folder.

5. Insert a blank floppy disk into the floppy drive (A: drive).

6. At the DOS command prompt, type **image C14-ea.ima a:** and press **Enter**.

Now you are ready to start your preferred computer forensics tool. If you're using DriveSpy, perform the following steps. If you're using another computer forensics tool, refer to the vendor's user manual. To use DriveSpy to examine a directory's content, follow these steps:

1. At the DOS command prompt, navigate to the Chap14\Chapter folder in your work folder. Type **drivespy** and press **Enter**.

2. At the DriveSpy SYS prompt, type **da** and press **Enter**. Then type **p1** and press **Enter**.

3. At the DAP1 prompt, type **dir /s** and press **Enter**. At the page mode prompt, type **n** to page through the file listings, and press any key to continue viewing each screen of files and directories. Note the cluster number for any directories displayed in the output. Directory entries have the letter "d" displayed under the Attrib column of the Dir output.

4. At the DAP1 prompt, type **cluster *x*** (*x* is the cluster location number where the directory is on the disk), and then press **Enter** to view the directory's contents.

5. In the cluster output screen, examine each file name listed to find any long file names, which you can use to determine whether any file was created and written from a Windows 95 or later OS. To exit the cluster view screen and return to DriveSpy's command shell, press **Esc**.

After you examine the content of the directory for this floppy disk, write a brief opinion report (one to three pages) of your findings. Give your expert opinion on which type of OS was used to create this floppy disk and the files it contains.

PREPARING FOR TESTIMONY

The types of testimony by professionals at any trial, deposition, or hearing can be divided into two categories: technical or scientific witness testimony and expert witness testimony. Computer forensics examiners need to be aware of the differences between these types of testimony as they prepare for any type of litigation. This section explains how to become an expert witness and how to avoid problems when giving testimony.

When cases go to trial, you as the forensic expert play one of two roles: You are called as a **technical or scientific witness** or as an **expert witness**. As a technical or scientific witness, you are only providing the facts you have found in your investigation. That is, you present any evidence you found that contributes to resolving the incident or crime. When you give technical or scientific testimony, you present this evidence and explain what it is and how it was obtained. You don't offer conclusions, only the facts.

However, as an expert witness, you have opinions about what you observe. You can base these opinions on experience, allowing you to use deductive reasoning with facts found during an investigation or examination of a digital system. In fact, it's your opinion that makes you an expert witness.

If you are called as a technical or expert witness in a computer forensics case, you need to thoroughly prepare for your testimony. Establish communication early on with your attorney. Learn the general concepts of the case before you start processing and examining the evidence. Keep in mind that criminal investigations have slightly different requirements than civil litigation needs; your attorney can give you specific guidelines. As an expert witness, you work for the attorney, not the client (plaintiff or defendant). The attorney and his or her client are dedicated to their case; if you discover negative findings, communicate them as soon as possible to the attorney.

When preparing to testify, confirm your findings with your own documentation and by corroborating with other computer forensics professionals. Return to the notes you took during your investigation. If you're working with electronic notes, use care in storing them. In your analysis and reporting, develop and maintain a standard method of processing to minimize or eliminate any confusion and to help you prepare for testimony later. Computer forensics is only now developing a peer review process as the number of examiners increases. To get peer review, often you have to search outside your region or approach the Federal Bureau of Investigation (FBI). Learn to take advantage of your professional network and request peer reviews to help support your findings.

Although you should recognize when conflict-of-interest issues apply to your case and discuss any concerns with the attorney who hires you, also be aware of a practice called **conflicting out**. This is an attempt to prevent another attorney from using you on an

14

important case and is most common in the private sector when you work as an independent consultant. Opposing attorneys might call to discuss the case with you, only to have you excluded from working for an attorney needing your services. By doing this, they have created at least the appearance of a conflict of interest for you and the other attorney trying the case. Avoid agreeing to review a case unless you are under contract and ready to process it. Also, avoid conversation with opposing attorneys—there's no such thing as an "off the record" conversation with opposing attorneys. Have a fee agreement ready to be e-mailed or faxed to the attorney to protect your livelihood from this abusive practice; this agreement documents that the attorney did not want to retain you, and if you are retained, it puts you in a better position to collect a fee.

Documenting and Preparing Evidence

Document your steps to make sure they are repeatable if challenged. When you gather and preserve technical evidence, make sure what you have done can be repeated. Without the ability to repeat your processes, your findings lose credibility as evidence. This guideline applies to all computer evidence. As emphasized in earlier chapters, always preserve the evidence you find and document how you preserved it. In addition, validate your tools and use MD5 or SHA-1 to perform hash checks on evidence before and after to ensure its integrity.

Do not create a formal checklist of your procedures or integrate a checklist into your final reports. Opposing counsel can easily challenge a checklist or use it during cross-examination to search for inconsistencies in your performance, compared to your documented organizational or personal procedures.

As a standard practice, collect your evidence and record the tools you used in designated file folders. This helps maintain the organization of your evidence and the tools you used. Follow a system in your office or laboratory to record where items are kept for each case and how documentation is stored.

Remember that the chain of custody of evidence supports the integrity of your evidence; do whatever you can to prevent contamination of the evidence. Document any lapse or gap in evidence preservation or custody. Lapses and gaps don't necessarily result in evidence being inadmissible, but they might affect the weight given to the evidence.

You can use the Internet to learn about opposing experts and to try to find their strengths and weaknesses in previous testimony. See how they present themselves and print their curriculum vitae, if possible. Your attorney might be able to get copies of depositions that opposing witnesses have given in other cases. As mentioned previously, many attorneys are members of organizations that maintain deposition banks containing thousands of depositions. Some organizations of digital investigators also maintain electronic mailing lists that you can use to query members about firms or expert witnesses.

When collecting evidence, be careful not to get too little or too much information. Remember that for litigation, you are responsible only for collecting what's asked for, no more. In some circumstances, collecting and identifying evidence on problems unrelated to the case could cause problems for your attorney.

NOTE   Make sure you note the date and time of your forensic workstation when initiating your analysis. If precise time is at issue, consider using an Internet clock, such as *www.time.gov*, or an atomic clock that's set several times each day by radio transmissions to verify the accuracy of your workstation's clock. Many retailers, such as Wal-Mart and Radio Shack, now sell atomic clocks.

Processing Evidence

As you process evidence, be sure to always monitor, preserve, and validate your work. Doing so helps ensure that it can be presented to best effect in court.

If you need a checklist to analyze evidence in a case, create it for a specific analysis, not a general one to be applied to other cases. If opposing counsel obtains a checklist through discovery that has been used on previous examinations and analysis, you can expect him or her to attempt to use your deviations from it against you in the current case.

Keep only successful output when running analysis tools; don't keep previous runs, such as those missing necessary switch settings or output settings of your software tools.

Whenever possible, use SHA-1 to validate your evidence because it uses a higher level of computation. Use MD5 or CRC-32 only if SHA-1 is unavailable. When examining evidence disks or files, perform an SHA-1 or a MD5 hash check before and after your examination of the evidence to ensure that nothing was altered during your data collection.

When searching for keyword results, rerun searches with well-defined search parameters. You might even want to state how the search parameters relate to the case, such as being business or personal names or nicknames. Narrow the search so that you eliminate false hits. Eliminate previous search results that contain false-positive hits from your final output.

When taking notes of your findings, keep them simple and specific to the investigation. You should avoid any personal comments or ideas in your note taking to minimize any need to explain to opposing counsel what you wrote.

When writing your report, list only the evidence that's relevant to the case. That is, list only the data you find that makes a difference in the outcome; do not include unrelated findings.

Serving as a Consulting Expert or an Expert Witness

Depending on the attorney's needs, you might need to provide only your opinion and technical expertise to the attorney instead of testifying in court. You might be hired as a consulting expert initially, but your role could become that of an expert witness later in the case. If that happens, all your previous work as a consulting expert is subject to discovery by opposing counsel.

14

Because your work might be discovered or formally requested by a court officer, do not record conversations or telephone calls. Doing so might create more work for you and the hiring attorney to explain than what's necessary for the case.

When presenting yourself to a federal court as an expert witness, federal rules require that you provide the following information:

- Four years of previous testimony you might have provided, which indicates that you have experience at trial
- Ten years of any published writings
- Previous compensation you might have received when giving testimony

When preparing for your testimony, learn about the victim, the complainant, opposing experts or technical and scientific witnesses, and the opposing attorney as soon as possible. Learn the basic points of the dispute. As you learn about the case for which you're testifying, take notes, but keep them in rough draft form, recording only the facts and keeping your notations to a minimum.

Define any procedures you use to conduct your analysis as scientific and conforming to the standards of your profession. Pointing to textbooks, technical books, articles by recognized experts, and procedures from responsible and authoritative agencies or companies are common ways to prove your conformity with scientific and professional standards.

When approached to give expert testimony, find out whether you are the first one asked. If you aren't the first person contacted, find out why other experts might have been contacted and not retained.

Creating and Maintaining Your CV

Your **curriculum vitae (CV)** tells your professional life story and is used to qualify your testimony. As a forensic specialist, keeping this document updated at all times is crucial to supporting your role as an expert. Organize your CV so that it shows you're continuously enhancing your skills through training, teaching, and experience.

In your CV, detail your job tasks to define specific accomplishments and list your basic and advanced skills. Also, indicate the professional training you have received. If the list of your training is lengthy or difficult to complete, introduce the list with language such as "Selected Training Attended." Be sure to include coursework sponsored by government agencies or organizations that train government agency personnel or courses sponsored or approved by professional associations, such as bar associations. Make sure your CV reflects you professionally. Unlike a job resume, it should not be geared for a specific trial.

Keep a separate list of books read on your specialized area of expertise, but don't include your reading list on the CV. Books listed on a CV might suggest that you approve of everything written in every book on the list.

Make sure you include a testimony log in your CV, which records every testimony you have given as an expert. Most of all, keep the CV current and date it for version control. If your

CV is more than three months old, you probably need to update it to reflect new cases and additional training.

Preparing Technical Definitions

Before you testify in court, prepare definitions of technical material so that you can provide them as answers when questioned by your attorney and the opposing attorney. When preparing your definitions, use your own words and language. You don't need to make the jury subject matter experts; you're simply explaining how a tool works.

The following are examples of definitions to prepare ahead of time for your testimony:

- Computer forensics
- CRC-32, MD5, and SHA-1 hash functions
- Image and bit-stream backups
- File slack and unallocated (free) space
- File date and time stamps
- Computer log files

TESTIFYING IN COURT

14

Before you are called to testify in court, become familiar with the usual procedures followed during a trial. First, your attorney demonstrates to the court that you are competent as an expert or technical witness. The opposing counsel might attempt to discredit you or might choose not to based on your past record. Your attorney then leads you through the evidence, and then opposing counsel cross-examines you. After your testimony, you might be called back to update your testimony, or you might be called as a rebuttal witness.

Understanding the Trial Process

The typical order of trial proceedings is as follows:

1. *Motions in limine*—Special hearing on admissibility of evidence or limitation of evidence (typically done a day or two before the beginning of trial, but always before trial begins). Effectively, it's a written list of objections to certain testimony or exhibits. It allows the judge to examine whether certain evidence should be admitted out of the jury's presence.

2. *Empanelling of the jury*—Includes voir dire of venireman, strikes, and seating of jurors.

3. *Opening statements*—Provide an overview of the case.

4. *Plaintiff*—Plaintiff presents the case.

5. *Defendant*—Defendant presents the case.

6. *Rebuttal*—Rebuttal from both plaintiff and defense.

7. *Closing arguments*—Statements that organize the evidence and the law.

8. *Jury instructions*—Instructions proposed by counsel and approved and read to the jury by the judge.

Qualifying Your Testimony and Voir Dire

During the qualification phase of your testimony, your attorney demonstrates your qualifications that make you an expert witness. It puts you above your competition and sets you apart from other expert witnesses with the jury. This qualification phase is called **voir dire** (from the French, literally "to see, to say").

The court might appoint its own expert witnesses. Court-appointed expert witnesses must be neutral in their initial position and opinion, and they must be knowledgeable about their profession. As an expert hired by the defense or plaintiff, you need to evaluate the court's expert. Make sure you brief your attorney on your findings and opinion of the court's expert to help your attorney better deal with the case and any testimony the court-appointed expert provides.

Opposing attorneys sometimes use the tactic of attempting to have you disqualified as a witness. At trial, the attorney who hired you qualifies you as an expert by guiding you through your CV. After your attorney has completed his or her examination on your qualifications, he or she asks the court to accept you as an expert on computer forensics. However, opposing counsel might object and is allowed to examine you also.

If you have especially strong qualifications and have been qualified as an expert on several occasions, opposing counsel might offer to accept you as an expert without your qualifications being formally stated. Generally, your attorney bypasses that offer in favor of impressing the jury with your qualifications.

Addressing Potential Problems

Early in direct examination, the attorney should ask you if you were hired to perform an analysis and to testify. The attorney might ask how much you charged for your services and whether you have already been paid; you should receive payment before testifying. If you have not been paid, it might appear that you have a contingent interest in the litigation. Fees and payment schedules are an appropriate subject area for examination. If your attorney doesn't ask you questions about payment, the opposing counsel will, and will attempt to make the most of it as an effort to discredit you or lessen your credibility as a witness.

Testifying in General

During the trial, be conscious of the jury, judge, and attorneys; try to learn their knowledge and attitudes related to computers and technology. If asked a question you cannot answer, respond by saying, "That is beyond the scope of my expertise" or "I was not requested to investigate that." These statements make it clear that you understand your limitations. Everybody has limitations; you won't seem less of an expert for knowing and expressing your limitations. If anything, expressing your limitations enhances your standing with a jury.

A scientific or technical witness testifies to facts. An expert witness gives an opinion for testifying. When you're serving in either capacity, be professional and polite when presenting yourself to any attorney or the court. If you don't understand a question or find it confusing, simply say, "Can you please rephrase the question?" Typically, this response gets the attorney to reorganize the question and is one method you can use to control the attorney. When presenting yourself, always acknowledge the jury and direct your testimony to the jury. Always put enthusiasm and sincerity in your testimony to keep the jury interested in what you have to say.

Be aware of leading questions, especially from the opposing attorney. An ambiguous question such as "Isn't it true that forensics experts always destroy their handwritten notes?" is an attempt to lead you to say something that could be construed as wrong. Leading questions such as this one are referred to as "setup questions."

When giving expert testimony, avoid overreaching opinions. Part of what you have to deliver to the jury is a person (you) they can trust to help them figure out something that's beyond their expertise. To overreach or overstate an opinion creates the potential for mistrust or doubt with the jury; like a teacher, you should admit your limitations and the limitations of your results.

When testifying, build repetition into your explanations and descriptions for the jury. To enhance your image with the jury, dress in a manner that conforms to the community's dress code. For example, clothing that is black, dark green, or yellow might not be appropriate. In a small town, dress like the local bank manager or in clothes similar to what the attorneys are wearing. If your testimony is being videotaped, avoid fine stripes in suits or ties.

If a microphone is present during your testimony, place it six to eight inches from you, and remember to project your voice so that your words are both recorded and heard by the jury.

If the question asked is awkwardly stated or you aren't sure of the intent, ask the attorney for clarification. If necessary, insert your comments in the question. In your speech, use simple, direct language to help the jury understand you. For example, use "test" instead of "analyze," as in "I ran a test on the files I found."

Use chronological order to describe events when testifying, and use hand gestures to help the audience understand what you are emphasizing. For example, point to graphics while talking. Also, make sure you use specific, articulate speech when speaking; for clarity, avoid contractions such as "can't or don't."

When asked a question by an attorney or the judge, turn toward the questioner, and then turn back to the jury to give the answer. If you're using technical terms, identify and define all the key terms for the jury, using analogies and graphics as appropriate. List any important technical elements, showing how you verified and validated each element. Speak clearly and

14

loudly enough so the jury can hear you, using a courteous tone. Do not use slang unless you are quoting a fact related to the case. Make sure the height of the witness chair makes you look presentable to the jury, and turn the chair so that it faces the jury.

When giving an opinion, cite the source of the evidence that the opinion is based on. Then express your opinion and explain your methodology—that is, how you arrived at your opinion.

Presenting Your Evidence

For direct examinations, state your opinion, identify evidence to support your opinion, and then relate the method you used to arrive at your opinion from your analysis. Restate your opinion, but never carry on with a lengthy build-up. Books and other documentation are useful but are not considered authoritative for testimony.

As an expert witness, you have to keep your audience in mind. You have a judge who is well educated, but not necessarily in the field of digital evidence. Jurors typically average just over 12 years of education and an eighth-grade reading level. The attorneys might have a thorough background or foundation in the field, but you are the expert with experience. You could also be dealing with an arbiter or mediator who may or may not have a background in computer forensics.

Consider the following questions when preparing your testimony:

- What is my story of the case?
- What can I say with confidence?
- What is the client's overall theory of the case?
- How does my opinion support the case?
- What is the scope of the case? Have I gone too far?
- Have I identified the client's needs?

You should have definitions ready for terms such as MD5, CRC-32, checksum, and SHA-1. You should familiarize yourself with the principles of electromagnetic theory to explain how data is stored on a disk drive. Learn how to describe the tools you use as a standardized practice or process flow for your work. Remember to state your descriptions so that a nontechnical person can understand them. Make sure you're knowledgeable about the fallibility of computer forensics to better resist counterattacks from opposing counsel. Lengthy explanations might be good for some jury cases but not for others, so seek your attorney's opinion.

When called on to provide testimony for a case, prepare it with the attorney who hired you and is trying the case. The following are specific questions you should prepare for:

- How is data (or evidence) stored on a hard disk drive?
- What is an image or a bit-stream copy of a disk drive?
- How is deleted data recovered from a disk drive?

- What are Windows temporary files and how do they relate to data or evidence?
- What are system or network log files?

When being called to testify, do not talk to anyone during court recess. If the opposing attorney sees you having a conversation with anyone, including the attorney you represent, the opposing attorney could cross-examine you again and demand that you explain and repeat your conversation. However, be aware that your attorney might want to notify you of any updates during breaks, so make sure you conduct any conferences in a private setting.

Helping Your Attorney

Talk to local attorneys to learn more about the type of people typically serving on a jury. Gauge your presentation to the jury's educational level, and incorporate appropriate analogies into your explanations.

When preparing your testimony for direct examination, develop a script and work with your attorney to get the right language that most effectively communicates your message to the jury.

Avoiding Testimony Problems

Always be an impartial expert witness, not an advocate. Be clear about your opinion, and define your boundaries of knowledge and ethics if necessary. Always build a business case for the justification of items such as graphics that improve your testimony, which could be considered an unnecessary expense. Build a case outline and summary for the attorney. You and the attorney can use this information to review your plan and to make sure he or she understands your level of knowledge about the case. Learn how you are expected to perform for your attorney and how you fit into the case. Make your best effort to coordinate your testimony with other experts your attorney has retained in support of the case. Make time with the attorney to ensure that he or she knows all the facts and your opinion. Above all, don't lie or misrepresent your expertise.

Take time to tutor the attorney in your area of expertise. To do this, you can create memorandums that list important items by bullets and build a glossary for technical terms.

Testifying During Direct Examination

Although many cases never make it to court, you provide direct testimony when you testify on behalf of the attorney who hired you. The direct examination is the most important part of testimony at a trial. Cross-examination is not as important, even if the opposing attorney is attempting to discredit you.

There are some effective direct testimony techniques you can use. State your background and qualifications that relate to why you are an expert able to give testimony. Provide a clear overview of your findings. Create a systematic and easy-to-follow plan for describing your evidence-collection methods. Balance between technical language and layperson language when describing complex matters. Remember to gauge your speech to the jury's educational level.

Be prepared by knowing the following terms and issues before giving testimony:

- *Independent recollection*—Things you know about this case and others without being prompted
- *Customary practice*—Procedures that are traditionally followed in similar cases
- *Documentation of the case*—The actual written records you have maintained

When questioned, give answers that bring attention to your factual findings and opinion, looking at the jury to keep them engaged with your answers. Remember to project your voice when speaking. Prepare with your attorney for your testimony, and before testifying, contribute to the examination plan your attorney is preparing. Your attorney uses these questions for his or her direct examination of you.

Practice testifying with your graphics, and always let the jury see your face when working with your graphics. If you have to draw something and explain it in detail, do one thing at a time—that is, draw your diagram or illustration, and then turn toward the jury and give your explanation. Keep in mind that you're basically instructing the jury in what you had to do to collect the evidence. Play the part of a good teacher for the jury.

When you meet before a trial or deposition to discuss the case, your attorney might advise you to be wary of your inclination to be helpful. This natural trait can hurt you when testifying. You should not volunteer any information or be overly friendly (or hostile) to the opposing attorney. Your attorney might also help you develop a theme to follow when presenting your testimony. Use your own words when answering questions. If you're asked whether you perform tasks the same way on every case, respond by saying, "That is my practice, to do it that way." In court, the best approach your attorney can take is to ask you "Then what?" and let you give your testimony.

Avoid vagueness. For example, don't use expressions such as "very large," "a long time," "very fast," and so forth. The appropriate terminology is to use precise numbers and units of measurement and to cite their statistical position, or the numbers' relationship to the mean.

Using Graphics During Testimony

Create graphical exhibits, such as charts and tables, that illustrate and clarify your findings. Make sure the jury can see your graphics, and face the jury as you present the graphics. Practice using charts for courtroom testimony. Your exhibits must be clear and easy to understand. Exhibits should be big and bold so that the jury can see them easily.

If necessary, make smaller copies of your graphics for each jury member so that they can see any details better. When talking about specific areas of your illustrations, use a pointer. When creating graphics, provide information the jury needs to know, such as how the mechanics of the hardware and software work, the role the evidence has in relation to the case, and an explanation of the evidence findings for the case.

As a general rule, visual information and memory retention is much weaker for audio and slightly stronger for visual. The most reliable method is combining audio and visual. Graphics that you prepare for trial should be big, bold, appealing, simple, and straightforward, with one item per graphic and only two dimensions. Each graphic should contain clear and understandable messages. It is the attorney's responsibility to ensure that graphical exhibits are admitted into evidence.

Prepare at least two copies of the graphics you use—one for your attorney and one for the opposing attorney. Review all graphics that you prepare for testimony with your attorney before trial. Do not include vendor logos on the charts, and create your own charts rather than use someone else's because you have to explain them yourself. Use two or more graphics for complex technical descriptions, with the first graphic providing an overview. Subsequent graphics should become more complex as needed to communicate the information.

Display the graphic during your testimony and face the jury to explain it. Use a pointer to direct their attention to the details of each point. If the graphic display is not near the jury box, ask the judge if you can move it so that the jury can see it better. If an attorney asks you questions as you explain the graphic, face the jury and answer the questions in full sentences. If you are right-handed, use your right hand to hold the pointer as you talk. Your left hand should be active, too; that is, gesture with that hand, making sure any gestures are above the waist. You can use your hands in addition to a pointer to help you emphasize certain information or direct attention to specific points. Make sure the jury sees you at all times and can see at what you are pointing when you're testifying. When standing in front of the jury with your graphics, leave your suit jacket unbuttoned and keep your elbows bent. Wear a dark suit with a white or light blue shirt. Men should wear conservative ties with a base color of red. For women who prefer to wear suits, conservative colors are advisable. If you prefer a dress, you should be able to move freely in it and sit and stand without worry. Another opinion on dress code for expert witnesses recommends dressing in the same fashion as the local bank manager. The reason is to influence the jury by associating your presence and persona with that of a respected figure in the community.

Testifying During Cross-examination

After your attorney has established your credentials and you have presented your evidence, the opposing attorney has an opportunity to ask questions about your testimony and evidence, a process called cross-examination. If the opposing attorney asks you something you do not know, a good answer is "I don't know." Never guess when you have no knowledge about a subject in question.

When answering questions from the opposing attorney, use your own words, not those of the opposing attorney. Certain words have additional meanings that an opposing attorney can easily exploit. For example, the word "suspicious" is more value laden than the more neutral "concerned."

During cross-examination, one trick opposing attorneys use is to interrupt you as you're answering a question. In a trial, a judge usually doesn't allow this, but in a deposition, there's no independent arbiter of procedure.

If the opposing attorney asks you a question such as "Did you use more than one tool to verify the evidence?" he or she is checking to make sure you validated the findings from one tool by using another tool. The following are other questions opposing attorneys often ask:

- What are the tools used and what are their known problems or weak features?

- Are the tools you used reliable? Are they consistent, and do they produce the same results?

- Have you been called on as a consultant on how to use tools from other professionals?

- Do you keep up with the latest technologies applied to computer forensics, such as by reading journal articles?

Some questions can cause conflicting answers. Be aware of questions that are posed to cause you to give conflicting answers. Your best offense for troublesome questions is to be patient with your answers. Speaking slowly also helps significantly. During examinations, lawyers are not supposed to ask another question until you have finished answering the current question. Shifting or turning toward the jury slowly when you give your response allows you to maintain control over the flow of the opposing attorney's examination.

In many instances, the opposing counsel uses rapid-fire questions meant to throw you off. Don't be afraid to regroup and restate your answers if you get confused during your testimony. The jurors will sympathize because typically they too are often confused by the opposing attorney's questions. If the opposing attorney causes you to turn away from the jury, take your time turning back toward the jury to answer the question.

If the opposing attorney declares that you are not answering the questions, he could be making an attempt to get you to change your testimony. You are not giving the answer he wants or he is attempting to get you to say something that contradicts part of your previous testimony. Don't take this personally, but think carefully about what the opposing attorney is trying to do.

Keep eye contact at all times with the jury. You might find yourself competing with the opposing attorney, but do your best to keep the jury's attention on you during your testimony. As the opposing attorney asks you questions, avoid flat yes or no answers; add the necessary facts to clarify your answer when appropriate. Make it a habit to insert your opinion or facts before the opposing attorney can hit you with the killer question, which is one you can't answer or deny. It's a question that can derail your testimony and the case for your client.

Sometimes opposing attorneys ask several questions inside one question; this practice is called compound questions. Your attorney should object to this question by calling it a compound question or by saying "Counsel has not allowed the witness to answer the question." If your attorney does not object, you can respond by saying "Could you please break your last question into individual questions?" Your response to these methods should challenge the opposing attorney to be more sensible, a response that often plays well with juries. Responding to a question with a sentence that communicates limitations or qualifications might be important in some circumstances, if a simple yes or no response can't answer the question completely and accurately.

Another tactic opposing attorneys use in cross-examinations is to make a speech and phrase it as a question. You have no obligation to respond to statements by opposing counsel. The judge usually catches this error, and your attorney should also object.

Some methods opposing attorneys use to challenge your credibility are putting words in your mouth and summarizing your testimony to fit their needs, creating assumptions or speculation, and controlling the pace of your testimony. Other tactics are stating minor inconsistencies that cause you to make conflicting statements and encouraging you to volunteer information. When in court or during a deposition, take your time to answer questions. Be courteous in your responses, and expand yes or no answers with qualifying information. Sound interested in what is being asked and said.

The more patient you are during the cross-examination, the better you will weather any possible attacks. When the opposing attorney becomes assertive or upset with your testimony, be as professional and courteous as possible. The opposing attorney might continue to lose control, which strengthens your image.

14

In general, maintain a vigorous demeanor and use energetic speech to make people want to listen to you. Build variety in your presentation to maintain the jury's interest. Be fluent, keep going, and stay comfortable during your testimony. Use extemporaneous speech; do not memorize your testimony.

Many factors contribute to your stress on the stand, including the judge, the attorneys, the jury, and the feeling of losing control. Do not feel you are responsible for the outcome. If you make a mistake, correct it, and get back on track with your testimony. You want to avoid losing control, which can be shown by any of the following behaviors:

- Being argumentative when being badgered by the opposing attorney or being nervous about testifying
- Having an unresponsive attorney who does not object to the opposing attorney's questions
- Having poor listening skills or using negative body language
- Being too talkative when answering questions
- Being too technical for the jury to understand your testimony
- Acting surprised and unprepared to respond when presented with unknown or new information

Never have unrealistically high self-expectations when testifying; everyone makes mistakes. Who controls the testimony is the most important part for the attorney. This applies for both direct examination and cross-examination. You can't remember everything. If you don't remember, simply say so to the attorney during the examination. The key to successful cross-examination is to continue selling yourself to the jury, no matter how much the opposing attorney tries to discredit you.

Exercising Ethics When Testifying

Be aware of negative influence from attorneys attempting to alter your opinion or fact-finding. Letting these negative influences alter your opinion and answers creates a failure on your part to remain ethical in your testimony. Explain yourself technically (describing the mechanical processes involved), not scientifically. You are not expected to explain the physics of magnetic fields, for example, but you might legitimately have to explain sectors, blocks, cylinders, and heads or the difference between a bit and a byte. If your attorney misunderstands the technology and asks a poorly worded question, reply "Can you repeat the question?" This response helps the attorney correct the question or retract it. (You can avoid this situation by preparing an examination plan that you and the attorney agree on and by reviewing the anticipated testimony.)

Understanding Prosecutorial Misconduct

If you are working for a prosecutor in a criminal case and believe you have found exculpatory evidence (evidence tending to exonerate or diminish the liability of a defendant), you have an obligation to ensure that the evidence is not concealed. Initially, you should report the evidence (emphasizing its exculpatory nature) to the prosecutor handling the case. If it's not disclosed to the defendant's counsel in a reasonable time, you can report this information to the prosecutor's supervisor, if he or she has one. If this still does not result in disclosure, you can report the lack of disclosure to the court (the judge). Do not directly communicate with the defense counsel; reporting evidence to the court fulfills your obligation. Document each attempt to induce disclosure and include your reasoning.

PREPARING FOR A DEPOSITION

A **deposition** differs from a trial testimony because there is no jury or judge. Both attorneys are present and ask you questions. The purpose of the deposition is for the opposing attorney to preview your testimony at trial. The attorney who requests a deposition usually establishes its location, which might be in an office or in your computer forensics laboratory.

There are two types of depositions: discovery and testimony preservation. A **discovery deposition** is part of the discovery process for trial. It is an examination under oath before trial with no judge present. The opposing attorney who requested the deposition frequently conducts the equivalent of a direct examination and a cross-examination.

A **testimony preservation deposition** is usually requested by your client to preserve your testimony in case of schedule conflicts or health problems. In some cases, you can set the deposition at your laboratory or have lab facilities available, which can make it easier to conduct demonstrations and produce better testimony.

Guidelines for Testifying at a Deposition

Overall, stay calm and convey a relaxed, confident appearance during a deposition. Maintain a professional demeanor and try not to be influenced by the opposing attorney's tone, expression, or tactics. Learn the name of the opposing attorney before the deposition so that you can respond to his or her questions with his or her name. Using the opposing attorney's name can help you control the deposition. Look the opposing attorney directly in the eyes, even if he or she attempts to avoid eye contact. During a deposition, opposing attorneys often interrupt you before you can complete your answer in an effort to confuse you. Be assertive in your responses. If possible, ask your attorney to videotape a practice session of you giving a deposition, and then evaluate your performance.

When sitting at a table in front of the opposing attorney, try to keep your hands on top of the table. Keep your hands away from your face; this behavior shows indecision and weakness. If you wear glasses, keep them on at all times, especially during videotaped depositions. Make sure your chair is at the best height possible to avoid sitting below the opposing attorney's eye level.

Here are some general rules to follow during depositions:

- Be professional and polite.
- Use facts when describing your opinion.
- Understand that being deposed in a discovery deposition is an unnatural process; it's intended to get you to make mistakes.

In general, take your time answering questions, making sure your answer is correct and you're stating it clearly. If you prepared a written report, the opposing attorney might attempt to use it against you by leading you to testify contrary to what you had previously written. If the attorney is concealing the report or any other document from your view, ask to see the document.

If your attorney objects to a question from the opposing attorney, pause and think of what direction your attorney might want you to go in your answer. Keep your answers short, in the form of phrases. Make the answers sound friendly, especially if you're being videotaped. To gain time and control, ask the opposing attorney questions. For example, ask the opposing attorney to repeat the question. When reviewing a report you have written and the opposing attorney asks you about something specific in the report, ask what page number he or she is referring to in the report. If you don't have the report in your hands, you can ask to review it.

14

Be prepared at the end of a deposition to spell any specialized or technical words you used. To aid court reporters, bring a list of technical or scientific words you frequently use, including definitions and correct spellings.

Recognizing Deposition Problems

Discuss any potential problems with your attorney before the deposition. Identify anything that might negatively affect your client and could be used by the opposing attorney. If you don't disclose this information, the opposing attorney will use it against you in court. Be prepared to defend yourself if there are possible problems. Avoid omitting information in your testimony; omissions can cause major problems. Although you don't have to volunteer more information than an attorney asks for, make sure you're telling the truth at all times. To respond to difficult questions that could jeopardize your client's case, pause before answering, allowing your attorney to object before you answer.

To avoid having the opposing attorney box you into a corner or lead you to contradict previous statements, answer only the questions you are asked, using short answers that are narrow in scope when possible. Recognize that excessively detailed questions from the opposing attorney are an attempt to get you to contradict yourself. Avoid trying to educate the opposing attorney, especially if the questions appear to be misguided—for example, beyond the scope of your expertise or the questions you were retained to answer. Feel free to give answers such as "I don't know" or "I don't understand." Keep in mind that you can correct any minor errors you make during your examination and reporting after you give your deposition. You'll be asked at the end of the deposition if you waive signature; if you want to review the deposition, you should not waive signature because you then get a chance then to review, correct, and sign the deposition. Also, discovery deposition testimony typically doesn't make it to the jury; however, it might be presented to the jury, usually as part of an attempt to discredit the witness. This process is called "publishing the deposition."

When asked whether you know about an opposing expert witness, your response should be as professional as possible. A good standard answer is "I have heard Mr. Smith is a competent examiner, but I have not reviewed his work." If you have specific and verifiable information that is damaging to the opposing expert's reputation, you can note it, but do it in an understated manner. This technique works best, especially if you have negative information about the opposing expert's skills or competency.

Public Release: Dealing with Reporters

Some legal actions generate interest from the news media, but you should avoid contact with them, especially during a case. If you are solicited for information or opinions by journalists (or anyone else), avoid saying anything; refer them to your client (the attorney who retained you). If you cannot avoid a journalist, consult with your attorney and determine how to address the situation. Plan to record any attempted interviews so that you have your own record of what occurred. (Note, however, that state laws on consent for recording vary.) This recording can be important if you are misquoted or quoted out of context. Reporters often look for a sensational sound bite or controversial quote.

You should avoid talking to the news media for the following reasons:

- Your comments could harm the case.

- It creates a record that can be used against you.

- You have no control over the context of the information the journalist publishes.

- You cannot rely on a journalist's promises of confidentiality. Journalists have been known to be aggressive in getting information. Their interests do not coincide with yours or your client's. Be on guard at all times, as your comments could be interpreted in a manner that taints your impartiality in a case and future cases. Even after the case is resolved, avoid discussing the details with the press.

CHAPTER SUMMARY

- When cases go to trial, you as the forensics expert play one of two roles: You are called as either a technical witness or an expert witness. As a technical or scientific witness, you are only providing the facts as you have found them in your investigation. However, as an expert witness, you have opinions about what you observe. In fact, it's your opinion that makes you an expert witness.

- If you are called as a technical or expert witness in a computer forensics case, you need to thoroughly prepare for your testimony. Establish communication early on with your attorney. When preparing to testify for any litigation, substantiate your findings with your own documentation and by collaborating with other computer forensic professionals.

- As you process evidence, be sure to always monitor, preserve, and validate your work. Doing so helps ensure that it can be presented in court. Then submit to your attorney all evidence you collected and analyzed. When writing your report, list only the evidence findings that are relevant to the case.

- When you are called to testify in court, your attorney examines you on your qualifications to inform the court that you are competent as an expert or a technical witness. The opposing counsel might attempt to discredit you or may choose not to based on your past record. Your attorney then leads you through the evidence followed by the opposing counsel cross-examining you. Redirect examinations and recross examinations of limited scope might follow.

- A deposition differs from a trial because there is no jury or judge. Both attorneys and a court reporter are present, and the attorney asks you questions. There are two types of deposition: discovery and testimony preservation.

- Know whether you are being called as a scientific/technical witness or expert witness (or both) and whether you are being retained as a consulting expert or an expert witness. Also, be familiar with the contents of your curriculum vitae.

- Reports should answer the questions you were retained to answer and minimize incorporation of information that doesn't support answering the specific questions.

14

❑ A well-defined report structure contributes to the readers' ability to understand the information you are communicating.

❑ Clarity of writing is critical to the success of a report. In addition, reports need to be grammatically sound, use correct spelling, and be free of writing errors. Avoid jargon, slang, or colloquial terms.

❑ Project objectivity; be detached in your observations for your report. Stand back from the details and synthesize what has (and has not) been learned about the problem, and determine what it all means.

KEY TERMS

conflicting out — When you already have knowledge or have rendered an opinion about a case before you are hired.

curriculum vitae (CV) — An extensive resume of your professional history that includes not only your education, training, work, and what cases you have worked on, but also training you have conducted, publications you have contributed to, and professional associations and awards.

deposed — To be called on to testify in a deposition.

deposition — A formal examination in which you are questioned under oath with only the opposing parties, your attorney, and a court reporter present. There is no judge or jury.

deposition banks — Libraries of previously given testimony that law firms have access to.

discovery — The efforts to obtain information before a trial by demanding documents, depositions, interrogatories (written questions answered in writing under oath), and written requests for admissions of fact.

discovery deposition — The opposing attorney sets the deposition and frequently conducts the equivalent of both direct and cross-examination. A discovery deposition is considered part of discovery. *See also* deposition.

examination plan — A document that lets you know what questions to expect when you are testifying.

expert witness — A person who has specialized knowledge in a field, acquired through experience, training, and/or education, and can offer an opinion about the facts in addition to stating observed facts.

high-risk documents — Documents containing sensitive information that could create an advantage for the opposing attorney.

lay witness — A witness whose testimony is based on observation; not considered to be an expert in a particular field.

spoliation — Destroying or concealing evidence; subject to sanctions.

technical (or scientific) witness — A person who has performed an examination or observed technical or scientific work. This person can testify to the observed facts, but does not offer an opinion in court.

testimony preservation deposition — This deposition is set by your attorney-client to preserve your testimony in case of schedule conflicts or health problems. In some cases, this deposition is conducted at your laboratory to make it easier to conduct demonstrations and improve your testimony. *See also* deposition.

voir dire — The process of qualifying a witness as an expert in his or her field. (From the French: literally, "to see, to say.")

REVIEW QUESTIONS

1. Which of the following rules or laws requires an expert to prepare and disclose a report?

    a. FRCP 26

    b. FRE 801

    c. neither of the above

    d. both of the above

2. The hypothetical question has traditionally been used in what context in litigation?

    a. to frame the factual context of the rendering of an expert witness's opinion

    b. to define the issues of the case for determination by the finder of fact (the jury or judge if there is no jury)

    c. to stimulate discussion between the consulting expert and the expert witness

    d. to deter the witness from expanding the scope of his or her investigation beyond the requirements of the case

3. If you were a lay witness at a previous trial, you should not list that case in your written report. True or False?

4. An example of a written report is:

    a. a search warrant

    b. an affidavit

    c. voir dire

    d. any of the above

5. Destroying a report before a final resolution has been reached is called what?

6. An expert witness can give an opinion if:

    a. The opinion, inferences, or conclusions depend on special knowledge, skill, or training not within the ordinary experience of laypersons.

    b. The witness is shown to be qualified as a true expert in the particular field of expertise.

    c. The witness testifies to a reasonable degree of certainty (probability) regarding his opinion, inference, or conclusion.

    d. all of the above

14

7. After the report is complete, you should:
   a. Run a spell check.
   b. Turn it in immediately.
   c. Check for grammar errors.
   d. Do both a and c.

8. Reports filed electronically in federal courts should be in what format?
   a. Word document
   b. Excel document
   c. PDF document
   d. HTML document
   e. any of the above

9. List two sources who can ask you questions in the courtroom in addition to the attorney who hired you.

10. Which of the following describes scientific or technical testimony?
    a. factual testimony describing the information recovered in a scientific or technical examination
    b. only evidence that conforms to the rules described in *United States v. Frye*
    c. only evidence that conforms to the rules described in *Daubert v. Merrill Dow*
    d. none of the above

11. Which of the following describes expert witness testimony?
    a. testimony designed to assist the finder of fact in determining matters beyond the scope of the knowledge of the ordinary person
    b. testimony that defines the issues of the case for determination by the finder of fact
    c. testimony that results in the expression of an opinion by a witness with scientific, technical, or other professional knowledge or experience
    d. a and c

12. When using graphics while testifying, which of the following guidelines apply?
    a. Make sure the jury can see your graphics.
    b. Practice using charts for courtroom testimony.
    c. Your exhibits must be clear and easy to understand.
    d. Make sure you have plenty of extra graphics, in case you have to explain more complex or supporting issues.
    e. a, b, and c

13. What kind of information do scientific or technical witnesses provide during a testimony?

    a. their professional opinion on the significance of evidence

    b. definitions of the issues to be determined by the finder of fact

    c. facts only

    d. all of the above

14. What expressions are acceptable to use in testimony to respond to a question for which you have no answer?

    a. No comment.

    b. That is beyond the scope of my expertise.

    c. I don't want to answer that question.

    d. I was not requested to investigate that.

    e. b and d

15. While working for a prosecutor, what do you think you should do if the evidence you found appears to be exculpatory and is not being released to the defense?

    a. Keep the information on file for later review.

    b. Bring the information to the attention of the prosecutor, his or her supervisor, or finally to the judge (the court).

    c. Destroy the evidence.

    d. Present the evidence to the defense attorney.

14

16. The names, addresses, and reports of which of the following people are routinely discoverable?

    a. expert witnesses

    b. technical witnesses

    c. expert consultants

    d. other attorneys who have worked on the case

    e. a and b

17. What should you do if you realize you have made a mistake or misstatement during a deposition?

    a. If the deposition is still in session, refer back to the error and correct it.

    b. Decide whether the error is minor, and if so, ignore it.

    c. If the deposition is over, make the correction on the correction page of the copy provided for your signature.

    d. Call the opposing attorney and inform him of your mistake or misstatement.

    e. a and c

18. List two types of depositions.

19. At trial as a technical, scientific, or expert witness, what must you always remember about your testimony?

   a. You are responsible for the outcome of the case.

   b. Your duty is to report your technical or scientific findings or render an honest opinion.

   c. Avoid mentioning how much you were paid for your services.

   d. all of the above

20. Voir dire is the process of qualifying a witness as an expert. True or False?

HANDS-ON PROJECTS

The Hands-on Projects in this chapter have you acting as an expert witness and rendering an opinion on a case. It is assumed at this stage that you know how to retrieve data from an image file and how to document your evidence. The current certification exams also take this approach.

HANDS-ON
PROJECTS

Project 14-1

Based on the scenario you worked with in Chapter 2, generate a three- to four-page report similar to the one generated in this chapter. The scenario concerns a company violations case involving George Montgomery. His supervisor seized a floppy disk from his desk at work. Please review the scenario in the "Examining a Company Policy Violation" section of Chapter 2 before writing the report. Make sure you include all the necessary parts of the report.

HANDS-ON
PROJECTS

Project 14-2

In this project, you examine the contents of a floppy disk and recover all data into a work folder. For additional information on this project, refer to Chapter 3 and Appendix B for FAT directory data structures.

For this project, you need:

❏ Cprj14-2.img from your student data files

❏ Digital Intelligence Image utility

❏ Computer forensics tool, such as DriveSpy, FTK, or other

❏ Blank floppy disk

❏ Disk editor, such as Hex Workshop, WinHex, Norton DiskEdit, or other

In this project, you need to collect the data on the floppy disk and place it in a work folder. Refer to previous chapters in this book for more detailed instructions on how to perform these steps.

1. Re-create the floppy image **Cprj14-2.img** from the Chap14\Projects folder to a blank floppy disk.

2. Create a target working directory on your investigation workstation.

3. Using your preferred computer forensics tool, extract all data from the floppy disk to the work folder. If you are using DriveSpy, use the DBExport command with the /MD5 and /HDR switches.

4. Attempt to open all graphics image files. If you cannot open one, analyze the file as described in the section on rebuilding file headers in Chapter 11.

5. Write a report of your findings, specifically stating all steps you took to recover the data.

Project 14-3

Contact the local FBI computer forensics lab and ask if you can get a copy of an affidavit of a case that has already closed. Write a one-page report critiquing the affidavit based on what was presented in the chapter. Did the FBI cover all the necessary items? Did the investigators retain their objectivity?

Project 14-4

In this project, you use FTK to analyze data from several floppy disks at one time. After completing the analysis, use FTK's Report Wizard to write a report stating your findings. For this project, you need the following:

❏ Cprj144a.img, Cprj144b.img, Cprj144c.img, Cprj144d.img, and Cprj144e.img from your student data files

❏ Digital Intelligence Image utility

❏ AccessData FTK (the demo version will work on this project)

❏ Five blank floppy disks to re-create the floppy image files

❏ Word processing program, such as Microsoft Word or OpenOffice.org Writer

To analyze the image files, boot your workstation to MS-DOS and follow these steps:

1. Re-create the five floppy disk image files (Cprj144a.img, Cprj144b.img, Cprj144c. img, Cprj144d.img, and Cprj144e.img) from the Chap14\Projects folder in your data files to floppy disks. (See previous chapters in this book on how to use the Digital Intelligence Image utility to complete this step.)

2. Create a work folder on your forensic workstation to process your analysis. (*Note*: Your work folder can be named **C14proj**.)

3. Use the Image utility to create separate images of each floppy, using the Raw data Image switch of /img and typing the following commands at a DOS command prompt. Note that for this exercise to work with FTK, you must give each image saved an extension of .001.

14

◻ For the first floppy, type **image a: C:*work folder*\Cprj14a.001 /img**, and then press **Enter**.

◻ For the second, third, fourth, and fifth floppies, type the following commands, and then press **Enter** after each one:

- **image a: C:*work folder*\Cprj144b.001 /img**

- **image a: C:*work folder*\Cprj144c.001 /img**

- **image a: C:*work folder*\Cprj144d.001 /img**

- **image a: C:*work folder*\Cprj144e.001 /img**

4. Using FTK, analyze the following elements for all floppy disks:

◻ All allocated and deleted files

◻ Header data values for all files

◻ MD5 hash values for all files

◻ Content of each directory

5. After examining each directory, determine what OS each file was created from, such as MS-DOS 6.22 or Windows 9x or later, and determine the dates and times each file was written to each floppy disk.

Use the following steps to analyze the files in FTK:

6. Start a new case for FTK.

7. Follow the FTK wizard. When you reach the Add Evidence dialog box, click the **Add Evidence** button. In the Add Evidence to Case dialog box, click the **Acquired Image of Drive** option button, and then click **Continue**. Navigate to and select all the *.001 files, click **Next**, and then click **Finish**.

8. From your findings, create a report with your preferred word processor that includes the following information:

◻ List each floppy disk with all directories and files it contains.

◻ Identify each file's possible origin, such as MS-DOS 6.22 or Windows 9x or later OS.

◻ List all files that might have been altered to appear to be a different file format.

◻ Give an opinion on what you have observed from this examination.

9. After you complete your narrative report, use the FTK Report Wizard to create a report. (See the FTK user manual, if necessary, for specific directions on how to use the Report Wizard and how to insert external data files.)

Project 14-5

In Chapter 5, you explored a situation in which a man was leaking information about a new bicycle design. Write a hypothetical situation that an attorney could ask you on the stand that would cover the particulars of the case without actually mentioning anything about the case.

Project 14-6

Contact your local county prosecutor's office and obtain an affidavit of a case that has already closed. Write a one-page report critiquing the affidavit based on what was presented in the chapter. Did the prosecutor's office cover all the necessary items? Do the investigators retain their objectivity?

Project 14-7

In this project, you use DriveSpy to analyze two different save-set image volumes from two different computers. After you have finished analyzing the two images, you need to compare the results from Hands-on Project 14-4. The goal of this project is to determine which data files found in Hands-on Project 14-4 came from which of these two save-set image volumes.

This project assumes you have completed Projects 14-2 and 14-4. This project also assumes you know how to configure additional disk drives on your workstation; if not, consult an A+ manual. For this project, you need the following:

▢ The case results from Hands-on Projects 14-2 and 14-4

▢ Image save-set files Cprj14_a.sav and Cprj14_b.sav from your student data files

▢ Digital Intelligence Image utility

▢ Disk-partitioning utility, such as Fdisk, Gdisk, or Partition Magic

▢ Five blank floppy disks to re-create the floppy image files

▢ One hard disk with two 50-MB partitions

▢ Word processing program, such as Microsoft Word or OpenOffice.org Writer, and spreadsheet program, such as Microsoft Excel or OpenOffice.org Calc

To re-create and analyze the image files, follow these steps:

1. Use a disk-partitioning utility to partition the target hard disk as a FAT16 disk with two partitions of 50 MB each.

2. Format both partitions.

3. Create a work folder on your forensic workstation to process your analysis

4. Run DriveSpy and restore each save-set image to the newly created partitions by using the WritePart command. (See Chapter 9 for more information on how to use the WritePart command.) Reboot your workstation when you are finished restoring the image files to both partitions.

14

5. Using DriveSpy, analyze for the following elements of each restored partition:

   ◻ All allocated and deleted files

   ◻ Header data values for all files

   ◻ MD5 hash values for all files

   ◻ Contents of each directory

   ◻ The OS each file was created from, such as MS-DOS 6.22 or Windows 9x or later

   ◻ The dates and times each file was written to each floppy disk

   Follow these steps to analyze the data and create a report:

6. Start a new case using DriveSpy, create an output file, and navigate to the investigation drive.

7. Extract and analyze all data from both partitions.

8. Create a report based on your findings, using your preferred word processor and including the following information:

   ◻ List each individual floppy with all directories and files it contains.

   ◻ Identify each file's possible origin, such as MS-DOS 6.22 or Windows 9x or later OS.

   ◻ List all files that might have been altered to appear to be a different file format.

   ◻ Give an opinion on what you have observed from this examination.

9. In your report, identify which files came from which partition. Give your expert opinion on your findings.

CASE PROJECTS

CASE PROJECTS

Case Project 14-1

In the kidnapping running case example, the investigator incorrectly combined evidence from several machines, but there was still enough evidence to locate the young lady. You need to put together the clues to show that she was enticed away by an older man on the Internet, bought a bus ticket to Oregon, and e-mailed her friend regularly about how things were progressing with him.

There are pictures of the man in the evidence. In the graphics analysis, there are several pictures of young women who may or may not be the missing young lady. You should make sure to use the bookmark feature in your software to produce the final report. Go through the list of documents and the bad extensions group, and find suspect files.

Finally, based on the original file sheet, you should generate a list of keywords and perform searches on them. Your final report should include the results.

Case Project 14-2

For the arson running case example, go through all the evidence you have collected in previous chapters (e-mail files in Chapter 13 and graphics files in Chapter 11, for example). Examine the evidence to determine whether any of it points to negligence on the part of the victims, such as the Wilbur's Mart store.

Case Project 14-3

The county prosecutor has hired you to investigate a case in which the county treasurer has been accused of embezzlement. As you collect the evidence, what should you keep in mind to ensure objectivity? Write a brief paper, no more than one page, outlining your tactics.

Case Project 14-4

Your computer investigation firm has been hired to verify the finding of the local police on a current case. Tensions over the case are running high in the city. What do you need to ask for from the police investigator, and what procedures should you follow? Write a one- to two-page report outlining what you need to do.

Case Project 14-5

A defense attorney asks you to review the report of another computer forensics technician's work on a criminal case. Write a two- to three-page paper on how you would approach a peer review of another technician's work.

CERTIFICATION TEST REFERENCES

IACIS CERTIFICATION

The International Association of Computer Investigative Specialists (IACIS) is a nonprofit organization formed to promote professional standards and to certify computer forensics examiners. Through IACIS, you can become a Certified Forensic Computer Examiner (CFCE). To qualify to take the CFCE exam, you must be an active law enforcement officer or other person qualified to be an IACIS member. For more information on qualification requirements, visit *www.cops.org*.

IACIS provides an extensive testing program to verify an individual's competence in performing a computing investigation. The examination process is not a training program; it's strictly a testing program. Applicants are screened before acceptance into the certification program, and IACIS is the sole decision maker for all applicants. IACIS offers two ways to obtain CFCE certification. The first is to attend an annual training conference that allows you to complete the certification in 12 months. The second is to apply for the examination through an external certificate program that requires completion within five months. Applying for the certification requires completing an application form and paying a fee at the time the application is submitted. For the latest information on fees for the CFCE, go to *www.cops.org/html/certification.htm*. If you are rejected for any reason, your fee is returned. If you're accepted into the program, a monitor (an IACIS CFCE member) directs you through the examination testing.

If you are accepted, you have to analyze six floppy disks, one CD, and one hard disk. The following are the requirements for the examinations:

- All disks must be examined.
- All technical matters must be solved for each disk.
- A report for each disk must be prepared and submitted to the monitor.
- All disks and reports must be submitted to the monitor within the specified completion time from the start of the testing process.

Sound forensic practices must be used for all disk examinations, including evidence control procedures and detailed written reports. Reports can be submitted to your monitor by e-mail and should be written in Microsoft Word or WordPerfect.

Reports for each disk need to contain the following information:

- Clear explanations of the procedures used to analyze the disks
- Clear explanations of what was found on each disk
- Exhibits of evidence recovered from the disks
- Detailed lists of evidence controls you have implemented for each disk examined

After you are accepted into this program, your monitor provides additional requirements, such as the type of software that can be used for each disk examination.

IACIS EXPECTATIONS FOR COMPUTER FORENSICS SKILLS

A

Tables A-1 through A-3 list the skills you need to master before taking the IACIS CFCE exam. These skills are divided into report writing, data analysis, and data acquisition proficiencies. For each skill, a corresponding chapter is listed where you can find specific information on how to perform these tasks.

Table A-1   Expected Skills for Report Writing

Skill	Covered in Chapter
Sanitizing target media with a wiping utility	Chapter 2
Maintaining chain-of-evidence procedures and documentation	Chapter 6
Writing a narrative report on how evidence was discovered	Chapter 14
Producing a formed conclusion	Chapter 14
Writing your stated opinion on the evidence you have found	Chapter 14

Table A-2   Expected Skills for Data Analysis

Skill	Covered in Chapter
Understanding file and RAM slack as well as unallocated disk space	Chapter 7
Reconstructing graphics files found in unallocated space	Chapter 11
Identifying files by header values	Chapter 10
Recovering deleted files	Chapter 10
Interpreting and forming a storyline of an examination and investigation	Chapters 10, 14
Understanding FAT file system directory structures and recovery	Chapter 7
Understanding data compression methods	Chapter 11
Searching disk data for specific hexadecimal values	Chapters 10, 14

Table A-3   Expected Skills for Data Acquisition

Skill	Covered in Chapter
Making a bit-stream image of a suspect disk	Chapter 9
Verifying the bit-stream image through algorithms	Chapters 9, 10

LOOKING UP URLS

Another skill IACIS CFCE examiners need, in addition to normal computer forensics skills, is knowing how to identify contact people or owners of Web sites. Part of the investigation and analysis process for the CFCE examination requires searching for information that supports the investigation and is not available on the supplied evidence disks. The primary source for this additional contributory evidence can be found on the Internet.

With any Web browser, finding a Web site's contact person or owner is easy. You can use a Whois Web page to get registration information about most Web pages. The following information is typically available at a Whois Web page:

- The assigned IP address for the Web site
- The Web site's contact person's name, address, e-mail, telephone number, and fax number
- Registration date and expiration date for the Web site
- The domain server for the IP address

From a Whois Web page, you can usually search for a site's registration by its domain name, InterNIC handle (that is, its identification), or contact person's name. For more information about Web site registrations, go to *www.internic.net*.

Several Web sites provide registration information for all sites. To locate these Web sites, search on "Whois" with any search engine to find a current list of Internet registration providers. Here are some easy-to-use Whois Web sites:

- *www-whois.internic.net/cgi/whois*
- *www.whois.net*
- *http://resellers.tucows.com/opensrs/whois/*

The output from a Whois inquiry for Course Technology's Web site is shown in Figure A-1.

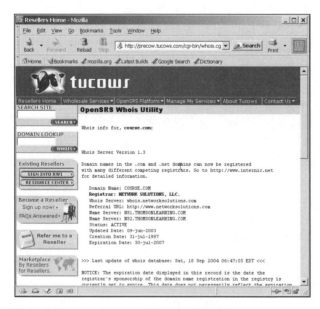

Figure A-1   Tucows Whois search results

B

COMPUTER FORENSICS REFERENCES

QUICK REFERENCES FOR COMPUTING INVESTIGATORS

This section contains references to the commands used with the software tools described in this book.

DriveSpy Command Switch References

Table B-1   DriveSpy Command Switches and Attributes

Category and Switch	Attribute	Description	Example
Wildcards	Asterisk (*)	Stand for one or more characters	To copy all .txt files to the Case_10 folder on Drive D: `Copy *.txt D:\Case_10\`
	Question mark (?)	Stand for a single character	To copy all files named Mydoc that have an extension beginning with "do" such as .doc and .dot: `Dir Mydoc.do?`
File attributes /A	A	Archived files	To list all the attributes of archived files: `Dir *.* /AA`
	D	Directories	To list only directories on a disk partition: `Dir /AD`
	E	Erased files	
	V	Disk volumes or partitions	
	S	System files	
	H	Hidden files	To copy hidden files: `Copy *.* /AH D:\Case_10\`
	R	Read-only files	

B

Table B-1 DriveSpy Command Switches and Attributes (continued)

Category and Switch	Attribute	Description	Example
Sorting /O	N	Sort by name	
	E	Sort by extension	
	G	Sort by directory	
	S	Sort by file size	
	D	Sort by the modification date and time	To get a directory listing sorted by date `Dir *.gif /OD`
	A	Sort by last access date	
	X	Sort deleted files when using the DIR command	
	-	Before an attribute, reverses the sort order	To display files by date and time in descending order: `Dir *.* /O-A`
Recursion /S		Lets you access subdirectory data when using other DriveSpy commands	To list the files in the current directory and all subdirectories: `Dir /S` To copy specific files from the current directories and all subdirectories: `Copy *.txt` `\D:\Case_10\ /S`
File types /T		Select specific file types that are predefined in DriveSpy.ini	To use the Unerase command to recover Excel spreadsheet files: `Unerase *.* /T:xls` `D:\Case_10\`
File groups /G		Access or recover predefined groups	To copy files defined in the Intel_Prop group: `Copy *.* /G:Intel_Prop` `D:\Case_10\`

NOTE

To negate the output of any attribute, place a hyphen in front of it. For example, Dir /-AD displays only files and no directories.

Table B-2 Wipe Command Switches

Switch	Description
Sector range, such as Wipe 0-1000	List specific sectors to overwrite
/L	Overwrite only a logical partition
/FREE	Overwrite only unallocated disk space
/SLACK	Overwrite only file slack space
/UNUSED	Overwrite unallocated and file slack space
/C: [value]	Overwrite a specified character value, which can be hexadecimal or decimal, as in /C:0xF6 or /C:246
/RAND	Random characters generated for the overwrite
/MBR	Overwrite the master boot record
/SA	Display the sector addresses while overwriting disk

UNIX and Linux Common Shell Commands

Table B-3 Standard UNIX and Linux Commands

Command	Switches	Description
cat file more file		Display the contents of a file (similar to the MS-DOS Type command)
dd	Use the man dd command to list the switch options available for this command	Create a bit-stream copy of a device to another device or image file
df bdf (HP-UX)	-k (Solaris)	Display information about the number of blocks that are allocated, used, and available for local and NFS-mounted partitions
find	Use the man find command to list the switch options available for this command	Find files matching a list of attributes, such as name, last modification time, and owner
netstat	-a	Display the systems connected via the network interface(s)
ps	-ef (Sys V) -ax (BSD)	Display a list of processes that are currently running
uname	-a	List the current name of system

Table B-4 Log and Data Files on UNIX and Linux Systems

Files	Description
Solaris systems	
/etc/passwd	Local account information
/etc/group	Local group information
/var/adm/sulog	Switch user log data
/var/adm/utmp	Current login information

Table B-4 Log and Data Files on UNIX and Linux Systems (continued)

Files	Description
/var/adm/wtmp/var/adm/wtmpx/var/adm/lastlog	Historical login information
/var/adm/loginlog	Login failure information
Messages	System log file
/etc/vfstab	Static information about file system
/etc/dfs/dfstab/etc/vfstab	Configuration files
HP-UX systems	
/etc/utmp	Current login information
/var/adm/wtmp/var/adm/wtmpx	Historical login information
/var/adm/btmp	Login failure information
/etc/fstab	Static information about file system
/etc/checklist	Static information about file system (version 9.x)
/etc/exports	Configuration files
syslog	System log file
AIX systems	
/etc/filesystems	Static information about file system
/etc/exports	Configuration files
/etc/utmp	Current login information
/var/adm/wtmp/etc/security/lastlog	Historical login information
/etc/security/failedlogin	Login failure information
IRIX systems	
/etc/fstab	Static information about file system
/var/adm/utmp/var/adm/utmpx	Current login information
/var/adm/wtmp/var/adm/wtmpx/var/adm/lastlog	Historical login information
/var/adm/btmp	Login failure information
/etc/fstab	Relevant file
/etc/exports	Configuration files
syslog	System log file
Linux systems	
/etc/exports	Configuration files
/var/run/utmp	Current login information
/var/log/wtmp/var/log/lastlog	Historical login information
/etc/fstab	Relevant files

SAMPLE SCRIPT FOR DRIVESPY

With the DriveSpy SaveSect and WriteSect commands, you can create multiple volume segments of disk drives and then re-create the saved volumes to a new target disk drive. Because the SaveSect and WriteSect commands work in Drive mode, they can copy and write data from non-FAT disk drives. For example, the sample script files in this section are for a Macintosh running O/S 8.2 on an 8 GB SCSI disk drive.

Figure B-1 shows the output of using the DriveSpy SaveSect command to create multiple volumes of a disk drive.

```
OUTPUT MAC_SAV.LOG
PAGE OFF
DRIVE 1
SAVESECT  00000000-00999999  MAC_SAV.000
SAVESECT  01000000-01999999  MAC_SAV.001
SAVESECT  02000000-02999999  MAC_SAV.002
SAVESECT  03000000-03999999  MAC_SAV.003
SAVESECT  04000000-04999999  MAC_SAV.004
SAVESECT  05000000-05999999  MAC_SAV.005
SAVESECT  06000000-06999999  MAC_SAV.006
SAVESECT  07000000-07999999  MAC_SAV.007
SAVESECT  08000000-08999999  MAC_SAV.008
SAVESECT  09000000-09999999  MAC_SAV.009
SAVESECT  10000000-10999999  MAC_SAV.010
SAVESECT  11000000-11999999  MAC_SAV.011
SAVESECT  12000000-12999999  MAC_SAV.012
SAVESECT  13000000-13999999  MAC_SAV.013
SAVESECT  14000000-14999999  MAC_SAV.014
SAVESECT  15000000-15999999  MAC_SAV.015
SAVESECT  16000000-16957030  MAC_SAV.016
```

Figure B-1   Output of DriveSpy SaveSect command

This script creates volume segments of 512,000,000 bytes each, with the exception of the last volume segment, which is only 489,999,872 bytes. This last segment is smaller because the end of the drive is at block position 16957030. Remember, each block is 512 bytes.

Figure B-2 shows the output of the DriveSpy WriteSect command to restore multiple volumes from a SaveSect script.

```
OUTPUT MAC_WRT.LOG
PAGE OFF
DRIVE 1
WRITESECT  MAC_SAV.000  00000000-00999999
WRITESECT  MAC_SAV.001  01000000-01999999
WRITESECT  MAC_SAV.002  02000000-02999999
WRITESECT  MAC_SAV.003  03000000-03999999
WRITESECT  MAC_SAV.004  04000000-04999999
WRITESECT  MAC_SAV.005  05000000-05999999
WRITESECT  MAC_SAV.006  06000000-06999999
WRITESECT  MAC_SAV.007  07000000-07999999
WRITESECT  MAC_SAV.008  08000000-08999999
WRITESECT  MAC_SAV.009  09000000-09999999
WRITESECT  MAC_SAV.010  10000000-10999999
WRITESECT  MAC_SAV.011  11000000-11999999
WRITESECT  MAC_SAV.012  12000000-12999999
WRITESECT  MAC_SAV.013  13000000-13999999
WRITESECT  MAC_SAV.014  14000000-14999999
WRITESECT  MAC_SAV.015  15000000-15999999
WRITESECT  MAC_SAV.016  16000000-16957030
```

Figure B-2   Output of the DriveSpy WriteSect command

OVERVIEW OF **FAT** DIRECTORY STRUCTURES

When Microsoft first created the MS-DOS operating system, data was stored on floppy disks. Because floppy disks have had a limited evolution in their maximum size, the addressable storage space is small compared to modern hard disks. All floppy disks for Microsoft OSs use the FAT12 file system (see Chapter 7 for additional information on FAT file systems). Because of the limited disk space and memory space on older computers, Microsoft engineered the FAT12 file system so that directory names could be only one to eight characters. File names could be only up to eight characters and zero to three characters for file extensions. The three characters for file extensions are used to identify the file type, such as .doc for a document file or .xls for a spreadsheet file.

When larger disk drives were developed, Microsoft re-engineered the FAT file system and created FAT16, which allows up to 2.0 GB of addressable storage space for disk drive partitions With further advances in disk technologies, Microsoft created FAT32, which can access up to 2.0 terabytes or more of storage space. Under MS-DOS 6.22, the same directory and file name convention from FAT12 was carried over to FAT16. For Windows 95 and newer OSs, FAT32 maintains both the MS-DOS eight-character maximum for file names and three characters for file extensions.

When Microsoft released Windows 95, it needed to allow for larger file names under FAT12 and FAT16. As a solution, Microsoft developed Virtual FAT (VFAT). VFAT provides two file names for every file within the directory file. The first name is the long file name that appears in what looks like a Unicode format. The Unicode format is displayed in a hexadecimal editor with null (00) values between each character. The second name is the short file name that follows the previously mentioned convention of eight-character file names and three-character extensions.

The purpose of having both a long file name and a short file name is to provide backward compatibility with older Microsoft operating systems and file systems. You can see an example of this file-naming method in Windows Explorer. Figure B-3 shows four files, three shorter than eight characters and one longer than eight characters. The first file, Market_Plan-31.txt, is over the eight-character maximum allowed under MS-DOS 6.22.

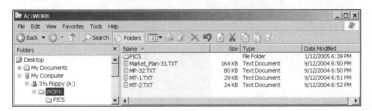

Figure B-3 Viewing file naming in Windows Explorer

When viewing the same folder with MS-DOS using the Dir command, the converted short file name appears as Market~1.txt (see Figure B-4).

```
A:\WORK>DIR

 Volume in drive A is APP_B
 Volume Serial Number is 1C36-19E4

 Directory of A:\WORK

 .              <DIR>              01-12-2005      06:39p
 ..             <DIR>              01-12-2005      06:39p
 PICS           <DIR>              01-12-2005      06:39p
 MARKET~1 TXT         167,123 09-12-2004      06:50p
 MP-32    TXT          78,985 09-12-2004      06:50p
 MT-1     TXT          28,533 09-12-2004      06:51p
 MT-2     TXT          23,802 09-12-2004      06:52p
          7 file(s)           298,443 bytes
                            1,157,005 bytes free


A:\WORK>
```

Figure B-4   Viewing file naming in MS-DOS with the Dir command

You can view the directory file and examine its content by using tools such as DriveSpy, FTK, EnCase, iLook, and others. Using DriveSpy, for example, to examine the directory structure requires locating the cluster position of the directory. Continuing with the example shown in previous figures, first you need to locate the cluster number for the Work directory by using the Dir command in DriveSpy (see Figure B-5). Next, to display the information listed in the directory file, use the Cluster command. For more information on using these commands in DriveSpy, refer to Chapter 10.

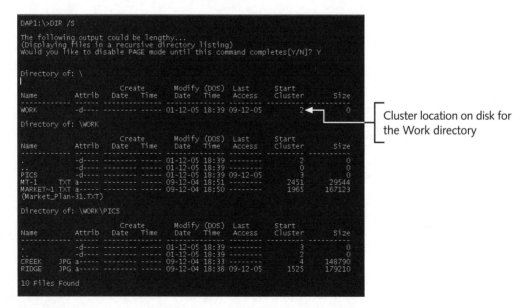

Figure B-5   Finding the Work directory cluster number in DriveSpy

FAT directories contain specific information about each file stored in them. All FAT directories start with the hexadecimal value of 2E followed by several hexadecimal 20 values. The hexadecimal 2E converts to the ASCII value of a period and the hexadecimal 20 represents a space.

Note that the cluster number for the Work directory is 2 in Figure B-5. To view the content of this cluster, type Cluster 2 and press Enter (see Figure B-6).

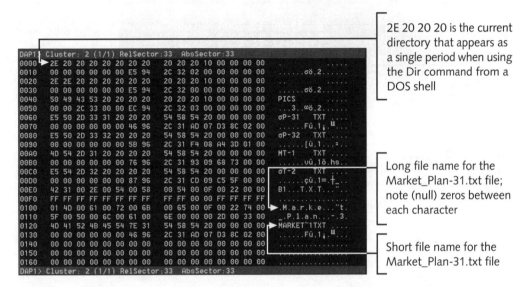

2E 20 20 20 is the current directory that appears as a single period when using the Dir command from a DOS shell

Long file name for the Market_Plan-31.txt file; note (null) zeros between each character

Short file name for the Market_Plan-31.txt file

Figure B-6 Viewing the directory cluster content in DriveSpy

Another useful tool designed to be run from Windows is the shareware program Directory Snoop from Briggs Software (*www.briggsoft.com*). Directory Snoop is a convenient GUI tool that enables you to inspect and recover deleted data from disks. Figure B-7 shows an example of using Directory Snoop for FAT file system partitions.

In the example shown in Figure B-7, note the missing long file name in the pane at the bottom. The lack of a long file name indicates that this floppy disk was formatted and data written to it from an MS-DOS 6.22 or older OS.

The deleted file is displayed with a ? above and with an E5 in the hexadecimal display below; the E5 (lowercase sigma) is not displayed in the Text Data field

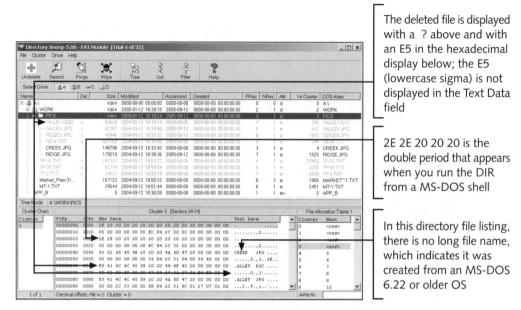

2E 2E 20 20 20 is the double period that appears when you run the DIR from a MS-DOS shell

In this directory file listing, there is no long file name, which indicates it was created from an MS-DOS 6.22 or older OS

Figure B-7 Directory Snoop

Following is the information listed for all files in the directory file:

- Long file name for Windows 95 or later formatted FAT disks
- Short file name (8.3 naming convention)
- Attributes assigned to the file
- Case and creation time in milliseconds
- Creation time of the file
- Creation date of the file
- Last access date of the file
- Starting cluster high-word for FAT32 file systems
- Modified time stamp
- Modified date stamp
- Starting cluster of the file (assigned by the FAT where all links to the file are listed)
- File size

When a file is deleted in a FAT directory, a hexadecimal E5 value is inserted in the first character position of the file's name (see callout in Figure B-7). If the file is renamed, a new entry containing the file's new name is created, and the old file name is marked as deleted with the E5 value, the same as though the file had been deleted. These entries are not typically deleted from the directory file. Several computer forensics tools and disk-editing tools can display the content of a directory file. As an example, Figure B-8 shows what a renamed file looks like in the directory file in a FAT12 disk in Directory Snoop.

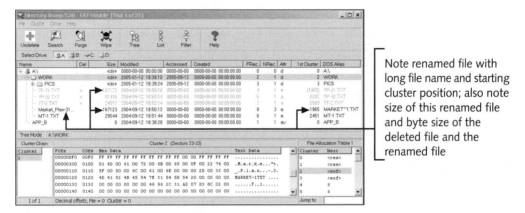

Note renamed file with long file name and starting cluster position; also note size of this renamed file and byte size of the deleted file and the renamed file

Figure B-8 Directory Snoop with a FAT12 disk

You can also reverse-engineer the starting cluster position and the file size. Within the directory file, these values are listed in hexadecimal format. To convert hexadecimal values to decimal, use the Windows scientific calculator in the following steps:

1. In Windows, click **Start**, point to **Programs** (**All Programs** in Windows XP), point to **Accessories**, and then click **Calculator**.

2. In the Calculator window, click **View**, **Scientific** from the menu.

3. In the Scientific Calculator window, click the **Hex** button.

4. Using the keyboard or the hexadecimal buttons, enter the hexadecimal value you want to convert, and then click the **Dec** button.

Figure B-9 shows the last four hexadecimal numbers as the byte size for the Market~1.txt file. When converting these numbers from hex to decimal, read the numbers from right to left. To find the decimal byte size, you type 00 02 8C D3 in a scientific calculator. Note that what's displayed with the Dir command or Windows Explorer might be slightly smaller than what's converted. Figure B-10 also shows the starting cluster number in hex for the Market~1.txt file. Note that to compute this value, you read right to left. To find the decimal cluster number value, you type 07 AD in a scientific calculator.

In Figure B-9, note the decimal value 1965. For all FAT directory entries, the file's starting cluster position is located at offset 1A hexadecimal or 26 decimal from the first position where the file's name is displayed. Remember, the first position where the file name appears has the starting value of zero. The file's byte size is located starting at offset 1C hexadecimal or 28 decimal. Note that these values are read from right to left.

Of special interest for an investigation is trying to determine the size of a file that has been deleted and overwritten by a newer file. Knowing the size of the previously deleted and overwritten file could provide subjective information that might contribute to a copy of the deleted file from another disk. It's subjective but might provide clues for the investigation.

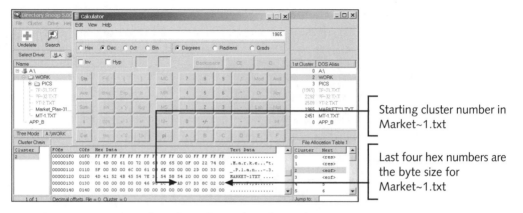

Figure B-9   Converting from hexadecimal to decimal

SAMPLE DOS SCRIPTS

In Chapter 7 you were introduced to DOS batch programming. This appendix shows two other useful batch program examples using the Goto, For...In...Do, and Choice commands. With these commands integrated into a batch program, you can manipulate data more reliably.

Goto is a simple branching command that instructs the batch file to jump to a predefined location. The predefined location is a unique name preceded with a colon, as in this example:

```
:go_loop
    echo sample goto loop
goto go_loop
```

A loop structure repeats one or more commands until a specified condition is met. The preceding Go_Loop command runs forever because it doesn't specify a condition that stops the loop. To specify a condition, you can use the If command. The If command tests three possible conditions: Errorlevel, the value of two strings to see whether they are equal, and whether a file exists.

The If Errorlevel command has five numeric error codes starting from zero (0). The following commands are the ones that return the error codes explained in Table B-5:

Backup	Diskcomp	Diskcopy
Format	Graftable	Keyb
Replace	Restore	Xcopy

Table B-5   Error Codes

Code	Result
0	Indicates a successful operation
1	Error of a read or write operation

Table B-5   Error Codes (continued)

Code	Result
2	The user initiated Ctrl+C (a common method to interrupt a command)
3	Fatal termination of read or write
4	Error during initialization

The following code is an example of how to use Errorlevel in a batch file with Xcopy. You can use the Xcopy command to copy files and any subfolders to a specified location.

```
xcopy c:\temp a:\
if errorlevel 1 goto go_error
Other code skipped when the above error is encountered.
:go_error
echo Command failed! Check for floppy in drive A
```

The following code uses Errorlevel with the Exist command. You use this command in the format If Exist *FileName* to verify whether *FileName* exists. If it does, the next command or function on the same line is performed. If *FileName* does not exist, the command on the same line is skipped, and the command on the next line is performed.

```
cd \mydocu~1
if exist text.doc goto go_del
Other code skipped when the above error is encountered.
:go_del
del text.doc
```

In MS-DOS, you can also compare strings. The following example shows how to use the If command to compare two values and then branch to another command:

```
rem test_if.bat
if "%1"=="" goto err_msg
if %1==copyfile goto go_copy
if %1==bye goto end
:err_msg
echo You need to enter something!
echo Run this batch file again!
goto :end
:go_copy
copy c:\temp\text.doc a:
:end
exit
```

To run this batch file, be sure to enter a matching parameter, as in the following code:

```
test_if copyfile
```

or

```
test_if bye
```

This example shows that if the user enters no parameters, which MS-DOS interprets as a null value, DOS tells the user to run the file again with the correct input. It stops running the file with the Exit command and returns to the MS-DOS prompt.

NOTE   MS-DOS parameters are case-sensitive. If you use all uppercase characters in a batch file, for example, you must type uppercase letters when you enter the parameters.

The For...In...Do command allows you to define a group of variables, and then process those variables to perform a specific task. A parameter can be also passed to refine the batch file. The double percent sign with a single letter (%%A) defines a variable in MS-DOS batch files, as in the following example:

```
Rem cpfloppy.bat
for %%a in (A: a: B: b:) do if "%%A"=="%1" goto cp_file
        echo You forgot to specify which floppy drive to use.
        echo Remember the floppy drive is either A: or B:
goto end
:cp_file
        echo You have selected the %1 drive.
        copy c:\temp\text.doc a:
:end
```

With the For command, a batch file repeats a command or function until the correct value is entered. In the preceding example, the For %%A command branches to the Do If statement if the user types the correct floppy drive letter. The allowed values for this example are a, A, b, and B. Use the Choice command if you want to build a batch file to accept input after the file has started running. Choice limits you to the options you have listed in the batch file and does not pass a parameter. This command also uses the Errorlevel command, although not like the other previously listed DOS commands. In the steps that follow, you create a batch file that uses these options to format a floppy disk. The Choice command can branch to up to 255 different labels that are defined in its key switch value. This is the syntax for the Choice command:

```
choice /C:key /N /S /T:choice,seconds prompt
```

Table B-6 defines each switch and option in the Choice command.

Table B-6   Switches and Options for the Choice Command

Switch or Option	Function
/C:key	Defines the keys, or labels, displayed at the Choice prompt
/N	Suppresses key list and question mark, which are normally displayed by the DOS prompt
/S	Makes the input at the Choice prompt case sensitive

Table B-6 Switches and Options for the Choice Command (continued)

Switch or Option	Function
/T:choice, seconds	Provides a delay in seconds for any previously defined /C:key value
prompt	Defines the choices for the user

The Errorlevel command has five basic responses from 0 to 4, as shown previously in Table B-4. Used with the Choice command, Errorlevel responds with exit codes, defined in Table B-7, to allow you to branch to a specific label.

Table B-7 Errorlevel Codes for the Choice Command

Code	Results
0	Terminated by user by pressing Ctrl+C or Ctrl+Break
1	First key parameter is selected with the /C:key switch
2	Second key parameter is selected with the /C:key switch
3–254	nth key parameter is selected with the /C:key switch
255	Error parameter is selected with the /C:key switch

The Choice command is an external MS-DOS command. Windows 9x stores the command in the Windows\Command folder; MS-DOS 6.22 stores it in the DOS directory. To build a batch file on a floppy disk, you must copy the Choice command to the disk along with the batch file. To use the Choice command in a batch file, follow these steps:

1. On a Windows 98 machine, open Notepad and create a new file named **MyChoice.bat**. Save the file in the AppB\Chapter folder in your work folder.

2. Type the following code in the document:

```
@echo off
cls
echo.
echo  *** Floppy Disk Format Batch Job ***
echo.
echo Choose the drive containing the disk you want to format.
echo.
echo Floppy disk drives available:
echo.
echo "A:"
echo "B:"
echo.
echo Select drive and type of format:
echo.
echo Option       Drive & Format
echo ------       ----------------
echo   A          A: Quick Format
```

```
echo    B           A: Unconditional Format
echo    C           A: Quick Format with System Files
echo    D           B: Quick Format
echo    E           B: Unconditional Format
echo    F           B: Quick Format with System Files
choice /c:ABCDEF "Choose Drive and Format option"
if errorlevel 255 goto Error
if errorlevel 6   goto F_for
if errorlevel 5   goto E_for
if errorlevel 4   goto D_for
if errorlevel 3   goto C_for
if errorlevel 2   goto B_for
if errorlevel 1   goto A_for
:Error
echo.
echo Run this batch file again,
echo but next time,
echo make a different selection.
echo.
goto end
:F_for
echo.
echo "B: Quick format with system files."
format b: /q /s
echo.
goto end
:E_for
rem "B: Unconditional format."
format b: /u
goto end
:D_for
echo "B: Quick format."
format b: /q
goto end
:C_for
echo "A: Quick format with system files."
format a: /q
goto end
:B_for
echo "A: Unconditional format."
format a: /u
goto end
:A_for
echo "A: Quick format."
pdblock 0
:end
```

3. Save the file and exit Notepad.

4. Open a command prompt window.

5. Using the **cd** command, navigate to the AppB\Chapter folder in your work folder.

6. Type **MyChoice.bat** and press **Enter**.

NOTE

The batch file displays commands on the screen that allow you to format the disk in the A: or B: drive in a variety of formats—quick, unconditional, or quick with system files.

7. In drive A: or B:, insert a floppy disk containing files you no longer need. Then type **c** or **f**, depending on the floppy drive you are using. Your choice is confirmed and the the floppy disk is formatted.

8. When the formatting process is over, close the command prompt window.

For more information on batch programming, see the "MS-DOS Reference Books" section in this appendix.

COMPUTER FORENSICS REFERENCES

This book is only the beginning of computer forensics and investigations. To master all levels of computing forensics, you should familiarize yourself with the works of many other authors who have made significant contributions to this profession. Listed here are several other books that can expand your technical skills and your understanding of computing investigation processes.

Caloyhannides, Michael A. *Computer Forensics and Privacy*. Artrech House Publishers, 2001 (ISBN 1580532837).

Carrier, Brian. *File System Forensic Analysis*, Addison-Wesley Professional, 2005 (ISBN 0321268172).

Casey, Eoghan, ed. *Digital Evidence and Computer Crime*. Academic Press, 2003 (ISBN 0121631044).

Casey, Eoghan, ed. *Handbook of Computer Crime Investigation, Forensic Tools and Technology*. Academic Press, 2002 (ISBN 0121631036).

Clark, Franklin and Ken Diliberto. *Investigating Computer Crime*. CRC Press, 1996 (ISBN 0849381584).

Icove, David, Karl Seger, and William VonStorch. *Computer Crime, A Crimefighter's Handbook*. O'Reilly & Associates, Inc., 1995 (ISBN 1565920864).

Kruse II, Warren G. and Jay G. Heiser, *Computer Forensics: Incident Response Essentials*. Pearson Education, 2001 (ISBN 0201707195).

Mel, H.X. and Doris Baker. *Cryptography Decrypted*. Addison-Wesley, 2001 (ISBN 0201616475).

Prosise, Chris, Kevin Mandia, and Matt Pepe. *Incident Response: Computer Forensics*. McGraw-Hill, 2002 (ISBN 007222696X).

Rosenblatt, Kenneth S. *High-Technology Crime*. KSK Publications, 1995 (ISBN 0964817101).

Sammes, Tom and Brian Jenkinson. *Forensic Computing, A Practitioner's Guide*. Springer-Verlag London Ltd., 2000 (ISBN 1852332999).

Stephenson, Peter. *Investigating Computer-Related Crime*. CRC Press, 2000 (ISBN 0-8493-2218-9).

MS-DOS Reference Books

The following books are good references on how to use MS-DOS and how to create your own DOS batch files. Some of these books might be out of print. If you cannot find them at a local bookstore, try searching for them on eBay or at *www.half.com*.

Cooper, Jim. *Special Edition Using MS-DOS 6.22, 3rd Edition*. Que, 2002 (ISBN 078972573).

Gookin, Dan. *DOS for Dummies, 3rd Edition*. Wiley Publishing, Inc., 1999 (ISBN 0764503618).

Menefee, Craig and Nick Anis. *Harnessing DOS 6.0, Batch File and Command Macro Power*. Bantam Computer Books, 1993 (ISBN 0553351885).

Procedures for Corporate High-Technology Investigations

PROCEDURES FOR INVESTIGATIONS

As an investigator, you need to develop formal procedures and informal checklists to cover all issues that are important to a high-tech investigation. Procedures are necessary to ensure that correct techniques are applied to an investigation. Use informal checklists to be certain that all evidence is collected and processed properly. This appendix lists some sample procedures that computing investigators commonly use in corporate investigations.

Employee Termination Cases

The majority of termination casework a corporate computing investigator performs involves employee abuse. Incidents that create a hostile work environment, such as viewing pornography in the workplace, and inappropriate e-mail messages are the predominant types of cases investigated. The following sections describe key points to consider when conducting an investigation that might lead to an employee's termination. Consulting with your organization's general counsel and Personnel Department for specific directions on how to handle these investigations is recommended. Your organization must have appropriate policies implemented, as described in Chapter 1.

Internet Abuse Investigations

The information in this section applies to an organization's internal private networks, not a public ISP. Consult with your general counsel after reviewing this list and to make changes according to the directions of your organization's attorneys to build your own procedures.

To conduct an investigation involving Internet abuse, you need the following:

- The organization's Internet proxy server logs
- Suspect computer's IP address; consult with your organization's network administrator
- Suspect computer's disk drive
- Your preferred computer forensic analysis tool (FTK, EnCase, DriveSpy, and so forth)

The following steps outline the recommended processing of an Internet abuse case:

1. Use the standard forensic analysis techniques and procedures described in this book for the disk drive examination.

2. Using tools such as Data Lifter or FTK's Internet Keyword Search option under the Tools menu, extract all Web page URL information.

3. If available, contact the firewall network administrator and request a proxy server log of the suspect computer's IP address for the date range of interest. Consult with your organization's network administrator to confirm that these logs are maintained.

4. Compare the data recovered from forensic analysis to the proxy server log data to confirm that they match.

5. If the URL data matches both the proxy server log and the forensic disk examination, continue analyzing the suspect computer's disk drive data, and collect any relevant downloaded inappropriate pictures or Web pages that support the allegation. If there are no matches between the proxy server logs, and the forensic examination shows no contributing evidence, report that the allegation is unsubstantiated.

NOTE Before conducting an Internet abuse case, research your state or country's privacy laws. Many countries have unique privacy laws that restrict the use of computer log data, such as proxy server logs or disk drive cache files, for any type of investigation. Some state or federal laws might supersede your organization's employee policies. Always consult with your organization's attorney. For companies with international business operations, jurisdiction is a problem; what is legal in the United States, such as examining and investigating a proxy server log, might not be legal in Germany, for example.

For investigations in which the proxy server log does not match the forensic analysis that found inappropriate data, continue the examination of the suspect computer's disk drive. Determine when inappropriate data was downloaded to the computer and whether it was through an organization's intranet connection to the Internet. Employees might have used their employers' laptop computers to connect to their own ISPs to download inappropriate Web content. For these situations, you need to consult your organization's employee policy guidelines for what's considered appropriate use of the organization's computing assets.

E-mail Abuse Investigations

E-mail investigations typically range from spam to inappropriate and offensive message content to harassment and threats. E-mail is subject to the same restrictions as other computer evidence data, in that an organization must have a properly defined policy as described in Chapter 1. The following list is what you need for an investigation involving e-mail abuse:

- An electronic copy of the offending e-mail message that contains message header data; consult with your e-mail server administrator

- If available, e-mail server log records; consult with your e-mail server administrator to see whether they are available

- For e-mail systems that store users' messages on a central server, access to the server; consult with your e-mail server administrator

- For e-mail systems that store users' messages on a computer as an Outlook .pst or .ost file, for example, access to the computer so that you can perform a forensic analysis on it

- Your preferred computer forensic analysis tool, such as FTK or EnCase

This is the recommended procedure for e-mail investigations:

1. For computer based e-mail data files, such as Outlook .pst or .ost files, use the standard forensic analysis techniques and procedures described in this book for the disk drive examination.

2. For server-based e-mail data files, contact the e-mail server administrator and obtain an electronic copy of the suspect and victim's server e-mail folder or data.

3. For Web-based e-mail investigations, such as Hotmail or Yahoo! mail, use tools such as FTK's Internet Keyword Search option under the Tools menu to extract all related e-mail address information.

4. Examine header data of all messages of interest to the investigation.

Attorney-Client Privileged Investigations

When conducting a computer forensic analysis under attorney-client privilege (ACP) rules for an attorney, you must keep all findings confidential. The attorney you're working for is the ultimate authority over the investigation. For investigations of this nature, attorneys typically request that you extract all data from the disk drive or drives. It is your responsibility to comply with the attorney's directions. Because of the large quantities of data a disk drive can contain, the attorney will want to know about everything on the disk drive or drives of interest.

Many attorneys like to have printouts of the data you have recovered, but printouts can presents problems when you have log files that are several thousand pages of data or CAD drawing programs that can be read only by proprietary programs. You need to persuade and educate many attorneys on how digital evidence can be viewed electronically. Learn how to teach attorneys and paralegals how to sort through data files so you can help them efficiently analyze the huge amounts of data a forensic examination produces.

You can encounter problems if you find data in the form of binary files, such as CAD drawings. Examining these types of files requires using the CAD program that created them. In addition, engineering companies often have specialized drafting programs. Discovery demands for lawsuits involving a product that caused injury or death requires extracting design plans for attorneys and expert witnesses to review. You will be responsible for locating the programs for these design plans so that attorneys and expert witnesses can view these files.

The following list shows the basic steps for conducting an ACP case:

1. Request a memorandum from the attorney directing you to start the investigation. The memorandum must state that the investigation is privileged communication and list your name and any other associates' names assigned to the case.

2. Request a list of keywords that are of interest to the investigation.

3. When you have received the memorandum, initiate the investigation and analysis. Any findings you have made before receiving the memorandum are subject to discovery by the opposing attorney.

4. For disk drive examinations, make two bit-stream image copies of the disk and one logical copy with a tool such as Norton Ghost. For each bit-stream image copy, use different imaging tools, such as EnCase for the first and DriveSpy's SaveSect or SafeBack for the second. If you have large enough storage disk drives, make each bit-stream image uncompressed to ensure that if any bit-stream images become corrupt, you can still examine the uncorrupted areas with your preferred forensic analysis tool.

5. If possible, run MD5 or SHA hashes on all files on the original and re-created disks. Typically, attorneys want to view all data even if it's not relevant to the case. Many GUI forensic tools perform this task during bit-stream imaging of the disk drive.

6. Methodically examine every portion of the disk drive (both allocated and unallocated data areas) and extract all data.

7. Run keyword searches on allocated and unallocated disk space. Follow up the search results to determine whether the keyword hit contains information that supports the case.

8. For Windows OSs, use specialty tools to analyze and extract data from the Registry file, such as AccessData's Registry Viewer, or one of the many Registry viewer programs, such as RegdatXP. Use the Find function in the Registry viewer to search for keywords of interest to the investigation.

9. If necessary, reconstruct the original drive so that you can boot it using the logical image save. If you don't have the original computer, creating a bootable drive might be difficult because many OSs rely on specific vendor hardware configurations. Reconstructing a computer so that you can boot it can provide additional information that might not be available when examining with a computer forensics tool.

10. For binary data files such as CAD drawings, locate the correct software product and, if possible, make printouts of the binary file content. If the data files are too large, load the specialty application on a separate workstation with the recovered binary files so that the attorney can view them.

C

11. For unallocated data (file slack space or free space) recovery, use a tool that removes or replaces nonprintable data, such as NTI's Filter_I program.

12. Consolidate all recovered data from the evidence bit-stream image into well-organized folders and subfolders. Store the recovered data output using a logical and easy-to-follow storage method for the attorney or paralegal.

Here are some other guidelines to remember for ACP cases:

- Minimize all written communications with the attorney; use the telephone when you need to ask questions or provide information related to the case.

- Any documentation written to the attorney must contain a header stating it is "Privileged Legal Communication—Confidential Work Product" as defined under the attorney-work-product rule.

- Assist the attorney and paralegal in analyzing the data.

If you have difficulty complying with the directions or don't understand the directives from the memorandum, contact the attorney and explain the problem. Always keep an open line of verbal communication with the attorney during these types of investigations. If you're using e-mail to communicate with the attorney, use encryption such as PGP or another security e-mail service for all messages.

Media Leak Investigations

For the corporate computing and network environment, controlling sensitive data can be difficult. Disgruntled employees, for example, might send an organization's sensitive data to a news reporter. The reasons for media leaks range from employees' efforts to embarrass management to a rival conducting a power struggle between competing internal organizations. Another concern is the premature release of information about new products, which can disrupt operations and cause market share loss for a business if it's made public too soon. Media leak investigations can be time consuming and resource intensive. Because management wants to find who leaked information, scope creep during the investigation is not uncommon.

Consider the following for media leak investigations:

- Examine e-mail, both the organization's e-mail servers and private e-mail accounts (Hotmail, Yahoo!, and so on) on company-owned computers.

- Examine Internet message boards (such as Yahoo!); research the Internet for any information about the company or product. Use Internet search engines to run word searches related to the company, product, or leaked information. For example, you might search for "graphite-composite bicycle sprocket" for a bicycle manufacturer that was the victim of a media leak about a new product in development.

C

- Examine proxy server logs to check for log activities that might show use of free e-mail services, such as Hotmail or Yahoo! mail. Track back to the specific workstation where these messages originated and perform a forensic analysis on the disk drives to help determine what was communicated.

- Examine known suspects' workstations, perform computer forensics examinations on persons of interest, and develop other leads of possible associates.

- Examine all company telephone records for any calls to known media organizations.

The following list outlines steps to take for media leaks:

1. Interview management privately to get a list of employees who have direct knowledge of the sensitive data.

2. Identify the media source that published the information.

3. Review company telephone records to see who might have had contact with the news service.

4. Obtain a listing of keywords related to the media leak.

5. Perform keyword searches on proxy and e-mail servers.

6. Discreetly conduct forensic disk acquisitions and analysis of employees of interest.

7. From the forensic disk examinations, analyze all e-mail correspondence and trace any sensitive messages to other people who have not been listed as having direct knowledge of the sensitive data.

8. Expand the discreet forensic disk acquisition and analysis for any new persons of interest.

9. Consolidate findings and periodically review to see whether new clues can be discovered.

10. Routinely report findings to management and discuss how much further to continue the investigation.

Industrial Espionage Investigations

Industrial espionage cases, similar to media leaks, can be time consuming and are subject to the same scope creep problems. This section offers some guidelines on how to deal with economic espionage investigations. Be aware that industrial espionage cases that deal with foreign nationals might be violations of the International Traffic in Arms Regulations (ITAR) or Export Administration Regulations (EAR). For more information on ITAR, see the U.S. Department of State's Web site (*www.NameOfState.gov*; substitute the actual state for *NameOfState*) or perform a Web search for "International Traffic in Arms Regulations." For EAR information, see the U.S. Department of Commerce Web site (*www.doc.gov*) or perform a Web search for "Export Administration Regulations."

Unlike the other corporate investigations covered in this appendix, all suspected industrial espionage cases should be treated as criminal investigations. The techniques described here are for the private network environment and internal investigations that have not yet been reported to law enforcement officials. Make sure you do not become an agent of the police by filing a complaint of a suspected espionage case before substantiating the allegation. The following list includes staff you might need when planning an industrial espionage investigation. This list isn't exhaustive, so be creative and apply your talents to improve on these recommendations.

- The computing investigator who is responsible for disk forensic examinations
- The technology specialist who is knowledgeable of the suspected compromised technical data
- The network specialist who can perform log analysis and set up network sniffers to trap network communications of possible suspects
- The threat assessment specialist (typically an attorney) who is familiar with federal and state laws and regulations related to ITAR and industrial espionage

In addition, consider the following guidelines when initiating an international espionage investigation:

- Determine whether this investigation involves a possible industrial espionage incident, and then determine whether it falls under ITAR or EAR.
- Consult with corporate attorneys and upper management if the investigations must be conducted discreetly.
- Determine what information is needed to substantiate the allegation of industrial espionage.
- Generate a list of keywords for disk forensics and sniffer monitoring.
- Make a list and collect resources needed for the investigation.
- Determine the goal and scope of the investigation; consult with management and the company's attorneys on how much work you should do.
- Initiate the investigation after approval from management, and make regular reports of your activities and findings.

The following are planning considerations for industrial espionage investigations:

- Examine all e-mail of suspected employees, both company-provided e-mail and free Web-based services, such as Hotmail or Yahoo! mail.
- Search Internet newsgroups, such as Yahoo! message boards, for any postings related to the incident.
- Initiate physical surveillance with cameras on people or things of interest to the investigation.

- If available, examine all facility physical access logs for sensitive areas, which might include secure areas where smart badges or video surveillance recordings are used.

- If there is a suspect, determine his or her location in relation to the vulnerable asset that was compromised.

- Study the suspect's work habits.

- Collect all incoming and outgoing telephone logs to see whether any unique or unusual places were called.

When conducting an industrial espionage case, follow these basic steps:

1. Gather all personnel assigned to the investigation and brief them on the plan and the concerns.

2. Gather the resources needed to conduct the investigation.

3. Start the investigation by placing surveillance systems, such as cameras and network sniffers, at key locations.

4. Discreetly gather any additional evidence, such as the suspect's computer disk drive, and make a bit-stream image copy for follow-up examination.

5. Collect all log data from networks and e-mail servers, and examine them for unique items that might relate to the investigation.

6. Report regularly to management and corporate attorneys on your investigation's status and current findings.

7. Review the investigation's scope with management and corporate attorneys to determine whether it needs to be expanded and more resources added.

INTERVIEWS AND INTERROGATIONS IN HIGH-TECHNOLOGY INVESTIGATIONS

Becoming a skilled interviewer and interrogator can take several years of experience. Typically, a corporate computing investigator is a technical person acquiring the evidence for an investigation. Many large organizations have full-time security investigators who have many years of training and experience in criminal and civil investigations and interviewing techniques. Few of these investigators have any computing or network technical skills. Because of this, you might be requested to assist in interviewing or interrogating of a suspect when you have performed a forensic disk analysis on that suspect's machine.

An interrogation is different from an interview. Interviews are usually information collection from a witness or suspect about specific facts related to an investigation. An interrogation is the process of trying to get a suspect to confess to a specific incident or crime. An investigator might change from an interview to an interrogation when talking to a suspect.

Your role as a computing investigator is to instruct the investigator who is conducting the interview on what questions to ask and what the answers should be. As you build rapport with the investigator, he or she might ask you to question the suspect. Watching a skilled interrogator is a unique learning experience in human relations skills.

If you are asked to assist in an interview or interrogation as a computer investigator, prepare yourself by answering the following questions:

- What questions do I need to ask the suspect to get the vital information about the case?

- Do I know what I'm talking about, or will I have to research the topic or technology related to the investigation?

- Do I need additional questions to cover other indirect issues related to the investigation?

Common interview and interrogation errors include being unprepared for the interview or interrogation and not having the right questions or enough questions to increase your depth of knowledge. Make sure you don't run out of conversation topics; you need to keep the conversation friendly to gain the suspect's confidence. Avoid doubting your own skills, which might show the suspect you lack confidence in your ability.

Ingredients for a successful interview or interrogation require the following:

- Being patient throughout the entire session

- Repeating or rephrasing questions to zero in on the specific facts from a reluctant witness or suspect

- Being tenacious

Glossary

4-mm DAT — Magnetic tapes that store about 4 GB of data, but like CD-Rs, are slow to read and write data.

absolute sector — The actual count of each sector of data, starting at the very beginning of the disk drive. Absolute sector 0 (zero) is typically the same location as the Master Boot Record (MBR) of a disk drive. The Sector command in DriveSpy's Drive mode displays the absolute sector values of the disk drive.

Advanced SCSI Programming Interface (ASPI) — Provides several software drivers that allow for communication between the OS and the SCSI component.

affidavit — The document, given under penalty of perjury, that an investigator creates detailing his or her findings. In many cases, this document is used to justify issuing a warrant or to deal with abuse in a corporation.

algorithm — A short mathematical procedure or procedural steps used to solve a problem.

allegation — A charge made against someone or something before proof has been found.

allocated data — Data on a drive that has not been deleted or written over.

allocation blocks — The number of logical blocks assembled in the Macintosh file system when a file is saved.

American Society of Crime Laboratory Directors (ASCLD) — A national society that sets the standards, management, and audit procedures for labs used in crime analysis, including computer forensics labs used by the police, FBI, and similar organizations.

American Standard Code for Information Interchange (ASCII) — A coding scheme using seven or eight bits that assigns numeric values to up to 256 characters, including letters, numerals, punctuation marks, control characters, and other symbols.

amorphic — A condition achieved when a laser heats the Metal PC layer to 600° Celsius.

approved secure container — A fireproof container that is locked by key or combination.

areal density — The number of bits per square inch of a platter.

attribute type code — In NTFS, the code assigned to file attributes such as the file name and security information.

authorized requester — In a corporation or company entity, the person who has the right to request an investigation, such as the chief security officer or chief intelligence officer.

Autoexec.bat — An automatically executed batch file containing customized settings for MS-DOS, including the default path and environmental variables, such as temporary directories.

Automated Fingerprint Identification Systems (AFIS) — A computerized system for identifying fingerprints that is connected to a central database for identifying criminal suspects and reviewing thousands of fingerprint samples at high speed.

B*-tree — A file system used by the Mac OS that consists of nodes, which are objects, and leaf nodes, which contain data.

bad block inode — In the Linux file system, the inode that tracks the bad sectors on a drive.

Berkeley Software Distribution (BSD) UNIX — A variation of UNIX created at the University of California, Berkeley.

bitmap image — A representation of a graphics image in a grid-type format.

bit-stream copy — A bit-by-bit copy of the data on the original storage medium.

bit-stream image — The file used to store the bit-stream copy.

bookmark — A marker or address that identifies a specific place or location for subsequent retrieval.

Boot.ini — Specifies the Windows path installation, along with a variety of other startup options.

BootSect.dos — If the machine has a multiple booting system, NTLDR reads BootSect.dos, which is a hidden file, to determine the address of the sector location of each OS. *See also* NT Loader (NTLDR).

bootstrap process — Information contained in ROM that the computer accesses during its startup process; this information tells the computer how to access the OS and hard drive.

brute-force attack — The process of trying every combination of characters—letters, numbers, and special characters typically found on a keyboard—to find a matching password or passphrase value for an encrypted file.

business case — Justification to upper management or a lender for purchasing new equipment, software, or other tools when upgrading your facility. In many instances, a business case shows how upgrades will benefit the company.

carving — The process of removing an item from a group of items. *See also* salvaging.

catalog — An area the Macintosh file system uses to maintain the relationships between files and directories on a volume.

Certified Computer Crime Investigator, Advanced Level — A certificate awarded by HTCN upon successful completion of appropriate exams. Requires a bachelor of science degree, three years of investigative experience, and four years of experience related to computer crimes.

Certified Computer Crime Investigator, Basic Level — A certificate awarded by the HTCN upon successful completion of the appropriate exams. Requires a bachelor of science degree, two years of investigative

experience, and 18 months of experience related to computer crimes.

Certified Computer Forensic Technician, Advanced Level — A certificate awarded by the HTCN upon successful completion of its requirements. Same requirements as the Certified Computer Crime Investigator, Advanced Level, but all experience must be related to computer forensics.

Certified Computer Forensic Technician, Basic Level — A certificate awarded by the HTCN upon successful completion of its requirements. Same requirements as the Certified Computer Crime Investigator, Basic Level, but all experience must be related to computer forensics.

Certified Electronic Evidence Collection Specialist (CEECS) — A certificate awarded by IACIS upon completion of the written exam.

Certified Forensic Computer Examiner (CFCE) — A certificate awarded by IACIS upon completion of the correspondence portion of testing.

Chain Directory Entry (CDE) — A DriveSpy command that displays all directory cluster positions.

Chain FAT Entry (CFE) — A DriveSpy command that displays all the clusters in a chain that start at a specified cluster.

chain of custody — The route evidence takes from the time the investigator obtains it until the case is closed or goes to court.

client/server architecture — A network architecture in which each computer or process on the network is either a client or a server. Clients are the systems that request services from the server. A server has systems that process the requests from clients.

clump — In the Macintosh file system, a contiguous allocation block. Clumps are used to keep file fragmentation to a minimum.

clusters — Storage allocation units composed of sectors. Clusters are 512, 1024, 2048, or 4096 bytes long.

Command.com — Provides a prompt when booting to MS-DOS mode.

computer forensics — Applying scientific methods to retrieve data and/or information that can be used as evidence.

computer forensics lab — A computer lab dedicated to computing investigations; typically has a variety of computers, OSs, and forensic software.

Computer Forensics Tool Testing (CFTT) — A project created by the National Institute of Standards and Technology to manage research on computer forensics tools.

computer forensics workstation — A workstation set up to allow copying of forensic evidence, whether on a hard drive, floppy, CD, or Zip disk. It usually has various software preloaded and ready to use.

computer investigations — Detailed examination and collection of facts and data from a computer and its operating system.

Computer Technology Investigators Northwest (CTIN) — A nonprofit group based in the Seattle–Tacoma, WA, area composed of law enforcement members, private corporation security professionals, and individual security professionals whose aim is to improve the quality of high-technology investigations in the Pacific Northwest.

computer-generated records — Data generated by the computer, such as system log files or proxy server logs.

computer-stored records — Digital files generated by a person, such as electronic spreadsheets.

Config.sys — A text file containing commands typically run only at system startup to enhance the computer's DOS configuration.

configuration management — The process of keeping track of all upgrades and patches you apply to your computer's OS and applications.

conflicting out — When you already have knowledge or have rendered an opinion about a case before you are hired.

constant angular velocity (CAV) — CD players that are 12X or faster use this system to read CDs.

constant linear velocity (CLV) — CD players slower than or equal to 12X use this method to read CDs.

continuation inode — Contains information such as the mode and file type, the quantity of links in the file or directory, the file's or directory's access control list (ACL), the least and most significant bytes of the ACL UID and GID, and the file or directory status flag.

covert surveillance — Observing people or places without being detected, often using electronic equipment such as video cameras or key and screen capture programs.

criminal case — A case in which criminal law must be applied.

criminal law — Statutes applicable to a jurisdiction that state offenses against the peace and dignity of the jurisdiction and the elements that define those offenses.

curriculum vitae (CV) — An extensive resume of your professional history that includes not only your education, training, work, and what cases you have worked on, but also training you have conducted, publications you have contributed to, and professional associations and awards.

Cyclic Redundancy Check (CRC) — A mathematical algorithm that translates a file into a unique hexadecimal code value.

cylinder — The intersection of tracks on two or more disk platters.

data block — In the Linux file system, a cluster of hard disk sectors, normally 4096 or 8192 bytes.

data compression — A complex algorithm used to reduce file size.

data fork — The part of the Macintosh file structure that contains a file's actual data.

data recovery — A specialty field in which companies retrieve files that were deleted accidentally or purposefully.

data recovery lab — An alternate name for a computer forensics lab.

deposed — To be called on to testify in a deposition.

deposition — A formal examination in which you are questioned under oath with only the opposing parties, your attorney, and a court reporter present. There is no judge or jury.

deposition banks — Libraries of previously given testimony that law firms have access to.

designator — The 0x before each value that tells DriveSpy the following value is a hexadecimal number.

device driver — Contains instructions for the OS for hardware devices, such as the keyboard, mouse, and video card.

digital hash — A unique value that identifies a file.

disaster recovery — A specialty field in which companies perform real-time backups, monitoring, data recovery, and hot site operations.

discovery — The efforts to obtain information before a trial by demanding documents, depositions, interrogatories (written questions answered in writing under oath), and written requests for admissions of fact.

discovery deposition — The opposing attorney sets the deposition and frequently conducts the equivalent of both direct and cross-examination. A discovery deposition is considered part of discovery. *See also* deposition.

distributed denial-of-service (DDoS) attacks — In these attacks, an Internet attacker uses other online machines, unbeknownst to them, to launch an attack. These machines are known as zombies.

DOS protected-mode interface (DPMI) — Used by many computer forensics tools that don't operate in the Windows environment. It allows DOS programs to access extended memory while protecting the system. (See *www.windowsitlibrary.com/Content/175/09/5.html* for more details.)

dotted quad — A term used to refer to the IP addressing scheme of Web sites, routers, and similar devices.

double-indirect pointers — The pointers in the second layer or group of an OS.

drive slack — Any information that had been on the storage device previously. It can contain deleted files, deleted e-mail, or file fragments. Both file slack and RAM slack constitute drive slack. *See also* file slack and RAM slack.

Encrypted File System (EFS) — A combination of symmetric key and public/private key encryption first used in Windows 2000 on NTFS-formatted disks. The file is encrypted with a symmetric key, and then a public/private key is used to encrypt the symmetric key. (See *www.serverwatch.com/tutorials/article.php/2106831* for more details.)

end user — The person who uses a software product. In most cases, this person has less expertise than the software designer.

end-of-file (EOF) marker — The code 0x0FFFFFFF is typically used with FAT file systems to show where the file ends.

enterprise environment — A large corporate computing system that can include one or more formerly independent systems.

erasable programmable read-only memory (EPROM) — A memory chip for a hardware device that can be reprogrammed with new instructions.

ergonomics — The proper placement of machinery, office equipment, and computers to minimize physical injury or repetitive-motion injuries. It's also the study of designing equipment to meet the human need of comfort while allowing for improved productivity.

evidence bag — A nonstatic bag used to transport floppy disks, hard drives, and other computer components.

evidence custody form — A printed form indicating who has signed out and been in physical possession of evidence.

evidence floppy disk — The original disk on which electronic evidence was found.

examination plan — A document that lets you know what questions to expect when you are testifying.

exculpatory — Evidence that indicates the suspect is innocent of the crime.

exhibits — Items used in court to prove a case.

expert witness — A person who has specialized knowledge in a field, acquired through experience, training, and/or education, and can offer an opinion about the facts in addition to stating observed facts.

Extended Format (HFS+) — Used by Mac OS 8.1 and higher, the primary difference between HFS and HFS+ is that HFS was limited to 65,536 blocks per volume, and HFS+ raised this number to more than four billion. HFS+ supports smaller file sizes on larger volumes, resulting in more efficient disk usage.

extensive-response field kit — A portable kit designed to process several computers and a variety of operating systems at a crime or incident scene involving computers. This kit should contain two or more different types of software or hardware computer forensics tools, such as extra disk drives and magnetic tape drives.

extents overflow file — Used by Macintosh File Manager when the list of a file's contiguous blocks becomes too long. The list's overflow is placed in the extents overflow file. Any file extents not in the MDB or VCB are contained here.

false-positive hits — A system incorrectly provides a positive validation when, in fact, it is false.

File Allocation Table (FAT) — The original Microsoft file structure. It's written to the outermost track of a disk and contains information about each file stored on the drive. The variations are FAT12, FAT16, and FAT32.

[File Groups] — The section of DriveSpy.ini where you can list all the extensions or file headers for graphics files or spreadsheets.

[File Headers] — The section of DriveSpy.ini that contains the hexadecimal number values for many known file types. These hexadecimal numbers are the header data contained in the first several bytes of all specialized data files, such as Microsoft Word documents or Excel spreadsheets and any associated templates.

File Manager — In the Macintosh file system, this utility handles reading, writing, and storing data to physical media. It also collects data to maintain the HFS and is used to manipulate files, folders, and volumes.

file slack — The slack space created when a file is saved. If the allocated space is larger than the file, the remaining space is slack and can contain passwords, logon IDs, and deleted e-mail.

file system — Gives an OS a road map to data on a disk.

Finder — Works as part of the Macintosh OS to keep track of files and maintain the user's desktop.

firmware — The software program that's loaded into a memory chip, such as an EPROM.

forensic copy — An exact copy of an evidence disk used during the actual investigation.

Forensic Software Testing Support Tools (FS-TST) — A collection of programs that analyze the capability of disk-imaging tools.

Fourth Amendment — The Fourth Amendment to the United States Constitution in the Bill of Rights dictates that the government and its agents must have probable cause for search and seizure.

free space — Space on a drive that is not reserved for saved files.

geometry — The internal organization of a drive.

Get FAT Entry (GFE) — A DriveSpy command that displays the FAT entry for a specified cluster.

GNU General Public License (GPL) — An agreement that defines Linux as open-source software, meaning that anyone can use, change, and distribute the software without owing royalties or licensing fees to another party.

GroupWise — The Novell e-mail server software, a database server similar to Microsoft Exchange and UNIX Sendmail.

gzip — A UNIX/Linux command that compresses image files and minimizes your storage needs.

Hal.dll — The Hardware Abstraction Layer dynamic link library tells the OS kernel how to interface with the hardware.

hardening — A process of ensuring network security, which includes tasks as simple as applying updated OS patches and as complex as using layered network defense strategies.

hazardous material (HAZMAT) — Chemical, biological, or radiological substances that can cause harm to people.

head — The device that reads and writes data to a disk platter.

head and cylinder skew — A method manufacturers use to minimize lag time. The starting sectors of tracks are slightly offset from each other to move the read-write head.

header node — Stores information about the B*-tree file in the Macintosh file system.

Hierarchical File System (HFS) — The system the Mac OS uses to store files, consisting of folders and subfolders, which can be nested.

High Performance File System (HPFS) — The file system IBM uses for its OS/2 operating system.

High Tech Crime Network (HTCN) — A national organization that provides certification for computer crime investigators and computer forensics technicians.

High Technology Crime Investigation Association (HTCIA) — A nonprofit association for solving international computer crimes.

high-risk documents — Documents containing sensitive information that could create an advantage for the opposing attorney.

honeypot — A computer set up to lure an attacker.

honeywall — An intrusion prevention and monitoring system that watches what an attacker does.

hostile work environment — An environment in which a person cannot perform his or her assigned duties because of the actions of others. In the workplace, these actions include sending threatening or demeaning e-mail or a co-worker viewing hate sites.

image file — A file created by the Image tool from Digital Intelligence.

inculpatory — Evidence that indicates a suspect is guilty of the crime with which he or she is charged.

index node — Stores link information to the previous and next node in the Macintosh file system.

indirect pointers — The pointers in the first layer or group of an OS.

industrial espionage — Selling sensitive company or proprietary information to a competitor.

Info2 file — In Windows NT, 2000, and XP, the control file for the Recycle Bin.

initial-response field kit — A portable kit containing only the minimum tools needed to perform disk acquisitions and preliminary forensic analysis in the field.

innocent information — Data that does not contribute to evidence of a crime or violation.

inode — A key part of the Linux file system that contains UIDs, GIDs, modification times, access times, creation times, and file locations. Links attribute records to other attribute records within the Master File Table.

International Association of Computer Investigative Specialists (IACIS) — An organization created to provide training and software for law enforcement in the computer forensics field.

International Organization of Standardization (ISO) — An organization set up by the United Nations to ensure compatibility in a variety of fields, including engineering, electricity, and computers. The acronym is the Greek word for equal.

International Organization on Computer Evidence (IOCE) — A group that sets standards for recovering, preserving, and examining digital evidence.

Internet service provider (ISP) — A local or national service that provides a connection to the Internet.

Io.sys — This MS-DOS file communicates between a computer's BIOS and hardware and with MS-DOS code.

journal — A notebook or series of notebooks in which you record the techniques you used and the people who assisted you with specific types of investigations.

key escrow — A technology designed to recover encrypted data if users forget their passphrase or if the user key is corrupted after a system failure.

keyed hash set — A value created by an encryption utility's secret key.

keyword search — Finding files or other information by supplying characters, words, or phrases to a search tool.

Known File Filter (KFF) — A program database updated periodically by AccessData that contains the hash values of known files, such as MSWord.exe, or illicit items floating on the Web. It's used to quickly identify the files for evidence or eliminate them from the investigation if they are legitimate files.

lay witness — A witness whose testimony is based on observation; not considered to be an expert in a particular field.

layered network defense strategies — An approach to network hardening that places the most valuable data at the innermost perimeter of a network.

leaf nodes — The bottom-level nodes of the B*-tree system that contain data in the Macintosh file system.

[License] — The section of the DriveSpy.ini file that contains the product license code and owner's name for DriveSpy.exe.

limiting phrase — A phrase in a search warrant that limits the scope of a search for evidence.

line of authority — The people or positions specified in a company policy who have the right to initiate an investigation.

litigation — The legal process leading to a trial with the purpose of proving criminal or civil liability.

logical address — When files are saved, they are assigned to clusters. The OS numbers these clusters starting at 2. The cluster number defines the logical address.

logical blocks — In the Macintosh file system, a collection of data that cannot exceed 512 bytes. They are assembled in allocation blocks to store files.

logical cluster number (LCN) — Used by the NTFS Master File Table (MFT), it refers to a specific physical location on the drive. *See also* virtual cluster number (VCN).

logical EOF — In the Macintosh file system, the number of bytes that contain data.

lossless compression — A compression method in which no data is lost. With this type of compression, a large file can be compressed to take up less space, and then decompressed without any loss of information.

lossy compression — A compression technique that can lose data but not perceptible quality when a file is restored. Files that use lossy compression include JPEG and MPEG.

low-level investigations — Corporate cases that require less effort than does a major criminal case.

malware — Any type of intrusive code that is used to attack a system including viruses, worms, virus-worms, Trojans, and so on.

map node — Stores the node descriptor and a map record in the Macintosh file system.

Master Boot Record (MBR) — On Windows and DOS computer systems, this boot disk file contains information about the files on a disk and their locations, size, and other critical items.

Master Directory Block (MDB) — On older Macintosh systems, the location where all volume information is stored. A copy of the MDB is kept in the next-to-last block on the volume.

Master File Table (MFT) — Used by NTFS to track files. It contains information about access rights, date and time stamps, system attributes, and parts files.

meta-data — In NTFS, this term refers to information stored in the MFT.

metafiles — Combinations of bitmap and vector images.

Msdos.sys — A hidden text file containing startup options for Windows 9x. Note that in MS_DOS 6.22 and earlier, it was not a text file, but an actual OS executable.

multi-evidence form — An evidence custody form used to list all items associated with a case. *See also* single-evidence form.

multiple data streams — Ways in which data can be appended to a file (intentionally or not). In NTFS, data streams become an additional data attribute of a file.

National Institute of Justice (NIJ) — The research, development, and evaluation agency of the U.S. Department of Justice dedicated to researching crime control and justice issues.

National Institute of Standards and Technology (NIST) — A unit of the U.S. Commerce Department formerly known as the National Bureau of Standards; NIST promotes and maintains measurement standards.

network address translation (NAT) — Using non-routable IP addresses on your LAN to hide the number of computers or nodes on your network.

network operating system (NOS) — An OS product used with network servers; includes products such as UNIX, Windows Server 2003, and Novell NetWare.

network forensics — Monitoring network intrusions and illicit activity, including Internet usage.

network intrusion detection and incident response — Detecting attacks from intruders by using automated tools; also includes the manual process of monitoring network firewall logs.

New Technology File System (NTFS) — Created by Microsoft to replace FAT. NTFS uses security features, allows for smaller cluster sizes, and uses Unicode, which makes it a much more versatile system. NTFS is used mainly on newer OSs, such as Windows 2000, 2003, and XP.

non-keyed hash set — A hash set used to identify files or viruses.

nonresident attributes — When referring to the NTFS MFT, all data that's stored in a location separate from the MFT.

nonstandard image file format — A less common graphics file format, including proprietary formats, newer formats, formats that most image viewers don't recognize, and formats related to old or obsolete technology.

notarized — Having a document witnessed and a person clearly identified as the signer before a notary public.

NT Loader (NTLDR) — A program that loads Windows NT. It's located in the root folder of the system partition. *See also* Bootsect.dos.

NTBootdd.sys — A device driver that allows access to SCSI or ATA drives that aren't referred to in the BIOS.

NTDetect.com — A command file that identifies hardware components during bootup and sends the information to NTLDR.

Ntoskrnl.exe — The kernel for Windows XP.

offset — A value added to a base address to produce a second address.

Open Firmware — The platform-independent boot firmware used on Macintosh systems to gather information, control devices, and load the OS.

packet sniffers — Devices and/or software used to examine network traffic. On TCP/IP networks, they examine packets, hence the term.

PageFile.sys — At startup, data and instruction code are moved in and out of PageFile.sys to optimize the amount of physical memory (RAM) available during startup.

partition — A logical drive on a disk. It can be the entire disk or a fraction thereof.

Partition Boot Sector — The first data set of an NTFS disk. It starts at sector [0] of the disk drive and can expand up to 16 sectors.

partition gap — Partitions created with unused space or voids between the primary partition and the first logical partition.

password dictionary — A collection of words or phrases that might be passwords for an encrypted file. Password recovery programs can use a password dictionary to compare potential passwords to an encrypted file's password or passphrase hash values.

password protected — Files and areas of any storage media can have limited access by requiring a password to prevent unintentional use.

password-cracking software — Software used to match the hash patterns of passwords or simply guess the words by using common combinations or standard algorithms.

PDBlock — A program designed to prevent writing to a disk drive.

PDWipe — A program used to overwrite hard disk drives, overwriting all data on the drive.

personal digital assistant (PDA) — One of several pocket-sized computers that store addresses, notes, and calendars. One popular brand is Palm.

person of interest — Someone who might be a suspect or someone with additional knowledge that can provide enough evidence for probable cause for a search warrant or arrest.

phase change alloy — The Metal PC layer of a CD-RW that allows it to be written to several times.

physical address — The actual sector in which a file is located. Sectors reside at the hardware and firmware level.

physical EOF — In the Macintosh file system, the number of allocation blocks assigned to the file.

pixel — A small dot used to create images; the term comes from "picture element."

plain view doctrine — When conducting a search and seizure, objects in plain view of a law enforcement officer who has the right to be in position to have that view are subject to seizure without a warrant and may be introduced as evidence.

police blotter — A journal of criminal activity used to inform law enforcement personnel of current criminal activities.

Post Office Protocol version 3 (POP3) — A protocol used to retrieve e-mail messages from an e-mail server.

private key — In encryption, the key used to decrypt the file.

probable cause — Indication that a crime has been committed, evidence of the specific crime exists, and the evidence for the specific crime exists at the place to be searched.

professional conduct — Behavior expected of an employee in the workplace or other professional setting.

professional curiosity — The motivation for law enforcement and other professional personnel to examine an incident or crime scene to see what happened.

protected-mode GUI — Provides the same items for Windows that Config.sys provided for DOS. It loads all the device drivers. (See *www.windowsitlibrary.com/Content/175/09/5.html* for more details.)

proxy server — A server computer that connects a local area network (LAN) to the Internet.

public key — In encryption, the key used to encrypt a file; it's held by a certificate authority, such as a global registry, network server, or company such as VeriSign.

RAM slack — The slack space in the last sector of a file. Any data currently residing in RAM at the time the file is saved can appear in this area, whether the information was saved or not. It can contain logon IDs, passwords, and phone numbers for dial-ups.

raster image — A bitmap file that organizes pixels in rows; usually created when a vector image is converted to a bitmap image.

rasterize — To convert a bitmap file to a raster file for printing.

recovery certificate — A method NTFS uses so that a network administrator can recover encrypted files if the file's user/creator loses his or her private key encryption code.

redundant array of independent disks (RAID) — A configuration of two or more hard drives with redundant storage features so that if one drive fails, the other drives can take over.

Registry — In Windows, the Registry contains information about hardware, network connections, user preferences, installed software, and other critical information. Use Regedit or Regedt32 from the Run dialog box to access the Registry.

relative sector — The actual count of each sector of data on a partition. Relative sector 0 (zero) starts at the very beginning of the disk partition. The Sector command in DriveSpy's Partition mode displays the relative sector values of the disk partition.

resident attributes — When referring to the MFT, all attributes stored in the NTFS MFT. *See also* Master File Table (MFT) and New Technology File System (NTFS).

resolution — Density of pixels on the screen.

resource fork — The part of the Macintosh file system that contains the resource map, header information for the file, window locations, executable code, and icons.

right of privacy — When employees think their transmissions at work are protected.

risk management — Involves determining how much risk is acceptable for any process or operation, such as replacing equipment.

root kit — A prebuilt package of programs that allows an intruder to install a network sniffer and obtain user IDs and passwords to your most sensitive systems.

router — A network device that connects a number of local area networks together.

salvaging — Another term for carving used outside North America; the process of removing an item from a group of items. *See also* carving.

Scientific Working Group on Digital Evidence (SWGDE) — A group that sets standards for recovering, preserving, and examining digital evidence.

scope creep — An unexpected situation or condition that increases the level of work.

screen resolution — The density of pixels displayed on your monitor.

[Search] — The section of the DriveSpy.ini file where you can specify what keywords you want to search for in an image file or document.

search and seizure — The legal act of acquiring evidence for an investigation. *See* Fourth Amendment.

search warrants —Legal documents that allow law enforcement to search an office, place of business, or other locale for evidence relating to an alleged crime.

Second Extended File System (Ext2fs) — The file system most used by Linux today.

sector — An individual section on a track, typically made up of 512 bytes.

secure facility — A facility that can be locked and provides limited access to the contents of a room.

Set command — When used at the command line with no switches or attributes, this command displays all current system-root paths.

silver-platter doctrine — The policy of submitting to the police by an investigator who is not an agent of the court when a criminal act has been uncovered.

Simple Mail Transfer Protocol (SMTP) — A protocol used for sending e-mail messages between servers.

single-evidence form — A form that dedicates a page for each item retrieved for a case. It allows the investigator to add more detail about exactly what was done to the evidence each time it was taken from the storage locker. *See also* multi-evidence form.

slack space — Space on a disk between the end of a file and the allotted space for that file.

small computer system interface (SCSI) — An input/output standard protocol device.

sniffing — Detecting data transmissions to and from a suspect's computer and a network server to determine the type of data being transmitted over a network.

sparse evidence file recovery — Creating files from separate large portions of data to streamline data analysis. When the volume of data is exceptionally high, only data from files users have accessed is recovered.

special-interest groups (SIGs) — Associated with various operating systems, these groups maintain electronic mailing lists and might hold meetings to exchange information about current and legacy operating systems.

spoliation — Destroying or concealing evidence; subject to sanctions.

standard image file format — An image file format that most or all graphics programs can open.

steganalysis — The practice of detecting and decoding steganography.

steganography — A cryptographic technique for embedding information into something else (such as an image or a sound file) for the sole purpose of hiding that information from casual observers.

technical (or scientific) witness — A person who has performed an examination or observed technical or scientific work. This person can testify to the observed facts, but does not offer an opinion in court.

TEMPEST — An unclassified term that refers to facilities that have been hardened so that electrical signals from computers, the computer network, and telephone systems cannot be easily monitored or accessed by someone outside the facility.

testimony preservation deposition — This deposition is set by your attorney-client to preserve your testimony in case of schedule conflicts or health problems. In some cases, this deposition is conducted at your laboratory to make it easier to conduct demonstrations and improve your testimony. *See also* deposition.

track density — The space between tracks on a disk. The smaller the space between tracks, the more tracks on a disk. Older drives with wider track densities allowed wandering.

tracks — The individual concentric circles on a disk platter.

triple-indirect pointers — The pointers in the third layer or group of an OS.

unallocated disk space — All data area on the disk that does not contain an active file. The data in this area includes but is not limited to deleted files.

Unicode — A character code representation that's replacing ASCII. It's capable of representing more than 64,000 characters and non-European-based languages.

Uniform Crime Report — Information collected at the federal, state, and local levels to determine the types and frequencies of crimes committed.

UTF-8 (Unicode Transformation Format) — One of three formats Unicode uses to translate the many languages of the world for digital representation.

vector image — An image based on mathematical equations.

vector quantization (VQ) — A form of vector image that uses an algorithm similar to rounding off decimal values to eliminate unnecessary data.

virtual cluster number (VCN) — When a file is saved in the NTFS, it's assigned both a logical cluster number and a virtual cluster number. The logical cluster number is a physical location; the virtual cluster number consists of chained clusters. *See also* logical cluster number (LCN).

voir dire — The process of qualifying a witness as an expert in his or her field. (From the French: literally, "to see, to say.")

volume — Any storage media, such as a floppy disk, a partition on a hard drive, the entire drive, or several drives. On Intel systems, a volume is any partitioned disk.

Volume Bitmap — A system application used to track blocks that are in use and blocks that are available.

Volume Control Block (VCB) — Contains information from the MDB and is used by File Manager in the Macintosh file system.

Volume Information Block (VIB) — Another name for the Master Directory Block. *See* Master Directory Block (MDB).

vulnerability assessment and risk management — Determining the weakest points in a system, and then calculating the return on investment to decide which ones have to be fixed.

warning banner — Text that appears on computer screens when people log on to a company computer; this text states the ownership of the computer and appropriate use of the machine or Internet access.

write-blocker — A hardware device or software program that prevents a computer from recording data on an evidence disk. Software write-blocker programs typically alter Interrupt 13 write functions to a disk drive in a PC's BIOS. Hardware write-blockers are usually bridging devices located between a disk drive and the computer.

zombie — A computer used without its knowledge or consent in a DDoS attack.

zoned bit recording — How most manufacturers deal with a platter's inner tracks being physically smaller than the outer tracks. Grouping the tracks by zones ensures that the most storage space is used. Inner tracks contain fewer sectors than the outer tracks.

Index

DIGITAL INTELLIGENCE, INC. DRIVESPY™ AND IMAGE
120 DAY TRIAL END-USER LICENSE AGREEMENT

YOU SHOULD CAREFULLY READ THE FOLLOWING TERMS AND CONDITIONS BEFORE BREAKING THE SEAL ON THE DISC ENVELOPE OR INSTALLING THE SOFTWARE. AMONG OTHER THINGS, THIS AGREEMENT LICENSES THE ENCLOSED SOFTWARE TO YOU AND CONTAINS WARRANTY AND LIABILITY DISCLAIMERS. BY USING THE DISC AND/OR INSTALLING THE SOFTWARE, YOU ARE ACCEPTING AND AGREEING TO THE TERMS AND CONDITIONS OF THIS AGREEMENT. IF YOU DO NOT AGREE TO THE TERMS OF THIS AGREEMENT, DO NOT BREAK THE SEAL OR USE THE DISC. YOU SHOULD PROMPTLY RETURN THE PACKAGE UNOPENED. THIS TRIAL END-USER SOFTWARE LICENSE AGREEMENT (THE "AGREEMENT" OR "LICENSE") IS A LEGAL AGREEMENT BETWEEN YOU (BOTH THE INDIVIDUAL INSTALLING THE PRODUCT AND ANY LEGAL ENTITY ON WHOSE BEHALF SUCH INDIVIDUAL IS ACTING) ("YOU" OR "YOUR") AND DIGITAL INTELLIGENCE, INC., A WISCONSIN CORPORATION ("DIGITAL INTELLIGENCE"), FOR DIGITAL INTELLIGENCE SOFTWARE PRODUCT(S), WHICH INCLUDES COMPUTER SOFTWARE AND ASSOCIATED MEDIA, AND ALL ACCOMPANYING MANUALS AND OTHER DOCUMENTATION, WHETHER PRINTED, "ONLINE", ELECTRONIC OR OTHERWISE (THE "SOFTWARE").

LICENSE: DIGITAL INTELLIGENCE GRANTS YOU A PERSONAL, NON-EXCLUSIVE, NON-TRANSFERABLE, NON-SUBLICENSABLE, LIMITED, TRIAL USE LICENSE TO USE THE SOFTWARE IN ACCORDANCE WITH THE END-USER DOCUMENTATION AND SUBJECT TO THE TERMS AND CONDITIONS, INCLUDING USE RESTRICTIONS, SPECIFIED BELOW.

You shall have the right to use the Software (a) only in object code form, (b) for personal purposes only for a single user on a single computer, (c) solely with the publication with which the Software is included, and (d) only for a one hundred twenty (120) day period (the "Trial Period") from the date you first use the Software. You may not distribute copies of the Software or use it after the Trial Period. You shall limit the use of the Software to a single machine at any given time. You shall not permit or allow any third party to use or have access to the Software, whether by timesharing, networking or any other means. Although this Agreement expressly permits the use of the Software on multiple machines, that usage must not be performed concurrently. In the event that multiple, simultaneous usage by a single individual or an organization is desired, a multiple-user license must be obtained in the amount equal to, or greater than, the maximum number of machines which will be operating the Software simultaneously. If You are an entity, Digital Intelligence grants You the right to designate one individual within your organization to have the right to use the Software in the manner provided above.

You are prohibited from and shall not cause or permit any third party to (a) transfer, sell, sublicense, assign or otherwise convey the Software, (b) timeshare, rent or market the Software, (c) use the Software for or as part of a service bureau, (d) distribute the Software in whole or in part, (e) use the Software for or as part of any third party training, and/or (f) use the Software for any other use not expressly permitted by this Agreement. Any attempt to transfer, sell, sublicense, assign or otherwise convey any of the rights, duties or obligations hereunder is void. You are prohibited from and shall use the Software solely for internal data processing operations, and shall not use the Software for processing data of a third party or for any commercial or production use. If You desire to use the Software for any use other than the use allowed under this Agreement, You must contact DIGITAL INTELLIGENCE to obtain the appropriate licenses. You may possess and use the Software only in machine-readable form. You have no right to receive, use or examine any source code or design documentation relating to the Software. You are prohibited from and shall not cause or permit the reverse engineering, disassembly, decompilation, modification or creation of derivative works based on the Software. You may not (or allow any third party to) incorporate any portion of the Software into any other software or create a derivative work of any portion of the Software, or develop any other product containing any of the concepts and ideas contained in the Software. You are prohibited from and shall not copy or duplicate the Software except as follows: You may make one copy of the Software in machine readable form solely for back-up purposes. No other copies shall be made without DIGITAL INTELLIGENCE's prior written consent. You are prohibited from and shall not: (a) remove any product identification, copyright notices, or other notices or proprietary restrictions from the Software, or (b) run any benchmark tests with or of the Software. This Agreement does not authorize You to use any DIGITAL INTELLIGENCE name, trademark or logo.

COPYRIGHT/OWNERSHIP OF SOFTWARE: The Software is the confidential and proprietary product of DIGITAL INTELLIGENCE and is protected by copyright and other intellectual property laws. You acknowledge that the Software constitutes proprietary information and trade secrets of DIGITAL INTELLIGENCE and its licensors, whether or not any portion thereof is or may be the subject of a valid copyright or patent. You acquire only the right to use the Software and do not acquire any rights, express or implied, in the Software or media containing the Software other than those specified in this Agreement. DIGITAL INTELLIGENCE, or its licensor, shall at all times, including but not limited to after termination of this Agreement, retain all rights, title, and interest, including intellectual property rights, in the Software and media.

WARRANTY DISCLAIMER: THE SOFTWARE IS PROVIDED "AS IS" AND DIGITAL INTELLIGENCE SPECIFICALLY DISCLAIMS ALL WARRANTIES OF ANY KIND, EITHER EXPRESS OR IMPLIED (STATUTORY OR OTHERWISE), INCLUDING, BUT NOT LIMITED TO, THE IMPLIED WARRANTIES OF MERCHANTABILITY, SATISFACTORY QUALITY, NON-INFRINGEMENT AND FITNESS FOR A PARTICULAR PURPOSE. DIGITAL INTELLIGENCE DOES NOT WARRANT, GUARANTEE OR MAKE ANY REPRESENTATIONS REGARDING THE USE, OR THE RESULTS OF THE USE, OF THE SOFTWARE IN TERMS OF CORRECTNESS, ACCURACY, RELIABILITY, CURRENTNESS OR OTHERWISE, AND DOES NOT WARRANT THAT THE OPERATION OF THE SOFTWARE WILL BE UNINTERRUPTED OR ERROR FREE. DIGITAL INTELLIGENCE EXPRESSLY DISCLAIMS ALL WARRANTIES NOT STATED HEREIN, NO ORAL OR WRITTEN INFORMATION OR ADVICE GIVEN BY DIGITAL INTELLIGENCE OR OTHERS SHALL CREATE A WARRANTY OR IN ANY WAY INCREASE THE SCOPE OF THIS LICENSE, AND YOU MAY NOT RELY ON ANY SUCH INFORMATION OR ADVICE.

LIMITATION OF LIABILITY: IN NO EVENT SHALL DIGITAL INTELLIGENCE BE LIABLE FOR ANY DIRECT, INDIRECT, INCIDENTAL, SPECIAL OR CONSEQUENTIAL DAMAGES, OR DAMAGES FOR LOSS OF PROFITS, REVENUE, DATA OR DATA USE, INCURRED BY YOU OR ANY THIRD PARTY, WHETHER IN AN ACTION IN CONTRACT OR TORT, EVEN IF DIGITAL INTELLIGENCE HAS BEEN ADVISED OF THE POSSIBILITY OF SUCH DAMAGES. SOME JURISDICTIONS DO NOT ALLOW THE EXCLUSION OF IMPLIED WARRANTIES OR LIMITATION OR EXCLUSION OF LIABILITY FOR INCIDENTAL OR CONSEQUENTIAL DAMAGES SO THE ABOVE EXCLUSIONS AND LIMITATION MAY NOT APPLY TO YOU. WITHOUT PREJUDICE TO THE FOREGOING, IF WE ARE NONETHELESS DETERMINED TO BE LIABLE TO YOU UNDER OR IN CONNECTION WITH THIS LICENSE, OUR ENTIRE LIABILITY, AND YOUR EXCLUSIVE REMEDY UNDER THIS AGREEMENT SHALL NOT EXCEED THE AMOUNT OF THE LICENSE FEES YOU HAVE PAID TO DIGITAL INTELLIGENCE UNDER THIS AGREEMENT.

TERMINATION: This Agreement and Your license to use the Software shall terminate upon expiration of the Trial Period. You may terminate this license at any time by discontinuing use of and destroying the Software together with any copies in any form. This license will also terminate if You fail to comply with any term or condition of this Agreement. Upon termination of the license, You agree to discontinue use of and destroy the Software together with any copies in any form. The Warranty Disclaimer, Limitation of Liability and Export Administration sections of this Agreement shall survive termination of this Agreement.

NO TECHNICAL SUPPORT: DIGITAL INTELLIGENCE is not obligated to provide and this Agreement does not entitle You to any updates or upgrades to, or any technical support or phone support for, the Software.

EXPORT ADMINISTRATION: You acknowledge that the Software, including technical data, is subject to United States export control laws, including the United States Export Administration Act and its associated regulations, and may be subject to export or import regulations in other countries. You agree to comply fully with all laws and regulations of the United States and other countries ("Export Laws") to assure that neither the Software, nor any direct products thereof, are (a) exported, directly or indirectly, in violation of Export Laws, either to countries or nationals that are subject to United States export restrictions or to any end user who has been prohibited from participating in the Unites States export transactions by any federal agency of the United States government; or (b) intended to be used for any purposes prohibited by the Export Laws, including, without limitation, nuclear, chemical or biological weapons proliferation. You acknowledge that the Software may include technical data subject to export and re-export restrictions imposed by United States law.

RESTRICTED RIGHTS: The Software is provided with Restricted Rights. The Software is a commercial product, licensed on the open market at market prices, and was developed entirely at private expense and without the use of any Government funds. Any use, modification, reproduction, release, performance, display, or disclosure of the Software to any Government entity shall be governed solely by the terms of this Agreement and shall be prohibited except to the extent expressly permitted by the terms of this Agreement, and no license to the Software is granted to any Government entity requiring different terms. Use, duplication or disclosure of the Software by the United State government is subject to the restrictions set forth in the Rights in Technical Data and Computer Software Clauses in DFARS 252.227-7013(c)(1)(ii) and FAR 52.227-19(c)(2) as applicable. Manufacturer is DIGITAL INTELLIGENCE, INC., 1325 Pearl Street, Waukesha, WI 53186.

MISCELLANEOUS: This Agreement and all related actions thereto shall be governed by the internal laws of the State of Wisconsin. DIGITAL INTELLIGENCE may audit Your use of the Software. If any provision of this Agreement is held to be invalid or unenforceable, the remaining provisions of this Agreement will remain in full force. This Agreement and all of the terms, provisions and conditions hereof shall be binding upon and inure to the benefit of the parties hereto and their respective successors and permitted assigns.

YOU ACKNOWLEDGE THAT YOU HAVE READ THIS AGREEMENT, UNDERSTAND IT, AND AGREE TO BE BOUND BY ITS TERMS AND CONDITIONS. YOU FURTHER AGREE THAT IT IS THE COMPLETE AND EXCLUSIVE STATEMENT OF THE AGREEMENT BETWEEN DIGITAL INTELLIGENCE AND YOU.

DIGITAL INTELLIGENCE and DRIVESPY are trademarks of DIGITAL INTELLIGENCE, INC.